ISBN 978-0-260-60657-0
PIBN 10959208

~~1268~~ No. 3512. 1269

IN THE

United States Circuit Court of Appeals

FOR THE NINTH CIRCUIT

PACIFIC LIVE STOCK COMPANY (a Corporation), *Plaintiff in Error,* vs. THE WARM SPRINGS IRRIGATION DISTRICT (a Municipal Corporation), *Defendant in Error.*	

BRIEF FOR PLAINTIFF IN ERROR.

JOHN L. RAND,
P. J. GALLAGHER,
W. H. BROOKE,
EDWARD F. TREADWELL,
Attorneys for Plaintiff in Error.

No. 3512.

IN THE

United States Circuit Court of Appeals

FOR THE NINTH CIRCUIT

PACIFIC LIVE STOCK COMPANY (a Corporation),

Plaintiff in Error,

vs.

THE WARM SPRINGS IRRIGATION DISTRICT (a Municipal Corporation),

Defendant in Error.

BRIEF FOR PLAINTIFF IN ERROR.

Statement of the Case.

This is an action brought by The Warm Springs Irrigation District to condemn a certain ranch of defendant, Pacific Live Stock Company, known as its Warm Springs Ranch, as a reservoir site for the use of the plaintiff. The plaintiff's complaint (Trans., pp. 7-14) alleges the organization of the plaintiff irrigation district, the corporate capacity of the defendant, the intention of the plaintiff to irrigate thirty thousand acres or more of land, the making of surveys and the location of a dam site and reservoir. It then alleges that the dam site is fourteen hundred feet south of the south line of the defendant's property, but that the plaintiff has located "the highest flow line" upon the defendant's land, and that

> "such lands lie in such position with reference to said dam and reservoir site as that about two thousand five hundred (2,500) acres of said land as hereinafter particularly described will be submerged at said high flow line by waters to be stored by the said dam and reservoir of the plaintiff, and that practically the whole of said lands are needed by and are necessary for the purposes of the plaintiff, and it is necessary that plaintiff should have, and it requires, all of said lands for such public use for irrigation purposes."

After describing the lands of defendant and the failure to agree as to the value thereof, it prays that "said lands" be condemned, and so forth. The complaint contains no allegation of any appropriation made by the plaintiff of any waters to be stored in the reservoir, nor does it allege any application made by the plaintiff to the State Engineer for a permit to appropriate any such water. The defendant moved the court for an order requiring the plaintiff to make its complaint more definite and certain in the following particulars:

> "1. By alleging whether it seeks to acquire the fee simple title to said land, or merely an easement over the same.
>
> "2. By alleging wherein it is necessary for the plaintiff to acquire the fee simple title to said land rather than an easement thereon.
>
> "3. By alleging what portion of the said land will be overflowed by the plaintiff." (Trans., pp. 23-24.)

The defendant also demurred to the complaint on the ground that the same did not state facts sufficient to constitute a cause of action against the defendant, and that the defendant had not the legal capacity to maintain the action. (Trans., pp. 26-27.)

It will be seen that by the motion to make the complaint more definite and certain the defendant raised the point that the complaint did not show whether an easement or the fee was desired to be acquired, and that there was nothing in the complaint showing that a fee was necessary, as it was only desired to overflow the land to a certain extent which could as well be accomplished by acquiring an easement.

The motion and demurrer were overruled. (Trans., p. 28.) The defendant answered (Trans., pp. 29-42), alleging that the plaintiff had never appropriated any water for the reservoir in question nor obtained any permit from the State Engineer to appropriate or reservoir any waters. (Trans., p. 30.) The answer also denied that the lands were necessary for the purposes of the plaintiff, "and it also alleges that the said plaintiff only requires at most an easement in and over the said lands for the purposes aforesaid." (Trans., p. 31.) The answer alleged that the lands were of the value of three hundred thousand dollars; that the lands were a part of a larger tract of land, about one thousand acres of which were not taken by the condemnation, and that those lands would be damaged in the sum of ten thousand dollars by being severed from the lands taken. (Trans., pp. 35-36.) It also alleged that the lands were suitable to be used as a reservoir site, and that the defendant owned other lands shortly down the river, known as the Harper Ranch, and that by reservoiring the waters in this reservoir they could be used for the further development of the Harper Ranch, and that by severing this land from the other property owned by the defendant there would be additional damage in the sum of one hundred thousand dollars caused to the defendant. (Trans., pp. 36-37.) It was also alleged by an amendment to the answer that at the time of the commencement of the action there was a thousand tons of hay upon the land which it had been intended to feed during the winter of 1919-20, and that on account of the condemnation it would be necessary to remove that hay, causing a loss of seventy-five hundred dollars. (Trans., pp. 40-41.) The defendant filed a reply which did not put in issue the allegation of the answer to the effect that the plaintiff only required at most an easement in the land, but denied all the other allegations of the answer. (Trans., pp. 43-45.)

The case was tried before the court sitting without a jury. The court fixed the value of the property at ninety thousand dollars. The court allowed nothing by way of damages to the thousand acres of land which were not taken, and allowed no damages in connection with the removal of the hay. (Trans., p. 51.) In its opinion the court said:

> "It is not necessary nor do I deem it proper to determine at this time whether such appropriation will amount to the taking of the fee or only an easement. Judgment will follow the language of the statute appropriating the property for reservoir purposes. (Sec. 6886, Lord's Oregon Laws.) The legal effect can be determined when the question arises, if it ever does." (Trans., pp. 51-52.)

Formal findings were filed, finding that it is necessary that plaintiff should have "said lands for such public use for irrigation purposes"; finding that the plaintiff on February 14, 1916, had made application to the State Engineer for a permit to appropriate the necessary waters; findings that the defendant would not be damaged with respect to the thousand acres of adjoining land, nor with respect to the hay on the property, and finding the market value of the lands to be ninety thousand dollars. (Trans., pp. 52-60.)

Judgment was entered on these findings by which the lands were appropriated "for a public use for reservoir and irrigation purposes and as a part of its irrigation system forever, and the same and the whole thereof shall be and is the property of plaintiff." (Trans., pp. 61-64.)

The defendant moved for a new trial, specifying that the decision was against law, and also insufficiency of the evidence with respect to all material findings in the case, and, among other things, contending that the undisputed evidence in the case showed that the highest use to which the land was adapted was for reservoir purposes, and that for that purpose the land was worth two hundred and fifty thousand dollars; that the ranch for hay and stock purposes was worth at least one hundred and forty thousand dollars; that damages should be allowed for the separation of the land from the neighboring land, and for the removing of the hay; that the court erred in permitting certain witnesses for the plaintiff to testify as to the value of the land, as they were not competent, and also that the court erred in finding that it was necessary for the plaintiff to take the land for the reason that it was apparent that it was only necessary to take an easement. (Trans., pp. 64-67.) This motion was denied. (Trans., pp. 28-29.)

All the proceedings on the trial were thereupon embodied in a bill of exceptions and are brought here by writ of error.

Assignment of Errors.

1. The court erred in overruling and denying the defendant's motion to make the complaint more definite and certain, for the reason that the said complaint did not set forth whether the plaintiff sought to acquire the fee simple title to the land described in the complaint or an easement therein, and it was impossible to determine from the said complaint whether the said plaintiff sought to acquire an easement in said land or the fee simple title thereto.

2. The court erred in overruling the demurrer to plaintiff's complaint, for the reason that said complaint did not set forth that the said plaintiff had made any appropriation of the waters of the Malheur River, or of any waters for the said reservoir, or that it had obtained from the authorities of the State any permit for the appropriation of any waters for said reservoir.

3. The court erred in granting judgment in said cause without deciding or specifying whether the plaintiff acquired thereby the fee simple title of the said land, or only an easement therein.

4. The court erred in granting judgment to the plaintiff, for the reason that it appeared on the trial

that the said plaintiff had not, prior to the commencement of said action, appropriated any water of the Malheur River, or obtained from the State Engineer of the State of Oregon any permit for such appropriation.

5. The court erred in permitting the plaintiff to show what particular lands would be overflowed, for the reason that the complaint should have indicated the lands which were intended to be overflowed, and in this particular defendant states that the complaint did not show what particular lands would be overflowed by the plaintiff, and the defendant moved to make the complaint more definite and certain in that particular, which motion was overruled by the court, and thereafter, over the objection of the defendant, permitted the plaintiff to show what lands would be and what lands would not be overflowed by it.

6. The court erred in overruling defendant's objection to the following question propounded to the witness J. C. Foley:

> "Q. Do you know of the sale in your neighborhood at a price which any way assisted you in reaching your conclusion as to the price of this ranch?"

And in this regard the defendant states that the said witness, J. C. Foley, was a witness called on behalf of the plaintiff, for the purpose of testifying to the value of the lands described in said complaint, and by the said question the said witness was permitted on direct examination to testify to the sale of other pieces of land and the prices at which the same were sold.

7. The court erred in overruling the defendant's objection to the following question propounded to the witness J. C. Foley:

> "Q. How much did that soil produce to the acre?"

And in this behalf defendant states that the said witness, J. C. Foley, was a witness called on behalf of the plaintiff, for the purpose of testifying to the value of the lands described in the said complaint, and by this question was permitted to testify and did testify on direct examination to the productivity of other lands, as to the sale of which he was permitted to testify.

8. The court erred in overruling defendant's objection to the following question propounded to the witness James Morfit:

> "Q. State what the fair market value of that thirteen hundred acre fenced ranch is."

And in this regard defendant states that the said witness, James Morfit, was a witness called on behalf of plaintiff, for the purpose of testifying to the value of the lands involved in this suit, and by said question was permitted on direct examination to testify to specific sales and the value of specific lands not involved in said suit.

9. The court erred in overruling the defendant's objection to the following question propounded to the witness James Morfit:

> "Q. How does it compare as range and pasture land with range and pasture lands you saw on the Warm Springs Ranch in November?"

And in this regard defendant states that the said witness, James Morfit, was a witness called on behalf of plaintiff, for the purpose of testifying as to the value of the lands described in the said complaint, and by this question was permitted to testify as to the range and pasture on certain specific lands other than the lands described in the complaint, and to give the value and productivity of such specific tracts of land.

10. The court erred in overruling the objections of the defendant to the qualifications of the witness C. C. Hunt to give an opinion as to the value of the said property, and in this regard defendant states that the said witness, C. C. Hunt, was a witness called on behalf of plaintiff, for the purpose of testifying as to the value of the land described in the complaint, and he did testify as to such value, and it appeared on the examination of the said witness that he lived one hundred and sixteen miles away from the said property, and had never seen it, except on two occasions in the winter time, after this litigation arose, when he went there for the express purpose of examining the same, and he testified that he had never owned any land within one hundred and sixteen miles of this land, had never bought or sold any land within one hundred and sixteen milees of this land, did not know the sale price of any land within one hundred and sixteen miles of this land, had never wintered any cattle on the ranch and had never wintered any cattle within one hundred and sixteen miles of the Warm Springs Ranch, and did not know the number of cattle wintered nor the amount of hay produced on it from year to year, nor had he ever bought

or sold any hay within one hundred and sixteen miles of the Warm Springs Ranch, and did not know the value or price of the hay on the ranch, and thereupon the defendant objected to the testimony of said witness, and objected that he was not qualified to give an opinion as to the value of said property, which objection was overruled.

11. The court erred in overruling the objections of the defendant to the qualifications of the witness J. F. Weaver to testify and give an opinion as to the value of said land, and in this regard defendant states that the said witness, J. F. Weaver, was a witness called on behalf of plaintiff, for the purpose of testifying as to the value of the land described in the complaint, and he did testify as to such value, and it appeared on the examination of the said witness that he lived one hundred miles away from the said property, and had never seen it, except on two occasions in the winter time, after this litigation arose, when he went there for the express purpose of examining the same, and he testified that he had never owned any land within one hundred miles of this land; had never bought or sold any land within one hundred miles of this land; did not know the sale price of any land within one hundred miles of this land; had never wintered any cattle on the ranch and had never wintered any cattle within one hundred miles of the Warm Springs Ranch, and did not know the number of cattle wintered nor the amount of hay produced on it from year to year, nor had he ever bought or sold any hay within one hundred miles of the Warm Springs Ranch, and did not know the

value or price of the hay on the ranch, and thereupon the defendant objected to the testimony of said witness, and objected that he was not qualified to give an opinion as to the value of said property, which objection was overruled.

12. The court erred in overruling the objections of the defendant to the qualifications of the witness E. M. Greig to testify and give an opinion as to the value of said land, and in this regard defendant states that the said witness, E. M. Greig, was a witness called on behalf of plaintiff, for the purpose of testifying as to the value of the land described in the complaint, and he did testify as to such value, and it appeared on the examination of the said witness that he lived one hundred miles away from the said property, and had never seen it, except on two occasions in the winter time, after this litigation arose, when he went there for the express purpose of examining the same, and he testified that he had never owned any land within one hundred miles of this land, had never bought or sold any land within one hundred miles of this land, did not know the sale price of any land within one hundred miles of this land, had never wintered any cattle on the ranch and had never wintered any cattle within one hundred miles of the Warm Springs Ranch, and did not know the number of cattle wintered nor the amount of hay produced on it from year to year, nor had he ever bought or sold any hay within one hundred miles of the Warm Springs Ranch, and did not know the value or price of the hay on the ranch, and thereupon the defendant objected to the testimony of said witness,

and objected that he was not qualified to give an opinion as to the value of said property, which objection was overruled.

13. The court erred in overruling the objections of the defendant to the admission in evidence of the application and permit of the plaintiff to appropriate water, for the reason that the said matter was not within any issue framed by the pleadings, and the same was done after the filing of this suit, and in this regard the defendant states that, notwithstanding this court overruled the demurrer to the complaint, and, although there is no allegation of the appropriation of any water by the plaintiff, the court permitted the defendant to introduce into evidence an alleged appropriation of the said water by the plaintiff, made after the commencement of this action.

14. The court erred in limiting the damages to the plaintiff to the value of the said land for agricultural purposes, and in this regard defendant states that the undisputed evidence in the suit was that the highest use to which the said land was adapted was as a reservoir site, and that for such purpose it had a value of two hundred and fifty thousand dollars, and the evidence was undisputed.

15. The court erred in limiting the defendant's damages to the sum of ninety thousand dollars as the value of the said ranch, for the reason that the evidence showed that the said ranch was of the value of one hundred and forty-three thousand dollars for agricultural purposes and of the value of two hundred and fifty thousand dollars for reservoir purposes, and the evidence is insufficient to justify the finding

that the said ranch was worth only ninety thousand dollars.

16. The court erred in failing to give the defendant damages caused by the separation of said land from other land owned by the defendant, and in this regard the defendant states that the evidence showed that the said defendant was the owner of one thousand acres of land immediately adjoining the land so taken, which was acquired, owned and used in connection with the said land, and for the purpose of supplying water to the cattle wintered upon the said land, and that the said land would be damaged in the sum of ten thousand dollars by being separated in ownership from said ranch, and the evidence is insufficient to justify the finding that the said land will not be so damaged.

17. The court erred in failing to give the defendant damages in the sum of seventy-five hundred dollars, which will be caused to it in case the said land is taken, by reason of the fact that it will be necessary for the defendant to remove one thousand tons of hay therefrom and to make preparations for feeding the same, and in this regard defendant states that the evidence showed that the said ranch was used as a stock ranch for the wintering of cattle in the winter time, and that defendant had thereon about one thousand tons of hay, which it intended to feed during the winter season of 1919-20, and by reason of the taking of said property in December, 1920, it would be necessary to remove said hay therefrom and make preparations for feeding the same at some other point, at an additional expense of seventy-five hundred dollars.

18. The court erred in finding that the defendant was not damaged with respect to the one thousand tons of hay on said ranch, and in failing to give the defendant damages therefor, and in this regard defendant states that by reason of the taking of the said ranch and the necessity of removing the hay therefrom, the hay on the said ranch was damaged in the sum of seventy-five hundred dollars and reduced in value to that extent, all of which was caused by the taking of said property.

19. The court erred in failing to give the defendant damages in the sum of one hundred thousand dollars, or in any other sum, caused by the separation of the said ranch from the Harper Ranch owned by the defendant, and in this regard defendant states that the evidence showed that the said defendant was the owner of a ranch, known as the Harper Ranch, situated below the said Warm Springs Ranch, and which could be irrigated by water reservoired in the Warm Springs Reservoir, and that the defendant, by the taking of the said ranch, would be deprived of the opportunity to so reservoir the water for the irrigation of the said Harper Ranch, to defendant's damage in the sum of one hundred thousand dollars, which was shown by undisputed evidence.

20. The court erred in finding that it was necessary to a public use that the plaintiff acquire the said property, for the reason that it appeared by the evidence that it was only necessary for the said plaintiff to acquire an easement therein, and no evidence whatever was introduced showing that it was necessary for the plaintiff to acquire the fee simple title to said property. (Trans., pp. 506-515.)

Argument.

I.

(a) The plaintiff only required an easement in the lands of the defendant, and it could not condemn a greater interest therein under the laws of the State of Oregon.

(b) If the laws of the State of Oregon did permit the plaintiff to acquire the fee when it only needed an easement for reservoir purposes, such laws would be in violation of the Constitution of the United States in that they would take defendant's property without due process of law in violation of the Fourteenth Amendment to the Constitution of the United States.

(c) The court erred in not sustaining the motion to make the complaint more definite and certain and thereby compelling the plaintiff to allege whether it sought the fee simple title to the land or only an easement therein.

(d) The court erred in failing to adjudge the particular interest in the land which it was necessary for the plaintiff to acquire.

In regard to all of these points it should be stated that the pleadings and the evidence show that the only use which the district intends to make of these lands is to flood them by constructing a dam below these lands across the Malheur River, and thus back the water up over those lands during the high stages of the river during the months of February, March and April, where they will be held until the latter part of the irrigation season, being largely drawn out during the months of July, August and September. According to the testimony of the plaintiff, even at the highest flow line there will be one hundred and fifty-eight acres of the land which will never be overflowed. (Trans., p. 87.) It must be obvious that as the water is drawn out more and more of the land will be uncovered, and as this ranch is situated in a range country it is obvious that the land so uncovered could be used for grazing purposes. It must be equally obvious that so far as the district is concerned, all it requires is the right to flood this land, which is merely an easement, and that for that purpose it does not require the fee.

While it does not appear in the record in this case, it might be stated that after this condemnation both the plaintiff and the defendant saw that it would be entirely feasible to enjoy the grazing privileges on this land without in any way interfering with its use for reservoir purposes, and, therefore, the plaintiff undertook to lease the grazing privileges to a sheep concern for the sum of fifteen thousand dollars. The defendant, on the other hand, claimed that the district had only acquired an easement by its condemnation, and therefore sought to enjoy the grazing privileges itself, and brought a suit in the United States District Court to enjoin the district and its lessee from interfering with it in that regard. In that case on an application for a temporary injunction Judge Bean held that the judgment in condemnation only gave the district an easement, and that the defendant was still the owner of the fee and entitled to graze the land. We attach as an appendix hereto a copy of Judge Bean's decision in that matter. The case has since been tried and finally decided in favor of the Pacific Live Stock Co.

If that decision is adhered to and affirmed on appeal these errors, of course, will become unimportant, but, as we cannot anticipate the result in that regard, we here present our authorities in support of our contentions.

I. The statutes should not be construed as permitting the taking of the fee simple title where an easement is all that is necessary.

II. The plaintiff cannot constitutionally take the fee simple title where an easement is all that is required, even if the legislature does authorize the taking of the fee.

III. The statutes of Oregon do not authorize the taking of the fee where only an easement is required.

Lord's Oregon Laws, sec. 6866;
Statutes of Oregon, 1919, chap. 267;
15 Cyc. 1018;
Washington Cemetery vs. *Prospect Park,* 68 N. Y. 591;
Nichols on Eminent Domain, sec. 358;
Nichols on Eminent Domain, sec. 150;
Lewis on Eminent Domain, sec. 449;
10 R. C. L., p. 88;
2 Kinney on Irrigation, sec. 1098;
1 Farnham on Water Rights, sec. 99a;
Clark vs. *Worcester,* 125 Mass. 226;
Reed vs. *Board of Park Commissioners,* 100 Minn. 167, 110 N. W. 1119;
Bowden vs. *York Shore Water Co.,* 114 Me. 150, 95 Atl. 779;
West Skokie Drainage Dist. vs. *Dawson,* 243 Ill. 175, 90 N. E. 377, 17 Amr. Cas. 776;
Lazarus vs. *Morris,* 212 Pa. 128, 61 Atl. 815;

Shreveport & R. R. Val. Ry. Co. vs. *Hinds,* 50 La. Ann. 781, 24 So. 287;
Idaho-Iowa Lateral & Reservoir Co. vs. *Fisher,* 27 Ida. 695, 151 Pac. 998;
Hunter vs. *Matthews,* 1 Rob. (Va.) 469;
O. R. & N. Co. vs. *Oregon Real Estate Co.,* 10 Or. 444;
Clark vs. *City of Portland,* 62 Or. 124;
Oregonian Ry. vs. *Hill,* 9 Or. 377;
Oregon vs. *Portland Gen. Elec.,* 52 Or. 502;
Oswego vs. *Cobb,* 66 Or. 587;
Lyford vs. *Laconia,* 75 N. H. 220, 72 Atl. 1085, 22 L. R. A. (N. S.) 1063;
Miller vs. *Coms'r of Lincoln Park,* 278 Ill. 400, 116 N. E. 178;
Newton vs. *Manufacturers' Ry.,* 115 Fed. 781;
McCarty vs. *S. P. Co.,* 148 Cal. 211, 82 Pac. 615;
Union Pacific Ry. vs. *Colorado Postal Tel. Cable Co.,* 30 Colo. 133, 69 Pac. 564;
People vs. *Blake,* 19 Cal. 579.

IV. These rules have been expressly applied to reservoirs.

Bowden vs. *York Shore Water Co.,* 114 Me. 150, 95 Atl. 779;
Idaho-Iowa Lateral & Reservoir Co. vs. *Fisher,* 27 Ida. 695, 151 Pac. 998;
Hunter vs. *Matthews,* 1 Rob. (Va.) 469.

V. Defendant was entitled to a clear description of the exact estate which plaintiff sought to acquire.

2 Lewis on Eminent Domain (3rd ed.), sec. 551.

II.

The court erred in admitting the testimony of the witnesses Hunt, Weaver and Greig as to the value of the ranch in question, for the reason that said witnesses are not qualified to give an opinion as to the value thereof.

As we shall point out more in detail later, the defendant produced twelve witnesses, all of whom testified that this property was worth over one hundred and forty thousand dollars for agricultural purposes, and, as we shall point out, practically all of these witnesses were men who had lived most of their lives within a few miles of this property, had known this property most of their lives, had ridden over it, were familiar with climatic conditions of the vicinity, range conditions, water conditions, and the value of hay and pasture in the vicinity of the property, as well as the value of the property itself. The plaintiff, to contradict this testimony, called three men who had formerly been in the employ of the defendant, namely, John Gilcrest, John C. Foley and George Love; one witness (James Morfit), who testified he was "not very much familiar" with the country, but who attempted to figure a value of the ranch from what cattle he thought it would carry from inspecting it; two sheep men, to-wit, Allen and McEwan, who were accustomed to hit the grazing land about the ranch pretty hard with their sheep, and one storekeeper (Drinkwater). As we shall point out later, there were many things connected with the testimony of these witnesses which very much weakens, if it does not entirely destroy, their testimony, and, as we shall point out, the trial judge did not place any dependence upon it. This left as the main reliance of the plaintiff three witnesses, Hunt, Weaver and Greig, and the opinion of the court, which is in the record, shows expressly that it was on their testimony that the court largely based its conclusion. (Trans., pp. 49-50.) In fact, the judge, among other things, said:

> "None of the witnesses on either side, testifying as to value, except Messrs. Gilcrest, Hunt, Greig and Weaver, had an intimate acquaintance with the property or had made a careful examination thereof for the purpose of qualifying to testify as to value."

The fact of the matter is that the three witnesses in question were appointed by the district after this controversy arose to make an appraisement of the property. Prior to their appointment as such "appraisers" they had no more knowledge of the ranch than they had of the Sahara Desert. In fact, they had never seen it, nor had they been anywhere near it. Having been appointed to make this investigation, they could not find time to make it until in December, 1918, and then went to the ranch when it was raining and the ranch was covered with snow, and there spent two days in going over the ranch in that condition. A few days before the trial in November, 1919, they again returned to the ranch for one day. We may be willing to admit that they made "a careful examination thereof *for the purpose of qualifying to testify as to value,*" but we deny that they were qualified to testify to value, for the reason that qualification as to value depends on knowledge of the property and its surroundings, residence in the neighborhood, the ownership of like property in the neighborhood, the sales of other property in the vicinity, and things of that kind, and a person can not qualify himself to testify as to value by going and looking at the property after a dispute has arisen as to its value.

Qualifications of the Witness Hunt.

The testimony of the witness Hunt is found at page 382 of the transcript. He testified on direct examination that he lived at Nyssa, which is on the line between Oregon and Idaho, and is situated twelve miles south of Ontario and sixteen miles south of Vale and one hundred and sixteen miles from the land in question. Before living there he lived at Umatilla. He first saw the Warm Springs Ranch on the 18th of December, 1918, and he spent two days on the property. He placed his value on it right while he was on the ground. The weather was cold and there had been a snowfall over the valley. He went back again on the 20th of October, 1919. On this qualification the defendant objected to the witness testifying (Trans., p. 388), and then further examined him as to his qualifications (Trans., p. 389), and he testified that he lived one hundred and sixteen miles from the Warm Springs Ranch; that he had never been there before his visit when he valued the land in December, 1918. He had gone through the Malheur country twice on his way to Burns, just traveling through, but on neither occasion did he see the Warm Springs Ranch.

"I have never owned any property up anywheres near the vicinity of this Warm Springs Ranch. I have never bought or sold any property up there. I do not know of any sales up there, or the prices at which any property sold in that vicinity. The closest piece of ranch property to this Warm Springs Ranch as to which I know the selling price was the place that Morfit sold over on Willow Creek. That is about ninety miles from the Warm Springs Ranch. I learned about that shortly after the sale was made about two years ago. I don't remember who told me about it. I have been to the Morfit property, but never examined it. I really have no definite knowledge as to the character of the property or its value. I cannot say that I know of any other piece of property which I know the sale value of anywhere near this Warm Springs Ranch. The Morfit place is as close as any that I know of. I never bought any hay in the vicinity of the Warm Springs Ranch. The closest to this ranch that I ever bought any hay would be where I live, which would be one hundred and sixteen miles, and the same would be true as to the sale of hay. I have never wintered any cattle or ranged any cattle anywhere near around this ranch. In fact, I never ranged any cattle at all. I bought and sold cattle. I owned ninety acres. They are enclosed alfalfa ranches. They are in a high state of cultivation. They would not be regarded as range country; of course, the land is all open back of us. I live just on the line of Idaho. (Trans., pp. 389-390.)

Qualifications of the Witness Greig.

The testimony of Greig is found at page 428. The witness Greig testified that he had lived at Ontario since 1905, and prior to that had lived in northern Iowa. He testified that he had very little business in what is called the Malheur Valley above Vale. He owned some property near Nyssa and some property at Dead Ox Flat. He was not familiar with the Warm Springs Ranch until December 19, 1918, "but I have heard of the ranch practically ever since I have been in eastern Oregon."

> "Thereupon counsel for the defendant objected on the ground that no foundation had been laid for it; that it did not appear the witness had any knowledge of the Warm Springs Ranch prior to the time he visited it in the winter of 1918, and again in the winter of 1919; that it did not appear he had any knowledge of any sales of any land in the vicinity, or any lands closer than one hundred miles from the Warm Springs Ranch, or that he had ever farmed it or run cattle on it, or anywhere else in the vicinity, or that he had any knowledge sufficient to enable him to testify on the subject, which objection was overruled and defendant duly excepted to." (Trans., p. 440.)

On cross-examination the witness further testified:

> "I am not in the cattle business and never have been. The closest piece of property which I own to the Warm Springs Ranch is probably eighty or ninety miles away in a straight line, I think. My land is practically along the Snake River. I have never raised any cattle in this country at all or anywhere else in the valley. I have never sold any land in the immediate vicinity of the Warm Springs Ranch, but I have sold land around Vale; that it is in the neighborhood of eighty miles from the ranch. I have never bought any hay any place—I never sold any hay up there. The closest I ever sold any hay was in the Snake Valley." (Trans., p. 442.)

Qualifications of the Witness Weaver.

The testimony of Weaver is found at page 407. He likewise lived at Ontario and had also lived on Willow Creek about fifty-five miles northwest from Ontario. As to the Warm Springs Ranch he testified:

> "I don't know very much about the Warm Springs Ranch belonging to the defendant. I have been there a couple of times, but not when it was anything of a ranch, and I don't really know very much about it, except hearsay. I first saw it in the fall of 1883; there wasn't any ranch there at that time; I think there was a little cabin, possibly there was some location stakes, foundations laid there with willows. I never saw the ranch after that time at any time while I was riding through that country. I never got to the Warm Springs Ranch; I didn't see it again until December, 1918. My work as a cattleman didn't take me over the range very much from Agency on south. I wasn't over that country very much, but between that and the Willow Creek country I was very familiar with it. I have heard of cattle ranches being sold in this range that I have described, but I never did charge my mind with it so as to remember and I couldn't be accurate about the prices nor making the deals." (Trans., p. 409.)

On this testimony defendant objected to his qualifications as follows:

> "Thereupon counsel for the defendant objected on the ground that no proper foundation had been laid for the question and on the ground that the witness had not been shown to be competent or to have knowledge of the ranch for any length of time sufficient for him to know its value, nor any

knowledge of market prices of land in that vicinity." (Trans., pp. 414-415.)

Argument.

It results that two of these witnesses had never seen this ranch until the day they went up there and examined it and placed a value upon it, and the third witness had gone through that country in 1883, when it was all in an Indian Reservation and when there was no ranch there but "a little cabin, possibly there were some location stakes, foundations laid there with willows." From that time he had never seen it until he went to value it when covered with snow in December, 1918. During that time the testimony shows how that ranch and that vicinity had been developed; how ditches had been constructed; the land planted to alfalfa, grain and other crops; the land fenced and used to winter large numbers of cattle, valuable water rights acquired, and during all of this period this witness had known nothing whatever of the ranch. The other witnesses owned no land within ninety to one hundred and sixteen miles of the ranch; had bought and sold no land in the vicinity; knew nothing about the selling prices of any land in the vicinity, and had bought and sold no hay in the vicinity, nor had they wintered any cattle in that vicinity.

The evidence clearly shows the importance of location and the exceptional warm winter on this ranch which made it more valuable than lands even fifteen miles away and the fact that hay on that ranch on account of its proximity to the range was worth several dollars a ton more than hay down in Nyssa and at the railroad. These were all matters of which these witnesses could have no knowledge because they never lived in the vicinity, nor had their business ever taken them to the vicinity.

The case is exactly the same, therefore, as if in a case involving the value of land in Portland men who had lived all their lives at Eugene should come in and testify as to value; men who had never seen the land; knew nothing of the sale price of land in the vicinity; who had never bought or sold any land in the vicinity; who had never owned any land in the vicinity, but who were simply selected to come up from Eugene and examine the land in a snowstorm and place a value upon it.

It would be the same as men at Santa Cruz or Sacramento attempting to testify to the value of real estate in San Francisco after they had testified that they had never been in San Francisco; had never seen the land; knew nothing of the sale price of the land; knew nothing of the production of the land; and, in fact, knew nothing about it until they were selected to come down and place a value upon it.

It seems to us that the trial court not only erred in permitting these persons to testify, but having permitted them to testify, gave an entirely unwarranted weight to the fact that they made during their two days' stay a more or less careful examination of the land. In other words, the defendant's witnesses had known this land ever since they were boys; they had gone back and forth over it riding over it and getting their cattle out; they had lived within a few miles of it all their lives; they had seen the crops grown upon it; they knew what land of the same character sold for; they owned the same kind of land in the same vicinity; they knew what cattle had been wintered upon it; they knew what crops had been produced upon it, but before testifying they again visited the ranch to see what, if any, changes might have been made in it, and because they only stayed on that occasion one day, while these two men who knew nothing of the property at all stayed two days, the court in its opinion states that these men were the only ones "who had made a careful examination thereof for the purpose of qualifying to testify as to value." We do not doubt that they made all the effort they could to qualify, but qualification as to value of land does not come from a two days' stay upon it in a snowstorm. The privilege which the law gives to certain classes of people to testify as to their opinion as to value is based upon the fact that they have known the land; that they have lived near it or been in business near it; that they have gathered the knowledge as to the price at which lands of that character are bought and sold for, or it is based on the fact that they themselves have owned land in the immediate vicinity, of which they are presumed to know the value, and it has never been held that a man, no matter how smart he may be, can come from some remote territory, knowing nothing about the land or the conditions surrounding it, and by merely making an examination of it qualify himself as a witness.

Central Pac. Railroad Co. vs. *Pearson,* 35 Cal. 247, 261-2;
Reed v. *Drais,* 67 Cal. 491;

Standard Furniture Co. vs. *City of Seattle,* 57 Wash. 290, 106 Pac. 491;
Chansky vs. *Williams Construction Co.,* 114 N. Y. Suppl. 687;
Ross vs. *Commissioners of Palisades Interstate,* 90 N. J. L. 461, 101 Atl. 60;
Brown vs. *New Jersey Short Line Railway,* 76 N. J. L. 795, 71 Atl. 271;
Walsh vs. *Board of Education,* 73 N. J. L. 643, 64 Atl. 1088;
Friday vs. *Pennsylvania Ry. Co.,* 204 Pa. St. 405, 54 Atl. 339;
New York etc. Co. vs. *Fraser,* 130 U. S. 611, 32 L. ed. 1031;
Oregon Pottery Co. vs. *Kern,* 30 Ore. 328, 49 Pac. 917;
Michael vs. *Crescent Pipe Line Co.,* 159 Pa. St. 99, 28 Atl. 204;
Swan vs. *Middlesex,* 101 Mass. 173;
San Diego Land D. Co. vs. *Neale,* 88 Cal. 50, 67.

III.

The court erred in permitting witnesses for the defendant to testify as to the sale prices of specific pieces of property not involved in the case.

The witness, J. C. Foley, resided in the extreme westerly portion of Harney Valley, which is over seventy miles distant from the land in controversy. He testified that he based his value of the land on what lands were selling for in Harney Valley and the sale of the Vischer Ranch to Mr. Peterson. (Trans., p. 327.) Thereupon, over the objection of the defendant, he was permitted to testify to the price at which a particular ranch sold in his neighborhood and also the amount that that ranch produced per acre. (Trans., p. 328.)

James Morfit was likewise a witness for the plaintiff and testified that he lived on Willow Creek, which would be about sixty-six miles from the Warm Springs Ranch. He testified that he owned thirteen hundred acres of pasture land, and over the objection of the defendant he was permitted to testify to the fact that it was for sale and as to his opinion as to its market value, and also as to how it compared with the Warm Springs Ranch. (Trans., p. 352.)

These rulings, we respectfully submit, were erroneous. It is a well-settled rule that on cross-examination of a witness in order to test his testimony the adverse party may cross-examine him as to his knowledge of specific sales of other properties, but on direct examination or redirect examination such a method of examination is entirely improper.

> *Central Pacific R. R. Co.* vs. *Pearson,* 35 Cal. 247;
> *Reclamation District No. 73* vs. *Inglin,* 31 Cal. App. 495, 160 Pac. 1098;
> *Oregon R. & N. Co.* vs. *Eastlack,* 54 Ore. 196;
> *Pac. Ry. & Nav. Co.* vs. *Elmore Packing Co.,* 60 Ore. 534.

While the authorities in the different states are in conflict on this subject we respectfully submit that the rule relied upon by us is the correct one. For the cases pro and con see

> 2 Lewis on Eminent Domain (3rd ed.), sec. 662;
> 16 Cyc., p. 1138.

The reason of this rule is that it would introduce

into the case a collateral issue which the adverse party could not well be prepared to meet.

In other words, near the end of the trial of this case at Portland, the plaintiff had a witness testify as to the value of a piece of land in Harney Valley which the witness himself testifies is "about the most inaccessible place in the United States" (Trans., p. 331), and also has this witness testify as to what that land produced per acre, and had another witness give like testimony as to land on Willow Creek in Malheur County.

It would be practically impossible without an elaborate trial for the adverse party to present to the jury the surroundings which might produce the value testified to by the witness as to the particular tracts of land. It would be necessary to go into the question of their water rights, their climate, their location with respect to range and transportation, and these are all things that the adverse party could not reasonably be prepared to do, and if it was attempted it would distract the attention of the jury from the real issue in the case.

The prejudicial character of this testimony is clear, for the witness Foley directly testified that he had based his opinion as to the value of the lands involved in this case on the sale of this particular piece of land in Harney Valley (Trans., pp. 327-328), and, he having testified to the actual sale of that land and that it was in his opinion better than the land of the defendant, the prejudicial effect produced by this testimony can readily be seen.

IV.

The court erred in refusing the defendant damages caused by the separation of the thousand acres of land of defendant from the land taken.

The evidence on this subject is to the effect that the Warm Springs Ranch is a ranch situated in the midst of a grazing country where there is a large amount of public or government range. The cattle are wintered on the ranch and in the summer time enjoy the range, and they cannot enjoy the range unless they have means of obtaining water. For this purpose isolated tracts are acquired in the range in order to enable the cattle to obtain water. About a thousand acres of those isolated tracts situated from two to four miles from the Warm Springs Ranch were owned by the defendant. The testimony all showed that they were immediately tributary to that ranch and owned for the purpose of protecting the cattle which wintered at that ranch and ranged on the adjoining range in the summer time. The testimony as to the damage which would be caused to these lands by the taking away of the Warm Springs Ranch was as follows:

The witness Jones testified that they would depreciate in value one-half. (Trans., p. 151.)

The witness Sitz testified that the value would be decreased one-third or one-half, or maybe more. (Trans., pp. 162-163.)

The witness Fairman testified that they would be depreciated fifty per cent. (Trans., p. 167.)

The witness Altnow testified that they would be

depreciated but he could not say to what extent. (Trans., p. 174.)

The witness Dunton testified that it would reduce the value of those lands pretty near the full value. (Trans., p. 178.)

The witness Woodard testified that the lands would be depreciated one-half anyway. (Trans., p. 187.)

The witness Goodman testified that if this ranch was taken the outlaying pieces would not be worth anything. (Trans., pp. 191-192.)

The witness Blackwell testified that they would be depreciated one-half. (Trans., p. 198.)

The witness Spurlock testified that it would detract from their value, but he could not say how much. (Trans., p. 213.)

The witness Peterson testified that they would be depreciated fifty per cent. (Trans., pp. 254-255.)

The witness Olsen testified to the ownership of these tracts by the Pacific Live Stock Company. (Trans., p. 245.)

The testimony generally in the record is that land of this kind is worth about ten dollars an acre, and, assuming that it was depreciated one-half, the defendant should have been allowed five thousand dollars damages with respect thereto.

The only testimony on this subject by the defendant was as follows:

The witness Love on direct examination had testified that he did not see how the taking of this land could decrease the value of this land (Trans., p. 336), but on cross-examination he admitted that those lands were more valuable in connection with the Warm

Springs Ranch and would bring more money in connection with that ranch. (Trans., p. 340.)

The witness Gilcrest gave his opinion that they would not depreciate because the cattle could still range there in the summer time. This is obviously answered by the defendant's witness Love that they would be more valuable if the cattle after ranging there could have the Warm Springs Ranch at which to winter, and this must be obvious.

The same may be said of the testimony of the witness Allen (Trans., p. 357), and the testimony of the witness McEwan, both of whom had been using these lands for watering their sheep.

It seems to us that there is no substantial conflict in the evidence, and that it clearly appears that these watering holes and isolated tracts are owned as a part of the ranch itself, and are more valuable connected with it than in any other way. The fact that these lands are not physically contiguous to the lands condemned is not material. If they are in the immediate neighborhood and are owned and operated as one property the damage to them by the severance may be recovered.

15 Cyc., pp. 729-733.

V.

The court erred in not allowing the defendant damages caused by the fact that it had a thousand tons of hay on the ranch which it would have to remove on account of the condemnation.

The judgment in condemnation in this case was

actually entered December 9, 1919, and by paying the damages assessed in court the plaintiff was then entitled to possession. (Trans., pp. 64, 524-525.)

The defendant in the previous summer had produced a thousand tons of hay which was then stacked on the property, and it was the intention to feed it during the winter of 1919-20. Obviously, there were only three things that could be done to save this hay:

(1) To bale it and take it to the railroad and sell it. The evidence shows that that would be practically prohibitive, as the cost of baling it and carrying it would absorb the value of it before it reached the market.

(2) To move it far enough off of the property so that it would not be flooded, and there make new arrangements for feeding it during the winter season.

(3) By bringing to the ranch immediately a large amount of cattle and have them consume the hay before the ranch was flooded.

This latter alternative would only be available from a legal standpoint in case the plaintiff only acquired an easement in the land. If it acquired the fee, of course, the defendant would have to vacate at once. Testimony was introduced as to the additional expense that would be caused by proceeding in either of these ways, and the evidence clearly showed that the expense would exceed the amount prayed for, namely, seven thousand five hundred dollars. The testimony on this subject is as follows:

The witness Jones testified that if it could be fed on the ranch it was worth eighteen dollars a ton, and that if it was hauled he would not give five dollars a ton for it. (Trans., pp. 151-152.)

The witness Fairman testified that the cost would be five dollars a ton or five thousand dollars. (Trans., pp. 168-169.)

The witness Altnow testified it would cost from six to seven dollars a ton or six or seven thousand dollars. (Trans., pp. 104-105.)

The witness Duntan testified that it would cost ten dollars a ton or ten thousand dollars. (Trans., p. 178.)

The witness Woodard testified that it would cost ten dollars a ton or ten thousand dollars. (Trans., p. 187.)

The witness Goodman testified it would cost eight dollars a ton or eight thousand dollars. (Trans., p. 192.)

The witness Blackwell testified that it would depreciate the hay five dollars a ton or five thousand dollars. (Trans., p. 199.)

The witness Newell testified that it would cost five dollars a ton or five thousand dollars. (Trans., p. 223.)

The witness Olsen testified what the loss would be in case a large number of cattle were brought in there to feed up the hay immediately before the land was flooded. He testified that it would cause a loss of six thousand five hundred dollars. (Trans., p. 248.)

There is no testimony contradicting this except the testimony of the witness McEwan, who testified that if he owned the hay he would take a chance on feeding it. (Trans., p. 372.) On cross-examination, however, he admitted that the hay would be very much more valuable if it was not to be flooded; at least three dollars a ton. (Trans., pp. 373-374.)

The court, in its opinion, stated:

> "I have not included the hay now on the property. It is not sought to be condemned. It is personal property and will be no more affected by the judgment in this case than any other personal property belonging to the defendant now on the ranch." (Trans., p. 51.)

It seems to us that this is not an ordinary case of personal property on property condemned. Generally such property can readily be removed and, at any rate, has a ready market value. But this is a case of an isolated ranch; in a territory where hay is grown to be fed on the ranch where it is grown; where it is not feasible to market it, and it has no market value if it has to be carried to the railroad. This is, therefore, a direct loss proximately caused by the condemnation and is a proper element of damages.

> *Oregon & Cal. R. R. Co.* vs. *Barlow,* 3 Ore. 311;
> 15 Cyc., pp. 741, 733.

VI.

The court erred in not allowing the defendant the value of this ranch based on its adaptability to use as a reservoir—the testimony being undisputed as to the value of the ranch for reservoir purposes in the sum of two hundred and fifty thousand dollars.

Only two witnesses testified as to the value of this ranch as a reservoir site. These witnesses were E. G. Hopson (Trans., p. 92), an engineer who had for many years been in charge of the government reclamation work and who examined for the government the Warm Springs reservoir site and laid out the project which was finally taken over by the Warm Springs Irrigation District, and W. C. Hammatt (Trans., p. 124), an engineer of extensive experience in the Western States in irrigation matters, and both of whom had personal knowledge of this reservoir site. Both of these witnesses testified that they considered that for reservoir purposes the property was worth two hundred and fifty thousand dollars. It is unnecessary to review that testimony, as their competency to testify was not questioned, and their testimony on that subject is not disputed by any witnesses, nor did the plaintiff make any attempt whatever to controvert their testimony, evidently taking the position that value for reservoir purposes was not recoverable.

All of the other witnesses in the case who testified to value based their testimony entirely upon the agricultural uses of the land, and expressly testified that they did not undertake to testify as to the value of the land for reservoir purposes. (Jones, Trans., p. 157; Sitz, p. 162; Fairman, pp. 167-169; Altnow, p. 175; Duntan, p. 185; Woodard, p. 185; Goodman, p. 191; Blackwell, p. 199; Hanley, p. 206; Robertson, p. 209; Spurlock, p. 213; Daly, p. 227; Peterson, p. 254; Morfit, p. 351; McEwan, p. 371; Hunt, p. 402; and Greig, p. 461.) It should be noted that while these witnesses did not attempt to value the land for reservoir purposes, they testified that it had been considered as a reservoir site for over twenty years.

The plaintiff took the position that the value of the land for reservoir purposes, for which it was being condemned, could not be recovered, and based its contention on the decision in the case of *United States* vs. *Seufert Bros. Co.,* 78 Fed. 520. We are confident that that case does not in any way sustain the contention of the plaintiff, and that if it did it would be contrary to numerous decisions of the Supreme Court of the United States.

The following cases clearly demonstrate our right to recover the value of this land, considering the highest use to which it can be put, which obviously under the testimony is to use it as a reservoir site:

> *United States vs. Chandler-Dunbar Power Co.,* 229 U. S. 53, 33 Sup. Ct. 667;
> *Oregon R. & Nav. Co.* vs. *Taffe,* 67 Ore. 102;
> *Brown* vs. *Forest Water Co.,* 213 Pa. St. 440, 62 Atl. 1078;
> *Alloway* vs. *Nashville,* 88 Tenn. 510, 135 S. W. 123;
> *U. S.* vs. *Great Falls Mfg. Co.,* 112 U. S. 846, 28 L. ed. 846;
> *San Diego Land Co.* vs. *Neale,* 78 Cal. 63, 88 Cal. 50;
> *Spring Valley Water Co.* vs. *Drinkhouse,* 92 Cal. 528;
> *In re Bensel,* 206 Fed. 369;
> *Gibson* vs. *Norwalk,* 13 Oh. C. C. 437;
> *Moulton* vs. *Newburyport Water Co.,* 137 Mass. 163;
> *Sargent* vs. *Merrimac,* 196 Mass. 171, 81 N. E. 970;
> *Mississippi etc. Co.* vs. *Patterson, 98* U. S. *403*, 25 L. ed. 206.

VII.

The demurrer to the complaint should have been sustained because the complaint did not allege any appropriation by the plaintiff of any water for the reservoir, nor any application to the State Engineer for a permit to reservoir the water. The court also erred in permitting proof of an alleged appropriation without any pleading thereof.

As we have already pointed out, the complaint alleged no appropriation by the plaintiff, nor did it allege any application to the State Engineer for a permit to appropriate or reservoir the water. It seems to be pretty well settled that where a person seeks to condemn property and it is necessary to obtain a franchise or permit from some official before it can use the property, he must obtain the same in advance and allege the obtaining thereof in his complaint.

> *Minn. Canal & Power Co. vs. Fall Lake Boom Co.,* 127 Minn. 23, 148 N. W. 561.

Notwithstanding the lack of allegation on this subject, the court in its findings found that such a permit had been obtained. (Trans., pp. 57-58.) The facts in this matter are that the State Engineer withdrew this water for the benefit of the United States on April 8, 1914. (Trans., pp. 80-81.) Thereafter, on March 5, 1919, the State Water Board assigned these withdrawal orders to the Warm Springs Irrigation District. (Trans., pp. 82-83.) Later the plaintiff attempted to introduce two documents certified by the State Engineer in the form of applications to appropriate water by the Warm Springs Irrigation District and endorsed as having been received in the office of the State Engineer on February 14, 1916 (Trans., pp. 463-469), but it was made to appear that this paper was simply made up a few days before the trial, and that the original paper was merely a withdrawal of the water for the government, and no paper at that time was filed in the name of the Warm Springs Irrigation District. (Trans., p. 471.)

The defendant relies on chapter 87 of the Laws of 1913. That act provides for co-operation between the state and national governments for the purpose of making investigations of the water resources of the State, and section 3 permits the State Engineer to withdraw water from appropriation pending the investigation. That act does not constitute the withdrawal of the water as an appropriation, nor does it authorize the assignment of any such withdrawal. In fact, if anything, the withdrawal would seem to be an absolute impediment to any appropriation by the Warm Springs Irrigation District. At all events, it did not constitute an appropriation by that district, and the mere writing up of an application to appropriate water a few days before the trial and having it certified to by the State Engineer as having been filed in 1916 could not constitute an appropriation by the Warm Springs Irrigation District, particularly when that district was not incorporated until the 29th day of May, 1918. (Trans., p. 74.) In other words, the plaintiff produces a document purporting to be an application to appropriate water by the Warm

Springs Irrigation District, solemnly certified to by the State Engineer as having been filed in 1916, when their own witness testified that he made it up himself a few days before the trial in 1919, and the Warm Springs Irrigation District was not even in existence until 1918.

VIII.

There was a conflict in the evidence as to the value of the Warm Springs Ranch for agricultural purposes; the witnesses for plaintiff testifying it was worth about fifty-five thousand dollars; the witnesses for defendant testifying it was worth about one hundred and forty-five thousand dollars; and the court fixing the value at ninety thousand dollars. We recognize that the evidence being conflicting the decision on that subject will not be reviewed by this court, but for the purpose of showing the importance of the errors committed by the court, particularly in the admission of evidence, we here briefly review the testimony as to the agricultural value, showing that a large preponderance of the evidence showed a value of over one hundred and forty-five thousand dollars for agricultural purposes.

The witness Hopson, who had investigated this project for the government and on behalf of the government collected the data for the co-operative report as to this project, testified that the agricultural value of this land was $143,350. (Trans., p. 102.)

W. C. Hammatt, a civil engineer, testified that its agricultural value was $161,913.05. (Trans., p. 131.)

William Jones testified to its agricultural value, based on its production, at $146,500. (Trans., p. 147.)

The witness Sitz testified to its agricultural value, based on its production, at $160,000. (Trans., p. 160.)

The witness Fairman testified to its agricultural value at $146,000. (Trans., p. 166.)

The witness Altnow testified to its agricultural value at $133,770. (Trans., p. 174.)

The witness Dunton testified to its agricultural value at $151,295. (Trans., p. 178.)

The witness Woodard testified to its agricultural value at $160,000. (Trans., pp. 186-187.)

The witness Goodman testified to its agricultural value at $140,995. (Trans., p. 191.)

The witness Blackwell testified to its agricultural value at from $125,000 to $150,000. (Trans., p. 198.)

The witness Hanley testified to its agricultural value at $190,000. (Trans., pp. 205-206.)

The witness Robertson testified to its agricultural value at $133,920. (Trans., p. 209.)

The witness Spurlock testified to its agricultural value at $149,600. (Trans., p. 213.)

The witness Davis testified to its agricultural value at $154,000. (Trans., p. 216.)

The witness Daly testified to its agricultural value at $175,000. (Trans., p. 227.)

The witness Howard testified to its agricultural value at $150,000. (Trans., p. 237.)

The witness Drake testified to its agricultural value at $192,000. (Trans., p. 242.)

The witness Cox testified to its agricultural value at $180,000. (Trans., p. 250.)

The witness Peterson testified to its agricultural value at $143,000. (Trans., p. 254.)

The witness Gault testified to its agricultural value at $145,917.50. (Trans., p. 259.)

Most of these witnesses lived from fifteen to twenty-five miles away from this property, and had done so for a great many years. They knew the climate, the range conditions, the water supply, the sale price of land, the sale price of hay, the number of cattle wintered upon it, and its production.

As opposed to this the defendant called the witness Gilcrest, who had formerly been a superintendent of the company, and who was so bitter against the company that he had even refused to testify in proceedings to determine the company's water rights, and the trial judge in his opinion states:

> "His testimony and estimate of value, however, must, I think, be weighed in the light of his present attitude towards the company." (Trans., p. 50.)

The witness Foley, who had formerly been an assistant superintendent of the company, but who had not seen the ranch for many years, and when he saw it it was only used for pasture, testified:

> "I never did consider that ranch as having any value beyond winter pasturage, and have had no occasion to change my mind. (Trans., p. 325.)
>
> * * * * * * * *
>
> "Mr. Hope asked me to come as a witness. He came to my ranch and asked me my idea of the ranch, and I gave it to him. I have had this idea of the value of this ranch for about twenty-five years." (Trans., p. 329.)

It is obvious from this that without seeing the ranch for twenty-five years, during which it had been developed into an alfalfa ranch, this witness gave his estimate of its value.

The witness Love was likewise a discharged employee of the company. He testified that the property was worth from sixty to seventy thousand dollars. (Trans., p. 335.) He admitted, however, on cross-examination, that he had been asked by the company to testify in the case, and in answer to that request he asked that he be employed as general assistant superintendent of the company. (Trans., p. 338.) He told the representative of the company at that time that he thought the ranch was worth from seventy to ninety thousand dollars. (Trans., p. 339.) Certainly the testimony of such a witness is not of persuasive value.

The witness Morfit, who testified that he did not know much about the country (Trans., p. 341), attempted to place a value on it by figuring what profit he would make by placing fifteen hundred head of cattle upon it. (Trans., p. 345.) He estimated that he would make a profit of $14,400. (Trans., p. 346.) On cross-examination it was shown that on his own figures he would have in fact made a profit of $26,630, which, even if capitalized at ten per cent, would have amounted to $260,000. (Trans., pp. 349-351.)

The testimony of the witness Allen (Trans., p. 353) and the witness McEwan (Trans., p. 365) can be explained by the fact that they were sheep men with the inherent dislike for the plaintiff engaged in the cattle business.

The witness Drinkwater was merely a storekeeper.

In connection with his testimony, however, it developed that he had no information as to the water rights of the property. He admitted that if it had water rights for eleven hundred and forty-three acres it would be very valuable, as he only figured water for five hundred acres. (Trans., p. 379.) As we showed that the ranch did in fact have water rights to that extent, this entirely destroys his testimony. (Trans., pp. 263-265.)

It also appeared that the people associated with Drinkwater owned eighty acres of land in the canyon immediately north of the defendant's ranch. According to his testimony this had twelve to fifteen acres under ditch, the balance being hill land. This he was selling to the district at $3,350. Eighty acres just like it of the company's land the district appraised at three dollars an acre or two hundred and forty dollars, and, in fact, it developed that as a matter of fact that the few acres on this eighty acres which were supposed to be under ditch were partially on the company's land and not on this land. (Trans., pp. 489-490.)

The only other witnesses for the defendant were the witnesses Hunt, Weaver and Greig, all of whom testified to the lowest figures of any of the witnesses, namely, $50,877.25. We have already reviewed their testimony and showed that they were not qualified to testify, and still the opinion of the trial judge clearly shows that he was more impressed with their testimony than any of the other witnesses in the case.

In view of this situation, it is obvious that the errors in admitting their testimony, as well as the errors in permitting other witnesses for the defendants to testify as to the amount of specific sales of other lands, were extremely prejudicial.

Range Conditions.

The following testimony shows the favorable location of this ranch with regard to a very large public range:

Jones	Transcript, p.	148
Sitz	" "	160
Altnow	"	173
Blackwell	"	196
Robertson	"	208
Davis	" "	215
Drake	"	242

Water Rights.

The following testimony shows the water supply to which this ranch is entitled. The adjudication decree in the matter of the waters of Malheur River adjudicates water for eleven hundred and forty three acres from the ditches on both the east and west sides of the ranch. This is extremely important because both the witness Hunt (Trans., p. 395) and the witness Greig (Trans., p. 446) showed that they based their valuation on a very much less quantity of water, and the same is true as to the witness Drinkwater. The witness Sitz (Trans., p. 161) and the witness Fairman (Trans., p. 168) testified as to the supply of water, and the witness Armstrong testified as to the right of the company in the East Side Ditch. (Trans., p. 118.)

Climatic Conditions and Winter Feeding.

The favorable location of the Warm Springs Ranch for winter feeding is established by all of the testimony, which shows that the ranch is so situated that it is much warmer than the surrounding country, and that they can begin feeding the cattle there ~~earlier~~ later and leave off much ~~later~~ earlier than in any other part of the country. (See testimony of Jones, Trans., p. 148; Sitz, p. 160; Fairman, p. 167; Goodman, p. 191; Robertson, p. 208; Davis, p. 215; Newell, p. 221; Daly, p. 230; Miller, p. 311; Howard, p. 238; Drake, p. 242, and Peterson, p. 254.)

Classification of Lands and Crops.

The property is fully equipped with farm buildings and improvements at a value of ten thousand dollars or upwards (Trans., pp. 100, 127); has ditches on it which the witness Gilcrest himself testified cost over twenty thousand dollars (Trans., p. 315), and the following classification made by defendant shows the character of the crops raised:

Garden	4	acres
Alfalfa	303	"
Clover	73	
Native Meadow	184	
Rye Grass	198	"
Sage and Greasewood	453	"
Willow and Thicket	70	
Total	1,285	"

Non-irrigable hill land.	1,275	"
	2,560	"

(Trans., pp. 96-99.)

A like classification by the plaintiff is even more favorable to the defendant:

268 acres of alfalfa land.
201 acres wild hay land.
40 acres mixed hay land.
65 acres plowed land.
335 acres rye pasture.
20 acres rye pasture.
1,251 acres fenced greasewood.
475 acres unfenced land.

Total, 2,655 acres. (Trans., p. 392.)

Evidence of Other Sales.

The evidence in the record of sales of other properties in the vicinity all tends to show that defendant's land was under-valued.

William Jones testified to one hundred and sixty acres of land selling for ten thousand dollars just above Drewsey. (Trans., p. 156.)

The witness Altnow testified that any good alfalfa land was worth one hundred and fifty dollars an acre; that he knew of sales around Ontario for three or four hundred dollars an acre; that Mr. Howard bought a ranch in the neighborhood at one hundred and fifty dollars an acre; that land sold at Agency in the neighborhood of one hundred and fifty dollars an acre; that a small ranch of one hundred and sixty acres sold for fourteen thousand dollars; not all alfalfa, had a lot of pasture land and wild grass. (Trans., p. 175.)

The witness Woodard testified to the sale of three hundred and twenty acres for thirty thousand dollars and only about half of it was improved. The balance was not any better than the hill land around the Warm Springs Ranch. (Trans., p. 188.)

The witness Davis testified that he sold a place to Mr. Howard above Drewsey containing three hundred acres for thirty thousand dollars and only one hundred and fifty acres of it was producing hay. The balance of it was common raw land. (Trans., p. 117.)

The witness Daly testified to this same sale (Trans., p. 230), and likewise the witness Howard (Trans., p. 238.)

The witness Love testified that raw sagebrush land without any water was selling around Vale from eighty to one hundred and twenty-five dollars an acre; that the only prospect it had of getting water was what water it would get from the Warm Springs reservoir and the purchaser would have to pay for that. (Trans., p. 337.)

The witness Hunt testified that around his place alfalfa land sold for from one hundred and seventy-five dollars to three hundred dollars an acre. (Trans., p. 400.)

The witness Weaver admitted that there was no difference whatever between the company's land which the plaintiff's witnesses appraised from one dollar and a quarter to ten dollars an acre and the

Drinkwater eighty immediately adjoining it, which was sold for thirty-three hundred dollars. (Trans., p. 419.)

Greig sold his alfalfa ranch at two hundred and forty-one dollars an acre and another one at one hundred and seventy-four dollars an acre, and he admitted that alfalfa land was selling as high as four hundred dollars an acre. (Trans., p. 443.)

In view of these facts we respectfully submit that there was at all events a sharp conflict in the evidence as to the value of this ranch for agricultural purposes; that the evidence largely predominated in favor of the defendant, and that for that reason the errors complained of were extremely prejudicial, and that the judgment should be reversed and a new trial granted.

Respectfully submitted,

JOHN L. RAND,
P. J. GALLAGHER,
W. H. BROOKE,
EDWARD F. TREADWELL,
Attorneys for Plaintiff in Error.

APPENDIX.

In the District Court of the United States for the District of Oregon.

PACIFIC LIVE STOCK COMPANY,
Complainant,
vs.
WARM SPRINGS IRRIGATION DISTRICT ET AL.,
Defendants.

Portland, Oregon, Monday, February 9, 1920.
R. S. BEAN, District Judge:

In December, 1919, judgment was entered in this court appropriating to defendant, its successors and assigns, certain lands belonging to the plaintiff for reservoir purposes. Thereafter the defendant, assuming that it thus obtained the fee simple to such lands and the improvements thereon, entered into a contract with the defendant Stanfield for the sale to him of the improvements and for the leasing to him of so much of the land as will not be covered from time to time by the water of the defendant's reservoir. The object of this suit is to enjoin the performance of such contract.

The question thus presented is whether under the laws of this state the defendant acquired, by the judgment of condemnation, a mere easement in the property or the fee simple title. There is nothing in the complaint in the condemnation suit indicating an intention to condemn the fee, or anything more than the right to overflow the land for reservoir purposes, nor does the judgment in terms award anything more.

The laws governing the organization of Irrigation Districts provide that the Board of Directors thereof may acquire by lease, purchase or condemnation lands and water rights, easements and other property necessary for the construction, use, supply, maintenance, repair and improvement of any canal or canals, or works proposed to be constructed by said Board, and may also so acquire lands and all necessary appurtenances for reservoirs and the right to store water. In acquiring the property and rights by condemnation, the Board shall proceed in the name of the District under the provisions of the laws of the state. The legal title to all property so acquired shall be vested in the Irrigation District, and be held by it in trust for the uses and purposes set forth in the law. (Laws 1917, 743; Laws 1919, 443.)

The general laws of the state provide for the acquisition of lands or easements therein by condemnation and declare that upon the payment into court of the damages assessed the court shall give judgment appropriating the lands, properties, rights, easements, etc., to the corporation, and thereafter the same shall be the property of such corporation. (Lord's Ore. Laws, sec. 6866.)

There are no express words in any of these statutes authorizing the acquisition by condemnation of the fee to land intended for reservoir purposes, and it will not be implied that any greater interest or estate can be thus taken than is necessary to satisfy the requirements of the District. The purposes of the statute and the needs of the District are fully satisfied by the taking of an easement or right to overflow the land, and that is all in my judgment the defendant acquired or could have acquired by the judgment of condemnation. (*Oregonian Ry. Co.* vs. *Hill,* 9 Ore. 377; *O. R. N. Co.* vs. *Oregon Real Estate Co.,* 10 Ore. 444; 15 Cyc. 1018.) The title to the land in question and the improvements thereon remained in the plaintiff, subject to the right of the Irrigation District to use and occupy the same for reservoir purposes. (15 Cyc. 1021.)

It is claimed that chapter 138 of the laws of 1919 empowers the District to make the contract in question. That statute has no bearing on the instant case. It simply authorizes an Irrigation District to sell and dispose of property acquired by gift, purchase or by right of eminent domain which, by reason of a subsequent change in the plans of the District or other reason, is no longer necessary for the purposes for which it was acquired. No such state of facts appear here. There has been no change in the plans of the District since the judgment of condemnation by which it no longer requires the use of the property for the purposes for which it was condemned.

Injunction will issue as prayed for.

IN THE

United States Circuit Court of Appeals

FOR THE NINTH CIRCUIT

PACIFIC LIVE STOCK COMPANY, a Corporation,
Plaintiff in Error,

vs.

THE WARM SPRINGS IRRIGATION DISTRICT, a Municipal Corporation,
Defendant in Error.

BRIEF FOR DEFENDANT IN ERROR

Upon Writ of Error to the District Court of the United States for the District of Oregon.

ED. R. COULTER,
H. C. EASTHAM,
ALLEN H. McCURTAIN,
THOMAS G. GREENE,
Attorneys for Defendant in Error.

THE IVY PRESS, PORTLAND

[illegible]

Names and addresses of Attorneys upon this writ of error:

EDWARD F. TREADWELL,
1323 Merchants Exchange Bldg., San Francisco, Cal.

JOHN L. RAND,
Baker City, Oregon,

P. J. GALLAGER,
Ontario, Oregon,

W. H. BROOKE,
Ontario, Oregon,
For Plaintiff in Error.

EDWARD F. COULTER,
Weiser, Idaho,

HARRY C. EASTHAM,
Vale, Oregon,

ALLEN H. McCURTAIN,
Henry Bldg., Portland, Oregon,

THOMAS G. GREENE,
Henry Bldg., Portland, Oregon,
For Defendant in Error.

No. 3512

IN THE

United States Circuit Court of Appeals

FOR THE NINTH CIRCUIT

PACIFIC LIVE STOCK COMPANY, a Corporation,
Plaintiff in Error,

vs.

THE WARM SPRINGS IRRIGATION DISTRICT, a Municipal Corporation,
Defendant in Error.

BRIEF FOR DEFENDANT IN ERROR

STATEMENT

In 1895 the legislature of Oregon passed an act providing for the organization of irrigation districts as public bodies and agencies of the State with the powers of taxation, eminent domain, and other attributes of municipal corporations, to be managed and conducted for the public benefit (Lord's Oregon Laws, Secs. 6167-6217). The law was adopted from the California act of 1887 known as the Wright Act. It has been amended from time to time to keep step with the growth of public sentiment on the subject of water conservation, and with the development of irrigation projects through public instrumentalities, and was re-enacted, with various amendments adopted *ad interim*, in 1917 (General Laws of Oregon 1917, Chap. 357, pp. 743-781).

The following is a brief outline of the act, with quotation of such sections as are deemed necessary to the decision of this case:

Section 1 provides for organization of an irrigation district whenever fifty or a majority of the owners of land irrigated or susceptible of irrigation desire to purchase, construct and operate works, or to assume as principal or guarantor indebtedness on account of district lands to the United States under the Federal reclamation laws, and sets out the procedure necessary.

Sections 2 to 13 provide for a hearing on the petition by the county court, notice of election for organization of the district, conduct of said election, canvass of votes by the county court, certification of the result, election and qualification of officers of the district, organization, meetings and quorum of the board of directors.

Section 14 authorizes and empowers the board to take conveyances in the name of the district; to maintain actions and suits, and the court shall therein "take judicial knowledge of the organization of, and boundaries" of irrigation districts.

Section 15 contains directions for surveys and plans, appointment of engineer, adoption in whole or in part of any surveys, plans and specifications which may have been made, submission thereof to and approval by State Engineer.

Sections 16 and 17 provide for advertising proposals for work, and letting contracts, and prohibit any director or officer from being personally interested in any such contract.

Section 18 provides for contract with the United States to acquire control over Government land within the district and of complying with the provisions of the Act of Congress to promote reclamation of arid lands, approved August 11, 1916; to assume as principal or guarantor indebtedness to the United States; to pledge its bonds, etc., and "any property acquired by the district may be conveyed to the United States insofar as the same may be needed by the United States for the construction, operation and maintenance of works for the benefit of the district under any contract that may be entered into with the United States pursuant to this Act."

Sections 19 to 23 prescribe procedure for bond elections, sale of bonds, payment and redemption of bonds and interest coupons, contract with the United States, etc.; sections 24 to 27 provide for assessment and taxation; section 28 for method of payment of claims; section 29, qualification of voters, and section 30, contest of elections.

Section 31, as amended by an act of the legislative assembly of 1919 (General Laws of Oregon 1919, Chap. 267, p. 443 effective May 22, 1919) confers powers of eminent domain and is as follows:

> Section 2. That section 31 of Chapter 357 of the general laws of Oregon for the year 1917 be, and the same hereby is, amended so as to read as follows:
>
> Sec. 31. Eminent Domain. This board and its agents and employes shall have the right to enter upon any land to make surveys, and may locate the necessary irrigation or drainage works and the line for any canal or canals, and the necessary branches for the same, on any lands which may be deemed best for such location. Said board shall also have the right to acquire, either by lease, purchase, condemnation, or other legal means, all lands and waters and water rights, rights of way, easements and other property, including canals and works and the whole of irrigation systems or projects constructed or being constructed by private owners, necessary for the construction, use, supply, maintenance, re-

pair and improvement of any canal or canals and works proposed to be constructed by said board, and shall also have the right to so acquire lands, and all necessary appurtenances for reservoirs and the right to store water in constructed reservoirs, for the storage of needful waters, or for any other purposes reasonably necessary for the purposes of said district. The property, the right to condemn which is hereby given, shall include property already devoted to public use which is less necessary than the use for which it is required by the district, whether used for irrigation or any other purpose. The right of way is hereby given, dedicated and set apart, to locate, construct and maintain said works over and through any of the lands which are now or may be the property of this state. In the acquisition of property or rights by condemnation, the board shall proceed in the name of the district under the provisions of the laws of the state of Oregon.

The use of all water required for the irrigation of the lands of any district formed under the provisions of this act, together with all water rights and rights to appropriate water, rights of way for canals and ditches, sites for reservoirs, and all other property required in fully carrying out the provisions of this act, is hereby declared to be a public use more necessary and more beneficial than any other use, either public or private, to which said water, water rights, rights to appropriate water, lands or other property have been or may be appropriated within said district.

The legal title to all property acquired under the provisions of this act shall immediately and by operation of law vest in such irrigation district, and shall be held by such district in trust for and is hereby dedicated and set apart to the uses and purposes set forth in this act; and said board is hereby authorized and empowered to hold, use, acquire, manage, occupy, possess and dispose of said property as herein provided.

The remaining sections of the act, 32 to 50, are not material to any question raised by the assignments of error.

The defendant in error was duly created and organized under the provisions of this law, and whatever question there may have been respecting the legality and regularity of its organization was set at rest by the Supreme Court of the State of Oregon in the case of *Herrett v. Warm Springs Irrigation District,* 86 Or. 343, affirming an adjudication to that effect made by the Circuit Court of the State of Oregon for Malheur County, Oregon. Since the decision in that case, the same court has held that proceedings for the confirmation of the organization of an irrigation district and the issuance of its bonds, under the law above referred to, are in the nature of proceedings in rem, and that the Supreme Court on appeal from a decree of confirmation must examine every question presented by the record whether discussed in the briefs or not (*Board of Directors of Medford Irr. Dist. v. Hill* (Or.), 190 Pac. 957, decided July 6, 1920).

For over a quarter of a century plaintiff in error was the owner of a tract of some 2500 acres of land (Transcript pp. 98, 268) situated in the Warm Springs Valley along the Malheur River in Harney and Malheur Counties, Oregon, which it operated as a cattle ranch. The tract is about five miles long following the main direction of the river, and varies in width from one-quarter of a mile to over a mile (Exhibits 2, 9, 11). In its natural state the land lying near the river is covered with a growth of willows and water grasses. Further away from the stream the vegetation consists of rye grass, greasewood and sagebrush, growing sparser and in patches as the higher levels are reached until the hill sides are practically barren of all growth except for a short time in the spring. During summer, autumn and early winter the Malheur River is a small stream, carrying only a few inches of water, but the rains and melting snows of the mountains where it has its source in late winter and spring give it an enormous flow. For the purpose of storing, conserving and utilizing the surplus water, otherwise wasted, for diversion to arid lands at a season void of natural irrigation, the Warm Springs project was formed.

In the early '90s the Pacific Live Stock Company, then controlled by the late Henry Miller, of Miller & Lux, made strenuous efforts to bring the land under cultivation. These efforts were continued at great expense for many years but were unsuccessful owing to the nature and topography of the soil. The story of man's struggle with adverse natural conditions is related graphically by John Gilchrist (Transcript, pp. 272-294, 304-308, 313-316) who was superintendent of this and nineteen other cattle ranches of the company in Oregon and twenty in Nevada for twenty-five years, and the facts and circumstances testified to by him are practically uncontroverted. Never more than a few hundred acres were brought under cultivation and for several years prior to the time of the trial of this cause there were only about 360 acres (alfalfa and garden) which could be called under cultivation (Exhibits A, 11; Trans. pp. 96, 126, 174, 193, 210, 213, 227, 246, 267, 392, 405, 415).

A short distance below the tract the Malheur River enters a narrow canyon at which point the Irrigation District constructed its dam to a height sufficient to store 170,000 acre feet of water. The dam is constructed on government land 1400 feet south of the south line of the lands condemned. With the reservoir full the water will overflow all of the lands of plaintiff in error appropriated in this action except about 158 acres (Exhibits 1, 2, 9; Trans. p. 87) which comprise the isolated outlying fractional portions of 40-acre subdivisions on the hill lands situated above the irregular high water flow line, as shown on the map prepared by the engineer (Exhibit 9).

The Irrigation District began action to condemn the lands first in 1916 but dismissed it in 1917 (Trans. 33, 243-244). That case reached the Oregon Supreme Court on the question of attorney's fees and was disposed of before the commencement of the present suit (*Warm Springs Irrigation District v. Pacific Live Stock Co.* 89 Or. 19) and has nothing to do herewith.

The present action was begun in the State Circuit Court for Malheur County, Oregon, July 3, 1919, but was removed to the Federal Court (Trans. 14-22) where the Company interposed a motion to make the complaint more definite (Trans. 23) and a demurrer (Trans. 26), both of which were overruled (Trans. 28).

The complaint is in the usual form and alleges the facts required by the statute to be stated. Section 31 (Laws of Oregon 1917, p. 763) above quoted provides *inter alia*:

> "In the acquisition of property or rights by condemnation the board shall proceed in the name of the district under the provisions of the laws of the State of Oregon."

Section 6859, Lord's Oregon Laws, as amended by Chapter 175, Laws of 1913 (Laws of Oregon 1913, p. 315) provides:

> "Whenever any corporation authorized as in the provisions of this act, to appropriate lands, rights of way, right to cut timber, or other right or easement in lands, is unable to agree with the owner thereof as to the compensation to be paid therefor, or if such owner be absent from this state,

such corporation may maintain an action in the circuit court of the proper county, against such owner, for the purpose of having such lands" * * * appropriated to its own use, and for determining the compensation to be paid to such owner therefor."

Section 6860, Lord's Oregon Laws, provides: "Such action shall be commenced and proceeded in to final determination in the same manner as an action at law, except as in this title otherwise specially provided."

Section 6862 Lord's Oregon Laws, provides: "The complaint shall describe the land, right or easement sought to be appropriated with convenient certainty."

By stipulation the cause was tried to the court, a jury being waived (Trans. 47), and in a memorandum opinion handed down November 24, 1919, the trial judge announced his conclusions appropriating the lands to defendant in error and fixing the market value thereof (Trans. 48-52). Special findings of fact on the issues, along with conclusions of law were made and filed December 2 (Trans. 52-60), and judgment thereon was entered December 9, 1919, giving plaintiff in error $90,000, besides attorney's fees, costs and disbursements amounting in all to $97,240.40 and appropriating the lands therein described to defendant in error (Trans. 61-64). In the course of the trial it developed that the Southwest quarter of the Northwest quarter and the Northwest quarter of the Southwest quarter of section 2, Township 22 South, range 36 East in Harney County, described in the last six lines of paragraph VI of the complaint (Trans. 11) would not be reached by the highest flow line of water in the reservoir, and the said 80 acres were omitted from the judgment of condemnation (Trans. 63).

During the pendency of said action plaintiff in error

began a suit on the equity side of the Federal Court to enjoin the district from proceeding with the erection of its reservoir dam, and the court therein required the district to furnish security "for such damages or compensation as should, in said suit or in any other action or proceeding, be awarded to defendant (plaintiff in error) for the taking of or injury to the lands" described in the condemnation action, including costs. In accordance with such order the district deposited with the clerk of the court below as custodian certificates of deposit issued by the Anglo and London-Paris National Bank of San Franisco, Cal., amounting to $200,000. In its findings and judgment in this case, as well as in the decree in the equity case which was tried at the same time, the trial court made appropriate disposition of said fund by directing that $97,240.40 thereof be converted into bank certificates of deposit to the credit of and payable to the order of defendant (plaintiff in error) and deliverable to it on demand (Trans. 59, 63). Although the writ and assignment of errors raise no question on this point, it may be remarked to complete the history of the case that the deposit was made as directed, certificates of the Anglo and London-Paris National Bank being converted into certificates of the Bank of California, both parties stipulating thereto and agreeing that the same shall be deemed as payment of the amount of the judgment into court in compliance with Section 6866 Lord's Oregon Laws, and without prejudice (Trans. 524). Said section reads as follows: "Upon the payment into court of the damages assessed by the jury, the court shall give judgment appropriating the lands, property, rights, easements, crossing, or connection in question, as the case may be, to the corporation, and thereafter the same shall be the property of such corporation."

The Pacific Live Stock Company tendered no findings of fact either before or after judgment and requested no particular findings at any time. One month after the court announced its decision the plaintiff in error filed a motion for a new trial on grounds substantially similar to those advanced as the basis of the writ (Trans. 64-67). The motion was denied.

In 1913 (General Laws of Oregon, Chapter 87, p. 141) the legislature of Oregon passed an emergency act which has a bearing on assignments of error 2, 4 and 13. After providing for co-operation between the State and Federal authorities in the investigation, development and control of the natural resources of the state in land, water and power, and authorizing the State Engineer on behalf of the State to enter into a contract with any federal department or bureau having jurisdiction in such matters for the execution of surveys and investigations, and the preparation of plans, specifications, estimates and other data by co-operation between the State and such federal department or bureau, and for a report of all such surveys and investigations, the act further provides as follows:

> Section 3. The State Engineer, on behalf of the State, is hereby authorized and required to withdraw and withhold from appropriation any unappropriated water which may be required for project under investigation or to be investigated under the provisions of this act. If the project is found to be feasible, he shall withhold the same from appropriation until the money expended in the investigation of such project shall be repaid to the co-operating parties in proportion to the amount contributed by each. No permit to appropriate water which may be in conflict with any such project under investigation shall be approved by the State Engineer, nor shall any assignment of plans and in-

formation or any part thereof be made except upon consideration and other by the State Water Board after full hearing of all interested parties.

May 5, 1913, in pursuance of the power thus granted, and in the name of the State of Oregon, John H. Lewis, who was then State Engineer of Oregon, entered into a contract with the United States by Franklin K. Lane, Secretary of the Interior, for the joint survey and investigation and for preparation of plans and estimates for the Warm Springs project. The contract was approved by the Governor of Oregon (Trans. 81) and thereupon, in co-operation with the United States Reclamation Service a co-operative survey and report was made and compiled by the State of Oregon and the United States government. To secure the expense of the investigation the Warm Springs Irrigation District deposited $4,724.61 for the State of Oregon and $14,724.61 for the Federal Government in the United States National Bank of Vale, Oregon (Trans. 82, 86, 91; Exhibit 21). The report of that co-operative work is Exhibit 1 in this case (Trans. 74, 75).

On April 26, 1909, by order of the Reclamation Service, Department of the Interior, all public land in the Warm Springs Reservoir site was withdrawn from public entry under the Act of Congress of June 17, 1902; and on March 25, 1911, an order signed by the Director of the Geological Survey, approved by the Secretary of the Interior, was issued reciting that there is ample water in the Malheur River and its tributaries for the irrigation of approximately one hundred thousand acres, and recommending the withdrawal of certain reservoir sites. Attached thereto was an order dated March 31, 1911, signed by William H. Taft, President of the United States, withdrawing from entry the public land in the Warm Springs Reservoir site (Trans. 83, 84).

On April 8, 1914, on behalf of the State of Oregon, the State Engineer withdrew and withheld three hundred thousand acre feet of the waters of the Middle Fork of the Malheur River to be stored in Warm Springs Reservoir for irrigation purposes; and on February 16, 1916, the same official withdrew and withheld from appropriation eight hundred second-feet of water of Malheir River and tributaries for irrigation, power and domestic purposes which may be required for the Warm Springs Reservoir project. Both of these withdrawals were made in accordance with said chapter 87 of the laws of Oregon for 1913, above referred to, and with the aforesaid contract between the Federal Government and the State of Oregon (Trans. 80, 81, 87; Exhibits 3 and 4).

The district made application to the State Water Board for the assignment of the plans, information and water rights withdrawn by the State Engineer as above stated, and the said Water Board in accordance with the above quoted section of Chapter 87, General Laws of Oregon 1913, duly approved and ordered the assignment of said water rights to the district March 5, 1919 (Trans. 82, 83, 90, 91, 465; Exhibits 5, 21). Owing to regulations of the State Engineer's office requiring applications for permits to specify the number of acres in each 40-acre tract proposed to be irrigated, and in order to avoid the confusion of filing a number of applications to conform to changes in the boundary of the district, the original applications were filed tentatively as of April 8, 1914, and February 14, 1916, but were completed and approved by the State Engineer on November 18, 1919, as shown by the testimony of John H. Lewis (Trans. 471-474; Exhibit 21).

ARGUMENT

For convenience and brevity the twenty assignments of error (Trans. 506-515) may be grouped and discussed under three general heads: THE COMPLAINT, involving assignments 1, 2, 3, 4, 5, 13 and 20, which predicate error upon the action of the trial court in overruling demurrer and denying motion to make more definite, and raises questions of the character of title, quantity of interest in and description of the particular lands sought to be condemned, and the contention that it was incumbent upon defendant in error, as a condition precedent to the exercise of its power of eminent domain to appropriate lands for a reservoir site, to show that it possessed rights to the waters of the Malheur River; THE TESTIMONY, comprising assignments 6 to 12 inclusive, of which 6, 7, 8 and 9 challenge the admission of certain evidence as to the value of the lands, and 10, 11 and 12, which go to the qualifications of certain witnesses; THE FINDINGS, under which may be grouped assignments 14 to 19 inclusive which attack the court's discretion and judgment in weighing a mass of conflicting testimony as to the value of the lands and amount of damages to be awarded.

The Complaint.

The Oregon statute on this subject is simplicity itself: "The complaint shall describe the land, right or easement sought to be appropriated with convenient certainty" (L. O. L. Sec. 6862). The public irrigation code (L. O. L. Secs. 6167-6217, as amended and reenacted by Chap. 357, Laws of Oregon, 1917, heretofore referred to will be searched in vain for any requirement that an irrigation district organized thereunder shall, in a complaint for the condemnation of any lands, rights or easements, allege anything more than a description with *convenient* certainty of the property sought, and the use or purpose for which it is needed. The Oregon Supreme Court has held that in condemnation cases no other judgment than the particular kind of judgment the law authorizes can be rendered (*Oregonian Ry. Co. v. Hill,* 9 Or. 377), from which it necessarily follows of course that the plaintiff in eminent domain proceedings cannot by an averrment in the complaint enlarge the power of the court nor alter the conclusion to be embodied in the judgment. The terms of the judgment are set forth in the statute: "Upon the payment into court of the damages assessed by the jury, the court shall give judgment appropriating the lands, property, rights, easements, crossing or connection in question, as the case may be, to the corporation, and thereafter the same shall be the property of such corporation." (L. O. L. Sec. 6866). The learned trial judge therefore, in his decision, properly remarked: "It is not necessary nor do I deem it proper to determine at this time whether such appropriation will amount to the taking of the fee or only an easement. Judgment will follow the language of the statute appropriating the property for reservoir purposes. The legal effect can be determined when the question arises, if it ever does" (Trans. 51-52). Error is predicated on this ruling by assignment 3, but the question of whether defendant in error got a fee or an easement does not arise on this review. The question here is, ought the complaint to allege, in the language of assignment 1, "whether the plaintiff sought to acquire a fee simple title to the land or an easement therein." It is not necessary for plaintiff in condemnation proceedings to set forth whether an easement or a fee in the land is sought (15 Cyc. 857). To claim a fee simple title would be useless unless the court had power to adjudge it in terms, and since the court's only power is to pass the particular kind of judgment authorized by law the pleader cannot, as a condition of maintaining the action, be required to pray for any other kind. His function is to state the facts upon which the conclusion sanctioned by the statute may follow. Plaintiff in error tried hard to make the court and the defendant in error commit themselves on this point. The defendant in error was frequently challenged to declare whether it was seeking a marketable title or a mere easement with right of reverter in the Live Stock Co. Had it done so and elected either, and had the court passed judgment accordingly, it can not be doubted, in view of the rule in Oregon above cited, that plaintiff in error would have complained that the court had no power in this proceeding to determine whether the Irrigation District took an absolute title or an easement.

The complaint avers inter alia the purpose of the district to be the constructing, equipping, maintaining and operating an irrigation system consisting of dams, reservoirs, canals, flumes and ditches for general irrigation purposes by the public and for public use, and for storing water for future use by the public and especially by owners of land within the boundaries of the district (paragraph III, Trans. 8); the adoption of a location and surveys for a reservoir dam necessary for the convenient use of the district to enable it to fulfill the purpose of its organization to maintain and operate a public irrigation system by storing waters; that said dam is situated about 1400 feet south of the south line of defendant's lands and is to be 107 feet high, giving a highest flow line contour at an elevation of 3420 feet, or thereabouts; that defendant's lands lie in such position with reference to said dam and reservoir site that about 2500 acres thereof will be submerged at said high flow line by waters stored by the said dam and reservoir (paragraphs IV and V, Trans. 8-10). Then follows a particular description by legal subdivisions of defendant's lands required for said use comprising approximately 2500 acres (paragraph VI, Trans. 10), and the statement, substantially in the language of the statute (Section 6859 L. O. L.), that plaintiff has negotiated in vain with defendant for the purpose of agreeing upon the compensation to be paid for said lands, offering $55,000 therefor and defendant demanding $143,000 (paragraphs VII and VIII, Trans. 11-12). The concluding paragraph and prayer of the complaint (Trans. 12-13), in connection with the allegations of the public purposes and objects of plaintiff's organization and the use to be made of the lands, express all that the law anywhere requires and gave the defendant ample notice of plaintiff's demand and of the issues to be met, namely: "That plaintiff desires to appropriate said lands to its use as hereinabove mentioned (*i. e.* reservoir site for storage of waters), and brings this action to have the damages to the defendant owner of said lands assessed, and to acquire the said lands for the uses and purposes herein set forth. Wherefore plaintiff prays that the said lands * * * hereby sought to be obtained, be condemned to the use of the plaintiff herein for the purposes set forth; * * * and that plaintiff have judgment against the defendant appropriating said lands to its use."

The defendant could not have been misled because all of its testimony was directed to the full value of the lands for any and all purposes, and to the amount which should be paid to it for taking the lands. There will be found no evidence in the record of any valuation of an easement in the lands. Nor was the court misled, for in fixing the amount of compensation to be allowed defendant for the property the trial judge remarked: "The same considerations are to be regarded as in a sale between private parties. The owner is entitled to the full value of the property taken, and that is what it fairly may be believed that a purchaser in fair market conditions would give for it in fact (citing *N. Y. v. Sage,* 239 U. S. 661). Its adaptability for the purposes for which it can be used most profitably is to be considered as far as the public would have considered it if the land had been offered for sale in the absence of an attempt to exercise the power of eminent domain" (Trans. 49). This, and finding XI "that the market value of the lands of defendant * * * which the plaintiff seeks to condemn for a public use, is, and at the time of the commencement of this action was, $90,000 (Trans. 58), makes it clear that, regardless of the character of title or quantity of interest actually acquired in the lands by the judgment of condemnation, defendant was in no degree prejudiced by failure of the complaint to allege whether plaintiff sought an absolute title or a mere easement, because in either event defendant was given the full value of the lands, which ought to preclude lamentation and cavil on its part respecting questions of pleading and procedure in this case.

Now, the plaintiff paid that award and got an appropriation of the lands to its use for reservoir purposes in connection with its public irrigation system. It may or may not be that the judgment of condemnation does in fact and in law give the district an absolute marketable title to those lands so that it may lease or pasture such portions thereof as may from season to season not be overflowed, and may sell and convey the whole or any part thereof, and that the holders of its mortgage bonds, in case of default in payment, may obtain a title freed from any right of reversion in the Pacific Live Stock

Co. for non-user, misuser or abandonment, but this is not the time to discuss that question. As Judge Bean well said concerning it: "The legal effect can be determined when the question arises if it ever does."

The question of the legal effect of that judgment has arisen. A suit was brought on the equity side of the court below by the Pacific Live Stock Company against Warm Springs Irrigation District and others less than a month after the entry of the judgment under review in this case, wherein the only point in issue is whether or not the Irrigation District, by the condemnation proceedings under the laws of Oregon acquired title to the lands or only an easement. An application for a temporary injunction resulted in the memorandum opinion quoted in the Appendix to the brief of plaintiff in error. Since then a trial has been had and a final decree entered in accordance with the prayer of the plaintiff. From that decree defendants are prosecuting an appeal to this court where the question will in due course formally be presented for determination. By the adoption of the course suggested in Judge Bean's opinion and the bringing of a plenary suit to determine the legal effect of the judgment in the condemnation case, plaintiff in error ought to be foreclosed from presenting the same question on this review. It has no place herein—indeed, this is practically conceded at the top of page 17, brief of plaintiff in error. But since it has been dragged in and stressed by citation of authorities in the body of the brief for plaintiff in error, and given factitious emphasis by an Appendix, perhaps the defendants in error may be excused for indulging in an Addenda comprising a statement of their position and anticipating somewhat the argument when the cause comes regularly before this court. But as concerns the merits of the instant case the point is reserved.

The record herein discloses confusion and inconsistency on the part of plaintiff in error. Paragraph 6 of its motion for a new trial alleges (Trans. 67): "The court erred in finding that it *was* necessary for the plaintiff to *take said land* for the reason that it only appeared that it was necessary to *take an easement therein,* and the court also erred in *failing to find* whether it was necessary to take the said *land* or only an *easement* therein, and also erred in failing to find and adjudge whether plaintiff took an *easement* or *fee simple* of said land." Assignment of error 3 says: "The court erred in granting judgment in said cause *without deciding or specifying* whether the plaintiff acquired thereby the *fee simple* title of the said land or only an *easement therein*" (Trans. 507), while assignment 20 (Trans. 514) alleges: "The court erred in finding that it *was* necessary to a public use that the plaintiff acquire the said *property,* for the reason that it appeared by the evidence that it was only necessary for the said plaintiff to acquire an *easement* therein, and no evidence whatever was introduced showing that it was necessary for the plaintiff to acquire the fee simple title to said property." In short, no matter what finding the court might have made on this subject, it would, according to defendant's incongruous contentions, have been wrong. But since the court followed the doctrine of the Oregon case above cited (9 Or. at page 384) and entered the only judgment it was authorized to render in condemnation proceedings, defendant's quarrel is with the law and not with the court. Any other judgment would be without authority of law and a nullity. The only possible inquiry respecting the findings is whether they sustain the judgment rendered, and the discussion of that question more appropriately comes under another division of this argument.

Assignments 2, 4 and 13 present the point that it

was incumbent upon plaintiff, as a condition precedent to its right to condemn lands for a reservoir site, to allege and prove that it had first appropriated waters of the Malheur River. Defendant's position appears to be, in other words, that a public irrigation district cannot condemn a place to store waters until it has acquired waters to store. If the statute explicitly so provided that would be true whether logical or not; but since the law is silent on the subject it is just as reasonable to say that the district has no power to appropriate waters until it has first acquired a place to store waters. The question does not seem important. Whether a man builds a barn before he buys the horse, or acquires the horse first; whether a railroad acquires locomotives or a roundhouse first; whether the expectant parents buy the cradle first or await the arrival of the baby, is all one in the general result. Reservoir, barn, roundhouse and cradle have their place in the general scheme and it makes no difference whether the things to be stored in them come first or last. Of course the legislature could make the prior acquirement of water right by a public irrigation district an essential prerequisite to the exercise of the right of eminent domain to appropriate a reservoir site, or vice versa. Such a provision would be without apparent sense or reason, but these are not always valid grounds for disregarding the law and doubtless under the rule that eminent domain statutes are strictly construed such an act would be given effect. It is sufficient to say, however, that the Oregon legislature has not done so. The act will be searched in vain for any requirement that the district shall acquire or possess a place to store waters before proceeding to condemn water rights or that it must have water before condemning a place to store water. The general effect of its provisions rebuts even an inference to that effect as is shown by section 31 hereinbefore quoted. In the same sentence granting power to condemn all lands, waters, water rights, rights of way, easements and other property, including canals and works constructed and being constructed by private owners, occurs the clause: "and shall *also* have the right to so acquire (*i. e.* by lease, purchase, condemnation, or other legal means) *lands and all necessary appurtenances for reservoirs* and the right to store water in constructed reservoirs, for the storage of needful waters," etc. The same section gives, dedicates and sets apart any lands which are now or may be the property of the State of Oregon to the district for purposes of location, construction and maintenance of said works over and through the same.

The case of *City of Helena v. Rogan*, 26 Mont. 452; 68 Pac. 798, 801, although not directly in point, is analogous in principle. Proceedings were commenced to condemn water rights in streams situated some distance from the city for the purpose of establishing a municipal water supply system. It seems the defendants raised the point that the complaint failed to allege that the city had obtained or was able to get a right of way to convey the water from the streams to the city. The court said:

> "Is it fatal to omit from the complaint an allegation that the city has a right of way from the creek to the city, or that it is able to get one? It does not appear to be necessary so to allege. It is not any concern of the owners of the property whether the water comes to Helena or not. It would hardly be necessary to allege and prove that the city has engaged the services of a competent civil engineer, and put him under bonds to lay out a feasible route, and to direct and superintend the laying of the pipes so well and faithfully that the water will actually run to Helena, before the own-

ers of the property sought may be required to part with it for a public use. What rights and remedies a city taxpayer, as such, may have in case the plant is foolish, or impossible of execution, is another question; but this we do not now consider."

In *Prescott Irrigation Co. v. Flathers,* 20 Wash. 454; 55 Pac. 635, a private irrigation company, organized for profit, sought to condemn a right of way for a canal to convey waters from the Touchet River. The answer alleged that plaintiff had not purchased nor condemned the rights of the riparian owners on the stream below the head of the ditch. The trial court held that it was necessary for the plaintiff to show that it had acquired water from all the riparian owners of the whole river before proceeding to appropriate a right of way for its canal. In short, that it must have water rights before it could condemn a right of way for a canal in which to convey the water. This ruling was reversed by the Supreme Court which held that under a statute "declaring that irrigation companies shall be deemed public carriers, subject to legislative regulation, such a company is not required to show that it has acquired the right to take waters from a stream from which it proposes to get its supply, from riparian owners, as a prerequisite to its right to condemn land for a right of way."

The case of *Willen v. Hensley School Township,* 175 Ind. 486; 93 N. E. 657, is more closely in point. The school trustees began condemnation proceedings for a school house site and defendant advanced the contentions that the petition should show what steps had been taken to build upon the land after its condemnation, or allege that the trustees had been authorized to create or incur indebtedness for the school house, or that the township intended in good faith to construct a school house thereon. It was held that good faith is presumed and it is not necessary to allege any of said matters. The case of *Minnesota Canal & Power Co. v. Fall Lake Boom Co.,* 127 Minn. 23; 148 N. W. 561, cited by plaintiff in error on this point, does not appear to throw any light on the question.

In the instant case the State itself may be said to have appropriated waters for the plaintiff by the passage of Chap. 87 of the Laws of 1913, under section 3 of which, heretofore quoted, the State Engineer withdrew from general appropriation the waters of the Malheur River for the use and benefit of the Warm Springs Irrigation District; and on March 5, 1919, before the commencement of this action the State Water Board authorized the issuance of a permit to the district covering the water so withdrawn and appropriated (Trans. 464-469, Exhibit 21). It is contended at page 40 of the brief for plaintiff in error that the filing of an application in 1916 could not constitute an appropriation by the Warm Springs Irrigation District for the reason that it was not in existence until 1918. The record does not confirm this statement. The answer alleges that in 1916 the District offered $25,000 for the land and defendant offered to sell it to plaintiff for $173,643.50 (Trans. 32, 33) and A. R. Olsen, the representative of the Live Stock Co. testified that the District began the first condemnation action in September, 1916 (Trans. 243, 244). It appears from the decision of the Oregon Supreme Court in *Herrett v. Warm Springs Irrigation District,* 86 Or. 343, at pages 347 to 352, that proceedings to organize the District were initiated March 2, 1916, and completed May 29, 1916, and confirmed accordingly. The withdrawals of the State Engineer, under the provisions of the law quoted, of unappropriated waters of the Malheur River for the Warm Springs Project were effective to fix priority, and the permit of the State Water Board dated March 5, 1919, relating to such withdrawals, for all practical purposes gave to the Warm Springs Irrigation District, organized in March-May, 1916, rights to waters of the stream which were unappropriated at the time of the withdrawals by the State Engineer, April 8, 1914, and February 16, 1916,—certainly such rights as justified it in bringing this action July 3, 1919, to condemn lands for a reservoir site to store waters. This is not a contest between adverse claimants to water rights, and hence the matter of perfecting the application by giving an accurate description of every forty acre tract within the boundaries of the district proposed to be served, as required by the regulations of the State Engineer's office, is in immaterial detail. The fact that it was not done in this case until November, 1919, can not affect the rights of the District in the proceeding. It suffices that the application, permit and appropriation were completed before the trial, and by relation the rights of the District were fixed as of the dates of the original withdrawals for its project. The ultimate facts were found by the trial court (Finding IX, Trans. 57), but assignment 13 (Trans. 512) charges error in the admission of the testimony on the ground that it is not within any issue framed by the pleadings. If that be true, then the evidence in question is immaterial; and since the cause was tried to the court without a jury plaintiff in error could not have been prejudiced by its admission. "When a judge hears a case without a jury," says Woods, Circuit Judge, in *Oates v. U. S.* 147 C. C. A. 207, 233 Fed. 201, at page 205, "he is supposed to act only on proper evidence, and if on review it is found that the evidence properly admitted justifies the decree it ought to be affirmed and it ought not to be reversed." The same decision quotes the rule laid down by Chief Justice

Marshall in *Field v. U. S.* 9 Pet. 202, 9 L. ed. 94, as follows: "As the cause was * * * not tried by a jury, the exception to the admission of evidence was not properly the subject of a bill of exceptions. But if the District Court improperly admitted the evidence, the only effect would be that this court would reject that evidence, and proceed to decide the cause as if it were not on the record. It would not, however, of itself constitute any ground for a reversal of the judgment." The same court in *Arthurs v. Hart,* 17 How. 6, 15 L. ed. 30, draws a clear distinction, where trial by jury has been waived, between the admission of evidence and the refusal of proper evidence, and reaffirms the doctrine of *Field v. U. S. supra.* To the same effect is

U. S. v. Ballinger, 35 App. D. C. 436.
Lynch v. Grayson, 5 N. Mex. 509; 25 Pac. 998.
Mitchell v. Beckman, 64 Cal. 123; 28 Pac. 112.

This doctrine is in harmony with the general rule of practice in condemnation cases as stated and supported by citation of numerous cases in 7 Enc. Pl. & Prac. 650: "Errors and irregularities which have prejudiced no rights of the appellant will not be regarded on his appeal, even though the rights of other parties who do not appeal may have been adversely affected. This rule is frequently applied in cases where improper but harmless evidence was admitted, or where faulty but harmless instructions were given in the court below."

It cannot be said, however, that either the testimony or the finding on this subject is irrelevant. Both possibly may be immaterial, in the sense of being nonessential because, as above shown, there is no requirement of law, nor rule of pleading of which we are aware, that makes such facts jurisdictional. Under the averments of paragraphs III and IV of the complaint (Trans. 8) and the specific denials in paragraphs III and IV of the answer (Trans. 30), however, they are at least pertinent if not highly important. It is also to be noted that no exception was taken by plaintiff in error to the finding which was based upon the evidence in question.

Assignment 5 (Trans. 507) challenges the ruling of the trial court respecting designation of the lands to be overflowed. The contention seems to be that the complaint must allege with precise exactness the boundaries of the land to be taken and that the proof must be limited strictly to the description thus given. The provision of the statute heretofore quoted does not warrant a rule of such harshness. The law contemplates no more than a reasonable exactitude in the description and evidently recognizes occasions for some latitude dependent upon the conditions and circumstances of particular cases. It calls for a description of the property sought to be appropriated with "*convenient* certainty" (L. O. L. Sec. 6862, *supra*). That is to say, such description as it is convenient for the plaintiff to make at the time of filing its complaint. The general rule appears to be that a corporation having the power to exercise the right of eminent domain must be permitted, in a modified degree, to determine for itself the amount of land necessary for the use for which it is sought to be taken. It is entitled to a reasonable latitude and discretion so long as it seeks in good faith to appropriate land for a public purpose, and may anticipate future growth and expansion. These rights of course are subject to the power of the court to prevent an abuse, but, as was said by the Supreme Court of the United States in a case involving the sale of surplus water stored by a public service company on lands condemned for reservoir purposes (*Kaukauna W. & P. Co. v. Green Bay & M. Canal Co.*, 142 U. S. 254; 35 L. Ed. 1004):

"So long as the dam was erected for the bona fide purpose of furnishing an adequate supply of water for the canal and was not a colorable device for creating a water power, the agents of the State are entitled to great latitude of discretion in regard to the height of the dam and the head of water to be created; and while the surplus in this case may be unnecessarily large, there does not seem to have been any bad faith or abuse of discretion on the part of those charged with the construction of the improvement. Courts should not scan too jealously their conduct in this connection if there be no reason to doubt that they were animated solely by a desire to promote the public interests, nor can they undertake to measure with nicety the exact amount of water required for the purposes of the public improvement."

2 Nichols on Em. Domain, pp. 150, 177, 181, 190, 203.

Lewis on Em. Domain, Secs. 239, 279.

Bell v. Mattoon Waterworks Co., 245 Ill. 544; 137 Am. S. R. 338; 19 Ann. Cas. 153.

Neitzel v. Spokane Int. Ry. Co., 80 Wash. 30; 141 Pac. 186.

Vallejo & N. R. Co. v. Home Savings Bank, 24 Cal. App. 166; 140 Pac. 974.

The case of *Eastern Oregon Land Co. v. Willow River L. & I. Co.*, 122 C. C. A. 636, 204 Fed. 516, is pertinent. Although the question there arose under an Oregon statute (L. O. L. Secs. 6525 et. seq.) giving right of eminent domain to private corporations in respect of irrigation projects, the rule ought to be at least as liberal regarding public irrigation districts. We quote from page 524, 205 Fed.:

"Without merit, also, is the contention that the plaintiff should be denied the right to condemn the right of way described in the complaint, for the reason that the route thereof varies from that which is described in the notice of April 7, 1908. It is not the intention of the law that the appropriator, when it resorts to condemnation proceedings, shall be held to the exact line of the route described in its notice, or in the map of its general route. The law of 1891 provides that the notice shall contain 'a general description of the course of said ditch or canal or flume,' and further provides that a map shall be filed 'showing the general route.' The statute, therefore, does not require that the corporation shall, in its appropriation notice, fix upon a precise line, from which it shall not thereafter deviate in the slightest degree. The very language of the statute shows that the law is complied with if the notice and map contain no more than a general description. The notice in this case complies with the statute. It gave what it declared to be the 'general courses and direction.' Having given such a general description of the course of its ditch, a corporation, when it comes into court in a condemnation suit for its right of way, is required for the first time to define the definite line of its ditch. That was done in the present case, and the defendant can claim no prejudice to it from the fact that the description in the notice was but the general description which is required by the act."

True, this comment relates to a statute containing different language, but in principle a description with "convenient certainty" required by Sec. 6862, L. O. L., would seem to impose no greater precision of pleading than the words from the act of 1891 quoted in the foregoing opinion.

But perhaps the most effectual confutation of the fifth assignment of error is to be found in the record. The complaint, after alleging the adoption of surveys and reports, location of dam to be constructed to a height of about 107 feet, giving the contour of highest flow line at an elevation of 3420 feet or thereabouts, avers that defendant's lands "lie in such position with reference to said dam and reservoir site as that about two thousand five hundred acres of said land as hereinafter particularly described will be submerged at said high flow line by waters to be stored by the said dam and reservoir of the plaintiff, and that practically the whole of said lands are needed by and are necessary for the purposes of the plaintiff, and it is necessary that plaintiff should have, and it requires, all of said lands for such public use for irrigation purposes" (Trans. 11-12). Then follows a particular description of the lands by legal subdivisions of the Government survey, the whole constituting a description of the lands sought to be taken with as much certainty, under the circumstances and the nature of the use and taking, as the plaintiff could conveniently allege at the time, which is all the statute requires. Paragraph V of the answer (Trans. 31) puts some of the statements in issue but *"admits that said dam is so located that it will submerge all the land described in said complaint."* Since the judgment condemned no lands of defendant which were not so described—in fact, omitted eighty acres therein described as heretofore stated—defendant's admission cuts the ground from under the fifth assignment of error. The complaint does *"indicate"* (to adopt defendant's phraseology) "the lands which were *intended to be overflowed,"* and, according to the express admission of the answer *does* "show *what particular lands would be overflowed."* Hence, there was no error in overruling demurrer to the complaint, and in denying motion to make the complaint more definite and certain in that particular.

The Testimony.

Assignments 6 to 9 (Trans. 507-509) present the question of whether a witness to the value of lands may on direct examination be interrogated respecting other sales to test his knowledge and judgment, and ascertain the basis of his opinion. Had the witnesses been asked these questions on cross-examination, or had the court propounded them in the course of the direct examination, there would be no room for discussion. The court or jury is entitled to know the worth of a witness' estimate as to value. It can be ascertained only by knowing from what standpoint the estimate is made, and upon what facts, experience and observations his opinion is founded. The questions objected to were proper for that purpose and defendant's criticism therefore goes only to the time when the questions were put. The conduct of a trial and the order in which the testimony is introduced are matters in the discretion of the trial court and its rulings in that respect will not be disturbed on appeal except for an abuse of discretion. No such showing is attempted to be made, nor, inasmuch as the case was tried without a jury, could there be any such showing. The trial judge himself may have wanted to ask the questions objected to—he could properly have anticipated counsel for the plaintiff in propounding the questions. Counsel for defendant doubtless would, on cross-examination, have asked those or similar questions designed to test the knowledge and credibility of the witnesses. Then why quibble over the time or order of their asking?

But aside from this, the questions were proper. In *Lynch v. United States*, 71 C. C. A. 59, 138 Fed. 535, a witness called by the plaintiff was interrogated similarly to the witnesses in this case on direct examination as to specific sales. Objection was made on the same grounds urged here, and this court, affirming the lower court, held that the question was proper and the testimony admissible for the purpose of ascertaining what knowledge the witness had on the subject, and was relevant to the question as to his qualification. Although the rule is different in some states, the great weight of authority sustains the position of this court in the case above cited, as appears from the text and citation of cases in 1 Jones Commentaries on the Law of Evidence, Sec. 168, pp. 854-860, and in volume II of the same work, Sec. 363, pp. 877-880. Another writer expresses the rule thus: "Where a witness is called upon to express an opinion, either as to the value or to the damages or benefits resulting from the improvement, it is proper, *either in the direct* or cross-examination, to test the value of his opinion by requiring him to state the elements of his calculation, although the evidence adduced by the answers may be inadmissible as independent evidence" (5 Enc. of Ev. p. 211).

There is another good reason why no error can be predicated on assignments 6 to 9. It is to be found in the argument hereinbefore presented on another point in connection with citation of *Oates v. U. S.* 147 C. C. A. 207, 233 Fed. 201; *Field v. U. S.*, 9 Pet. 202, 9 L. Ed. 94 and other cases. As the cause was not tried by a jury the trial judge is presumed to have passed judgment only on evidence properly admitted, and exceptions to the admission of the testimony in question are not properly the subject of a bill of exceptions. It makes no difference whether the evidence was admissible or not, because plaintiff in error was not prejudiced by its admission. The admission of immaterial or irrelevant evidence is harmless error where it does not affect the finding (*Weems v. George,* 13 How. 190, 14 L. Ed. 108; *Union Consol. Mining Co. v. Taylor,* 100 U. S.

37, 25 L. Ed. 541; *Reed v. Stapp,* 3 C. C. A. 244, 52 Fed. 641).

Assignments 10, 11 and 12 (Trans. 509-511) charge the trial court with error in overruling defendant's objections to the qualifications of the witnesses C. C. Hunt, J. F. Weaver and E. M. Gregg, who testified as to the value of the lands. The qualification of a witness is always a question for the court (1 Jones on Ev., Sec. 363, p. 879). The credibility of the witness and the weight to be given to his testimony are questions for the jury. The weight and credence to be given to the testimony of the witness named were matters of argument to be addressed to the triers of fact (*Congress Etc. Co. v. Edgar,* 99 U. S. 645, 25 L. Ed. 487). The admission of the testimony rested solely in the judicial discretion of the court (*N. Y. Evening Post v. Chaloner,* C. C. A. 265 Fed. 204, 216, Feb. 18, 1920). No exception is taken to the admission of the testimony, the objection going only to the qualification of the witnesses. In a good many jurisdictions the ruling of the trial court on the competency of a witness to give opinion testimony is not subject to review (Rodgers on Expert Testimony, Sec. 22) and in the jurisdictions where such ruling is reviewable it is only done where the court has committed a plain and palpable error in matter of law.

The rule as laid down in *Stillwell Mfg. Co. v. Phelps,* 130 U. S. 520, 32 L. Ed. 1035, where the lower court had excluded the testimony of a witness called on a question of value, may be said to be as well settled as any question of federal trial practice. Mr. Justice Gray, speaking for the court, said:

> "No error is shown in the exclusion of Geissner's testimony as to the rental value of a mill which he had never seen and knew nothing of. Whether a witness called to testify to any matter of opinion has such qualifications and knowledge as to make

his testimony admissible is a preliminary question for the judge presiding at the trial; and his decision of it is conclusive, unless clearly shown to be erroneous in matter of law."

This rule has been affirmed many times. In *Iron Co. v. Blake,* 144 U. S. 476, 36 L. Ed. 510, the court said:

"How much knowledge a witness must possess before a party is entitled to his opinion as an expert is a matter which, in the nature of things, must be left largely to the discretion of the trial court, and its ruling thereon will not be disturbed unless clearly erroneous."

This court, in *Union Pac. Ry. Co. v. Novak,* 9 C. C. A. 629, 61 Fed. 573, said:

"The question whether a witness is shown to be qualified to testify to any matter of opinion is always a preliminary question for the judge presiding at the trial, and his decision thereon is conclusive, and will not be reversed unless manifestly erroneous, as matter of law."

The following cases approve and reaffirm the rule:

Island etc. Co. v. Tolson, 139 U. S. 551, 35 L. Ed. 270.

Gila Valley Co. v. Hall, 232 U. S. 94, 58 L. Ed. 521.

St. Louis & S. F. Ry. Co. v. Bradley, 4 C. C. A. 528, 54 Fed. 630, 633.

Bradford Glycerine Co. v. Kizer, 51 C. C. A. 524, 113 Fed. 894.

U. S. v. German, 115 Fed. 987, 989.

Kenney v. Meddaugh, 55 C. C. A. 115, 118 Fed. 209, 220.

Williamson v. Berlin Mills Co., C. C. A. 190 Fed. 1, 3.

St. Louis I. M. & S. Ry. Co. v. Reed, C. C. A. 216 Fed. 741, 743.

It should be remembered that in connection with plaintiff's averment of an attempt to agree with defendant on amount of compensation to be paid for the lands, there is an allegation that plaintiff offered $55,000 and that the reasonable and market value was no greater than that sum (Trans. 12). The answer admits the offer but alleges that the same "was not made in good faith nor was the said amount the amount which said plaintiff believed to be the value of said property but said sum offered was a mere sham for the purpose of enabling said plaintiff to institute this action and at said time said plaintiff well knew that the said land was worth vastly more than said sum" (Trans. 32).

These statements raised an issue upon which it was incumbent for plaintiff to present proofs. The attempt to agree with the owner in condemnation cases is a statutory requirement and an offer must be made in good faith. Prior to bringing the action in July, 1919, the directors of the district had selected and requested Messrs. Hunt, Weaver and Gregg, disinterested farmers and men of affairs who had resided and operated in that part of the country for several years (Trans. 382-383, 407-408, 428-429) to go upon the lands of defendant and make an examination and report their appraisement of the value thereof (Trans. 92). They did so and appraised the property at $50,877.75 (Trans. 392, 415, 440). The district then offered defendant $55,000 for its lands. The testimony of the three appraisers was relevant and material on the issue of bona fides of the plaintiff in its effort to agree on value with the defendant and of its offer to pay $55,000 as the fair, reasonable value thereof, irrespective of the qualifications of the witnesses, as tending to show that the offer was not sham nor the amount fixed arbitrarily and at haphazard, but was the result of an independent and disinterested appraisement.

The remark of Judge Morrow of this court in the decision in the case of *Lynch v. United States*, 71 C. C. A. 59, 138 Fed. 535, fits this point like a glove. Change of names and amounts makes a paraphrase more than merely apropos: "It is evident that the defendant was not prejudiced by the testimony of Hunt, Weaver and Gregg that the property was worth *$50,877.75*, since the only inference that can be drawn from the testimony is that the trial judge fixed the value at *$90,000*."

Moreover, even if the trial court erred in admitting the testimony of said witnesses a reversal could be justified only by invoking what Judge Coxe in ***Press Pub. Co. v. Monteith***, 103 C. C. A. 502-508, 180 Fed. 356, 362, called the "archaic" rule that if error be discovered, no matter how trivial, prejudice must be presumed. There is no showing here that the rights of plaintiff in error were injuriously affected by the alleged error. Prejudice will not be presumed, and if a just result, which is the object of all litigation, was reached there was no error (*Miller v. Continental Shipbuilding Corporation*, C. C. A. 265 Fed. 158, 164, March 12, 1920; *Hoogendorn v. Daniel*, 120 C. C. A. 537, 202 Fed. 431). Findings will not be set aside for the admission of incompetent evidence if there be other competent evidence to support the conclusion, unless it appears that the court in making its decision relied upon such irrelevant evidence (*Grayson v. Lynch*, 163 U. S. 468, 41 L. Ed. 230; *Miller v. Houston Co.*, 5 C. C. A. 134, 55 Fed. 366).

The Findings.

Assignments 14 to 19 inclusive (Trans. 512-514) in substance challenge the action of the court, as a trier of facts, in fixing the amount of damages or value of the property at $90,000 instead of $143,000 or $250,000 or some other amount greater than $90,000.

Assignment 18 (Trans. 514) presents one feature not common to the others of this group. It refers to hay which had been cut by defendant during the season of 1919 and was stacked on the property at the time of the trial. Plaintiff had no use for it and did not seek to condemn it. It was dragged into the case by an amendment to the answer filed after the trial was commenced (Trans. 40-42). The author of the article on Eminent Domain in 15 Cyc. 899, lays down the rule that if other property than that described in the complaint is brought into the case on cross petition, it is incumbent on the party thus bringing it in to show in the first instance that it was taken or damaged. No such showing was made. There was some testimony to the effect that if defendant had to move the hay out of the way of advancing flood waters some expense would be incurred, but that contingency was not shown to be imminent. There was also testimony to the effect that the hay could advantageously be fed to the defendant's live stock before the occasion for moving it arose. The trial judge appears to have considered it in arriving at his conclusion, for he said: "I have not included the hay now on the property. It is not sought to be condemned. It is personal property and will be no more affected by the judgment in this case than any other personal property belonging to the defendant, now on the ranch."

In view of assignments 1, 2, 3 and 20 (Trans. 506, 514) and the great pother made by plaintiff in error over the failure of the district to allege whether it sought the title or only an easement in the lands, a resort to the *tu tuoque* argument may be excused. If the complaint is deficient in that respect why, when defendant pitched that thousand tons of hay into the case with its answer, did it not allege whether it was necessary for the district to acquire the ownership thereof or a mere easement therein? Some further mention of the hay will be found in the Addenda to this brief. It has no further importance here, if it ever had any.

If the errors alleged in assignments 14 to 19 are to be considered it necessitates the examination and weighing by this court of 425 pages of testimony contained in the record (Trans. 74-499). It is possible that each member of this court would arrive at a conclusion different from that of the trial judge and different from each other. On the question of damages and value the defendant called twenty-four witnesses, and their opinions varied from $133,770 to $405,000 (Trans. 92-265, 474-498). The plaintiff called twelve witnesses whose estimates varied from $50,877.75 to $65,040. As the trial judge remarked in his memorandum opinion:

> "None of the witnesses on either side, testifying as to value, except Messrs. Gilchrest, Hunt, Gregg and Weaver, had an intimate acquaintance with the property or had made a careful examination thereof for the purpose of qualifying to testify as to value. Gilchrest is perhaps more familiar with it than any other witness. He was superintendent of the defendant for many years and as such developed the property to its present state. His testimony and estimate of value, however, must, I think, be weighed in the light of his present attitude towards the company. Messrs. Hunt, Gregg and Weaver were exceedingly intelligent and fair witnesses. They live, however, many miles from the property and I am persuaded their estimate of its value was

unconsciously colored by the time at which they made their examination and a comparison of it with property with which they were more intimately acquainted and accustomed to cultivate and deal in. None of the witnesses for the defendant had anything but a general knowledge of the property, its production or the nature and character of the soil. They spent a few hours riding over it in an automobile a short time before the hearing, and formed their opinions from a cursory examination and their general knowledge of it and the country and the business carried on there. I have not the slightest doubt that each and every witness was entirely sincere and intended to and did give to the court his best opinion and judgment on the subject based on his qualifications to do so. But I am equally convinced that defendant's witnesses placed the value too high, and those of the plaintiff too low." (Trans. 49-50.)

Gilchrist testified that $59,715 was the fair value and market price of the land (Trans. 310-311), and Hunt, Gregg and Weaver placed the value at $50,877.75 (Trans. 392, 415, 440). The court found the market value of the lands to be $90,000 (Trans. 58). With equal consistency the plaintiff could fairly predicate error on this finding as being $40,000 in excess of the true and just amount as shown by its witnesses. If, by the judgment of condemnation plaintiff acquired nothing but a bare easement in the lands, as claimed by the defendant, then $90,000 is certainly too much. There was no testimony whatever on the value, market or otherwise, of a mere easement in the lands. All of the witnesses on both sides were interrogated respecting elements of value which could only be predicated upon a transfer of the entire title. That the court's conclusion was drawn accordingly is apparent from the language of his opinion: "After a careful consideration of all the evidence and the argument of counsel, I have concluded that considering the property as a whole, the improvements thereon, the relation of the several parts to each other, its location, situation, character and adaptability to the various uses to which it can be put, that $90,000 is the fair and reasonable value thereof, and what it may fairly be believed one desiring and able to purchase would give for it if it were offered in the market."

Had there been no special findings the general finding would have precluded any review except as to the rulings of the court in the progress of the trial. The fact that the court made special findings does not alter the rule that they have the effect of a verdict of a jury and are conclusive if there be any evidence to support them, and the review is limited to a determination of the sufficiency of the facts as found by the court to support the judgment.

U. S. Rev. Stat. Secs. 649, 700; 6 Fed. Stat. Ann. 2d Ed. p. 205.

Pac. Postal Tel. Cable Co. v. Fleischner, 14 C. C. A. 166; 66 Fed. 899.

King v. Smith, 49 C. C. A. 46; 110 Fed. 95.

U. S. v. U. S. Fidelity & Guar. Co., 235 U. S. 512; 59 L. Ed. 696.

Adamson v. Gilliland, 242 U. S. 350; 61 L. Ed. 356.

Los Angeles G. & E. Corp. v. Western Gas Const. Co., 124 C. C. A. 200; 205 Fed. 707, 715.

Central etc. Co. v. Dunkley Co., 159 C. C. A. 648; 247 Fed. 790.

Stanley v. Board etc., 121 U. S. 535; 30 L. Ed. 1000.

Streeter v. Sanitary Dist., 66 C. C. A. 190; 133 Fed. 124.

U. S. Fidelity & G. Co. v. Board, 76 C. C. A. 114; 145 Fed. 144.

None of the assignments question the sufficiency of the findings to support the judgment, the contention being merely insufficiency of evidence to support the finding of ultimate facts. If the ultimate facts found have any support in the evidence it follows that the judgment is sound. The only possible inquiry then is whether the record contains any legal evidence tending to sustain the ultimate facts found. If there is, then the findings will not be disturbed. This court is not charged with the duty of weighing testimony nor of measuring preponderance. A special finding is unassailable when it depends upon conflicting testimony or upon the credibility of witnesses. A special finding of fact is inconclusive upon the appellate court only when, upon a fair examination of the whole record, it can be said that there is no evidence tending to support such finding.

Dooley v. Pease, 180 U. S. 126; 45 L. Ed. 457.

Eastern Oregon Land Co. v. Willow River L. & I. Co., 122 C. C. A. 636; 204 Fed. 516.

Sayward v. Dexter, 19 C. C. A. 176; 72 Fed. 758, 769.

San Fernando Copper Mining Co. v. Humphrey, 64 C. C. A. 544; 130 Fed. 298.

Ware v. Wunder Brewing Co., 87 C. C. A. 235; 160 Fed. 79.

Syracuse Township v. Rollins, 44 C. C. A. 277; 104 Fed. 958.

Pabst Brewing Co. v. E. Clemens Horst Co. (C. C. A. 9th Cir.), 264 Fed. 909.

Security Nat. Bank v. Old Nat. Bank, 154 C. C. A. 1; 241 Fed. 6.

Since, then, as Judge Gilbert said in the case of *San Fernando Copper Mining & R. Co. v. Humphrey, supra,* it is not the province of this court "to review the evidence further than may be necessary to discover that the case is not one wherein there was no evidence to justify the finding," little remains to be said on behalf of defendant in error. A mere reading of the testimony, we apprehend, will be all that the court will find necessary to discover that there was ample evidence on both sides to justify any finding on the question of damages from $50,000 up to some of the absurdly high estimates of defendant's witnesses. More than one reference has been made herein to the testimony of Mr. Gilchrist, who, as the learned trial judge remarked, "is perhaps more familiar with it than any other witness. He was superintendent of the defendant for many years and as such developed the property to its present state. His testimony and estimate of value, however, must I think be weighed in the light of his present attitude towards the company." Gilchrist said the property was fairly worth a certain sum. Many other witnesses testified to smaller and greater sums. The trial judge weighed the evidence and reached a conclusion greater than Gilchrist or any of the plaintiff's witnesses, and less than any of the defendant's witnesses save perhaps one. His award is nearly twice the average of plaintiff's witnesses and about half the average of defendant's witnesses. Here, then, is a problem whose solution depends upon the preponderance of testimony and the credibility of witnesses—two elements respecting which no Federal Court of review has any function or duty whatever. In reaching his conclusion the trial judge manifestly must have been influenced by those proper considerations open only to one who has the advantage of seeing the witnesses and hearing them testify. The atmosphere of the case, the psychology of the trial, the demeanor, manner and emphasis of the witnesses—these and many other things which do not register in the record make his decision final on all questions of fact about which there is any conflict. The instant case affords a peculiarly apt demonstration of the soundness of the rule.

Plaintiff in error, at page 41 of its brief, concedes that this court, in view of the conflict of evidence on the questions of value and damages, can not review the testimony; but it proceeds, nevertheless, with extensive citation thereto and comment thereon "for the purpose of showing" says the brief, "the importance of the errors committed by the court." It is claimed that the importance of the alleged errors is shown by the fact that a "large preponderance of the evidence showed a value of over $145,000 for agriculutral purposes." Perhaps; but it was up to the trial judge to credit as much or as little of that evidence as he saw fit. Similarly as to defendant's witnesses. Neither side "has anything" on the other in this respect. Counsel for plaintiff in error ought not to appropriate for their witnesses more than their fair share of the compliment paid by the trial judge when he said in his opinion that: "I have not the slightest doubt that each and every witness was entirely sincere and intended to and did give the court his best opinion and judgment on the subject based on his qualifications to do so. But I am equally convinced that defendant's witnesses placed the value too high, and those of the plaintiff too low." None of them were liars but some of them may have been more or less crazy in the head.

But this is not the way to demonstrate errors of law occurring at the trial. Those errors, if any were committed, do not depend upon the result of the court's judgment upon the facts. Whether a court errs in settling the pleadings or in the admission of evidence does not remain an open question until the verdict is returned. A party can not speculate with the rules of law, and argue that because the judgment in his favor is not as large as he thinks it ought to be, the importance of alleged errors is thereby magnified to proportions that warrant a reversal. Were this a sound argument the converse would be true, with the result that an error of law is never an error of law when the party is satisfied with the judgment. The defendant in error is not satisfied with the amount of the judgment. We think it is too large, but it does not follow that there was reversible error. If we got nothing but an easement in that land; nothing but a right of periodic aqueous possession whose extent depends wholly upon seasonal meterological conditions; become trespassers every time we plant our feet an inch above the constantly advancing or receding water line of our reservoir; if, from March to June, we are to soak the sagebrush, greasewood flats of those desert hills with our stored water and make them thrive with grasses and pasturage from July to January to the greater profit of the Pacific Live Stock Company than it ever realized from the entire ranch, then it was not damaged $97,000 worth by the limited, conditional and restricted appropriation, and we no longer *think* the judgment was too large, we *know* it. But, as heretofore stated, the matter of easement or fee title not being in this case there was no error and the judgment should be affirmed.

ED. R. COULTER,
H. C. EASTHAM,
ALLEN H. MCCURTAIN,
THOMAS G. GREENE,
Attorneys for Defendant in Error.

ADDENDA

It would save time and reduce the labor of the court could the two causes be submitted together, but, for lack of time, it is doubtful if the record in the equity case will reach the court before the date set for the argument in the condemnation action.

Judgment in the latter was entered December 9, 1919. On January 3, 1920, the Pacific Live Stock Co. filed in the court below its bill of complaint against the Irrigation District, its directors and secretary and Gerald Stanfield, to whom the District had leased part of the condemned lands, alleging in substance that the Irrigation District acquired only an easement in the lands theretofore appropriated in said condemnation action, and praying for an injunction restraining defendants from removing the improvements, feeding upon or depasturing said lands, or interfering with the alleged right of complainant to feed upon and depasture the same, and for a decree adjudging the Irrigation District to be the owner of only an easement therein. An answer was filled February 6, which denied the equities of the bill, set up the proceedings, findings and judgment in the condemnation case (discussed in the foregoing brief) and a lease to defendant Gerald Stanfield of the outlying corners and a strip lying between high flood line and low water mark of the reservoir site varying in width with the rise and fall of stored waters.

An application was made for a temporary injunction and on February 9, 1920, Judge Bean granted the same in the memorandum decision quoted in the Appendix to brief of plaintiff in error. An amended answer was filed June 14, 1920, wherein, as a further defense, it is alleged in substance that after the said judgment of condemnation the board of directors of the District found and determined that portions of said land would not be needed for the purposes of the District during parts of each year and thereupon leased such portions to defendant Gerald Stanfield for pasturage purposes subject to the use thereof at all times for the storage of waters by the Irrigation District.

The cause was tried June 22, 1920. Plaintiff admitted the new matter set up in the amended answer. Its superintendent testified in substance that it continued to occupy the premises after the judgment of condemnation and fed the thousand tons of hay complained of in its seventeenth assignment of error and at pages 33 to 36 of its brief to its own cattle on the lands in question before the water in the reservoir reached the hay; that it had removed some of the buildings to other lands owned by it and had torn down and removed beyond high water other structures including fencing, and that the receding waters of the reservoir had left the land more productive and in better condition for pasturage purposes than it was before the overflow. The defendants showed that some 50,000 acre-feet of water had been stored during the season, covering about 1860 acres of the 2500 acres described in the condemnation suit.

On August 23, 1920, the trial judge directed a decree substantially as prayed for injoining defendants from interfering with the removal by plaintiff of said buildings, fences, barns, sheds, corrals, etc., and from pasturing or otherwise using and enjoying the pasturage and feed growing upon said lands at times when the same or any part thereof are not flooded and when such use and enjoyment by plaintiff will not interfere with the use of said premises for reservoir purposes.

The court's memorandum opinion on final hearing is as follows:

"The questions raised on the final hearing of this

suit are substantially the same as those presented in the application for a preliminary injunction. I have examined them aided by the elaborate briefs of counsel and feel constrained to adhere to the views expressed in the injunction hearing. For the reasons given in the memorandum then filed a decree will be entered in favor of plaintiff as prayed for."

Petition for appeal, order allowing the same and bond on appeal from said decree were filed September 15, 1920, and citation on appeal issued.

The single question is whether by its condemnation of the land and payment of the judgment the Irrigation District obtained a title to the lands or a mere easement therein, and the answer must be found in the Oregon Laws. At pages 17 and 18 of its brief plaintiff in error cites many authorities but they are in point if, and only to the extent that, they interpret and apply statutes identical with those of Oregon, or announce general principles applicable alike to all eminent domain statutes. In this memorandum it is not necessary to take the time and space required to analyze and comment upon them in detail, the purpose hereof being merely to define the position and contention of the Irrigation District. The Oregon cases cited are in point only on three general propositions too well settled to require citation, namely: (a) The legislature cannot authorize any corporation to appropriate the property of an individual without just compensation first assessed and tendered; (b) cannot authorize a *private* corporation such as a railroad to acquire by condemnation a title freed from a public use; (c) while statutes providing for condemnation should be strictly construed, they should also be construed so as to effectuate the purpose for which they were enacted and give effect to all the provisions of the law (*Oswego D. & R. Co. v. Cobb,* 66

Or. 587, 598; 1 Lewis Em. Dom. 3d Ed. Sec. 338; Nichols on Em. Dom. Sec. 358).

On this text the argument for the Irrigation District proceeds. We contend that an interpretation of the Oregon statute, giving effect to all its provisions, so as to effectuate the purpose for which it was enacted, vests public irrigation districts with the title to lands condemned for reservoir sites.

The Warm Springs Irrigation District is a public corporation. It is an arm of the state, and although in some respects resembles a private corporation, is vested by law with all the rights, powers and privileges of the state in respect of the acquisition of private property for public use.

> Laws of 1917, Chap. 357, Secs. 1, 14, 31, pp. 743, 751, 763.
>
> Laws of 1919, Chap. 267, Sec. 2, p. 443.
>
> Herrett v. Warm Springs Irrigation District, 86, Or. 343.
>
> In re Madera Irrigation District, 92 Cal. 296, 14 L. R. A. 755, 27 Am. S. R. 106.
>
> Turlock Irr. Dist. v. Williams, 76 Cal. 360.
>
> Board of Directors v. Peterson, 64 Or. 46, 51.

Its status when exercising the right of eminent domain may therefore be said to be on a higher plane than that of a private corporation, organized for private gain. An unqualified fee cannot be taken by condemnation by a *private* corporation without *express* authority of a statute, whereas, in the case of a municipal corporation, the language of the statute granting the right of condemnation, although not in express terms mentioning a fee simple estate, may be broad enough to vest an absolute title without being technical in its terms.

> Brooklyn Park Commissioners v. Armstrong, 45 N. Y. 234, 6 Am. Rep. 70.

Hudson & M. R. Co. v. Wendel, 193 N. Y. 166.

It is not necessary that the authority to take a fee be given to a public corporation in express terms, or that exact or technical language should be used in the enabling act, in order that the fee or the whole title of the owner pass by the condemnation proceedings. In the absence of express and precise provisions, the intention of the act and the construction to be put upon its terms may be gathered from the general scope and tenor. If the legislative intention to vest the fee is thus made clear and this intention is consistent with the language employed, effect will be given to the intention.

Driscoll v. City of New Haven, 75 Conn. 92; 52 Atl. 618, 620.

Newton v. Perry, 163 Mass. 319; 39 N. E. 1032.

1 Lewis on Eminent Domain 3d Ed., Secs. 388, 389, pp. 709, 710.

2 Nichols on Eminent Domain 2d Ed., Sec. 358, p. 989.

Ward v. Boston Street Com., 217 Mass. 381.

In re City of New York, 217 N. Y. 1.

Mills on Eminent Domain 2d Ed., Sec. 49, p. 153.

In the absence of constitutional restrictions, the legislature is the exclusive judge of the extent, degree, and quality of interest which are proper to be taken. Courts can determine questions of public use, but the legislature alone can say what estate shall be taken.

Secombe v. Milwaukee etc. R. R. Co., 23 Wall. 108; 23 L. Ed. 67.

Shoemaker v. U. S., 147 U. S. 282, 298; 37 L. Ed. 170, 184.

Sweet v. Rechel, 159 U. S. 380; 40 L. Ed. 188.

U. S. v. Gettsburg Elec. Ry. Co., 160 U. S. 668, 685; 40 L. Ed. 576, 582.

Adirondack Ry. Co. v. State, 176 U. S. 335, 349; 44 L. Ed. 492, 500.

Sears v. Akron, 246 U. S. 242, 251; 62 L. Ed. 688, 698.

Burnett v. Commonwealth, 169 Mass. 417.

Hellen v. Medford, 188 Mass. 42; 69 L. R. A. 314, 316; 108 Am. S. R. 459.

Davis v. Hallock, 44 Or. 246; 252.

Shasta Power Co. v. Walker, 149 Fed. 568, 570.

Cooley, Const. Lim., 7 Ed. 809.

Note, 22 L. R. A., N. S. 76.

Lewis, Em. Dom., Secs. 277, 596.

When and what estate shall be taken is a question of policy over which the courts have no supervision. If the statute authorizes the taking of a fee, it cannot be held invalid, or that an easement only was acquired thereunder, on the ground that an easement only was required to accomplish the purpose which the legislature had in view. That is a legislative and not a judicial question.

Brooklyn Park Com. v. Armstrong, 45 N. Y. 234; 6 Am. Rep. 70.

Sweet v. Buffalo etc. Co., 79 N. Y. 293.

Driscoll v. New Haven, 75 Conn. 92.

Clendaniel v. Conrad, 3 Boyce (Del.), 549; Ann. Cas. 1915 B 968, 985.

U. S. Pipe Line Co. v. Del. L. & W. R. R. Co. 62 N. J. L. 254; 42 L. R. A. 572, 578

15 Cyc. 1018.

We are not now concerned with private irrigation companies, nor with rights of way for ditches, railroads or canals, nor with city parks, streets, docks or highways. The inquiry relates solely to a reservoir site for a public irrigation district. Applying the above stated general principles to the construction of the laws of

Oregon, did the Warm Springs Irrigation District acquire the title to the lands in question for a reservoir site, or did it acquire only an easement for that purpose?

The law quoted in extenso in the foregoing brief applies only to such public bodies. Section 31 of the act, which confers the power of eminent domain was amended March 3, 1919, and provides inter alia:

> "Said board shall also have the right to acquire, either by lease, purchase, condemnation, or other legal means, all lands and waters and water rights, rights of way, easements and other property including canals and works and the whole of irrigation systems or projects constructed or being constructed by private owners, necessary for the construction, use, supply, maintenance, repair and improvement of any canal or canals and works proposed to be constructed by said board."

Here is ample power to take any form of property or rights in property, whether lands, water, water rights, rights of way, easements or other property necessary for an irrigation system; but the legislature evidently intended to grant unquestioned power to appropriate for *reservoirs for the storage of waters* not merely *easements* or rights *in* land, *but the land itself* as distinguished from an easement or right enumerated in the first part of the section. To that enumeration the legislature added the significant clause:

> "and shall *also* have the right to so acquire *lands,* and all necessary appurtenances for *reservoirs* and the right to store water in constructed reservoirs, for the storage of needful waters, or for any other purposes reasonably necessary for the purposes of said district."

There is a further distinction made in said section between easements or rights of way, and lands; for after granting rights of way over state lands it declares the use of water for irrigation, together with all water rights, rights of way for canals and ditches, *sites for reservoirs,* etc., to be a public use more necessary and more beneficial than any other use, either public or private, to which said water, water rights, rights to appropriate water, *lands* or other property may have been or may be appropriated.

The section then provides:

> "The *legal title* to all property acquired under the provisions of this act shall immediately and by operation of law vest in such irrigation district, *and shall be held by such district in trust* for and is hereby dedicated and set apart to the uses and purposes set forth in this act; and said board is hereby authorized and empowered to *hold, use, acquire, manage, occupy, possess* and *dispose* of said property as herein provided."

"All property" and "said property," the legal title to which is vested in the district to be held in trust by it, and to be managed, occupied, possessed and disposed of by the board, include, of course, the kinds of property mentioned in the first part of the section, that is to say, *first* "all lands and waters and water rights, rights of way, easements and other property, including canals and works and the whole of irrigation systems or projects constructed or being constructed by private owners, necessary for the construction, use, supply, maintenance, repair and improvement of any canal or canals and works proposed to be constructed by said board;" *second* "and also *lands* and all necessary appurtenances for *reservoirs* for the storage of needful waters," etc.

The last clause of Sec. 31, vesting legal title to all property acquired in the irrigation district to be held in trust for and to the uses and purposes set forth in the act, and empowering the board to hold, use, acquire, manage, occupy, possess and dispose of said property, clearly contemplates absolute ownership of some of the property at least. The language is too broad to refer only to easements and rights in property, and puts the district in a position analogous to a municipality which acquires land for a public park of which it has been said:

> "The legal title became vested in the city, not for its own use in a corporate capacity, but in perpetual trust for the use of all who at any time might enjoy the benefit of a public park."
> Holt v. Somerville, 127 Mass. 408, 411.

Certainly, there is nothing in the section that reserves any right to the original private owner of the site for a reservoir in land taken for that purpose. The legal title to the site so taken is in the district in trust but the original owner is not one of the cestui que trustent.

It is clear that the legislature intended to distinguish lands and ownership of lands and the right to acquire and hold title to lands, from rights *in* or *over* lands and the acquirement of easements therein. A water right, right of way, an easement, in or over canals and works, and the irrigation system or project of a private owner might be sufficient for the necessities of the irrigation district for "any canal or canals and works proposed to be constructed by said board." Up to this point in the statute the power conferred comprehends the acquirement by the district of title to the property or title to an easement therein as may be needed. But the ensuing clause: *"and shall also have the right to so acquire* (i. e. by condemnation) *lands* and all necessary appurtenances *for reservoirs"* makes no reference to easements or rights in lands.

"Lands" of course includes any lesser estate than fee simple therein, but all parts of the section must be given a meaning if possible, and when the law speaks of taking lands, rights of way and easements for *canals and works* in one clause and follows this with a grant of power to *acquire lands* for a *reservoir,* not mentioning any lesser interest than the whole estate in the lands as was done in the preceding clause, the legislature must have contemplated that the use of land by a public corporation as a reservoir site for the storage of waters would be inconsistent with retention of any interest therein by the private owner, and intended the district to take the absolute title. The legislature must have thought that an easement in land for a reservoir site and storage of waters—a use in its nature fixed, unchangeable and permanent—would not satisfy the requirements of the public; that such a use would be continuous and peculiarly exclusive, and therefore unequivocally provided for condemnation of "lands," the entire estate of the private owner, both legal and equitable, for reservoir sites for the storage of needed waters.

That there should be no doubt of its intention to vest the ownership in fee of any lands acquired by an irrigation district, and of the right of the district to sell or otherwise dispose of the same, the legislature itself placed an interpretation upon the law above quoted by the passage of the act of February 25, 1919, being Chapter 138, Laws of 1919, page 193, as follows:

> "AN ACT To authorize drainage and irrigation districts to sell or dispose of real property acquired for the uses and purposes of said district.
>
> *Be it Enacted by the People of the State of Oregon:*
>
> Section 1. Whenever any drainage or irrigation district heretofore or hereafter created shall have acquired any lands, by gift, purchase or by the right of eminent domain or otherwise, for the uses and purposes of the said district and shall thereafter by reason of a change of its plans or for any other reason shall determine that all or any part

> thereof is no longer necessary for the uses or purposes for which it has been acquired, said district is hereby given the right to sell or dispose of said lands or any part thereof, either at private or public sale, and the officers of said district otherwise authorized to excute conveyances shall have the authority to make such conveyance."

This act is contemporaneous with and relates to the same subject as the other act quoted, passed at the same session of the legislature. It is a familiar rule in Oregon and perhaps everywhere, that contemporaneous statutes and acts relating to the same subject where not repugnant or inconsistent with each other, are in *pari materia,* and are to be construed as though their several provisions were incorporated together and constituted one entire act for the purpose of arriving at the intent of the legislature. (*Miller v. Tobin,* 16 Or. 540, 556; *Smith v. Kelly,* 24 Or. 464, 474; *Stoppenback v. Multnomah County,* 71 Or. 493, 509.) This rule is particularly applicable when in the case of two enactments one is the complement of the other (*Stoppenback v. Multnomah County, supra*).

It is to be noted that the act refers only to *lands* acquired by gift, purchase, or by eminent domain or otherwise. Rights of way and easements are not mentioned. Whether the legislature also intended to confer power of sale or other disposition of such rights in property as easements, is beside the question here. The act speaks of lands acquired by eminent domain or by any of the other methods enumerated, and gives the district absolute power of sale and disposal—a power consistent only with ownership of the fee. If the legislature had not intended by Sec. 31 of the Act of 1917 and 1919, to vest absolute title to lands acquired by the district by condemnation, the words: "or by right of eminent domain," in the act approved February 25, 1919, last quoted, are superfluous and meaningless. It is not necessary to cite authority on the proposition that every word and clause of a statute must be given effect if possible, and the clause in question is in complete harmony with the provision of Sec. 31 granting power to acquire by lease, purchase, condemnation or other legal means "lands for reservoirs." Grant of the right to sell and dispose of lands acquired by the right of eminent domain is the corollary of the grant of power to acquire, and raises an implication so strong as to amount to a positive declaration that the original grant of power to acquire by condemnation meant to acquire the fee. The legislature indubitably must have meant that condemnation of a reservoir site gives the district title thereto, otherwise the grant of power to sell or dispose of it "*or any part thereof,* either at private or public sale" and "to execute conveyances," means nothing. That those words mean nothing is unthinkable because the very title of the act is declaratory of their import. Nor is the power to sell and convey in anywise made to depend on how or by what method the district acquired title. Whether obtained by gift, purchase or condemnation, the right to sell remains.

If, therefore, following the well settled rule, the act of February 25, 1919, be read as a part of Section 31 first above quoted, treating the two as constituting one act, we have the following expression of the legislative intention:

> "This board and its agents and employes shall have the right to enter upon any land to make surveys, and may locate the necessary irrigation or drainage works and the line for any canal or canals, and the necessary branches for the same, on any lands which may be deemed best for such location. Said board shall also have the right to acquire, either by lease, purchase, condemnation, or other legal means, all lands and waters and water rights,

rights of way, easements and other property, including canals and works and the whole of irrigation systems or projects constructed or being constructed by private owners, necessary for the construction, use, supply, maintenance, repair and improvement of any canal or canals and works proposed to be constructed by said board, and shall also have the right to so acquire lands, and all necessary appurtenances for reservoirs and the right to store water in constructed reservoirs, for the storage of needful waters, or for any other purposes reasonably necessary for the purposes of said district. The property, the right to condemn which is hereby given, shall include property already devoted to public use which is less necessary than the use for which it is required by the district, whether used for irrigation or any other purpose. The right of way is hereby given, dedicated and set apart, to locate, construct and maintain said works over and through any of the lands which are now or may be the property of this state. In the acquisition of property or rights by condemnation, the board shall proceed in the name of the district under the provisions of the laws of the state of Oregon."

* * * * *

"The legal title to all property acquired under the provisions of this act shall immediately and by operation of law vest in such irrigation district, and shall be held by such district in trust for and is hereby dedicated and set apart to the uses and purposes set forth in this act; and said board is hereby authorized and empowered to hold, use, acquire, manage, occupy, possess and dispose of said property as herein provided."

"Whenever any drainage or irrigation district heretofore or hereafter created shall have acquired any lands, by gift, purchase or by the right of eminent domain or otherwise, for the uses and purposes of the said district and shall thereafter by reason of a change of its plans or for any other reason shall determine that all or any part thereof is no longer necessary for the uses or purposes for which it has been acquired, said district is hereby given the right to sell or dispose of said lands or any part thereof, either at private or public sale, and the officers of said district otherwise authorized to execute conveyances shall have the authority to make such conveyance."

Thus far we have considered the Act of February 25, 1919, only as to its effect as an aid to the construction of Sec. 31 of the Acts of 1917 and 1919, and without regard to the exercise by the district of the power of sale therein conferred. Our contention is that said act must be considered in any inquiry as to whether the legislature intended by Sec. 31 to vest in the district a transferable title, freed from reversion, of lands condemned for a reservoir site. It is too plain for argument that if Chapter 138 *supra* had given irrigation districts power to sell and dispose of such lands as had been acquired by *gift or purchase,* but without mention of lands acquired by right of eminent domain, the legislative interpretation would be just the opposite of what the district contends. The district needed no legislative grant of power to sell and dispose of that which had been given to it, or property it had purchased and paid for; and since the act extends the power to sell and dispose of lands acquired "by the right of eminent domain" the same as of lands acquired by gift, purchase or otherwise, there seems to us no room for any doubt that condemnation of land for a reservoir site gave the district a marketable title the same as purchase of the lands would have done.

But the admitted facts bring the district within the provisions of the act giving it the right, when *"for any reason"* it shall determine that any part of the land acquired is no longer necessary for the uses and purposes for which it was acquired, to sell or dispose any part of said land. It determined that some portion of said land would not be overflowed during the 1920 season and would therefore not be needed for the storage of waters. The right to sell and dispose includes the right to lease, and hence the district leased to defendant Stanfield that portion of the land which from year to year might not be overflowed. There may be some years when practically the whole of the land will be overflowed. In other years, like 1920, the water may cover little more than two-thirds of the land. The lessee takes those chances, and the district obtains a fixed rental which is a substantial help in meeting the interest on its bonds. In this connection, and as an aid to the construction of the act, one of the reasons that influenced the legislature in passing the act of February 25, 1919, as a complement of the eminent domain section, may be adverted to.

On the day after the approval of that act by the governor there was filed in the office of the Secretary of State, House Joint Resolution No. 32, proposing an amendment to the Oregon Constitution to be known as Article XIb (Laws of Oregon, 1919, page 848), for the purpose of providing funds for the payment by the state, for a period not exceeding five years, of interest on bonds theretofore or thereafter issued by irrigation and drainage districts. Since the state purposed to pledge its credit to guarantee for five years the payment of interest on Irrigation District bonds the legislature quite naturally reinforced and broadened the rights and powers of the districts with a view, no doubt, of affording them every opportunity of paying their way so as to obviate as much as possible the necessity of resort to the state guaranty. The proposed amendment was submitted to the people at the election, June

3, 1919, and was adopted by a substantial majority. It became effective by proclamation of the governor June 23, 1919 (Laws of Oregon, Special Session 1920, pages 5-10).

Regardless of whether Section 31 of the act of 1917, as amended in 1919, vests the district with the title to the lands condemned for reservoir purposes, the district has brought itself within the provisions of the act of February 25, 1919 (Laws of 1919, Chapter 138) and its disposal of portions of the land not needed for water storage, being in strict accordance with that act, should be ratified.

If plaintiff still owns the fee in those lands and defendant has nothing but an easement therein to the extent only of water impounded above its dam, the resulting consequences are unique. It creates an ambulatory, peripatetic, periodic, migratory sort of use; an easement that runs up and down hill according to the fall of snow or rain in the mountains miles away; a meterological easement that appears with storms, thaws and floods, and vanishes with cold and drought. The fee simple title and use claimed by plaintiff in such parts of the reservoir site as may not from day to day be covered by stored water is similarly afflicted with a sort of legal St. Vitus dance, and hops up and down over the grease wood convolutions of Warm Springs ranch close upon the heels of defendant's fleeing easement. The evidence shows that this year at high water defendant flooded about 1860 acres of the 2500 which it condemned, leaving plaintiff (according to its contention) with the fee and right of possession and use of some 700 acres. Evaporation and withdrawal have caused the waters to recede each day adding many acres to plaintiff's growing title and reducing defendant's easement by as much. When the floods come next February and March the operation will be reversed, and in the course of nature it is possible that plaintiff's agitated title may give way to defendant's perambulating easement over some 2400 acres; and so, according to plaintiff's schedule, this fantastic race between a fee simple title and an easement is to go on forever. Said Falstaff in *Henry IV*: "Old father antic the law," and at that he knew nothing of the shimmy nor of its performance by a fee title and an easement.

Chapter 138, Laws of 1919, authorizes the district to sell or dispose of lands not only when by reason of a change in its plans they are no longer necessary for the uses or purposes for which acquired, but *"for any other reason."* Whether or not the board acted wisely in leasing the marginal land is a question that cannot be raised by the plaintiff. The board's action in that behalf can be questioned, if at all, only by the taxpayers in the district or by the State of Oregon. Similarly as to whether authority to "sell or dispose of" includes power to lease. If defendant acquired title to the lands it is no concern of plaintiff what disposition is made of them.

The doctrine is generally prevalent that where the acquisition of lands by exercise of eminent domain is made by a public corporation in good faith for a public purpose, a reasonable discretion and latitude (subject of course to review by the courts) as to the amount to be taken, may be exercised; and that the municipality may anticipate future growth and expansion.

Neitzel v. Spokane Int. Ry. Co. (Wash.), 141 Pac. 186.

2 Nichols on Eminent Domain, pp. 150, 177, 181, 190, 203.

The condemnation case was tried on the supposition that plaintiff therein sought the property in perpetuity; all of the testimony went to the entire value of the property; the Live Stock Co. centered a mass of evidence on the market value of the lands, buildings and other improvements; the court considered "the property as a whole, the improvements thereon, the relation of the several parts to each other, its location, situation, character and adaptability to the various uses to which it can be put" and found that $90,000 was the fair and reasonable value thereof, that is, what "one desiring and able to purchase would give for it if it were offered on the market." It cannot be believed that any one desiring to *purchase the property* would give that sum for the sort of title which it is now claimed the district obtained—a mere fluctuating, ambulatory easement in the land with reversion of the fee to the Live Stock Company the instant water shall cease to be stored thereon.

One of the uses for which the lands was adaptable, considered by the court, was that of grazing or pasturage for live stock. It is the one on which the Live Stock Company laid greatest stress and directed most of its testimony, and must be assumed as the principal element considered in fixing the amount of the judgment. It is that use of the varying area not flooded by impounded waters which the district now seeks to make as an incident of the main object and purpose in condemning the lands for a reservoir site. The judgment followed the statute, appropriated the lands to the district as a part of its irrigation system forever, and decreed the lands and the whole thereof to be its property. It paid the price, and thereby got what the legislature by Sec. 31, Chapter 357, Laws of 1917 (Sec. 2, Chapter 267, Laws 1919) intended it to get, the absolute title, and thereafter by virtue of the power granted to it by Chapter 138, Laws of 1919, it disposed of such portions thereof as it found for the time being no longer necessary for the storage of water, retaining title and right of resumption of possession and use as the necessities of the district may require.

Defendant paid the full market value of the lands including the buildings and other improvements affixed thereto. In the condemnation proceeding it occupied the position of purchaser and the Live Stock Company that of seller. The district holds under a statute conveyance and its title is, in legal phrase, by purchase (*Burt v. Merchants Insurance Co.,* 106 Mass. 356; 8 Am. Rep. 339, 342). The seller has taken and appropriated some of defendant's property. Those buildings and other improvements were bought and paid for by defendant as a part of the lands condemned (*Jackson v. State,* 213 N. Y. 34; 106 N. E. 758; Ann. Cas. 1916C. 779 and *Note;* L. R. A, 1916D 492 and *Note*). In addition to converting property which it claims to be worth many thousand dollars it also claims right of possession and use of a large part of the lands with reversion of the whole. Every element of equity in this case is on the side of the defendant.

Pursuant to authority of the statute which created it defendant has borrowed, and investors have loaned it, large sums of money on the faith and credit of its ownership of the lands, and the bonds issued and purchased are on the statutory guarantee that: "In addition to the provisions for the payment of said bonds and interest by taxation and other provisions of this act, *all the property of the district, including irrigation and other works, shall be liable for* the indebtedness of the district."

Chapter 357, Sec. 22, Laws 1917, p. 757.

Should the district default, and the bondholders or the United States take possession, as provided in said section, would they be compelled to operate the system forever in case the district did not pay? If they sold the property to liquidate the debt would the purchaser be bound to operate the irrigation project on penalty of forfeiture for misuser, nonuser, or abandonment? Would the doctrine of reverter apply in favor of the Pacific Live Stock Company as against a purchaser—whether bondholder or the United States—in case of foreclosure? These questions must all be answered in the affirmative if plaintiff is to prevail in this case, because the legislature has given bondholders and purchasers no better title than it has given the district. The provision with reference to the rights of creditors, however, afford strong support to our contention that the law gives the district absolute title. The right to pledge, sell, dispose of and convey property, granted by express unequivocal terms of the statute can mean nothing else, and completely destroy the doctrine of reverter.

> "When only an easement is taken," says Mr. Mills, "it is presumed that the full value is not given and that the owner receives a lesser amount when there is reserved to him the chance of a reversion on a discontinuance of the public use."
>
> Mills on Eminent Domain, Sec. 50, p. 156.

If the act provides that full value should be given for lands, and that lands so taken should be pledged to secure payment of bonds, it must be inferred that a fee was taken.

> Mills on Eminent Domain, Sec. 50, p. 157.
> Brooklyn Park Com. v. Armstrong, 45 N. Y. 234.

When, as in this case, the district acquired the legal title to lands by operation of a law which at the same time in unequivocal terms granted express power to mortgage, sell, dispose of and convey the same; and when, as in this case, the district has paid to the plaintiff full compensation, fairly estimated and without deduction or allowance for right of user or reversion, it would be violative not only of well settled rules of construction but of the principles of justice itself to decree that anything less than a fee simple title passed and is now held by defendant.

If the law is otherwise, then on behalf of the Warm Springs Irrigation District and its taxpayers we join with counsel for the Pacific Live Stock Company in asking for a reversal of the judgment fixing the damages in the condemnation case because we are confident that on a retrial thereof neither the judge who tried it nor any jury would render a verdict of $90,000 or anywhere near that amount for a mere easement in that 2500 acres of land.

Respectfully submitted,

Ed. R. Coulter,
H. C. Eastham,
Allen H. McCurtain,
Thomas G. Greene,
Solicitors for Defendants and Appellants.

No. 3513

United States

Circuit Court of Appeals

For the Ninth Circuit.

AMERICAN MERCHANT MARINE INSURANCE COMPANY OF NEW YORK, a Corporation,

Appellant,

vs.

H. G. TREMAINE, S. L. BUCKLEY and JOHN DOE BUCKLEY, Doing Business Under the Firm Name and Style of BUCKLEY-TREMAINE LUMBER COMPANY,

Appellees.

Transcript of Record.

Upon Appeal from the United States District Court for the Western District of Washington, Northern Division.

Filmer Bros. Co. Print, 330 Jackson St., S. F., Cal.

United States
Circuit Court of Appeals
For the Ninth Circuit.

AMERICAN MERCHANT MARINE INSURANCE COMPANY OF NEW YORK, a Corporation,

Appellant,

vs.

H. G. TREMAINE, S. L. BUCKLEY and JOHN DOE BUCKLEY, Doing Business Under the Firm Name and Style of BUCKLEY-TREMAINE LUMBER COMPANY,

Appellees.

Transcript of Record.

Upon Appeal from the United States District Court for the Western District of Washington, Northern Division.

Filmer Bros. Co. Print, 330 Jackson St., S. F., Cal.

INDEX TO THE PRINTED TRANSCRIPT OF RECORD.

[Clerk's Note: When deemed likely to be of an important nature, errors or doubtful matters appearing in the original certified record are printed literally in italic; and, likewise, cancelled matter appearing in the original certified record is printed and cancelled herein accordingly. When possible, an omission from the text is indicated by printing in italic the two words between which the omission seems to occur.]

Names and Addresses of Counsel.

B. S. GROSSCUP, Esq., Solicitor for Plaintiff,
Perkins Building, Tacoma, Washington.

W. CARR MORROW, Esq., Solicitor for Plaintiff,
Perkins Building, Tacoma, Washington.

HAROLD M. SAWYER, Esq., Solicitor for Plaintiff,
Mills Building, San Francisco, California.

ALFRED T. CLUFF, Esq., Solicitor for Plaintiff,
Mills Building, San Francisco, California.

F. A. HUFFER, Esq., Solicitor for Defendant,
Henry Building, Seattle, Washington.

W. H. HAYDEN, Esq., Solicitor for Defendant,
Henry Building, Seattle, Washington. [1*]

No. 186–E.

Bill of Complaint.

Complainant complains and alleges:

I.

That the American Merchant Marine Insurance Company of New York is a corporation duly organized and existing under and by virtue of the laws of the State of New York and is a citizen of said State, and is authorized to do business as an insurance company in the State of Washington, and has fully complied with all the requirements of the laws of the State of Washington, and has paid its annual license fee last due.

*Page-number appearing at foot of page of original certified Transcript of Record.

II.

That the defendants, H. G. Tremaine and S. L. Buckley, are copartners doing business under the firm name and style of Buckley-Tremaine Lumber Company in the City of Seattle, in the State of Washington, and the defendant, H. G. Tremaine, is a citizen of the State of Washington.

III.

That on or about the third day of October, 1919, complainant insured for defendants, lumber on Scow F. L. B. No. 3 for October sailing, in tow of tug "Coutli" and/or other approved tug, at and from Craig, Alaska (in single tow), to Prince Rupert, B. C., thence (in double tow) to Seattle, Washington, in the sum of four thousand eight hundred seventy-five dollars ($4,875.00), which said lumber was valued at $17.50 per thousand feet; loss if any payable to the order of the assured in Seattle; copies of said insurance are hereto attached, marked Exhibits "A" and "B" and made a part of this complaint. [2]

IV.

That in the drafting and delivery of Exhibit "B" this complainant inadvertently and by mistake omitted to insert therein the sailing date or time within which said Scow F. L. B. No. 3 was required and warranted under said insurance to sail, and said defendants inadvertently and by mistake received, accepted, and ever since have retained and do now retain said Exhibit "B" so erroneously issued.

V.

That the sailing date set forth and agreed to in Exhibit "A" and inadvertently and by mistake omitted from Exhibit "B" was a material warranty by defendants, materially and substantially affecting the rights and obligations of the parties thereto, and particularly the rights and obligations of this complainant.

VI.

That complainant has no plain, speedy and adequate remedy in a court of law, and complainant further alleges that in equity and justice Exhibit "B" hereto attached ought to be reformed and corrected by inserting therein the words "October sailing." That the controversy in this suit is between citizens of different States, to wit, between a citizen of the State of New York and citizens of the State of Washington, and is one which can be fully determined between them in a District Court of the United States. That the amount involved, exclusive of interest and costs, exceeds the sum of $3,000.00.

WHEREFORE Complainant prays that said Exhibit "B" herein set forth be corrected and reformed by inserting therein the words "October sailing," and that complainant have such other and further relief as to the Court may seem just and equitable, and recover its costs herein expended.

B. S. GROSSCUP and
W. C. MORROW,
Attorneys for Complainant. [3]

Exhibit "A."

Seattle, Wash., Oct. 3d, 1919.

INSURANCE IS WANTED BY BUCKLEY-TREMAINE LUMBER COMPANY.

LOSS, IF ANY, payable to Them, or order.

FOR $7,875. ON Lumber VALUED AT $17.50 per M. Ft.

PER F. L. B. SCOW "No. 3" in single tow of Tug "COUTLI" at and from Craig, Alaska, to Prince Rupert, B. C., thence while in double tow of Approved Tug to Seattle, Wash. (Oct. Slg.)

This insurance is understood and agreed to be subject to English Law and usage to Liability for and settlement of any and all claims.

RATE—3%.

CONDITIONS—Insured only against the risk of Total and/or Constructive Total Loss but to pay any General Average and/or Salvage Charges that may be incurred.

ACCEPTED—PACIFIC MARINE INSURANCE CO.

$4,875.00—AMERICAN MERCHANT MARINE INS. CO. OF N. Y.

(M. D. C.) [4]

Exhibit "B."

CERTIFICATE OF INSURANCE.

To conform with the Revenue Laws of Great Britain, in order to collect a claim under this Certificate it must be stamped within ten days after its receipt in the United Kingdom.

Special Cargo
11123–C
No. ~~11261–C~~

Amount
$4,875.00
Rate 3%
Prem. $146.25

AMERICAN MERCHANT MARINE INSURANCE COMPANY OF NEW YORK,
SEELEY & CO., (MARINE) INC.,
Pacific Coast General Agents.

140 Sansome Street.
San Francisco, Cal.

Colman Bldg.
Seattle, Wash.

Board of Trade Bldg.
Portland, Ore.

Dominion Building
Vancouver, B. C.

Seattle, Wash., October 6, 1919.

THIS IS TO CERTIFY, that on the Sixth day of October, 1919, this Company insured for Buckley-Tremaine Lumber Company Four thousand eight hundred seventy-five dollars ($4,875.00) Dollars on Lumber, Valued at $17.50 per 1,000 feet on board Scow F. L. B. No. 3 in tow tug "COUTLI" and/or other approved tug at and from Craig, Alaska, (in single tow), to Prince Rupert, B. C., thence (in double tow) to Seattle, Wash., loss, if any, payable to the order of the assured in Seattle.

This insurance subject to conditions as stated below and on back hereof.

[Stamped across face:] Original. Original and duplicate issued, one of which being accomplished, the other to stand null and void.

MARKS AND NUMBERS.

CONDITIONS.

This certificate is subject to the full terms of the policy, BUT warranted by the assured free from loss or expense arising from capture, seizure, restraint, detention or destruction, or the consequence of any attempt thereat, whether lawful or unlawful, or whether by the act of any belligerent nations or by governments of seceding or revolting States, or by unauthorized or lawless persons therein, or otherwise, and whether occurring in a port of distress or otherwise, anything in this policy to the contrary notwithstanding, and free from all other consequences of hostilities whether before or after declaration of war.

Held covered at a premium to be arranged, in case of deviation or change of voyage or of any error or unintentional omission in the description of the interest, vessel or voyage, provided same be communicated to the assurers as soon as known to the assured.

Held covered on board craft and/or lighter to and from the vessel. Each craft and/or lighter to be deemed a separate insurance.

IT IS AGREED THAT THERE SHALL BE NO RETURN OF PREMIUM IF INTEREST INSURED BE LOST BY PERILS NOT INSURED AGAINST HEREUNDER.

In Case of Loss Apply to SEELEY & CO, (Marine), Inc., at Seattle, Wash.

CONDITIONS.

Warranted not to cover the interest of any alien

enemies including such persons, copartnerships or corporations, as now, or may hereafter, appear in any Enemy Trading List issued by the War Trade Board of the United States of America.

ENGLISH POLICY.

Insured only against the risk of total and/or constructive total loss, but to pay any General Average and/or Salvage Charges that may be incurred.

MDC.

This insurance is understood and agreed to be subject to English law and usage to Liability for and settlement of any and all claims.

MDC.

IN WITNESS WHEREOF, the said Company has caused these Presents to be signed by its President in the City of New York, but this certificate shall not be valid unless countersigned by the Company's duly authorized representative.

I. STEWART,
President.

T. M. LEE MARTIN,
Secretary.

Countersigned at Seattle, Wash., the 6th day of October, 1919.

SEELEY & CO. (Marine) Inc.,
By M. D. CALDER. [5]

The adventures and perils which the said Assurers are contented to bear and take upon themselves in this voyage are *of the seas, fires, men of war, enemies, pirates, rovers, assailing thieves, jettison, letters of mart or countermart, takings at sea, arrests, restraints and detainments of all kings, princes and peo-*

ple, of what nation, condition or quality soever, criminal barratry of the master and mariners, and all other like perils, losses and misfortunes, that have or shall come to the hurt, detriment or damage of the said goods and merchandise or any part thereof. And in case of any loss or misfortune, it shall be lawful and necessary to and for the assured, and the assured's factors, servants and assigns, to sue, labor and travel for, in and about the defense, safeguard and recovery of the said goods and merchandise or any part thereof, without prejudice to this insurance; nor shall the acts of the assured or assurers, in recovering, saving and preserving the property insured, in case of disaster, be considered a waiver or an acceptance of an abandonment; to the charges whereof, the said assurers will contribute according to the rate and quantity of the sum herein insured.

In case of loss, such loss to be paid in thirty days after proof of loss, and proof of interest in the merchandise hereby insured (the amount of premium if unpaid, being first deducted); Provided Always, and it is hereby further agreed, that if the assured shall have made any other assurance upon the premises aforesaid, prior in day of date to this certificate, then the said Assurers shall be answerable only for so much as the amount of such prior assurance may be deficient toward fully covering the premises hereby assured, and the said Assurers shall return the premium upon so much of the sum by it assured as it shall be by such prior assurance exonerated from. And in case of any assurance upon the said premises, subsequent in date to this certificate, the said Assurers shall nevertheless be answerable for the full extent of the sum by them subscribed hereto, without right to claim contribution from such subsequent assurers, and shall accordingly be entitled to retain the premiums by them received, in the same manner as if no such subsequent assurance had been made. Other insurance upon the premises aforesaid, of date the same day as this certificate, shall be deemed simultaneous herewith, and these assurers shall not be liable for more than a ratable contribution in the proportion of the sum by them insured to the aggregate of such simultaneous insurance.

The said merchandise is insured as under deck unless otherwise specified in this certificate. Only such merchandise as shall be stowed under the main deck shall be deemed stowed under deck. Cargo on deck free from claim for damage by wet, breakage, leakage or exposure, and liable only for absolute total loss or total loss of a part, if amounting to ten per cent.

Warranted by the assured, if loaded with grain, petroleum and heavy cargoes, to be loaded under the inspection of the surveyor appointed or approved by the Assurers for that purpose, and his certificate as to the proper loading and seaworthiness obtained.

Warranted not to abandon, in case of capture, seizure or detention, until after the condemnation of the property insured; nor until ninety days after notice of condemnation is given to the Assurers. Also warranted not to abandon in case of blockade, and free from any expense in consequence of capture, seizure, detention or blockade; but in the event of blockade, to be at liberty to proceed to an open port and there end the voyage, when and where all the liability of the Assurers shall cease. It is Also Agreed that the property be warranted by the Assured free from any charge, damage or loss which may arise in consequence of a seizure or detention for or on account of any illicit or prohibited trade, or any trade in articles contraband of war or the violation of any port regulation.

Warranted by the Assured free from damage or injury from dampness, change of flavor, or being spotted, discolored, musty or mouldy, except caused by actual contact of sea water, with the articles damaged, occasioned by sea perils. Not liable for leakage on molasses or other liquids, nor for breakage of glass, crockery or other bottled wares, unless occasioned by stranding or collision with another vessel. In case of loss or damage to any part of a machine, consisting, when complete for sale or use of several parts, the Assurers shall only be liable for the insured value of the part lost or damaged.

It is Agreed that upon the payment of any loss or damage, the Assurers are to be subrogated to all the rights of the Assured under their bills of lading or transportation receipts or contracts, to the extent of such payments.

This insurance is warranted to be in all cases null and void to the extent of any insurance by any carrier or bailee which would attach and cover said property if this certificate had not been issued, and to be null and void, as concerns loss or damage by fire on land, to the extent of any insurance against loss or damage by fire directly or indirectly covering upon the same property, whether prior or subsequent hereto in date or of the same date herewith, anything hereinbefore contained to the contrary notwithstanding; and it is also understood and agreed, that in case any agreement shall have been or shall be made or accepted by the Assured with any carrier or bailee by which it is stipulated or agreed that such or any carrier or bailee shall have, in case of any loss for which he may be liable, the benefit of this insurance, or exemption in any manner from responsibility grounded on the fact of this insurance, then and in that event the Assurers shall be discharged of any liability for such loss hereunder, but these Assurers, in these and all cases of loss or damage by perils insured against, shall be liable and owe actual payment for only what cannot be collected from the carrier, bailee, and/or other insurers of property lost or damaged, but also shall be chargeable with the direct pecuniary consequence to the Assured temporarily arising from delay in collection from said carrier and/or bailee and/or insurers, and the advancing for this purpose only, of funds to the Assured for his protection pending such delay, shall in no case be considered as affecting the question of the final liability of these Assurers and as soon as collection is made from the carrier, bailee and/or insurers, the right of the Assured to hold the sums so advanced by these Assurers shall discontinue and a portion thereof equal to the sum collected from such carrier, bailee and/or insurers, shall be repaid to these Assurers, but in case of final failure to collect from such carrier, bailee and/or other insurers a portion of the sums advanced by these Assurers, equal to the sum short collected from such carrier, bailee and/or other insurers, may be retained and applied in settlement of the actual liability of these Assurers thereby established, (provided always the loss shall constitute in other respects a claim under this insurance). In the event of loss or damage, this insurance shall be null and void in the extent of any payment made by any carrier, bailee, or other insurers whether liable or not.

Proofs of loss and all bills of expense must be approved by the Agent of these Assurers, if there be one at or near where the loss occurs, or the expenses are incurred, or if there be none in the vicinity, by the Correspondent of the National Board of Marine Underwriters, or by Lloyd's Agent; and such agent or correspondent must be represented on all surveys.

UNITED STATES OF AMERICA.

In the United States District Court for the Western District of Washington.

IN EQUITY.

No. 186–E.

Subpoena.

The President of the United States of America, to H. G. Tremaine and S. L. Buckley, Doing Business Under the Firm Name and Style of Buckley-Tremaine Lumber Company, GREETING:

YOU ARE HEREBY COMMANDED, That you be and appear in said District Court of the United

States aforesaid, at the courtroom of said Court, in the city of Seattle, on the 13th day of April, 1920, to answer a bill of complaint filed against you in said court by American Merchant Marine Insurance Company of New York, and to do and receive what the Court shall have considered in that behalf. And this you are not to omit under the penalty of the law.

WITNESS the Honorable JEREMIAH NETERER, Judge of said Court, and the seal thereof, at Seattle, Washington, this 24th day of March, 1920.

[Seal] F. M. HARSHBERGER,
Clerk.
By Leeta D. Manning,
Deputy Clerk.

MEMORANDUM PURSUANT TO RULE 12, SUPREME COURT U. S.

YOU ARE HEREBY REQUIRED to enter your appearance in the above mentioned suit on or before twenty days from the date of service, excluding the day thereof, at the Clerk's Office of said Court, pursuant to said bill; otherwise the said bill will be taken, *pro confesso.*

[Seal] F. M. HARSHBERGER,
Clerk.
By Leeta D. Manning,
Deputy Clerk. [6]

MARSHAL'S RETURN.

United States of America,
Western District of Washington,—ss.

I HEREBY CERTIFY, That I have served the within writ by delivering to and leaving a true copy thereof with H. G. Tremaine, one of the partners of the firm.

JOHN M. BOYLE,
United States Marshal.
By Thos. Waters,
Deputy.

Mch. 24th, 1920.
Fees: $2.12. [7]

No. 186.

Praecipe for Appearance.

To the Clerk of the Above-entitled Court:

Please enter our appearance as solicitors for the defendant H. G. Tremaine. Service of all subsequent papers except writs and process may be made upon the undersigned as solicitors for said defendant at the address below given.

HUFFER & HAYDEN,
Solicitors for Defendant H. G. Tremaine.

Office and Postoffice Address: 527 Henry Building, Seattle, Washington. [8]

No. 186.

Motion to Dismiss Bill of Complaint.

Comes now H. G. Tremaine, one of the defendants in the above-entitled action, and a copartner with F. L. Buckley, doing business under the firm name and style of Buckley-Tremaine Lumber & Timber Company (the bill of complaint herein incorrectly designating the defendant F. L. Buckley as S. L. Buckley, and the firm name and style of Buckley-Tremaine Lumber & Timber Company now being incorrectly designated both in the bill of complaint and in the exhibits attached thereto as Buckley-Tremaine Lumber Company), and moves the Court to dismiss the bill of complaint herein upon the ground and for the reason that said bill of complaint shows upon its face by reference to Exhibit "A," that the said Exhibit "A" was preliminary to and an application for insurance as evidenced by the policy set forth as Exhibit "B"; that a copy of such application was not delivered with the policy to defendants and that the said application makes none of its statements or representations therein contained warranties, and the alleged phrase of said application sought by complainant to be incorporated in and made a warranty in said policy has no place in, and should not be inserted in said policy of insurance.

II.

That the said policy of insurance, marked Exhibit "B" and attached to the bill of complaint, does not by its terms make the said application, marked Exhibit "A," a part thereof, or contain any provision that any of the terms, phrases, or language used in the said application should become a warranty in the said policy or form a part thereof. [9]

III.

That the said application, marked Exhibit "A," was before the complainant prior to the writing of the said policy of insurance, and the bill of complaint fails to show that there was any mutual mistake, and complainant herein is estopped from demanding the relief prayed for and attempting to modify said policy of insurance, after complainant delivered said policy to assured, and the same was accepted by the assured, without a copy of said application being attached thereto or any statement in said application being made a warranty either by said application or said policy.

IV.

That there is an insufficiency of fact to constitute a valid cause of action in equity against the defendant.

V.

That there is an adequate remedy at law.

HUFFER & HAYDEN,
Solicitors for Defendant H. G. Tremaine.

Service of the within motion to dismiss is hereby admitted this 13th day of April, 1920.

GROSSCUP & MORROW,
Attorney for Complainant. [10]

No. 186.

Hearing on Motion to Dismiss.

Now on this 26th day of April, 1920, this cause comes on for hearing on motion to dismiss, the plaintiff represented by Grosscup & Morrow and the defendants by Huffer & Hayden, whereupon the motion is treated as a demurrer and same is confessed. Amended complaint to be filed by April 29, 1920.

Equity Journal 1. [11]

No. 186.

Order Permitting Plaintiff to File Amended Bill of Complaint.

On this 26th day of April, 1920, upon motion made by Grosscup & Morrow, attorneys for the above-named plaintiff, for an order, before the hearing on defendants' motion to dismiss, for leave to file an amended bill, and it appearing to the Court a proper matter therefor, it is

ORDERED that plaintiff be and it is hereby permitted to file its amended bill of complaint and it is ordered to serve and file same by Thursday, April 29, 1920, and further hearing upon this cause is continued until Monday, May 3, 1920.

JEREMIAH NETERER,
Judge.

Approved:
GROSSCUP & MORROW.
HUFFER & HAYDEN,
For Deft. H. G. Tremaine. [12]

No. 186—IN EQUITY.

First Amended Bill of Complaint.

American Merchant Marine Insurance Company of New York, a corporation duly organized and existing under and by virtue of the laws of the State of New York and with its principal place of business in the City and County of New York, a citizen of the United States and a citizen and resident of the said

State of New York, alleges as its first amended complaint, filed herein by leave of Court first duly had and obtained, against H. G. Tremaine, a citizen of the State of Washington, and a resident of the Northern Division of the Western District thereof, and S. L. Buckley and John Doe Buckley, whose true name is to this plaintiff unknown, aliens, and subjects of the King of Great Britain and Ireland, and citizens and residents of the Provinces of British Columbia and Ontario, Dominion of Canada, respectively, as follows, that is to say:

I.

At all the times herein mentioned the plaintiff has been and it now is a corporation duly and regularly incorporated, organized and existing under and by virtue of the [13] laws of the State of New York, and at all of said times it was and it now is a citizen of the United States and a citizen and resident of the said State of New York with its principal business in the City of New York in said State of New York.

At all the times herein mentioned the plaintiff has been and it now is duly authorized to do business in the State of Washington by virtue of strict compliance with the laws of said State governing the right of foreign corporations to transact business therein.

At all the times herein mentioned the defendants H. G. Tremaine, S. L. Buckley and, as plaintiff is informed and believes, one John Doe Buckley, were and they now are copartners doing business under the firm name and style of Buckley-Tremaine Lumber Company, having a principal place of business in the

City of Seattle, State of Washington.

At all the times herein mentioned the defendant H. G. Tremaine was and he now is a citizen of the United States and a citizen and resident of the State of Washington, residing in the Northern Division of the Western District thereof.

At all the times herein mentioned the defendants S. L. Buckley and John Doe Buckley were and they now are aliens, subjects of the King of Great Britain and Ireland and citizens and residents of the Provinces of British Columbia and Ontario, Dominion of Canada, respectively.

II.

The grounds upon which the jurisdiction of this Court in this cause depend are that this is a suit of a civil nature in equity where the matter in controversy exceeds, exclusive of interests and costs, the sum or value of three thousand dollars ($3,000.00), and is between a citizen of the State of [14] New York on the one hand and a citizen of the State of Washington and aliens, citizens or subjects of a foreign state on the other.

III.

On the 3d day of October, 1919, in the City of Seattle, State of Washington, the defendant made application in writing to the plaintiff for insurance in the sum of seven thousand eight hundred and seventy-five dollars ($7,875.00) on certain lumber in which the defendant had an insurable interest, while on board S. L. B. Scow No. 3 in single tow of tug "Coutli" at and from Craig, Alaska, to Prince Rupert, B. C., and thence in double tow of approved tug to Seattle, Washington, voyage actually to commence in October, 1919. Thereafter the plaintiff insured the said lumber in the sum of four thousand eight hundred and seventy-five ($4,875.00) dollars for the voyage set forth in the said application, and as evidence of its acceptance of the said application and of the effecting of the insurance as aforesaid, the plaintiff endorsed in writing its acceptance of insurance in the said sum of four thousand eight hundred and seventy-five dollars ($4,875.00) upon the said application. A copy of the application of the defendants with the acceptance of the plaintiff endorsed thereon (commonly called the cover note or cover slip) is hereunto annexed, made a part hereof and marked Exhibit "A."

IV.

At all times herein mentioned there has been and there now is a universal and long established custom and usage among underwriters of marine insurance and purchasers of such insurance that when insurance is sought by a purchaser, the latter prepares an application in writing setting forth the [15] nature of the risk, the amount of insurance desired, and any special terms, conditions and warranties upon which the risk is predicated, which said application is presented to the underwriter who rejects the same or accepts the risk in whole or in part, indicating his acceptance by endorsing on the said application over his signature the portion of the amount of insurance applied for which the said underwriter is willing to accept. As soon thereafter as the same can be prepared, the underwriter executes to the applicant a formal policy or certificate of insurance embodying therein all the terms, conditions and warranties contained in the said cover note, which said policy or certificate when delivered to the assured supersedes and takes the place of said cover note. Such usage and custom was at all the times herein mentioned and now is known to the defendants and to each of them and the application of the 3d day of October, 1919, hereinabove in paragraph III hereof described, was presented by the defendants to the plaintiff and accepted by the plaintiff in accordance with the said custom and usage.

V.

On the 6th day of October, 1919, in accordance with the said custom and usage, the plaintiff executed and delivered to the defendants its certificate of insurance No. 11123–C, in the usual form, which said certificate of insurance contains all of the terms, conditions and warranties set forth in the said cover note, except as hereinafter alleged. A copy of the said certificate of insurance so executed is hereunto annexed, made a part hereof and marked Exhibit "B." The defendants thereupon accepted the said certificate of insurance in substitution of the said cover note in accordance with [16] the said custom and usage.

VI.

In drafting the said certificate, the scrivener employed by the plaintiff, by accident and mistake, failed to incorporate in the said certificate, the provision contained in the said cover note to the effect that the voyage of the scow from Craig, Alaska, to Prince

Rupert, B. C., should commence during the month of October, 1919. Thereupon the representative of the plaintiff in Seattle, Washington, without knowledge of the said omission, and believing that the said certificate of insurance did in fact contain all the provisions of the said cover note, by accident and mistake signed the said certificate and caused the same to be forwarded to the defendants.

VII.

As the plaintiff is informed and believes and therefore alleges, the defendants, also believing that the said certificate did in fact contain the said omitted provision, and did in fact contain all the provisions set forth in the said cover note, by accident and mistake accepted the said certificate of insurance in the form written in substitution of the said cover note, or the defendants, knowing that the said omitted provision was in fact not incorporated in the said certificate, and that the same was omitted therefrom by accident and mistake and without the knowledge of the plaintiff or of the plaintiff's representative, failed and neglected to disclose the fact of such omission to the plaintiff.

VIII.

Said omitted provision constituted a material express warranty by defendants materially and substantially affecting [17] the rights and obligations of plaintiff, and, by reason of the said omission by accident and mistake as aforesaid, the said certificate of insurance failed to express the contract of insurance between the plaintiff and the defendants, and in order to express such contract, the certificate of insurance should be in words and figures identical with those set forth in a form hereunto annexed and made a part hereof, marked Exhibit "C."

IX.

The plaintiff has no plain, speedy and adequate remedy at law in the premises.

Forasmuch as plaintiff can have no relief, except in this court, the defendants, S. L. Buckley, H. G. Tremaine and John Doe Buckley, and each of them, may, according to their best belief, full, true, direct and perfect answer make to the matters hereinabove stated and charged; but not under oath, an answer under oath hereby being with respect to each of said defendants expressly waived.

AND the plaintiff humbly prays that on final hearing of this cause this Honorable Court may be pleased to grant to it, in the alternative, the following relief, that is to say:

1. That the defendants, and each of them, may be decreed to surrender to the clerk of this court for cancellation the original certificate of insurance of which Exhibit "B" is a copy, upon condition that the plaintiff shall simultaneously with the entry of the decree herein execute and deposit with said clerk for delivery to the defendants, a new certificate in lieu of the original which shall be in words and figures identical with the words and figures of Exhibit "C"; or, [18]

2. In the event that the defendants, or either of them, shall fail or refuse to obey such order or decree as may be entered pursuant to the first of these prayers, then that the defendants, and each of them, may

be enjoined and restrained from commencing in any court any action at law and/or suit in equity and/or admiralty designed or intended to enforce against plaintiff any liability arising out of or connected with the execution and delivery of plaintiff to defendants of said original certificate of insurance of which said Exhibit "B" is a copy, without first complying with the direction of such order or decree as may be entered pursuant to the first of these *prays;* or,

3. That plaintiff may have such other and further, or other or further, relief, orders and decrees as in equity and good conscience may seem meet to this Honorable Court.

B. S. GROSSCUP and
W. C. MORROW,
Solicitors for Plaintiff. [19]

Exhibit "A."

MATHER & CO.,
811 First Avenue,
Seattle, Wash.

Seattle, Wash., October 3d, 1919.

INSURANCE IS WANTED BY—BUCKLEY-TREMAINE LUMBER COMPANY.

LOSS, IF ANY, Payable to Them, or order.

FOR $7,875. ON Lumber VALUED AT $17.50 per M. feet.

PER F. L. B. SCOW "No. 3" in single tow of TUG "COUTLI," at and from Craig, Alaska to Prince Rupert, B. C., thence while in double tow of Approved Tug to Seattle, Wash., (Oct. Slg.)

RATE—3%.

This insurance is understood and agreed to be subject to English Law and usage as to Liability for and settlement of any and all claims.

CONDITIONS—Insured only against the risk of Total and/or Constructive Total Loss but to pay any General Average and/or Salvage Charges that may be incurred.

ACCEPTED—PACIFIC MARINE INSURANCE CO.

$4875.00—AMERICAN MERCHANT MARINE INS. CO., of N. Y. [20]

Exhibit "B."

CERTIFICATE OF INSURANCE.

To conform with the Revenue Laws of Great Britain, in order to collect a claim under this Certificate it must be stamped within ten days after its receipt in the United Kingdom.

Special Cargo. Amount
No. 11123-C $4875.00
Rate 3%
Prem. $146.25

AMERICAN MERCHANT MARINE
INSURANCE COMPANY OF NEW YORK
SEELEY & CO., (MARINE) Inc.,
Pacific Coast General Agents

140 Sansome Street Colman Bldg.
San Francisco, Cal. Seattle, Wash.
Board of Trade Bldg. Dominion Building
Portland, Ore. Vancouver, B. C.

Seattle, Wash., October 6, 1919.

THIS IS TO CERTIFY, that on the sixth day of

October, 1919, this Company insured for Buckley-Tremaine Lumber Company, Four Thousand, Eight Hundred Seventy-five Dollars ($4,875.00), on Lumber, original. Valued at $17.50 per 1,000 feet, on board Scow F. L. B. No. 3 in tow tug "Coutli" and/or other approved tug at and from Craig, Alaska (in single tow) to Prince Rupert, B. C., thence (in double tow) to Seattle, Wash., loss, if any, payable to the order of the assured in Seattle.

This insurance subject to conditions as stated below and on back hereof.

[Stamped across face]: Copy. Not Negotiable. Original and Duplicate Issued. One of which Being Accomplished, the Other to Stand Null and Void.

MARKS AND NUMBERS.

CONDITIONS.

This certificate is subject to the full terms of the policy, BUT warranted by the assured free from loss or expense arising from capture, seizure, restraint, detention or destruction, or the consequence of any attempt thereat, whether lawful or unlawful, or whether by the act of any belligerent nations or by governments of seceding or revolting states, or by unauthorized or lawless persons therein, or otherwise, and whether occurring in a port of distress or otherwise, anything in this policy to the contrary notwithstanding, and free from all other consequences of hostilities whether before or after declaration of war.

Held covered at a premium to be arranged, in case of deviation or change of voyage or of any error or unintentional omission in the description of the interest, vessel or voyage, provided same be communicated to the assurers as soon as known to the assured.

Held covered on board craft and/or lighter to and from the vessel. Each craft and/or lighter to be deemed a separate insurance.

IT IS AGREED THAT THERE SHALL BE NO RETURN OF PREMIUM IF INTEREST INSURED BE LOST BY PERILS NOT INSURED AGAINST HEREUNDER.

IN CASE OF LOSS APPLY TO Seeley & Co. (Marine), Inc., at Seattle, Wash.

CONDITIONS.

Warranted not to cover the interest of any alien enemies including such persons, copartnerships or corporations, as now, or may hereafter, appear in any Enemy Trading List issued by the War Trade Board of the United States of America.

ENGLISH POLICY.

Insured only against the risk of total and/or constructive total loss, but to pay any General Average and/or Salvage Charges that may be incurred.

This insurance is understood and agreed to be subject to English Law and usage as to Liability for and settlement of any and all claims.

IN WITNESS WHEREOF, the said Company has caused these Presents to be signed by its President and attested by its Secretary in the City of New York, but this certificate shall not be valid unless countersigned by the Company's duly authorized representative.

I. STEWART,
President.

T. M. LEE MARTIN,
Secretary.

Countersigned at Seattle, Wash., the 6th day of October, 1919.

SEELEY & CO., (Marine), Inc.,
By M. D. CALDER,

Exhibit "C."

CERTIFICATE OF INSURANCE.

To conform with the Revenue Laws of Great Britain, in order to collect a claim under this Certificate it must be stamped within ten days after its receipt in the United Kingdom.

Special Cargo. Amount
#11123–C $4,875.00
Rate 3%
Prem. $146.25

AMERICAN MERCHANT MARINE
INSURANCE COMPANY OF NEW YORK
SEELEY & CO., (MARINE) Inc.,
Pacific Coast General Agents

140 Sansome Street Colman Bldg.
San Francisco, Cal. Seattle, Wash.
Board of Trade Bldg. Dominion Building
Portland, Ore. Vancouver, B. C.

Seattle, Wash., Oct. 6th, 1919.

THIS IS TO CERTIFY, that on the sixth day of October, 1919, this Company insured for Buckley-

Tremaine Lumber Company, Four Thousand, Eight Hundred Seventy-five and 00/100 Dollars, on Lumber. Original, valued at $17.50 per 1,000 feet, on board Scow F. L. B. #3, in tow tug "Coutli" and/or other approved tug, at and from Craig, Alaska—October sailing (in single tow) to Prince Rupert, B. C., thence in double tow to Seattle, Wash., loss, if any, payable to the order of assured in Seattle.

This insurance subject to conditions as stated below and on back hereof.

[Stamped across face]: Copy. Not Negotiable. Original and Duplicate Issued. One of which Being Accomplished, the Other to Stand Null and Void.

MARKS AND NUMBERS.

CONDITIONS.

This certificate is subject to the full terms of the policy, BUT warranted by the assured free from loss or expense arising from capture, seizure, restraint, detention or destruction, or the consequence of any attempt thereat, whether lawful or unlawful, or whether by the act of any belligerent nations or by governments of seceding or revolting states, or by unauthorized or lawless persons therein, or otherwise, and whether occurring in a port of distress or otherwise, anything in this policy to the contrary notwithstanding, and free from all other consequences of hostilities whether before or after declaration of war.

Held covered at a premium to be arranged, in case of deviation or change of voyage or of any error or unintentional omission in the description of the interest, vessel or voyage, provided same be communicated to the assurers as soon as known to the assured.

Held covered on board craft and/or lighter to and from the vessel. Each craft and/or lighter to be deemed a separate insurance..

IT IS AGREED THAT THERE SHALL BE NO RETURN OF PREMIUM IF INTEREST INSURED BE LOST BY PERILS NOT INSURED AGAINST HEREUNDER.

IN CASE OF LOSS APPLY TO Seeley & Co. (Marine), Inc., at Seattle, Wash.

CONDITIONS.

Warranted not to cover the interest of any alien enemies including such persons, copartnerships or corporations, as now, or may hereafter, appear in any Enemy Trading List issued by the War Trade Board of the United States of America.

Insured only against the risk of total and/or constructive total loss, but to pay any General Average and/or Salvage Charges that may be incurred.

This insurance is understood and agreed to be subject to English Law and usage as to Liability for and settlement of any and all claims.

IN WITNESS WHEREOF, the said Company has caused these Presents to be signed by its President and attested by its Secretary in the City of New York, but this certificate shall not be valid unless countersigned by the Company's duly authorized representative.

I. STEWART,
President.

T. M. LEE MARTIN,
Secretary.

Countersigned at Seattle, Wash., the 6th day of October, 1919.

SEELEY & CO., (Marine), Inc.,

By ——————.

Rec'd copy of foregoing First Amended Complaint by the receipt of a true copy thereof, together with true copies of the exhibits recited therein as being attached thereto, hereby is admitted in behalf of all parties entitled to such service by law or by rules of Court, this 28th day of April, 1920.

HUFFER & HAYDEN,

Attorney for H. G. Tremaine, Defendant, [21]

IN EQUITY—No. 186.

Motion to Dismiss First Amended Bill of Complaint.

Comes now, H. G. Tremaine, one of the defendants in the above-entitled and numbered action, and a copartner with F. L. Buckley, doing business under the firm name and style of Buckley-Tremaine Lumber & Timber Company (the first amended complaint herein incorrectly designating the defendant, F. L. Buckley as S. L. Buckley, and the firm name and style of Buckley-Tremaine Lumber & Timber Company as Buckley-Tremaine Lumber Company, both in the bill of complaint and the exhibits attached thereto), and moves the Court to dismiss the first amended complaint herein upon the ground and for the reason that said bill of complaint shows upon its face, by reference to Exhibit "A" that the said Exhibit "A" was preliminary to and an application for insurance as evidenced by the policy set forth as Exhibit "B";

that a copy of such application was not delivered with the policy to defendants, and that the said application makes none of its statements or representations therein contained warranties, and the alleged phrase of said application sought by complainant to be incorporated in and made a warranty in said policy has no place in, and should not be inserted in said policy of insurance.

II.

That the said policy of insurance, marked Exhibit "B" and attached to the said bill of complaint, does not by its terms make the said application, marked Exhibit "A," a part thereof, or contain any provision that any of the terms, phrases, or language used in the said application should become a warranty in the said policy or form a part thereof.

III.

That the said application, marked Exhibit "A," was before the complainant prior to the writing of the said policy of insurance, [22] and the said bill of complaint fails to show that there was any mutual mistake, and complainant herein is estopped from demanding the relief prayed for and attempting to modify said policy of insurance after complainant delivered said policy to assured and the same was accepted by the assured, without a copy of said application being attached thereto or any statement in said application being made a warranty either by said application or said policy.

IV.

That there is an insufficiency of fact to constitute a valid cause of action in equity against defendant.

V.

That there is an adequate remedy at law.

VI.

That said first amended complaint shows upon its face that complainant's alleged cause of action is based wholly upon a usage and custom which is contrary to statutory law and fatal to the relief prayed for; that said usage and custom is so pleaded that, being incompetent, irrelevant and immaterial, it cannot be stricken from said bill of complaint without destroying the whole thereof.

VII.

That said first amended complaint shows upon its face that it is a different cause of action against different parties defendant than those named in the original bill of complaint, the defendant H. G. Tremaine appearing specially for the purpose of objecting to the jurisdiction of the Court herein to require him to plead or answer to said first amended complaint without service of process thereunder.

HUFFER & HAYDEN,

Solicitors for Defendant, H. G. Tremaine. [23]

Due service of the within motion to dismiss is hereby admitted this 30th day of April, 1920.

GROSSCUP & MORROW,

Attorneys for Pltf. [24]

No. 186

Hearing on Motion for Order Dismissing First Amended Bill of Complaint.

Now on this 3d day of May, 1920, this cause comes

on for hearing in open court on Motion for Order Dismissing First Amended Complaint, Grosscup & Morrow appearing for Plaintiff and Huffer & Hayden for the Defendants, whereupon the motion is argued by respective counsel and taken under advisement by the court.

Equity Journal 1. [25]

No. 186—E.

Decision.

Filed May 6, 1920.

Messrs. GROSSCUP & MORROW, Solicitors for Plaintiff.

Messrs. HUFFER & HAYDEN, Solicitors for Defendants.

NETERER, District Judge.

The plaintiff seeks to correct certificate of insurance issued to the defendant "Per Lumber on F. L. B. Scow No. 3," in single tow of Tug "Coutli" at and from Craig, Alaska, to Prince Rupert, B. C., thence while in double tow of approved tug to Seattle, Washington, by inserting in the certificate of insurance: "October Sailing." It is alleged that by inadvertence and mistake, the certificate was issued without including these words which were endorsed upon the application for insurance. The application for insurance is not signed by the insured. It is dated October 3, 1919. The certificate of insurance was issued October 6, 1919. The defendants have moved to dismiss upon the ground that the petition does not state facts upon which to predicate any relief.

It does not appear from the complaint that the

application is made a part of the certificate, or the basis for its insurance; nor does the language of the certificate comprehend or have relation to the amendment sought. The application for insurance was made in Seattle, and the certificate was issued in Seattle. The contract is made pursuant to the laws of Washington, although there is endorsed upon the certificate that as to liability for and settlement of any and all claims, it should be subject to English law and usage; but no English law and usage is pleaded; nor is this a proceeding in settlement of any claim in the policy. The Insurance Code of Washington, Sec. 5069-31, L. 11, p. 195, Sec. 31, provides that:

> "Every contract of insurance shall be construed according to the terms and conditions of the policy, except where the contract is made pursuant to a written application therefor, and such written application is intended to be made a part of the insurance contract, and the insurance company making such insurance contract unless as otherwise provided by this act, shall deliver a copy of such application with the policy to the assured, and thereupon, such application shall become a part of the insurance contract, and failing so to do, it shall not be made a part of the insurance contract."

The statute must be complied with, or the application cannot be considered. Joyce on Insurance, Sec. 190, and cases cited. Section 6059--179 has no application. The motion is sustained.

JEREMIAH NETERER,

Judge. [26]

Cases cited by Plaintiff:

6059-179 Equity Insurance Co. v. Hern, 20 Wall. 494.

Kilbourn v. Sunderland, 130 U. S. 505.

Taylor v. Merchants Ins. Co., 9 Howard 191.

Western Assur. Co. v. Ward, 75 Fed. 338.

26 Cyc. p. 569, Sec. 3, Subdiv. 2.

p. 613, Sec. 6, Subdiv. d.

Joyce on Ins., Vol. 5, Sec. 309.

Cases cited by defendants:

Minor, Conflict of Laws, p. 411, Sec. 172.

R. & B. Code, Sec. 6059-31.

1 Joyce, Ins. 481, Sec. 186.

498, Sec. 190.

501, Sec. 190-b.

502, Sec. 190-c.

503, Sec. 190-e.

513, Sec. 190-t.

522, Sec. 194.

530, Sec. 194.

637, Sec. 247.

640-1, Sec. 249.

258, Sec. 66.

154, Sec. 31. [27]

IN EQUITY—No. 186.

Judgment of Dismissal.

This cause came on to be heard on this day upon motion of the defendant H. G. Tremaine to dismiss the first amended complaint in equity of the plaintiff with prejudice, and the plaintiff declining to further plead, the motion is granted.

It is therefore hereby ORDERED, ADJUDGED AND DECREED that the first amended complaint in equity be, and the same is hereby dismissed as to Tremaine with prejudice, upon the ground that it does not state a cause for equitable relief; and that the said defendant do have and recover his costs and disbursements herein to be taxed; to which the plaintiff excepts, and exception is noted.

Done in open court this 17th day of May, 1920.

JEREMIAH NETERER,
Judge. [28]

IN EQUITY—No. 186

Assignment of Errors.

And now on the 18th day of May, A. D. 1920, comes the plaintiff herein, American Merchant Marine Insurance Company of New York, by B. S. Grosscup, W. Carr Morrow, Harold M. Sawyer and Alfred T. Cluff, its solicitors, and says that the decree in said cause is erroneous and against the just rights of plaintiff, for the following reasons, that is to say:

FIRST. Because the District Court of the United States for the Western District of Washington, Northern Division, erred in ordering and directing the dismissal of plaintiff's suit and in holding that plaintiff was not entitled to the relief prayed for in its bill of complaint and in holding that the first amended complaint herein did not state facts sufficient to entitle plaintiff to equitable relief, or any relief, and the District Court erred in rendering judgment for the defendant, H. G. Tremaine, [29] in said cause, because said first amended complaint does state facts sufficient to entitle plaintiff to equitable relief in that it appears from said first amended complaint herein that prior to the issuance and delivery by plaintiff to defendants of the certificate of insurance embodied in Exhibit "B" and attached to and made a part of said first amended complaint, there existed between plaintiff and defendants a valid and mutually enforceable contract embodied in Exhibit "A" and attached to and made a part of said first amended complaint, all the terms and provisions of which were in accordance with the custom set forth in said first amended complaint intended by the plaintiff and defendants to be incorporated in said Exhibit "B," and that by reason of the mutual mistake of plaintiff and defendants, there was omitted from said Exhibit "B" when the same was delivered pursuant to said custom by plaintiff to defendants, a material term, condition and warranty contained in said existing contract in which omission defendants knowingly and fraudulently acquiesced.

SECOND. The District Court erred in holding that Section 6059--31 of Remington & Ballinger's Annotated Code of the State of Washington (Laws of 1911, Chap. 49, Sec. 31, Pg. 195) precluded the plaintiff from obtaining any relief without compliance with said Section, for the reason that said Section has no application to the facts alleged in said first amended complaint and does not apply to contracts of marine insurance.

THIRD. The District Court erred in holding that Section 6059--31 of Remington & Ballinger's Annotated [30] Code of the State of Washington (Laws of 1911, Chap. 49, Sec. 31, Pg. 195) precluded the plaintiff from obtaining any relief without compliance with said section, for the reason that said section merely prescribes a rule of evidence for determining the construction of an insurance policy in an action brought by the assured to recover thereon.

FOURTH. The District Court erred in holding that Section 6059--31 of Remington & Ballinger's Annotated Code of the State of Washington (Laws of 1911, Chap. 49, Sec. 31, Pg. 195) precluded the plaintiff from obtaining any relief without compliance with said section, for the reason that said section is merely a statutory extension of the parol evidence rule.

FIFTH. The DistrictCourt erred in holding that Section 6059--31 of Remington & Ballinger's Annotated Code of the State of Washington (Laws of 1911, Chap. 49, Sec. 31, Pg. 195) precluded the plaintiff from obtaining any relief without compliance with said section, for the reason that said section does not preclude examination of the antecedent contract set forth in the said first amended complaint for the purpose of determining in a court of equity whether or not a subsequent formal certificate of marine insurance issued pursuant to said custom and in which it was intended by the parties hereto that said antecedent contract should be merged shall be reformed so as to express accurately all of the terms, condition and warranties of said antecedent contract.

SIXTH. The District Court erred in holding that Section 6059--31 of Remington & Ballinger's Annotated Code [31] of the State of Washington (Laws of 1911, Chap. 49, Sec. 31, Pg. 195) precluded the plaintiff from obtaining any relief without compliance with said section, for the reason that said section applies only to a case where the application for insurance is not accepted unless and until there is a delivery of a policy, and has no application to a case where the application has been accepted and there is an existing and mutually enforceable contract between the parties prior to and independently of the subsequent delivery of any certificate of insurance.

SEVENTH. The District Court erred in holding that Section 6059--31 of Remington & Ballinger's Annotated Code of the State of Washington (Laws of 1911, Chap. 49, Sec. 31, Pg. 195) precluded the plaintiff from obtaining any relief without compliance with said Section, for the reason that said section does not apply to a case where the antecedent contract is embodied *verbatim* in the certificate of insurance with the exception of material portions of said antecedent contract omitted by reason of mutual mistake and fraudulent acquiescence therein.

EIGHTH. The District Court erred in holding that Section 6059--31 of Remington & Ballinger's Annotated Code of the State of Washington (Laws of 1911, Chap. 49, Sec. 31, Pg. 195) precluded the plaintiff from obtaining any relief without compliance with said section, for the reason that said section cannot control the practice or prescribe rules of evidence in or for the governance of the equity courts of the United States of America.

WHEREFORE said plaintiff prays that said decree be reversed and that the District Court be directed [32] by the Circuit Court of Appeals for the Ninth Circuit to enter a decree denying the motion of said defendant, H. G. Tremaine, to dismiss said first amended complaint.

B. S. GROSSCUP,
W. CARR MORROW,
HAROLD M. SAWYER,
ALFRED T. CLUFF,
Solicitors for Plaintiff.

Service of the within and foregoing assignment of errors by the receipt of a true copy thereof hereby is admitted in behalf of all parties entitled to such service by law or by rules of court this 18th day of May, 1920.

HUFFER & HAYDEN,
Attorneys for Deft. H. G. Tremaine. [33]

IN EQUITY—No. 186.

Petition for Appeal to the United States Circuit Court of Appeals for the Ninth Circuit.

The above-named plaintiff, American Merchant Marine Insurance Co. of New York, conceiving itself aggrieved by the Decree made and entered on the 17th day of May, 1920, in the above-entitled cause, does hereby appeal from said decree to the United

States Circuit Court of Appeals for the Ninth Circuit, for the reasons specified in the assignment of errors which is filed herewith; and it prays that this appeal may be allowed, that citation be issued as provided by law, and that a transcript of record, proceedings and papers, upon which said decree was made, duly authenticated, may be sent to the United States Circuit Court of Appeals for the Ninth Circuit.

And said plaintiff further prays that the proper order touching the security required of it to perfect its appeal be made, and, desiring to supersede the execution of the decree, said plaintiff here tenders bond with sufficient surety in such amount as the Court may require for such purpose, and prays that with the allowance of the appeal a supersedeas be issued.

B. S. GROSSCUP,
W. CARR MORROW,
HAROLD M. SAWYER,
ALFRED T. CLUFF,
Solicitors for Plaintiff. [34]

Service of the within and foregoing Petition for Appeal by the receipt of a true copy thereof, hereby is admitted in behalf of all parties entitled to such service by law or rules of court, this 18th day of May, 1920.

HUFFER & HAYDEN,
Attorneys for Deft. H. G. Tremaine. [35]

IN EQUITY—No. 186.

Order Allowing Appeal and Fixing Cost and Supersedeas Bond.

There having been presented to the Court the petition of appeal of American Merchant Marine Insurance Co. of New York, plaintiff herein, from the Decree made and entered in this court on the 17th day of May, 1920, and said plaintiff having petitioned that a supersedeas may issue suspending the execution of said decree pending said appeal;

It is here and now ORDERED AND ADJUDGED that said petition of appeal be and it hereby is allowed.

It is further ordered that the bond with sufficient sureties for cost and supersedeas be, and the same is, hereby fixed in the sum of fifty-five hundred dollars, to be conditioned as required by law.

Done in open court this 18th day of May, 1920.

JEREMIAH NETERER,
Judge.

Service of the within and foregoing order by the receipt of a true copy thereof hereby is admitted in behalf of deft. H. G. Tremaine, this 18th day of May, 1920.

HUFFER & HAYDEN,
Attys. for Deft. H. G. Tremaine. [36]

No. 186—IN EQUITY.

Supersedeas and Cost Bond on Appeal.

KNOW ALL MEN BY THESE PRESENTS, That we, American Merchant Marine Insurance

Company of New York, a corporation, as principal, and American Surety Company of New York, a corporation, as surety, are held and firmly bound unto H. G. Tremaine in the full and just sum of five thousand five hundred dollars ($5,500), to be paid to the said H. G. Tremaine, his heirs, executors, administrators and assigns, to which payment well and truly to be made, we bind ourselves, our successors and assigns, jointly and severally, firmly by these presents.

IN TESTIMONY WHEREOF, American Merchant Marine Insurance Company of New York has caused this instrument to be executed on its behalf and in its name by C. H. Williamson, its General Agent, and American Surety Company of New York has likewise caused this instrument to be executed on its behalf and in its name by S. H. Melrose, its resident vice-president, its corporate seal to be hereon set and the same to be attested by C. N. Bertch, [37] its resident Assistant Secretary, all on this 29th day of May, in the year of our Lord, one thousand nine hundred and twenty.

WHEREAS, lately at a District Court of the United States, for the Western District of Washington, Northern Division, in a suit pending in said Court between American Merchant Marine Insurance Company of New York, as plaintiff, and H. G. Tremaine, S. L. Buckley and John Doe Buckley, doing business under the firm name and style of Buckley-Tremaine Lumber Company, as defendants, a decree was rendered against said American Merchant Marine Insurance Company of New York, and said American Merchant Marine Company of New

York having obtained an allowance of an appeal and filed a copy thereof in the clerk's office of the said Court to reverse the decree in aforesaid suit, and a citation directed to the said H. G. Tremaine citing and admonishing him to be and appear in the United States Circuit Court of Appeals for the Ninth Circuit, at the City of San Francisco, in the State of California, on the 16th day of June, 1920, and within thirty days from and after the date of said citation.

NOW, the condition of the above obligation is such, that if the said American Merchant Marine Insurance Company of New York shall prosecute its said appeal to effect, and answer all damages and costs if it fails to make its plea [38] good, then the above obligation to be void; else to remain in full force and virtue.

AMERICAN MERCHANT MARINE INSURANCE COMPANY OF NEW YORK.

By (Signed) CHAS. H. WILLIAMSON,
General Agent.

AMERICAN SURETY COMPANY OF NEW YORK.

By S. H. MELROSE,
Resident Vice-President.

[Seal] Attest: C. N. BERTCH,
Resident Asst. Secretary.

Approved this 1st day of June, 1920.

JEREMIAH NETERER,
District Judge.

Received copy of the within this 1st day of June, 1920.

HUFFER & HAYDEN,
Attorneys for Defendant Tremaine. [38a]

No. 186—IN EQUITY.

Stipulation Re Motion to Strike Defendant's Praecipe for Additional Record.

IT IS STIPULATED AND AGREED by and between counsel for the respective parties undersigned that the transcript on appeal may show that the plaintiff moved to strike the defendant H. G. Tremaine's praecipe for additional record, on the ground and for the reason that the additional papers and journal entries requested in said praecipe were immaterial to the issue and unnecessary for the determination of said case on appeal; that said motion was heard by the Court on June 7, 1920, and an order entered denying said motion.

This stipulation to be included in the transcript on appeal in lieu of said motion and journal entries denying the same.

Dated June 7, 1920.

HAROLD M. SAWYER,
ALFRED T. CLUFF,
B. S. GROSSCUP,
W. C. MORROW,
Solicitors for Plaintiff.
HUFFER & HAYDEN,
Solicitors for Defendant.

Filed June 7, 1920.

No. 186.

Hearing on Motion to Strike Praecipe for Additional Record.

Now, on this 7th day of June, 1920, this cause comes on for hearing in open court on motion to strike praecipe for additional record, and after argument by respective counsel, the motion is denied by the Court and exception allowed.

Journal 8. [40]

IN EQUITY—No. 186.

Praecipe for Transcript of Record.

To the Clerk of the Above-Entitled Court:

You are requested to take a transcript of the record and transmit the same to the United States Circuit Court of Appeals for the Ninth Circuit, omitting all captions and endorsements, verifications, etc., but containing all proofs of service, and to include in such transcript of record the following and no other papers, that is to say:

1. First amended complaint.
2. Motion of defendant, H. G. Tremaine, to dismiss first amended complaint.
3. Opinion of Court sustaining said motion.
4. Decree dismissing said first amended complaint.
5. Assignment of errors.
6. Petition for appeal.
7. Order allowing appeal and fixing amount of cost of supersedeas bond.
8. Cost and supersedeas bond.

9. Citation and proof of service.
10. Praecipe and proof of service.
11. Your certificate.
12. Stipulation re motion to strike defendant's praecipe.
13. Order denying said motion.

B. S. GROSSCUP,
W. CARR MORROW,
HAROLD M. SAWYER,
ALFRED T. CLUFF,
Solicitors for Plaintiff. [41]

I waive the provisions of the Act approved February 13, 1911, and direct that you forward typewritten transcript to the Circuit Court of Appeals for printing as provided under Rule 105 of this court.

HAROLD M. SAWYER,
Of Solicitors for Plaintiff.
HUFFER & HAYDEN,
Attys. for Deft. Tremaine.

Service of the within and foregoing praecipe by the receipt of a true copy thereof hereby is admitted in behalf of H. G. Tremaine, this 18th day of May, 1920.

HUFFER & HAYDEN,
Attys. for Deft. H. G. Tremaine. [42]

No. 186.

Praecipe for Additional Record.

To the Clerk of the Above-entitled Court:

You are requested to include the following additional papers and journal entries in the transcript of record on appeal to the United States Circuit Court of Appeals for the Ninth Circuit, omitting captions, endorsements and verifications, but containing all proofs of service:

1. Original bill of complaint.
2. Subpoena.
3. Marshal's return on subpoena.
4. Appearance of defendant H. G. Tremaine.
5. Motion to dismiss of defendant H. G. Tremaine.
6. Journal entry of April 26th, showing above motion treated as demurrer—Confessed. Amended complaint to be filed by April 29th, 1920.
7. Order granting leave to file amended complaint.
8. Journal entry of May 3d showing hearing on motion to dismiss first amended complaint; advisement.

HUFFER & HAYDEN,
Solicitors for Defendant H. G. Tremaine. [43]

United States District Court, Western District of Washington, Northern Division.

No. 186—E.

AMERICAN MERCHANT MARINE INSURANCE CO. OF NEW YORK, a Corporation,
Plaintiff,

vs.

H. G. TREMAINE, S. L. BUCKLEY and JOHN DOE BUCKLEY, Doing Business Under the Firm Name and Style of BUCKLEY-TREMAINE LUMBER CO.,
Defendants.

Certificate of Clerk U. S. District Court to Transcript of Record.

United States of America,
Western District of Washington,—ss.

I, F. M. Harshberger, Clerk of the United States District Court, for the Western District of Washington, do hereby certify this typewritten transcript of record consisting of pages numbered from 1 to 43, inclusive, to be a full, true, correct and complete copy of so much of the record, papers, and other proceedings in the above and foregoing entitled cause, as is required by praecipes of counsel filed and shown herein, as the same remain of record and on file in the office of the clerk of said District Court, and that the same constitute the record on appeal herein from the judgment of said United States District Court for the Western District of Washington to the United States Circuit Court of Appeals for the Ninth Circuit. [44]

I further certify the following to be a full, true and correct statement of all expenses, costs, fees and charges incurred and paid in my office by or on behalf of the appellant and appellee for making record, certificate or return to the United States Circuit Court of Appeals for the Ninth Circuit in the above-entitled cause, to wit:

FOR APPELLANT:

Clerk's fee (Sec. 828, R. S. U. S.) for making record, certificate or return, 68 folios at 15¢........................$10.20

Certificate of clerk to transcript of record 4 folios at 15¢........................ .60

Seal to said certificate........................ .20

FOR APPELLEE:

Clerk's fee (Sec. 828 R. S. U. S.) for making record, certificate or return, 27 folios at 15¢........................$ 4.05

I hereby certify that the above costs for preparing and certifying record for appellant amounting to $11.00 and for appellee amounting to $4.05, have been paid to me by solicitors for appellant and appellee, respectively.

I further certify that I hereby attach and herewith transmit the original Citation issued in this cause.

IN WITNESS WHEREOF, I have hereto set my hand and affixed the seal of said District Court at Seattle, in said District, this 12th day of June, 1920.

[Seal] F. M. HARSHBERGER,

Clerk United States District Court. [45]

In the District Court of the United States for the Western District of Washington, Northern Division.

IN EQUITY—No. 186.

AMERICAN MERCHANT MARINE INSURANCE CO. OF NEW YORK, a Corporation,
Plaintiff,

vs.

H. G. TREMAINE, S. L. BUCKLEY and JOHN DOE BUCKLEY, Doing Business Under the Firm Name and Style of BUCKLEY-TREMAINE LUMBER CO.,
Defendants.

Citation and Notice on Appeal.

To H. G. Tremaine, S. L. Buckley and John Doe Buckley, and to F. A. Huffer and W. H. Hayden, Solicitors for H. G. Tremaine, GREETING:

YOU ARE HEREBY NOTIFIED that in a certain cause in equity in the District Court of the United States for the Western District of Washington, Northern Division, wherein American Merchant Marine Insurance Co. of New York is plaintiff, and H. G. Tremaine, S. L. Buckley and John Doe Buckley, doing business under the firm name and style of Buckley-Tremaine Lumber Co., are defendants, an appeal has been allowed the plaintiff therein to the United States Circuit Court of Appeals for the Ninth Circuit.

You are hereby cited and admonished to be and appear in said court at the city of San Francisco,

State of California, on the 16th day of June next, to do and receive what may appertain to justice to be done in the premises.

Given under my hand at the city of Seattle, in the Ninth Circuit, this 18th day of May, in the year of our Lord one thousand nine hundred and twenty.

[Seal] JEREMIAH NETERER,

Judge of the District Court of the United States, for the Western District of Washington, Northern Division. [46]

[Endorsed]: No. 186. In the United States District Court, Western District of Washington, Northern Division. American Merchant Marine Insurance Company of New York, a Corporation, Plaintiff, vs. H. G. Tremaine, S. L. Buckley and John Doe Buckley, Doing Business Under the Firm Name and Style of Buckley-Tremaine Lumber Company, Defendants. Citation. Filed in the United States District Court, Western District of Washington, Northern Division. May 18, 1920. F. M. Harshberger, Clerk. By S. E. Leitch, Deputy.

Service of the within and foregoing Citation and Notice by the receipt of a true copy thereof hereby is admitted in behalf of defendant H. G. Tremaine, this 18th day of May, 1920.

HUFFER & HAYDEN,

Attorneys for Deft. H. G. Tremaine. [47]

[Endorsed]: No. 3513. United States Circuit Court of Appeals for the Ninth Circuit. American Merchant Marine Insurance Company of New York, a Corporation, Appellant, vs. H. G. Tremaine, S. L.

Buckley and John Doe Buckley, Doing Business Under the Firm Name and Style of Buckley-Tremaine Lumber Company, Appellees. Transcript of Record. Upon Appeal from the United States District Court for the Western District of Washington, Northern Division.

Filed June 15, 1920.

F. D. MONCKTON,

Clerk of the United States Circuit Court of Appeals for the Ninth Circuit.

By Paul P. O'Brien,

Deputy Clerk.

IN THE

United States Circuit Court of Appeals

For the Ninth Circuit

AMERICAN MERCHANT MARINE INSURANCE COMPANY OF NEW YORK (a corporation),
Appellant,

vs.

H. G. TREMAINE, S. L. BUCKLEY and JOHN DOE BUCKLEY, doing business under the firm name and style of BUCKLEY-TREMAINE LUMBER COMPANY,
Appellees.

BRIEF FOR APPELLANT.

HAROLD M. SAWYER,
ALFRED T. CLUFF,
Mills Building, San Francisco,
Solicitors for Appellant.

PERNAU-WALSH PRINTING CO.

No. 3513

IN THE

United States Circuit Court of Appeals

For the Ninth Circuit

American Merchant Marine Insurance Company of New York (a corporation), *Appellant,*

vs.

H. G. Tremaine, S. L. Buckley and John Doe Buckley, doing business under the firm name and style of Buckley-Tremaine Lumber Company, *Appellees.*

BRIEF FOR APPELLANT.

Statement of the Case.

This cause arises upon an appeal taken by American Merchant Marine Insurance Company of New York from a decree made in the court below dismissing its first amended complaint praying reformation in equity, upon the ground that it did not state a cause for equitable relief (Tr. 36, 37).

Appellant was plaintiff in the court below and appellee was one of three parties defendant sued as copartners. For the sake of simplicity, the terms "plaintiff" and "defendant" will be used in this brief to describe appellant and appellee respectively, unless the context indicates otherwise.

The original complaint (Tr. 1-12) was attacked by a motion to dismiss (Tr. 14, 16), which was confessed by plaintiff (Tr. 16) but at the same time leave to amend was sought and obtained (Tr. 17) and, within the time limited by the court, plaintiff duly filed its first amended complaint (Tr. 17-31). Nothing turns upon the pleadings prior to the first amended complaint and they need not be further considered.

The amended complaint was likewise attacked by a motion to dismiss (Tr. 31, 33), and, after hearing (Tr. 33, 34), the motion was granted (Tr. 34, 36). Thereafter, plaintiff having declined to plead further, a decree was entered dismissing the first amended complaint with prejudice (Tr. 36, 37), to which an exception was duly noted and allowed (Tr. 37). Immediately thereafter this appeal was taken and perfected.

The purpose of the suit is to reform a contract of marine insurance entered into in the City of Seattle, Washington, between plaintiff as insurer and a copartnership composed of H. G. Tremaine, the appellee, F. L. Buckley, and John Doe Buckley, doing business under the firm name and style of Buckley-Tremaine Lumber & Timber Company. The contract in suit was executed in the name of Buckley-Tremaine Lumber Company, and the firm name was thus designated in both the original and first amended complaints.

The original complaint named only two partners as defendants, H. G. Tremaine, the appellee, and F. L. Buckley, erroneously described as S. L. Buckley. At the time of the filing thereof, plaintiff did not know of the existence of any other partner, but during the framing of the first amended complaint, plaintiff learned that there was a third partner and joined him therein as an additional partner defendant under the name of John Doe Buckley, his true name being unknown to plaintiff.

The motion to dismiss the original complaint and also the motion to dismiss the first amended complaint was made by defendant H. G. Tremaine only. Up to the time when the decree was rendered, it proved impossible to obtain personal service upon the other two defendant partners named in the first amended complaint. Neither of them have made any appearance in the suit.

The issue involved in this appeal is solely a question of law, namely, the sufficiency of the first amended complaint. As an aid to the proper understanding of this issue and for the purpose of serving the convenience of the court, we shall summarize the allegations of the first amended complaint (Tr. 17-31).

After alleging the corporate character of the plaintiff and its qualification to do business in

Washington, the complaint describes the personnel of the partnership and sets up the jurisdictional allegations. It then states the facts which are substantially as follows:

> On October 3rd, 1919, the defendant partners made a written application for insurance on a cargo of lumber in the sum of $7,875. Plaintiff accepted the application for $4,875 and its acceptance was endorsed upon the application. The contract of insurance thus effected provided that the scow which was to carry the lumber should sail from Craig, Alaska, during the month of October, 1919. This contract, consisting of the application and the acceptance of plaintiff endorsed thereon, is commonly called a cover note or cover slip, and is embodied in Exhibit "A" of the amended complaint (Tr. 24, 25).
>
> There is a universal and long established custom among underwriters and purchasers of insurance that when insurance is sought by a purchaser, the latter prepares an application in writing setting forth the nature of the risk, the amount of insurance desired, and any special terms, conditions and warranties upon which the risk is predicated, which application is presented to the underwriter who rejects the same or accepts the risk in whole or in part, indicating his acceptance by endorsing on the said application over his signature, the portion of the amount of insurance applied for which

he is willing to accept. As soon thereafter as the same can be prepared, the underwriter executes to the applicant a formal policy or certificate of insurance embodying therein all the terms, conditions and warranties contained in the said cover note, and the policy or certificate delivered to the assured supersedes and takes the place of the cover note. This usage was known to the defendant and the application of October 3rd, 1919, was presented by the defendant to the plaintiff and accepted by the plaintiff in accordance therewith.

On October 6th, 1919, plaintiff, pursuant to the custom executed and delivered its certificate of insurance in the usual form to the defendant, which contained all the terms, conditions and warranties set forth in the cover note except that the scrivener employed by the plaintiff, by accident and mistake, failed to incorporate in the certificate the provision contained in the cover note to the effect that the voyage of the scow from Craig, Alaska, should commence in the month of October, 1919. Plaintiff's representative in Seattle executed and delivered the certificate to defendant under the belief that the certificate contained all the provisions of the cover note.

The defendant accepted the certificate under a like belief, or knowing that the certificate did not contain the said omitted provision, and that the same had been omitted by accident and mistake and without the knowledge of plaintiff and its representative, failed to disclose the omission to plaintiff.

The omitted provision constituted a material express warranty by defendants materially and substantially affecting the rights and obligations of plaintiff, and by reason of the said omission, the certificate failed to express the contract of insurance between the parties and in order to express such contract, it should contain the omitted provision.

The above constitute the facts alleged in the first amended complaint upon which the plaintiff's right to reformation is predicated. It is plaintiff's contention that the facts show either a material mutual mistake, or a material mistake of plaintiff coupled with knowing and fraudulent acquiescence therein by defendants, in either of which cases the certificate should be reformed.

This position is tacitly conceded by defendant because his whole case against the sufficiency of the first amended complaint is based upon plaintiff's failure to allege compliance with Sec. 31 of Chapter 49 of the Laws of Washington for 1911, which reads as follows:

> "Every contract of insurance shall be construed according to the terms and conditions of the policy, except where the contract is made pursuant to a written application therefor, and such written application is intended to be made

a part of the insurance contract, and the insurance company making such insurance contract, unless as otherwise provided by this act, shall deliver a copy of such application with the policy to the assured, and thereupon such application shall become a part of the insurance contract, and failing so to do it shall not be made a part of the insurance contract" (Laws 1911 Chap. 49, Sec. 31, page 195).

It is admitted that the first amended complaint does not alleges that a copy of the cover note was delivered to the assured with the policy, but it is the contention of plaintiff that this statute has no application to the facts alleged in the first amended complaint and that therefore no allegation of compliance therewith is necessary.

Specification of Errors Relied Upon and Intended to be Urged.

Plaintiff specifies the following as errors relied upon and intended to be urged for the reversal of the decree herein, that is to say:

ERROR OF THE DISTRICT COURT IN DISMISSING THE FIRST AMENDED COMPLAINT (Assignment of Errors, Tr. 37-41).

This error is the only one raised by the record but it has been assigned in several different forms in order that all questions involved in the issue may be brought to the attention of the court. The eight assignments of error simply present the reasons why and the particulars in which the decree of the court below is erroneous. These reasons are as follows:

I. Disregarding for the moment the Washington statute, the first amended complaint states facts sufficient to constitute a cause of suit in equity entitling plaintiff to the relief of reformation in some appropriate form. This is the substance of the first assignment of error (Tr. 37, 38).

The remaining assignments of error merely set forth the reasons why the Washington statute is inapplicable to the case and why there is no need to allege compliance therewith in a complaint for reformation which is otherwise sufficient.

II. The Washington statute has no application to suits in equity for reformation, whereas the statute as construed and applied by the court below has abolished the doctrine of reformation in contracts of marine insurance.

(1) The statute is merely a legislative extension of the "parol evidence rule". This rule has no application to suits in equity for reformation and consequently the statutory extension can not be applied where the rule itself is inapplicable. This is the theory upon which the fourth and fifth assignments of error are framed (Tr. 39, 40).

(2) The Washington statute does not in terms apply to the case at bar. This point is made by the third assignment of error (Tr. 39).

III. The Washington statute has no application to contracts of marine insurance, for;

(1) Such contracts are governed by the general maritime law of which the law of marine insurance is a part, and the requirement of the statute is not and never has been any part of the law of marine insurance.

(2) The general maritime law of the United States, including as part thereof, the law of marine insurance, is binding upon all courts, whether of admiralty, common law or equity.

(3) It is beyond the power of the state of Washington to change the law of marine insurance, and hence the statute should not be construed as affecting such a change by making its terms applicable to marine insurance, or, if no other construction is possible, the statute must be held unconstitutional to that extent.

These points are embraced within the scope of the second assignment of error (Tr. 38, 39).

IV. The Washington statute has no application in the equity courts of the United States. The jurisdiction of such courts can neither be expanded nor contracted by state legislation, and the jurisdiction to reform contracts cannot be abridged by a state statute which in effect prescribes a rule of evidence and thereby abolishes the equitable remedy of reformation. This is the point raised in the eighth assignment of errors (Tr. 40, 41).

Brief of Argument.

1. DISREGARDING THE WASHINGTON STATUTE, THE FIRST AMENDED COMPLAINT STATES FACTS SUFFICIENT TO CONSTITUTE A CAUSE OF SUIT IN EQUITY ENTITLING PLAINTIFF TO THE RELIEF OF REFORMATION IN SOME APPROPRIATE FORM (First Assignment of Error, Tr. 37, 38).

The only question before the court on this appeal is one of law. Does the first amended complaint state facts sufficient to constitute a cause of suit for reformation? There are no questions of fact in the case. The facts are the allegations contained in the complaint, all of which are admitted by the motion to dismiss, which, under the new equity rules, takes the place of and operates with the same effect as the former demurrer.

Equity Rules of the Supreme Court, Rule 29.

The facts alleged show that the cover slip constituted a definite concluded contract of marine insurance, upon which, had no subsequent certificate been issued, an action for a loss within the contract could have been maintained.

Kerr v. Union Marine Insurance Co., 124 Fed. 835;
Ibid., 130 Fed. 415;
26 Cyc. 569, note 88.

The facts also show that the contract was to be followed by and merged in a certificate, which was intended by the parties to embrace all the stipulations of the existing contract. They show that a material term, condition and warranty contained in the original contract was omitted from the certificate by accident and mistake with the result that the certificate does not express the contract of the parties.

Under all the authorities these facts are sufficient to entitle plaintiff to reformation of the certificate.

> "One of the most common classes of cases in which relief is sought in equity on account of a mistake of facts is that of written agreements either executory or executed. Sometimes by mistake the written agreement contains less than the parties intended, sometimes it contains more, and sometimes it simply varies from their intent by expressing something different in substance from the truth of that intent. In all such cases if the mistake is clearly made out by proofs entirely satisfactory, equity will reform the contract so as to make it conformable to the precise intent of the parties."

1 Story's Equity Jurisprudence, (14th Ed.) Sec. 224.

> "Reformation is appropriate, when an agreement has been made, or a transaction has been entered into or determined upon, as intended by all the parties, interested, but in reducing such agreement or transaction to writing, either through the mistake common to both parties, or through the mistake of the plaintiff accompanied by the fraudulent knowledge and procurement of the defendant, the written instrument fails to express the real agreement or transaction. In such a case the instrument may be corrected so that it shall truly represent the agreement or transaction actually made or determined upon according to the real purpose and intention of the parties."

2 Pomeroy's Equity Jurisprudence, (3rd Ed.) Sec. 870.

"There are certain principles of equity applicable to this question, which, as general principles, we hold to be incontrovertible. The first is, that where an instrument is drawn and executed, which professes, or is intended, to carry into execution an agreement, whether in writing or by parol, previously entered into, but which, by mistake of the draftsman, either as to fact or law, does not fulfill, or which violates the manifest intention of the parties to the agreement, equity will correct the mistake, so as to produce a conformity of the instrument to the agreement."

Mr. Justice Washington, speaking for the court in the case of

Hunt v. The Administrators of Rousmaniere, 1 Peters 1, at page 11; 7 L. Ed. 27 at 32.

Andrews v. Essex Co., 1 F. C. 374;

Hearne v. Equitable Safety Ins. Co., 11 F. C. 6300;

North American Ins. Co. v. Whipple, 18 F. C. 10,315;

Oliver v. Mutual Commercial Marine Ins. Co., 18 F. C. 10,498;

Western Assurance Co. v. Ward, 75 Fed. 338;

Providence Steam Engine Co. v. Hathaway Mfg. Co., 79 Fed. 512;

Trenton Terra Cotta Co. v. Clay Shingle Co., 80 Fed. 46;

New York Life Ins. Co. v. McMaster, 87 Fed. 63;

Equitable Safety Ins. Co. v. Hearne, 20 Wall. 494; 22 L. Ed. 398;

5 Joyce on the Law of Insurance, Sec. 3509 and following;

17 The Laws of England by Lord Hallsbury, page 403, Sec. 788 and notes;

26 Cyc., pages 569, 570 and 613.

Aside from the attack based upon the effect of the Washington statute, defendant in his motion to dismiss (Tr. 31-33) challenges the sufficiency of the first amended complaint upon the following grounds which will be discussed in the order enumerated:

1. Exhibit "A" of the first amended complaint (Tr. 24) was preliminary to and an application for insurance as evidenced by the certificate or policy set forth in Exhibit "B" of the complaint (Tr. 25).

2. The application did not make any of its statements or representations therein contained warranties.

3. The omitted phrase sought to be made a warranty has no place in the policy.

4. The certificate or policy did not make the application a part thereof or provide that any of the terms, phrases or language used in the application should become a warranty in the policy or form a part thereof.

5. The complaint fails to show a mutual mistake and plaintiff is estopped by delivery of the certificate or policy to assured and the acceptance thereof by the assured.

6. There is an adequate remedy at law.

7. The first amended complaint shows upon its face that it is a different cause of action against different parties defendant than those named in the original complaint.

The first four points can be grouped and discussed as one. It is true that defendant made an application, but after it was accepted by plaintiff and the acceptance was endorsed thereon, the so-called application was no longer a mere unaccepted continuing offer, which is precisely what an application is in legal effect, but became a contract, commonly called a cover note or cover slip. Such indeed is the precise allegation of paragraph III. of the first amended complaint, the material portions of which read as follows:

> "* * * the defendant made application in writing for insurance in the sum of seven thousand eight hundred and seventy-five dollars ($7,875.00) * * *. Thereafter the plaintiff insured the said lumber in the sum of four thousand eight hundred and seventy-five dollars ($4,875.00) * * *, and as evidence of its acceptance of the said application and of the effecting of the insurance, the plaintiff endorsed in writing its acceptance * * * upon the said application. A copy of the application of the defendants with the acceptance of the plaintiff endorsed thereon (commonly called the cover note or cover slip) is hereunto annexed, made a part hereof and marked Exhibit 'A'."

These are allegations of offer and acceptance from which one and only one legal conclusion can be drawn, namely, that the cover note constitutes a contract; and these allegations of fact are admitted by the motion. Throughout the entire motion to dismiss (Tr. 31-33) much emphasis is placed upon the so-called application, doubtless in support of defendant's attempt to bring the case within the scope of the Washington statute; but defendant entirely overlooks the fact that as a matter of law, the original application became by acceptance thereof merged in the cover note as a contract, and that thereafter there was no application but a completed contract.

Plaintiff's entire case rests upon the fact that there was a preliminary but nevertheless binding contract between the parties, and because a part of that contract, intended by both parties to be incorporated in the certificate, was omitted therefrom by accident and mistake, plaintiff brought this suit. Probably this first point is preliminary and intended to lay a foundation for the objection based on the Washington statute. In any event, however, it is merely a restatement of paragraph III of the first amended complaint, and a specific admission of the fundamental fact upon which the case of plaintiff rests.

It is also true that the application did not designate any of its statements as warranties, and neither did the certificate make the application a part thereof, or provide that any part of the application should be a warranty. But the complaint alleges in paragraph IV a universal usage to the effect that all of the terms and provisions of the cover note were to be embodied in the certificate, and that the dealings between the parties were had in accordanc with and pursuant to this usage. The motion admits the usage and that the parties acted with reference thereto.

The motion is a specific admission that all the terms, conditions and warranties of the cover note were *intended by both parties* to be incorporated in the certificate, which is the foundation of the plaintiff's case. It is not necessary to determine at this time what the effect of incorporation therein is, or whether parts of the certificate can be construed as representations merely or as warranties. The sole purpose of the suit is to get the terms, and all the terms, of the cover note into the certificate. Once this is done, there is no need for this court in this suit to construe the certificate as reformed.

Defendant's first four objections amount to nothing but the denial of facts alleged in the complaint and admitted by the motion itself.

With regard to the point that the complaint does not allege facts showing a mutual mistake, it is sufficient to say that the allegations of the mutual mistake as set forth in paragraphs VI, VII and VIII of the first amended complaint (Tr. 21, 22) are well and sufficiently pleaded under the authorities.

> "The allegations that the terms of the contract were agreed upon, that they were to be put in writing by plaintiff, that both plaintiff

> and defendant executed the writing under the mistaken impression that it did conform to the prior verbal agreement, fully meet the objection that the bill states merely a case of unilateral mistake in making a proposition" (Brown, District Judge, in *Providence Steam Engine Co. v. Hathaway Mfg. Co.*, 79 Fed. 512 at 516).

Furthermore the first amended complaint is a bill with a double aspect, and it is alleged in paragraph VII thereof that either both plaintiff and defendant believed the certificate did contain the omitted provision, or that defendants, knowing of the omission and that it was made by accident and mistake on the part of plaintiff and without its knowledge, failed and neglected to disclose the fact of such omission to the plaintiff. This is a sufficient allegation of unilateral mistake by plaintiff coupled with fraud on the part of defendant. The word "fraud" does not appear in the complaint, but the facts upon which fraud is predicated are sufficiently pleaded.

> "There is, however, one equivalent which may be substituted for mutual mistake. Common honesty forbids a man to obtain or perfect rights with knowledge that the other party is laboring under a mistake. Equity will not permit him to reap the fruits of his dishonest silence. It will not avail him to say that the error ceased to be mutual because he discovered the mistake which he failed to correct. Such conduct amounts to fraud. If, then, by reason of mistake on the one hand, and knowledge of the error on the other, the writing fails to express the prior bargain correctly, equity

will reform just as readily as if there had been mutual mistake" (*23 Har. Law Rev.*, 618, 619).

Essex v. Day, 52 Conn. 483;

Roszell v. Roszell, 109 Ind. 354; 10 N. E. 114;

Welles v. Yates, 44 N. Y. 525;

James v. Cutler, 54 Wis. 172; 10 N. W. 147;

Venable v. Burton, 129 Ga. 537; 59 S. E. 253.

As far as any estoppel arising out of the delivery of the certificate is concerned, there can be none under the facts pleaded. The entire transaction from first to last was intended by both parties to be in harmony with the custom set out in paragraph IV of the first amended complaint (Tr. 20). That custom contemplated the subsequent delivery of a certificate which should embrace all the terms, conditions and warranties of the cover slip, and the delivery of a certificate which through mistake omitted a material term, condition or warranty of the cover slip cannot work an estoppel. If such were the rule, the whole doctrine of reformation would be reduced to a theoretical right incapable of enforcement, for in every case there is a delivery of an erroneous instrument, out of which the necessity for reformation arises.

The defendant also urges that there is an adequate remedy at law. It is true that under some circumstances there may be some remedy at law. Reformed procedure in many states permits of equitable relief in law actions. This situation always obtains in any reformation suit, but the remedy at law is not as complete, thorough going and effective as in equity. The jurisdiction to reform is essentially equitable and the fact that some degree of relief may also be obtained in some law courts is not sufficient to deprive a court of equity of its ancient and indisputable jurisdiction of a reformation suit. The remedy at law which will oust a court of equity of jurisdiction means a remedy known to the common law at the time the constitution was adopted, and not some remedy created by statute passed subsequent to that time. Procedural statutes permitting equitable defences in law actions are all of recent date.

Western Assurance Company of Toronto v. Ward, 75 Fed. 338;
Tayloe v. Insurance Company, 9 How. 390; 13 L. Ed. 187;
Kilbourne v. Sunderland, 130 U. S. 505; 32 L. Ed. 1005.

The last of the minor objections raised by defendant to the first amended complaint is that it shows upon its face that it is a different cause of action against different parties defendant than those named in the original bill of complaint. Coupled with this objection in the motion is a statement that defendant H. G. Tremaine appears specially for the purpose of objecting to the jurisdiction of the court to require him to plead or answer the first amended complaint without service of process thereunder.

The theory upon which a defendant may at one and the same time enter a general appearance and subject himself to the jurisdiction of the court for the purpose of attacking the sufficiency of the complaint, and then limit his appearance in the manner attempted by this defendant is beyond our comprehension. The defendant H. G. Tremaine is and always has been subject to the jurisdiction of the court since the service of the original subpoena upon him, and it is now too late for him to make a special appearance. Furthermore, it is submitted that the reason why he seeks to make a special appearance is not well founded.

The equity rules specifically provide for amendments at any and every stage of the proceedings, and the allowance thereof is wholly within the discretion of the court, and is not subject to review. *Equity Rule 19.*

> "These rules, 19 and 28, covering the subject of amendments to the bill, supplant former equity rules 28, 29, 30, 45 and 46, and their apparent effect is to greatly broaden the power of the courts in permitting amendments at any or all stages of the proceeding.
>
> An examination of the decisions on this point under the former rule, however, discloses the fact that the courts have always considered that the power of a court of equity to grant amendments is wholly discretionary, and that in furtherance of justice they will not consider themselves hampered by the particular rules in court."

Montgomery's Manual of Federal Procedure (2nd. Ed.), page 345.

Furthermore, the cause of action stated in the original complaint is precisely the same cause of action as is stated in the first amended complaint. The purpose of both is to procure reformation of the same instrument upon the same basic facts, and the first amended complaint is nothing but a more detailed and explicit statement of the identical cause of suit set up in the original complaint. It is against the same partnership and the only new party added by the first amended complaint is an additional partner whose existence was unknown to the plaintiff at the time the original complaint was filed.

Further discussion of this branch of the case can serve no useful purpose, for the sufficiency of the first amended complaint cannot be successfully challenged on any of the grounds thus far considered. As a pleading, the complaint responds to every test, either of principle or authority, and must, independently of the Washington statute, constitute the statement of a sufficient cause of suit in equity, justifying the relief of reformation in some appropriate form.

II. THE WASHINGTON STATUTE HAS NO APPLICATION TO SUITS IN EQUITY FOR REFORMATION, WHEREAS THE STATUTE AS CONSTRUED AND APPLIED BY THE COURT BELOW HAS ABOLISHED THE DOCTRINE OF REFORMATION IN CONTRACTS OF MARINE INSURANCE.

(1) The statute is merely a legislative extension of the "parol evidence" rule. This rule has no application to suits in equity for reformation and consequently the statutory extension can not be applied where the rule itself is inapplicable. This is the theory upon which the fourth and fifth assignments of error are framed (Tr. 39).

The real question at issue in this case is the scope and effect of the Washington Statute. This is the sole question considered by the court below in his decision, and the one upon which the case was expressly decided.

The statute has already been quoted (brief page 6) and need not be repeated. It provides in substance that when a contract of insurance is construed, the court must look solely to the terms and conditions of the policy itself, unless, (1) the contract is made pursuant to a written application; (2) the application is intended to be made a part of the contract, and (3) a copy of the application is delivered to the assured with the policy. Then, and only then, the application becomes a part of the contract and may be considered with the policy for the purposes of construction. By necessary implication nothing other than a written application can ever be considered, and then only when made in accordance with the statute.

The learned district judge said in his decision (Tr. 35), after quoting the exact language of the statute, "the statute must be complied with, or the application cannot be considered", and sustained the motion to dismiss.

The only authority adduced by the court in support of his contention is *Joyce on Insurance,* Sec. 190, and cases cited. We have carefully examined that section and all of the cases referred to in the notes and have been unable to discover a single authority which even remotely justifies application of the statute to a reformation suit. We have also made an extended search for cases in point in every jurisdiction where similar legislation has been adopted, and our researches have not disclosed a single case in which such a statute has been applied to defeat a suit for reformation otherwise well founded. There are literally hundreds of cases in the books involving the construction and application of these statutes for they have been adopted quite generally throughout the United States, but all are practically without exception, actions at law on the policy. None involve reformation in equity.

Hence it cannot be said that the decision of the court below finds any support in the authorities.

Neither is it justified on principle. The statute in question is nothing but a legislative extension of the "parol evidence" rule. This rule is in force in every common law jurisdiction, either as the result of statutory enactment or judicial decision. Nothing in our law is more fundamental than this rule, that the terms of a written instrument cannot be altered, varied or contradicted by parol evidence. The effect of the rule is to preclude proof of any antecedent agreement or understanding between parties which would alter, vary or contradict the terms of their subsequent formal written agreement. The word "parol" means extrinsic for it includes both verbal and written evidence. The formal and final written instrument is supposed to express the entire contract, and if it were not for the parol evidence rule the value and certainty of written agreements would be destroyed.

But the parol evidence rule has no application to a suit for reformation. The sole purpose of such a suit is to alter, vary and contradict the terms of the written instrument, and the justification is that the written instrument does not express the real contract which the parties actually made. Unless parol, that is, extrinsic evidence were admissible in equity, it would be absolutely impossible to reform any document, because all the evidence which will prove that the document does not express the real contract must necessarily be extrinsic, and it must, if the suit is to be effective, result in altering, varying and contradicting the terms of the written instrument. To assert, therefore, that the parol evidence rule is applicable to a suit in equity for reformation is to deny the very existence of the entire doctrine of reformation. As Lord Hardwicke observed in the case of *Baker v. Paine,* 1 Ves. Sen.

457; 27 Eng. Rep. 1140, "How can a mistake in an agreement be proved but by parol evidence?"

It is well settled that parol or extrinsic evidence is admissible in the federal courts of equity in a reformation suit.

Andrews v. Essex Co., 1 F. C. 374;
Hearne v. Equitable Safety Ins. Co., 11 F. C. 6300;
North American Ins. Co. v. Whipple, 18 F. C. 10,315;
Oliver v. Mutual Commercial Marine Ins. Co., 18 F. C. 10,498;
Western Assurance Co. v. Ward, 75 Fed. 338;
Providence Steam Engine Co. v. Hathaway Mfg. Co., 79 Fed. 512;
Trenton Terra Cotta Co. v. Clay Shingle Co., 80 Fed. 46;
New York Life Ins. Co. v. McMaster, 87 Fed. 63;
Equitable Safety Ins. Co. v. Hearne, 20 Wall 494; 22 L. Ed. 398.

The Washington statute was framed to correct an evil which was beyond the reach of the parol evidence rule. It is well known that the legislation was aimed at the custom of life insurance companies to put in their blank forms of application long and intricate questions and statements to be answered or made by the applicant, printed usually in very small type and the relevancy and materiality not always apparent to the inexperienced. The subsequent policy when issued usually contained a statement that the application was made a part thereof. As the result of this practice, the insurance company was always able to rely upon the application as a part of the contract because it was made so by reference. The application therefore was not extrinsic evidence but an integral part of the contract, and there was no way to exclude it under the parol evidence rule. This resulted in much injustice and led to the adoption of the Washington and other similar statutes.

The effect of the statute is to extend the salutary principle which is at the foundation of the parol evidence rule. That rules provides that no extrinsic evidence shall be introduced, meaning thereby anything that is not expressly included in the final instrument, but it does not apply to matters incorporated by reference. The statute goes one step further. It adopts the parol evidence rule bodily by declaring that the contract shall be construed solely according to the terms and conditions of the policy or final instrument. Had it stopped there it would have amounted merely to a statutory enactment of the parol evidence rule. But its chief aim was to exclude evidence of matters which were made a part of the contract merely by reference contained in the policy, and for the understanding of which it was necessary to examine other instruments. The desired result is accomplished awkwardly and by implication. After providing that the terms and conditions of the policy shall constitute the sole criterion for determining what the contract is, an exception to the rule is created. The exception provides that under certain circumstances, namely, when a copy of the application is delivered with the policy, the former as well as the latter shall be a part of the contract of insurance. In brief, the statute excludes everything which will alter, vary or contradict the terms and conditions of the policy, except a written application, and then only when a copy thereof is delivered with the policy.

We have already seen that the parol evidence rule cannot be applied to reformation suits without abolishing the doctrine. The same result will be accomplished by applying to such suits the statutory extension of that rule.

If the statute applies, it will operate to exclude all evidence of whatever character that will prove mistake and thus alter, vary or contradict the policy. The only evidence extrinsic to the policy which is permitted by the statute is the application when a copy thereof is delivered with the policy.

It must be remembered that the sole purpose of this suit for reformation suit is to make the certificate speak the real contract of the parties as expressed in the cover slip, and thus enable the insurer, if sued upon the unreformed certificate, to deny that he made any such contract as is expressed therein, and, in support of his denial, to introduce the reformed certificate as evidence of what the real contract was.

The court below says that a marine insurance certificate cannot be reformed unless a copy of the cover note was delivered with the certificate. In other words, no term omitted from the cover slip can by reformation be added to the certificate, unless both were delivered together.

But had both been delivered together, the cover slip would have been a part of the contract just as much as the certificate. By force of the statute the term contained in the cover slip would have been part of the contract in spite of the fact that it was omitted from the certificate. The sole purpose of the reformation suit would have been accomplished by the operation of the statute, and the suit would have been needless.

On the other hand, when, as in the case at bar, a copy of the cover slip is not delivered with the certificate, the latter cannot be reformed. As the need for reformation will never exist if both instruments are delivered together, and can arise only in the case where no copy of the coverslip has been delivered, it follows that the court below has abolished the doctrine of reformation in cases of insurance by applying the statute to suits of that character.

We submit, therefore, that if the parol evidence rule itself is not applicable in a suit in equity for reformation, the statutory extension of that rule must likewise be inapplicable under the same circumstances. The logic is the same in both cases, and should lead to the same result in either. There is no escape from the conclusion that any application of the statute to reformation suits necessarily results in the abolition of the entire doctrine of reformation in cases of insurance contracts.

(2) The Washington Statute does not in terms apply to the case at bar. (Third Assignment of Error—Tr. 39).

In the discussion of this point particular attention should be paid to the precise language of the statute. In the first place, the statute is a rule of construction, for it provides that every contract of insurance shall be *construed* according to the terms and conditions of the policy. This appears to be a statutory declaration that no extrinsic evidence shall be introduced for the purpose of construing the policy. The suit at bar neither involves nor requires any construction of the policy. The problem is not to determine the meaning of any of the terms of a complete written instrument, but to embody in that instrument all the terms which the parties intended to include therein. No question of construction can arise until the problem presented by this suit has first been solved. Therefore, the operation of the statute is plainly excluded by its own terms.

III. THE WASHINGTON STATUTE HAS NO APPLICATION TO CONTRACTS OF MARINE INSURANCE FOR:

(1) Such contracts are governed by the general maritime law of which the law of marine insurance is a part, and the requirement of the statute is not

and never has been any part of the law of marine insurance.

(2) The general maritime law of the United States, including as part thereof the law of marine insurance, is binding upon all courts, whether of admiralty, common law or equity.

(3) It is beyond the power of the State of Washington to change the law of marine insurance, and hence the statute should not be construed as affecting such a change by making its terms applicable to marine insurance, or, if no other construction is possible, the statute must be held unconstitutional to that extent.

These points are embraced within the scope of the second assignment of error (Tr. 38, 39).

Throughout the discussion of this point, it must not be forgotten that prior to the issuance of the certificate which the first amended complaint seeks to reform, the cover slip constituted a valid and binding contract of marine insurance between the parties. Had a loss occurred prior to the issuance of the certificate plaintiff would have been liable on the contract in the law courts.

But not only was the cover slip a contract, it was a maritime contract, and as such if a loss had occurred before the certificate was issued, plaintiff would have been liable therefor in admiralty, as well as at common law.

> *Kerr v. Union Marine Ins. Co.*, 124 Fed. 835; Ibid., 130 Fed. 415.

Inasmuch therefore, as it is a maritime contract, it is governed not by the law of Washington, the place where it was made, but by the general maritime law. The same thing is true of the certificate, that is, it was a maritime contract and governed in all particulars by the general maritime law and not by the law of the State of Washington.

These principles are clearly established by the case of *Union Fish Company v. Erickson,* 248 U. S. 308; 63 L. Ed. 261. This was a suit in admiralty upon a verbal contract made in California for the employment of libellant as a skipper upon a fishing voyage in Alaskan waters. It was objected by the respondent that the contract was governed by the law of California where it was made and that it was void because it was not in writing, as required by the Statute of Frauds of California, but the court held that it was a maritime contract governed by the general maritime law and that the local statute of the place where made had no application.

Mr. Justice Day, speaking for the court, said:

> "In entering into this contract, the parties contemplated no services in California. They were making an engagement for the services of the master of the vessel, the duties to be performed in the waters of Alaska, mainly upon the sea. The maritime law controlled in this respect, and was not subject to limitation because the particular engagement happened to be made in California. The parties must be presumed to have had in contemplation the system of maritime law under which it was made" (248 U. S. 313; 63 L. Ed. 263).

It is submitted that this case is a conclusive authority that the Washington statute does not apply to the facts alleged in the first amended complaint. Both the cover slip and the certificate are maritime instruments executed by the parties in contemplation of the general maritime law, and the local statute has no application to the case.

Nor is the Union Fish Company case distinguishable because of the fact that it arose in admiralty, for the general maritime law governs in every court, whether it be of admiralty, common law or equity. Such is the precise holding of the Supreme Court in the case of *Chelentis v. Luckenbach Steamship Co.,* 247 U. S. 372; 62 L. Ed. 1171.

This was an action at law by an injured seaman to recover damages by way of idemnity. Under the general maritime law he was entitled only to maintenance and cure, whereas under common law he could recover full indemnity. The court held that upon the facts presented in the case, the seaman's rights, in whatever court that they might be asserted, were such as were prescribed by the laws of the sea.

It must therefore be taken as settled by the decisions of the Supreme Court that there is a general maritime law of the United States which is binding upon all courts when dealing with maritime matters.

The conclusion is irresistible that in the light of the foregoing principles it was never the intention of the Legislature of the State of Washington, that this statute should apply to contracts of marine insurance. The court below, however, has held that the statute does apply to such contracts, a construction of the statute which necessarily renders it unconstitutional because legislation with respect to the general maritime law is not within the legitimate scope of state legislative power.

Southern Pacific Co. v. Jensen, 244 U. S. 205; 61 L. Ed. 1086.

In the Jensen case, the majority of the Supreme Court says that state legislation with respect to martime matters is invalid "if it works material prejudice to the characteristic features of the general maritime law, or interferes with the proper harmony and uniformity of that law in its international and interstate relations" (244 U. S. 216; 61 L. Ed. 1098). A majority of the court were of opinion that the Workmen's Compensation statute of the State of New York was state legislation of this precise character and the statute was held unconstitutional insofar as it purported to cover maritime matters.

The business of marine insurance is world-wide, involving transactions and risks on all the waters of the earth. It is in no sense a local or municipal matter. To hold that the State of Washington may prescribe the methods by which such contracts shall be made and to punish infractions of its statutes by forfeiture of valuable and universally recognized rights, is to invite every state to indulge in similar legislation.

The chaotic condition resulting from such legislation is precisely what a majority of the Supreme Court had in mind when the opinion in the Jensen case quoted with approval the following remarks of Mr. Justice Bradley in *The Lottawanna,* 21 Wall. 558; 22 L. Ed. 654:

> "That we have a maritime law of our own, operative throughout the United States, cannot be doubted. The general system of maritime law which was familiar to the lawyers and statesmen of the country when the Constitution was adopted, was most certainly intended and referred to when it was declared in that instrument that the judicial power of the United States shall extend 'to all cases of admiralty and maritime jurisdiction' * * *. One thing, however, is unquestionable: the Constitution must have referred to a system of laws co-extensive with and operating uniformly in the whole country. It certainly could not have been in the intention to place the Rules and limits of maritime law under the disposal and regulation of the several States, as that would have defeated the uniformity and consistency at which the Constitution aimed on all subjects of commercial character affecting the intercourse of the States with each other or with foreign States." (21 Wall. 574; 22 L. Ed. 662.)

Marine insurance is one of the most ancient branches of the general maritime law and the methods by which it is effected, though often beyond the ken of laymen, are well known to the shipping world. They have undergone practically no modification in the last two hundred years. The course of dealing between insurers and those purchasing insurance has crystalized into a universal usage which is set forth in the fourth paragraph of the first amended complaint (Tr. 20). To permit state legislatures to tinker with this ancient and settled usage pursuant to which contracts of marine insurance have been made, construed and enforced in the four corners of the earth, strikes at the very heart of the shipping world. Insurance is of the essence of every maritime transaction and of all sea borne commerce, and in no department of maritime law is there greater necessity for harmony and uniformity.

Inasmuch, therefore, as the contract between the parties in this suit is a maritime contract which is governed by the general maritime law and not by the local law, it is entirely competent for the parties to contract with reference to the universal and settled usages of marine insurance. It is alleged that they did so contract and the allegation is admitted by the motion.

The local law has nothing to do with the case. The Washington Legislature doubtless knew the limitations upon its power, and therefore the statute should not be given a construction which necessarily renders it unconstitutional. The court below has not only attributed to the legislature an intention to vitiate the settled marine insurance law of the ages, but has declared that such a result can be lawfully accomplished. It is respectfully submitted that his decision can be supported neither by principle nor authority. If the statute can be given no construction other than that placed upon it by the learned District Judge, it is plainly void.

IV. THE WASHINGTON STATUTE HAS NO APPLICATION IN THE EQUITY COURTS OF THE UNITED STATES.

The jurisdiction of such courts can neither be expanded nor contracted by state legislation, and the jurisdiction to reform contracts cannot be abridged by a state statute which in effect prescribes a rule of evidence and thereby abolishes the equitable remedy of reformation. This is the point raised in the eighth assignment of error (Tr. 40, 41).

It is well settled that the jurisdiction of the Federal Courts depends exclusively upon the Constitution of the United States and appropriate legislation of Congress. No state can contract or expand the jurisdiction as thus established, nor prescribe rules of procedure or evidence applicable in the federal courts.

By Sec. 721 of the Revised Statutes, Congress has to a limited extent adopted the laws and practice of the several states for the government of the federal courts when sitting purely as courts of law.

> "The laws of the several States, except where the Constitution, treaties, or statutes of the United States otherwise require or provide, shall be regarded as rules of decision in trials at common law, in the courts of the United States, in cases where they apply" (R. S. Sec. 721).

But this statute applies only to courts of law. Courts of equity and admiralty are not included. As far as courts of equity are concerned, their jurisdiction and practice is governed by that of the English High Court of Chancery at the time the Constitution was adopted. It might perhaps be competent for Congress to change the situation as it has done by Sec. 721, with respect to the law courts, but suffice it to say it has never done so. Clearly, the state legislatures have no power in the premises.

Burt v. Keyes, 4 F. C. 2,212;
Lamson v. Mix, 14 F. C. 8,034;
Davis v. James, 2 Fed. 618;
Strettell v. Ballou, 9 Fed. 256;
Mississippi Mills v. Cohn, 150 U. S. 202; 37 L. Ed. 1052.

It must be conceded, therefore, that if the Legislature of Washington had enacted a statute which provided in terms that no federal court of equity shall hereafter entertain a suit to reform an insurance policy, the statute would be void. Reformation of instruments is an ancient head of equity jurisdiction and as courts of equity the federal courts have exercised the power since the foundation of our government.

It will be recalled that at an earlier point in this brief, the argument was advanced that the Washington statute could not be applied to suits in equity without abolishing the doctrine of reformation itself.

It follows, therefore, that the application of the statute to reformation suits commenced in the federal equity courts, must of necessity, completely deprive them of the power to reform insurance contracts. The statute will operate directly upon the jurisdiction of the federal equity courts, and will in effect, destroy an essential part thereof.

If such a result could not be accomplished by the Washington Legislature directly, which must be conceded, it cannot be accomplished indirectly. If the Washington Legislature can prescribe rules of evidence applicable to the federal equity courts, the necessary effect of which must be to exclude any and all evidence upon which their equitable jurisdiction of reformation can be exercised, it has destroyed the jurisdiction itself.

Should such a statute as the one under consideration be held applicable to the federal courts of equity, then there is no limit to the power of state legislatures with respect to federal equity jurisdiction. By prescribing rules of procedure and evidence the entire equity jurisdiction could ultimately be completely abolished.

In view of these considerations, it is unthinkable that the Washington Legislature ever intended the statute to apply to reformation suits, or to suits of that character in the federal courts. If such was the intention the statute is clearly unconstitutional.

Courts have ever been reluctant to construe statutes in such fashion as to render them void, especially when any other construction is possible. Yet this is precisely what the court below has done. Its decision in effect declares that the Washington Legislature has precluded a federal equity court, sitting in Washington, from reforming a marine or any insurance policy made in that state.

The mere statement of the proposition demonstrates the error into which the learned District Judge has fallen, and emphasizes anew the conclusion that his decree should be reversed.

In conclusion it is respectfully submitted that, independently of the Washington statute, the first amended complaint constitutes a sufficient statement of a cause of suit for reformation in equity, and that the statute, if properly construed has no application to the case, or if applicable in terms and by necessary construction is unconstitutional and void.

The decree should be reversed and the cause remanded to the District Court for further proceedings and with instructions to deny defendant's motion to dismiss the first amended complaint.

Dated, San Francisco,
September 1, 1920.

HAROLD M. SAWYER,
ALFRED T. CLUFF,
Solicitors for Appellant.

No. 3513

IN THE

UNITED STATES CIRCUIT COURT OF APPEALS

FOR THE NINTH CIRCUIT

AMERICAN MERCHANT MARINE INSURANCE COMPANY OF NEW YORK (a corporation),
Appellant,

vs.

H. G. TREMAINE, S. L. BUCKLEY and JOHN DOE BUCKLEY, doing business under the firm name and style of BUCKLEY-TREMAINE LUMBER COMPANY,
Appellees.

BRIEF FOR APPELLEE, H. G. TREMAINE

FRANK A. HUFFER,
WILLIAM H. HAYDEN,
GERALD H. BUCEY,
527 Henry Building, Seattle, Wash.,
Solicitors for Appellee H. G. Tremaine.

THE BELL PRESS, TACOMA, WASH.

No. 3513

IN THE

UNITED STATES CIRCUIT COURT OF APPEALS

FOR THE NINTH CIRCUIT

AMERICAN MERCHANT MARINE INSURANCE COMPANY OF NEW YORK (a corporation),
Appellant,

vs.

H. G. TREMAINE, S. L. BUCKLEY and JOHN DOE BUCKLEY, doing business under the firm name and style of BUCKLEY-TREMAINE LUMBER COMPANY,
Appellees.

BRIEF FOR APPELLEE, H. G. TREMAINE

In answer to the brief of appellant herein, and in support of the decree of the district court granting appellee's motion and dismissing appellant's first amended bill of complaint, we respectfully submit the following points and authorities:

I. IRRESPECTIVE OF THE PROVISIONS OF THE WASHINGTON STATUTE, THE AMENDED BILL OF COMPLAINT DOES NOT STATE FACTS SUFFICIENT TO CONSTITUTE A VALID CAUSE OF ACTION IN EQUITY AGAINST DEFENDANT, OR TO ENTITLE PLAINTIFF TO THE RELIEF SOUGHT.

(1) **The bill of complaint fails to show that plaintiff has been or will be injured by reason of the omission from the insurance policy of the clause in question. or to show any need or reason for equitable relief.**

It is essential to a cause of action in equity that there be some damage to the plaintiff, either suffered or threatened.

> "Courts of equity will not exercise their powers for the enforcement of right or prevention of wrong in the abstract and where no actual benefit is to be derived by the party who seeks to exercise such right, nor injury suffered by the wrong complained of."

Goodrich vs. Moore, 72 Am. Dec. 75.

10 R. C. L., 369.

Although plaintiff's amended bill of complaint was filed herein on April 28th, 1920, (Tr. 31), almost seven months after the policy was issued, (Tr. 21) and almost six months after the expiration of the period during which it is alleged the vessel was to sail with the insured cargo, (Tr. 20) it does not show either that the vessel failed to sail within the required time, or that any loss has occurred or may occur, on account of which plaintiff has been or may be injured. Plaintiff has failed to show, either that it would be benefited by the granting of the relief prayed for, or that it would be injured without such relief. It asks a court of equity to reform a contract without any showing whatever that it has suffered or will suffer any loss or damage on account of such contract in its present form. It is thus presenting for determination a purely speculative and abstract proposition, which a court of equity will not entertain.

It is alleged in the complaint (Tr. 20) that the terms of the contract entered into on October 3rd, 1919, between plaintiff and defendants provided that the scow, carrying the insured cargo, should sail during the month of October; but it is nowhere alleged, and there is nothing in the complaint to show, that the scow did not sail during that month, and certainly there is no presumption that it did not. If the contract provided for October sailing, as the complaint alleges, then, in the absence of any statement or showing to the contrary, it must be presumed that defendants complied with the terms of that contract and that the scow did sail in October. And if the scow with the insured cargo actually sailed in October, in compliance with the alleged terms of the contract, then it necessarily follows that plaintiff could not be injured by the mere fact that such provision for October sailing had been omitted from the policy, even if such provision were intended to be inserted therein as a warranty. Plaintiff has therefore failed to show wherein it is injured by this omission from the policy or to show any equitable reason why the policy should be reformed as prayed for.

Furthermore, the bill of complaint does not state or show that any loss has occurred, or may occur, with respect to the insured cargo, or that plaintiff has been or may be required to pay any sum or discharge any obligation whatever on account of the policy of insurance in question. If no loss has occurred or may occur, then there could be no damage to plaintiff by reason of the omission from the policy of the provision for October sailing. If, for instance, the vessel has arrived safely, the policy is terminated, and a reformation of it is a futile thing. Plaintiff fails to show either that a loss has occurred or that the voyage has not yet terminated and that a loss may occur.

There is, of course, no presumption that loss has occurred. If there be any presumption it would be to the contrary. And in this connection the court will consider the fact that plaintiff's amended bill of complaint was filed, as above stated, nearly seven months after the date of issuance of the policy in question, and almost six months after the expiration of the period during which it is alleged the scow should sail, and yet it does not contain one word to indicate that any loss has occurred—that the voyage has not been safely completed. After such a lapse of time, this silence certainly tends strongly to create or corroborate the presumption that no loss has occurred and that the voyage has been safely completed. Certainly, in the face of this, plaintiff can not expect a court of equity to indulge in any presumption that a loss has occurred or may occur, in order to supply to its complaint an essential element of its right to the equitable relief sought.

(2) The bill of complaint does not sufficiently show whether the phrase "Oct. Slg." appearing in the application was intended by both parties to be a warranty, or a representation, and, if the latter, that it was material.

To make the facts stated in a bill of complaint sufficient to authorize a court of equity to reform a contract by inserting *somewhere* therein certain words, intended by both parties to be inserted, but omitted by mistake, it must affirmatively appear that the minds of the parties met as to the connection and relation in which the words were to be used—as to the *legal significance and force* they should have when inserted; or, in other words, that the minds of the parties met upon the *same thing in the same sense.*

Plaintiff in this action seeks to have a policy of insurance reformed, in accordance with what it alleges was the actual intention of the parties, by inserting therein the words "October sailing," which words, it alleges, appeared in the application for the insurance (Tr. 19, 20) and were intended by the parties to be included in the policy, but were omitted by mistake (Tr. 21). Plaintiff does not state what kind of term or obligation of the policy it was intended by the parties that these words should express, whether a representation or a warranty. It is not enough to say that these words should be in the policy; their intended force and significance therein must be shown, and it also must be clearly shown that the purpose indicated was the exact purpose and significance that both parties intended. Plaintiff in its bill of complaint has not only failed to indicate definitely in what particular legal sense these words should be embodied in the policy, but it has failed to show that this particular legal sense was actually intended by both parties.

The importance of definitely showing the intended character of these words in the insurance policy is all the more appreciated when we consider the essential difference, in nature and legal effect, between a provision in a policy of insurance constituting a warranty and that which constitutes a representation. A warranty is in effect a condition precedent to the validity of the policy, and if not strictly adhered to avoids the policy; and this is true whether or not the thing warranted is in fact material to the risk. If it has been agreed upon by the parties as a warranty its materiality is conclusively presumed on account of such agreement. Moreover, to constitute a warranty, the provision must appear in the policy.

> *Joyce on Insurance* (2nd ed.) secs. 1882, 1951, 1962.

A representation, on the other hand, does not affect the validity of the policy unless it be actually material to the risk or has induced the insurer to accept the risk.

> *Joyce on Insurance* (2nd ed.) secs. 1882, 1892-3.

If plaintiff in this action seeks to show that the words "October sailing" were intended as a warranty, then it must definitely so allege. This it has failed to do. The only allegations in the complaint which at all relate to the nature of this phrase are those contained in paragraphs III and VIII (Tr. 19, 22). In paragraph III plaintiff merely alleges (Tr. 19, 20) that defendants made an application in writing for insurance, which plaintiff accepted. This application is then set forth in Exhibit "A" (Tr. 24). It contains the words, "Oct. slg."; but nothing appears thereon to indicate that such words were intended as warranty, and plaintiff does not allege that it was so intended by both parties. Certainly the mere fact that such statement appears in the application does not make it a warranty. There is not only no such presumption, but the contrary presumption is well established.

In the first place a statement in an application can not in any event become a warranty, unless and until it is incorporated in the insurance policy. This rule is an absolute and unfailing one.

Joyce on Insurance (2nd ed.) sec. 1949.

In the second place, a statement, even when contained in the policy, will be presumed or construed to be a representation rather than a warranty in every case unless the intention to make it a warranty clearly appears. Warranties are not favored by construction.

Joyce on Insurance (2nd ed.) secs. 1949-50.

Moulor vs. Insurance Co., 28 U. S. (L. ed.) 449.

Plaintiff in paragraph VIII (Tr. 22) alleges that "said omitted provision constituted a material express warranty by defendants materially and substantially affecting the rights and obligations of plaintiff." But this is a mere statement of a legal conclusion. It is not equivalent to, and does not dispense with the necessity of a statement of facts showing that it was agreed and intended by both parties that such provision should be a warranty. Plaintiff's allegations, therefore, utterly fail to show a mutual intention and agreement that this provision should constitute a warranty.

If, on the other hand, plaintiff seeks to have the provision for October sailing inserted in the policy as a representation, then it must show that such provision is either material to the risk, or induced plaintiff to accept the risk. For, if this provision is merely a representation which has no material bearing on the risk and did not induce plaintiff to accept the risk, then no reason exists for seeking the aid of a court of equity to insert it in the policy. It is incumbent upon plaintiff to show by definite allegations of fact, either that the risk was less upon a vessel sailing in October than upon one sailing at a subsequent time; that the rate of premium was less, or that without such a representation plaintiff would not have accepted the risk. The bill of complaint is entirely lacking in such allegation.

Joyce on Insurance (2nd ed.) sec 1892.

The only allegation whatever in the complaint

relating to the materiality of this provision for October sailing is the broad, general statement, above quoted, to the effect that the omitted provision materially and substantially affects the rights and obligations of plaintiff. This statement is not only a mere conclusion, but fails to even indicate how or in what manner its rights and obligations are affected. Before a court of equity will reform a contract by inserting therein a provision alleged to have been omitted by mistake, it must be shown in what manner and for what reason the party seeking such reformation has been or will be injured by the omission. If the omitted provision is immaterial and of no consequence, a court of equity will not exercise its powers to perform the useless function of inserting it in the policy. Plaintiff has totally failed to show the materiality of this omitted provision and the relief prayed for should be denied.

(3) The amended bill of complaint does not contain a sufficient allegation as to the existence cf a mutual mistake to entitle plaintiff to reformation of the policy.

It is a fundamental rule of pleading, whether at law or in equity, that facts must be stated and not mere conclusions. It is also a well-established rule that the facts must be definitely stated. Especially is this true where fraud or mistake is alleged. The fraud or mistake must be stated with particularity.

> "It is elementary that a complainant in equity must allege with particularity every material fact necessary for him to prove to establish his right to the relief prayed."

Wilson vs. Ice Company, 206 Fed. 738.

Story's Equity Pleading, sec. 241.

Equity Rule 25.

Montgomery's Federal Procedure (2nd ed.) 319.

The amended bill of complaint in this case not only fails to state with definiteness and particularity facts showing the existence of a mutual mistake, but it alleges instead of facts mere speculations or conclusions, and even these are conflicting and inconsistent.

The only allegation in the complaint with reference to any mistake on the part of defendants is that contained in paragraph VII (Tr. 22). Plaintiff there alleges:

"* * plaintiff is informed and believes * * the defendants * * *believing* that the *said certificates did in fact contain the said omitted provision* * * * by accident and mistake accepted the said certificate * * *or* the defendants, *knowing that the said omitted provision was in fact not incorporated* in the said certificate and that the same was omitted therefrom by accident and mistake * * *neglected to disclose the fact* of such omission to the plaintiff."

It will be noted that while plaintiff alleges on information and belief that defendant accepted the policy by accident and mistake *believing that it contained the omitted provision* and not knowing that it had been omitted, this statement is coupled with a directly refuting statement that defendant *did know the provision had been omitted* but fraudulently concealed its knowledge from plaintiff. Plaintiff in the same breath alleges good faith and bad faith on the part of defendants respecting the same transaction. It is thus apparent that plaintiff has not alleged the facts according to its knowledge, information or belief, but, having neither any knowledge, information or belief as to what the facts are, has indulged in speculation as to what they might be, and, as a result of such speculation, has alleged as facts the two alternative and inconsistent conclusions mentioned.

If under any circumstances it be permissible to base a cause of action such as this upon a mere conclusion, which we do not at all concede, it could only be in a case where the conclusion alleged constituted the only possible deduction from the facts stated. Any such justification is lacking in this case, for the reason that, in addition to the two conclusions asserted by plaintiff, there is a third, which, we submit, is far more logical and reasonable in view of the facts and circumstances stated in the complaint, and is more consistent with honesty and fair dealing, namely this: That defendants examined the policy when delivered to them, and noticed that the provision for October sailing had been omitted, but, knowing that the policy had been prepared by plaintiff, naturally and reasonably assumed that the omission was intentional and deliberate, and that plaintiff had considered the provision immaterial; which assumption is in accordance with the general rule of law referred to in another part of this brief. This conclusion does not involve any assumption of mistake or of fraud, and is entirely consistent with the transactions leading to the issuance of the policy. If conclusions are to be considered in determining the rights of the parties in this action, then we submit that this third conclusion is the most logical one, and necessarily precludes the relief sought by plaintiff.

We insist, however, that the rules of pleading should govern, and that according to such rules plaintiff's bill of complaint is fatally defective, in that it has failed to allege definitely and with particularity facts sufficient to show any mutual mistake with respect to the terms of the policy.

(4) Plaintiff is not entitled to the relief sought for the reason that its bill of complaint shows that it has been guilty of laches in bringing this action and that defendant has been prejudiced thereby.

It is a well settled rule of equity that an equitable remedy to which a party might otherwise be entitled will be denied to him whenever it appears that he has so long delayed the enforcement of his rights that the situation of the other party has been changed to his prejudice and the granting of the remedy would work an injustice upon such other party.

Pomeroy's Equity Jurisprudence (3d ed.) secs. 424, 897, 917.

Pomeroy's Equitable Remedies, sec. 21.

It is also incumbent upon a plaintiff seeking relief in equity to state facts showing that he has not been guilty of delay to the prejudice of defendant; and in cases where mistake or fraud is alleged, he must definitely state when and how he obtained knowledge thereof, why it was not obtained earlier, and the degree of diligence exercised by him to discover the mistake or fraud. Otherwise his bill will be dismissed.

Pomeroy's Equitable Remedies, secs. 21, 36.

Hubbard vs. Manhattan Trust Co., 87 Fed. 51 (59).

Cutter vs. Water Co., 128 Fed. 505 (509).

Wood vs. Carpenter, 25 U. S. (L. ed.) 807.

Hardt vs. Heidweyer, 38 U. S. (L. ed.) 548 (552).

Plaintiff in its bill of complaint alleges that the policy in question was executed and delivered to defendants on October 6, 1919 (Tr. 21). It also alleges that according to the terms of the application for the insurance the scow carrying the insured cargo was to sail during the month of October (Tr. 19, 20). It states that a mistake was made by it in omitting the provision for October sailing from the policy (Tr. 21), but makes no statement whatever as to when or in what manner it first discovered that the mistake had been made; neither does it state what degree of diligence it exercised to discover any mistake. It does not show that the mistake was not discovered by it until after the vessel carrying the insured cargo had sailed. If plaintiff discovered the alleged mistake at any time during the month of October, and before the vessel had sailed, and it intended to insist upon the provision for October sailing as an essential condition of the insurance, then as a matter of equity and fair dealing it owed a duty to defendants to seek such modification of the policy before the month of October expired, in order that defendants might not be misled by the silence and inaction of plaintiff into believing that they were protected by the policy of insurance delivered to them, the terms of which did not restrict the time of sailing to the month of October.

The necessity for prompt action to correct a mistake is especially applicable to a case like this one, where a policy of insurance is involved and plaintiff seeks to have it reformed to agree with the terms of the application, because of the strong presumption of law that a policy of insurance when issued supersedes the application and all prior agreements, and that any provision of the application inconsistent with or omitted from the policy is deemed to have been waived.

U. S. Cas. Co. vs. Charleston Co., 183 Fed. 238.

El Dia Ins. Co. vs. Sinclair, 228 Fed. 833.

Andrews vs. Ins. Co., Fed. Cas. 374.

Union Mutual Ins. Co. vs. Mowry, 24 U. S. (L. ed.) 674.

American Popular Life Ins. Co. vs. Day, 23 Am. Rep. 198.

The case of *Andrews vs. Insurance Company*, above cited, was a case, like the one at bar, where plaintiff sought to have a policy of marine insurance reformed to agree with the terms of the application, by inserting therein a clause relating to the voyage, which it was alleged had been contained in the application but omitted by mistake from the policy. The case was brought in a court of admiralty, and was dismissed for the reason that an admiralty court had no jurisdiction to entertain such a suit. The court, however, referred to the necessity of extreme caution in granting reformation in such cases, using the following language, which is so peculiarly applicable to the case at bar that we invite the court's attention to it:

> "It is not pretended that every thing contained in the memorandum was to be inserted in the policy. It is perfectly notorious that proposals of this nature often contain remarks, representations, and queries, for the information and guidance of the underwriters which cannot by any reasonable construction be supposed proper for insertion in the policy. In many instances the insertion would be absurd, and in some might be repugnant

> to the obvious intent of the parties in their final act. * * * It is not sufficient therefore to show that a clause is in the momorandum, to justify its insertion in the policy, unless from its nature and object it clearly formed a part of the contract. A clause may in the event become material and decisive of a right if inserted, which may nevertheless, at the time of the proposal, not have been contemplated by either party as a part of the policy. It might make all the difference between a representation and a warranty, a difference in many cases of the most serious importance."

We would call attention to the fact that this presumption above mentioned obtains irrespective of the provision of any statute, such as exists in the State of Washington. We shall, hereafter, refer to that statute and its effect upon this case.

II. PLAINTIFF'S VIOLATION OF THE PROVISIONS OF THE WASHNIGTON STATUTE PRECLUDES ITS RIGHT TO THE RELIEF SOUGHT.

The maxim of equity that he who comes into equity must come with clean hands requires a denial of equitable relief to one who has violated the law.

Plaintiff's amended bill of complaint states that it is a foreign corporation, and is "duly authorized to do business in the State of Washington by virtue of strict compliance with the laws of said State" (Tr. 18). One of the laws of the State of Washington governing such insurance companies is that contained in Sections 6059-31 of Remington's Code, which provides as follows:

> "Every contract of insurance shall be construed according to the terms and conditions of the policy, except where the contract is made pursuant to a written application therefor, and such written application is intended to be made a part of the insurance contract, and the insurance company making such insurance contract, unless as otherwise provided by this act, shall deliver a copy of such application with the policy to the assured, and thereupon such application shall become a part of the insurance contract, and failing so to do it shall not be made a part of the insurance contract."

Attention is directed to the fact that this section absolutely requires that *"the insurance company * * shall deliver a copy of such application with the policy to the assured* * * and *failing to do so, it shall not be made a part of the insurance contract.* From the bill of complaint it plainly appears that plainiiff did not deliver a copy of the application in question with the policy. Yet, having absolutely violated this positive requirement of the statute, plaintiff now comes into a court of equity asking that a provision of this application be made part of the insurance contract. As a violator of the law it does not come into this court with clean hands, and the relief it seeks should be denied.

Plaintiff argues that this statute prescribes merely a rule of evidence, and for that reason it can not have any effect in a federal equity suit, and can not apply to a suit for reformation of an insurance policy. On page 8 of plaintiff's brief, counsel makes the statement that the Washington statute is merely "a legislative extension of the parol evidence rule," but he cites no authority in support of this extraordinary statement. We say this statement is extraordinary, because nothing whatever is said in the statute about proof or evidence; but the statute in clear and definite terms imposes a duty or obligation upon insurance companies, namely, to deliver to the assured a copy of any application which is intended to be made a part of the insurance contract, and in case of failure so to do, excludes therefrom any and all provisions of the application.

The purpose of such laws, as stated in various decisions of the courts, is to require the entire insurance contract to be placed in the hands of the assured, that he may know what the exact terms of the completed contract are; and to place upon the insurance company the obligation of either including in such delivered contract all the terms it deems essential or be held to have waived such as are not included.

Rauen vs. Insurance Co., 106 N. W. 198 (Iowa).

Provident Co. vs. Puryear, 59 S. W. 15 (Kentucky.)

Failure of an insurance company to comply with the provisions of such a statute has been held to preclude its obtaining in a court of equity the cancellation of an insurance policy for fraud in its procurement.

> *New York Life Ins. Co. vs. Hamburger*, 140 N. W. 510 (Michigan.)

This last mentioned case as well as those above cited amply support the decision of the district court in dismissing plaintiff's bill of complaint.

III. AS TO APPELLANT'S CLAIM OF THE UNCONSTITUTIONALITY OF THE WASHINGTON STATUTE AS APPLIED TO THIS CASE.

Counsel contends that the statute of Washington, prescribing the form of contracts of marine insurance, does not apply to this case on the ground that, so to apply it, would tend to disturb the uniformity of the admiralty jurisdiction throughout the United States; and, to sustain this contention, he cites the case of *Union Fish Company vs. Erickson*, 248 U. S. 308, in which the court sustained a libel in admiralty brought by Erickson in a United States district court of California to recover damages from the owner of a vessel for breach of an oral contract for its use upon the seas in a commercial adventure, which contract was not to be performed within a year, and, such being the case, was, under the California statute of frauds, required to be in writing.

The fallacy of counsel's contention and the inapplicability of the *Erickson* case can be readily disclosed by the consideration of these facts:

Erickson was in a court of admiralty seeking an admiralty remedy for a breach of a maritime right; this appellant is here in a court of equity, seeking an equitable remedy for the enforcement of an equitable right.

The doctrine of the necessity of uniformity of admiralty jurisdiction and of admiralty rights throughout the United States, is not pertinent to the case of a suitor who invokes the jurisdiction of a court of *equity* to establish a merely *equitable* right. The very reason appellant has come into a court of equity is because the subject matter of its suit is not of a maritime character. That it is not of that character is established in the case of *Andrews vs. Essex Fire & Ins. Co.*, 1 Fed. Cas. No. 374, p. 885, which was an action in admiralty seeking reformation of a policy of marine insurance by inserting therein a clause specifying the voyage, which clause had been contained in the memorandum for the insurance, but, as was alleged, omitted from the policy through mistake. In the course of its opinion, the court said:

> "Courts of admiralty, in my view, have jurisdiction over maritime contracts WHEN EXECUTED, but not over contracts leading to the execution of maritime contracts * * * If the contract be an executed maritime contract, the jurisdiction attaches; and the admiralty may then administer relief upon that contract according to equity and good conscience. The law looks to the proximate and not to the remote cause as a source of jurisdiction, and deals with it only when it has as-

> sumed its final shape as a maritime contract. It has been said that the memorandum in the present case is an executed maritime contract, equivalent to a policy; but I understand it to be *nothing more than an agreement for a policy;* and if no policy had been executed, this court, as a court of admiralty, would not have had jurisdiction to enforce it."

The doctrine of the above case has been followed in the following cases, to-wit:

Williams vs. Ins. Co., 56 Fed. 159.

United T. & L. Co., vs. N. Y. & B. T. Line, 185 Fed. 386.

Rea. vs. "Eclipse," 34 U. S. (L.ed) 269.

In the *Erickson* case, the libelant was suing upon an executed maritime contract, claiming damages on account of the wrongful interruption by respondent of a marine adventure. In this action, appellant is asking to have a *certain piece of paper*, purporting to contain the terms of a contract of marine insurance, brought into court and the language thereof changed by the insertion of certain words. Such a suit relates merely to the *making* of a maritime contract and not to the enforcement of one. The making of such a contract, whether solely by the manual acts of the parties, or partly by such acts and partly by the interposition of a court of equity, is purely a land transaction, as much so as the making of a deed of land or of a bill of sale of personal property, or of a policy of insurance on a brick block.

It is true that, in making a contract of marine insurance, the parties contemplate a future marine adventure. So, also, do the parties to a contract for the building of a ship; but no one would contend that a suit for the reformation of a contract to build a ship lies in the field of admiralty law either substantive or adjective, or that it was not competent for the state in which the ship was to be built to prescribe the form of a ship building contract, or to define the rights of the parties thereto in case such form was departed from in any specified particular on the ground that to do so would disturb the uniformity of our admiralty system.

While the above is a conclusive answer to counsel's contention, it is also well to note the following distinctions between the *Erickson* case and this case:

1. In the court's opinion in the *Erickson* case occurs this language:

> "In intering into this contract, the parties contemplated no service in California. They were making an engagement for the services of the master of the vessel, the duties *to be performed in the waters of Alaska, namely, upon the sea.* The maritime law controlled in this respect and was not subject to limitations because the engagement happened to be made in California."

The insurance policy before the court was not only made in the state of Washington, but was to be performed in that state, as is indicated by this language:

"Loss, if any, payable to the order of assured in Seattle, Washington."

We thus have a contract made in Seattle, Washington, *and to be performed in Seattle, Washington.*

2. Besides, as we have before stated, the first amended complaint, alleges that appellant is a corporation of the state of New York, and was at all of the times mentioned in the bill, duly authorized to do business in the state of Washington by virtue of strict compliance with the laws of that state governing such foreign corporations. Appellant had no right to do business in the state of Washington, except upon the conditions prescribed by the legislature of that state; and when appellant entered the state of Washington for the purpose of writing insurance therein, it agreed to comply with the statutes of that state relating thereto, and, among other things, agreed that, whenever it issued a policy of insurance, it would deliver therewith a copy of the application, and, also that, if it failed so to do, such application would be considered no part of the insurance contract. Even if appellant had been a natural person and a resident of the state of Washington, writing such a contract, and as such, had been exempt from the application of the statute on the constitutional grounds expounded by counsel, yet there is no rea-

son why, being as it in fact is and was, a foreign corporation entitled to write insurance only on the conditions prescribed by the state law, it could not, in consideration of a license to do business in the state, waive those constitutional admiralty rights and agree to be governed in the matter of writing policies of marine insurance by state laws in conflict therewith.

IV. EVEN HAD THE BILL OF COMPLAINT BEEN SUFFICIENT IN OTHER RESPECTS TO ENTITLE PLAINTIFF TO THE RELIEF SOUGHT, IT WAS PROPERLY DISMISSED BECAUSE PLAINTIFF'S FAILURE TO BRING ALL THE ESSENTIAL PARTIES BEFORE THE COURT RENDERS IMPOSSIBLE THE GRANTING OF ANY RELIEF.

The amended bill of complaint shows (Tr. 18) that this action is against three defendants, namely, "H. G. Tremaine, * * S. L. Buckley, and John Doe Buckley," who are co-partners constituting the firm of Buckley-Tremaine Lumber Company, and is for the purpose of reforming a policy of insurance, set forth in Exhibit "B" (Tr. 25), which was issued in favor of said defendants and delivered to them on October 6, 1919. (Tr. 21). The complaint therefore clearly shows that the policy sought to be reformed is the contract and property of the three defendants named.

The records also shows that only one of these above defendants, H. G. Tremaine, has been served or made any appearance herein. (Tr. 13). The record fails to show why the other defendants have not been served, or whether plaintiff ever expects to obtain service upon them. When the motion to dismiss was heard on April 26th, 1920, (Tr. 16) the original bill of complaint had been served upon defendant Tremaine only, (Tr. 13) yet no continuance was asked on that account, nor was the lack of such service at all referred to; and when the hearing was had on the motion to dismiss the amended bill of complaint, on May 3, 1920, (Tr. 33) still no service had been made upon the other defendants, and no continuance was asked on that account, or any reference made to that fact by plaintiff. While counsel make the assertion on page 3 of their brief that "up to the time when the decree was rendered, it proved impossible to obtain personal service upon the other two defendants," there is nothing whatever in the record to justify this statement.

At the hearing upon the motion to dismiss the amended bill, appellant should, if it expected to obtain service on the other defendants, have asked the court to defer action on the motion until such service was obtained; and if it was found impossible to obtain such service the bill was subject to dismissal for that reason alone. But, instead of asking for time to complete service, or making any other counter application, appellant refused to plead further and stood uncompromisingly on the record as it then was. (Tr. 37).

It is obvious that the relief sought, which involves the surrender for correction of a policy of insurance, cannot possibly be granted where the policy in question is the property of and in the possession of three persons, only one of whom is before the court and amenable to its decree.

To allow plaintiff the relief prayed for, in view of the circumstances stated, must either result in a decree which can bind only one of three essential parties and can never be enforced,—a futile act which equity abhors—, or in permitting plaintiff to prosecute its suit against each of three essential parties separately, or piece-meal, thus multiplying litigation, a thing equally opposed to the principles of equity.

It is a settled rule in equity, which should be applied in this case, that if all the necessary parties are not before the court, either by service of process or by voluntary appearance, and the interests of those present and those absent are inseparable, the bill must be dismissed.

20 Ruling Case Law, 704, and cases cited.

Mallow vs. Hinde, 6 U. S. (L.ed.) 599 (600).

Barney vs. Baltimore, 18 U. S. (L.ed.) 825 (826).

The Matter of Change of Voyage Covered by Adjustment of Premium.

The policy contains this provision:

"Held covered at a premium to be arranged, in case of *deviation or change of voyage* or

> of any error or unintentional omission in the description of the interest, vessel or *voyage*, provided same be communicated to the insurrer as soon as known to the assured."

Nothing is alleged in the amended bill to show why the above provision could not have been applied to the present case.

In view of the general rule of the law that any provision in an application for insurance which has been omitted from the policy is presumed to have been considered immaterial or to have been waived, and, also, of the stringent provisions of the Washington statute now before the court, designed to prevent such controversies as this and also *particularly* unconscionable defenses by insurance companies, do the allegations of the amended bill, especially considering their lack of candor, definiteness and certainty, appeal to the conscience of the court as sufficient to entitle appellant to any relief?

Respectfully submitted,

FRANK A. HUFFER,
WILLIAM H. HAYDEN,
GERALD H. BUCEY,
Solicitors for Appellee H. G. Tremaine.

No. 3513

IN THE

United States Circuit Court of Appeals

For the Ninth Circuit

AMERICAN MERCHANT MARINE INSURANCE COMPANY OF NEW YORK (a corporation), *Appellant,*

vs.

H. G. TREMAINE, S. L. BUCKLEY and JOHN DOE BUCKLEY, doing business under the firm name and style of BUCKLEY-TREMAINE LUMBER COMPANY, *Appellees.*

REPLY BRIEF FOR APPELLANT.

HAROLD M. SAWYER,
ALFRED T. CLUFF,
Mills Building, San Francisco,
Solicitors for Appellant.

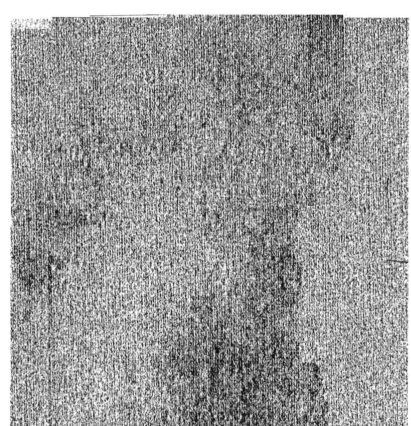

No. 3513

IN THE

United States Circuit Court of Appeals

For the Ninth Circuit

AMERICAN MERCHANT MARINE INSURANCE COMPANY OF NEW YORK (a corporation), *Appellant,*

vs.

H. G. TREMAINE, S. L. BUCKLEY and JOHN DOE BUCKLEY, doing business under the firm name and style of BUCKLEY-TREMAINE LUMBER COMPANY, *Appellees.*

REPLY BRIEF FOR APPELLANT.

Pursuant to leave of court first had and obtained, the following reply to the brief of appellee herein is submitted on behalf of appellant.

I. FAILURE TO ALLEGE COMPLIANCE WITH THE WASHINGTON STATUTE IS THE SOLE GROUND ASSIGNED IN THE OPINION OF THE COURT BELOW FOR DISMISSING THE COMPLAINT, AND, IF THAT STATUTE IS NOT APPLICABLE TO THE CASE, THE DECREE SHOULD BE REVERSED WITH LEAVE TO PLAINTIFF TO AMEND ITS COMPLAINT SO AS TO MEET ANY VALID OBJECTION NOW RAISED BY DEFENDANT.

As was stated in plaintiff's opening brief, the sole question at issue in this case is the construction and application of the Washington statute, for that was the only question passed upon by the District Court.

In his brief in this court defendant has, however, devoted more than half his space to pointing out other alleged defects in the complaint. Because of these defects he urges that, regardless of the statute, the complaint is still insufficient and therefore the decree must be affirmed.

This argument proceeds upon the tacit admission that the statute has no application to the case, and it will be met upon that basis. But even if it be assumed for the sake of argument that the complaint is defective in other respects, it does not follow that the decree should be affirmed, especially in view of the fact that all of the alleged defects can be cured by amendment.

Rule 19 of the Equity Rules of the Supreme Court provides for the allowance of amendments at any time, and requires the court, at every stage of the proceedings, to disregard any error or defect in the proceeding which does not affect the substantial rights of the parties.

Equity Rule 19.

It would have been useless, after the court below based its decision on the statute, to amend the complaint, for no amendment which plaintiff could have framed would have obviated the effect of the decision. Furthermore, plaintiff was, in the light of an opinion based solely upon the statute, justified in assuming that its complaint was sufficient in all other respects.

There were then only two courses open to plaintiff, either to abandon its suit or to appeal from the decree. If, therefore, on the appeal this court is of opinion that the statute has no application to the case, the complaint should not be dismissed because of any other defect therein which can be cured by amendment. On the contrary, the decree should be reversed and leave given plaintiff to file such amended complaint as will conform to the views of this court.

Had the court below held that the statute was inapplicable, but nevertheless dismissed the complaint because of other defects curable by amendment, plaintiff would undoubtedly have been permitted to amend. The fact that plaintiff was forced to take an appeal before it could be determined that the statute was inapplicable, should not deprive plaintiff of the privilege of amendment which could have been exercised had no appeal been necessary.

Should this court hold that the statute has nothing to do with the case and yet affirm the decree because of other amendable defects in the complaint, plaintiff will have been penalized for failing to amend at a time when nothing could have been accomplished by amendment, and will have been robbed of the fruits of a necessary and successful appeal.

II. DISREGARDING THE WASHINGTON STATUTE, DEFENDANT'S OTHER CRITICISMS OF THE COMPLAINT ARE NOT WELL FOUNDED, AND, EVEN IF JUSTIFIED, ALL OF THEM CAN BE OBVIATED BY AMENDING THE PLEADING.

Independently of the statute, defendant asserts that the complaint is insufficient in several particulars which will be discussed in the order of their enumeration in defendant's brief. Again, however, we desire to emphasize the fact that the only real question in this case is the statute. If the District Court is correct and the decree is affirmed because of the statute, this suit is ended. But if this court is of opinion that the statute has nothing to do with the case, we do not think a meritorious suit should be brought to an abrupt conclusion solely because of technical and amendable defects in pleading. Hence we hesitate to burden the court with a lengthy discussion involving nothing but hair splitting distinctions over technical niceties of pleading. There is a real controversy concerning the merits of this case. If the complaint in its present form is certain enough so that the defendant is distinctly informed of the nature of the case which he is called upon to meet, it is sufficient. On the other hand, any allegations necessary to obviate the exceedingly technical objections now raised by defendant can be supplied by amendment. In any event, plaintiff should be permitted to try its case upon this or some amended pleading.

We submit that the present complaint is sufficient. It sets forth with precision the contract that was made as expressed in the certificate (Exhibit "B", Tr. 25). With equal precision it sets up the contract both parties intended to make (Exhibit "C", Tr. 28). It alleges wherein the contract made differs from the one intended, and that the intention of both parties was frustrated by mistake or fraud. Under all the authorities these allegations constitute a sufficient and complete statement of a cause of suit.

Cases cited Opening Brief, pages 12, 13.

Defendant urges that the complaint is insufficient for the following reasons:

1. The complaint fails to show that plaintiff has been or will be injured, or the need or reason for equitable relief.

This objection seems to us little short of puerile and we hesitate to dignify it by any extended discussion. Here is a case which has been so hard fought that it is in the Circuit Court of Appeals even before issue joined on a mere question of pleading. Yet defendant endeavors with medieval scholasticism to convince this court that the complaint presents nothing but a "purely speculative and abstract proposition". The learned Senior Judge of this circuit during oral argument remarked, "I assume a loss has occurred". We do not suggest there is any such presumption of law nor do we seek to construe the remark as committing the court in advance of decision. But the observation is an apt commentary upon defendant's contention that the parties and their counsel have engaged in this litigation as an intellectual diversion.

Of course a loss has occurred, and the fact can be alleged by amendment. But the point we are making is that no amendment is necessary.

If, after having largely abandoned the statute as his real position, the defendant seeks to rest his case on other alleged technical deficiencies in the complaint, we can match technicality with technicality.

The certificate as it stands amounts to an open policy, apparently covering the voyage whenever it may be made. Under it, for all that appears, defendant may dispatch the scow at any time, next week or next month, and, if a loss occurred, hold the plaintiff to a contract of indemnity, which the complaint alleges was never intended by the parties.

Surely such a situation, apparent on the face of the complaint, constitutes sufficient showing that plaintiff "has been or will be injured" and conclusively demonstrates the "need or reason for equitable relief".

To meet this case defendant falls back on presumption. First he denies to plaintiff the benefit of any negative presumption that the scow did not sail in time, and then claims for himself an affirmative presumption not only that the scow has already sailed, but that she sailed in October, 1919. As a matter of law there is no presumption either way.

Furthermore, even though no presumption may be entertained in behalf of a pleading, certainly none will be to defeat it.

However, if the injury to plaintiff and the need for equitable relief do not sufficiently appear upon the face of the complaint, it can be amended to show that the scow did not sail until the second week in November, 1919; that thereafter a claim was made for a total loss of its cargo; that shortly after the decree of the District Court was entered, defendant and his two partners brought suit in admiralty in the same District Court upon the very certificate plaintiff is seeking to reform; and that the admiralty suit has been stayed pending the determination of this suit.

2. The complaint does not sufficiently show whether the omitted phrase was intended by the parties to be a warranty, or a representation, and, if the latter, that it was material.

Whether the omitted phrase constitutes a warranty or a representation is a question of construction, which can only arise when some court is called upon to determine the meaning and legal effect of a contract in which the phrase appears. The certificate as it stands contains no such phrase. Because it doesn't, this suit was filed. The problem presented by this suit is merely to determine whether or not the omitted phrase, whatever its meaning and effect, should be inserted in the certificate. This problem involves no question of construction and none can arise until this case is determined.

Without pressing the argument further, suffice it to say that if the court thinks defendant's point is well taken, the objection is easily met by amendment.

3. The complaint does not contain a sufficient allegation as to the existence of a mutual mistake.

This criticism seems to be based upon the fact that the complaint is a bill with a double aspect. Paragraph VII (Tr. 22) charges mutual mistake and, in the alternative, unilateral mistake, coupled with fraud by defendant. It is elementary that reformation will be allowed in either case. Under such circumstances a bill with a double aspect has the sanction of authority and is the approved practice of a careful pleader.

> *Brown v. New York Life Ins. Co.,* 68 Fed. 785.

The test of mutual mistake is not found in the mere allegation that the mistake was mutual, but rather in the question, "Is the contract the one both parties meant to make?" Judged by this criterion, it is submitted, that the complaint clearly shows that the parties did not intend to make any such contract as is expressed in the certificate in its present form.

But again, the objection involves nothing that cannot be met by amendment, should the court be impressed with defendant's point.

4. The complaint shows laches in bringing suit and that defendant has been prejudiced thereby.

In view of the discussion of this subject which took place during oral argument between the writer and the learned Senior Judge, we feel justified in giving the question more than passing consideration.

The gist of laches, estoppel and analogous matters is not mere lapse of time, but resulting prejudice. Laches has nothing to do with the Statute of Limitations which involves merely the passage of time, but is founded on the principle that equity will not grant relief when the defendant has justifiably altered his position in complete ignorance of the facts upon which relief is sought. In every instance the question of laches must be determined upon the facts and circumstances of the particular case, and no general rule can be laid down.

In this case defendant claims he has been prejudiced by delay; that he has changed his position in reliance upon a condition which plaintiff now seeks to alter. Obviously the only prejudicial change of position which he can claim must rest upon an admission or statement that he dispatched the scow later than October, 1919, in reliance upon a certificate which contained no limitation on the sailing date.

We are, however, testing the sufficiency of a complaint and not determining the validity of a defence. Hence every single element of laches must be found in the complaint. All that appears is the mere lapse of time which in itself does not constitute laches. The resulting prejudice flows only from a late sailing, a fact not apparent on the face of the complaint. This indispensable element of laches is entirely lacking and is supplied only by defendant's argument. So technically laches does not appear on the face of the bill, and, if it exists at all, must be raised by answer.

Another element of laches is ignorance of the facts upon which relief is predicated and justifiable reliance upon a condition which is for the first time controverted by the complaint. This element of laches is completely negatived by the complaint.

Paragraph VII (Tr. 22) contains alternative allegations of mutual mistake, or unilateral mistake coupled with fraud, which have already been mentioned in another connection.

The allegation of mutual mistake charges in substance that defendant accepted the certificate believing that it required an October sailing. This allegation is admitted by the motion. If such was defendant's belief, he could not have permitted the scow to sail later than October without a conscious knowledge that he was deliberately disregarding what he believed to be the requirements of his contract. There is no reliance upon the certificate for its supposed terms have been ignored. In order to supply the missing element of laches (reliance on the certificate) defendant must deny the allegation that he believed the certificate required an October sailing. This he can do by answer, and, it may be, he can establish laches as a defence. But inasmuch as he has not done so, but, on the contrary, has by his motion admitted a specific allegation which shatters the entire theory of laches, he has demonstrated by his own argument that laches does not appear on the face of the bill.

The other alternative allegation is that defendant knew all the time that the certificate did not contain the October sailing clause; that plaintiff thought it did, and that it was omitted by accident and mistake. These allegations are likewise admitted as an alternative by the motion, as well as the further significant fact that defendant failed to disclose the omission to plaintiff.

If, then, defendant dispatched his scow later than October, he did so with the conscious and deliberate intent of entrapping plaintiff into a liability which was never contemplated by either party to the contract. This is not laches on the part of plaintiff, but unconscionable fraud on the part of defendant. Here again, laches may be a real defence, but it must be established by a denial and not by an admission of the allegations under attack.

The complaint does not say that both the alternative allegations are true, but only that one or the other was the fact. An admission of either is a complete refutation of defendant's entire argument. His point is merely a premature attempt to present his case on the merits.

> *Providence Steam Engine Co. v. Hathaway Mfg. Co.,* 79 Fed. 512, at 516, 517.

Furthermore, the courts of this circuit are reluctant to dismiss a bill for laches unless it clearly and unmistakably appears in the complaint, and prefer to reserve the question until final hearing on the merits.

> *Durham v. Fire & Marine Ins. Co.,* 22 Fed. 468, at 469 (U. S. C. C. D. Oregon).

Defendant also urges that plaintiff's delay operates as a waiver of any provision of the cover note which is inconsistent with or was omitted from the certificate. But his cases all lay down the rule that the presumption of waiver governs only in the absence of fraud, misrepresentation and mistake. Obviously the presumption is inapplicable to a suit for reformation, the gist of which must be either fraud or mistake.

In the same connection defendant calls attention to the case of *Andrews v. Essex Co.* (1 F. C. 374), in which it was said that "it is not pretended that everything contained in the memorandum was to be inserted in the policy." The application of the quoted language is not apparent, for it is alleged in paragraph IV of the complaint (Tr. 20) that the entire transaction was governed by a custom and usage, one of the essential elements of which was that *all the terms, conditions and warranties of the cover note were to be inserted in the certificate.* This was the alleged intention of both parties and is admitted by the motion.

However, if the court should be of opinion that, unless explained, the delay in bringing suit constitutes laches, the objection can be easily overcome by amendment. Such amendment, if required, will show that immediately after the delivery of the certificate, plaintiff in the usual course of business filed all the papers away and had no occasion to refer to them until November 25, 1919, when defendants made a claim for total loss under the certificate; that up to that time plaintiff believed the certificate contained the October sailing clause and assumed that the risk had been run off in accordance with the real contract of the parties; that the omission of this clause from the certificate was not discovered until claim for loss was made, at which time plaintiff informally denied liability on the certificate because the scow did not sail in October; that formal claim was made on December 19 or 20, 1919, and formally denied March 8, 1920; and that this suit was filed on March 24, 1920.

III. THE WASHINGTON STATUTE.

It was contended in plaintiff's opening brief that the statute has no application to suits in equity for reformation because, (1) it is a statutory extension of the parol evidence rule and neither the rule nor its extension can be applied in such suits without abolishing the doctrine of reformation itself; because (2) it is a rule of construction and hence inapplicable to suits of this character in which no question of construction is involved; because (3) it has no application to contracts of marine insurance for the reason that the general maritime law cannot be changed by state legislation; and because, (4) regardless of any other consideration, it cannot be applied in a reformation suit on the equity side of the Federal courts without in effect impairing their jurisdiction.

In reply to these contentions defendant urges the following points which will be discussed in the order of their enumeration in his brief:

1. Plaintiff does not come into court with clean hands because it did not comply with the statute.

This argument assumes that the statute commands plaintiff in every instance to deliver a copy of the application with every policy issued by it. But the most superficial examination of the statute negatives any such idea. The statute merely lays down a rule for determining the construction of an insurance policy in any proceeding in which its construction is properly involved. Rules of construction are addressed to courts, not to parties. The only way in which a rule of construction can be "violated" is by disregarding it, and the only person who can be deemed to have violated it is a judge who ignores it in construing an insurance policy properly before him.

Moreover, even if the statute were addressed to plaintiff, it does not follow that plaintiff was bound to obey it. When plaintiff qualified as a foreign corporation to do business in Washington it did not agree to obey all the laws of Washington, but only those which were constitutional and applicable under proper construction. For example, it did not agree to obey any law which forbade it to remove cases into the Federal Court. Such a statute is a nullity because unconstitutional. If, therefore, the instant statute is void when construed and applied as it was by the District Court, plaintiff's failure to deliver a copy of the cover note with the certificate does not furnish any support for defendant's assertion that plaintiff does not come into court with clean hands.

As to the suggestion that plaintiff waived its right to question an unconstitutional statute by accepting the privilege of doing business in Washington, we can only urge that such a motion does the utmost violence to fundamental principles and is entirely unsupported by authority or reason.

2. The statute does not prescribe any rule of evidence nor is it an extension of the parol evidence rule.

In discussing this point defendant relies upon the fact that the statute says nothing about proof or evidence. In other words, it does not bear the label we put on it in the opening brief.

Without any desire to be flippant, the language of a noted raconteur furnishes an apposite answer to defendant's criticism of the label. Any liquid which looks like gin, tastes like gin, acts like gin, and, upon analysis is found to possess the chemical constituents of gin, is gin, regardless of any label on the bottle.

In the opening brief we made a somewhat painstaking analysis of the statute, and endeavored to show that it operated not only as a rule of evidence, but as a complete abolition of the entire doctrine of reformation when applied in suits of that character. It is submitted that the analysis is ample warrant for labelling the statute a rule of evidence.

Defendant offers no criticism of the analysis nor does he question the reasoning upon which our conclusions are based. He contents himself with the remark that our characterization of the statute as a rule of evidence is "extraordinary", and rests his argument upon the bald assertion, unsupported either by principle or authority, that the statute was properly applied by the District Court.

Plaintiff's contention that the decree of the District Court amounts to acquiescence in the destruction of its equitable jurisdiction by state legislation, is left absolutely unanswered.

There is no case in the books which holds that the statute has any application to a reformation suit. Up to the present time no one but defendant has thought that state legislatures have by passing this and similar statutes intended to destroy the doctrine of reformation, and no one has had the temerity to assert that such legislation could constitutionally accomplish such a result in the Federal equity courts.

3. The statute is not unconstitutional, and its application to a suit in equity for reformation does not disturb the uniformity of admiralty jurisdiction.

The argument proceeds upon a complete misconception of plaintiff's opening brief, and clearly demonstrates that defendant has confused the distinction between the general maritime law and admiralty procedure and practice.

The constitution, as interpreted by the Supreme Court in the *Jensen* case (244 U. S. 205; 61 L. Ed. 1086), not only prohibits the states from disturbing the uniformity of admiralty jurisdiction, procedure and practice, but also precludes them from changing the general maritime law. That is, both adjective and substantive maritime law are withdrawn from the scope of legitimate state legislation.

Defendant urges that the *Erickson* case (248 U. S. 308; 63 L. Ed. 261) merely decided that the California Statute of Frauds could not govern the making of a maritime contract when sued upon in admiralty in the Federal court. He then draws the conclusion that as this case is in equity, the application of the Washington statute herein cannot be regarded as tending to disturb the uniformity of admiralty jurisdiction or practice and procedure.

This conclusion is an example of the familiar practice of knocking down a man of straw. The only reason for citing the *Erickson* case in the opening brief was to show that the formation of a maritime contract is governed by the general maritime law, and not by the local statute. Then we cited the *Chelentis* case (247 U. S. 372; 62 L. Ed. 1171) to establish that the maritime law must be applied to maritime transactions in every court, whether of admiralty, common law or equity. We next set forth the general maritime law governing the making of contracts of marine insurance. This is the law which, under the doctrine of the *Erickson* and *Chelentis* cases, must be applied even in a court of equity. And lastly we cited the *Jensen* case (supra) to show that the general maritime law cannot be changed by state legislation.

Our conclusion was that the instant statute was never intended by the Washington legislature to apply to contracts of marine insurance, because the legislature must have known the limitations upon its power and cannot be presumed to have adopted an unconstitutional act. Hence, as the statute does change the general maritime law if applied to contracts of marine insurance, we urged that the decision of the District Court not only imputed an unconstitutional intent to the legislature, but amounted to a declaration that such an intent can be given effect.

It has never been suggested that the application of the statute in this equity case will destroy the uniformity of admiralty jurisdiction, procedure or practice in the Federal courts. Moreover, we stated expressly in the opening brief (page 32) that the *Erickson* case (supra) could not be distinguished nor its authority diminished because it arose in the admiralty court; for, as the *Chelentis* case shows, the general maritime law governs in every court regardless of its character and jurisdiction. The *Erickson* case (supra) was but a link in the chain of argument, and, while it can be differentiated from this case, none of the distinctions drawn by defendant undermine the argument in the slightest degree.

Our whole contention upon this branch of the case was and is that the Washington statute should not be construed as applicable to contracts of marine insurance, and, if no other construction is possible, the statute is unconstitutional. The authority for this assertion is the *Jensen* case (supra), holding that the general maritime law cannot be changed by state statute. Although defendant devoted four pages of his brief to an analysis of the *Erickson* case, he failed even to mention the *Jensen* case or the *Chelentis* case. He has made no answer to the main contention and the argument of the opening brief remains unimpaired.

The only attempt to answer the argument involves an effort to show that the cover note is not a maritime contract, but merely a preliminary agreement which will result in the conclusion of such a contract when the certificate is issued. It is true that there is a dictum to that effect in the early case of *Andrews v. Essex Co.* (1 F. C. 374), but this dictum has long since been overruled by more recent cases. *Kerr v. Union Marine Ins. Co.* (124 Fed. 835) is a clear-cut decision that a cover note is a maritime contract, and the decision is not contradicted by any later case. The cases cited by defendant in his brief (page 21) did not involve suits on cover notes, and hence are not in point.

Defendant also attempts to draw an analogy between a cover note and a contract to build a ship, and because, as he says, both are non-maritime, state legislation with regard to either is valid. The analogy fails because the premise is false. A cover note is a maritime contract as we have just seen, whereas a contract to build a ship is not.

However, plaintiff's argument does not rest upon the fact that the cover note is a maritime contract, for, irrespective of the cover note, there can be no doubt that a policy or certificate of marine insurance is of maritime character. The fact that the cover note is also a maritime contract is but additional evidence that the whole transaction is maritime in its nature, and hence beyond the legitimate scope of state legislation.

IV. PLAINTIFF'S FAILURE TO BRING ALL THE ESSENTIAL PARTIES BEFORE THE COURT RENDERS IMPOSSIBLE THE GRANTING OF ANY RELIEF.

There are three partners named as defendants in the complaint. The defendant H. G. Tremaine is a citizen of Washington and appellee herein. The other two partners are Canadians, non-resident aliens. They had not been served nor had they made any personal appearance when the decree of the District Court was made.

It is admitted that no final decree awarding relief to plaintiff can be made until all three partners are before the court. But the decree in this case does not involve the merits, it was not made after final hearing, and it cannot be final unless, of course, the statute is thought to end the litigation.

The rule that all indispensable parties must be before the court means only that no relief can be granted by final decree which will bind them in their absence. This rule is clearly enunciated in the only two cases cited by defendant in support of his contention that the bill must be dismissed at this time because of the absence of indispensable parties.

In *Mallow v. Hinde* (12 Wheat. 193; 6 L. Ed. 599) the cause had been set down for final hearing on the merits on bill and answer. The absence of indispensable parties at this stage of the suit inevitably resulted in the dismissal of the bill, but without prejudice.

In *Barney v. Baltimore* (6 Wall. 290; 18 L. Ed. 825) the situation was slightly different. Jurisdiction depended solely on diversity of citizenship. Certain indispensable parties were residents of the District of Columbia, and as such not citizens of any state. Inasmuch as there is no jurisdiction based solely on diversity of citizenship when any indispensable party is a resident of the District of Columbia, the bill was necessarily dismissed, and of course without prejudice. But the dismissal was based not on the absence of indispensable parties at a preliminary stage of the proceedings, but because of the fundamental lack of jurisdiction which could not have been cured even if they had been served or had personally appeared.

The case at bar is not for final hearing on the merits and hence is distinguishable from *Mallow v. Hinde* (supra). It is also distinguishable from *Barney v. Baltimore* (supra) because in that case there was a fundamental lack of jurisdiction which neither service nor appearance could cure, whereas in this case the jurisdiction will be complete as soon as the other two defendants are personally served or voluntarily appear.

The phraseology of defendant's objection closely follows the rule laid down in his cases, but the wording itself shows that his position is untenable and that the rule does not apply at this stage of the proceedings. He says the absence of his partners "renders impossible the granting of any relief." But we have not yet progressed to the point where any relief is sought or can be granted. If defendant's motion in the court below had been denied, no relief would have been granted to plaintiff. The defendant would merely have been required to answer. Again, no decree that his court can make on this appeal will result in granting plaintiff the relief prayed for. This case is not on final hearing and the decree cannot settle the merits.

The motion to dismiss based on the Washington statute constituted an attack which, unless successfully parried, meant an immediate end of the whole case. But as the merits are not and cannot be involved, the absence of the other two partners at this stage of the proceedings is wholly immaterial.

If the decree is reversed, it will be time enough to bring the non-resident partners into court. Defendant's discussion implies that this will prove an impossible task. His position as the close business associate of the two Canadians doubtless leads him to believe that they either intend, or can be induced by him, to evade service successfully. Suffice it to say that we are prepared to meet this issue when it arises. Notwithstanding defendant's confident belief to the contrary, when this case comes on for final hearing the decree will not fail for lack of indispensable parties. Jurisdiction of the Canadians will be obtained speedily if the decree is reversed by this court.

In any event, in view of the fact that this is not a final decree on the merits, the objection based on failure to serve the Canadian partners, does not require that the decree be affirmed and the complaint dismissed.

V. THE MATTER OF CHANGE OF VOYAGE COVERED BY ADJUSTMENT OF PREMIUM.

The certificate contains the following provision:

> "Held covered at a premium to be arranged, in case of deviation or change of voyage or of any error or unintentional omission in the description of the interest, vessel or voyage, provided same be communicated to the insurer as soon as known to the assured."

Defendant wants to know why this provision could not be applied to the case and why something wasn't said about it in the complaint.

The most obvious answer is that the clause is dependent upon notice from defendant to plaintiff. If notice was given, let the defendant allege it. It is purely matter of defence and no concern of the plaintiff nor part of its case.

This point is but another illustration of defendant's constant effort to try his case on the merits in this court by complaining of plaintiff's failure to allege defensive matter in the complaint.

VI. COSTS.

If the court be of opinion that the Washington statute is inapplicable, plaintiff will have prevailed in this appeal, even though the complaint may contain other defects which may require amendment. The statute is the gist of the case and the decision of the District Court blocked the further prosecution of the cause unless an appeal was taken. If then the statute is inapplicable, plaintiff is entitled to proceed either upon this or an amended complaint. We have endeavored to show that this complaint is sufficient and such is our confident belief, but even though the court be of a contrary opinion, plaintiff should be permitted to amend. In any event, if the court decides that the statute is inapplicable, plaintiff must be deemed to have prevailed in its appeal, and should be allowed costs in both courts.

In conclusion we submit that the decree of the District Court should be reversed and the cause remanded for further proceedings; that the District Court should be directed to deny defendant's motion to dismiss and require him to answer the first amended complaint herein; or, in the event this court is of opinion that the complaint contains amendable defects, that the District Court be directed to sustain the motion with leave to plaintiff to amend the complaint. Plaintiff should be allowed the costs of both courts.

Dated, San Francisco,
October 20, 1920.

Respectfully submitted,

HAROLD M. SAWYER,
ALFRED T. CLUFF,
Solicitors for Appellant.

No. 3514

United States

Circuit Court of Appeals

For the Ninth Circuit.

GEORGE E. KNOWLTON and JERRY KNOWLTON,

Plaintiffs in Error,

vs.

THE UNITED STATES OF AMERICA,

Defendant in Error.

Transcript of Record.

Upon Writ of Error to the United States District Court for the District of Oregon.

No. 3514

United States
Circuit Court of Appeals
For the Ninth Circuit.

GEORGE E. KNOWLTON and JERRY KNOWLTON,

Plaintiffs in Error,

vs.

THE UNITED STATES OF AMERICA,

Defendant in Error.

Transcript of Record.

Upon Writ of Error to the United States District Court for the District of Oregon.

INDEX.

Names and Addresses of Attorneys of Record.

MESSRS. MANNING & BECKMAN,
Fenton Building, Portland, Oregon.
For the Plaintiffs in Error.

MR. LESTER W. HUMPHREYS,
United States Attorney.

MR. HALL S. LUSK,
Assistant United States Attorney, Portland, Oregon.

For the Defendant in Error.

In the District Court of the United States for the District of Oregon.

UNITED STATES OF AMERICA,

Plaintiff,

vs.

GEORGE E. KNOWLTON and
JERRY KNOWLTON,

Defendants.

Citation on Writ of Error.

United States of America,
District of Oregon,—ss.

To the United States of America, and to Lester W. Humphreys, United States Attorney for the District of Oregon, GREETING:

You are hereby cited and admonished to be and appear before the United States Circuit Court of Appeals for the Ninth Circuit, at San Francisco, California, within thirty days from the date hereof, pursuant to a writ of error filed in the Clerk's office of the District Court of the United States for the District of Oregon, wherein George E. Knowlton and Jerry Knowlton are plaintiffs in error and you are defendant in error, to show cause, if any there be, why the judgment in the said writ of error mentioned should not be corrected and speedy justice should not be done to the parties in that behalf.

Given under my hand, at Portland, in said District, this 19th day of April, in the year of our Lord one thousand nine hundred and twenty.

R. S. BEAN, Judge.

Due service of the within citation accepted this 19th day of April, 1920.

HALL S. LUSK,

Asst. U. S. Attorney.

[Endorsed]: United States District Court, District of Oregon. Filed April 19, 1920, G. H. Marsh, Clerk.

In the United States Circuit Court of Appeals for the Ninth Clrcuit.

Writ of Error.

GEORGE E. KNOWLTON and
JERRY KNOWLTON,

Plaintiffs in Error,

vs.

THE UNITED STATES OF AMERICA,

Defendant in Error.

The United States of America,—SS.

The President of the United States of America, to the Judges of the District Court of the United States for the District of Oregon, GREETING:

Because in the records and proceedings, as also in the rendition of the Judgment of a plea which is in the District Court before the Honorable ROBERT S. BEAN, one of you, between the United States of America, plaintiff and defendant in error, and George E. Knowlton and Jerry Knowlton, defendants and plaintiffs in error, a manifest error hath happened to the great damage of the said plaintiffs in error, as by complaint doth appear; and we, being willing that error, if any hath been, should be duly corrected, and full and speedy justice done to the parties aforesaid, and, in this behalf, do command you, if judgment be therein given, that then, under your seal, distinctly and openly, you send the record and proceedings aforesaid, with all things concerning the same, to the United States Circuit Court of Appeals for the Ninth Circuit, together with this writ, so that you have the same at San Francisco, California, within thirty days from the date hereof, in the said Circuit Court of Appeals to be then and there held; that the record and proceedings aforesaid, being then and there inspected, the said Circuit Court of Appeals may cause further to be done therein to correct that error, what of right and according to the laws and customs of the United States of America should be done.

WITNESS the Honorable EDWARD DOUGLAS WHITE, Chief Justice of the Supreme Court of the United States, this 19th day of April, 1920.

[Seal] G. H. MARSH,

Clerk of the District Court of the United States for the District of Oregon.

I hereby certify that the foregoing writ of error

was duly served upon the District Court of the United States for the district of Oregon by filing with me, as the Clerk of said Court, a duly certified copy thereof on this 19th day of April, 1920.

G. H. MARSH,
Clerk of the District Court of the United States for the District of Oregon.

[Endorsed]: Filed April 19, 1920. G H Marsh, Clerk United States District Court, District of Oregon.

BE IT REMEMBERED, that on the 28th day of June, 1919, there was filed in the United States District Court for the District of Oregon an Indictment, in words and figures as follows, to-wit:

In the District Court of the United States for the District of Oregon.

UNITED STATES OF AMERICA,

vs.

GEORGE E. KNOWLTON, alias George W. Wilson,
FLORENCE MAY KNOWLTON, alias Florence Wilson,
JERRY KNOWLTON, alias Jerry Smith, alias James King,

Defendants.

Indictment for Violation of Section 37 of the Federal Penal Code and Section 5 of the Act of

Congress approved March 3, 1917, known as the "REED AMENDMENT" (37 Stat. 1069).

United States of America,
District of Oregon,—ss.

The Grand Jurors of the United States of America for the District of Oregon, duly impaneled, sworn and charged to inquire within and for said district, upon their oaths and affirmations, do find, charge, allege and present:

COUNT ONE:

That GEORGE E. KNOWLTON, alias George W. Wilson; FLORENCE MAY KNOWLTON, alias Florence Wilson; JERRY KNOWLTON, alias Jerry Smith, alias James King, the defendants above named, on, to-wit: the first day of January, 1919, the exact time and place thereof being to the Grand Jurors unknown, did then and there knowingly, wilfully and feloniously conspire, combine, confederate and agree together with, between and among themselves and with divers other persons to this Grand Jury unknown, to commit the acts made offenses and crimes by the laws of the United States, to-wit: Section Five of the Act of Congress approved March 3, 1917, known as the Reed Amendment, that is to say: That the said above named defendants did then and there knowingly, unlawfully, wilfully and feloniously conspire, combine, confederate and agree together with, between and among themselves and with divers other persons to this

Grand Jury unknown, to enter into, devise and execute and did devise and execute a plot and scheme to order, purchase and cause intoxicating liquors for beverage purposes to be transported in interstate commerce, to-wit: from the State of California to the State and District of Oregon and to and into a State, the laws whereof then and there prohibited the manufacture and sale therein of intoxicating liquors for beverage purposes and which intoxicating liquors so as aforesaid to be ordered, purchased and caused to be transported as aforesaid, were not to be and were not so ordered, purchased and caused to be transported in interstate commerce as aforesaid for scientific, sacramental, medicinal and mechanical purposes, or for any purpose other than for beverage purposes in violation of the said Act of Congress as aforesaid.

That it was a part and portion of said unlawful, wilful and felonious conspiracy, so entered into as aforesaid by the above named defendants, that said plot and scheme to violate said Reed Amendment as aforesaid was to be carried out, carried on and effected by the following means, methods and plans, that is to say: That at certain cities, towns and places in the State of California, the exact cities, towns and places therein being to this Grand Jury unknown, the said defendants were to order and purchase intoxicating liquor for beverage purposes from persons whose names are to this Grand Jury unknown. That such intoxicating liquor, so ordered and purchased as aforesaid, was thereupon and thereat to be placed in and about certain automobiles and in and about certain receptacles therein specially provided therefor, and that said automobiles containing said intoxicating liquor as aforesaid, were to be hauled and driven by said defendants to and into certain cities, towns and places in the State and District of Oregon, the exact cities, towns and places therein being to this Grand Jury unknown. That upon the arrival of said automobiles containing said intoxicating liquor as aforesaid and so hauled and driven to and into the State of Oregon as aforesaid, the said defendants were to receive, conceal and store the said intoxicating liquor, which said intoxicating liquor was to be thereafter sold and distributed in various cities in said State of Oregon, the exact places of sale and distribution thereof being to this Grand Jury unknown; that the said wilful, unlawful and felonious conspiracy, so entered into by the above named defendants as aforesaid, continued from the date of the conspiracy as aforesaid up to and including the 15th day of June, 1919. That at and during all the times between said dates as aforesaid, said unlawful, wilful and felonious conspiracy was continually in existence and in operation and that at and during all of said times, all of the above named defendants as aforesaid, continued to wilfully, unlawfully and feloniously conspire, combine, confederate and agree together to commit the said crime herein set forth.

And the Grand Jurors aforesaid, upon their oaths and affirmations aforesaid, do further find, charge, allege and present:

1. That in pursuance and in furtherance of said unlawful, wilful and felonious conspiracy, combination, confederation and agreement and to effect the object thereof, the said defendants on, to-wit: the 6th day of June, 1919, at Portland, in the State and District of Oregon, caused certain automobiles to be taken and driven from said City of Portland, in the State of Oregon, to a certain point in the State of California, the exact place thereof being to the Grand Jurors unknown, which said automobiles, so taken and driven as aforesaid, were to be used by said defendants in conveying intoxicating liquors for beverage purposes, which said intoxicating liquors as aforesaid, were to be ordered and purchased in the State of California and which said automobiles, so to be used as aforesaid, were to be thereafter driven from the State of California to the State of Oregon.

2. That in furtherance and in pursuance of the said unlawful and felonious conspiracy, combination, confederation and agreement and to effect the object thereof, said defendant George E. Knowlton, alias as aforesaid, and Florence May Knowlton, alias as aforesaid, on to-wit: the 10th day of June, drove a certain automobile, to-wit: a Stutz automobile bearing an Oregon license number, to-wit: 35,-

447, which said automobile then and there contained a quantity of intoxicating liquor for beverage purposes, to-wit: 234 quarts of whiskey, which said automobile containing said intoxicating liquor as aforesaid was by said above named defendants, driven from a point in California, the exact place thereof being to the Grand Jurors unknown, to Lakeview in the State and District of Oregon.

3. That in furtherance and in pursuance of the said unlawful and felonious conspiracy, combination, confederation and agreement and to effect the object thereof, said defendant Jerry Knowlton, alias as aforesaid, on to-wit: the 10th day of June, drove a certain automobile, to-wit: a Mercer automobile bearing a California license number, to-wit: 308789, which said automobile then and there contained a quantity of intoxicating liquor for beverage purposes, to-wit: 201 quarts of whiskey, which said automobile containing said intoxicating liquor as aforesaid was by the said above named defendant, driven from a point in California, the exact place thereof being to the Grand Jurors unknown, to Lakeview in the State and District of Oregon.

4. That in furtherance and in pursuance of the said unlawful and felonious conspiracy, combination, confederation and agreement and to effect the object thereof, the said defendants George E. Knowlton, alias as aforesaid, Florence May Knowlton, alias as aforesaid, and Jerry Knowlton, alias as aforesaid, on to-wit: the 10th day of June, 1919,

at a point about twenty-five miles from Lakeview, in the State and District of Oregon, had in their possession a quantity of intoxicating liquor for beverage purposes, to-wit: 435 quarts of whiskey, which said intoxicating liquor was packed in and about two certain automobiles then and there being driven by and in the custody and under the control of the said defendants, and which said intoxicating liquor so packed and contained in said automobiles as aforesaid, had theretofore and on said 10th day of June, 1919, been transported in interstate commerce, to-wit: from the State of California to the State of Oregon aforesaid.

All of which is contrary to the form of the statute in such case made and provided and against the peace and dignity of the United States of America.

And the Grand Jurors aforesaid, upon their oaths and affirmations aforesaid, do further find, charge, allege and present:

COUNT TWO:

That GEORGE E. KNOWLTON, alias George W. Wilson; FLORENCE MAY KNOWLTON, alias Florence Wilson; JERRY KNOWLTON, alias Jerry Smith, alias James King, the defendants above named, on to-wit: the 10th day of June, 1919, did knowingly, wilfully and unlawfully, order, purchase and cause to be transported in interstate commerce, to-wit: from the State of California to Portland, in the State and District of Oregon and within the jurisdiction of this Court, a quantity of intoxicating liquor for beverage purposes, to-wit: 435 quarts of whiskey, which said intoxicating liquor as aforesaid, so caused to be transported in interstate commerce as aforesaid, was transported to and into a state, to-wit: Oregon, the laws whereof then and there prohibited the manufacture and sale therein of intoxicating liquor for beverage purposes, and which intoxicating liquor so as aforesaid, ordered, purchased and caused to be transported in interstate commerce as aforesaid, was not ordered, purchased and caused to be transported in interstate commerce as aforesaid for scientific, sacramental, medicinal and mechanical purposes, or for any purpose other than for beverage purposes, contrary to the form of the statute in such cases made and provided and against the peace and dignity of the United States of America.

Dated at Portland, Oregon, this 28th day of June, 1919.

A TRUE BILL.

WALTER GADSBY,
Foreman, United States Grand Jury.
BARNETT H. GOLDSTEIN,
Assistant United States Attorney.

[Endorsed]: Filed June 28, 1919, in open court, G. H. Marsh, Clerk.

Record of Arraignment.

AND AFTERWARDS, to-wit: on Saturday, the 19th day of July, 1920, the same being the ——— JUDICIAL day of the Regular July term of said Court; present the Honorable ROBERT S. BEAN, United States District Judge, presiding, the following proceedings were had in said cause, to-wit:

In the District Court of the United States for the District of Oregon.

The United States of America,

vs.

George E. Knowlton, alias George W. Wilson, Florence May Knowlton, alias Florence Wilson, and Jerry Knowlton, alias Jerry Smith, alias James King.

Now at this day come the plaintiff by Mr. Barnett H. Goldstein, Assistant United States Attorney, and the defendants, eGorge E. Knowlton, Florence May Knowlton and Jerry Knowlton, each in his own proper person and by Mr. John J. Beckman, of counsel. Whereupon said defendants being duly arraigned upon the indictment herein state to the Court that their true names are George E. Knowlton, Florence May Knowlton and Jerry Knowlton.

Record of Plea.

AND AFTERWARDS, to-wit: on Monday, the 11th day of August, 1919, the same being the 31st

JUDICIAL day of the Regular July Term of said Court; present the Honorable ROBERT S. BEAN, United States District Judge, presiding, the following proceedings were had in said cause, to-wit:

In the District Court of the United States for the District of Oregon.

The United States of America,
vs.
George E. Knowlton, et al.

Now, at this day, come the plaintiff by Mr. Charles W. Reames, Assistant United States Attorney, and the defendant Jerry Knowlton, in his own proper person and by Mr. John J. Beckman, of counsel, whereupon said defendant being duly arraigned upon the indictment herein, for plea thereto says he is not guilty.

Record of Plea.

AND AFTERWARDS, to-wit: on Tuesday, the 19th day of August, 1919, the same being the 38th JUDICIAL day of the Regular July Term of said Court; present the Honorable ROBERT S. BEAN, United States District Judge, presiding, the following proceedings were had in said cause, to-wit:

In the District Court of the United States for the District of Oregon.

The United States of America,

vs.

George E. Knowlton, Florence May Knowlton, et al.

Now, at this day, come the plaintiff by Mr. Bert E. Haney, United States Attorney, and the defendants George E. Knowlton and Florence May Knowlton, each in his and her own proper person, and by Mr. John J. Beckman, of counsel, whereupon said defendants for plea to the indictment herein each say that they are not guilty.

Record of Empanelling Jury.

AND AFTERWARDS, to-wit: on Tuesday, the 25th day of November, 1919, the same being the 20th JUDICIAL day of the Regular November Term of said Court; present the Honorable ROBERT S. BEAN, United States District Judge, presiding, the following proceedings were had in said cause, to-wit:

In the District Court of the United States for the District of Oregon.

The United States of America,

vs.

George Knowlton, alias Geo. W. Wilson, Florence May Knowlton, alias Florence Wilson, Jerry Knowlton, alias Jerry Smith, alias James King.

Now at this day come the plaintiff by Mr. Barnett H. Goldstein, United States Attorney, and Mr. John C. Veatch, Assistant United States Attorney, and the defendants above named each in his own proper person and by Mr. John J. Beckman and Mr. John Manning, of counsel. Whereupon this being the day set for the trial of this cause now come the following named jurors to try the issues joined, viz.: C. Lewis Mead, Frederick E. Vrooman, X. M. Morgan, Alton W. James, Austin D. Parker, A. W. Bunn, Harry C. Moore, James W. Mason, C. M. Stites, Richard E. Ward, M. Z. Donnell and J. D. Smith, Sr.; twelve good and lawful men of the district who, being accepted by both parties and being duly impaneled and sworn, proceed to hear the evidence adduced.

Record of Verdict.

AND AFTERWARDS, to-wit: on Wednesday, the 26th day of November, 1919, the same being the 21st JUDICIAL day of the Regular November Term of said Court; present the Honorable ROBERT S. BEAN, United States District Judge, presiding, the following proceedings were had in said cause, to-wit:

In the District Court of the United States for the District of Oregon.

The United States of America

vs.

Geo. E. Knowlton, alias Geo. W. Wilson, Florence May Knowlton, alias Florence Wilson, Jerry Knowlton, alias Jerry Smith, alias James King.

And thereafter, said plaintiff being present by Mr. Barnett H. Goldstein, United States Attorney, and Mr. John C. Veatch, Assistant United States Attorney, and said defendants being present each in his own proper person and by Mr. John J. Beckman and Mr. John Manning, of counsel, said jury returns to the Court the following verdict, viz.:

"We, the Jury duly impaneled to try the above entitled cause, do find the defendant George E. Knowlton, alias George W. Wilson, disagree as charged in Count One of the Indictment, and guilty as charged in Count Two of the Indictment; and we find the defendant Florence May Knowlton, alias Florence Wilson, disagree as charged in Count One of the Indictment, and guilty as charged in Count Two of the Indictment, and we do further find the defendant Jerry Knowlton, alias Jerry Smith, alias James King, disagree as charged in Count One of the Indictment, and guilty as charged in Count Two of the Indictment herein.

Dated at Portland, Oregon, this 26th day of November, 1919.

AUSTIN D. PARKER, Foreman."

which verdict is received by the Court and ordered to be filed.

Record of Sentence.

AND AFTERWARDS, to-wit: on Wednesday, the 10th day of December, 1919, the same being the 32nd JUDICIAL day of the Regular November Term of said Court; present the Honorable ROBERT S. BEAN, United States District Judge, presiding, the following proceedings were had in said cause, to-wit:

In the District Court of the United States for the District of Oregon.

The United States of America

vs.

George E. Knowlton, Florence May Knowlton, and Jerry Knowlton.

Now at this day come the plaintiff by Mr. Barnett H. Goldstein, Assistant United States Attorney, and the defendants each in his own proper person and by Mr. John Manning and Mr. J. J. Beckman, of counsel. Whereupon this cause comes on to be heard upon the motions of said defendants in arrest of judgment and for a new trial herein. And the Court, having heard the arguments of counsel, and being fully advised in the premises,

IT IS ORDERED AND ADJUDGED that the motion of Florence May Knowlton for a new trial herein be and the same is hereby allowed, and that the verdict of the jury heretofore filed herein be and the same is hereby set aside as to her. And

IT IS FURTHER ORDERED AND ADJUDGED that the motions of George E. Knowlton and Jerry Knowlton in arrest of judgment and for a new trial herein be and the same are hereby denied. Whereupon on motion of said plaintiff for judgment against the said defendants George E. Knowlton and Jerry Knowlton upon the verdict of the Jury heretofore filed herein.

IT IS ADJUDGED that said George E. Knowlton and Jerry Knowlton each be imprisoned in the county jail of Multnomah County, Oregon, for the term of six months, and that each of them stand committed until this sentence be performed or until he be discharged according to law.

In the District Court of the United States for the District of Oregon.

UNITED STATES OF AMERICA,
Plaintiff,

vs.

GEORGE E. KNOWLTON and JERRY KNOWLTON,
Defendants.

Petition for Writ of Error.

To the Honorable CHARLES E. WOLVERTON

and ROBERT S. BEAN, Judges of the above entitled Court:

And now comes George E. Knowlton and Jerry Knowlton, the defendants herein, and by their attorneys, Manning & Beckman, respectfully show that on the 26th day of November, 1919, a jury duly empaneled herein found your petitioners guilty of the violation of the Act of Congress approved March 3rd, 1917 (37 Stat. L. 1069), known as the Reed Amendment, upon which said verdict sentence was passed and final judgment entered against your petitioners on the 10th day of December, 1919.

Your petitioners feeling themselves aggrieved by said verdict and judgment in which judgment and proceedings had prior thereto, certain errors were committed to the prejudice of these defendants, all of which will more fully appear from the bill of exceptions and the assignment of errors filed with this petition, do herewith petition the Honorable Court for an order allowing them to prosecute a writ of errors to the United States Circuit Court of Appeals for the Ninth Circuit under the rules and laws of the United States in such case made and provided.

WHEREFORE, these defendants pray that a Writ of Error may issue in this behalf out of the United States Circuit Court of Appeals for the Ninth Circuit for the correction of the errors so complained of and that an order be made approving the bond of your petitioners and staying all further proceedings until determination of such Writ of Error by said Circuit Court of Appeals, and that a transcript of the records, proceedings and papers in this cause, duly authenticated, may be sent to the United States Circuit Court of Appeals for the Ninth Circuit.

GEORGE E. KNOWLTON,
JERRY KNOWLTON,
Defendants.
MANNING & BECKMAN,
Attorneys for Defendants.

State of Oregon,
County of Multnomah,—ss.

Due and legal service of the foregoing petition is hereby accepted at the City of Portland, this 19th day of March, 1920.

HALL S. LUSK,
Asst. United States Attorney.

[Endorsed]: United States District Court, District of Oregon. Filed April 19, 1920. G. H. Marsh, Clerk.

In the District Court of the United States for the District of Oregon.

UNITED STATES OF AMERICA,

Plaintiff,

vs.

GEORGE E. KNOWLTON and JERRY KNOWLTON,

Defendants.

Assignment of Errors.

George E. Knowlton and Jerry Knowlton, the defendants in the above entitled action and plaintiffs in error herein, having petitioned for an order from said Court permitting them, and each of them, to procure a Writ of Error to this Court directed from the United States Circuit Court of Appeals for the Ninth Circuit from the judgment and sentence made and entered in said cause against the said plaintiffs in error, and each of them, and petitioners herein now make and file with the said petition the following assignment of errors herein upon which they, and each of them, will rely for a reversal of the said judgment and sentence upon the said writ, and which said errors, and each and every of them, are to the great detriment, injury and prejudice of the said plaintiffs in error, and each of them, and in violation of the rights covererd upon them, and each of them, by law; and plaintiffs in error say that in the record and proceedings of the above entitled cause upon the hearing and determination thereof in the District Court of the United States for the District of Oregon there are manifest errors in this, to-wit:

I.

That the Court erred in over-ruling the following motion made by the defendant, George E. Knowlton, at the close of the Government's case:

> "I also move the Court to instruct the jury to bring in a verdict of acquittal as to Count 2, the violation of the Reed Amendment. First, for the reason that there has been no proof that these defendants, or any of them, ordered, purchased, or caused to be transported in interstate commerce any intoxicating liquor from California into Oregon; nor has there been any proof of the purpose for which the intoxicating liquors were to be used; and I might also say there is a variance between the indictment and the proof. The indictment says they ordered, purchased and caused to be transported in interstate commerce from the State of California to Portland, in the State and District of Oregon. The Grand Jury having alleged definitely that they were transporting this to Portland, I think they are confined to that allegation. There has been no proof whatsoever that these liquors, if there were any at all, were to be transported to Portland, or anywhere near Portland, or that these people had ever been in Portland."

To which ruling of the Court the defendant duly excepted.

II.

That the Court erred in over-ruling the motion for a directed verdict made by the defendant, Jerry Knowlton, which said motion is the same motion as fully recited in assignment of errors number I. To which ruling of the Court the said defendant duly excepted.

III.

That the Court erred in over-ruling the motion of the defendant, George E. Knowlton, for a directed verdict, made at the close of all the testimony in the case, which said motion is the same as the motion fully recited in assignment of errors number I. To which ruling of the Court the said defendant duly excepted.

IV.

That the Court erred in over-ruling the motion of the defendant, Jerry Knowlton, for a directed verdict, made at the close of all the testimony in the case, which said motion is the same as the motion fully recited in assignment of errors number I. To which ruling of the Court the said defendant duly excepted.

V.

That the Court erred in refusing the requests

of the defendants, George E. Knowlton and Jerry Knowlton, and each of them, to instruct the jury as follows:

"Circumstantial evidence is the evidence of certain facts from which are to be inferred the existence of other material facts bearing upon the question at issue or fact to be proved. This evidence is legal and competent, and, when of such a character as to exclude every reasonable doubt of defendants' innocence, is entitled to as much weight as direct evidence. When a conviction is sought on circumstantial evidence alone, it must not only be shown by preponderance of evidence that the facts are true, but they must be such as are absolutely opposed, upon any reasonable ground of reasoning with the innocence of the accused, and incapable of explanation upon any reasonable hypothesis other than that of the guilt of the accused. The degree of certainty must be equal to that of direct testimony and, if there is any single fact proved to your satisfaction by a preponderance of evidence which is inconsistent with defendants' guilt, this is sufficient to raise a reasonable doubt, and the jury should acquit the defendant. In order to justify the inference of legal guilt from circumstantial evidence, the proof must be absolutely incompatible with the innocence of the accused, and incapable of explanation upon any other reasonable hypothesis than that of his guilt. If there is any reasonable doubt as to reality of the connection of the circumstances of evidence with the facts to be proved, or as to the completeness of the proof, or as to the proper conclusion to be drawn from the evi-evidence, it is safer to err in acquitting than in convicting."

To which refusal of the Court to so instruct the jury, the said defendants, and each of them, duly excepted.

VI.

The Court erred in over-ruling the motion of the defendants, George E. Knowlton and Jerry Knowlton, and each of them, for a new trial, which motion was as follows:

"Comes now George E. Knowlton and Jerry Knowlton, the above named defendant, each for themselves, by their attorneys, Manning & Beckman, within the time allowed by Court, and move the Court for a new trial on behalf of each of said defendants, upon the following grounds and for the following reasons:

I.

That count 2 of the indictment does not state facts sufficient to constitute a crime.

II.

That the Court erred in refusing to direct a

verdict of not guilty, as to each of the said defendants, at the close of the government's evidence.

III.

That the Court erred in refusing to direct a verdict of not guilty as to each of said defendants, at the close of all the evidence.

IV.

That the evidence was insufficient to justify a verdict of guilty against George E. Knowlton on count 2 of the indictment.

VI.

That the evidence was insufficient to justify a verdict of guilty against Jerry Knowlton on count 2 of the indictment.

VII.

That the verdict of the jury against George E. Knowlton was against the law as laid down by the Court.

IX.

That the verdict of the jury against Jerry Knowlton was against the law as laid down by the Court."

Assignment VII.

That the Court erred in over-ruling the motion of the said defendants, George E. Knowlton and Jerry Knowlton, and each of them, for an order arresting judgment, which said motion was as follows:

"And now after verdict against the defendants, George E. Knowlton and Jerry Knowlton, and before sentence, come the said defendants, and each of them for themselves, by their attorneys, Manning & Beckman, and move the Court here to arrest judgment herein and not pronounce judgment against the said defendants, or either of them, for the following reasons:

I.

That count 2 of the indictment does not state facts sufficient to constitute a crime.

II.

That the Court erred in refusing to direct a verdict of not guilty, as to each of the said defendants, at the close of the government's evidence.

III.

That the Court erred in refusing to direct a verdict of not guilty, as to each of the said defendants, at the close of all of the evidence.

IV.

That the evidence was insufficient to justify a verdict of guilty against George E. Knowlton on count 2 of the indictment.

VI.

That the evidence was insufficient to justify a verdict of guilty against Jerry Knowlton on count 2 of the indictment.

VII.

That the verdict of the jury against George E. Knowlton was against the law as laid down by the Court.

IX.

That the verdict of the jury against Jerry Knowlton was against the law as laid down by the Court."

Assignment VIII.

That the Court erred in entering a judgment of conviction and sentencing each of the said defendants to confinement in the County Jail of Multnomah County, Oregon, for a period of six months.

WHEREFORE, on account of the errors above assigned, the said judgment against each of the said defendants ought to have been given for the said defendants, and each of them, and against the United States of America, now the said defendants, and each of them, pray that the judgment of the said Court be reversed and the sentence herein imposed upon the said defendants, and each of them, be set aside, and that this cause be remanded to the said District Court and such directions be given that the above errors may be corrected and law and justice done in the matter.

Dated this 19th day of April, 1920.

MANNING & BECKMAN,
Attorneys for Defendants.

Service acknowledged April 19th, 1920.

HALL S. LUSK,
Assistant United States Attorney.

[Endorsed]: United States District Court, District of Oregon. Filed April 19, 1920. G. H. Marsh, Clerk.

In the District Court of the United States for the District of Oregon.

UNITED STATES OF AMERICA,
Plaintiff,

vs.

GEORGE E. KNOWLTON and
JERRY KNOWLTON,
Defendants.

Order Allowing Writ of Error.

Now, at this day, come the defendants in the above entitled cause by Manning & Beckman, their counsel, and present to the Court their petition praying for the allowance of a Writ of Error to be issued out of the United States Circuit Court of Appeals for the Ninth Circuit to review the judgment of this Court entered in said cause, and move the Court for an order allowing the said petition:

On consideration whereof, IT IS ORDERED that the Writ of Error issue as prayed for in said petition.

It is further ORDERED that all proceedings in the above entitled District Court be stayed, superseded and suspended until the final disposition of the Writ of Error in the aforesaid United States Circuit Court of Appeals for the Ninth Circuit, upon each defendant filing an undertaking in the sum of Fifteen Hundred ($1,500.00) Dollars to be approved by the Court.

Dated at Portland, Oregon, this 19th day of April, 1920.

R. S. BEAN, Judge.

[Endorsed]: United States District Court, District of Oregon. Filed April 19, 1920. G. H. Marsh, Clerk.

In the District Court of the United States for the District of Oregon.

UNITED STATES OF AMERICA,
Plaintiff,

vs.

GEORGE E. KNOWLTON and
JERRY KNOWLTON,
Defendants.

Bond of Defendant, George E. Knowlton, on Writ of Error.

KNOW ALL MEN BY THESE PRESENTS, That we, George E. Knowlton, as principal, and John Rometsch and Alfred A. Closset, as sureties, are held and firmly bound unto the United States of America in the penal sum of One Thousand Five Hundred ($1,500.00) Dollars, for the payment of which, well and truly to be made, we bind ourselves and each of us, our heirs, executors, administrators, successors and assigns, forever firmly by these presents.

Sealed with our seals and dated and signed this 9th day of April, 1920.

WHEREAS, at the November term, 1919, of the District Court of the United States for the District of Oregon, in a cause therein pending, wherein the United States was plaintiff and the said George E. Knowlton was defendant, a judgment was rendered against the said defendant on the 10th day of December, 1919, wherein and whereby the said defendant was sentenced to be imprisoned in the County Jail of Multnomah County at Portland, Oregon, for the period of six months, and the said defendant has prayed for and obtained a Writ of Error from the United States Circuit Court of Appeals for the Ninth Circuit to review the said judgment and sentence in the aforesaid action, and the citation directing the United States to be and appear in the said United States Circuit Court of Appeals for the Ninth Circuit at San Francisco, California, thirty days from and after the date of said citation has issued, which citation has been duly served.

NOW, THE CONDITION OF THIS OBLIGATION IS SUCH, That if the said George E. Knowlton shall appear either in person or by attorney in the said Circuit Court of Appeals for the Ninth Circuit on such day or days as may be appointed for the hearing of said cause in said Court, and prosecute his writ of error and abide by the orders made by the said United States Circuit Court of Appeals, and shall surrender himself in execution as said Court may direct, if the judgment and sentence against him shall be affirmed, then this obligation shall be void, otherwise to be and remain in full force and effect.

IN WITNESS WHEREOF, we have hereunto set our hands and seals this 9th day of April, 1920.

JERRY KNOWLTON, (Seal)
Principal.

JOHN ROMETSCH, (Seal)
Surety.

ALFRED A. CLOSSET, (Seal)
Surety.

United States of America,
District of Oregon,—ss.

We, John Rometsch, residing at 300 Benton Street, Portland, Oregon, each being first duly sworn, for himself says: That I am a resident and freeholder in the State of Oregon, and that I am worth the sum of One Thousand Five Hundred ($1,500.00) Dollars over and above all my just debts and liabilities, and exclusive of property exempt from execution.

JOHN ROMETSCH.

Subscribed and sworn to before me this 9th day of April, 1920.

G. H. MARSH,

Clerk United States District Court, District of Oregon.

United States of America,
District of Oregon,—ss.

I, Alfred A. Closset, residing at 514 Hancock Street, Portland, Oregon, being duly sworn, depose and say that I am one of the sureties in the foregoing bond, that I am a resident and freeholder within said District, and that I am worth, in property situated therein, the sum of Fifteen Hundred ($1,500.00) Dollars, over and above all my just debts and liabilities, exclusive of property exempt from execution.

ALFRED A. CLOSSET.

Subscribed and sworn to before me this April 14th, 1920.

G. H. MARSH,
Clerk United States District Court, District of Oregon.

The above bond approved April 19, 1920.

R. S. BEAN,
U. S. District Judge.

[Endorsed]: Filed April 19, 1920. G. H. Marsh, Clerk.

In the District Court of the United States for the District of Oregon.

UNITED STATES OF AMERICA,
Plaintiff,

vs.

GEORGE E. KNOWLTON and JERRY KNOWLTON,
Defendants.

Bond of Defendant, Jerry Knowlton, on Writ of Error.

KNOW ALL MEN BY THESE PRESENTS, That we, Jerry Knowlton, as principal, and John Rometsch and A. A. Clossett, as sureties, are held and firmly bound unto the United States of America in the penal sum of One Thousand Five Hundred ($1,500) Dollars, for the payment of which, well and truly to be made, we bind ourselves and each of us, our heirs, executors, administrators, successors and assigns, forever firmly by these presents.

Sealed with our seals and dated and signed this 9th day of April, 1920.

WHEREAS, at the November term, 1919, of the District Court of the United States for the District of Oregon, in a cause therein pending, wherein the United States was plaintiff and the said Jerry Knowlton was defendant, a judgment was rendered against the said defendant on the 10th day of December, 1919, wherein and whereby the said defendant was sentenced to be imprisoned in the County Jail of Multnomah County at Portland, Oregon, for the period of six months, and the said defendant has prayed for and obtained a Writ of Error from the United States Circuit Court of Appeals for the Ninth Circuit to review the said judgment and sentence in the aforesaid action, and the citation directing the United States to be and appear in the said United States Circuit Court of Appeals for the Ninth Circuit at San Francisco, California, thirty days from and after the date of said citation has issued, which citation has been duly served.

NOW, THE CONDITION OF THIS OBLIGATION IS SUCH, That if the said Jerry Knowlton shall appear either in person or by attorney in the said Circuit Court of Appeals for the Ninth Circuit on such day or days as may be appointed for the hearing of said cause in said Court, and prosecute his writ of error and abide by the orders made by the said United States Circuit Court of Appeals, and shall surrender himself in execution as said Court may direct, if the judgment and sentence against him shall be affirmed, then this obligation shall be void, otherwise to be and remain in full force and effect.

IN WITNESS WHEREOF, we have hereunto set our hands and seals this —— day of April, 1920.

JERRY KNOWLTON (Seal).
Principal.
JOHN ROMETSCH (Seal).
Surety.
ALFRED A. CLOSSET (Seal).
Surety.

United States of America,
District of Oregon,—ss.

We, John Rometsch, residing at 300 Benton St., Portland, Oregon, first duly sworn for himself says: That I am a resident and freeholder in the State of Oregon, and that I am worth the sum of One Thousand Five Hundred ($1,500.00) Dollars over and above all my just debts and liabilities, and exclusive of property exempt from execution.

JOHN ROMETSCH.

Subscribed and sworn to before me this 9th day of April, 1920.

G. H. MARSH,
Clerk United States District Court, District of Oregon.

United States of America,
District of Oregon,—ss.

I, Alfred A. Closset, residing at 514 Hancock Street, Portland, Oregon, being duly sworn, depose and say that I am one of the sureties in the foregoing bond, that I am a resident and freeholder within said District, and that I am worth, in property situated therein, the sum of Fifteen Hundred ($1,500.00) Dollars, over and above all my just debts and liabilities, exclusive of property exempt from execution.

ALFRED A. CLOSSET,

Subscribed and sworn to before me this 14th day of April, 1920.

G. H. MARSH,

Clerk United States District Court, District of Oregon.

The above bond approved April 19, 1920.

R. S. BEAN,

U. S. District Judge.

[Endorsed]: Filed April 19, 1920. G. H. Marsh, Clerk.

In the District Court of the United States for the District of Oregon.

UNITED STATES OF AMERICA,

Plaintiff,

vs.

GEO. E. KNOWLTON and JERRY KNOWLTON,

Defendants.

BILL OF EXCEPTIONS.

BE IT REMEMBERED, that on the 24th day of

November, 1919, at a stated term of said Court, beginning and held in Portland, Oregon, before the Hon. Robert S. Bean, District Judge, presiding, the above entitled cause came on to be heard before said Court and the jury impaneled therein. The United States appearing by Mr. B. H. Goldstein, Assistant United States Attorney for said District; and the defendants appearing in person, and represented by their counsel, Mr. John Manning and Mr. John J. Beckman. Florence Knowlton, wife of defendant Geo. E. Knowlton, was also a defendant.

WHEREUPON the following proceedings were had:

T. M. Word, a witness on behalf of the Government, after being duly sworn, testified as follows: That he was a special agent of the Department of Justice and had been since November 1, 1918. In June, 1919, he was at Lakeview, Oregon, and on the 10th of said month left the said city at four o'clock A. M. in company with the sheriff of Lake County, Mr. Woodcock and wife, a 13-year-old boy and a prisoner. They were in an automobile and were going to Bend and Portland. On the road to Bend, about 20 to 23 miles north of Lakeview, the witness saw two automobiles on the right hand side of the road, and he asked the sheriff to stop so he could examine the machines and ascertain if there were any "booze" in them; he looked the machines over and took the names of same; one had a California license and one an Oregon license; one of the cars was of the Stutz make and the other was a Mercer. George Knowlton and his wife, Florence, were asleep in the front seat of the Stutz car, and defendant Jerry Knowlton was in the back part of the Mercer. The witness then testified: "I woke up the people in the Stutz car and asked them how much liquor they had'. and he said he only had a small amount for his own use, and I said how much, and I think they said about 15 or 20 cases, and then I awoke them; I got them out of the machine and got the man out of the other machine. The one in the Stutz car gave his name as Geo. W. Wilson, the one in the Mercer car gave me the name of James King. Then I looked in and under the mattress and I saw that both of them was loaded with liquor, and the sheriff got out and came over with me at the time I took the number of the machines, and then I told them that I was a special agent for the government, and told them who I was, and they knew of me; they had lived here."

The witness then testified that he took Mrs. Wilson out of the Stutz car and put her into the car with the sheriff's wife, his son and the prisoner, and put the sheriff into the Stutz car and started on toward Bend. In the Mercer car there was a wide mattress over the top and some blankets over that and a box of food and clothing, and the other car had some blankets over it, and some gunny sacks. The place where the defendants were found was about 35 miles from the California State line in the State of Oregon. When the several machines above mentioned got near Paisley they all stopped and Mrs. Wilson got out of the sheriffs' car in which she was riding, saying that she felt sick. She then got into the Stutz car with her husband and the sheriff; afterward the car stopped and George Knowlton and the sheriff got out, and then Mrs. Knowlton started to run away with the machine. We pursued her in Jerry's car, Jerry driving, for some distance, about five or six miles, when we caught up with her. Then they all went back to the main road and Jerry Knowlton took out a box of provisions from his machine and made some coffee, and I ate a beef heart sandwich; the provisions were in a wooden box; "there were quite a lot of sandwiches, and there was some kind of stuff in it, I don't remember."

Q. Did you notice what kind of liquor they had there?

A. Yes, they had some Sunnybrook, some brandy and some old Sage pints and quarts.

"We then proceeded to Bend; we left there about a quarter to eight, and the sheriff left me there and came with his prisoner and family to Portland. The sheriff at Bend came to the hotel and we took the liquor to the jail, unloaded and counted it; there were 234 bottles in the Stutz car and 201, I think, in the Mercer; I am not sure. Some of the bottles was whiskey, and a few bottles of brandy and a few bottles of gin. The bottles had revenue stamps on them. We unloaded the Stutz liquor in one cell and the Mercer in another cell and turned it over to the sheriff for the night and put the men in jail. We left Bend at 2:20 the next day and went to The Dalles. I took George Knowlton with me and Jerry Knowlton went with another person."

The witness then testified that upon arriving at The Dalles he took George Knowlton in a restaurant with him, and left the Stutz car containing the liquor in front of the restaurant, where he could watch same. While in the restaurant a man got into the machine and witness ran out of the restaurant and fired several shots and hit a building. The car was later recovered about 26 miles from The Dalles near Dufur; the booze had been taken out and the car left stranded. The Mercer car came from Bend by another road and got as far as the Deschutes river; then witness went up with the Stutz car and loaded the stuff out of the Mercer car and brought it to The Dalles.

ON CROSS EXAMINATION the witness testified that at the time Mrs. Knowlton got out of the sheriff's car, as stated in his direct examination, she complained that the Ford, the sheriff's car, was hard riding and that she was not feeling well. The prisoner in the Ford car riding with her was a wife murderer and was being taken to the state penitentiary to serve a sentence upon conviction for that crime. Several bottles were offered in evidence containing liquor, and the witness stated that this came from the Mercer car. No bottles out of the Stutz car were produced in evidence, nor were any of them in possession of witness.

Q. Then you don't know whether he, George Knowlton, had whiskey, brandy, gin, or any thing in his car, except you know he had bottles?

A. I know he had whiskey and gin.

Q. Did you see, as a matter of fact, any of it?

A. No; I never touched it.

Q. How do you know he had whiskey?

A. I can tell a bottle of whiskey when I see it.

Q. I know you can tell a bottle from the label on the bottle, but is that proof to you; would you swear to it that it was whiskey?

A. I can swear that he begged me all night to let him open a bottle and let him take a drink.

Q. That is all right, but I am asking you if you can swear positively that he had whiskey in that bottle? A. I just told you.

Q. You didn't taste it?

A. No, I never tasted it.

Q. And he might have had a bottle of liquor?

A. He begged me to take a drink with him, but I would not do it.

Q. Did he have a bottle open? A. Yes.

Q. Did he take a drink?

A. I don't remember; I don't think he took a drink that night.

Witness further testified that he had never seen the defendants in the State of Califorina.

Q. Then you don't know from whom they bought this liquor, do you?

A. No, they did not tell; they told, like all the rest of them, that they bought it in Oregon.

The witness further testified that he did not have a bottle of any description from the Stutz car; that the defendants had a fishing basket and some fishing tackle with them.

E. E. WOODCOCK, called as witness on behalf of the Government, and being sworn, testified as follows:

That he was the sheriff of Lake County, Oregon; that on June 10, 1919, he accompanied special agent, Tom Word, from Lakeview to Bend; that he was on his way to Salem with a prisoner; that he was accompanied by his wife and son, the said prisoner and Tom Word; they were all riding in a Ford; they left Lakeview at four A. M. and about 25 miles north of Lakeview they saw two big machines by the side of the road; that they thereupon stopped and Word and he jumped out of the Ford; he stepped to one machine and Word to the other; the side curtains were all down and the occupants were asleep; they woke them up and asked them what they were loaded with, and they said they had a little booze for their own use; the machines were heavily loaded with booze; the occupants of the car were George Knowlton and his wife in one car, and Jerry Knowlton in the other car. We placed them under arrest and decided to bring them to Portland. The prisoner who was being taken to the penitentiary, was put into the Ford car with witness's wife and boy and Mrs. Knowlton. The witness got into one of defendants' cars and Tom Word into the other. The witness stated that he tasted some whiskey from a bottle which was in the Stutz car.

ON CROSS EXAMINATION the witness said that the prisoner having been convicted of murder, he was taking him to the penitentiary. At the time he stopped to look at the cars belonging to defendants, he and Special Agent Word were looking for certain other automobiles, but not these. Both George Knowlton and Jerry Knowlton told the witness and Tom Word that they bought the liquor which was in their cars from some one in Oregon a short while before; they said there was no Federal charge against them as they got the liquor in Oregon. As far as the witness knew, they might have got it in Oregon.

ON RE-DIRECT EXAMINATION, the witness

testified that the road where the defendants were found was the main traveled road from Lakeview to Bend. Lakeview is 15 miles from the nearest California point; the nearest California town to Lakeview is Fairport; the nearest large California town on the road to Lakeview is Alturas, which is about 45 miles from the boundary line of Oregon.

ON RE-CROSS EXAMINATION, the witness testified that there were no other roads running into the road where the defendants were found north of Lakeview, except roads leading from ranches. There are two roads leading from Lakeview to Paisley, Oregon, and there are also roads from Klamath Falls, Oregon, to Lakeview and from Silver Lake, Oregon, to Lakeview.

H. W. LAUGENOUR, a witness called on behalf of the government, being first duly sworn, testified as follows:

That in the month of June, 1919, he was at Davis Creek, California; this town is about 25 miles north of Alturas and about 12 or 15 miles south of the Oregon State line; the witness further testified that on June 9, 1919, two men and a woman came into his store at Davis Creek; he identified Jerry Knowlton as being one of the men, and a spectator among the audience in the court room (and not one of the defendants) as the other man, and was not able to identify the woman; the woman had on a khaki uniform when he saw her in the store and wore leather leggings; the taller of the men, whom the witness identified as Jerry Knowlton, came to the counter and purchased some sardines, sausages, cheese and oranges; afterward he saw two machines through the window of his store, one of which he described as a Stutz and the other as a Mercer. The witness was in the automobile business from 1903 to 1912.

Q. When was it this took place?

A. Some time near lunch; I don't know exactly.

ON CROSS EXAMINATION, the witness testified that these people were strangers to him; that he had never seen them before; that the government special agent called upon him and showed him photographs of the defendants; witness stated that he was unable to identify the wife of George Knowlton (who was one of the defendants being tried), as the woman he saw in the store. When the witness went to the window to look at the automobile, some one having called his attention to them, they were from 75 to 100 feet away on a side street, one on each side; they were not on the street in front of his store. The front ends of the cars were not facing him, and he got a side view of them.

EUGENE B. ASH, called as a witness on behalf of the Government, and being sworn, testified as follows:

June 9, 1919, as near as he could recall, he was in the garage business in that town; that on said date,

That he lived at Alturas, California; that on between 1 and 2 o'clock in the afternoon, a Mercer car drove into his garage with defendant, Jerry Knowlton, therein; he wanted to know if witness could fix the car, and witness found a broken frame on it, which he repaired. The witness knew that the car was heavily loaded because it broke through the floor at one place; the car was fixed about 10 P. M. of the same day. After the car was finished Jerry Knowlton took out a "partly drank" bottle of brandy, and the witness, his father and Jerry Knowlton finished up the bottle of brandy and the bottle was left in the shop. As near as witness could recollect Knowlton went around to the right hand side of the car and reached in and pulled the bottle out; the witness never paid particular attention to how he got the bottle. The back of the car seemed to be pretty well filled up, but it was covered over and witness did not know what was inside. The witness identified the bottle which he said he thought was the same one which had been left in the shop from which they had partaken, as aforesaid. Next day the witness' brother threw the bottle outside, and when Special Agent Word came he looked about for it and found it; the label on the bottle was Three Star Claremont Brandy. Defendant Jerry Knowlton was at the garage most of the time while the car was being repaired.

ON CROSS EXAMINATION, the witness testified that it was not against the law to have liquor in California at that time; that the brother of witness threw the bottle from which they all partook outside the shop in a corner between two buildings and that was the way he came to find it afterward when the agent wanted to know if he could find it; that this was some time afterward. Witness never had the bottle in his possession from the time it was thrown out of the shop, as above stated, until Mr. Word came and interviewed him, when it was turned over to Mr. Word. Witness could not identify the bottle as being the identical one, but that it was just like the one from which they drank.

On further cross examination, witness testified that the Mercer car would weigh about 4200 or 4300 pounds; that the garage had a wooden floor which was old; and that before this time a two-ton truck had also broken through the floor. The building was about 10 or 15 years old and the floor was the same age as the building.

T. M. WORD, again called as witness by the Government, testified that he had procured the bottle from the witness Ash, and that it was the same one concerning which testimony had been given by Mr. Ash, whereupon the same was offered and received in evidence. Mr. Word called upon Mr. Ash and obtained the bottle about two months after the arrest of the defendants; the witness said that Mr. Ash had said that his brother had put the bottle outside, and that Ash then went outside accompanied by the witness and picked up the bottle off the ground at a place between two buildings.

F. L. KESER, a witness called on behalf of the Government, being sworn, testified as follows:

That on June 9, 1919, he was in business at Alturas, California, the name of his business being the Alturas Tire & Battery Co.; that on said date he recalled a Stutz car being there; that a man and woman were in same and the woman was dressed in a khaki suit. He saw the Stutz car between ten and eleven o'clock on the morning of that date; he repaired a tire and furnished gasoline for the people in the Stutz car. The back of the car was piled up level with the back seat and covered over with a blanket or canvas. The witness was unable to identify any of the defendants as being the persons who were in the Stutz car at that time.

ON CROSS EXAMINATION, the witness testified that it was not an unusual thing to see a car covered up and full of valises, bedding, etc., when driven by tourists. The witness did not recognize the defendant George Knowlton or his wife, or defendant, Jerry Knowlton, as being any of the parties who were in or were driving the Stutz car. He expressly stated that Mrs. Florence Knowlton was not the woman that he had reference to. The witness distinctly remembered the Stutz car by the way it was painted. It had white wire wheels and was of a kind of maroon color with gold stripes and the lights were painted white. Witness was not absolutely sure the color was maroon, but knew the same was red.

HENRY KOCK, called as witness on behalf of the Government, being sworn, testified as follows:

That he lived in Alturas, California, and in June 1919, was running a lunch counter there; that on the 8th or 9th of June two men came to his lunch counter and purchased 20 sandwiches—ten beef heart and ten pork sandwiches; the sandwiches were placed in a small spaghetti box. Witness recognized Jerry Knowlton as being one of the men who purchased the sandwiches, but could not state as to who the other man was. The witness thought that Jerry Knowlton came in a machine because he heard fellows make the remark about two nice big machines. He did not see the machines nor who occupied them.

ON CROSS EXAMINATION, witness stated that the sale of sandwiches was for cash. He stated that Jerry Knowlton was not pointed out to him, but he was shown Jerry's picture by Mr. Word in California, and also since he came to Portland to testify as a witness. The witness was also unable to recognize George Knowlton as being present at the time said sandwiches were sold. Witness was busy waiting on other customers at time of sale and it probably took him half an hour before the sandwiches were put up and delivered, at the time his attention was divided between different customers. Witness further testified that Mr. Word came to California and showed him a picture and said, Did you ever see this man in here? And I said, I think

I have; and he said look again, and I looked again and said, I am very sure this is the man I sold sandwiches to.

Q. Never saw the man in your life before?

A. No sir; but when I see a man's picture I can pretty near recognize him.

Q. You never thought of this man from the time he bought the sandwiches and went out, until Mr. Word came in and asked you if you recognized the picture?

A. No, sir; the sandwiches were purchased between eleven and one o'clock in the day time and on the 8th or 9th of the month.

Witness kept no track of the number of sandwiches sold, except an item in his account book that there were 20 sandwiches sold on the 8th and 9th of June, without itemizing the particular kind.

The Government then rested.

Exception I.

WHEREUPON the defendants, in due and proper season, by their counsel, then moved the Court for an instructed verdict as follows:

"I also move the Court to instruct the jury to bring in a verdict of acquittal as to Count 2, the violation of the Reed Amendment. First, for the reason that there has been no proof that these defendants, or any of them, ordered, purchased, or caused to be transported in interstate commerce any intoxicating liquor from California into Oregon; nor has there been any proof of the purpose for which the intoxicating liquor was to be used; and I might also say there is a variance between the indictment and the proof. The indictment says they ordered, purchased and caused to be transported in interstate commerce from the State of California to Portland, in the State and District of Oregon. The Grand Jury having alleged definitely that they were transporting this to Portland, I think they are confined to that allegation. There has been no proof whatsoever that these liquors, if there were any at all, were to be transported to Portland, or any where near Portland, or that these people had ever been in Portland.

COURT: I don't think it necessary to take up any more time on that. In my judgment there is sufficient evidence in this case to call upon the jury to determine these disputed questions raised by the plea of not guilty, and under these circumstances it would not be proper or just for the Court to comment upon the testimony in any shape or form. The motion, therefore, will be overruled without any further comment.

MR. BECKMAN: Exception, if Your Honor please.

COURT: Certainly.

The defendant then called T. M. WORD as a witness, he having been previously sworn, and he testified as follows.

That on the 10th day of June, 1919, when he arrested the defendant he took charge of the Stutz car and brought the same to Portland, put it in Therklesen's garage, where it had been ever since and was at the time of trial; that it had been in the Government's possession ever since the said arrest, and nothing had been done to it, either by himself or on behalf of the Government, in the way of painting, or otherwise, since the arrest.

L. E. THERKELSEN, being called as witness by defendants, being sworn, testified as follows:

That he was in the automobile business in Portland and that Mr. Word had placed in his possession a Stutz car owned by defendant George Knowlton, with instructions to keep the same until he heard from Mr. Word; and that ever since the same had been in his possession there had been nothing done to it in the way of painting; that the color of the wheels of the car was black and the body red; that there were no gold stripes, or any other stripes. The fenders were black and the body painted red.

Thereupon the defendants rested.

Exception II.

Whereupon the following proceedings were had;

the defendants, in due and proper season by their counsel, made the following motion:

MR. BECKMAN: I desire at this time to renew my motion for a directed verdict as to each count in the indictment on the same ground and for the same reasons that I stated in my motion at the close of the Government's case, with the understanding that this motion at this time covers all the objections made at that time.

WHEREUPON the Court over ruled said motion, and the defendants requested and were allowed an exception.

Exception III.

WHEREUPON the defendants in proper time and season requested the Court to instruct the jury as follows:

Circumstantial evidence is the evidence of certain facts from which are to be inferred the existence of other material facts bearing upon the question at issue or facts to be proved. This evidence is legal and competent, and, when of such a character as to exclude every reasonable doubt of defendants' innocence, is entitled to as much weight as direct evidence. When a conviction is sought on circumstantial evidence alone, it must not only be shown by preponderance of evidence that the facts are true, but they must be such as are absolutely opposed, upon any reasonable ground of reasoning with the innocence of the accused, and incapable of explanation upon any reasonable hypothesis other than that of the guilt of the accused. The degree of certainty must be equal to that of direct testimony and, if there is any single fact proved to your satisfaction by a preponderance of evidence which is inconsistent with defendants' guilt, this is sufficient to raise a reasonable doubt, and the jury should acquit the defendant. In order to justify the inference of legal guilt from circumstantial evidence, the proof must be absolutely incompatible with the innocence of the accused, and incapable of explanation upon any other reasonable hypothesis than that of his guilt. If there is any reasonable doubt as to reality of the connection of the circumstances of evidence with the facts to be proved, or as to the completeness of the proof, or as to the proper conclusion to be drawn from the evidence, it is safer to err in acquitting than in convicting.

WHEREUPON the Court declined, neglected and refused to instruct the jury as was requested, and through the failure, neglect and refusal of the Court to so instruct, the defendants, in due and proper time and manner, requested, and were allowed an exception as to said requested instruction.

WHEREUPON the Court instructed the jury as follows:

"Gentlemen of the Jury:

A law of the United States provides that whoever shall order, purchase or cause intoxicating liquors to be transported in interstate commerce, except for scientific, sacramental or medicinal purposes, into any state or territory, the laws of which state or territory prohibit the manufacture or sale therein of intoxicating liquors shall be punished as provided in the statute. To come within the provisions of this statute it is necessary that the transportation of intoxicating liquors be from one state into another state, the laws of which prohibit the manufacture or sale. The laws of Oregon prohibit the manufacture and sale of intoxicating liquors and, therefore, it is a violation of this statute for any person to transport from another state into Oregon intoxicating liquors. Another statute of the United States provides that if two or more persons conspire either to commit an offense against the United States or to defraud it in any manner and one or more of such parties do any act to effect the object of the conspiracy, each of the parties shall be guilty of the crime and punished as provided in the statute.

The indictment in this case charges the three defendants on trial, in the first count, with violation of Section 37, and in count two with the violation of the statute that I first read to you.

The first count in the indictment charges in substance that in January, or about January, 1919, the three defendants entered into a conspiracy or unlawful agreement to transport into this state from the State of California intoxicating liquors, and that in pursuance of such agreement and understanding, and in furtherance of such unlawful conspiracy, the two defendants, George Knollton and Florence Knollton, drove a certain automobile described in the indictment as a Stutz machine, which contained a quantity of liquor, from a point in California, the exact place thereof to the Grand Jury unknown to Lakeview in the State of Oregon. Again another act alleged to have been in furtherance of this conspiracy was that upon the same date the defendant, Jerry Knollton drove a certain automobile, described in the indictment as a Mercer machine, containing intoxicating liquors from the State of California into Oregon. And, third, that in pursuance of this alleged conspiracy the three defendants had in their possession some twenty-five miles from Lakeview a certain quantity of intoxicating liquor.

The second count of the indictment charges the three defendants with wilfully and unlawfully transporting or causing to be transported from the State of California into Oregon a quantity of intoxicating liquors described in the indictment as 435 quarts.

The defendants have each entered a plea of not guilty, and that plea controverts and is a denial of every material allegation in the indictment, and imposes upon the government the duty of proving such allegations to your satisfaction beyond a reasonable doubt before you will be justified in finding the defendants, or either of them, guilty. The defendants in this case, as in all criminal cases, come before this jury clothed with the presumption of innocence, and the presumption continues with them throughout the trial until it is overcome by the testimony. In other words, it is not incumbent upon a defendant charged with a criminal offense to prove his or her innocence, but it is the duty of the Government, or the state as the case may be, to prove the guilt, and that beyond a reasonable doubt.

By a reasonable doubt, I do not mean a mere possible doubt; I do not mean a doubt such as a juror can conjure up in his own mind without any basis for it, but I mean a real substantial doubt, based whether upon the testimony or the want of testimony, and being such a doubt as would cause a reasonably prudent man to hesitate to act in his own most important affairs. And, if, after you have considered all of the evidence in this case, you entertain such a doubt, the defendants are entitled to the benefit of it and an acquittal.

Proof sufficient to justify a conviction in a criminal cases must be of a clear and convincing character. It is not sufficient to base a verdict upon mere conjecture, speculation or inference, not justified by the proof in the case, but it must be upon real substantial testimony that satisfies the minds of the jurors of the guilt of the defendants beyond a reasonable doubt.

As I have said, the first count in the indictment charges the defendants with the crime of conspiracy. A conspiracy is a mere unlawful agreement or understanding between two or more persons to commit an offense against the United States, and in this particular instance to commit the offense charged, which is alleged to have been the transportation of liquor from California into Oregon. Direct and positive proof of a conspiracy is not required. It may be shown by circumstances, by association, by co-operation, but there must be a unity of action and in pursuance of some plan or scheme entered into between the parties, and in this case, unless you believe there has been such an understanding or agreement between these parties, then the charge of conspiracy is not made out.

Conspiracy alone does not constitute a crime, but it is necessary in order to complete the offense that one or more of the conspirators do some act to effect the object thereof or in furtherance of the conspiracy as charged in this indictment, as I have already called to your attention, and if you believe from the evidence, beyond a reasonable doubt that these people entered into, either positively or impliedly, an understanding or agreement that they should transport intoxicating liquors from California into Oregon, and that in pursuance of that agreement and in furtherance thereof one of them drove an automobile containing liquor across the line, that would constitute an overt act within the statute and complete the offense; and the same may be said as to either of the other two overt acts. It is not necessary for the Government to prove all three of them, but any one of them would satisfy that requirement of the statute.

The next count in the indictment is a direct charge that these parties transported intoxicating liquors from California into the State of Oregon, and that is a straight charge which has been denied by the plea of not guilty, and is for you to determine from the testimony.

Now, Gentlemen, the questions involved in this case under the rules as I have and shall give them to you are questions of fact, and all questions of fact are to be determined by this jury.

The Court over ruled a motion for a directed verdict, in your presence. You are not to infer from that, that in the opinion of the Court there is sufficient evidence to justify a conviction in this case. Under the system of administration of the law prevailing in this country it is the duty of the Court to determine all questions of law, and the exclusive duty of the jury to determine all questions of fact, and all that was implied or can be implied from the action of the Court in over-ruling the motion for a directed verdict is that in its judgment there was at least some evidence to go to the jury upon the questions involved in this controversy, and the Court has no more right to invade your province and undertake to determine a disputed question of fact than you have a right to invade its province and undertake to determine a question of law. The duties of each are separate and distinct and one has no right to assume to perform the duties of the other. Therefore, no inference is to be drawn by this jury as against the defendants from the action of the Court in overruling the motion for a directed verdict.

You are the exclusive judges of all questions of fact in the case and of the credibility of all witnesses. Every witness is presumed to speak the truth. The presumption, however, may be overcome by the manner in which a witness testifies, by his appearance upon the witness stand, by contradictory testimony, or by evidence effecting his reputation or standing. You have heard these witnesses testify; you have noticed their appearance upon the witness stand, and now it is for you, and you alone, to determine what weight and credit is to be given to the testimony, judging from their appearance, their manner of testifying, their powers of observation, and all the circumstances surrounding their testimony, and from that determine what credit shall be given to it.

The Government relies to a considerable extent on what is known as circumstantial evidence. This character of evidence is competent and is often resorted to in the trial of criminal cases. When a conviction is sought upon it, it should not only show that the circumstances testified to are true, but that they are not capable of reconciliation or being reconciled with the theory of the defendants' innocence. It is the duty of the jury in considering the testimony in the case, if you care to reconcile it with the theory of the defendants' innocence. The degree of certainty when circumstantial evidence if relied upon must be equal to direct testimony, and if there is any fact proved to your satisfaction by a preponderance of the evidence which is inconsistent with guilt, and that is a material fact in the chain of circumstances, then that will be sufficient to raise a reasonable doubt, and the defendant would be entitled to the benefit of it.

It is in evidence that George Knollton and Florence Knollton, two of the defendants, are husband and wife, and as far as the question of conspiracy is concerned they are to be considered as one, so that before you could find the defendants guilty on the first count of the indictment, it will be necessary for you to find there was co-operation, understanding and agreement between the two Knollton brothers.

The defendants have not testified in the case; they were not obliged to, not required to, and no inference is to be drawn against them because they did not testify; they had a perfect right to refrain from doing so, and to say to the Government, as the law says they may, "You charged me with this crime and it is your duty to prove it, and to prove it beyond a reasonable doubt," and no unfavorable inference or deduction is to be inferred or assumed against the defendants because of their failure to testify.

There are two counts in this indictment. It will be necessary for this jury to pass upon each one, and to find a verdict of either guilty or not guilty, as you may think the testimony warrants.

You have no concern, of course, with the punishment that may follow the verdict in case you should find the defendants guilty. It is your duty under the testimony and under your oaths to say whether they are guilty or not, and if you believe they are, beyond a reasonable doubt, then it is your duty to say so, leaving the question of punishment, whatever it may be, to the Court. If, on the other hand, you are not able to say beyond a reasonable doubt that they are guilty, or if you have a reasonable doubt upon that subject, you should give them the benefit of it and acquit.

MR. BECKMAN: I also want to call the Court's attention to the early part of the instructions regarding what is alleged in Count 1 of the indictment. I believe the Court told the jury as to overt acts 2 and 3, the indictment reads that defendant George Knollton and Florence Knollton drove a car to Oregon; I think the indictment limits it to Lakeview, Oregon.

COURT: I make that correction; I notice it says they drove across the Oregon line to Lakeview.

MR. BECKMAN: As to Count 2 of the indictment, the Court said that they bringing the whiskey from California into Oregon. I think the indictment says from California to Portland in the State of Oregon.

COURT: It does say that.

MR. BECKMAN: They are required to prove it as alleged.

COURT: It says from California to Portland in the State of Oregon.

And the foregoing instructions are all the instructions given by the Court to the jury at said trial.

Exception IV.

Thereafter, within the time allowed by the Court, the defendants moved the Court as follows:,

"Comes now George W. Knowlton, Florence May Knowlton and Jerry Knowlton, the above named defendants, each for themselves, by their attorneys, Manning & Beckman, within the time allowed by Court, and move the Court for a new trial on behalf of each of said defendants, upon the following grounds and for the following reasons:

I.

That count 2 of the indictment does not state facts sufficient to constitute a crime.

II.

That the Court erred in refusing to direct a verdict of not guilty, as to each of the said defendants at the close of the Government's evidence.

III.

That the Court erred in refusing to direct a verdict of not guilty as to each of the said defendants, at the close of all the evidence.

IV.

That the evidence was insufficient to justify a verdict of guilty against George E. Knowlton on count 2 of the indictment.

V.

That the evidence was insufficient to justify a verdict of guilty against Florence May Knowlton on count 2 of the indictment.

VI.

That the evidence was insufficient to justify a verdict of guilty against Jerry Knowlton on count 2 of the indictment.

VII.

That the verdict of the jury against George E. Knowlton was against the law as laid down by the Court.

VIII.

That the verdict of the jury against Florence May Knowlton was against the law as laid down by the Court.

IX.

That the verdict of the jury against Jerry Knowlton was against the law as laid down by the Court.

Thereafter the Court heard arguments of counsel upon the said motion and sustained the same as to defendant Florence May Knowlton, and overruled the same as to the defendants George E. Knowlton and Jerry Knowlton, to which action of the Court, the two last named defendants were duly allowed an exception.

Exception V.

Thereafter, within the time allowed by the Court the defendants moved the Court for an arrest of judgment as follows:

AND now after verdict against the defendants

George E. Knowlton and Florence May Knowlton and Jerry Knowlton, and before sentence, come the said defendants, and each of them for themselves, by their attorneys, Manning & Beckman, and move the Court here to arrest judgment herein and not pronounce judgment against the said defendants, or either of them, for the following reasons:

I.

That count 2 of the indictment does not state facts sufficient to constitute a crime.

II.

That the Court erred in refusing to direct a verdict of not guilty, as to each of the said defendants, at the close of the Government's evidence.

III.

That the Court erred in refusing to direct a verdict of not guilty, as to each of the said defendants, at the close of all of the evidence.

IV.

That the evidence was insufficient to justify a verdict of guilty against George E. Knowlton on count 2 of the indictment.

V.

That evidence was insufficient to justify a verdict of guilty against Florence May Knowlton on count 2 of the indictment.

VI.

That the evidence was insufficient to justify a verdict of guilty against Jerry Knowlton on count 2 of the indictment.

VII.

That the verdict of the jury against George E. Knowlton was against the law as laid down by the Court.

VIII.

That the verdict of the jury against Florence May Knowlton was against the law as laid down by the Court.

IX.

That the verdict of the jury against Jerry Knowlton was against the law as laid down by the Court.

Thereafter the Court heard the arguments of counsel upon said motion, and allowed the said motion as to defendant Florence May Knowlton, and over-ruled the said motion as to defendants George E. Knowlton and Jerry Knowlton, to which action of the Court the last two named defendants were allowed an exception.

Exception VI.

Thereafter, the Court entered a judgment of conviction and sentenced the defendants, George E. Knowlton and Jerry Knowlton, to confinement in the County Jail of Multnomah County, Oregon for a period of six months.

It is certified that the foregoing is all of the testimony, evidence, records and exceptions in said case material to the exceptions herein noted.

Thereafter, within the time allowed by the Court, the defendants, George E. Knowlton and Jerry Knowlton, presented this, their Bill of Exceptions, which is hereby allowed.

Dated this 19th day of April, 1920.

R. S. BEAN,
District Judge.

Due service of the within Bill of Exceptions is hereby accepted this 19th day of April, 1920.

JOHN C. VEATCH,
Assistant United States Attorney.

[Endorsed]: United States District Court, District of Oregon. Filed April 19, 1920. G. H. Marsh, Clerk.

In the District Court of the United States for the District of Oregon.

UNITED STATES OF AMERICA,
Plaintiff,

vs.

GEORGE E. KNOWLTON and
JERRY KNOWLTON,
Defendants.

Sitpulation as to Record.

It is hereby stipulated by and between the United States of America, by John C. Veatch, Assistant United States Attorney for the District of Oregon, and George E. Knowlton and Jerry Knowlton, the defendants, by Manning & Beckman, their attorneys, that the following documents, papers and records in the case of the United States of America vs. George E. Knowlton and Jerry Knowlton shall be included in the transcript of record in the said cause, and that the same are all the necessary documents, papers and records to be considered in reviewing the said case on writ of error, to-wit:

Indictment.
Bill of Exceptions.
Assignments of Error.
Petition for Writ of Error.
Order Allowing Writ of Error.
Citation.
Writ of Error.
Arraignment and Plea.

Impaneling of Jury.
Verdict.
Judgment.
Bond.

It is further hereby stipulated between the respective parties hereto that the foregoing printed record now tendered to the Clerk of the above entitled Court for his certificate, and filed in the above cause, is a true transcript of the record in said cause, and that the said Clerk may certify said transcript to the United States Circuit Court of Appeals for the Ninth Circuit, without comparing the same with the original record which is on file herein.

Dated this 17th day of May, 1920.

JOHN C. VEATCH,
Attorneys for Plaintiff.
MANNING & BECKMAN,
Attorneys for Defendants.

[Endorsed]: Filed May 17, 1920. G. H. Marsh, Clerk.

In the District Court of the United States for the District of Oregon.

UNITED STATES OF AMERICA,

Plaintiff,

vs.

GEORGE E. KNOWLTON and
JERRY KNOWLTON,

Defendants.

Order Under Rule 16 Enlarging Time to June 15, 1920, to File Record Thereof and to Docket Case.

Now at this time, upon motion of defendants, by their attorneys, Manning & Beckman, the time within which the defendants are allowed to file their transcript of record and docket said cause in the United States Circuit Court of Appeals for the Ninth Circuit is hereby extended to and including the 15th day of June, 1920.

Dated at Portland, Oregon, this 17th day of May, 1920.

R. S. BEAN, Judge.

In the District Court of the United States for the District of Oregon.

UNITE DSTATES OF AMERICA,
Plaintiff,

vs.

GEORGE E. KNOWLTON and
JERRY KNOWLTON,
Defendants.

United States of America,
District of Oregon,—ss.

I, G. H. Marsh, Clerk of the District Court of the United States for the District of Oregon, do hereby certify that the foregoing printed transcript of record on writ of error in the case of George E. Knowlton and Jerry Knowlton, plaintiffs in error, vs. United States of America, defendant in error, is a true transcript of the record in said cause in said Court. This certificate is made without comparing the said transcript of record with the original record in said cause, pursuant to the stipulation of the parties therein that this record may be certified to by me to be a true copy, without comparison.

IN TESTIMONY WHEREOF, I have hereunto set my hand and the seal of said Court in said District this —— day of May, 1920.

....Clerk.

No. 3514

United States Circuit Court of Appeals

For The Ninth Circuit

GEORGE E. KNOWLTON and JERRY KNOWLTON
Plaintiffs in Error,

vs.

UNITED STATES OF AMERICA,
Defendants in Error

Brief of Plaintiffs in Error

Upon Writ of Error to the United States District Court for the District of Oregon

JOHN MANNING and JOHN J. BECKMAN,
Both of Portland, Oregon,
Attorneys for Plaintiffs in Error.

LESTER W. HUMPHREYS, United States Attorney for Oregon, and HALL S. LUSK, Assistant United States Attorney, both of Portland, Oregon, Attorneys for Defendants in Error.

No. 3514.

United States Circuit Court of Appeals

For The Ninth Circuit

GEORGE E. KNOWLTON and JERRY KNOWLTON
Plaintiffs in Error,

vs.

UNITED STATES OF AMERICA,
Defendants in Error

Brief of Plaintiffs in Error

Upon Writ of Error to the United States District Court for the District of Oregon

JOHN MANNING and JOHN J. BECKMAN,
Both of Portland, Oregon,
Attorneys for Plaintiffs in Error.

LESTER W. HUMPHREYS, United States Attorney for Oregon, and HALL S. LUSK, Assistant United States Attorney, both of Portland, Oregon, Attorneys for Defendants in Error.

LIST OF CASES CITED IN THIS BRIEF

STATEMENT OF THE CASE

The indictment against the appellants, George E. Knowltown and Jerry Knowlton contains two counts, the first being a charge of conspiracy to violate the Reed Amendment, and the second being a charge of was no verdict on the first count. but the appellants violation of the provisions of the said Act itself. There was found guilty on the second count. Florence Knowlton, wife of George E. Knowlton, jointly indicted with appellants, was found guilty, but the verdict as against her was set aside by the court. Motions for a new trial and arrest of judgment were overruled as to appellants and judgment was imposed, that they each be imprisoned in the Multnomah County Jail for a term of six months.

The indictment upon which conviction was had, charged that on June 10, 1919, George E. Knowlton and Jerry Knowlton did knowingly, wilfully and unlawfully order, purchase and cause to be transported in interstate commerc from the State of California to Portland in the State of Oregon, 435 quarts of intoxicating liquor, to-wit: whiskey, for beverage purposes, and that such intoxicating liquor was transported into Oregon, the law of which State prohibited the manufacture and sale therein of intoxicating liquor for beverage purposes, and that the said intoxicating liquor was not ordered, purchased and caused to be transported in interstate commerce for scientific, sacramental, medicinal or mechanical purposes, or for any other than for beverage purposes.

There is a marked distinction between the amount and character of the proof affecting each of the appellants, and we will therefore review the evidence as to each separately.

Testimony as to George E. Knowlton.

T. M. Word, a government agent, testified that in the early morning of June 10, 1919, while traveling on the road from Lakeview, Ore., to Bend, Ore., in company with the Sheriff of Lake County, Ore., and others, he came across two automobiles standing at the road side and stopped to look them over. One of the automobiles was of the Stutz make and the other was a Mercer. One machine had a California license and one an Oregon license, but the witness did not state which one had the Oregon license. In the Stutz car was George E. Knowlton and his wife, asleep, and Jerry Knowlton was in the back part of the Mercer. The government agent awakened George E. Knowlton and his wife and asked them how much liquor they had and they replied that they had a small amount for their own use, about fifteen or twenty cases. George E. Knowlton gave his name as George W. Wilson and Jerry Knowlton said his name was James King. The place where these automobiles were found was between twenty to twenty-three miles north of Lakeview, and about thirty-five miles from the California State line. At Bend the Sheriff and the Government agent took 234 bottles of liquor from the Stutz car. The witness said that some of the bottles were filled with whisky, and a few bottles of brandy and a few bottles of gin. The bottles had revenue stamps on them. Shortly afterwards, at The Dalles, while the government officer and the prisoners were dining in a restaurant, some unknown person got into the Stutz machine and drove it away, and the car was later found abandoned and the liquor had disappeared. There was no liquor offered in evidence as coming from the Stutz car, nor was any of it in the possession of the witness at the time of the trial. The government agent could only testify that George E. Knowlton had whisky in his car from the appearance of the bottles. He never tested the liquor, nor is there any evidence that it was at any time tasted by anyone or shown to be intoxicating liquor. The government agent said that he had never seen either George E. Knowlton or Jerry Knowlton in the State of California; that he did not know from whom they bought the liquor, and that they told him they bought it in Oregon. Witness further said that both of the defendants had a fishing basket and some fishing tackle with them. (Transcript pp. 44 to 48).

F. E. Woodcock, county sheriff, corroborated the government officer with respect to finding the automobiles on the road, and that the occupants of the machines said that they had a little booze for their own use. He further said that both of the defendants told him and the government agent, that they had bought the liquor which was in their cars from some one in Oregon, a short while before. As far as he knew they might have gotten it in Oregon. He furthed testified that the road upon which the defendants were found was the main traveled road from Lakeview to Bend; that Lakeview is fifteen miles from the nearest California point; the nearest California town to Lakeview is Fairport; the nearest large California town on the road to Lakeview is Alturas, which is about forty-five miles from the boundary line of Oregon; that there were no other roads running into the road where the defendants were found north of Lakeview, excepting roads leading from ranches. There are two roads leading from Lakeview to Paisley, Oregon, and there are also roads leading from Klamath Falls, Oregon, to Lakeview and from Silver Lake, Oregon, to Lakeview, Oregon. (Transcript pg. 49).

There was no evidence whatsoever to show that George E. Knowlton ordered or purchased any intoxicating liquor whatever in the State of California at any time or had anything to do with the ordering or purchasing of any liquor. There is further no evidence whatsoever that the liquor found in his car had ever been transported from California or had in fact ever been in California.

There was some attempt to show that George E. Knowlton had been in California, but this failed. The witness, Laugenour, testified, that on June 9, 1919, near lunch time, two men and a woman came into his store at Davis Creek, which is a town in California, twenty-five miles north of Alturas. He identified Jerry Knowlton as being one of the men and a spectator among the audience in the court room, and not one of the defendants, as the other man and was not able to identify the woman, who, he said, wore a khaki uniform at the time. He said that Jerry Knowlton purchased some provisions; that he saw two machines through the window, at a glance, and said that one was a Stutz and the other a Mercer. An inspectiion of his cross-examination will show that he really had no opportunity to observe the makes of these cars, and that he merely had a fleeting glimpse of two machines. (Transcript pg. 51)

Another witness, Mr. Keser, testified that on June 9, 1919, at Alturas, he furnished a Stutz car with gasolene; that there was a man and a woman in the Stutz car, the woman being dressed in a khaki suit. The back of the car was piled up level with the back seat and covered with a blanket or canvas. On cross-examination he said that it was not an unusual thing to see a car so covered up and filled with bedding, etc., driven by tourists. He could not identify George E. Knowlton as being the man in the car and positively stated that his wife, Florence Knowlton, was not the woman he had reference to. The Stutz car he saw had white wire wheels and was a kind of maroon color, gold stripes and the lights painted white. It was later shown that the Stutz car owned by George E. Knowlton was a different one. because the wheels of the car were black and the body red and there were no stripes---gold or otherwise, and the fenders were black. (Transcript pg. 55.)

Another witness, Henry Kock, also testified that he recognized Jerry Knowlton in his restaurant and that Jerry had come in with another man to purchase sandwiches, but he could not recognize the other man and was unable to recognize George E. Knowlton as being in his place of business. (Transcript pg. 56.)

This was all the proof offered to connect George E. Knowlton with the crime charged in the indictment. There was no proof to show that he had ever been in California at any time.

Testimony As to Jerry Knowlton.

The testimony of the government agent and the sheriff with respect to finding the two cars on the road is the same as that against George E. Knowlton, and it will not be necessary to repeat it. There is this additional testimony, however.

The government agent said that in the Mercer car there was a wide mattress over the top and some blankets over that and a box of food and clothing. On the road later, Jerry Knowlton took out a box of provisions from his machine and made some coffee. The provisions were in a wooden box, the government agent ate a beef heart sandwich. The government agent further testified that there were about 201 bottles in the Mercer car. Several bottles were offered in evidence containing liquor and the government agent said that these came from the Mercer car. Jerry Knowlton told the sheriff and the government agent that they bought the liquor which was in his car from some one in Oregon, a short while before. (Transcript pp. 44 to 50.)

We have already referred to the testimony of the witness Laugenour, who said that he identified Jerry Knowlton as being the person who was in his store on June 9, 1919, about lunch time, and purchased some provisions, in company with two other unidentified persons. (Transcript pg. 51.)

We have also referred to the testimony of witness Kock, who said that on the 8th or 9th of June, 1919, between 11 A. M. and 1 P. M., two men came into his lunch counter at Alturas, California, and purchased twenty sandwiches, ten beef heart and ten pork sandwiches; that the sandwiches were placed in a spaghetti box; that Jerry Knowlton was one of the men, but he could not identify the other. The sandwiches were purchased between eleven and one o'clock in the day time, on the 8th or 9th of June. This witness was aided in identifying Jerry Knowlton by being shown his picture by the government agent in California and again when he came to Portland to testify in the case. (Transcript pg. 56).

The witness Ash, testified that on June 9, 1919, between one and two o'clock in the afternoon, a man drove into his garage at Alturas for the purpose of having a broken frame repaired. He identified this man as Jerry Knowlton, he said the car was heavily loaded, because it broke through the floor at one place, but later said that a Mercer car would weigh about 4200 pounds; that the garage had a wooden floor, which was old, and that before this time a two ton truck had broken through it. The car was not fixed until about ten P. M. of the same day. After the car was finished Jerry Knowlton went around to the right hand-side of the car and reached in and pulled out a bottle of brandy which had been partly consumed. The witness never paid any attention to how he got the bottle. The back of the car seemed to be pretty well filled up, but it was covered over and the witness did not know what was inside. The contents of this bottle were wholly consumed by the witness, his father and Jerry Knowlton, and the bottle left lying in the shop. (Transcript pg. 52.)

This was all the evidence against Jerry Knowlton. There was no evidence whatsoever that he either ordered or purchased any liquor at any place in California, at any time; there was no evidence that he ever had any liquor in California, except the single bottle which was consumed in the shop at Alturas. There was no evidence that the liquor found in his car was ever at any time in California or that he brought it from California. There was no evidence tending to show that he did not buy it in Oregon, as he claimed to the officers.

The above, we think, is a fair statement of all the testimony in the case, as shown by the Bill of Exceptions, which contains all of the testimony material to the exceptions taken and noted therein. (Transcript pg. 75.)

The principal exception taken in the case and the one upon which appellants base their argument, is the refusal of the court to direct a verdict of acquittal, after the close of the evidence, bcause there had been no proof of the offense charged in the indictment. (Transcript pp. 57-58.)

SPECIFICATIONS OF ERROR

I.

The court erred in refusing to direct a verdict for the defendant, George E. Knowlton, at the close of all the testimony in the case, upon the said defendant's motion. Assignment of Errors I, III, VI, VII, and VIII.

II.

The court erred in refusing to direct a verdict for the defendant, Jerry Knowlton, at the close of all the testimony in the case, upon the defendant's motion. Assignment of Errors, II, IV, VI, VII and VIII.

POINTS AND AUTHORITIES.

An inference from facts proved, in order to justify a conviction, must be inconsistent with innocence. The facts proved must reasonably justify the inference and the accused cannot be convicted on mere conjecture or suspicion.

16 Corpus Juris, 760, Sec. 1560.

In order to sustain a conviction on circumstantial evidence all the circumstances proved must be consistent with each other, consistent with the hypothesis that accused is guilty and at the same time inconsistent with the hypothesis that he is innocent and with every other rational hypothesis, except that of guilt,

16 Corpus Juris, 763, Sec. 1568.

The facts which form the basis of the corpus delicti must be proved by either direct or presumptive evidence of the most cogent and irresistible kind.

16 Corpus Juris, 771, Sec. 1579.

Circumstantial evidence alone is insufficient to establish the corpus delicti where it suggests a theory as consistent with the absence as with the existence of crime.

White vs State 18 Ga., A. 214, 89 S. E. 175.

Evidence of facts that are as consistent with innocence as with guilt is insufficient to sustain a conviction. Unless there is substantial evidence of facts which exclude every other hypothesis but that of guilt, it is the duty of the trial judge to instruct the jury to return a verdict for the accused, and where all the substantial evidence is as consistent with innocence as with guilt, it is the duty of the appellate court to reverse a judgment against him.

Union Pacific Coal Company, vs U. S. 173;

Fed. 737, at 740;

Isbell vs U. S. 227 Fed. 788,at 792;

Wright vs U. S. 227 Fed. 855;

Scoggins vs U. S. 255 Fed. 825;

Goff vs U. S. 257 Fed. 294.

Moral probability, however strong, cannot take the place of legal evidence, and inferences which the jury may draw in a case must be based upon facts which of themselves tend to establish the guilt of the accused.

Wolf vs U. S. 238 Fed. 902, at 906.

ARGUMENT

In order to convict either of the defendants upon the indictment in this case it was incumbent upon the government to prove beyond a reasonable doubt that on some date within the statute of limitations the defendants, or either of them, did knowingly order, or purchase, or cause to be transported in inter-state commerce from California into Oregon, a quantity of intoxicating liquors, for beverage purposes and not for any of the excepted purposes mentioned in the Statute. All of these elements of the crime must be proved.

As will be seen from an inspection of the record,

the only evidence against George E. Knowlton consists of the fact that he was found, together with his wife, in an automobile, on a road about twenty miles or more north of Lakeview, Oregon, and about forty miles north of the Californa line. There are a number of other roads joining the said road leading from ranches and from several towns in Oregon, at points south of where they were found. There is no testimony that he or his wife were ever in California, or that he transported or caused to be transported, any liquor from California to Oregon. Further, there is no substantial testimony in the record to show that the liquor that he had in his car was intoxicating liquor and no testimony to show what or where his destination was, or whether it was Oregon or Washington or Idaho, or some other State. Further, there was no testimony to show that he had any previous association with the other defendant, Jerry Knowlton, or that they were together for any length of time previous to the occasion of their arrest by the government agent. The facts are just as consistent with his innocence as with his guilt. If he actually had any intoxicating liquor in his car, which the government failed to prove, it is just as consistent to conclude that he obtained it some place in Oregon as in California; there is no legal presumption that he obtained it in California. There is no more than a probability or a possibility that he transported intoxicating liquor from California. As far as the evidence shows it is just as likely that he obtained the liquor at Lakeview, Klamath Falls, or some other place in Oregon.

It is true there is some testimony to the effect that the day before his arrest, Jerry Knowlton was in the State of California. but there is absolutely no proof that he ordered, purchased or caused to be transported any intoxicating liquor from California to Oregon, nor is there any proof that he ever had any intoxicating liquor at any place, except in Oregon, and it is just as consistent to draw the conclusion that he bought it in the last mentioned State as that he bought it in the State of California. In fact, the jury had no substantial evidence, whatsoever, before them upon which to conclude that he purchased the liquor in California or transported it from that State to Oregon. In fact, the evidence of both the sheriff and the government agent is to the effect that he told them he had purchased the liquor in the State of Orgon, and there appears to be no evidence in the record to the contrary.

The test laid down by the authorities, that there must be substantial evidence of facts which exclude every other hypothesis but that of guilt, has not been met by the government. There may be a moral probability of guilt, but that cannot take the place of legal evidence.

In the case of Isbell vs U. S. 227 Fed. 788, above cited, one Isbell was convicted for introducing intoxicating liquor into the State of Oklahoma from without that State. The evidence showed that the defendant was a drayman and one Hostetter had employed him to haul household goods from Chetopa, Kansas, to Tiff

City, Missouri, across a part of Oklahoma. He was arrested at Vinita, Oklahoma, and a number of barrels of whisky and wine, marked "household goods" were confiscated, some of the barrels of wine were marked "for Mrs. Isbell". The defendant claimed to be ignorant of the contents of the freight he was hauling. In this case the defendant was found with the liquor in the State into which the introduction of liquor was forbidden; it was shown that he came from another State, and yet the court held that the evidence was insufficient and reversed the conviction, because the destination of the liquor was not proven to be in Oklahoma.

In Goff vs U. S. 257 Fed. 294, above cited, the defendant, as in the last case, was convicted of introducing liquor into Oklahoma, formerly Indian Territory. He was found by officers in Nowata, Oklahoma, a point about twenty-four miles from the Kansas line, traveling in a Ford car, equipped with a false bottom, having concealed in and about the car more than 280 pints of whisky and some beer. There was no proof that he could not have obtained this supply of liquor in Oklahoma. The appellate court reversed the conviction in this case, because the corpus delicti was not proved. This case is very much like the one at bar.

In Wolf vs U. S. 238 Fed. 902, above cited, the defendant, Sam Wolf, was indicted, with others, for concealing assets in bankruptcy; Sam Wolf was the president of the bankrupt concern. It was shown that at least he was in a position to know of certain concealment of assets of the bankrupt concern, but the court held that this was not enough and reversed the conviction, saying that the conviction rested wholly on inference and conjecture, and that moral probability, however strong, could not take the place of legal evidence, and inferences which the jury might draw must be based upon facts which of themselves tend to establish the guilt of the accused. This case, we think, is very much in point, because the convictions in the case at bar are based wholly upon conjecture. The fact that the defendants had in their possession a quantity of intoxicating liquor at a point forty miles north of the California line, raises no inference, legal or otherwise, that they transported the same from California.

In Duff vs U. S. 185 Fed. 101, the defendant was convicted of refilling a bottle containing distilled spirits, which had been filled and stamped under the revenue law, without removing and destroying the stamp previously affixed. The evidence showed that the revenue officers found such bottles in the defendant's premises unlawfully refilled and that the defendant was one of three persons who had a special tax stamp for the saloon in question, there was no evidence to show who refilled the bottle. The appellate court reversed the conviction in this case because the evidence was insufficient.

In the case of Scoggins vs U. S. 255 Fed. 825, where the defendant was convicted of selling whisky without having paid the revenue tax, the testimony showed the transaction by the witness with the defendant in which there appeared to be some doubt as to whether a sale actually took place or whether the transfer of the liquor was a gift and because there was no substantial evidence of all the requisites of a sale, the judgment was reversed.

In Stager vs U. S. 233 Federal 510, the defendant, a federal official, was convicted of conspiring with others, to divulge confidential information regarding invoices and appraisements, contrary to the regulations of the Treasury Department. The evidence showed no more than an opportunity to commit the crime, that such information was divulged, and the possibility that defendant might have divulged it. The appellate court reversed the conviction on the ground that the evidence was insufficient.

This last mentioned case, we think, is in many ways parallel to the one at bar. The only evidence offered at the trial was to show that there was some liquor found in Oregon in two automobiles, and that the defendants had an opportunity to have brought it from California or that it was possible for them to have done so, but no evidence to show that they did.

In the case of Martin vs U. S. 264 Fed. 950, defendant was convicted of having transported intoxicating liquor from Missouri to Nebraska. The evidence showed that a quantity of whisky was found in his residence in Nebraska, also that he had pleaded guilty to a complaint in the State court to a state of facts equivalent to the charge in the federal indictment. The court reversed this conviction because the evidence was insufficient, in that there was no proof of the corpus delicti corroborating the extra judicial admission.

In the light of the above authorities, we think there is no question but that the trial court should have upon the motion of the defendants, directed a verdict of acquittal as to each of them, because the indictment against them was not proven and the corpus delicti was not established.

Wherefore, appellants pray that the judgment against them, and each of them, be reversed and that they be granted a new trial.

Respectfully submitted.

MANNING & BECKMAN,

Attorneys for Appellants, George E. Knowlton and Jerry Knowlton.

No. 3514.

United States Circuit Court of Appeals

For The Ninth Circuit

GEORGE E. KNOWLTON and
JERRY KNOWLTON,
Plaintiffs in Error,

vs.

UNITED STATES OF AMERICA,
Defendant in Error.

Brief of Defendant in Error

Upon Writ of Error to the United States District Court for the District of Oregon.

No. 3514.

United States Circuit Court of Appeals

For The Ninth Circuit

GEORGE E. KNOWLTON and JERRY KNOWLTON,
Plaintiffs in Error,

vs.

UNITED STATES OF AMERICA,
Defendant in Error.

Brief of Defendant in Error

Upon Writ of Error to the United States District Court for the District of Oregon.

JOHN MANNING and JOHN J. BECKMAN,
Both of Portland, Oregon,
Attorneys for Plaintiffs in Error.

LESTER W. HUMPHREYS, United States Attorney for Oregon, and HALL S. LUSK, Assistant United States Attorney, both of Portland, Oregon, Attorneys for Defendant in Error.

INDEX.

List of Cases and Authorities Cited in This Brief.

STATEMENT OF FACTS.

George E. Knowlton and Jerry Knowlton, brothers, were convicted under an indictment charging them with violation of the Reed amendment. The specific charge was the transportation of intoxicating whiskey from the State of California into the State of Oregon, the laws of which prohibited the manufacture and sale therein of intoxicating liquor for beverage purposes.

The Defendants were arrested by Government Special Agent Tom Word on June 10, 1918, in Oregon, about 35 miles from the California State line. Word at the time was bringing a prisoner from Lakeview, Oregon, to Portland, accompanied by E. E. Woodcock, Sheriff of Lake County. When the Government Agent came upon them, George Knowlton and his wife, Florence, were asleep in a Stutz automobile, and Jerry Knowlton was in a Mercer car drawn up on the side of the road to Bend. Both automobiles were loaded with liquor. The defendant George Knowlton, stated to the officer that they had a little liquor for their own use—about 15 or 20 cases—which they had bought in Oregon. (Transcript pp. 44-51).

The defendants both told the Government Agent and Sheriff Woodcock that they bought the liquor which was in the cars from some one in Oregon; and that there was no Federal charge against them. (Transcript p. 50).

On June 9, 1918, two men and a woman came into the store of H. W. Laugenour, at Davis Creek, California, which is 25 miles north of Alturas, California, and 12 or 15 miles south of the Oregon State line. One of these men, identified by Laugenour as Jerry Knowlton, came to the counter and bought some provisions. Laugenour was unable to identify the woman, and picked out a spectator among the gathering in the court room as the other man. Afterwards Laugenour, who had been in the automobile business from 1903 to 1912, saw through the store window two automobiles, one a Stutz, the other a Mercer. (Transcript, pp. 51 and 52).

The road where the defendants were found is the main traveled road from Lakeview to Bend. Lakeview is 15 miles from the nearest California point, and the nearest large California town on the road to Lakeview is Alturas, which is 45 miles from the boundary line of Oregon. (Transcript, p. 51).

On June 9, 1919, between 1 and 2 o'clock p. m., Jerry Knowlton drove a heavily loaded Mercer car into the garage of Eugene B. Ash, at Alturas, California. Ash repaired a broken frame on the car, and Jerry Knowlton gave him a drink out of a partially filled bottle of brandy which he pulled out of the car. The back of the car seemed to be pretty well filled up, but it was covered over and witness Ash did not know what was inside. (Transcript, p. 53).

On the same day, June 9, 1919, between 10 and 11 a. m., F. L. Kiser, who conducted the Alturas Tire & Battery Co., at Alturas, repaired a tire and furnished gasoline for a Stutz car, in which were a man, and a woman dressed in a khaki suit. The back of the car was flled up level with the back seat and covered over with a blanket or canvas. Keser did not recognize the Defendant George Knowlton or his wife, or Defendant Jerry Knowlton as the persons who were in or driving the Stutz car, and stated that Florence Knowlton was not the woman. The Stutz car, he testified, had white wire wheels, the lights were painted white, and the car was of a kind of maroon color—"witness was not sure the color was maroon, but knew it was red." (Transcript, p. 55).

In June, 1919, Henry Koch was running a lunch counter at Alturas, and on the 8th or 9th of June two men came to his counter and purchased twenty sandwiches—ten beef heart and ten pork. One of these men Koch recognized as Jerry Knowlton, but he could not say who the other man was. Koch thought that Jerry Knowlton came in a machine, because he had heard fellows make a remark about two big machines. (Transcript, p. 56).

Shortly after the defendants were arrested, they had lunch, and Jerry Knowlton took out a box of provisions from his machine, and the Government Agent ate a beef heart sandwich. (Transcript, p. 46).

It was also proven that after the Defendants werearrested Mrs. George Knowlton attempted to escape in the Stutz car; (transcript, p. 46); and that when the Government Agent with his prisoners arrived at The Dalles, and went into a restaurant with George Knowlton, a stranger drove off with the Stutz car, which was later recovered about 26 miles from The Dalles, all the liquor having been taken out and the car left stranded. (Transcript, page 47).

The foregoing is a summary of the testimony for the Government.

The defendants introduced no evidence, except that L. L. Therkelsen, who was in possession of the Stutz car at the time of the trial, and who testified that the color of the wheels of the car was black and of the body red; that there were no stripes on it and that the fenders were black. (Transcript, page 59).

POINTS AND AUTHORITIES.

I.

It is not every hypothesis, but every reasonable hypothesis but that of guilt, that the circumstantial evidence must exclude; the evidence need not demonstrate the guilt of defendant beyond the possibility of his innocence; and if the circumstances as proved produce a moral conviction to the exclusion of every reasonable doubt, they need not be absolutely incompatible, on any reasonable hypothesis with the innocence of accused.

16 Corpus Juris, 765.

II.

The evidence in a criminal case need not exclude the possibility of innocence.

United States vs. Green, 220 Fed. 973.

III.

The general rule is now well settled that in all criminal cases the corpus delicti may be established by circumstantial evidence.

Dimmick vs. United States, 137 Fed. 257—
C. C. A. 9th Circuit.
16 Corpus Juris, 772.

IV.

A jury in a criminal case is not restricted to palpable facts, but may consider all the inferences which reasonably may be drawn from the facts proven.

United States vs. Wilson, 176 Fed. 806.

V.

If an inference of guilt may be fairly drawn, the evidence meets the test of legal sufficiency, and its credibility must be determined by a jury.

United States vs. Green, 220 Fed. 973.

VII.

When the reasonableness of the only hypothesis of innocence propounded presents at least a question upon which men of ordinary intelligence might ordinarily differ, then the rule that to justify conviction of crime the evidence must be such as to exclude every reasonable hypothesis but that of guilt, is to be applied, not by the court, but by the jury.

Glass vs. United States, 231 Fed. 65.

Chambers vs. United States, 237 Fed. 513.

VII.

The identity of accused is not an element of the corpus delicti.

16 Corpus Juris, 772.

VIII.

The evidence in this case was sufficient to justify the verdict as to both Defendants.

Berryman vs. United States, 259 Fed. 208.

Laughter vs. United States, 259 Fed. 94, 100.

ARGUMENT.

But one question is presented by the brief of plaintiffs in error, namely: The sufficiency of the evidence to justify the verdict.

I.

Taking up first the case of Jerry Knowlton, we believe that it can readily be shown that the evidence was ample under any standard of proof adopted by the courts. Jerry was found asleep soon after 4 o'clock in the morning of June 10, 1919, in the Mercer car at a point on the road to Bend, Oregon, about 35 miles from the California State line. His brother, George, and the latter's wife, were found at the same time and place under like circumstances in the Stutz car. Both cars were loaded with intoxicating liquor, a fact which the men admitted. Some of this liquor from the Mercer car was introduced in evidence. On June 9, 1919, Jerry Knowlton bought some provisions in a store at Davis Creek, a town about 12 or 15 miles South of the Oregon State line, and about 25 miles north of Alturas; another man and a woman were with him; and Laugenour, the storekeeper, who had been in the automobile business for nine years, saw two automobiles outside, which he described as a Stutz and a Mercer.

On the same day, June 9, Jerry Knowlton drove the Mercer car into a garage at Alturas, and had some repairing done. His car was heavily loaded—so much so that it broke through the floor of the garage. He took a "partly drank" bottle out of the car and gave a drink to the garage man, Eugene B. Ash. Ash described the back of the car as pretty well filled up, but it was covered over and he did not know what was in it. This corresponds with Government Agent Word's testimony that in the Mercer car there was a wide mattress over the top and some blankets over that.

On June 8th or 9th, according to the testimony of Henry Kock, two men and a woman came to his lunch counter at Alturas and bought ten beef heart and ten pork sandwiches. He identified Jerry Knowlton as one of the men, and he thought Knowlton came in an automobile because he heard some remarks made at the time about two nice big machines. It was a beef heart sandwich which the defendant gave Agent Word when they had lunch together.

The **corpus delicti** in this case is the transportation of intoxicating liquors from California into Oregon. Plaintiff in error, Jerry Knowlton, says that that has not been established. We submit that it has been established.

We know from the authorities that the corpus delicti may be shown by circumstantial evidence. We know further that where the proof is by circumstantial evidence, it is not every hypothesis, but every reasonable hypothesis that the circumstantial evidence must exclude before a judgment of conviction is warranted.

Now, the circumstances adduced in this case were, in a word, these: That Jerry Knowlton was in Alturas, California, about 45 miles from the Oregon State line, with a heavily loaded Mercer automobile, on the afternoon of June 9; that the automobile was so covered up that its contents could not be seen; that Jerry Knowlton took a bottle of brandy out of the automobile; that on the same afternoon he was in Davis Creek, California, about 25 miles closer to the Oregon State line with the same automobile; and that early on the morning of June 10, shortly after 4 o'clock in fact, he was in Oregon, about 35 miles from the California State line, with the same automobile, heavily loaded with liquor—201 bottles, to be accurate.

The natural and reasonable inference from those facts is that Jerry Knowlton brought the liquor with him from California; that the load which made his automobile so heavy as to break through the floor of the garage at Alturas was precisely the same load as that which the officers found in his car on the road to Bend. This is not conjecture or suspicion, but deduction from proven facts.

There is a hypothesis, of course, which is consistent with Jerry Knowlton's innocence. There usually is such a hypothesis in circumstantial evidence cases, but the evidence in a criminal case need not exclude the possibility of innocence. United States vs. Green, 220 Fed. 973. It might be predicated that some time between the afternoon of June 9 and the early morning of June 10, Jerry Knowlton came from Alturas into Oregon, and after arriving in the State obtained the liquor and went to sleep on the road to Bend. But that is not a hypothesis which would appeal to a reasonable man; on the contrary, it is forced, and especially does it seem so when we reflect that Oregon was a "dry" state, where it was difficult and unlawful, and California was a "wet" state where it was easy and lawful to obtain intoxicating liquors.

Is it the law, that the Court must in such a state of facts peremptorily deny to the jury the right to say which is the reasonable deduction from the proven circumstances? We believe not.

"If an inference of guilt may be fairly drawn," it is said in United States vs. Green, 220 Fed. 973, "the evidence meets the test of legal sufficiency, and its credibility must be determined by a jury."

In Glass vs. U. S. 231 Fed. 65, the court was asked to give this instruction:

> "If there are any number of theories fairly deducible from the evidence which are compatible with guilt, and a single theory fairly compatible with innocence, the jury must adopt the theory of innocence."

"The defendant," it was said, "has not indicated the source of the proposition. We imagine that it was intended to embody the principle of the rule that to justify conviction of crime, the evidence must be such as to exclude every reasonable hypothesis but that of guilt. (Isbell vs. U. S. 227, Fed. 788). While such a rule is recognized, the question is always present—by whom is it to be applied? In some cases no doubt by the court, but certainly not in such a case as this where the reasonableness of the only hypothesis of innocence propounded presents at least a question upon which men of ordinary intelligence might honestly differ. Hart vs. United States, 84 Fed. 799. The trial court was therefore right in leaving the jury to determine whether the defense that the goods were sold before bankruptcy and the proceeds applied to the payment of the defendant's debts, was reasonable or not. The jury found that it was unreasonable, thereby destroying the 'single theory fairly compat--ible with innocence.' "

An attempt is made in the brief of counsel for plaintiff in error to deduce something from the fact that Jerry Knowlton claimed to the officers when convicted that he bought the liquor in Oregon, and that there was no evidence tending to show that he did not buy it in Oregon. It was not necessary for the Government to undertake the proof of that kind of a negative, except to the extent of showing by the circumstances that the defendant had the liquor in California and therefore must have transported it into Oregon. But, it is worthy of note, and proper to remark, since counsel appears to be relying on this self-serving declaration as evidence in their own behalf, that no such evidence was offered at the trial, and in fact no evidence whatever was given by defendants to explain away the incriminating circumstances.

II.

The case as to George Knowlton differs from

that as to Jerry in that no witness was able to identify him as the man who was seen in the Stutz car in California. But two men and a woman came into H. W. Laughenour's store at Davis Creek, on June 9, when Jerry bought the sandwiches, and outside of the store were a Mercer automobile and a Stutz automobile. A Stutz car, with a man and woman in it, obtained gasoline from the garage of F. L. Keser in Alturas on the morning of June 9. Two men, one of whom was Jerry Knowlton, bought sandwiches from Henry Kock at his lunch counter in Alturas on June 8th or 9th, and Kock heard some talk in that connection about two nice big machines.

Keser testifed that the back of the Stutz car was piled up level with the back seat and covered over with a blanket or canvas. The Stutz car when found by the officers, had some blankets over it and a gunny sack, and George Knowlton and Florence, his wife, were asleep in the front seat.

From the foregoing it is plain that a man and a woman and a Stutz car accompanied Jerry Knowlton to Davis Creek; and that a man and a woman in a Stutz car were in Alturas on the same day that Jerry Knowlton was there in his Mercer; and a man was with Jerry Knowlton when he bought sandwiches from a lunch counter at Alturas.

And when the defendants were found on the road to Bend, on the very next morning, George Knowlton and his wife were sleeping in the Stutz car, which in a general way corresponded to the description given by F. L. Keser of the car for which he had furnished gasoline and mended a tire. While it is true that there is a discrepancy as to some details between Keser's description of George Knowlton's car and the testimony on that point of L. E. Therkelsen for the Defendants, this can be taken as nothing more than a commentary on the fallibility of human testimony, memory and powers of observation. The value of Keser's testimony was a matter to be weighed by the jury, which, despite this discrepancy, evidently believed that the Stutz car he described was the same Stutz car in which George Knowlton and the intoxicating liquor were found.

The man who accompanied Jerry Knowlton was not a resident of Alturas or Davis Creek, for he was unknown to the witnesses from either of those places. He was a stranger. Now, even in the face of the failure of the Government to identify that man by any witness able to say that it was George

Knowlton, the brother of Jerry, are the jury to be told that they must ignore the cogent force of the circumstances pointing to the conclusion that George Knowlton was with Jerry Knowlton in Alturas and Davis Creek, on the theory that it is equally possible that he joined his brother Jerry after the latter came into Oregon. To adopt the latter theory, the jury must conclude that a man and a woman—not George and Florence Knowlton—in a Stutz car were with Jerry in Davis Creek and in Alturas on June 9th, that they left him before the early morning of the following day, and that sometime during the night of June 9-10, George and Flonence came along in another—or perhaps the same Stutz car and went to sleep with George on the road to Bend. Such a theory is not only not rational, but borders closely on the absurd.

It only remains then to consider whether there was any substantial evidence to show that George Knowlton transported intoxicating liquor from California into Oregon. It will be remembered that Keser testified that the back of the Stutz car for which he furnished gasoline, was piled up level with the back seat and covered over with a blanket or canvas. Now, the Government Agent, testified that the Stutz car had some blankets over it and some gunny sacks. There were 234 bottles of liquor in it.

That the Stutz car was loaded with something when in Alturas is evident. The purpose of covering the contents with a blanket was of course concealment. Men don't cover their ordinary legitimate baggage in that manner, and this was a circumstance to be considered by the jury.

As to the rest, while there was no direct evidence, as in the case of Jerry Knowlton, of the presence of liquor in the Stutz car while in California, the argument already advanced as to the rational conclusion to be drawn from the proven facts, applies equally to the case of George Knowlton, and it was for the jury to determine whether the hypothesis that the liquor was obtained in Oregon between the time that the defendants left Davis Creek and the time they went to sleep on the road to Bend was a reasonable one.

It was, indeed, not necessary to prove that any liquor was actually transported in the Stutz car. If the proof of transportation in the Mercer car was sufficient, George Knowlton was in the position of one aiding and abetting the commission of the crime, and his conviction can be sustained on that theory.

The statement in counsel's brief that there was no substantial testimony to show that the liquor in the Stutz car—George Knowlton's—was intoxicating, is hardly correct. It is true that none of this liquor was introduced in evidence. That was impossible, as some one, evidently a confederate of the defendants, managed to make off with it at The Dalles. But Sheriff Woodcock testified that he tasted some whisky from a bottle in the Stutz car; and the defendants both admitted that it was liquor, which it need scarcely be stated, is common parlance for intoxicating liquor. And George Knowlton, testified Government Agent Word, "begged me all night to let him open a bottle and let him take a drink."

III.

Most of the principles of law cited in the brief of plaintiffs in error are incontestible. The cases relied on, however, do not admit of the application claimed for them. We shall notice only two, for the purpose of giving point to this statement.

In Goff vs. United States, 257 Fed. 294, there was no evidence apart from the admission of the defendant (which of course required corroborative proof) that the defendant's automobile was ever in another state.

In Isbell vs. United States, 227 Fed. 788, the questions were:

1. Did defendant know that he was transporting liquor? 2. Whether the defendant's destination was Oklahoma or Missouri, the rule being that to transport liquors **across** that part of Oklahoma which was formerly Indian Territory would not be a violation of the Act.

On the second question the only evidence was the fact that the liquor was siezed on the road from Chetopa, Kansas, to Vinita, Oklahoma, 18 miles from the former place and that two or three bottles of wine in Isbell's automobile were marked "for Mrs. Isbell." There was no evidence that the bottles were so marked by Isbell, or with his knowledge or consent. Isbell claimed that he had been hired to haul the goods from Chetopa, Kansas, to Tiff City, Mo.

"No witness came to testify that the destination of the goods was in the State of Oklahoma. All the witnesses testified that it was Tiff City, Mo., the route over which the goods were removed was not inconsistent with that tination, the marks "For Mrs. Isbell," on two or three wine bottles, unsupported by any proof tending to show who made them, do not rise to the dignity of evidence, and there was no substantiated evidence, nothing but suspicion, that the destination was Oklahoma, or that Isbell was consequently guilty."

The other cases cited by counsel, we believe are shown by the statements of their facts in the brief to have little if any bearing on the question at bar.

IV.

It is said at page 16 of the brief for plaintiffs in error that there was no evidence to show what the defendant's destination was. There was evidence, however, that the defendants were found in Oregon, and no claim whatever was made that Oregon was not their destination. On this point, as well as on the general questions of the sufficiency of the evidence, we quote from the opinion in Berryman vs. United States, 259 Fed. 208, where the defendants were convicted of violation of the Reed Amendment:

"Berryman and Gold claim that the evidence did not justify the submission of their case to the jury. Both of them testified on the trial that they had procured the liquor in Paducah, Ky., and were bringing it from that place. They lived in Memphis, where they were partners in operating a taxicab line, and they had driven from Memphis to Paducah for the purpose of getting the liquor. Their guilt, under their own statement, is not to be doubted, except for the fact that they also claimed that they had procured it for a man in Helena, Ark., and, that, when arrested they were making the through trip from Paducah to Helena for delivery there to him. If this was true, they were not guilty, since the sale of liquor in Arkansas was not prohibited. United States vs. Gudger (April 14, 1919) 249 U. S. 373, 39 Sup., Ct. 323, 63 L. Ed. 653. However, the facts brought out on cross-examination threw grave doubt upon the truth of so much of this story as involved the Helena destination, and the jury was under no obligation to believe it. From all the facts, it was an entirely legitimate inference that Memphis was the final destination of the liquor; and the jury may, of course, convict upon legitimate inferences, as well as upon direct testimony.

"In Tucker's Case, the additional point mainly urged against the judgment is that there was no sufficient proof of the corpus delicti to corroborate the defendant's confession. The proposition that there must be such corroborative evidence in order to justify a conviction is not questioned by the District Attorney, but he affirms the existence of such evidence. The testimony is that Tucker, at the time of his arrest, admitted that he got the liquor in Paducah and was carrying it to Memphis. It is said that this was the only evidence tending to show one element of the crime charged, viz. transportation across the state line into Tennessee, and that, since the crime was not complete without this interstate transportation, the commission of the crime had not been shown at all, except by this confession. Without going at all into the refinements of the legal rule, there are two answers to this contention, either of which is sufficient: The first is that the rear cushion of the automobile had been taken out, apparently to facilitate the packing of the load which was being carried, and Tucker had in his possession an express receipt therefor, issued at Paducah indicating that he had been in Paducah and delivered this cushion to an express company for transportation to Memphis. This distinctly tended to show that the journey on which he was then engaged began in Paducah.

"The other answer is that the liquor itself was there and was being transported, and its presence, in Tucker's charge, under these circumstances, was strongly corroborative of his statement that he had brought it across the state line. Especially is this true, in view of the fact that he could not have purchased it in Tennessee, nor could any one have delivered it to him in Tennessee, without violating the Tennessee law, and it is a fair presumption, and in Tucker's favor, that he procured it where he could easily do so without violating any state law, rather than where its acquisition must have been surreptitious, difficult of accomplishment and in defiance of the laws of the state. Rivalto v. United States, 259 Fed. 94-C.C.A.-(January 17, 1919), and see Robilio v. United States, 259 Fed. 101,-C.C.A. (March 5, 1919). This view also disposes of the contention that it was error to charge that the possession of the liquor gave the confession sufficient corroboration."

As further throwing light on the general question of the sufficiency of the evidence, we quote from Laughter vs. United States, 259 Fed. 94, 100; also a Reed Amendment case:

"In the Rivalto Case, No. 3221, the further specific objection is that there was no evidence to justify conviction. We think the circumstances sufficiently point to the conclusion that Rivalto participated in ordering or transporting or causing the transportation of a quantity of liquor which might have been for purposes of resale and which was taken from an interstate train on its arrival in Memphis. The only plausible objection to the sufficiency of proof is that this train had traveled for more than 100 miles and made several stops after it entered the state of Tennessee, and that there is nothing to show that the liquor was on board before the train came into the state. The train had come directly through from Cairo, Ill., where liquor could lawfully be bought. For it to have been purchased and loaded upon the train in Tennessee would necessarily have involved violation of the Tennessee laws, and to assume Tennessee origin would be to presume that at least one, and probably several offenses against Tennessee laws had been committed. The liquor was in bottles which bore labels purporting to show that it had been recently bottled for some dealer in Cairo. These labels were received in evidence without objection. The combined force of these circumstances was enough to justify the jury in thinking that the journey which ended in Memphis began in Cairo."

The evidence seems to us to be sufficient, and we believe that the judgment of conviction should be sustained.

Respectfully submitted,
LESTER W. HUMPHREYS,
United States Attorney.
HALL S. LUSK,
Assistant United States Attorney.
Attorneys for Defendant in Error.

No. 3515

In the United States
Circuit Court of Appeals
For the Ninth Circuit.

MARTIN TROGLIA,
Plaintiff in Error,
vs.
THE BUTTE SUPERIOR MINING COMPANY, a Corporation,
Defendant in Error.

In Error to
The District Court of the United States for the District of Montana.

TRANSCRIPT

WALKER & WALKER and
C. S. WAGNER,
Attorneys for Plaintiff in Error,
307 Daly Bank Bldg.,
Butte, Montana.

McKEE PRINTING CO., BUTTE, MONT.

No.________

In the United States Circuit Court of Appeals
For the Ninth Circuit.

MARTIN TROGLIA,
Plaintiff in Error,
vs.
THE BUTTE SUPERIOR MINING COMPANY, a Corporation,
Defendant in Error.

In Error to
The District Court of the United States for the District of Montana.

TRANSCRIPT

WALKER & WALKER and
C. S. WAGNER,
Attorneys for Plaintiff in Error,
307 Daly Bank Bldg.,
Butte, Montana.

INDEX

INDEX

In the District Court of the Second Judicial District of the State of Montana, in and for the County of Silver Bow

---

MARTIN TROGLIA,

Plaintiff,

vs. COMPLAINT.

THE BUTTE SUPERIOR MINING COMPANY, a Corporation,

Defendant.

I.

At all times herein mentioned plaintiff was the father of John Troglia, a minor child 11 years of age, and the defendant was and is a corporation organized and existing under and by virtue of the laws of the State of ~~Arizona~~ Montana and doing, inter alia, a general mining and milling business in Silver Bow County, Montana.

II.

Plaintiff alleges he brings this action against the defendant for damages for the death of his said minor child on or about the 13th day of June, 1918, approximately caused by the wrongful and negligent acts of the defendants as hereinafter set forth.

III.

Plaintiff alleges that prior to and on the 13th day of June, 1918, the defendant herein did keep and maintain an artificial dam or reservoir located, and being about one mile north of Meaderville in said county and state, to supply its mill with water, which said artificial dam and reservoir was of the following dimensions, to wit: About 100 feet long and about 75 feet wide, and varying in depth from 1 to 12 feet, and which had been prior thereto and was on said day filled with water. That said artificial dam and reservoir was not enclosed prior thereto or on said day with any fence or other barrier, but then was, and prior thereto had been, wholly unenclosed and open to the public generally, and on said day the said defendant carelessly and negligently suffered and permitted said artificial dam and reservoir to so be and remain open and exposed, and no watchman or person to warn minor children against trespassing was kept or maintained at or near said artificial dam and reservoir, or at all.

IV.

That said artificial dam and reservoir is contiguous to, and in close proximity with, a public highway, to wit, 25 feet therefrom, upon and over which, and upon and over the contiguous and adjacent lands many children passed to and fro at ~~all~~ the times herein ~~alleged~~ mentioned, particularly the son of plaintiff, John Troglia above mentioned, and his youthful companions and playmates. That said artificial dam and reservoir so, as aforesaid, carelessly and negligently kept and maintained by the defendant, became and was an enticing and alluring attraction to children generally as a swimming hole or bathing pond, and many children of the neighborhood including plaintiff's said son, John Troglia, did at divers times prior to the 13th day of June, 1918, go swimming or bathing at and in said artificial dam and reservoir, all of which was well known to the defendant, or by the exercise of ordinary care would have been known to it.

V.

That the said artificial dam and reservoir is fed from the waters of a creek or channel whose source of supply is found in the melting snows of the highlands nearby, and during the month of June of each year, and particularly during the month of June, 1918, the waters entering and contained in said artificial dam and reservoir were cold, chilly and of low temperature, to wit, of the temperature of 40 or 50 degrees Fahrenheit, all of which was well known to the defendant or which, by the exercise of ordinary care, would have been known to it.

VI.

That by virtue of the premises, the defendant well knew, or by the exercise of ordinary care would have known, that the said artificial dam and reservoir so, as aforesaid, kept and maintained by it was a dangerous instrumentality peculiarly attractive to children of tender years, and in its exposed and unguarded condition would, and did, allure children of tender years thereto, among them plaintiff's said minor son, John Troglia, for the purpose of making use of the same for swimming and bathing purposes, yet, notwithstanding the premises, the defendant failed and neglected to use ordinary care, or any care at all, to prevent children, and particularly the minor son of plaintiff, John Troglia, from making use of the said artificial dam and reservoir for swimming and bathing purposes, but carelessly and negligently suffered and permitted children, among them plaintiff's said minor son, John Troglia, to so make use of said artificial dam or reservoir for bathing and swimming purposes.

VII.

That on the 13th day of June, 1918, defendant knew, or by the exercise of ordinary care would have known, that plaintiff's said minor son, John Troglia, and his playmates and companions were lawfully upon the premises of defendant at said artificial dam and reservoir by and through an invitation implied by law, for that the said minor son of plaintiff, John Troglia, and his playmates and companions were on said day lured thereto by the peculiar and tempting attractiveness of the said artificial dam and reservoir as a swimming pool or bathing pond, that it then became and was the legal duty of defendant to warn plaintiff's said minor son and his playmates and companions of the dangers attendant upon going in swimming in the deep and cold waters of said artificial dam and reservoir and to forbid its use for such purposes and to order plaintiff's minor son, John Troglia, and his playmates and companions from the said artificial dam and reservoir and the premises of the defendant. But the said defendant on said day carelessly and negligently suffered and permitted the said minor son of the plaintiff, John Troglia, and his companions and playmates to go in swimming in the deep and cold waters of said artificial dam and reservoir, and while the said minor son of plaintiff, John Troglia, was so suffered and permitted to bathe in said deep and cold waters by and through the implied invitation of defendant, and by its careless and negligent acts, as aforesaid, the body of the said minor son of plaintiff, John Troglia, sank therein and he was drowned and he died therein.

VIII.

That the death of the said minor son of plaintiff, John Troglia, was proximately caused by the careless and negligent acts of defendant, as aforesaid, in suffering and permitting, and in failing to prevent, minor children to swim and bathe in the said artificial dam and reservoir, among them ~~and~~ the said John Troglia, and in suffering and permitting said artificial dam and reservoir to be and remain upon its premises in an open, exposed and unguarded condition while knowing, or by the exercise of ordinary care it would know, the same to be a dangerous instrumentality, and it was a dangerous instrumentality peculiarly attractive and alluring to minor children, and that by the implied invitation of the defendant, as aforesaid, it did entice and lure minor children, amongst them the said minor son of plaintiff, John Troglia, as aforesaid, to his death on said 13th day of June, as aforesaid, and whose death could have been prevented by the use and exercise of ordinary care by the defendant.

IX.

Plaintiff alleges that he was required to pay and did pay the sum of, to wit, seven hundred ($700.00) dollars to conduct the funeral and to inter and bury the remains and dead body of his said minor son, John Troglia, and that the sum so expended was the reasonable value of the services rendered for such purposes in the said County of Silver Bow.

X.

Plaintiff further alleges that by reason of the loss of the love, companionship and services of his said minor son, John Troglia, through his death by drowning occasioned by the careless and negligent acts of the defendants, he has suffered damage in the sum of twenty-five thousand ($25,000.00) dollars.

WHEREFORE, plaintiff prays judgment against the defendant in the sum of twenty-five thousand seven hundred ($25,700.00) dollars.

WALKER & WALKER and
C. S. WAGNER.

Duly verified.

(TITLE OF COURT AND CAUSE.)

DEMURRER.

Comes now the defendant above-named, Butte and Superior Mining Company, sued in said action as The Butte Superior Mining Company, a corporation, and demurs to the complaint of plaintiff herein on file, and for ground of demurrer alleges:

That said complaint does not state facts sufficient to constitute a cause of action against the defendant.

KREMER, SANDERS & KREMER,
Attorneys for Defendant.

United States District Court, Montana.

TROGLIA,

vs.

MINING CO.

It is believed the complaint meets the requirements of a cause of action upon its theory. 53 Mont. 152 U. S. 262. Demurrer overruled, 10 days for answer.

BOURQIN, J.

(TITLE OF COURT AND CAUSE.)

ANSWER.

Comes now the above-named defendant and for answer to plaintiff's complaint herein, admits, denies and alleges:

I.

Admits the allegations contained in paragraph I of plaintiff's complaint.

II.

Answering the allegations contained in paragraph II of plaintiff's complaint, this defendant admits that the plaintiff has brought this alleged action for the alleged death of his said minor child on or about the 13th day of June, 1918, but denies that said death was approximately or at all caused by the wrongful or negligent or any act or acts of the defendant as set forth in plaintiff's complaint, or at all.

III.

Answering the allegations contained in paragraph III of plaintiff's complaint, admits that the said defendant prior to and on the 13th day of June, 1918, kept and maintained an artificial dam or reservoir located and being about a mile north of Meaderville, in Silver Bow County, Montana, to supply its mill with water; admits that said dam and reservoir was of the approximate diminensions of 100 by 75 feet and varied in depth from 1 to 12 feet or thereabouts; admits that said dam and reservoir was prior to and on the 13th day of June, 1918, filled with water; denies that said artificial dam or reservoir was not inclosed prior thereto or on said day by any fence or other barrier; denies that said dam was open to the public generally, or at all ,and denies that on said day or at all the said defendant carelessly or negligently suffered or permitted said artificial dam or reservoir to be or remain open or exposed, and denies that no watchman or person to warn minor children, or others, against trespassing was kept or maintained at or near said artificial dam or reservoir; but in this connection this defendant avers that there was at said place at all times in the employ of the defendant an employe of the said company who protected said property against trespassers and who repeatedly warned children and others against trespassing upon or in said dam or reservoir, and who particularly warned the minor child of the plaintiff, to-wit: John Troglia; but that notwithstanding such repeated warning the said John Troglia and his associates continued trespassing upon and in said premises.

IV.

Answering the allegations contained in paragraph IV defendant admits that said artificial dam and reservoir is approximately 25 feet from a public highway, but in this connection avers that said public highway is seldom used and few people traverse the same; denies that over or upon said public highway or upon or over the contiguous or adjacent lands many children passed to and fro at the time mentioned in plaintiff's complaint, or at all; but in this connection avers that few, if any, children traversed said public highway save and except children trespassing upon the property of the defendant against the will and contrary to the wishes and warnings of the said defendant, notwithstanding the fact that the defendant had used reasonable care and caution to prevent said children trespassing upon its said property; denies that said highway was particularly used by said John Troglia, or his youthful companions or playmates, except when the said John Troglia and his companions or playmates were trespassing upon the premises of the defendant notwithstanding the protests of the said defendant and notwithstanding that the defendant actually protested against the said trespass and actually drove the said John Troglia and his playmates therefrom; denies that said artificial dam or reservoir was carelessly or negligently kept or maintained by the defendant; denies that the same became or was an enticing or alluring attraction to children or to children generally as a swimming pool or bathing pond, or at all, or that many, or any, of the children of the neighborhood or elsewhere, including plaintiff's minor son, John Troglia, or any other person, did at divers or any time prior to the 13th day of June, 1918, go swimming or bathing at or in said artificial dam or reservoir except when the said defendant was unable to prevent the same by the use of ordinary care and diligence and against the will of the defendant, and in this connection defendant avers that it repeatedly drove the said John Troglia and his companions and other children from said premisse through the agency of the person charged with the responsibility of protecting the said property of the said defendant against trespass, and particularly with the duty of preventing children and others from encroaching upon said premises; denies that all or any of said alleged acts of the said John Troglia and his associates, save as herein set forth, were well or at all known to the defendant, or by the exercise of ordinary care would have been known to it, and in this connection defendant avers that it at all times protested against the said trespass of the said John Troglia and his companions and frequently drove them from the said premises as aforesaid.

V.

Answering the allegations contained in paragraph

defendant admits that said artificial dam or reservoir is fed from the waters of a creek or channel whose source of supply is found in the melting snows of the mountains nearby; denies that during the month of June of each year, or particularly during the month of June, 1918, the waters entering or contained in said artificial dam or reservoir were cold or chilly, or of low temperature, or were of the temperature of 40° to 50° Fahrenheit; denies that it was well known to the defendant or would have been known to the defendant by the exercise of ordinary care on its part that the said waters were of such temperature; denies that the waters during the month of June, 1918, and particularly on the 13th day of June, 1918, were of any lower temperature than 60° Fahrenheit.

VI.

Denies that the said defendant well or at all knew, or by the exercise of ordinary care, or any care, would have known that the said artificial dam or reservoir kept or maintained by it was a dangerous instrumentality particularly or at all attractive to children of tender, or any, years; denies that the said dam or reservoir was or is an instrumentality particularly attractive to children of tender, or any years; denies that said dam or reservoir in its alleged exposed or unguarded condition would or did allure children of tender or any years thereto, or among them plaintiff's said minor son, John Troglia, for the purpose of making use of the same for swimming or bathing purposes, or otherwise, but in this connection states that contrary to the will and wish and warnings of defendant and notwithstanding the fact that he had been repeatedly driven therefrom the said John Troglia did attempt to use the same for swimming or bathing purposes; denies that the defendant failed or neglected to use ordinary care or care of any kind to prevent children, or particularly the minor son of plaintiff John Troglia of making use of said artificial dam or reservoir for swimming or bathing purposes, but in this connection defendant avers that it used every means possible for preventing the use of the same for said purposes by the said John Troglia and other children by repeatedly warning them to remain away from said premises and driving them therefrom; denies that the said defendant carelessly or negligently suffered or permitted children or other persons or particularly plaintiff's minor son John Troglia, to make use of said artificial dam or reservoir for bathing or swimming purposes, but in this connection this defendant specifically alleges that it did not suffer or permit children or any person or persons or the plaintiff's minor son John Troglia to make use of said artificial dam or reservoir for bathing or swimming purposes, but particularly forbade swimming or bathing in the same.

VII.

Denies that on the 13th day of June, 1918, defendant knew, or by the exercise of ordinary care, would have known, that plaintiff's minor son John Troglia, or his playmates or companions, were lawfully upon the premises of plaintiff at said artificial dam or reservoir by or through an invitation implied by law, or otherwise; denies that the said John Troglia, or his playmates or companions, were upon said premises lawfully or by or through an invitation implied by law or at all; denies that on said day the said John Troglia or his playmates or companions were lured thereto by the peculiar or tempting or any attractiveness of said artificial dam or reservoir as a swimming pool or bathing pond, or otherwise; denies that it became or was the legal duty or any duty of defendant to warn said plaintiff's said minor son or playmates or companions, of the dangers, if any, of going in swimming in the deep or cold waters of said artificial dam or reservoir; but in this connection avers that it did warn children against going in swimming in sad waters and did repeatedly drive them from the said premises; denies that it was the duty of the said defendant to forbid its use for said purpose or to order plaintiff's minor son John Troglia or his playmates or companions from the artificial dam or reservoir or the premises of the defendant, but in this connection defendant particularly avers that it did forbid its use for said purpose and did order plaintiff's minor son John Troglia and his playmates from the said dam and reservoir and from the said premises of defendant; denies that said artificial dam or reservoir was tempting or attractive as a swimming pool or bathing pond, but avers that the said artificial dam or reservoir was not attractive as a swimming pool or bathing pond, but notwithstanding that fact upon the said day the said John Troglia trespassed upon said premises against the will and wish of the said defendant and was drowned in said pond; denies that the said defendant on said day, or any other day, carelessly or negligently suffered or permitted the said minor son John Troglia or his companions or playmates to go in swimming in the said deep or cold or any waters or any waters of said artificial dam or reservoir, or at all; denies that said waters were cold; denies that while the said minor son of plaintiff John Troglia was suffered or permitted to bathe in said deep or cold waters or any water, or at all, by or through the alleged implied, or any invitation of defendant or by the alleged carless or negligent acts of the defendant, or at all, the body of the said minor son of plaintiff John Troglia sank therein or was drowned or he died therein; denies that said waters were cold; admits that the said John Troglia was drowned in said artificial poor or reservoir and died therein, but defendant avers that it was not through any act of carelessness or negligence on the part of the defendant.

VIII.

Answering the allegations containe din paragraph 8 this defendant denies that the death of the said minor son of plaintiff John Troglia was proximately or at all caused by the careless or negligent act or acts of defendant in suffering or permitting or in failing to prevent minor or any children to swim or bathe in said artificial dam or reservoir (among them the said John Troglia), or in suffering or permitting said artificial dam or reservoir to be or remain upon its premises in an open or exposed or unguarded condition, or otherwise, or at all; denies that the said defendant knew or by the exercise of ordinary care would have known the same to be a dangerous instrumentality; denies particularly that it was a dangerous instrumentality peculiarly or at all attractive or alluring to minor or any children; denies that by the alleged implied invitation or any invitation of the defendant, it did entice or lure minor or any children, amonk them the said minor son of plaintiff John Troglia to his death on said 13th day of June aforesaid, or any other time; denies that the said death could have been prevented by the use of exercise of ordinary care by the said defendant, and in this connection the said defendant particularly denies that it was guilty of any carless or negligent act whatsoever, or that it did suffer or permit the minor son of the plaintiff to bathe in said dam or reservoir; denies particularly that it failed to guard or protect said reservoir; denies particularly that said dam was an instrumentality particularly attractive or alluring to minor or any children; and in this connection defendant avers that it guarded said dam and reservoir by human agency so as to prevent trespass thereon by any persons whatsoever, but that notwithstanding the same the said John Troglia did trespass thereon.

IX.

Answering the allegations contained in paragraph IX denies that it has any knowledge or information thereof sufficient to form a belief.

X.

Answering the allegations contained in paragraph X, defendant denies that by reason of the loss of the love or companionship or services of said minor son of plaintiff John Troglia through his death by drowning, the said plaintiff has suffered damages in the sum of Twenty-five Thousand ($25,000.00) Dollars, or any other sum, or at all; denies particularly that said death was occasioned by any carless or negligent act or acts of the defendant, and denies that by reason of any carless or negligent act or acts of the defendant the said plaintiff has suffered damage in the sum of Twenty-five Thousand ($25,000.00) Dollars, or any other sum, or at all.

XI.

Further answering plaintiff's complaint, defendant denies each and every allegation therein contained not hereinbefore specifically admitted or denied.

XII.

Further answering plaintiff's complaint, this defendant alleges that the said plaintiff, Martin Troglia, was and is the father of the said John Troglia, a minor of the age of eleven (11) years referred to in plaintiff's complaint: that the said Martin Troglia was guilty of carlessness and negligence in not forbidding said John Troglia from exposing himself to the danger of trespassing upon and swimming in the artificial dam or lake constructed by the defendant upon its said premises for the purpose set forth in plaintiff's complaint and the character of which plaintiff well knew or could have known by the exercise of ordinary care and diligence; that the said Martin Troglia, as father and guardian and protector of said child, negligently and carelessly permitted the said John Troglia to enter upon said premises of the said defendant and swim in said artificial pond or lake, and that the said Martin Troglia, by the exercise of ordinary care could have prevented the said John Troglia from swimming in said artificial lake, and thereby could have prevented the said John Troglia from drowing therein, the said Martin Troglia knowing or by the exercise of ordinary care and diligence could have known that said John Troglia was trespassing and swimming in said artificial dam or reservoir, and that had the said Martin Troglia not been guilty of the said negligent and careless acts in so permitting or causing his son to trespass upon and swim in said artificial lake, the death of the said John Troglia would not have happened by drowning in said artificial lake aforesaid; that it was the duty of the said Martin Troglia to shield his said minor child from danger and by failing to prevent the said John Troglia from trespassing upon the premises of plaintiff and swimming in said artificial dam or lake, the said Martin Troglia contributed to the injury and death of his said child and that the said Martin Troglia thereby became i pari delicto by reason of his said carless and negligent acts.

WHEREFORE, defendant having fully answered prays that it be dismissed hence with its costs.

KREMER, SANDERS & KREMER,
Attorneys for Defendant.

Duly verified.

(TITLE OF COURT AND CAUSE.)

REPLY.

Now comes the plaintiff above named and for reply to the answer of the defendant on file herein admits, denies and alleges:

I.

Denies as alleged in paragraph three of said answer that at the time and place alleged the said defendant protected the said property against trespassers or warned children and others against trespassing upon or in said dam or reservoir, and denies the said defendant particularly or at all warned the minor child of plaintiff, John Troglia, and denies that, notwithstanding such alleged warning, the said John Troglia and his associates continued trespassing upon or in said premises.

II.

Replying to the allegations of paragraph four of said answer, plaintiff denies that the said John Troglia and his youthful playmates and companions were trespassing upon the property of the defendant and against the will and contrary to the wishes and warnings of the defendant or at all, and alleges in this connection that the defendant failed to use reasonable care and caution to prevent said children trespassing or entering into and upon the said premises, and at all times alleged in said complaint the said John Troglia and his youthful playmates and companions were at and upon said premises by the implied invitation of the defendant as alleged in plaintiff's complaint, and denies that the said defendant actually protested or protested at all against any trespass or drove the said John Troglia and his playmates and companions, or any or either of them, therefrom.

III.

Replying to the sixth paragraph of defendant's answer, this plaintiff denies that the said John Troglio and his playmates or companions, or any or either of them, were upon the premises of the defendant, as alleged in the answer, contrary to the will and wish and warnings of the defendant, or otherwise, than by the implied invitation of the defendant as alleged in plaintiff's complaint, and denies that the said John Troglio had been repeatedly driven therefrom, and denies that the defendant used every means possible, or reasonable means, or any means at all, for preventing the use of the said artificial pond and reservoir for swimming and bathing purposes.

IV.

Replying to the seventh paragraph of defendant's answer, this plaintiff denies that the defendant did forbid the use of said artificial dam and reservoir for swimming and bathing purposes, and denies that he did order plaintiff's minor son, John Troglio, and his playmates and companions from said dam and reservoir and from the premises of the defendant.

V.

Replying to the 8th paragraph of ~~the~~ defendant's answer, this plaintiff denies that the defendant guarded the said dam or reservoir, and denies that the said John Troglio did trespass thereon, but avers that the said John Troglio was lawfullly upon the premises of the defendant at the times alleges in the complaint of plaintiff by and through the implied invitation of the defendant.

VI.

Replying to the 12th paragraph of defendant's answer, this plaintiff denies that he was guilty of carelessness or negligence in not forbidding the said John Troglio from exposing himself to the dangers attendant upon going in swimming or using the said artificial pond or reservoir for swimming or bathing purposes, and denies that this plaintiff carelessly or negligently permitted his said son, John Troglio, to enter upon said premises of the said defendant and swim in the said artificial pond or lake, and denies that plaintiff by the exercise of ordinary care or any care could have prevented the said John Troglio from drowning therein, and denies that this plaintiff by the exercise of ordinary care or diligence, or any care or diligence at all, could or would have known that his said minor son would not have happened in said artificial dam or reservoir if this plaintiff had used ordinary care and diligence to prevent his said son from swimming or bathing therein, and denies that plaintiff contributed in any degree to the injury or death of his said child, and denies that plaintiff became or was in pari delicto in any degree whatsoever by reason of any carless or negligent acts upon his part, ~~are~~ or at all, and alleges that the death of his said minor son was proximately caused as alleged in his complaint.

WHEREFORE, plaintiff having fully replied to the answer of the defendant on file herein prays judgment according to his complaint.

Attorneys for Plaintiff.

Duly verified.

(TITLE OF COURT AND CAUSE.)

Friday, November 21st, 1919.
Before Hon. G. M. Bourquin, Judge, and a Jury.

Appearances:

For Plaintiff,
WALKER & WAGNER.
For Defendant,
KREMER, SANDERS & KREMER.

TRANSCRIPT OF TESTIMONY.

G. H. MACDOUGALL, Reporter.

Be it remembered that this cause came regularly on for hearing before the above entiled court of Friday, Nov. 21st, 1919, before Hon. G. M. Bourquin, Judge of said court; the plaintiff being present in person and by counsel, Walker, Walker, [redacted]r & Wagner, Esq. The defendant being present by counsel, Kremer, Sanders & Kremer, Esqs. Whereupon a jury having been duly impanneled and sworn to try the cause the following proceedings were had to-wit:

By the consent, and by permission of the court, the first paragraph of plaintiff's complaint was amended by inserting the words "Arizona," instead of "Montana," on the fourth line thereof.

MARTIN TROGLIO,

Plaintiff, after being duly sworn in his own behalf, testified as follows:

DIRECT EXAMINATION.

BY MR. WAGNER:

Q. State your name, age and residence to the stenographer.

A. Martin Troglio, Meaderville, Montana, 8 Webster street.

Q. You are the plaintiff in this action, are you?

MR. SANDERS: If your Honor please, at this time the defendant desires to object to any testimony in the case in support of the allegations of the complaint, on the following grounds and for the following reasons, to-wit:

That the complaint does not state facts sufficient to constitute a cause of action, nor does it state actionable negligence against the defendant. That the artificial dam and reservoir mentioned in plaintiff's complaint was not such an attractive nuisance or alluring attraction as to bring it within the rule that renders a person liable to children of tender years, or to the plaintiff in this case for maintaining such dam and reservoir as charged in plaintiff's complaint as being an attractive nuisance; that the defendant was not guilty of actionable negligence in maintaining the same unenclosed by a fence or other barrier, or for suffering or permitting the same to remain open or exposed without watchmen or persons to warn minor children, or particularly plaintiff's minor son, against trespassing at, near or in the same. That the artificial dam or reservoir mentioned in plaintiff's complaint was not such a dangerous instrumentality as comes within the doctrine of attractive nuisances, whereby children of tender years are allured thereto to their injury or death.

The attorneys for both sides agree that if this complaint does not state facts sufficient to constitute a cause of action as an attractive nuisance, a complaint can not be drawn referring to reservoirs which does. It seems to me it would be well to discuss the law.

THE COURT: No; I will overrule the objection at present and we can take it up again.

To which ruling of the Court in overruling said objection, defendant, by counsel, then and there duly excepted.

Q. You are the plaintiff in the case?

A. Yes, sir.

Q. Did you know of the existence of the swimming pond which is mentioned in this complaint prior to the time your son was drowned in it?

A. I never went up there before and I never saw that dam before. Even at that day he was drowned I never went there.

Q. Your boy was drowned in that dam, was he?

A. He was drowned in the dam.

Q. Do you remember the date?

A. The date was the 13th of June, 1917.

Q. How old was your boy at that time?

A. Eleven years old.

Q. What was he doing then, going to school or what?

A. Well, he had just quit the school.

Q. Do you remember the day that school closed?

A. Well, I dont remember exactly; I think the school closed on the 10th of June.

Q. Do you know, and did you know at that time that your boy was going in swimming at this pond?

A. No, I never knowed he was going up there, for I never knowed the dam was built.

Q. What was your occupation at that time?

A. Well, I was sick; I could not work, and I was home; I was helping a fellow raise up the house, just showing him to raise up the house. I couldn't work no more and I was sick, and he came there and asked me to show him how to raise the house, and I was doing that.

Q. When did you first learn that your boy was drowned in the dam?

A. Well, they sent down a little kid, smaller than him to buy something in the store, and he came back with nothing, and he came back and says: "Papa, John is pretty near dead."

Q. Just tell when you learned about it; you learned about it shortly after the boy was drowned.

A. Yes, I just know about five o'clock in the evening.

Q. And you buried the boy, did you; you had a funeral, did you?

A. Yes, I had a funeral.

Q. Do you recall what it cost you to bury the boy?

A. It cost me about five hundred dollars or more.

Q. That was the charge that was made for the funeral services was it?

A. Well, I didn't pay all the funeral expenses myself; the older boy is in the mine; he was doing the paying.

Cross-examination waived.

Witness excused.

JOSEPH BERTOGLIO,

A witness for plaintiff, after being duly sworn, testified as follows:

DIRECT EXAMINATION.

BY MR. WAGNER:

Q. State your name, age and residence to the stenographer.

A. Joseph Bertoglio, 63 Ella street; age fifteen.

Q. Did you know the little Troglio boy?

A. Yes, sir.

Q. The one that was drowned in the dam?

A. Yes, sir.

Q. Were you present at the time that he was drowned?

A yes sir.

Q. Now, just state to the Court and jury what happened.

A. Well, we were there going in swimming, and

we got out, and me and another boy—another of my playmates were dressing up, and all of a sudden we heard two of them calling for help, and we went to get the one that was closest, and before we had time to get him he was down already.

Q. How long were you there that day?

A. Just about half an hour.

Q. Do you know how long John Troglio had been in swimming before he drowned?

A. No, sir.

Q. How long had you seen him there?

A. As soon as I came from school I went there. They did not go to school that day.

Q. You saw John's body sink in the water, did you?

A. Yes, sir.

Q. Did he say anything before he drowned?

A. Just hollered twice: "Help".

Q. Who else was in the dam at the time?

A. Well, that other boy that was drowned in there; they were the only two.

Q. How many boys were in swimming there that day?

A well I don't know

Q. Can you estimate how many boys were in there?

A. Eleven or twelve.

Q. Had you been in swimming yourself?

A. Yes, sir.

Q. How many times had you been in swimming there before that time?

A. That season?

Q. How many boys had you seen in swimming in there?

A. Oh, pretty many.

Q. That season, yes.

A. I had been there two times before.

Q. Was there a watchman or a boss around there?

A. There was just a pumpman there.

Q. Was anybody in charge of the dam?

A. I don't know.

Q. What was the closest place where an employe of the Butte & Superior was?

A. Well, in the pump room.

Q. How far is that from the dam?

A. Fifteen or twenty yards.

Q. Did that man ever protest against the boys swimming in the dam?

A. Not while I was there.

MR. KREMER: That is objected to on the ground that it is negative testimony.

Which objection was by the Court overruled.

To which ruling of the Court in overruling said objection, defendant, by counsel, then and there duly excepted.

Q. Did the watchman there at the station consent to the boys going in swimming?

A. He never said nothing.

MR. KREMER: That is objected to as calling for a conclusion.

THE COURT: The objection is overruled. The

answer that he already made manifested that he understood the question.

Q. What did the boys usually do when they went in swimming there?

MR. SANDERS: That is objected to as assuming a state of facts not shown. There is no testimony that they usually went in swimming.

Which obection was by the Court overruled.

To which ruling of the Court in overruling said objection, defendant, by counsel, then and there duly excepted.

MR. SANDERS: For the preservation of the record we also desire to object to any testimony tending to establish the fact that boys congregated at or near the reservoir or ever entered it, as incompentent, irrelevant and immaterial under the allegations of this complaint, for the reason that the artificial dam and reservoir was not such an attractive nuisance at to bring it within the rules which render a person liable to children of tender years or to the plaintiff in this case for maintaining the dam as an attractive nuisance.

Which objection was by the Court overruled.

To which ruling of the Court in overruling said objection, defendant, by counsel, then and there duly excepted.

A. They just swim around, and sometimes I have seen them when they used to be cold, they used to go in and get warm in the pump room.

Q. Did the watchman or the man in charge of the pump station there know that the boys went in swimming?

A. Yes, sir.

Q. Did he ever protest against it?

A. No, sir.

Q. I will ask you to state if it is not a fact that the boys who went in swimming in that pond frequently went to the pump station to get warm while they were disrobed?

MR. SANDERS: That is objected to on the ground that it is leading.

THE COURT: The objection is sustained. He has already answered that they did and that is enough, without repitition.

Q. Was there any enclosure around this pond?

A. No, sir.

Q. Was it near a public highway?

MR. SANDERS: We object to this character of testimony with respect to an enclosure or fence for the reason that, in view o fthe character of the alleged attractive nuisance, the same being a reservoir, that there was no legal duty imosed by the law upon the defendant o close the reservoir by a fence, or to refrain from permitting it to remain open or unenclosed, nor was there a duty devolved by law on the defendant to maintain a watchman to prevent minor children or the deceased son of the plaintiff herein fro mentering the reservoir for the purpose of swimming or otherwise.

THE COURT: All those matters will be determined from all the testimony and evidence in the case. At this time the objection is overruled.

To which ruling of the Court in overruling said objection, defendant, by counsel, then and there duly excepted.

A. Yes, sir.

Q. How far was the public road from this dam or reservoir?

MR. SANDERS: That is objected to on the ground that it is incompetent, irrelevant and immaterial.

Which objection was by the Court overruled.

To which ruling of the Court in overruling said objection, defendant, by counsel, then and there duly excepted.

A. In one place it was about ten yards, probably out where the stream was coming in; and if you go down closer it was about fifteen.

Q. Do you know whether or not that public road was travelled very much?

A. No, sir.

Q. Where did the public road lead to?

A. It led up to just a few mines that was up there.

Q. Please mention the points and the places that this highway led to.

MR. SANDERS That is objected to on the ground that it is immaterial. It is not a proximate cause or a proximate issue in this case, the presence or absence of a public road.

Which objection was by the Court overruled.

To which ruling of the Court in overruling said objection, defendant, by counsel, then and there duly excepted.

A. It led to the Butte & Bacorn min, and to the Butte & Great Falls, and a ranch.

Q. How frequently during 1918, prior to the 13th of June, did the boys go swimming there?

MR. SANDERS: To which we object on the ground that there was no duty that devolved upon the defendant in this case to protect the pond from intrusion by boys, nor was this such an attractive nuisance as comes within the law as to attractive nuisances. With the understanding and consent of counsel, we will refrain from further objections, and may it be inserted in the record that all this line of testimony is deemed introduced over this objection?

THE COURT: If there is no duty, and none is proven, your case is won without a single objection. You may put in as many as you please or desire. The objection is overruled.

To which ruling of the Court, in overruling said objection, defendant, by counsel, then and there duly excepted.

A. That season they had started going there about two weeks. Some kids were going there two weeks already.

Q. Do you know whether the boys that went swimming there were forbidden to swim in the pond?

A. No, sir.

MR. SANDERS: That is objected to on the ground that it is repittion.

THE COURT: Well, I don't know. He spoke of the pumpman and no one else. The answer may stand.

To which ruling of the Court in overruling said objection, defendant, by counsel, then and there duly excepted.

Q. Did the watchman at the pump station permit the boys to go in swimming there?

MR. SANDERS: That is objected to on the ground that it is repitition.

Which objection was by the Court sustained.

To which ruling of the Court in sustaining said objection, by counsel, then and there duly excepted.

CROSS EXAMINATION.

BY MR. KREMER:

Q. How many times had you been there before the 13th of June with young Troglio, the boy that was drowned?

A. Twice.

Q. Was he an intelligent boy?

Q. In what grade was he at school?

A. I don't know.

Q. Could he read, do you know?

A. I think he did.

Q. Did you see signs there?

A. Yes, sir.

Q. Just tell the jury what kind of signs they were and what was upon the signs?

A. One sign there was "No trespassing," and the other one was "Private Property," and the other one was "Ten feet deep; keep off."

Q. And you saw the Troglio boy drown, did you not?

Q. How far did drown from the place where this sign was "Danger, ten feet deep; keep out."?

A. I don't know.

Q. Well, do you know where the sign was?

A. Well, I don't remember exactly now.

Q. Can you tell us about how far it was; just your best judgment; how many feet?

A. I don't know.

Q. Ten feet?

A. I don't know.

Q. Well, I don't want to argue with you, but was it closer to ten or fifteen feet where this sign was?

A. Well, it was just about fifteen or sixteen feet.

Q. And you had been swimming in there, in that deep water?

A. Yes, sir.

Q. And you had been swimming that day with young Troglio?

A. Yes, sir.

Q. Could he swim?

A. Yes, sir.

Q. He was a fairly good swimmer, was he not?

A. Well; he could swim.

Q. Had you boys been driven off of there that day?

A. No, sir.

Q. Now, do you remember a raft that somebody built and put on that pond?

A. Well, I remember the raft, yes, sir.

Q. Do you remember who broke it up?

A. No, sir.

Q. You know it was broken up, dont you?

A. No, sir.

Q. Didn't you see the broken raft lying there on the side of the bank?

A. No, sir.

Q. Just tell us what day—you say you had been there twice before this day during that year?

A. Yes, sir.

Q. And how many days before the 13th was the day that you made your last visit before this day that the boy was drowned?

A. I went there twice after school.

Q. And about how far apart were those visits?

A. I don't know.

Q. Was Troglia there both days?

A. I just saw him the last day.

Q. How do you know that boys had been going there for two weeks before this day, if you had only been up there twice?

A. Because the boys told me they were going swimming.

Q. Just what the boys told you. Just tell us what you know yourself, Joseph. Now, do you remember the sheriff going down there?

A. Yes, sir.

Q. And running everybody out of there?

A. He didn't run them out of there; he just told them to wear tights.

Q. The sheriff told them to wear tights?

A. Yes, sir.

Q. Do you know Mr. Melia?

A. No, sir.

Q. He was the man that came there.

A. No; Mr. Borich came there.

Q. Borich and Melia both came there?

A. No; they told us we had to wear tights when we went in swimming.

Q. You were there when they were there?

A. Yes; that was the season before.

Q. It was not this season?

A. No, sir.

Q. As a matter of fact, the season before the place was nothing like the condition it is in today or was in 1918?

A. No, sir.

Q. The condition is entirely different there?

A. Yes, sir.

Q. Between 1917 and 1918 the whole dam had been built there, had it not?

A. Yes, sir.

Q. And the whole condition had been changed.

A. Yes, sir.

Q. It was in the spring, wasn't it, that they built that dam, the spring of 1918

?A. Well, I don't know when they built it.

Q. But it was after the swimming season, as you boys call it, the summer time

A. The season before that they had started to build it already.

Q. But the water was nothing like it was on the 13th of June, 1918?

A. No, sir.

Q. Just describe those signs to the jury; were they on signs painted upon white boards in big, black letters?

A. Yes, sir.

Q. All of them?

A. Yes, sir.

Q. There was one over by the pump house, wasn't there? Q There was on by the dam

a. yes sir.

A. Yes, sir.

And there was one out in the stream there, where you said it was within fifteen or sixteen feet of where Troglio was drowned, which said "Danger; ten feet deep; keep out."?

A. Yes, sir.

Q. There was another down at the dam where the water came in?

A. Yes, sir.

Q. And then there was another away over on the bank on the other side of the dam?

A. That is all I can remember, is four.

Q. Five?

A. Four.

Q. You do remember four, but you can't remember more?

A. Yes, sir.

RE-DIRECT EXAMINATION.

BY MR. WAGNER:

Q. The boys didn't pay any attention to the signs, did they?

A. ~~Yes~~ No, sir.

Q. They went in swimming, anyway?

A. Yes, sir.

MR. SANDERS: That is objected to on the ground that it is leading.

Which objection was by the Court sustained.

To which ruling of the Court in sustaining said obection, plaintiff, by counsel, then and there duly excepted.

Q. The watchman at the pump house never objected to you boys going in swimming?

MR. SANDERS: That is objected to on the ground that it is repetition.

Which objection was by the Court sustained.

To which ruling of the Court in sustaining said objection, palintiff, by counsel, then and there duly excepted.

Witness excused.

ANTONE DONETTI,

A witness for plaintiff, after being duly sworn, testified as follows:

DIRECT EXAMINATION.

BY MR. FRANK WALKER:

Q. What is your name?

A. Antone Donetti.

. Where do you live?

A. 59 Front street, Meaderville.

Q. You attend school do you?

A. Yes, sir.

Q. Where?

A. Butte Business College.

Q. Did you know John Troglio in his lifetime?

A. Yes, sir.

Q. Did you know him on or about the 13th of June, 1918?

A. Yes, sir.

Q. How old was he at that time?

A. Eleven.

Q. Did you go to the same school with him or not?

A. Yes, sir, at that time.

Q. Were you in the same grade?

A. No, sir; I was in a grade ahead of him, I think.

Q. What grade was he in, do you know?

A. He was passed in the seventh.

Q. And he was then eleven years of age?

A. Yes, sir.

Q. What school was this, Antone?

A. The Franklin school.

Q. That is one of the public schools of the county of Silver Bow, state of Montana?

Q. Yes, sir.

Q. When you say he was past the seventh; what do you mean by that; that he was entering into the eighth grade?

A. No, sir; he was going from the sixth to the seventh.

Q. When was it that he had passed from the sixth grade into the seventh?

A. It was some time in June; I think it was the 13th, that same day that he was drowned.

Q. He had passed his grade that same day?

A. Yes, sir; I am not sure what day.

Q. The 13th day of June was the last day of school for that season?

A. Yes, sir; it was on a Friday, I think.

Q. You were in the grade above him?

A. Yes, sir.

Q. Had you ever been in any of the same classes with him at all?

A. No, sir.

Q. What have you to say, Antone, with reference to whether or not John Troglio was a bright boy or otherwise.

A. Well, he was bright, for he was eleven years, and in the seventh grade.

Q. What have you to say with reference to his physical condition for a boy of eleven years?

A. Well, he was not very tall, but he was strong and husky.

Q. Did yo u)ake part in any athletics with him at all?

A. No, sir.

Q. Do you know whether or not he took part in any?

A. Well, he was in the races at the school.

Q. He used to indulge in races at the school?

A. Yes, sir.

Q. Was he or was he not as well proportioned as the average boy of eleven years who attended the Franklin school with him?

A. Yes, sir, and a little bit better.

Q. What have you to say with reference as to whether or not he was as bright as the average boy of eleven years in the county of Silver Bow, state of Montana?

A. Yes, he was as bright as any of them.

Q. Do you know where this artificial pond or dam is located that belongs to the Butte & Superior Mining Company?

A. Yes, sir.

Q. I will ask you whether or not you were around or about those premises on the 13th of June, 1918?

A. Yes, sir, I was there when he drowned.

Q. Did you see John Troglio there?

A. Yes, sir.

Q. Were you there when John Troglio came up on the scene?

A. No sir; he was there before I was.

Q. What was John doing when you came upon the scene?

A. Well, he was playing with a little gun he had.

Q. Was he in the water at the time?

A. No, sir.

Q. Did you see John when he entered the water?

A. Yes, sir.

Q. Were you there when he undressed?

A. Yes, sir; he was undressed when I was there; that is, he had his shirt on, that is all.

Q. Did he remove his shirt before he went in the water?

A. Yes, sir.

Q. Did you see him do that?

A. Yes, sir.

Q. What part of the dam with reference to the directions, north and south and east and west, did he enter?

A. Well, he entered the eastern part of it, the shallow spot.

Q. He entered from the eastern shore?

A. Yes, sir.

Q. Was there any remark made to him by anybody at the time that he entered?

A. No, sir.

Q. I will ask you were you right near him at the time he entered the water?

A. Well, when he went in swimming I was about fifteen feet from him, facing the opposite way.

MR. KREMER: We have a map here.

MR. FRANK WALKER: It is satisfactory to the plaintiff that this map be admitted at this time, if it meets with the approval of the Court.

MR. KREMER: I think it will indicate the conditions very well.

Q. Did you go in the pond that day yourself?

A. Yes, sir.

Q. At what time with reference to when John Troglio went in?

A. It was about four o'clock; close to four o'clock the last time he went in.

You say that you were there when John went in?

A. Yes, sir, while I was there.

Q. Was that the first time, or did he go in and come out again?

A. I don't know whether it was the first time but while I was there it was the first time.

Q. That was the only time he went in while you were there?

A. Yes, sir.

Q. What time of the day was that?

A. That was close to four—about half past three, and then he went in again at the last.

Q. What time had school closed that day?

A. Ten-thirty, I think.

O. In the morning?

A. Yes, sir; it was the last day.

Q. I will ask you at what point John went into the pond with reference to this pump station or pump house referred to in the testimony?

A. Well, it was closer to the pump house where he went in; it was the eastern part, and the pump was southeast from the pond.

Q. Could you say, approximately, how far he was from the pump station when you saw him enter the pond?

A. Oh, just about twenty-five feet where he entered.

Q. Did you see him swim around the pond after he went in?

A. Yes, sir.

Q. I will ask you whether or not there was anything—any fence or any character or kind of abstruction to prevent John Troglio from entering the pond?

A. No, sir.

MR. SANDERS: We desire this line of testimony to go in under the same objection that we made to the former testimony, that it was not the duty of the defendant to provide any fence.

THE COURT: If you want to object to all the evidence, the objection is overruled.

To which ruling of the Court in overruling said objection, defendant, by counsel, then and there duly excepted.

Q. Is there any kind of enclosure about this dam?

A. No, sir; there was only a bank to hold the water, that is all.

Q. That was the only thing that surrounded it of any kind or character?

A. Yes, sir.

Q. Did you see any person, any man connected with the Butte & Superior Company, around or about the premises the day this accident happened?

A. Well, there was the pump man.

Q. Did you see him there that day?

A. Yes, sir.

Q. Did you see him there at the time John Troglio entered the pond or not?

A. Well, he came after he was drowned and tried to get him out.

Q. Did you see him before John drowned?

A. No, sir.

Q. How many times, if at all, had you been at this pond prior to June, 13th, 1918, and during this season?

A. Twice, I think; it was after school.

Q. When was it with reference to this day?

A. Well, between the first and the thirteenth.

Q. You were there twice before June 13th?

A. Yes, sir.

Q. Or was it twice including June 13th?

A. No, this was the third time.

Q. On the other two occasions had you seen any boys in the water there?

A. Well, there was two boys with me; we just went there to take a bath, about ten or fifteen minutes.

Q. Did you see the pump man there on either of those occasions?

A. No, sir.

Q. Did you ever see the pump man there at any time when you went in the pond or enclosure?

A. Only the day of the drowning.

Q. Were you up around the pond at any time other than these two times that you testified that you went into the dam?

A. Well, I just passed there on a bicycle; I never stopped there.

Q. During the month of June?

A. Yes, sir.

Q. Did you see any boys in there as you passed?

A. No, sir; this was about five o'clock in the evening.

Q. And there was nobody there?

A. No, sir.

Q. Do you know where this highway is, the public highway near the pond and west or northwest of the pond?

A. No, it is west; northwest; it is right near the house, Folger's house.

Q. Have you ever seen any person or persons use that road during the month of June, 1918?

A. Yes, sir.

Q. I will ask you whether there were many persons or few who used that road?

A. It was just an automobile that I saw, and a few grocery wagons.

Q. I will ask you if there any house in the immediate vicinity of this highway?

A. Yes, sir; there is six or seven houses.

Q. Where were you at the time that John Troglio sank?

A. Well, I was right on the embankment, facing the opposite way.

Q. Did you see him at any time immediately prior to his drowning?

A. Well, I saw him—I went after one boy, I and another boy, and when I got out I seen him just go down; that is all I saw.

THE COURT: I don't imagine there is any dispute about this drowning having occurred?

MR. WALKER: I take it, your Honor, that the map is introduced in evidence.

THE COURT: Yes.

Q. Will you take your pencil and mark the point about where John Troglio was situated at the time that he was drowned in the pond.

A. It was about up here.

Q. Put an A there.

(Witness marks the letter A on the map).

Q. Do you know how deep the water of the pond was at about that place?

A. Well, close to eight feet, I guess, or more.

Q. Do you know how tall John Troglio was on the 13th of June, 1918?

A. About four feet, six.

Q. About how many boys were in swimming in this pond on the 13th of June, 1918?

A. Oh, about twelve or fourteen.

Q. I will ask you whether or not the boys were quiet or whether or not they were making any noise, shouting or playing or calling?

A. Well, they were not making much noise; those in the water, they would holler once in a while, playing around.

Q. I will ask you whether or not they hollered to each other?

A. No, sir.

Q. Did you hear any calling of one boy to another or any laughter or anything?

A. No, sir.

Q. You went there on three occasions during the month of June, 1918, you say?

A. Yes, sir.

Q. Did anybody on any of those occasions forbid you from going on the premises?

A. No, sir.

CROSS EXAMINATION.

BY MR. KREMER:

Q. You say that John Troglio went in twenty-five feet from the pump house?

A. Yes, sir.

Q. How deep was the water there?

A. Well, about eight feet, I guess.

Q. What did he do, dive in?

A. No; he just walked out till it got deeper than he swam out.

Q. He was a good swimmer, was he?

A. Yes, sir, for his size he was a good swimmer.

Q. And you had been swimming with him twice before that?

A. Not with him; it was the first time I was with him.

Q. Wasn't he there when you were there?

A. No, sir.

Q. You went there, then, with the Bertoglio boy who just left the stand?

A. No; I was there the day he drowned, but not the other times.

Q. I meant upon the other occasions?

A. No, sir.

Q. You say he was drowned right where this mark of "A" is made or just about there?

A. Yes, sir.

Q. Now, isn't that just about exactly the place where that sign is that reads: "Danger, keep out; ten feet deep"?

A. No, the sign is on the opposite side of the gate.

Q. Isn't that sign right there?

A. No, sir; there is no sign in the water; the sign is on the embankment.

Q. Sure of that?

A. Yes, sir; the sign is away outside of the water on each side of it, but not in the water.

Q. How many signs do you remember there?

A. Four or five.

Q. Can you tell us where they are?

A. Well, there is one: "No trespassing," right on the dam there.

Q. Here?

A. Yes, sir.

Q. And this other one right close to the gate there?

A. Right about here.

Q. Then there is two: "Ten feet deep," on each side, and down here do you remember one down here?

A. Yes, I believe there was one on the upper side there.

Q. In fact, there were signs all around you?

A. There are four or five, I am sure.

Q. And it would be impossible for a boy to go up there and go in swimming in that pond without seeing those signs, wouldn't it?

A. Well, I don't know; they could see them, all right, because they ought to see one of them.

Q. And you are sure that John Troglio saw the sign, are you?

A. Well, I don't know if he saw it or not. He never said anything about it, but he was supposed to see it; he passed there.

Q. He went in right there by the sign, didn't he?

A. Yes; I don't think he paid any attention to them.

Q. You don't think he paid any attention to the signs?

A. None of the boys did.

Q. They knew they were there?

A. Yes, sir.

Q. You knew they were there?

A. Yes, sir.

Q. You paid no attention to them?

A. Oh, well, I read them once in a while.

Q. You know that John Troglio could read, don't you?

A. Yes, sir.

Q. He was a bright boy, you say?

A. Yes, sir.

Q. How long had you been there before he was drowned?

A. You mean that same day?

Q. Yes.

A. I came there about two-thirty.

Q. And he was drowned about what time?

A. About four.

Q. Had he been going in and out of the water?

A. Yes; he would go in for ten minutes at a time, or fifteen and then come out.

Q. He had been swimming there for a couple of hours?

A. Yes, sir.

Q. Did you tell me whether he was a good swimmer or not; you said he was good for his size?

A. Yes, sir.

Q. Did he dive into the deep water?

A. No, sir; he would just go out where it is shallow and swim out to the deep, and then swim back again.

Q. You saw him swimming there in the deep water, and you did not see any difficulty in his swimming, did you?

A. No, sir.

Q. He was considered as good a swimmer as the rest of the boys, wasn't he?

A. Not quite, but he was a good swimmer.

WITNESS EXCUSED.

HUGO GIACHETTI, a witness for plaintiff, after bein gduly sworn, testified as follows:

DIRECT EXAMINATION.

BY MR. WALKER:

Q. What is your name?

A. Hugo Giachetti.

Q. Where do you live?

A. 65 Atlantic street.

Q. You are attending school, are you?

A. Yes, sir.

Q. How old are you?

A. Fourteen.

Q. I will ask you if you knew John Troglio in his lifetime?

A. Yes, sir.

Q. You knew him on the 13th of June, 1918?

A. Yes, sir.

Q. Were you attending school with him that time or not?

A. Yes, sir.

Q. Did you attend the same school?

A. Yes, sir.

Q. Were you in the same grade?

A. Yes, sir.

Q. I will ask you whether or not you were around and about the pond, the artificial pond, that is maintained by the Butte & Superior north of Meaderville on the 13th of June, 1918?

A. I was there that day, but I was not there when he was drowned.

A. Had you been there prior to the 13th of June?

A. Yes, sir.

Q. How often prior to that?

A. Oh, once that day.

Q. How often prior to the 13th of June; how many times before that?

A. Two times.

Q. When was that?

A. That was on Saturday, and on Sunday, you know, we would go out and go swimming.

Q. And during the month of June you had been there twice before the 13th of June?

A. Yes, sir.

Q. Did you go in the water?

A. Yes, sir.

Q. Do you know where this pump station is near the pond?

A. Yes, sir.

Q. Do you know who maintains that?

A. The pump man.

MR. KREMER: The Butte & Superior maintains that pump station.

Q. Did you see the pumpman there at any time while you were in the water?

A. Yes, sir; he used to go in the pump room to go to work.

Q. Did yo u go into the pump room during the month of June, 1918, to get warm?

A. Yes, sir, on Sundays we used to go in and get warm, and also to see the funny papers.

Q. Can you say what the pump man was doing at those times?

A. He was attending to the engine, to the pumps.

Q. At the time that you went into the pump room were you dressed; did you have your clothes on or were you naked?

A. Naked.

Q. I will ask you whether or not you saw the pumpman at any time when you were in the water?

A. No, sir.

Q. Did you go immediately from the water to the pump room at any time during the month of June?

A. Yes, sir, on Sundays we used to go to see the funny pictures, and tried to get ahead of each other.

Q. How many of you were there that went in on the last occasion that you went into the pump room?

A. I don't know.

Q. The last time you went in there was prior to the 13th of June, 1918, wasn't it?

A. No, sir; it was the Sunday before.

Q. Do you know how many boys went into the pump room with you that day?

A. I don't know, sir.

Q. Were there more than one?

A. Yes, there was more than one; there was one looking at the funny pictures, and about two or three standing around to get next.

Q. What do you mean by getting next.

A. Next with the funny pictures.

Q. You mean taking your turns glancing at the papers?

A. Yes, sir.

Q. I will ask you whether or not, when you went into the pump room, immediately prior to June 13th, your body was wet or dry?

A. Wet.

Q. I will ask you what was the condition, if you

noticed of the bodies of the other boys with reference to being wet or dry?

A. The two that came in with me were wet, and the one that was looking at the funny pictures was dry.

Q. Did you have any conversation or did you hear any of the boys have a conversation with the pump man with reference to going from the pond or with reference to what you were doing or anything of that kind or character?

A. No, sir.

Q. Did the pumpman see you as you first came into the pump room?

A. Yes, sir.

Q. Did you boy sspeak to him at all?

A. Not while we were waiting for the funny pictures.

Q. Did you talk to him when you first came into the pump room?

A. No, si.r

Q. Did you say hello to him?

A. Oh, we said hello to him when he was through phoning. They phoned from the Superior down there to the pump room, and he came out and he said hello to these boys, and we answered him back and said hello.

Q. Where were you at that time?

A. We were just right in the door, and he got through phoning and he said hello, and we said hello, and that is all I said.

Q. That was immediately after you came from the pond?

A. Yes, sir.

Q. What have you to say with reference as to whether or not there was any barrier or fence at any point around or about this pond or artificial lake?

A. No, sir.

Q. Was there anything to hinder or keep a boy or anybody else from walking from the vicinity there right into the pond?

A. No, sir.

Q. Do you know where the public highway is located with reference to this pond?

A. Yes, sir.

Q. How far would you say it was located from the western or northern border of the pond?

A. Twenty-five to thirty feet.

Q. Did you see any person or persons using that road during the month of June, 1918?

A. Yes, sir.

Q. About how many people would you say that you sa wusing it?

A. Oh, there was a ranchman up there, and he used to always come down to Meaderville, and there was the boss that would be from the Bacorn with the automobile, he always used to come down there, too.

Q. In order to travel from Meaderville to the Butte& Bacorn mine I will ask you whether or not one had to use this highway?

A. Yes, sir.

Q. Did this serve as a highway to any other property except the Butte & Bacorn?

A. And the Butte & Great Falls.

Q. The Butte & Great Falls was away north and beyond the pond, was it?

A. Yes, sir.

Q. And did those persons travelling to the Butte & Great Falls use this highway as a means of traversing to that place?

A. Yes, sir.

Q. There are some houses, are there not, located in this immediate vincinity?

A. Yes, sir.

Q. Did you see John Troglio in the water on the 13th of June, 1918?

A. Yes, sir.

Q. Where were you when you last saw him?

A. I was on the bank.

Q. Had you been in the water this day yourself?

A. No, sir.

Q. Did you see John Troglio when he went into the water?

A. No, sir.

Q. You didn't observe that?

A. No, sir.

Q. Was there more than one watchman or pumpman at the same time at or about this pond during the month of June?

A. No, sir; there was just the pumpman.

Q. Did you ever see this pumpman or hear him converse with any of the boys at or near the pond during the month of June?

A. No, sir.

CROSS EXAMINATION.

BY MR. KREMER:

Q. This road leading up to the Great Falls and Bacorn was not traveled very much, was it; there was nobody working at the Great Falls in 1918, was there?

A. No, sir.

Q. And the only people at the Butte & Bacorn that used the road was the superintendent with the machine; the men went up on the track, didn't they?

A. Yes, sir.

Q. And that is about all it was used for, wasn't it?

A. Yes, sir.

Q. Do you remember the signs around that pond?

A. Yes, sir.

Q. How many do you remember?

A. Four or five.

Q. Will you tell the jury what was on those signs?

A. There was one: "No trespassing," and there was four: "Ten feet deep, keep off."

Q. Four of them?

A. Yes, sir.

Q. And you paid no attention to the signs?

A. No, sir.

Q. Was Troglio a good swimmer?

A. A good swimmer for his size.

Q. And he was pretty athletic, wasn't he, well developed?

A. Yes, sir.

Q. He was considered one of your strong boys in school, a good athlete?

A. Yes, sir.

Q. You were in the same room with him, so you heard him read?

A. Yes, sir.

Q. You know he could read?

A. Yes, sir.

Q. He was a bright boy?

A. Yes, sir.

Q. Do you know whether he saw these signs or not?

A. I don't know.

Q. Do you think it would be possible for a boy to go in swimming up there without seeing these signs?

A. No, sir.

Q. He was bound to see them?

A. Yes, sir.

Q. Now, on this Sunday when you were out there swimming, that was the Sunday before the 13th of June?

A. Yes, sir.

Q. What time was it when you went in that pond?

A. Two o'clock.

Q. Who was the man that was there?

A. I don't know.

Q. What kind of a looking man was he?

A. Skinny, and like an old man.

Q. Did he have a mustache?

A. No, sir.

Q. Asmooth face?

A. Yes, sir.

Q. A thin man?

A. Yes, sir.

Q. Do you know what they called him, his first name or any other name?

A. No, sir.

Q. Can you give us any other description than just a smooth faced, thin man; was he tall?

A. He was tall looking.

Q. Was he old or young?

A. Old.

Q. About how old?

A. About around the age of forty-five or forty-six.

Q. You went in there with the other boys; was Troglio with you?

A. No, sir.

Q. He was not there at all that Sunday?

A. No, sir.

Q. You never saw him in the pump house?

A. No, sir.

Q. And you had gone up there the day that he was there swimming and drowned, and then you went away?

A. I was not there at the moment he got drowned; I left about ten or fifteen minutes before he got drowned.

Q. And you saw him swimming out in the deep water?

A. No, sir.

Q. Where was he swimming when you were there, or was he swimming at all when you were there?

A. No, sir.

Q. He was out on the bank?

A. Yes, sir; he and I were playing with this cap gun that he had.

Q. But you had seen him swimming in the deep water before that?

A. No, sir.

Q. How did you know he could swim?

A. Well, the boys all told us that he could swim, and he used to runraces and everything.

Q. In the water?

A. Yes, and see how long he could stay under the water.

Q. He would see how long he could stay under the water?

A. Yes, sir.

Q. He was a fancy swimmer; by that I mean a swimmer that could do more than just go through the water?

A. Yes, sir.

Q. Did you ever see him make any high dives?

A. No, sir; he never used to dive.

Q. Do you know whether he was trying to stay under the water this day that you were there?

A. No, sir.

Q. Now, ho wmany houses are there?

A. Six or seven.

Q. Look at that map, and see if there are any other houses that are not shown on that map. There is the McLeod house right down here, isn't it?

A. Yes, sir.

Q. You know the McLeod house?

A. Yes, sir.

Q. And here is your pump station?

A. Yes, sir.

Q. Who lives here, do you know?

A. No, sir.

Q. Is that where the Allens live?

A. The Holters live down here, and the Allens live up there.

Q. That is all the houses about there; those three houses are the only ones that really are very close to the pond?

A. Yes, sir.

Q. Now, you went up there on those two occasions before the time that this Troglio boy was drowned?

A. Yes, sir.

Q. Who did you go with?

A. Myself and the boys that were up here before I was.

Q. Did I ask you whether Troglio was with you upon either one of those trips?

A. Yes sir. He was not with us either one of those trips.

RE-DIRECT EXAMINATION.

BY MR. WALKER:

Q. I will ask you did you see the watchman during any time of the year 1918 and prior to June 13th, talk to any of the boys as some of them were inswimming, and while he was at and near the pond?

A. No, sir.

Q. For the purpose of refreshing your memory I will ask you if the watchman of the Butte & Superior, or the pumpman, did not ask you why it was that he did not go in swimming?

A. Yes, sir.

MR. SANDERS: That is objected to on the ground that it is leading.

THE COURT: I think it is proper under the circumstances. The objection will be overruled.

To which ruling of the court in overruling said objection, defendant, by counsel, then and there duly excepted.

THE COURT: It is to direct his memory to the particular point. It is not very material otherwise.

A. Yes.

RE-CROSS EXAMINATION.

BY MR. KREMER:

Q. Was that the same watchman or pumpman?

A. Yes, sir.

Q. Was that that Sunday?

A. Yes, sir; he was with me that Sunday.

Q. It was the same Sunday that he spoke to your brother?

A. Yes, sir.

Q. It all happened that day?

A. Yes, sir.

Q. At the same time?

A. Yes, sir.

WITNESS EXCUSED.

THOMAS CIABATTARI, a witness for plaintiff, after being duly sworn, testified as follows:

DIRECT EXAMINATION.

BY MR. FRANK WALKER:

Q. Your name?

A. Thomas Ciabattari.

Q. How old are you?

A. Fourteen years old.

Q. Where do you live?

A. Meaderville.

Q. Do you go to school now?

A. Yes, sir.

Q. Did you know John Troglio in his lifetime?

A. Yes, sir.

Q. Did you know him on the 13th of June, 1918?

A. Yes, sir.

Q. Did you see him that day?

A. Yes, sir.

Q. I will ask you whether or not you have ever gone swimming in the pond known as the Butte & Superior pond north of Meaderville?

A. I did go swimming there.

Q. How many times did you go swimming there during the year 1918?

A. About two times.

Q. Was that before the 13th of June, 1918?

A. No.

Q. Do you remember the day that John was drowned?

A. Yes, sir.

Q. Was it before that time that you went in swimming there?

A. No, sir; it was after—I don't know what you mean.

Q. Was it afterwards that you went in?

A. Before he got drowned.

Q. Before he was drowned?

A. Yes, sir.

Q. How many boys went in with you?

A. I don't remember.

Q. Well, about how many; were there two or three or four or more?

A. About four or five.

Q. How many days before the 13th of June, before the day that John was drowned was it that you first went in during the season of 1918?

A. About once.

Q. What date was it, do you remember?

A. No, sir.

Q. Was it before or after the first of June?

A. Around the sixth of June I went.

Q. About a week before the 13th?

A. Yes, sir; and then I went the day he got drowned, but I came home about ten minutes before he got drowned.

Q. Did you know the pumpman that was in charge of the pump up there near the pond?

A. No, sir.

Q. Did you ever see him?

A. No, sir.

Q. Was John Troglio there with you the 7th of June?

A. Yes, sir—the 13th of June, you mean.

Q. The time before, was he there?

A. No, sir; I never seen him.

Q. Did you see him go into the water on the 13th of June?

A. No, sir.

Q. The day that he was drowned?

A. No, sir.

Q. Did you see him around there?

A. Yes, sir, he had a cap gun and we were playing with it.

Q. Was he dressed or undressed at that time?

A. He was undressed.

Q. How many boys were in the water when you left the pond?

A. About seven or eight.

Q. Did you know any of those boys?

A. Yes, sir.

Q. Some of them are the boys that have been on the witness stand?

A. Yes, sir.

Q. Did anybody connected with the Butte & Superior Mining Company, any pumpman or any watchman tell you not to go in the water that day?

A. No, sir.

Q. Did anybody tell you not to go into the water on the 7th or 6th of June, the time you went in before?

A. No, sir.

Q. I will ask you whether or not there was any fence or barrier to prevent you from going into the water?

A. No, sir; there was no fence there or nothing.

Q. Was there anything to prevent you from going into the water?

A. No, sir.

Q. Do you know where this road or highway is north and west of the Butte & Superior pond?

A. I think it is on the west of it.

Q. The road?

A. Yes, sir.

Q. Where does that road lead to, do you know?

A. The Butte & Superior mine, I think.

Q. Is that the same road that leads to the Butte & Bacorn?

A. Yes, the Butte & Bacorn; the same road goes right up to the Butte & Bacorn mine.

Q. This road that is north of the pond, where does that road lead to?

A. To the Butte & Superior mine.

Q. This road that is north of the pond, where does that road lead to?

A. To the Butte & Superior mine.

Q. You are sure of that?

A. Yes, sir.

MR. KREMER: He is right about that.

Q. And it also goes to the Butte & Bacorn?

A. Yes, sir—I mean it goes to the Butte & Bacorn mine.

Q. Does it go to the Butte & Superior?

A. I don't know. I meant to say it goes to the Butte & Bacorn.

Q. Did you ever see anybody on that road?

A. No, sir. There are some houses up there.

Q. Did you ever see anybody walking or driving on that road?

A. Yes, sir.

Q. How many people?

A. There was automobiles going up that road.

Q. Just automobiles, is that all?

A. And up on the side of the road there was roads leading off—away up around the houses.

Q. You left before John Troglio was drowned?

A. Yes, sir.

CROSS EXAMINATION.

BY MR. KREMER:

Q. The road to the Butte & Superior is the one that leads north; the Butte & Superior is far closer to town than the pond?

A. Yes, sir.

Q. You don't have to pass the pond to go to the Butte & Superior?

A. No, sir.

THE COURT: He corrected that and said he meant the Butte & Bacorn.

Q. Now, upon these two times that you went there before the 13th of June, who was with you?

A. Me and my brother Antone Ciabattari.

Q. Troglio wasn't with you?

A. No, sir.

Q. Just three of you in there swimming?

A. Yes, sir.

Q. You saw signs there, didn't you?

A. Yes, sir.

Q. You saw the signs there the day that the Troglio boy was drowned, didn't you?

A. Yes, sir.

Q. And what did the signs say?

A. "No trespassing" and "Danger, ten feet deep."

Q. How many of them, do you remember?

A. About four.

Q. And you paid no attention to the signs?

A. No, sir; I didn't understand the signs.

Q. You could read it where it said danger, ten feet deep and you couldn't understand it?

A. No, sir; I didn't even look at that.

Q. How do you know they were there?

A. That is what the boys would say.

Q. The boys said that they were there?

A. Yes, sir; well, I seen them, but I never used to read them.

RE-DIRECT EXAMINATION.

BY MR. FRANK WALKER:

Q. You didn't go into the water there on June 13th?

A. Yes, I went in about once or twice.

Q. Did you stay in very long?

A. About five or ten minutes.

Q. Why was it you came out then?

A. I came out.

Q. You came out right after you were in five or ten minutes?

A. Yes, sir.

Q. What was your reason for that?

A. I wanted to go and play.

Q. I will ask you whether or not this water was warm or cold?

A. It was kind of warm.

WITNESS EXCUSED.

Adjourned until Saturday morning at 9:30 A. M.

Saturday, Nov. 22nd, 1919, 9:30 A. M.

JOSEPH DARIN, a witness for plaintiff, after being duly sworn, testified as follows:

DIRECT EXAMINATION.

BY MR. FRANK WALKER:

Q. State your name.

A. Joseph Darin.

Q. What is your age?

A. Thirteen.

Q. Where do you live?

A. 69 Main street, Meaderville.

Q. Did you know young John Troglio in his lifetime?

A. Yes, sir.

Q. Do you know the artificial pond or reservoir as it is called here, which is located north or northeast of Meaderville?

A. Yes, sir.

Q. Did you ever go swimming in that pond prior to the 13th of June, 1918?

A. Yes, sir.

Q. How many times?

A. Once before that.

Q. When was that?

A. On the Sunday.

Q. The Sunday prior to the 13th of June?

A. Yes, sir.

Q. Is that the only other time that you had been in there?

A. Before he was drowned.

Q. Were you in there the year prior?

A. Yes, sir.

Q. How many times were you in there swimming the year prior?

MR. KREMER: That is objected to as incompetent. The condition is shown to have been changed entirely from the year before.

THE COURT: He may answer. I doubt if it is immaterial, but it may show that it is a place of common resort. Objection overruled.

To which ruling of the court in overruling said objection, defendant, by counsel, then and there duly excepted.

Q. Were you there during the year 1917?

A. Yes, sir; the year 1918.

Q. Were you there during the year 1917, the year prior to the year that John Troglio was drowned?

A. Yes, sir.

Q. How many times were you there during the year 1917?

A. Sometimes I would go there two times a day.

Q. Beginning what month in the year 1917?

A. I don't know.

Q. Were you there before school closed?

A. Yes, sir, in the night; many times I went there before the school closed.

Q. In 1917?

A. Yes, sir.

Q. And the school closed in the month of June, 1917, did it not?

A. Yes, sir.

Q. Were you there during the months of July and August or during the months of vacation?

A. During the months of vacation I was there.

Q. Was there any watchman or pumpman in the vicinity?

A. There was a pumpman in the pump station there.

Q. Did the watchman or the pumpman object to you boys going in swimming?

MR. KREMER: All this in 1917?

MR. WALKER: Yes.

MR. KREMER: We renew the objection as to what might or might not have been said or done by the pumpman or watchman in 1917, on the ground that it was the dam or pond referred to the compaint.

THE COURT: I think he may answer. Objection overruled.

To which ruling of the Court in overruling said objection, defendant, by counsel, then and there duly excepted.

A. Yes, sir. He did not tell us anything.

Q. Was the watchman about the premises at any time when you boys were in swimming?

A. Yes, sir.

Q. Did he see you while you were in swimming.

A. He did see us in there many times.

Q. What was the condition of this pond or dam, Joseph, in 1917 as compared with 1918; was there any material difference in the pond?

A. No, sir. They had made a new bank there to hold back the water.

Q. About how deep was the water in the immediate vicinity of the dam in 1917?

A. Oh, about six or seven feet?

Q. Was it the same in 1918 or different?

A. Different; it was deeper in 1918.

Q. Were there other boys with you when you were in swimming in 1917?

A. Yes, sir.

Q. About how many?

A. Oh, about six or seven.

Q. Did you boys play in the water when you were in the water?

A. Yes, sir.

Q. Did you call or shout at each other in playing your games?

A. We hollered to each other many times.

Q. Now, there is a road or highway near this point, is there not?

A. Yes, sir.

Q. And about how far from the western or northern border of the pond is this road?

other place it is right up to the bank, a few yards

A. Well, one place it is about fifteen feet, and the away from it.

Q. Is that road used by the people or is it used by automobiles or wagons?

A. Well, it is used by some automobiles, and the ranchers there, and there is a few houses there, and sometimes people walk on that road.

Q. To what point does that road lead?

A. To the Butte & Bacorn, up to the junction.

Q. Have you seen people passing over that road during 1917 and 1918?

A. I have seen some automobiles passing and wagons.

Q. Did you ever see any people walking on the road?

A. The ones that live in the houses.

Q. Now, during the year 1917 was there any fence or barrier around or about the borders or edge of this road?

A. No, sir.

Q. During the year 1918, Joseph, was there any fence or barrier or anything that would impede or stop one from going into the water?

A. No, sir.

Q. You were in the pond on the Sunday prior to June 13th, you say?

A. Yes, sir.

Q. Were you at any time during the year 1918 in the pump room?

A. Yes, sir.

Q. When and on what day?

A. Well, I cant tell you the date, but I was in there many times.

Q. Prior to June 13th the day John was drowned?

A. I wasn't in that day.

Q. Was it before that?

A. Yes, sir; that Sunday, I went in then.

Q. And when you went into the pump room were you dressed in your clothes, your suit and stockings and shoes, or were you naked?

A. I was dressed that time. I didn't go in that day.

Q. Was there any boys up there with you that day?

A. Yes, sir.

Q. Were they also in the pump room? A. Yes sir.

Q. How were they dressed?

A. They were dressed; there was only two of them there naked looking at the funny pictures.

Q. Who were those boys that were naked?

A. Well, I don't remember who they were.

Q. Did you see those boys go into the pump room?

A. Yes, sir.

Q. Were their bodies dry or wet?

A. Well, their bodies were dry, because they were in there looking at the paper. This man came in, and their bodies were dry then.

Q. Did you notice them as they came into the pump room, Joseph?

A. Yes, sir.

Q. What was the condition of their bodies then as to being dry or wet?

A. Well, they was wet when they came in; they just came out.

Q. Where was the pump man when they came in?

A. He was up back there; he seen us coming in. He was there, sitting down, reading the paper.

Q. Was he talking to any of you boys immediately after you came in or not?

A. He said hello to us, that is all.

Q. That was the only conversation that you had with the pump man?

A. Yes, sir.

Q. Were you there at this pond or dam on the 13th of June?

A. I was there, yes, sir, just before he got drowned.

Q. Were you there at the time that John Troglio ~~went away~~. was drowned

A. No; he was just going in the water when I ~~was drowned?~~ went away

Q. Do you know where the pump man was at the time that John Troglio went in the water?

A. When he went into the water the pump man was in the station there.

Q. Were you present at the time that John went into the pond?

A. Yes, sir.

A. How many boys were around and about the pond at that time?

A. Oh, there was about thirteen or fourteen boys.

Q. I will ask you what the boys were doing?

A. Well, there was some just come out of the water, and some going in and some going home with me.

Q. Were they playing any games in the water?

A. Well, just swimming around, that is all.

Q. Were they shouting and calling to each other?

A. They would shout, sure.

Q. And from the place that these boys were playing swimming how far is it to the pump house?

A. About seven or eight yards.

Q. Do you know whether or not the doors or the windows of the pump house were open or closed on the 13th of June?

A. Well, I know the door was open when I went by there.

Q. You were sure of that?

A. Yes, sir.

Q. You says there were several boys in the water this day?

A. Yes, sir.

CROSS EXAMINATION.

BY MR. KREMER:

Q. Did you see those signs up there?

A. Yes, sir.

Q. What was on the signs?

A. One says: "No trespassing," and there was three other, "Ten feet dep, keep away."

Q. Ten feet deep, keep out, danger?

A. There was a danger sign, yes, sir.

Q. Where were these signs?

A. There was one right there on the bank which said "No trespassing," and there were the other ones around the bank: "Ten feet deep, keep away."

Q. Where were the rest of them?

A. There was three of them around the dam, "Ten feet deep, keep away," and there was only one there that did not say ten feet, and it said: "No trespassing."

Q. Do you know what that meant?

A. Yes, sir.

Q. What did it mean?

A. Not to walk around there.

Q. So the signs ten feet deep, keep out meant that you must not walk around the pond?

A. The signs ten feet deep, keep out; danger, meant to keep away from there.

Q. Danger of what?

. "Danger, ten feet deep, keep away."

Q. Keep out out of the pond; you knew what that meant, didn't you?

A. Yes, sir.

Q. Did you keep out?

Q. No, sir.

Q. John Troglio was there with you on this Sunday, was he?

A. No, sir.

Q. But you went up there with him on the day that he was drowned?

A. I was not with him; he was just going in. He was there undressing to go in when I was coming home.

Q. Did you ever see him up there before?

A. Yes, sir.

Q. How many times during the year 1918?

A. Twice.

Q. Was he a good swimmer?

A. For his size he was.

Q. Was he as good a swimmer as you are?

A. Yes, better.

Q. Can you swim?

A. No, sir, not very good.

Q. And was he a strong, healthy, robust boy?

A. Healthy and strong for his size.

Q. How big was he?

A. Well, he is as big as I am.

Q. He was as big as you are now?

A. Yes, sir.

Q. Was he a bright boy?

A. Yes, sir.

Q. Did you go to the same school with him him?

A. Yes, sir.

Q. Were you in the same room?

A. No, sir.

Q. Was he behind you or ahead of you?

A. Two grades ahead of me.

Q. How old was he?

A. Eleven years old.

Q. And you are now thirteen?

A. Yes, sir.

Q. You were really older than he was?

A. Yes, sir.

Q. And he was two grades ahead of you?

A. Yes, sir.

Q. You know he could read, dont you?

A. Yes, sir.

Q. It would be impossible for a boy to go up there to go in swimming in that pond without seeing these signs, wouldn't it?

A. No, sir.

Q. He was bound to see the signs?

A. Yes, sir.

Q. Now, about this Sunday that you were there in the pump house, what kind of looking man was this pump man that you saw?

A. Well, I don't quite remember how he looked. He was a big, tall man, big and skinny.

Q. Was he young or old

A. Kind of old and kind of skinny.

Q. Skinny and old. What do you mean by old; can you tell us about how old. Did he have gray hair?

A. No, sir.

Q. Smooth face?

A. Yes, sir.

Q. Don't you know that the pump man that was on at two o'clock on the Sunday preceding the 13th of June was a man with a gray mustache?

A. I don't quite remember if it was him, if he had a gray mustache.

Q. Would you know his name if you heard it?

A. No, sir.

Q. Now, you spoke of the summer of 1917. In the spring of 1918 before the warm weather came isn't it a fact that they put in this dam that is shown there in the yellow on that map behind you?

A. Yes, sir.

Q. That dam deepened the water?

A. Yes, sir.

Q. This water in 1917 was only about three feet deep in that pond, was it not?

A. About five feet.

Q. No deeper than that?

A. Five or six feet.

Q. You have no means of knowing, except just simply swimming in the water just how deep it was?

A. Well, it was almost over my head at that time.

A. Well, you are not a very good swimmer?

A. No, sir.

Q. You didn't go in that deep water, did you?

A. No, sir.

Q. So you don't know how deep it is or was out there?

A. No, but I heard it was ten feet; I didn't go out there.

Q. I mean in 1917?

A. Oh, I was out there then, yes, sure.

Q. You did go out there?

A. Yes, sir.

Q. Even though you couldn't swim?

A. Yes, sir.

Q. Then, it was not over you head?

A. Almost over my head.

Q. Almost but not quite over your head?

A. No, sir.

RE-DIRECT EXAMINATION.

BY MR. FRANK WALKER:

Q. During the year 1917, Joseph, was there any place in that pond where the water was over your head?

A. Well, not quite; it was about up to my neck at that place there by the gate.

Q. Was there any place in the pond where the water was ~~not~~ over your head?

A. No, sir.

Q. You said on direct examination that the water was six or seven feet; what did you mean by that, Joseph?

A. Well, it was not quite that deep.

Witness excused.

NICHOLAS FABATZ,

A witness for plaintiff, after being duly sworn, testified as follows:

DIRECT EXAMINATION.

BY MR. FRANK WALKER:

Q. State your name.

A. Nicholas Fabatz.

Q. How old are you?

A. Thirteen.

Q. Where do you live?

A. 23 Lincoln avenue.

Q. You go to school, do you?

A. Yes, sir.

Q. Did you know John Troglio in his lifetime, the litt boy who was drowned?

A. No, sir.

Q. You didn't know him?

A. No, sir.

Q. Do you know this pond or dam owned by the Butte & Superior located north of Meaderville?

A. Yes, sir.

Q. Were you ever there the year before the year in which John Troglio was drowned?

A. Yes, sir.

Q. Were you there the year before the year that John was drowned?

A. Yes, sir.

Q. What year was John drowned in?

A. 1918.

Q. You were there around this pond in 1917?

A. Yes, sir.

Q. How many times?

MR. KREMER: We object to any testimony with reference to conditions of the pond in 1917, it being clearly shown that the conditions were entirely changed between 1917 and 1918.

THE COURT: Yes, but I think he can answer. It shows it a common resort and whether or not notice could be inferred from it, or whatever it is very material we will see when the testimony is all in. Objection overruled.

To which ruling of the Court in overruling said objection, defendant, by counsel, then and there duly excepted.

MR. KREMER: It may all go in under the same objection?

THE COURT: Yes.

A. About five or six times.

Q: Were there other boys with you at those times?

A. Yes, sir.

Q. How many boys, about?

A. About seven or eight.

Q. Did you go into the pond?

A. Yes, sir.

Q. Did the other boys go into the pond?

A. Yes, sir.

Q. Did you ever know John Troglio to see him?

A. No, sir.

Q. When you saw him you didn't know who John Troglio was at all?

A. No, sir.

Q. Did you know the pump man or the watchman that was working for the Butte & Superior, located

A. No, sir.

around the pond?

Q. Did you ever see him?

A. Yes, sir.

Q. Were you ever in the pump house during the year 1917?

A. No, sir.

Q. Did the pump man or watchman ever come to see you go into this pond?

A. In 1918 he did.

Q. Did he in 1917?

A. No, sir.

Q. When you boys went into the pond in 1917 did you play games in the water?

A. Yes, sir.

Q. Chase each other around?

A. Yes, sir.

Q. And shout or call out to each other?

A. We were not shouting, but we were talking.

Q. And the pump house was about how far from you when you were doing this talking?

A. About twenty-five feet.

Q. Did anybody interfere or prevent you from going into the water?

A. No, sir.

Q. Now, in the year 1917 was this pond or artificial lake any different than it was the year 1918?

A. Yes, sir.

Q. What was the difference?

A. It was deeper and bigger.

Q. In 1918 than it was in 1917?

A. Yes, sir.

Q. I will ask you how deep the water was in the year 1917 in that pond?

A. Four or five feet deep.

Q. Was there any place in the pond where the water was over your head?

A. No, sir.

Q. Did you walk all through the pond?

A. Yes, sir.

Q. And there was no place where it was over your head?

A. No, sir.

Q. Was there any barrier or fence around this place in 1917?

A. In -17?

Q. Was there any barrier or fence or anything to prevent fro nyone going from the ground or the borders of the pond into the water in 1918?

A. No, sir.

Q. How man times, if at all, were you around this pond or in it 1918?

A. That was my first time that year.

Q. Had you been up around there before that at all?

A. No, sir.

Q. You say you saw the watchman in there in 1918?

A. That is the first time I saw him there was when John Troglio was drownded.

Q. Was it before or after John Troglio was drowned that you saw the watchman?

A. Before.

Q. How long before, Nicholas?

A. About an hour before.

Q. Where was he then?

A. Who?

Q. The watchman?

A. He was over there watching us swimming.

Q. He was watching you swimming?

A. Yes, sir.

Q. How many boys were in swimming about that time?

A They was about four or five.

Q. Did the watchman say anything to the boys who were in swimming?

A. No, sir.

Q. Were you in swimming at the time?

A. Yes, sir.

Q. Who was there when you went in swimming?

A. There was one boy over there, Joe Bertoglio.

Q. Was the watchman there when you went in swimming?

A. Yes, sir.

Q. Did he tell you not to go in?

A. No, sir.

Q. After you were in did he tell you to come out?

A. No, sir.

Q. Did you see John Troglio around there this day?

A. Yes, sir.

Q. You saw John?

A. Yes, sir.

Q. How long prior to his death was it that you first saw him.

A. About two or three hours before.

Q. What was he doing around there?

A. He was playing with his gun.

Q. What sort of a gun was it?

A. A cap gun.

Q. Did you see John Troglio when he went into the water?

A. Yes, sir.

Q. Was the watchman there at that time?

A. No, sir.

~~No, sir~~.

Q. Where was the watchman then?

A. He went in the pump house.

Q. How many boys were in the water when John Troglio went in?

A. There was about four.

Q. Did you watch John Troglio after he went into the water?

A. Yes, sir.

Q. Did you see him when he was drowning?

A. Yes, sir.

Q. Now, just tell these gentlemen how it happened that John Troglio was drowned.

MR. SANDERS: That is objected to as immaterial. It is conceded.

Which objection was by the Court overruled.

To which ruling of the Court in overruling said objection, defendant, by counsel, then and there duly excepted.

A. He went from the low part and swam to the east part, and then he hollered for help a couple of times, and he was going up and down in the water, and the third time he went down under the water.

Q. How far were you from him at that time?

A. About fifteen feet.

Q. About where around the pond was it that he was drowned; about what point? Could you look at this map over there; do you understand this map?

A. Yes, sir.

Q. You recognize this part here marked with yellow or brown as the dam

A. Yes, sir.

Q. And this part in blue is the pond?

A. Yes, sir.

Q. Now, point out to these gentlement about where it was that John Troglio dropped into the water?

A. Right about here.

Q. Mark there with the letter 'B".

A. (Marking the letter "B".)

Q. About how deep was the water there, or do you know?

A. About ten feet; it was just a little past the gage at the time.

Q. W asthe water over your head at that place?

A. Yes, sir.

Q. Was it over John Troglio's head?

A. Yes, sir.

Q. Was there anybody near John Troglio at the time that he died?

A. No, sir.

Q. At the time that he went down, rather?

A. No, sir.

THE COURT: Wasn't it testified that there were two drowned there at once?

MR. WALKER: No; one witness brought out the fact that he brought a boy out.

MR. KREMER: Yes; the other boy was nearly drowned at just about the same time.

THE COURT: All right; I didn't know whether there were two boys struggling together or something.

Q. What was the first thing that attracted your attention to the fact that John Troglio was in trouble; what made you think that there was something wrong?

A. I thought he was only playing in the water when he was drowning.

Q. You thought he was only playing when you heard him shout?

A. Yes, sir.

Q. You didn't think he was drowning?

A. No, sir.

Q. When was it that you first realized or first knew that he was drowning?

A. When the boys swam for him and he went down before they got up to him.

Q. You were not in the pump house during the year 1918 were you?

A. No, sir.

Q. And this was the only time that you had been up at the dam?

A. Yes, sir.

CROSS EXAMINATION.

BY MR. KREMER:

Q. You thought that John was only playing when he was calling for help, because you knew he was a good swimmer?

A. Yes, sir.

Q. And he was a good swimmer?

A. Yes, sir.

Q. Strong?

A. Yes, sir.

Q. A healthy boy?

A. Yes, sir.

Q. A bright boy?

A. Yes, sir.

Q. Did you see those signs around there?

A. Yes, sir.

Q. What did they read?

A. "No trespassing;" "Danger, keep out;" and "Private property."

Q. "Ten feet deep"?

A. Yes, sir.

Q. Was that also on one of them?

A. Yes, sir; that is all I saw.

Q. Do you know what that meant, those signs; did you know what the signs meant?

A. Yes, sir.

Q. What did they mean?

A. To keep out; to keep out of the pond; and no trespassing is that no one is to go past that way, to go past the water.

Q. Well, you knew it meant, generally for you boys to stay away from there, didn't you?

A. Yes, sir.

Q. John could read, could he?

A. Yes, sir.

Q. How many times had you seen him going in and out of the water that day?

A. Twice.

Q. And each time he started out swimming fine and strong?

A. Yes, sir.

Q. Do you know what hapuened him out there in that deep water?

A. No, sir.

Q. When you last saw him in the water he was swimming along well and having no trouble?

A. Yes, sir.

Q. And how long had he been in the water when he hollered for help and sank?

A. About ten minutes.

Q. Now, referring to this pond in the year, 1917, that is, the year before the one when John was drowned, you say the water was not over your head in places?

A. No, sir.

Q. And you were a little bit smaller then than you are now?

A. Yes, sir.

Q. Have you any idea how much you have grown since the summer of 1917?

A. No, sir.

Q. A couple of inches?

A. Yes, sir.

Q. And do you know how tall you are now?

A. About four feet.

Q. I guess you are taller than that; just stand up so the jury may see you.

(Witness stood up.)

Q. In the year 1917 the water was not over your head in that pond?

A. No, sir.

Q. Now, what kind of looking man was this pump-man that you saw around there.

A. He had a little mustache.

Q. That is the man that was there at the time that Troglio was drowned?

A. Yes, sir.

Q. By the way, did you see a raft on the bank there, a broken raft?

A. Yes, sir.

Q. Tell the jury about the broken raft.

A. I just saw it there; I didn't know who broke it.

Q. Pulled out on the bank?

A. Yes, sir.

Q. What was that raft; what do you mean by a raft?

A. Like a little boat to ride on the water.

Q. Did you ever see the boys playing there with htat raft before?

A. No, sir.

Q. Were any of the planks gone off this raft when you saw it on the bank that day?

A. Yes, sir.

Q. Somebody had broken them off?

A. Yes, sir.

Q. Do you know who did it?

A. No, sir.

Q. How far from Meaderville is this pond.

A. About a mile.

Q. And where is it that you boys go to school?

A. It is in the McQueen Addition.

Q. How far is this pond from the school in the McQueen Addition?

A. It is further than from Meaderville to the pond.

Q. Over a mile?

A. Yes, sir.

Q. Where did John Troglio live?

A. I don't know.

Q. Well, you knew he lived in Meaderville?

A. Yes, sir.

Q. In order to go to this pond from either Meaderville or from the school, it was necessary for you boys to walk away from Meaderville or from the McQueen Addition, the school, over a mile before you could reach this pond at all?

A. Yes, sir.

Q. This pond was not along the way that you boys would usually go in going to school or coming from school or going home to Meaderville, was it?

A. No, sir.

Q. It was away out of the way?

A. Yes, sir.

Witness excused.

JOHN H. McINTOSH,

A witness for the plaintiff, after being duly sworn, testified as follows:

DIRECT EXAMINATION.

BY MR. TOM WALKER:

Q. Mr. McIntosh, besides being Fued Administrator, what, if any, position did you occupy in Silver Bow County, Montana, during the years 1918 and 1919?

A. Manager of the Associated Industries of Montana.

Q. And as such manager of the Associated Industries of Montana are you familiar with the going rate of wages for the various grades in the county of Silver Bow?

A. I am.

Q. It is your business to be familiar with them?

A. Yes, sir.

Q. Were you familiar with the going wage in 1918 and 1919 for an apprentice to mechanics and electricians, and elevator boys and newsboys and news carriers and boys who drive trucks, and the wage of miners and that sort of thing?

A. Yes, sir, generally familiar with them.

Q. What was the prevailing wage in 1918, and what is the prevailing wage in 1919 for news carriers?

A. News carriers draw a dollar a day or thirty dollars a month.

Q. And elevator boys?

A. Pardon me on that question I will make a correction about news carrier. News carriers during the summer draw thirteen dollars a month and fifteen dollars in winter. Elevator boys draw a dollar a day or thirty dollars a month.

Q. And apprentice helpers or apprentice to machinists?

A. Apprentices to mechanists draw one dollar less than journeymen, which during the past year has been for apprentices four dollars and seventy-five cents.

Q. That is for 1918 and 1919?

A. Yes, sir.

Q. And electrician's helpers?

A. The same applies in mechanics, in the different mechanical departments around the mines and smelters.

Q. For the years 1918 and 1919?

A. Yes. You will understand, Mr. Walker, that the wages are more or less movable, as they have been paid on a sliding scale according to the cost of copper.

Q. Are you familiar with the going wage for boys who drive these light Ford trucks around the city for the merchants?

A. Yes, sir.

Q. And what were they getting in 1918 and 1919.

A. There is a regular printed scale for all the boys and teamsters, and I happen to have that here. However, I will tell you that that is for boys under twenty years of age, which means probably boys from fourteen to twenty, very few under fifteen are employed at that work. For two horse teams they get two dollars and thirty-five cents a day, and general work, including produce and commission house drivers on those light trucks, four dollars and twenty-five cents, and it will range from four dollars to four dollars and thirty-five cents; not under four and not over four thirty-five.

Q. And for boys employed in and about the stores of the city, butcher shops and drug stores and grocery stores, etc., what is the going wage for them?

A. There is no fixed wage, because that work would be classed as odds and ends, and there is no union to cover it; but the rate for elevator boys is around thirty dollars a month or a dollar a day, and ranging from that wage up to drives for four dollars to four dollars and thirty-five cents a day, it would be somewhere between them, and striking mene average, I should say that the wage for boys for that kind of work would be around two dollars a day.

Q. And boys employed in the messenger service of the city?

A. I am not familiar with that; I am sorry that I cannot tell you.

Q. What was the prevailing wage of miners during the year 191 8 and 1919?

A. During 1918 and until early in this year it was five dollars and seventy-five cents per day for miners. It was reduced early in this year to four seventy-five, and is now five seventy-five again. The laborers get five dollars a day in the Butte district.

CROSS EXAMINATION.

BY MR. SANDERS:

Q. Mr. McIntosh, are you familiar with the age of elevator boys, the average age?

A. Captain, I cannot say that I am, further than just from observation. I don't believe there is any particular age limit. Sometimes men run elevators. In the office building in which I have an office there are are two boys engaged, one I should say is about fourteen and the other about sixteen or seventeen.

Q. Below fourteen they don't employ boys to run elevators?

A. I don't believe so.

Q. Not boys eleven years of age?

A. I don't believe so.

Q. Boys from fourteen to fifteen and on up?

A. I believe so, yes, sir.

Q. You say apprentices draw four dollars and seventy-five cents, is that your testimony?

A. Yes, when the journeymen's wages is five seventy-five the apprentices for most of the mechanical trades in town give a dollar less.

Q. Is there any custom or rule with reference to the age of apprentices; that is, below what age do they employ boys as apprentices?

A. I believe that varies with the unions, Captain, but I cannot say that I am familiar with the age. I am under the impression, however, that there is a minimum age limit, beyond which they will allow apprentices to work.

Q. They do not allow a bow below eighteen to work as an apprentice, do they?

A. I am not familiar with the union rules in that respect.

Q. There are no boys of the age of eleven employed as apprentices?

A. No, they wouldn't be of any use.

Q. They have to be boys of mature judgment before they are put in a position of that kind?

A. I should say so, though I cannot say what the minimum age is.

Q. Now, truck drivers; boys eleven years of age do not drive trucks in town, do they?

A. No.

Q . As a matter of fact, they are not permitted to lrive trucks, under the law, under the age of sixteen?

A. It either fifteen or sixteen; it is along there.

Q. And what do you say they get, truck drivers?

A. Not under four dollars and not to exceed four dollars and thirty-five cents a day.

Q. Now, about butcher shops? boys

A. Butcher shop boys, Captain, are in about the same classification as drivers for small grocery stores and in the wholesale district.

Q. From your observation do you know anything about the average age of those who are employed as butcher shop boys?

A. Well, from observation I would say that the average will range between fifteen and nineteen years.

A. And what have you to say about boys employed in drug stores?

A. You mean messenger boys and carriers of parcels and drivers?

Q. There was something mentioned by counsel about boys employed in drug stores; I presume messenger boys delivering drugs.

A. Yes, I would take it from observation that they run about the same as the average messenger boy or driver, possibly ranging from fifteen to nineteen.

Q. You say miners at the present time draw five dollars and seventy-five cents

A. Yes, sir.

Q. The wage was reduced to four dollars and seventy-five, and then it was raised?

A. Yes, sir; the apprentices draw a dollar less in most of the metal trades.

Q. In your experience in these positions which you have held, can you advise the jury about the average of miners; the average age at which men or boys are employed in the mines?

A. Occasionally you will see one under age, but they almost certainly average considerably above a man's majority.

Q. The average age of miners is above twenty-one years?

A. Oh, yes, considerably.

Q. And you have the same thing to say with reference to laborers?

A. Yes, sir.

RE-DIRECT EXAMINATION.

BY MR. TOM WALKER:

Q. What have you to say as to whether or not the tendency o fthe wage in all of those classes that you have mentioned is upward?

A. I don't quit catch the meaning of your question.

Q. What have you to say as to whether or not the tendency of these values that you have fixed, the scale of wages that you have fixed is one going upward?

A. You mean progressively with one's age?

Q. Yes, and with the difference of the times as you find them now.

A. Most assuredly it has been upward, yes, sir.

Q. Increasing

A. Yes, sir.

Witness excused.

ARTHUR W. MERKLE,

A witness for plaintiff, after being duly sworn, testified as follows:

DIRECT EXAMINATION.

BY MR. TOM WALKER:

Q. State your name.

A. Arthur W. Merkle.

MR. WALKER: It seems to be agreed between counsel for the plaintiff and defendant that the record may show that if Mr. Troglio was called to the stand, the father of the boy, John Troglio, he would testify that his age was forty-six.

MR. SANDERS: Yes, but not conceding that it is material or competent.

Q. What is your business or occupation?

A. State Manager of the Prudential Insurance Company of Montana.

Q. How long have you been engaged in the insurance business?

A. Four years.

Q. Where?

A. In the state of Montana.

Q. As such insurance man are you familiar with an ybook or standard of statistics which is used by the insurance companies generally throughout the United States?

A. Yes, I have the Stanley standard established by all the standard companies, which they call the Experience Table of Mortality.

Q. What is an annuity?

A. Well, a certain amount of money is paid into the insurance company, which assures a man a set income for life, a certain amount paid in one lump sum, which assures him of a certain amount during his lifetime.

Q. From your experience as an insurance man are you familiar with the period of life expectancy of men?

A. I can quote from the tables I mentioned, yes, sir.

Q. Have you that table with you?

A. Yes, sir.

Q. What have you to say would be the expectancy of a man twenty years of age?

MR. SANDERS: That is objected to as incompetent, irrelevant and immaterial in this case.

Which objection was by the Court sustained.

To which ruling of the Court in sustaining said objection, plaintiff, by counsel, then and there duly excepted.

Q. What have you to say from that table as to what is the expectancy of life of a man forty-six years of age?

MR. SANDERS: The same objection.

TH ECOURT: I cannot see how it is material.

MR. WALKER: It is merely to show the expectancy of man. Also the expectancy of a boy of twenty, because the insurance tables do not go below that age, down to a boy of eleven. It is to prove our damage.

THE COURT: What would be the rule of damage?

MR. WALKER: The damage would be the damages that he suffered from the death.

THE COURT: These expectancies are not material.

MR. WALKER: Only as a guide.

THE COURT:Oh, no. Objection overruled.

To which ruling of the Court in overruling said objection, defendant, by counsel, then and there duly excepted.

A. 23.81 years.

THE COURT: You may repeat the question as to the boy.

Q. What is the expectancy of a boy twenty years of age?

A. 42.20 years.

Q. Have you any figures showing the expectancy of life of a boy of eleven, and if not, why?

A. Well, I have never heard of a table where they have arrived at anything for a boy from eleven to twenty years, for the reason, I imagine, that owing to the many illnesses that the younger people are subject to, it would be hard to figure.

Q. You do not accept risks from boys under that age?

A. Well, they do, but not on an examination. They don't do it in this state.

Q. What would it cost for an annuity for a man twenty years of age of six hundred dollars per annum?

A. $12,136.00.

Q. And what would it cost to get an annuity of six hundred dollars per annum for a man forty-six years of age?

A. $8,994.00.

Cross examination waived.

WITNESS EXCUSED.

JOHN R. REED, a witness for plaintiff, after being duly sworn, testified as follows:

DIRECT EXAMINATION.

BY MR. TOM WALKER:

Q. State your name.

A. John R. Reed.

Q. What is your business?

A. Undertaker.

Q. Are you acquainted with Martin Troglio, the plaintiff in this case?

A. I have seen him, yes, sir.

Q. You are the manager and president of the Sherman & Reed Company?

A. Yes, sir.

Q. I will ask you whether or not your company during the month of June, 1918, prepared for burial and buried John Troglio, the minor child of Martin Troglio?

A. Yes, sir.

Q. What were the expenses entailed by Martin Troglio with your company for the burial of this minor son, John Troglio?

A. Two hundred and forty-three dollars.

Q. What did that include, Mr. Reed?

A. That included the casket, the outside box, the care of the body, the hearse coach and four cabs, four limousines, the paper notice, the grave, and the ground and the opening of the grave, and three cards of thanks after the funeral.

Q. Did that include the lot in the cemetery?

A. Yes, sir.

Q. You paid for that out of this sum?

A. Yes, sir.

Q. What have you to say with reference to whether or not the sum you have just mentioned was a reasonable sum for the burial of a child of that age during the month of June, 1918, in the County of Silver Bow County, Montana.

A. That was a reasonable charge.

Cross examination waived.

WITNESS EXCUSED.

MARTIN TROGLIO, plaintiff, recalled in his own behalf:

DIRECT EXAMINATION.

BY MR. FRANK WALKER:

Q. What have you to say, Martin, with reference to whether or not your son, John, was a loving and affectionate boy?

MR. SANDERS: That is objected to on the ground that it is incompetent, irrelevant and immaterial.

THE COURT: Oh, it might have its bearing on the question of how much the boy would contribute to the father. If he was an affectionate boy the inference might probably be that he would contribute more than otherwise. The objection is overruled.

To which ruling of the court in overruling said objection, defendant, by counsel, then and there duly excepted.

A. My boy could help me now this day to make my living, because I am sick; I couldn't do nothing in the mine, and no work at all, and he could help me.

MR. SANDERS: That is objected to.

MR. WALKER: That may be stricken.

THE COURT: It is stricken.

Q. What have you to say about his being loving, and having regard and care for you?

A. He was regard and care; he was the best I have. Any time I go out and come back he was just like a man that never see me for ten or fifteen years, and he just love me all the time I come home from work or anything.

Q. What have you to say with reference to whether or not he was obedient and obeyed your commands and directions?

MR. SANDERS: The same objection.

Which objection was by the court overruled.

To which ruling of the court in overruling said objection, defendant, by counsel, then and there duly excepted.

Q. Did he do what you told him to do?

A. He do everything I told him; everything I told him he was doing.

Q. What have you to say with reference to whether or not he helped you about the house or yard?

A. Well, he was doing anything the best he can, sawing wood, and I had a couple of cows, and sometimes he would come and help me to milk the cow and do anything he can to help; he was good at that.

CROSS EXAMINATION.

BY MR. KREMER:

Q. Have you any other children?

A. Yes, sir.

Q. How many?

A. I have got six children.

Q. How old is your oldest?

A. The oldest one is twenty-three.

Q. That is Pete?

A. That is Pete.

Q. What does Pete do?

A. Well, he is running a butcher shop.

Q. Down in Meaderville?

A. Yes, sir.

Q. Now, your next child?

A. The next child is a girl; she is Mary.

Q. And how old is she?

A. Well, she is twenty.

Q. Then, the next one?

A. The next one is sixteen.

A. A girl.

Q. She goes to school?

A. Well, she just quit the school this year.

Q. What is she doing?

A. Well, working around the house.

Q. Then, your next one?

A. The next is twelve, a girl.

Q. She is going to school?

A. Going to school.

Q. Does Pete own this butcher shop?

A. Well, Pete don't own the butcher shop; he owns part, and his partner owns the other.

PLAINTIFF RESTED.

MR. SANDERS: Comes now the defendant and moves the court to direct the jury to return a verdict on behalf of defendant and dismiss the action for the following reasons:

That the said complaint does not set forth sufficient to constitute a cause of action nor any actionable negligence on the part of the defendant; that the dam or reservoir mentioned in plaintiff's complaint is not such an attractive nuisance as to bring it under the rule that renders the defendant laible to children of tender years for maintaining such dam or reservoir, as charged in the plaintiff's complaint as being an attractive nuisance; that the defendant is notliable for maintaining the same without any fence or without a watchman to warn minor children from trespassing in the same; that the artificial reservoir is not within the doctrine of attractive nuisances, whereby children of tender years are allured thereto to their injury; that in this case defendant had no further duty to the plaintiff or the minor son of plaintiff than not to wilfully or ~~wrongfully~~ injure them. That it is the theory or assumption of the plaintiff, as appears from the plaintiff's complaint, that it is a duty that devolves on the defendant by law to enclose that dam by a fence or other barriers, and not to suffer the same to remain open, and that it was the duty of the defendant to provide a watchman to warn, either minor children generally or plaintiff's son particularly against entering the same to swim; that under the law none of such duties are required of such defendant. Actionable negligence arises only from the failure to perform a legal duty; that there is not sufficient competent evidence proving or tending to prove that the defendant was negligent in failing to guard a dangerous instrumentality, the dangers of which were concealed or hidden; that there is not sufficient competent evidence that the defendant had any knowledge of the presence of said minor son at or in said reservoir at or prior to the time that he was drowned; that there is not sufficient competent evidence that the defendant then knew or by the exercise of ordinary care could have known that said minor child was in peril or likely to be injured or drowned. That in the absence of actual knowledge on the part of the defendant or its servants or agents that said minor son was swimming in said pond, no duties devolve on the defendant as a matter of law to prevent his being there. That it has not been made to appear by sufficient competent evidence that the deceased son was incapable of appreciating the dangers that was in entering into said reservoir or in swimming therein, which must not only be alleged, but established by a preponderance of the evidence. On the other hand, the uncontradicted testimony on behalf of the plaintiff is that John Troglio, the deceased son, was a bright, intelligent boy for his age of eleven years, could read, and was a good swimmer for his age and an athlete. That there is not sufficient competent evidence herein warranting a recovery on the theory that the deceased was rightfully on the said premises of the defendant, either by invitation or license. And finally, there is no sufficient competent or substantial evidence to prove the negligence alleged.

Argument by counsel.

THE COURT: At the conclusion of the plaintiff's case the defendant moves the court to direct a verdict in its favor. That motion challenges the sufficiency of the evidence to sustain a verdict in favor of the plaintiff, if the jury should find one, and it immediately resolves itself into a question of law for the court to decide, whether or not the evidence is sufficient, if it went to the jury and the jury should find a verdict for the plaintiff, to sustain a verdict. If in the judgment of the court, as a question of law, the evidence is not sufficient to sustain a verdict for the plaintiff, if the jury should find one, then it is the duty of the court to direct a verdict in favor of the defendant, and in this case the court will do so, its judgment being that the evidence would not sustain a verdict for the plaintiff.

Briefly, in order that it may appear in the record, the court is satisfied that, as against a general demurrer the complaint states a good cause of action for the negligence of the defendant. It charges that the boy who was drowned was eleven years old; that the defendant built an artificial dam, a hundred by seventy-five feet, one to twelve feet deep, not enclosed, and no watchman, within twenty-five feet of a highway over which this boy and many other people were habited to pass; that the water was fifty degrees cold; that the defendant knew that this place would allure children to swim; that it was its duty to warn them of the danger; that they negligently suffered the boy and others to go swimming and bathing in the cold water, and while the boy who was drowned was bathing, he sank and was drowned. The general demurrer only challenged the general sufficiency, not in detail. Under that demurrer it might have been open to proof that this pond was one in the character of a deception; that this boy could not swim; that he was not of the average intelligence of his own age; that walking along the shore, wading, he suddenly stepped into a deep and obscure hole and was drowned, and other items of that sort might have been introduced in evidence under that complaint, which might well have warranted the case going to the jury for its determination. But when we come to the evidence we find a different situation. Here we find a boy—in the first place we find that it was not near a road that was habitually travelled by this boy and other boys, though that is not material in any phase of the case. After all the location of the pond only goes to what the defendant ought to anticipate and its knowledge, and that might have been well proven by other evidence in the case, as to what the defendant should have anticipated and its knowledge.

Here was a boy eleven years old. He was a strong boy for his age, somewhat athletic and a good swimmer, and a boy who was well able to read, and we find a number of signs there—none of those things appear in the complaint—we find also that the company had exercised some reasonable degree of care to warn people of the danger, and boys; that they placed a sign: "Danger, ten feet deep, keep off," "No trespassing," and the like, which this boy could read, or any other boy of his age.

Now, it appears from the evidence that the season before this accident happened—because the court will finally say in this case that nobody was guilty of any negligence, neither the company nor the boy—it was an accident pure and simple; the boy was conducting himself properly under the circumstances, being a strong boy and a boy well able to swim, and the fact is after all, when he did drown, it was because he had stayed around there, in and out of the water, so long that he was either exhausted, or what is more probable he was seized by cramps and sank, because the two boys that saw him when he drowned, say he had been there about two hours and before they had been there, and all that time in and out of the water; that he was swimming well before and at the time that he went down; that he swam from the low water out and over the deep water, and suddenly threw up his hands and hollered and sank. I think there can be only one inference, that he was seized with cramps.

But however that may be, the law is that every person must so care for his own and use his own that it causes no unnecessary harm to others, and that every one who his any sort of premises or business house or farm or, as in this case, a pond, or a mine, shall have it reasonable safe for the visits of any one who mthey invite there expressly or impliedly. That is the duty which the law imposes upon anybody, and the grade of that duty differs with different persons. A grown man who comes upon your premises, your duty is not so great toward him. A boy of twelve or fifteen or sixteen, your duty would be a little more than for a man, but not so great as it would be for children of three or four or five or six, if you invite them upon your premises expressly or impliedly. An express invitation, of course, means when yo utell them to come ;an implied invitation may arise out of the circumstances, if you have a place attractive to children especially, which has instrumentalities upon it with which they like to play, and if you have, then you ought to anticipate that they will come if you have, then you ought to anticipate that they will come if you place it near where there are large groups or numbers of children. If you place it where you know that children are accustomed to be and find it, then you have got to see to it that it is reasonably safe in due proportion to the helplessness or the sense of the child or the man. I still think that if it had appeared in evidence that little, children of three or four or five years of age were coming around this pond, if such a case had been made here, it would have been within the turntable doctrine. This is nothing more than a phase of the general law; it is part of the general law; it comes right back to the proposition that premises must be kept reasonably safe to those who are impliedly invited there. But there is great danger in carrying it too far. You may say that a man should not plant a tree in his yard because children might climb it and fall, and to a certain extent there may be some truth in that. For instance, if a man set up ladders outside of his house, and if he knows children are accustomed to climb up and play on his roof, if he lets little children not capable of caring for themselves, go up there, three or four or five or six years old, I imagine he still might be held liable, where he would not be for a child twelve or thirteen or fourteen or fifteen. Other circumstances might be imagined.

But to get right back to this case, here is a boy against whom the defendant, as the court sees it, neglected no ~~detail.~~ duty B. They had a pond there; every one has a right to have such things on their premises if they are useful, ~~within the bounds of the statute.~~ B. This boy was strong; he was able to swim, and apparently to swim for a long time. Defendant has no reason to anticipate that he was not able to care for himself; defendant had no reason to furnish him a guard nor a fence nor anything else. He was not negligent in going there, because you might then say that of any person if they go in bathing, that they are negligent, but they are not, if they are able to swim; they are able to take care of themselves. If misfortune comes to them, and anything happens, chance or anything else, or if they stay in till they are exhausted and they sink in deep water, it is an accident and nothing else, and the court places its decision in this case on that basis. The defendant was not negligent, consequently not negligent as far as this boy is concerned. Consequently the court will instruct the jury to return a verdict in favor of the defendant. The record is small in this case and can be readily carried further if counsel desires.

Exception of the plaintiff to the ruling of the court noted and thirty days extra time allowed plaintiff to prepare, serve and file a bill of exceptions.

I, George H. MacDougall, do certify that I am a reporter of many years' experience do hereby certify that I reported the above entitled cause in the United States Court, district of Montana, before Hon. George M. Bourquin, Judge thereof, and a jury, on the 21st and 22nd days of November, 1919, in Butte, Montana; that the above and foregoing transcript from page 1 to page ~~120~~ 89 inclusive, is a full, true and correct transcript of my shorthand notes of said testimony to the best of my skill and ability.

Witness my hand this 30th day of January, 1920.

G. H. McDOUGALL,
Reporter.

(TITLE OF COURT AND CAUSE.)

This cause coming on this day regularly further to be heard upon the application of the plaintiff by Messrs. Walker & Walker, his attorneys, appearing herein through I. Parker Veazey, Jr., an attorney acting for the plaintiff in the presentation of this motion at the instance of his said attorneys, for good cause shown;

IT IS HEREBY ORDERED that the time within which the plaintiff may prepare and serve his Bill of Exceptions to the rulings made, and the proceedings had on the trial of the above entitled cause be, and the same hereby is, extended to and including the first day of February, A. D. 1920.

Done in open court this 31st day of December, 1919, and ordered entered as above.

BOURQUIN,
Judge.

Service of the foregoing bill of exceptions acknowledged and copy received this.....30.....day of January, 1920. Subject to all legal objections and exceptions to be hereafter urged.

KREMER, SANDERS & KREMER,
Attorneys for Defendants.

The foregoing bill of exceptions is this 13th day of February, 1920, hereby signed, settled and allowed as true and correct and ordered filed.

BOURQUIN,
Judge.

No. 286.

Order Directing Verdict.

Counsel for respective parties present as before and trial of cause resumed. Thereupon Joseph Darin, Nicholas Faboltz, John H. McIntosh, Arthur W. Merkle, and J. R. Reed, were sworn and examined as witnesses for plaintiff and Martin Troglio recalled, whereupon plaintiff rested. Thereupon counsel for defendant moved the court to direct a verdict herein in favor of the defendant upon the ground that the complaint does not state facts sufficient to constitute a cause of action or any actionable negligence upon the part of the defendant which motion was duly argued, submitted to the court and taken under advisement, the jury being excused until 1:30 p. m. Thereupon after due consideration court ordered that defendant's said motion be and is granted, that a verdict in favor of the defendant and against the plaintiff be, and hereby is entered by the clerk and jury discharged from further consideration of the cause; to which ruling of the court the plaintiff then and there excepted the exception noted. Thereupon the plaintiff was granted thirty (30) days additional time within which to prepare and serve a Bill of Exceptions herein. ~~In re excuse of Jurors.~~ Entered in open court this [illegible]

~~Ordered that all trial jurors now in attendance be excused for the terms.~~

~~Court thereupon adjourned until 10 a. m. Monday next.~~

~~G. R. Garlow, Clerk,~~

~~By L. R. Polglase, Deputy.~~

Attest: G R Garlow Clerk
B. L R. Polglase Deputy

(TITLE OF COURT AND CAUSE.)

No. 286.

Judgment.

This cause coming on regularly for trial on the 21st day of November, 1919, in the above entitled court, plaintiff appearing in person and by counsel, Messrs. Walker & Walker and C. S. Wagner, Esq., and the defendant appearing by counsil Messrs. Kremer, Sanders & Kremer, ~~the~~ a jury of twelve (12) good and lawful men were duly impaneled and sworn to try said cause; whereupon witnesses upon behalf of plaintiff and [were duly sworn and testified on the witness stand in behalf of plaintiffs] counsel for plaintiff having announced in open court that they had rested their said case thereupon counsel for the defendant in open court moved for a directed verdict in said cause in favor of the defendant and against the plaintiff and said motion having been duly argued by respective counsel and considered by the court the same was on the 22nd day of November, 1919, by the court duly and regularly sustained.

And now upon consideration by the court of the premises it is hereby ORDERED, ADJUDGED, AND DECREED, that the said plaintiff have and recover nothing from the said defendant and that defendant have and recover of the plaintiff, its costs and disbursements incurred in said action and taxed at the sum of $54.00...........

Dated this 22nd day of November, 1919.
Entered November 26, 1919.

C. R. GARLOW, Clerk,
By L. R. POLGLASE, Deputy.

Attest ~~and~~ a true copy of Judgment.

C. R. GARLOW, Clerk,
By L. R. POLGLASE, Deputy.

(TITLE OF COURT AND CAUSE.)

Petition for Writ of Error.

To the Honorable George M. Bourquin, Judge of the District Court Aforesaid:

Now comes Martin Troglio, plaintiff above named, by Walker & Walker, and C. S. Wagner, his attorneys, and respectfully shows that on the 21st day of November, 1919, the court directed a verdict, by a jury duly impaneled against your petitioner and in favor of the Butte-Superior Mining Company, a corporation, defendant, and upon said verdict a final judgment was entered on the 26th day of November, A. D., 1920, against your plaintiff petitioner, and in favor of the defendant.

Your petitioner, feeling himself aggrieved by the said verdict and judgment entered thereon as aforesaid, herewith petitions the court for an order allowing him to prosecute a writ of error to the Circuit Court of Appeals of the United States for the ninth circuit under the laws of the United States in such cases made and provided.

Wherefore, premises considered, your petitioner prays that a writ of error do issue that an appeal in this behalf to the United States Circuit Court of Appeals aforesaid, sitting at San Francisco, in said circuit for the correction of the errors complained of and herewith assigned, be allowed and that an order be made fixing the amount of security to be given by plaintiff in error conditioned as the law directs, and upon giving such bond as may be required that all further proceedings may be suspended until the determination of said writ of error by the Circuit Court of Appeals.

WALKER & WALKER,
C. S. WAGNER,
Attorneys for Petitioner in Error,
307 Daly Bank, Butte, Mont.

(TITLE OF COURT AND CAUSE.)

Assignment of Errors

Number 286.

Now comes Martin Troglio, plaintiff in error, in the above entitled cause, and in connection with his petition for a writ of error in this cause assigns the following errors which plaintiff in error avers occurred on the trial thereof, and upon which he relies to reverse the judgment entered herein as appears of record:

1.

The court erred in granting a motion to return a verdict in favor of the plaintiff in this cause for the reason that the evidence conclusively shows that the plaintiff's deceased minor son was an infant, eleven years of age, at the time he was drowned in the artificial dam and reservoir, maintained by the defendant, and non sui juris, and was upon the premises of the defendant and swimming in said pond upon the invitation of the defendant and the question of his contributory negligence was, and is a question of fact to be resolved by the jury and not a question of law, to be determined by the court.

2.

The said court erred in charging the jury as follows: "If in the judgment of the court, as a question of law, the evidence is not sufficient to sustain a verdict for the plaintiff, if the jury should find one, then it is the duty of the court to direct a verdict in favor of the defendant, and in this case the court will do so, its judgment being that the evidence would not sustain a verdict for the plaintiff." Because the question of the negligence of the defendant and the contributory negligence of the plaintiff's deceased minor son were and are questions of fact to be resolved by the jury, and not questions of law, to be determined by the court.

3.

The said court erred in charging the jury as follows:

"Here we find a boy—in the first place we find that it was not near a roa dthat was habitually travelled by this boy and other boys, though that is not material in any phase of the case. After all the location of the pond only goes to what the defendant ought to anticipate and its knowledge, and that might have been well proved by other evidence in the case, as to what the defendant should have anticipated and its knowledge." Because the evidence conclusively shows that there was a Public Highway within twenty-five feet of the north edge of said artificial pond and that it, and the contiguous territory was habitually travelled by boys of tender age who were allured to said pond by its attractive characteristics for swimming and bathing purposes.

4.

The said court erred in charging the jury as follows:

"Here was a boy eleven years old. He was a strong boy for his age, somewhat athletic and a good swimmer, and a boy who was well able to read, and we find a number of signs there—none of these things appear in the complaint—we find also that the compan yhad exercised some reasonable degree of care to warn people of the danger, and boys; that they placed a sign: "Danger, ten feet deep, keep off." "No trespassing," and the like, which this boy could read, or any boy of his age." Because the evidence shows without contradiction, that defendant had a watchman in charge of a pump station located within twenty-five feet of said pond, who suffered and permitted children of tender years, including plaintiff's minor son to go swimming and bathing therein, without protest, but with acquiescence and consent of the defendant, whereby the signs adverted to were wholly disregarded by said children.

5

The said court erred in charging the jury as follows:

"Now, it appears from the evidence that the season before this acident happened—because the Court will finally say in this case that nobody was guilty of any negligence, neither the company nor the boy—it was an accident pure and simple; the boy was conducting himself properly under the circumstances, being a strong boy and a boy well able to swim, and the fact is after all, when he did drown, it was because he had stayed around there, in and out of the water, so long that he was either exhausted, or what is more probable, he was seized by cramps and sank, because the two boys that saw him when he drowned, say he had been there about two hours and before they had been there, and all that time in and out of the water; that he was swimming well before and at the time that he went down; that he swam from the low water out and over the deep water, and suddenly threw up his hands and hollered and sank. I think there can be only one inference, that he was seized with cramps."

Because the question as to whether the drowning was an accident or was due to defendant's negligence was, and is, a question of fact to be resolved by the jury and not one of law, to be determined by the court.

6

The said court erred in charging the jury as follows:

"A grown man who comes upon your premises, your duty is not so great towards him. A boy of twelve or fifteen or sixteen, your duty would be a little more than for a man, but not so great as it would be for children of three or four or five or six, if you invite them upon your premises expressly or impliedly."

7

The said court erred in charging the jury as follows:

"For instance, if a man set up ladders outside of his house, and if he knew children are accustomed to climb up and play on his roof, if he lets little children not capable of caring for themselves, go up there, three or four or five or six years old, I imagine he still might be held liable, where he would not be for a child twelve or thirteen or fourteen or fifteen. Other circumstances might be imagined."

The court erred in charging the jury as follows:

"But to get right back to this case, here is a boy against whom the defendant, as the court sees it, neglected no detail. They had a pond there; every one has a wriht to have such things on their premises if they are useful, within the bounds of the statute. This boy was strong, he was able to swim, and apparently to swim for a long time. Defendant had no reason to anticipate that he was not able to care for himself; defendant had no reason to furnish him a guard nor a fence nor anything else." Because the question as to whether said boy was sui juris, was a question of fact to be determnned by the jury, and not a question of law, to be determined by the court.

9

The said court erred in charging the jury as follows:

"He was not negligent in going there, because you might then say that of any person if they go in bathing, that they are negligent, but they are not, if they are able to swim; they are able to take care of themselves. If misfortune comes to them, and anything happens, chance or anything else, or if they stay in till they are exhausted and they sink in deep water, it is an accident and nothing else, and the Court places its decision in this case on that basis." Because questions of accident and negligence as disclosed by the evidence in this case, were and are questions of fact to be decided by the jury and not by the court.

The court erred in directing the jury to return a verdict in favor of the defendant as follows:

"The defendant was not negligent, consequently not negligent as far as this boy is concerned. Consequently the Court will instruct the jury to return a verdict in favor of the defendant."

WALKER & WALKER,
C. S. WAGNER,
Attorneys for plaintiff in error.
307 Daly Bank Bldg., Butte, Mont.

Read on application for Writ of Error.................... 1920.

....

(TITLE OF COURT AND CAUSE.)
(Prayer for Reversal)

To the Honorable, the Circuit Court of Appeals of the United States, for the Ninth District.

Now comes Martin Troglio, the plaintiff in error, and prays for a reversal of the judgment of the District Court of the United States for the District of Montana, which judgment was made, rendered and entered in the office of the Clerk of the District Court of the United States for the District of Montana, on or about the 26th day of November, 1919.

WALKER & WALKER,
C. S. WAGNER,
Attorneys for Plaintiff in Error.
307 Daly Bank Bldg., Butte, Mont.

(TITLE OF COURT AND CAUSE.)

No. 286.

Waiver of Citation.

Whereas in the above entitled cause the plaintiff has petitioned for a writ of error and accompanied the same with an assignment of errors and a prayer for the reversal of the judgment made, rendered, and entered in the above entitled cause on the 26th day of November, 1919.

It is stipulated and agreed by and between plaintiff and defendant through their respective attorneys that citation in error and notice thereof be and the same is hereby expressly waived.

WALKER & WALKER,
C. S. WAGNER,
Attorneys for Plaintiff in Error.
KREMER, SANDERS & KREMER,
Attorneys for Defendant in Error.

(TITLE OF COURT AND CAUSE.)
No. 286.

Order Granting Writ.

Now May 21, 1920; the plaintiff in the above entitled case having presented his petition for a writ of error to the Circuit Court of Appeals of the United States, in and for the Ninth District, accompanied with an assignment of errors and a prayer for the reversal of the judgment in the above entitled cause, made, rendered, and entered on the 26th day of November, 1920.

It is ordered that ~~the~~ a writ of error be granted as prayed for upon the furnishing of a good and sufficient bond in the sum of $300. dollars.

BOURQUIN,

Judge.

In the District Court of the United States for the District of Montana.

MARTIN TROGLIO,

Plaintiff in Error,

vs.

THE BUTTE-SUPERIOR MINING COMPANY, a corporation,

Defendant in Error.

THE WRIT OF ERROR.

UNITED STATES OF AMERICA—ss.

The President of the United States, Woodrow Wilson, to the Honorable George M. Bourquin, Judge of the District Court of the United States for the District of Montana, Greeting:

Because in the record and preceedings, as also in the rendition of the judgment of a plea which is in the said District Court before you between Martin Troglio, Plaintiff in Error, and The Butte-Superior

ANSWER OF COURT TO WRIT OF ERROR.

Mining Company, a corporation, Defendant in Error, a manifest error has happened to the damage of Martin Troglio, plaintiff in error, as by said complaint appears, and we being willing that error, if any hath been, should be corrected, and full and speedy justice be done to the parties aforesaid in this behalf, do command you if judgment be therein given, that under your seal you send the record and proceedings aforesaid, with all things concerning the same, to the United States Circuit Court of Appeals for the Ninth Circuit, together with this writ so that you have the same in San Francisco, in the State of California, where said court is sitting, within thirty days from the date hereof, in the said Circuit Court of Appeals to be then and there held, and the record and preceedings aforesaid being inspected, the said United States ~~Circuit~~ Court of Appeals may cause further to be done therein to correct the error what of right, and according to the laws and customs of the United States should be done.

Witness the Hon. Edward D. White, Chief Justice of the United States, this 25th day of May, A. D. 1920.

C. R. GARLOW,

(Seal) Clerk of the United States District Court for

the................................District of Montana.

In the District Court of the United States for the District of Montana.

MARTIN TROGLIO,
Plaintiff in Error,

vs.

THE BUTTE-SUPERIOR MINING COMPANY, a corporation,
Defendant in Error.

PRAECIPE FOR TRANSCRIPT.

To the Clerk of the above styled Court:

Please prepare transcript in above entitled case returnable to the Circuit Court of Appeals of the United States, for the Ninth district and include thereon the following papers, matters and things:

1.

Plaintiff's complaint.

2.

Defendant's demurrer to plaintiff's complaint.

3.

Order of the court over-ruling defendant's demurrer.

4.

Defendant's answer.

5.

Plaintiff's reply.

6.

Transcript of the testimony as settled and allowed by the court.

7.

Defendant's motion for a directed verdict.

8.

The charge of the Court granting said motion and directing the jury to return a verdict against the plaintiff and in favor of the defendant.

9.

The verdict of the jury.

10.

The judgment on the verdict.

11.

Plaintiff's petition for writ of error. Plaintiff's assignment of errors and prayer for ~~revisal~~ Reversal.

13.

Order granting the writ. and Writ

14.

Stipulation waiving citation and all minute entries and orders appearing in the above entitled cause together with the clerk's certificate, certifying to the correctness of the same.

Dated this 24th day of May, 1920.

Walker & Walker C. S. Wagner

Attorneys for Plaintiff in Error.

(TITLE OF COURT AND CAUSE.)

No. 286.

Clerk's Certificate.

United States of America,
............District of Montana.

I, C. R. Garlow, clerk of the United States District Court for the District of Montana, do hereby certify that the foregoing 137 pages presents a true, full and correct copy of the proceedings had and orders entered as therein stated in cause No. 286 wherein Martin Troglio was plaintiff, and the Butte-Superior Mining Company, a corporation, was defendant as the same appears of record and of file in this office, except that the original writ of error and waiver of citation therein at pages 000 and 000, respectively, all of which constitutes the entire transcript of the proceedings in the cause, as per praecipe therefor.

I further certify that a good and sufficient undertaking in due form of law in the sum of three hundred ($300.00) dollars proved by the judge of said court was duly and regularly filed. and costs amount of amounting to $62.60 and that the same have been paid

Witness my official signature and seal of said District at my office in the city of Butte, State of Montana, this the 12 day of June, A. D. 1920.

C. R. Garlow
Clerk.

By L. R. Polglase, Deputy.

No. 8515

In the United States
Circuit Court of Appeals
For the Ninth Circuit

MARTIN TROGLIA,
Plaintiff in Error,
vs.
THE BUTTE SUPERIOR MINING COMPANY, a Corporation,
Defendant in Error.

IN ERROR TO
THE DISTRICT COURT OF THE UNITED STATES FOR THE DISTRICT OF MONTANA

Brief of Plaintiff in Error

WALKER & WALKER and
C. S. WAGNER,
Attorneys for Plaintiff in Error
307 Metals Bank Bldg.,
Butte, Montana.

MURPHY-CHEELY PRINTING CO
BUTTE, MONT

No......................

In the United States
Circuit Court of Appeals
For the Ninth Circuit

MARTIN TROGLIA,
Plaintiff in Error,
vs.
THE BUTTE SUPERIOR MINING COMPANY, a Corporation,
Defendant in Error.

IN ERROR TO
THE DISTRICT COURT OF THE UNITED STATES FOR THE DISTRICT OF MONTANA

Brief of Plaintiff in Error

WALKER & WALKER and
C. S. WAGNER,
Attorneys for Plaintiff in Error
307 Metals Bank Bldg.,
Butte, Montana.

STATEMENT OF THE CASE

The above entitled action was commenced in the District Court of the Second Judicial District of the State of Montana, in and for the County of Silver Bow. The defendant in error, an Arizona corporation, filed its appearance and by stipulation of the parties the cause was removed to the District Court of the United States for the District of Montana.

Plaintiff brought this action against the defendant corporation for damages for the death of his minor son, on or about the 13th day of June, 1918, which he alleges was approximately caused by wrongful and negligent acts of the defendant substantially as follows:

That on and prior to the day when plaintiff's son met his death the defendant kept and maintained in Silver Bow County, Montana, an artificial dam or reservoir to supply its mill with water, it being engaged at the time in a general mining and milling business. The dam was about 100 feet long, 75 feet wide, and varied in depth from one to twelve feet, and was filled with water. This dam was not enclosed with fence or other barrier, but then was, and prior thereto had been, wholly unenclosed and open to the public generally, and defendant carelessly and negligently suffered and permitted the artificial dam and reservoir to be and remain open and exposed, with no watchman or person to warn minor children against trespassing at or near the same. That it was contiguous to a public highway, about 25 feet therefrom, and many children passed to and fro, including the minor son of plaintiff and his youthful companions and playmates.

That the dam and reservoir became and was an enticing and alluring attraction to children generally as a swimming hole and bathing pond, and many children of the neighborhood, including plaintiff's minor son, did at divers times prior to the 13th day of June, 1918, go swimming or bathing at and in the same, all of which was well known to the defendant, or by the exercise of ordinary care would have been known to it. It is then alleged that the dam or reservoir is fed from the waters of a creek or channel whose source of suply is found in the melting snows of the highlands nearby, and during the month of June of each year the waters therein contained are cold, chilly and of low temperature, that is to say of a temperature of 40 or 50 degrees Fahrenheit, this being known to the defendant.

It is then alleged that the defendant knew, or by exercise of ordinary care would have known, that the dam and reservoir adverted to and kept and maintained by it, was a dangerous instrumentality peculiarly attractive to children of tender years, among them plaintiff's minor son, for the purpose of making use of the same for bathing and swimming purposes; yet notwithstanding the premises, the defendant failed and neglected to use ordinary care or any care at all to prevent children, and particularly the minor son of plaintiff, from making use of the same for swimming and bathing purposes, but carelesly and negligently suffered and permitted children, among them plaintiff's minor son, to so make use of the same.

Further, that on the said day the defendant knew, or could have known by the exercise of ordinary care, that plaintiff's minor son and his playmates and companions were lawfully on the premises of said defendant at said dam or reservoir, by and through an invitation implied by law, for that plaintiff's minor son, and his playmates and companions were on said day lured thereto by the peculiar and tempting attractivness of the same as a swimming pool or bathing pond. It became and was the legal duty of the defendant to warn plaintiff's minor son and his playmates and companions of the dangers attendant on going in swimming in the deep and cold waters of said dam or reservoir and to forbid its use for such purposes and to order plaintiff's minor son and his playmates and companions from the same and from the premises of the defendant, but the defendant carelessly and negligently suffered and permitted plaintiff's minor son and his playmates and companions to go in swimming in the deep and cold waters of the same, and while plaintiff's minor son was so suffered and permitted to bathe in the same, by and through the implied invitation ofthe defendant, and by its careless and negligent acts, the body of plaintiff's minor son sank therein, and he was drowned and he died therein.

The proximate cause of the death is alleged to have been due to the careless and negligent acts of the defendant in suffering and permitting and in failing to prevent minor children to swim and bathe in the dam and reservoir, particularly the minor son of plaintiff, and in suffering and permitting the same to be and remain upon its premises in an open, exposed and unguarded condition, while in the exercise of ordinary care it would have known that it was a dangerous instrumentality peculiarly attractive and alluring to minor children, and that by the implied invitation of the defendant it did entice and allure children, and particularly the minor son of plaintiff, to his death on said day, and whose death could have been prevented by the use and exercise of ordinary care by the defendant.

General and special damages are prayed for. (Tr. 5-10).

A general demurrer was interposed which was, after argument and consideration by the Court, overruled upon the authority of Union Pacific Ry. Co. vs. McDonald, 152 U. S. 262, and Fusselman vs. Yellowstone Valley Co., 53 Mont. 254. (Tr. 11).

The answer of the defendant put in issue the allegations of the complaint, and alleged some affirmative matters which were met by reply, not necessary to be considered here.

On the 21st day of November, 1919, a trial was had by the Court sitting with a jury.

In support of the allegations of the complaint, plaintiff's proofs disclose that defendant's artificial dam and reservoir was of the size and depth substantially as alleged in the complaint on the 13th day of June, 1918 when plaintiff's minor son came to his death therein by drowning. It appears that in 1917 a smaller and shallower dam existed there and that it was enlarged and deepened sometime between the two seasons (Tr. 40-78-85-86-90). The witness Joseph Bertoglio testified the dam was distant from a public road about ten or fifteen yards (Tr. 35). The witness Antone Donetti testified that he saw grocery wagons going upon the road and an automobile and that there were six or seven houses in the immediate vicinity (Tr. 50). The witness Hugo Giachetti testified that the road was twenty-five to thirty feet from the western or northern border of the pond; it led to some mining properties beyond the pond (Tr.60-61) to the same effect as the testimony of Thomas Ciabattari (Tr. 71-72). There was no enclosure around the pond (Tr. 34-48-60-71-79). Four or five signs bearing the words "No Trespassing" "Private Property" and "Danger, ten feet deep, keep out" were posted about the reservoir (Tr. 37-53-54-62-73). The witness Joseph Bertoglio testified that the boys who went swimming there paid no attention to these signs (Tr. 42) to the same effect is the testimony of Thomas Ciabattari (Tr. 73-74) and Joseph Darin (Tr.83) and witness Joseph Bertoglio testified that a pump-room was located about fifteen or twenty yards from the dam in charge of an employee of the defendant but the pump-man never protested against boys swimming in the dam while the witness was there. When asked whether the watchman consented to the boys going in swimming this witness answered that the pumpman never said anything against it (Tr. 32). They were not forbidden to swim in the pond (Tr. 36). On the day of the drowning, the pumpman was there (Tr. 48-49-52). Hugo Giachetti testified that when the boys went in swimming they used to go into the pumproom on Sundays to look at the funny papers; at such times the watchman or pumpman would be attending to his duties and the boys would go in there naked and the pumpman never made protest of any kind (Tr. 57-59-67). The witness Hugo Giachetti testified that the watchman or pumpman saw the boys in swimming there many times but never made protest (Tr. 77) and was in the pump-room many times in 1918 prior to the 13th of June (Tr. 69) further, that the boys making use of the pond for swimming purposes would enter the pump-room with their bodies wet and naked, the pumpman would see them going in and would greet them by saying "hello" (Tr.80-81). The witness Nicholas Fabatz testified that the boys played games in the water and nobody interfered to prevent them from going in the water though the pump-room was twenty-five feet away in charge of a pumpman (Tr. 90). About an hour before the drowning, the pumpman was there watching the boys swim; at that time there were four or five boys in the pond but the watchman made no protest (Tr. 91-92). On the day of the drowning, as many as eleven or twelve or fourteen boys were in swimming at the pond (Tr. 31-51-68-70-81). The drowning occured late in the afternoon; the drowned boy had been there two or three hours (Tr. 54-92). Preceding the drowning, the deceased entered the shallow water about twenty-five feet from the pump house and swam out into the deep water where the drowning occured (Tr. 93). The boy called for help (Tr. 31). The witness Nicholas Fabatz standing nearby thought the boy was only playing in the water when the call for help came (Tr. 95). At the time of the drowning another boy was also apparently drowning but was rescued, (Tr. 94). Both during 1917 and 1918 prior to the drowning, this pond had been made use of by many boys for swimming purposes without protest, and with the knowledge and acquiescence of defendant's watchman or pumpman (Tr. 32-36-49-56-69-74-76-77-88). It was conceded the pump-room was maintained by defendant (Tr. 57). At the time of the drowning, deceased was about four feet six inches tall (Tr. 51) eleven years of age (Tr. 28) a fairly good swimmer (Tr. 38) and had just passed from the sixth to the seventh grade of the common schools (Tr. 43) and was a bright boy for his age (Tr. 44) but was at the reservoir without the knowledge or consent of his parents (Tr. 28-29). Proof of damage was received by the Court (Tr. 100-109).

At the conclusion of plaintiff's case, defendant moved the court to direct the jury to return a verdict for the defendant (Tr. 113-116); this motion was granted by the Court and the jury was instructed to return a verdict in favor of the defendant (Tr. 116-120). Judgment was duly entered upon the verdict (Tr. 124) and the usual proceedings had to bring the matter before this Court on writ of error Tr. 125-138). During the course of the Court's charge, the Court again reiterated its view that the complaint was sufficient to charge the defendant with negligence making use of the following language:

"Briefly, in order that it may appear in the record, the court is satisfied that, as against a general demurrer the complaint states a good cause of action for the negligence of the defendant. It charges that the boy who was drowned was eleven years old; that the defendant built an artificial dam, a hundred by seventy-five feet, one to twelve feet deep, not enclosed, and no watchman, within twenty-five feet of a highway over which this boy and many other people were habited to pass; that the water was fifty degrees cold; that the defendant knew that this place would allure children to swim; that it was its duty to warn them of the danger; that they negligently suffered the boy and others to go swimming and bathing in the cold water, and while the boy who was drowned was bathing, he sank and drowned. The general demurrer only challenged the general sufficiency, not in detail."

The reasons prompting the court to direct a verdict for the defendant appear in the charge (Tr.116-120) and more specifically in the assignment of errors (Tr. 127-132) which appear on the following pages of this brief.

ASSIGNMENT OF ERRORS

1.

The court erred in granting a motion to return a verdict in favor of the defendant in this cause for the reason that the evidence conclusively shows that the plaintiff's deceased minor son was an infant, eleven years of age, at the time he was drowned in the artificial dam and reservoir, maintained by the defendant, and non sui juris, and was upon the premises of the defendant and swimming in said pond upon the invitation of the defendant and the question of his contributory negligence was, and is a question of fact to be resolved by the jury and not a question of law, tó be determined by the court.

2.

The said court erred in charging the jury as follows:

"If in the judgment of the court, as a question of law, the evidence is not sufficient to sustain a verdict for the plaintiff, if the jury should find one, then it is the duty of the court to direct a verdict in favor of the defendant, and in this case the court will do so, its judgment being that the evidence would not sustain a verdict for the plaintiff." Because the quesiton of the negligence of the defendant and the contributory negligence of the plaintiff's deceased minor son were and are questions of fact to be resolved by the jury, and not questions of law, to be determined by the court.

3.

The said court erred in charging the jury as follows:

"Here we find a boy—in the first place we find that it was not near a road that was habitually travelled by this boy and other boys, though that is not material in any phase of the case. After all the location of the pond only goes to what the defendant ought to anticipate and its knowledge, and that might have been well proved by other evidence in the case, as to what the defendant should have anticipated and its knowledge." Because the evidence conclusively shows that there was a public highway within twenty-five feet from the north edge of said artificial pond and that it, and the contiguous territory was habitually traveled by boys of tender age who were allured to said pond by its attractive characteristics for swimming and bathing purposes.

4.

The said court erred in charging the jury as follows:

Here was a boy eleven years old. He was a strong boy for his age, somewhat athletic and a good swimmer, and a boy who was well able to read, and we find a number of signs there—none of these things appear in the complaint—we find also that the company had exercised some reasonable degree of care to warn people of the danger, and boys; that they placed a sign: "Danger, ten feet deep, keep off." "No trespassing," and the like, which this boy could read, or any other boy of his age." Because the evidence shows without contradiction, that defendant had a watchman in charge of a pump station located within tewnty-five feet of said pond, who suffered and permitted children of tender years, including plaintiff's minor son to go swimming and bathing therein, without protest, but with acquiescence and consent of the defendant, whereby the signs adverted to were wholly disregarded by said children.

5.

The said court erred in charging the jury as follows:

"Now, it appears from the evidence that the season before this accident happened—because the Court will finally say in this case that nobody was guilty of any negligence, neither the company nor the boy—it was an accident pure and simple; the boy was conducting himself properly under the circumstances, being a strong boy and a boy well able to swim, and the fact is after all, when he did drown, it was because he had stayed around there, in and out of the water, so long that he was either exhausted, or what is more probable, he was seized by cramps and sank, because the two boys that saw him when he drowned say he had been there about two hours and before they had been there, and all that time in and out of the water; that he was swimming well before and at the time that he went down; that he swam from the low water out and over the deep water, and suddenly threw up his hands and hollered and sank. I think there can be only one inference, that he was seized with cramps." Because the question as to whether the drowning was an accident or was due to defendant's negligence was, and is, a question of fact to be resolved by the jury and not one of law, to be determined by the court.

6.

The said court erred in charging the jury as follows:

"A grown man who comes upon your premises, your duty is not so great towards him. A boy of twelve or fifteen or sixteen, your duty would be a little more than for a man, but not so great as it would be for children of three or four or five or six if you invite them upon your premises expressly or impliedly."

7.

The said court erred in charging the jury as follows:

"For instance, if a man set up ladders outside of his house, and if he knew one's children are accustomed to climb up and play on his roof, if he lets little children not capable of caring for themselves, go up there, three or four or five or six years old, I imagine he still might be held liable, where he would not be for a child twelve or thirteen or fourteen or fifteen. Other circumstances might be imagined."

8.

The court erred in charging the jury as follows:

"But to get right back to this case, here is a boy against whom the defendant, as the court sees it, neglected no detail. They had a pond there; every one has a right to have such things on their premises if they are useful, within the bounds of the statute. This boy was strong, he was able to swim, and apparently to swim for a long time. Defendant had no reason to anticipate that he was not able to care for himself; defendant had no reason to furnish him a guard nor a fence nor anything else." Because the question as to whether said boy was sui juris, was a question of fact to be determined by the jury, and not a question of law, to be determined by the court.

9.

The said court erred in charging the jury as follows:

"He was not negligent in going there, because you might then say that of any person if they go in bathing, that they are negligent, but they are not, if they are able to swim; they are able to take care of themselves. If misfortune comes to them, and anything happens, chance or anything else, or if they stay in till they are exhausted and they sink in deep water, it is an accident and nothing else, and the Court places its decision in this case on that basis." Because questions of accident and negligence as disclosed by the evidence in this case, were and are questions of fact to be decided by the jury and not by the court.

The court erred in directing the jury to return a verdict in favor of the defendant as follows:

"The defendant was not negligent, consequently not negligent as far as this boy is concerned. Consequently the Court will instruct the jury to return a verdict in favor of the defendant."

ARGUMENT

The theory upon which this action is brought is that under the facts stated, defendant is liable in damages to the plainiff for the deah of his minor child by drowning in the artificial pond or reservoir of the defendant in Silver Bow County, Montana, on the 13th day of June, 1918, upon the turn-table or attractive nuisance doctrine.

As pointed out in the statement of facts, the court held the complaint to state facts sufficient to charge the defendant with actionable negligence, supporing its ruling by citing the cases of Union Pacific Ry. Co. vs. McDonald, 152 U. S. 262, and Fusselman vs. Yellowstone Valley Co., 53 Mont. 254. The Fusselman case is authority for the proposition that the attractive nuisance or turntable doctrine is recognized as being the law in the jurisdiction of Montana and that the doctrine extends to cases of this kind; the trial court, however, after holding the complaint as sufficient against atack by general demurrer, at the close of the trial ruled the plaintiff's proofs were not sufficient to justify recovery against the defendant. It is our contention that plaintiff proved by good, competent and sufficient evidence, every material allegation of the complaint and that the court committed reversible error in directing the jury to return a verdict against the plaintiff.

That the defendant maintained an attractive nuisance upon its premises as alleged in the complaint is substantiated by ample proof; that children of tender years were lured thereto for the purpose of using the same as a swimming hole cannot be gainsaid, and that the maintenance of the pond by the defendant as disclosed by the proof was a dangerous instrumentality is manifest from the fact that not only was plaintiff's minor son drowned on the day alleged but that another youngster with him was rescued from drowning. Its presence there in its unguarded condition and with defendant's watchman and pumpman present, tolerant and acpuiescent, was the very attraction which lured deceased to his death. It is true a number of signs or placards were posted at or near the pond warning against danger and that this fact is not alleged in the complaint but on the other hand the proof stands wholly without contradiction that the defendant kept and maintained a pump station within a few feet of the edge of the pond and a very short distance from the pond where the fatal drowning occured, and that this station was in charge of a watchman or pumpman in the employ of the defendant. This servant of the defendant not only did not warn the children of any dangers attendant upon going in swimming in the cold waters of the reservoir, but actually encouraged them to do so by permitting them to make use of the pump station for warming their bodies when chilled and drying and robing themselves therein and to use the place generally for the purposes of youthful pastimes and diversions. This watchman knew of the presence of the deceased at the pond on the day in question for the boy had been in and out of the water a number of times covering a period of two or two and one-half hours and about or within an hour before the fatal drowning occured, the pumpman stood there watching the boys swim; small wonder then that no attention was paid by the boys to the warnings appearingupon the signs and placards adverted to. The nature and instinct, the youthful passions and proclivities common in the majority of boys, especially healthy ones, often impels them for the sake of indulging in pleasurable pastimes to become wholly oblivious and unconscious of impending dangers which those of maturer years are chargeable with knowing as a matter of law.

We respectfully urge that the trial court erred in holding deceased to be sui juris as a matter of law. The general doctrine is, that the question of the negligence or contributory negligence of a child presents one of fact for the jury to pass upon and not one of law for the court to decide. In Kansas Central Railway Company vs. Fitzsimmons 21 Kansas 286, 31 American Reports 203, it was held that where a boy twelve years of age was injured while playing on a turntable left unlocked and unguarded in an open prairie where persons frequently passed, the question as to whether the child was sui juris was properly left to the jury to decide An extensive note accompanies the reported case in 31 American Reports, 203, to which atention is respectfully invited. In the jurisdiction of Montana in the case of Mason vs. N. P. Ry. Co. 45 Mont. 474, the plaintiff, a young lady sixteen years of age whilst driving along the public highway with her fifteen year old brother was injured by colliding with a railroad train at a crossing. The court in passing upon an instruction given by the trial court, used the following language:

' "The court gave the following instruction to the jury: "You are instructed that a child is bound to exercise only the care of (1) those of his own age and understanding, and if you find that the plaintiff and her brother, who was driving the carriage in which she was riding, were children at the time of the alleged injury, and that they exercised such care as a reasonable person of their respective ages would exercise under the circumstances of this case, then neither of them was guilty of contributory negligence which would defeat plaintiff's right to recover in this action." We think this instruction correctly stated the law. White's Supplement to Thompson on Negligence, section 309, thus states the rule: "The measure of responsibility of a person of immature years for contributory negligence is regarded as the average capacity of others of the same age, intelligence and experience, and this is to be considered with reference to the character of the danger to which he is exposed."

"In view of the immaturity of the plaintiff, we cannot say, considering the precautions which were actually taken to discover whether or not a train was approaching, and all the other facts and circumstances of the case, that she was guilty of contributory negligence as a matter of law, and we think the learned district judge erred in so holding. Whether or not she was guilty of contributory negligence was a question of fact to be determined by the jury; they decided the question in the negative, and that decision should stand so far as that feature of the appeal is concerned."

See also the following authorities: Brown vs.

Salt Lake City (1908) 33 Utah 222, 14 L. R. A. (N. S.) 619, 126 Am. St. Rep. 828, 93 Pac. 540, 14 Ann. Cas. 1004. Price v. Atchison Water Co. (1897) 58 Kan. 551, 62 Am. St. Rep. 625, 50 Pac. 450, 3 Am. Neg. Rep. 392. Indianapolis v. Williams (1915) 58 Ind. App. 447, 108 N. E. 387. Kansas City v. Siese (1905) 71 Kan. 283, 80 Pac. 626. Omaha v. Richards (1896) 49 Neb. 224, 68 N. W. 528. Union Pacific Railway Company v. David George McDonald 152 U. S. 262, 38 L. Ed. 434.
Sioux City & P. R. Co. v. Stout, 17 Wall. (84 U. S.) 657, 21 L. Ed. 745.

Conway v. Monida Trust Co. (1918) 47 Mont. 269.

The foregoing discussion presupposes the attractive nuisance or turntable doctrine has found recognition in the jurisdiction of Montana. In 1908 the Supreme Court, in the case of Gates vs. Northern Pacific Railway Company, 37 Mont. 103-116, had the following to say:

"It is my judgment that when the owner or occupier of grounds brings or artificially creates something thereon especially attractive to children, as shown by the nature of the thing itself and the fact that a child was, or children were, attracted to it, and leaves it so exposed that they are likely to come in contact with it, either as a plaything or an object of curiosity, and where their coming in contact with it or playing about it is obviously dangerous to them, the person so exposing the dangerous thing should reasonably anticipate the injury that is likely to happen to them from its being so exposed, and is bound to use ordinary care to guard it so as to prevent injury to them."

The Stout case, 84 U. S. 657, recognized as the leading "turntable" case, has been recognized by the Supreme Court of the State of Montana in the case of Fussleman vs. Yellowstone Valley Co., 53 Mont. 254, an action for damages for the drowning of a child in an irrigation canal; recovery, however, being denied because neither pleadings nor the proofs were sufficient to charge the defendant with liability. The case of Union Pacific Railway Co. v. McDonald 152 U. S. 262, relied upon by the trial court as authority for overruling defendant's demurrer to plaintiff's complaint extends the turntable doctrine to cases involving other dangerous instrumentalities. There can be no question therefore, but that the attractive nuisance and turntable doctrines constitute the rules of decision in the Montana jurisdiction.

Was the learned trial judge under these circumstances justified in holding the defendant company free from negligence as a matter of law? We contend not. A case very much in point it that of Price vs. Atchison Water Company 58 Kan. 551, 62 Am. St. Rep. 625. In that case, plaintiff's minor son, eleven years of age was drowned while playing at one of defendant's reservoirs, the reservoir in question was enclosed with a barb wire fence, ten to twelve wires high; there were two gates through the fence which were kept closed and two contrivances for stiles or sheds nailed to the adjacent trees and enclosing the fence wires and upon and over which boys climbed from the outside to get access to the reservoir; defendant had employed a watchman custodian at the grounds who was aware of the habits of the boys of the town to climb over the stiles or sheds and permitted them to do so without objection. Plaintiff's deceased son went with some companions to the reservoir in question to fish and play and was drowned. A demurrer to the evidence for insufficiency to prove a cause of action was sustained. Upon review by the higher court two questions were raised, and disposed of as follows:

"The contention arising upon the above state of facts divides itself into two principal questions: 1. Was the defendant in error negligent, as to the deceased boy, in maintaining the dangerous reservoir: and 2. Was the deceased guilty of contributory negligence in venturing upon the slanting walls and projecting apron? These are questions of fact, and they should have been left to the jury for determination. They are not questions of law for decision by the court."

In the course of the opinion, the court had the following to say:

"Counsel for defendant in error endeavors to distinguish the "turntable" and other like cases from the one under discussion, upon the ground that, in such first-mentioned cases, the dangerous instruments or places were not inclosed, so as to exclude or warn trespassers, while, in the present case, the reservoirs had been so fenced as to render access to them difficult to say the least, and in any event to operate as notice to stay on the outside because of the dangerous situation within. Whatever merit such precautionary measures might have under other circumstances, it is sufficient to say that in this case, they were not reasonably effective; because it was the daily habit of trespassing boys to mount the fence and frequent the reservoirs on the inside, and this habit was known to the company's responsible agent, and was not only tolerated but went unrebuked by him. Knowing the fence to be ineffective either as barrier or warning, it was the duty of the company to expel the intruders, or adopt other measures to avoid accident. Whatever advantage the defendant in error might have gained from the erection of a reasonably effective barrier or warning is neutralized by the facts of its knowledge that the boys did trespass, and its permission to them to do so. It is as though no fence at all had been erected."

Paraphrasing the latter portion of the foregoing excerpt, we may, we believe, say with entire propriety that whatever advantage the defendant in error might have gained from the erection of the signs at the reservoir where plaintiff's minor son was drowned was neutralized by the facts within defendant's knowledg that many boys of tender years did repeateldy make use of the said reservoir as a swimming hole, at no time rebuked by defendant's watchman but by him tolerated, humored, encouraged and entertained in the pump station of which he had charge, situated on the edge of the dam. It thus became indeed and was in fact an alluring attraction to the neighboring youngsters.

The very fact that defendant had erected signs and placards at or near the pond with such words imprinted thereon as "Danger," "Danger, ten feet deep, keep out" is ample proof of defendant's actual knowledge of the dangerous character of the pond as a swimming hole. The words "Ten feet deep, keep out" of themselves were sufficient to charge the defendant with knowledge, yes with an open admission that the pond was a dangerous instrumentality, particularly alluring to minor children for swimming and bathing purposes, else why did it cause signs bearing them to be erected there?

Prior to June 13th and after the enlargement of the dam, it had already been made use of by children for bathing purposes for at least two weeks, and on the day of the drowning as many as twelve or possibly fourteen young boys were there for that purpose; the public schools had closed that day and the drowned boy had just succeeded in passing from the sixth to the seventh grade in the common schools; the occasion made this particular day therefore, a grand holiday for the boys. True the Troglio boy could swim and had he been possessed of the discretion common in men of mature years, the drowning in all probability would not have occured. The court in its charge to the jury after hearing the facts attributed his death to exhaustion or cramps:

"It was an accident pure and simple; the boy was conducting himself properly under the circumstances, belng a strong boy well able to swim, and the fact is after all when he did drown, it was because he had stayed around there, in and out of the water, so long that he was either exhausted, or what is more probable he was seized by cramps and sank, because the two boys that saw him when he drowned say he had been there about two hours and before they had been there, and all that time in and out of the water; (Tr. 118).

If we are to accept the court's conclusion in this respect, then it is manifest that between the time he first entered the water and the time of the drowning pathological changes occured in his body, due to its temperature being lowered from normal, by reason of its repeated immersion and exertion in the water of the dam, resulting in exhaustion or cramps, and we respectfully submit that a boy of his years could not be charged, as a matter of law with knowledge of the consequences which might ensue from the repeated immersion and exertion of his body in waters concededly of a lower temperature than that of a human body. Had the drowned boy been younger, the court would have permitted the case to go to the jury, for in the charge we find this language:

"I still think that if it had appeared in evidence that little children of three or four or five years of age were coming around this pond, if such a case had been made here, it would have been within the turntable doctrine. This is nothing more than a phase of the general law; it is part of the general law; it comes right back to the proposition that premises must be kept reasonably safe to those who are impliedly invited there."

It would appear from the foregoing excerpts, that it was the court's conclusion that defendant in this case had discharged its duty towards plaintiff's intestate because the boy was eleven years old, strong, athletic and could swim, but that under precisely and exactly similar circumstances the case of negligence would have been made against the defendant had deceased been four or five years of age. Was the court justified in so holding? Had the defendant exercised ordinary or any degree of care to preserve the life of this youngster, and of his associates and companions, may we not here with entire confidence say that one word of protest from the watchman and pumpman in charge would most surely have prevented the fatal consequences suffered by this boy; indeed, we think we may go further and declare with equal confidence that the defendant was guilty of gross negligence in failing to require its servant in charge to do so. In any event, we earnestly maintain the situation presents an undisputed statement of facts from which different inferences might be drawn and therefore, resolveable by a jury and not by a court (See cases cited supra and Volume 8 Rose's notes page 176). The Supreme Court of Montana, in Conway v. Monida Trust Company 47 Mont. 269, made use of the following language:

"At what age a child becomes sui juris, so that negligence may be predicated of his acts, is a matter upon which authorities differ. By some it is held that a child of seven years of age is conclusively presumed incapable of contributory negligence. (Watson v. Southern Ry., 66 S. C. 47, 44 S. E. 375; Taylor

v. Delaware & Hudson Ry., 113 Pa. 162, 57 Am. Rep. 446, 8 Atl. 43; Chicago etc. Ry. Co. v. Welsh, 118 Ill. 572, 9 N. E. 197; Indianapolis etc. Ry. v. Pitzer, 109 Ind. 179, 194, 58 Am. Rep. 387, 6 N. E. 310, 10 N. E. 70) However that may be, the rule in this state is that contributory negligence is not to be inferred as a matter of law, even in the case of a much older child. (Mason v. Northern Pac. Ry. Co., 45 Mont. 474, 124 Pac. 271.)"

In the recent case of Sherris v. Northern Pacific Ry. Co. Decided in 1918, 55 Mont. 189, the Supreme Court of Montana, laid down the following rule:

"The general rule is that after a child has reached the age of fourteen years he is presumed, as a matter of law, to be capable of contributory negligence. (White's Supp. to Thompson on Neg., sec. 315; 20 R. C. L., p. 128.)

In the case of the City of Pekin vs. McMahon, (Ill. 27, L. R. A. 206) the Supreme Court of Illinois in 1895 reached the conclusion that liability attached to the defendant under facts similar and analogous to those in the case at bar and applying the turntable doctrine, made use of the folowing:

"The love of motion, which attracts a child to play upon a revolving turntable, will also attract him to experiment with a floating plank or log which he finds in a pond within his easy reach. The doctrine of the turntable cases is sustained by other cases where the injuries complained of were caused by agencies of a different character. Such are Mackey v. Vicksburg, 64 Miss. 777; Birge v. Gardiner, 19 Conn. 507, 50 Am. Dec. 261; Daley v. Norwich, 81 Ky. 638, 50 Am. Rep. 193; Hydraulic Works Co. v. Orr, 83 Pa. 332; Whirley v. Whiteman, 1 Head, 610."

The Supreme Court of South Carolina in Franks v. Southern Cotton Oil Co. 58 S. W. 960; 12 L. R. A., N. S. 468, held the defendant to be liable for the death of a child who went to its reservoir which defendant maintained in an open field in an unprotected condition where children were accustomed to resort and play. In reaching its conclusion the opinion of Mr. Chief Justice Cooley in Powers v. Harlow, 53 Mich. 507, 51 Am. Rep. 154, was quoted from as follows:

"Children, wherever they go, must be expected to act upon childish impulses; and others, who are chargeable with a duty of care and caution towards them, must calculate upon this, and take precautions accordingly. If they leave exposed to the observation of children anything which would be tempting to them, and which they, in their immature judgment, might naturally suppose they were at liberty to handle or play with, they should expect that liberty to be taken. Or, as was tersely and pithily expressed in the Minnesota case (Keffe v. Milwaukee & St. P. R. Co. 21 Minn. 207, 18 Am. Rep. 393): What an express invitation would be to an adult, the temptation of an attractive plaything is to a child of tender years* * * *If an owner sees fit to keep on his premises something that is an attraction and allurement to the natural instincts of childhood, the law, it is well settled, imposes upon him the corresponding duty to take reasonable precautions to prevent the intrusion of children, or to protect from personal injury such as may be attracted thereby."

An examination of the authorities discloses that in jurisdictions where the turntable doctrine has been extended to embrace other attractive nuisances a variety of instrumentalities has been embraced. It is not our contention that every unguarded pond, reservoir or other water course is or may become an attractive instrumentality alluring to children, but it is our contention that an artificial pond, reservoir or dam may become so, and in the instant case actually did become such. In humid regions where there is an abundance of moisture and consequently innumerable lakes, ponds, streams and water courses, a dam such as the one described in this case may not be attractive to children at all, furthermore, in such places, children of tender years presumably are early in life educated to the dangers attendant upon going in swimming; on the other hand, in arid regions of high altitude where moisture is scarce and natural lakes, ponds, streams and water courses are a rarity, the creation of an artificial pond such as that created and maintained by the defendant in this case is, and of necessity must be, a novelty and its very presence an enticing and alluring attraction to the youths of the community in which it is situated, and in the instant case did actually become so. The defendant having had actual notice of this condition and knowing the pond was habitually frequented by boys of immature years for swimming purposes owed more than a passive duty to them, such as the posting of signs and placards. In view of the fact that the premises were in charge of a watchman and pumpman the defendant owed to these youngsters the active duty to prohibit the use of the pond for the purposes which resulted in the death of plaintiff's intestate.

It is true that some courts deny the right of recovery in actions of this kind unless the injury for which damages is sought was wantonly inflicted, or was due to recklessly careless conduct on the defendant's part, but of these cases Thompson in his work on Negligence says:

"This cruel and wicked doctrine, unworthy of a civilized jurisprudence, puts property above humanity, leaves entirely out of view the tender years and infirmity of understanding of the child, indeed, his inability to be a trespasser in sound legal theory, and visits upon him the consequences of his trespass just as though he were an adult, and exonerates the person or corporation upon whose property he is a trespasser from any measure of duty which they would not owe under the same circumstances towards an adult." (1 Thomp. Neg. 2d ed. s 1026)

In conclusion, we respectfully submit the judgment of the trial court should be reversed and the cause remanded for a new trial.

Respectfully Submitted,

WALKER & WALKER,
C. S. WAGNER,

Attorneys for Plaintiff in Error.
307 Metals Bank Building,
Butte, Montana.

No. 3515

In the United States Circuit Court of Appeals For the Ninth Circuit.

MARTIN TROGLIA,

Plaintiff in Error,

vs.

THE BUTTE & SUPERIOR MINING COMPANY, a Corporation,

Defendant in Error.

Brief of Defendant in Error.

WALKER & WALKER and
C. S. WAGNER,
Attorneys for Plaintiff in Error.

KREMER, SANDERS & KREMER,
Attorneys for Defendant in Error,
O'Rourke Estate Building,
Butte, Montana.

McKEE PRINTING CO., BUTTE, MONT.

No. 3515

In the United States Circuit Court of Appeals For the Ninth Circuit.

MARTIN TROGLIA,

Plaintiff in Error,

vs.

THE BUTTE & SUPERIOR MINING COMPANY, a Corporation,

Defendant in Error.

Brief of Defendant in Error.

STATEMENT OF THE CASE.

The statement of the case on behalf of plaintiff in error consists of a review of the allegations of the complaint rather than one of the testimony. In view of the fact that the record is brief and the conditions surrounding the scene of the unfortunate accident may readily be understood we deem it unnecessary to point out in detail wherein the statement of opposing counsel is inadequate, but it is proper to invite the attention of the court to a few important facts.

The deceased minor was 11 years of age at the time of his death (R., p. 29). All of the witnesses agree that he was a bright youth, strong, athletic and physically above the average boy of his age; that he could read and was a good swimmer (R., pp. 84, 96, 45, 54, 63, 55, 83, 96). It further appears from the record that he had been swimming in the pond before the drowning for a couple of hours, going in for ten or fifteen minutes at a time (R., p. 55). He was considered one of the strong boys in school (R., p. 63). One of his playmates testified that he was a fancy swimmer and he was fond of seeing how long he could stay under water (R., p. 65).

The record further discloses that there were four or five signs in and on the banks of the pond reading variously: "NO TRESPASSING," "10 FEET DEEP—KEEP OFF," "DANGER—10 FEET DEEP," "10 FEET DEEP—KEEP OUT—DANGER" (R., pp. 53, 62, 73, 82). All of the boys knew the signs were there (R., p. 54).

The water was "kind of warm" at the time of the accident (R., p. 74), although the complaint alleges as part of the failure of duty of the defendant in error that it was its legal duty to warn plaintiff's minor son of the dangers attendant on going in swimming in the deep *and cold* waters (R., p. 8), and that the waters were cold, chilly and of low temperature—40 or 50 degrees, etc. (R., p. 7).

The record further discloses the fact that the pond in question was remote from the home of the deceased and from the school which he attended. The pond was about a mile from Meaderville, where deceased lived, and over a mile from the school in the Mc-

Queen Addition, where he went to school. In order to go to the pond from either Meaderville or the school it was necessary for this boy to walk away from Meaderville and from the McQueen Addition over a mile before he could reach the pond at all. It was not along the way that the boys usually traveled in going to or coming from school or in going home. "It was away out of the way" (R., p. 99).

It is further disclosed by the record in the case that the pond in question was not near a road that was habitually or at all travelled by the deceased or the other boys. It appears that there was a road nearby that led to two mines—the Butte & Bacorn and the Butte and Superior, and also to a ranch (R., p. 36). The use of this road was confined to comparatively few persons. The ranchman used it and the boss or superintendent of the Butte & Bacorn travelled over it in his automobile. In 1918 this road was not travelled very much (R., p. 62). There is other evidence that it was used by automobiles and wagons and by a few persons living in houses in the neighborhood (R., pp. 35, 50, 60, 61, 62, 72, 79, 99). There is absolutely no evidence in the case to substantiate the assertion of opposing counsel "that many children passed to and fro including the minor son of plaintiff and his youthful companions and playmates." (Brief of plaintiff in error, p. 3.)

Without unduly prolonging this statement, we submit the record in conjunction with the sketch of the pond which was introduced in evidence at the trial.

ARGUMENT.

It will serve no useful purpose to attempt to explain or reconcile the decisions of the courts in an effort accurately to define the legal status of the deceased at and immediately prior to his death with respect to whether he was technically a trespasser, a licensee or was present in the pond by invitation, express or implied. The weight of opinion is to the effect that the general rule that an owner of premises is under no legal obligation to trespassers or licensees to keep them in proper condition applies with equal force to children and adults. Those courts challenging the application of this general rule in cases involving children of tender years base their argument upon various grounds—the element of "attractive dangers" and knowledge, actual or implied, of the presence of the child, its tender years which constitute justification in departing from the rule in question, and other grounds. Some adopt the exception to the general rule on the ground of "implied intention" on the part of the owner. Some say that the exception is but an application of the maxim "sic utere, etc." Other courts base their reasoning on the ground of "implied invitation," while still others assert simply that the rule is an exception to the general rule born of necessity and adopted in the interest of humanity. An interesting review and criticism of the cases and the reasoning in support thereof are found in Bottum's Adm'r v. Hawkes, 79 Atl., 858 (Vt.).

This court, of course, is familiar with the origin

of the doctrine of "attractive nuisances." It was first announced in *Lynch* v. *Nurdin,* 41 E. C. L., 422; 1 Q. B. 29, 10 Am. Neg. Cases, 77 N. In this country it was first applied in the case of *Sioux City & Pacific Ry. Co.* v. *Stout,* 17 Wall (U. S.), 675, and later approved by the Supreme Court of the United States in *Union Pacific Ry. Co.* v. *McDonald,* 152 U. S., 262. All modern decisions agree that in recent years there has been and is now strong inclination on the part of all courts to restrict the rule rather than to extend it or to repudiate it altogether; and the Supreme Court of the State of Montana has unqualifiedly followed the trend of the courts in strictly limiting the scope of its application.

A REVIEW OF THE MONTANA DECISIONS.

In *Driscoll* v. *Clark,* 32 Mont., 172, it is said:

> "There seems, however, to be a growing tendency in the later cases to strictly limit the doctrine to cases falling within the facts disclosed by Railroad Co. v. Stout, or to renounce the doctrine altogether. (p. 181).
>
> * * * * * * *
>
> "It has been contended broadly that when an owner places or permits anything upon his property which is attractive to others, the invitation may be inferred as a fact by the court or jury. Now, since it is manifest that to some classes of persons, such as infants, the things ordinarily in existence and use throughout the country, such as rivers, creeks, ponds, wagons, axes, plows, woodpiles, haystacks, etc., are both attractive and

dangerous, it is clear that the adoption of such a broad contention would be contrary to reason, lead to vexatious and oppressive litigation, and impose upon the owners such a burden of vigilance and care as to materially impair the value of property and seriously cripple the business interests of the country. Therefore, it has been generally held that the invitation cannot be inferred in such cases. These cases rest upon the sound principle that, where the owner makes such use of his property as others ordinarily do throughout the country, there is not, in legal contemplation, any evidence from which a court or jury may find that he had invited the party injured thereon, though it be conceded that his property or something thereon was calculated to and did attract him. * * *

"The writer of this opinion does not hesitate to say that, in his judgment, the doctrine of the 'turntable cases' is against the weight of authority, and cannot be sustained upon principle or reason. See the following cases: Delaware etc. R. Co. v. Reich, 61 N. J. L., 635, 68 Am. St. Rep., 727, 40 Atl., 682, 41 L. R. A., 831; Turess v. New York etc. R., 61 N. J. L., 314, 40 Atl., 614; Walsh v. Fitchburg R. Co., 145 N. Y., 301, 45 Am. St. Rep., 615, 39 N. E., 1068, 27 L. R. A., 724; Daniels v. New York etc. R. Co., 154 Mass., 349, 26 Am. St. Rep., 253, 28 N. E., 283, 13 L. R. A., 248; Frost v. Eastern R. R., 64 N. H., 220, 10 Am. St. Rep., 396, 9 Atl., 790; Ryan v. Towar, 128 Mich., 463, 92 Am. St. Rep., 481, 87 N. W., 644, 55 L. R. A., 310; Uthermohlen v. Bogg's Run Co., 50 W. Va., 457, 88 Am. St. Rep., 884,

> 40 S. E., 410, 55 L. R. A., 911; Paolino v. McKendall, 24 R. I., 432, 96 Am. St. Rep., 736, 53 Atl., 268, 60 L. R. A., 133."

In the case of *Gates* v. *Northern Pacific Ry. Co.*, 37 Mont., 103, wherein it was sought to apply the doctrine of "attractive nuisances" to a worn out car, bottom side up on the sloping side of a railroad embankment in such a way as to fall upon and kill a child eleven years old, the court adhered to its earlier announced tendency and laid down the rule that to bring an action based on the doctrine of the "turntable cases" it was necessary for plaintiff to allege and prove not only that the car was especially attractive to children, but also, *that the child was too young to appreciate the danger, etc.* From a judgment for plaintiff defendant appealed and the Supreme Court of Montana, in reversing the lower court, said:

> "A peculiar situation appears from the record. Plaintiff relied upon the fact that the deceased was a child of such tender years that he was attracted to the car by its 'queer' appearance, and was therefore not technically a trespasser, and that he was unable to appreciate and understand the danger attendant upon the conditions surrounding him; yet the fact that he was so immature as to bring him within the rule of the *Stout Case* was neither alleged nor proved, and the court gave the jury an instruction on contributory negligence. The plaintiff testified that Amos, who was eleven years of age, was an active, robust boy, able to earn money. In the case of *Buch* v.

Amory Mfg. Co., 69 N. H., 257, 76 Am. St. Rep., 163, 44 Atl., 809, the court said: 'The plaintiff was an infant of eight years. The particular circumstances of the accident—how or in what manner it happened that the plaintiff caught his hand in the gearing—are not disclosed by the case. It does not appear that any evidence was offered tending to show that he was incapable of knowing the danger from putting his hand in contact with the gearing, or of exercising a measure of care sufficient to avoid the danger. Such an incapacity cannot be presumed. * * * An infant is bound to use the reason he possesses and to exercise the degree of care and caution of which he is capable. If the plaintiff could by the due exercise of his intellectual and physical powers have avoided the injury, he is no more entitled to recover than an adult would be under the same circumstances.'

"In view of the fact that the deceased was *prima facie* a trespasser, the burden rested upon the plaintiff to allege and prove facts that would remove that objection to a recovery, and bring the case within the principles laid down in the *Stout Case*. I do not mean to say—because the question is not before us—that a child so young that his trespass in pursuit of an especially attractive object might be excused, could not be guilty of contributory negligence. What I do say is that, where the trespasser is excusable on account of the tender years of the child, the fact should be alleged and some proof offered in support of it, unless the child is so very young that there can be no question of his lack of capacity."

In this last Montana decision the deceased minor was of the same age as John Troglia—11 years. The solitary fact of his age appears in the record but there is not a scintilla of evidence tending remotely to prove the essential ingredient that he was "too young to appreciate the danger" of going into the pond, rather the evidence is all the other way.

The Gates Case not only affirmed the earlier Driscoll-Clark case in limiting the application of the doctrine of the "turntable cases," but went further, as noted, in laying down the rule that it must not only be alleged, but established by evidence that the infant was too young to appreciate the danger.

In *Nixon* v. *Montana, etc. Ry. Co.,* 50 Mont., 95, the Supreme Court of Montana says:

> "The extent to which the 'turntable' doctrine has been accepted in this state and how it may be invoked are disclosed in Driscoll v. Clark, 32 Mont., 172, and in Gates v. Northern Pacific Ry. Co., 37 Mont., 103. * * *
>
> "As elucidating some of the circumstances to which this doctrine *cannot be applied* we incorporated in the Driscoll case certain expressions of the Supreme Court of Texas in *San Antonio, etc. Ry. Co.* v. *Morgan,* 92 Tex., 98, 46 S. W., 28, including the following: 'It has been contended broadly that when an owner places * * * anything upon his property which is attractive to others and *one is thereby induced to go thereon,* the invitation may be inferred as a fact by the court or jury. Now, since it is manifest that to some classes of persons, such as infants, the

things ordinarily in existence and use throughout the country, such as rivers, creeks, *ponds,* wagons, axes, plows, woodpiles, haystacks, etc., are both attractive and dangerous, it is clear that the adoption of such a broad contention would be contrary to reason, lead to vexatious and oppressive litigation, and impose upon the owners such a burden of vigilance and care as to materially impair the value of property and seriously cripple the business interests of the country. Therefore it has been generally held that the invitation cannot be inferred in such cases.' "

Herefrom it will be noted that the Supreme Court of the State of Montana, in adopting the views of the Supreme Court of Texas, with respect to the inapplicability of this doctrine to ponds has specifically held that in Montana this doctrine finds no application in the case of a pond or reservoir.

The next Montana case is that of *Fusselman* v. *Yellowstone Valley, etc. Co.,* 53 Mont., 254, which, when examined, does not in any way suggest any departure by the Supreme Court of this state from the rule laid down in the Driscoll-Clark case, for in the Fusselman case it appears that the judgment of the lower court in favor of the defendant was affirmed solely because of the insufficiency of the evidence with respect to where and the circumstances under which the death occurred and the consequent failure to establish actionable negligence by substantial proof. However, we invite the attention of the court to the rule announced in the Fusselman case, as follows:

> "To state a cause of action under the doctrine of the turntable cases it is not enough for the complaint to show that the premises were attractive to children, or that children generally were attracted thereto, but it must show that the attraction lured the injured child there with the result complained of, the facts pleaded disclosing the causal connection between the negligent act and the injury."

A search of the record fails to disclose that John Troglia ever saw or knew of the existence of the pond until the occasion of his death, although the complaint alleges in effect that he had frequently bathed therein (R., p. 7). He was then seen there carrying a gun (R., pp. 45, 70, 72). It is reasonable to presume that he left his home, a mile away, to go shooting, ignorant that the pond existed. It can scarcely be contended, within the rule announced in the Fusselman case, that the pond "lured the injured child there with the result complained of." Certainly it could not be said that if A had a dangerous bomb (assuming that the same constituted an attractive nuisance), in his cellar and a child of tender years in ignorance of its existence gained access to the cellar and was killed by tampering with it, such attraction could be held to have lured the child to his death.

From the foregoing review of the Montana decisions it appears that the highest court of this state has unequivocally adopted the rule restricting the application of the doctrine of "attractive nuisances" and has even gone further in holding that at least with respect to an infant of the age of eleven years there must be substantial evidence that the child was too young to appreciate the danger and that the attraction in fact lured the child to his death. Herein all of the evidence without contradiction is to the effect that John Troglia was a bright boy, strong and husky, an athlete, runner and fancy swimmer, could read and generally speaking was above the average physically and mentally—certainly not a showing indicative of any incapacity to appreciate the danger of going into the pond in question. Moreover, there is absolutely no evidence that John Troglia was lured to the pond, for so far as the record discloses he never knew that such a pond existed until he was found playing with a gun upon its banks.

An extended examination of modern decisions demonstrates that the rule applicable to what is known as the "turntable cases" finds no application to a case of this kind.

A pond or reservoir is not a dangerous instrumentality within the meaning of the rule as is abundantly and exhaustively shown, both directly and indirectly, by textwriters and the decisions of the courts. Our assertion, of course, is made advisedly upon the record in the instant case. The question here presented is not whether the defendant in error is liable (a) by reason of a trap or pitfall upon his property which may produce death or injury; (b) a hidden or concealed danger; or (c) a dangerous agency in close proximity, or so near a highway that in the use of the highway an accident may occur; but is, whether this pond of water not shown in any particular to differ from a natural body of water was an attractive nuisance such as must subject the defendant in error to liability for the death of the deceased minor child. It was a pond, artificial admittedly, but to all intents and purposes quite like a natural lake presenting only those dangers that in law are considered to be obvious even to those of tender years.

One of the latest expositions of the modern tendency of courts upon this subject is to be found in 20 Ruling Case Law "Negligence," Section 85, page 96:

> "85. WATERS.—Ponds, pools, lakes, streams, and other waters embody perils that are deemed to be obvious to children of the tenderest years; and as a general proposition no liability attaches to the proprietor by reason of death resulting therefrom to children who have come upon the land to bathe, skate, or play. In a recent case the court said: 'That a pond of water is attractive to boys for the purpose of play, swimming and fishing no one will deny. But its being an attractive agency is not sufficient to subject the owner to liability. It must be an agency such as is likely, or will probably, result in injury to those attracted to it. That many boys every year lose their lives by drowning is a matter of common knowledge. But the number of deaths in comparison to the total number of boys that visit ponds, lakes, or streams for purposes of play, swimming and fishing is comparatively small. It would be extending the doctrine too far to hold that a pond of water is an attractive nuisance, and therefore

comes within the turntable cases. Accordingly, a right of recovery has been denied in the case of children eleven, ten, nine, eight, seven, six, and even five years of age. Although a property owner may know of the habit of children to visit waters upon his premises, he is as a rule under no obligation to erect barriers or take other measures to prevent them being injured thereby. According to some of the decisions, if a pond or pool is in close proximity to the highway, a recovery may be had for the drowning of a young child who has fallen therein; but the weight of authority appears to hold to the contrary, except where the facts bring the case within the rule respecting pitfalls adjacent to highways. And there would seem to be no room to doubt but what a pond on an unfenced city lot, formed by surface water on account of the damming up of a natural drain therefor, by the dumping of trash and dirt into it by city authorities, without the knowledge of the owner, who did not know of the existence of the pond, will not render him liable for the drowning of a boy while playing on the pond. In the case of wells, cisterns, conduits, sluices, and the like, it is very plain that the rules above stated have only a limited application, if any at all. The danger from such places differs from that embodied by ordinary ponds and pools, inasmuch as the peril of the former often is concealed or not to be appreciated by the childish mind. Consequently, while a drowning in a pond does not, ordinarily, give rise to a right of action, it not infrequently has been held that the drowning of a child in a well, cistern, or the like, constitutes a ground for recovery. And it has been held that where a conduit that easily can be guarded is permitted to remain unprotected with knowledge that children resort to it, a recovery is properly allowed. But recent cases hold that the owner of a mill race about which children are accustomed to play because of its attractive character is not bound to protect it to prevent accidents to the children, and therefore is not liable for the death of a child who falls into it and is drowned."

"c. PONDS, RESERVOIRS OR STREAMS. As to ponds or reservoirs the weight of authority is that they are not to be classed with turntables and that the owner of premises on which a pond or reservoir is situated is under no obligation to keep the premises guarded against the trespass of children. So it has been held that a properly constructed drain, made for the purpose of carrying off surface water, is not such a contrivance as would be so inviting to a child that the owner would be liable for his death by drowning, due to his playing in the drain during or just after a very heavy rain."

29 Cyc., page 464, "c."

Even in many of the states where the "turntable" doctrine is approved, the courts thereof decline to extend the application of the rule to cases involving ponds or reservoirs.

See *Savannah etc.* v. *Beavers* (Ga.), 39 S. E., 82, which was a case of a five-year-old boy drowned in a pool formed in an excavation on the premises of the defendant; *Stendall* v. *Boyd* (Minn.), 75 N. W., 735, which was a case of a boy not quite five years old, drowned in a quarry on the premises of the defendant; *Moran* v. *Pullman Palace Car Co.* (Mo.), 36 S. W., 659, which was a case of a nine-year-old boy drowned in a quarry filled with water; *Dobbins* v. *Ry. Co.* (Texas), 41 S. W., 62, which was a case of a three-year-old child drowned in a pool of water on a right-of-way of the defendant; *Richards* v. *Connell* (Neb.), 63 N. W., 915, which was a case of a ten-year-old boy drowned in a pond on defendant's premises; *Peters* v. *Bowman* (Cal.), 47 Pac., 113, which was a case of an eleven-year-old boy drowned in a pond of surface water. There are cases which extend the application of the rule to wells, underground conduits and other like bodies of water or streams which by virtue of their construction constitute traps or pitfalls, but we submit that the overwhelming weight of modern authority denies the application of the doctrine of "attractive nuisances" to ponds or reservoirs which to all intents and purposes are similar to natural bodies of water and present none of the characteristics that are concealed, such as for instance, an unguarded well, or the open mouth of a sewer, or conduit into which children might slip or fall, oblivious to the presence of these dangerous instrumentalities.

There is no evidence that there was any latent or hidden danger present other than that which is inseparably connected with any ordinary body of water. It is charged that the water was extremely cold, but the evidence is that it was "kind of warm" (R., p. 74). There is, we submit, absolutely nothing to be found in the record to justify the contention that its then condition was inherently dangerous or obviously or unusually alluring.

> "The doctrine of responsibility for having on one's premises an inviting or attractive danger to children is confined to cases where the dangerous agency is so *obviously* tempting to children that the owner is guilty of negligence for failing to observe and guard against the temptation and danger."
>
> *Tomlinson* v. *Vicksburg S. & R. Ry. Co.* (La.), 79 So., 174.

In the case of *Martin* v. *Northern Pacific Ry. Co.*, 51 Mont., 31, 41, the Supreme Court of the State of Montana discussing the doctrine of implied invitation in a case of an alleged attractive nuisance, says:

> "A swing or rose garden might be peculiarly attractive to children of tender years, but it would overturn every rule of law upon the subject to hold that the owner of private grounds, who maintains exposed thereon either the garden or the swing, by implication invites every child of the community upon his property. Upon the theory of implied invitation—the only one upon which the instruction" (under discussion) "could be applicable at all—it is erroneous in omitting the very essential element of knowledge on the part of the landowner, that the device is *inherently* dangerous, that it is unusually alluring to children of tender years, etc."

Nothing in the record remotely establishes the essential fact that this particular pond was inherently dangerous or that it was obviously or unusually alluring to the deceased son of plaintiff in error.

We have hereinbefore asserted that the overwhelming weight of authority denies the application of the rule of the turntable cases to ponds or reservoirs and we, therefore, are impelled to cite cases in such number as will justify our assertion; and in so doing we take the liberty of quoting therefrom for the purpose of presenting the reasoning of the courts in denying the application of the rule.

In *Zartner* v. *George* (Wis.), 145 N. W., 971, the court in denying the application of the doctrine to a pond, says:

> "The language in Ryan v. Towar, 128 Mich., 470, 55 L. R. A., 310, 92 Am. St. Rep., 481, 87 N. W., 646, is quite suggestive of the necessity of drawing a line limiting liability to trespassers within the bounds of what is reasonable and practical. The court, in commenting upon the case of Kansas C. R. Co. v. Fitzsimmons, 22 Kan., 686, 31 Am. Rep., 203, said: 'Here we have the doctrine of the Turntable Cases carried to its natural and logical result. We have only to add that every man who leaves a wheelbarrow, or a lawn mower, or a spade upon his lawn; a rake, with its sharp teeth pointing upward, upon the ground or leaning against a fence; a bed of mortar prepared for use in his new house; a wagon in his barnyard, upon which children may climb, and from which they may fall; or who

turns in his lot a kicking horse or a cow with calf—does so at the risk of having the question of his negligence left to a sympathetic jury. How far does the rule go? Must his barn door, and the usual apertures through which the accumulations of the stable are thrown, be kept locked and fastened, lest twelve-year-old boys get in and be hurt by the animals, or by climbing into the haymow and falling from beams? May a man keep a ladder or a grindstone or a scythe or a plow or a reaper without danger of being called upon to reward trespassing children, whose parents owe, and may be presumed to perform, the duty of restraint? Does the new rule go still further, and make it necessary for a man to fence his gravel pit or quarry? And, if so, will an ordinary fence do, in view of the known propensity and ability of boys to climb fences? Can a man nowadays safely own a small lake or fishpond? And must he guard ravines and precipices upon his land? Such is the evolution of the law, less than thirty years after the decision of Sioux City & P. R. Co. v. Stout, 17 Wall., 656, 21 L. ed., 745, when, with due deference, we think some of the courts left the solid ground of the rule that trespassers cannot recover for injuries received, and due merely to negligence of the persons trespassed upon.' To this the court might have added that there is a growing tendency to make everybody responsible for the safety of children except their parents."

In the case of *Thompson* v. *Baltimore & Ohio Railroad Co.* (Pa.), 218 Pennsylvania State, 444, Vol.

11 American & English Annotated Cases, page 899, the court says:

> "Whether an owner of land who makes changes on it in the course of its beneficial use, which tend to attract children and to expose them to danger, is under a duty to take special precautions for their safety, is a question on which there is a conflict of authority. That such a duty exists has been asserted in some jurisdictions and denied in others. The earlier cases on the subject followed Sioux City, etc. R. Co. v. Stout, 17 Wall. (U. S.), 657, but the tendency of the later decisions is decidedly against the imposition of such a duty; some of the courts that adopted the ruling in Sioux City, etc. R. Co. v. Stout, have since repudiated it, and others have followed it with hesitation or have limited its application to a particular class of improvements.
>
> "The establishment of such a duty would create a restraint which in some cases would amount to a prohibition, upon a mode of beneficial use of land, for the protection of intruders and intermeddlers. It is difficult to see any ground upon which such a duty can be placed. An owner is not liable for leaving his land in its natural shape. Why should he be held liable for placing structures upon it which are harmless in themselves and are necessary for the lawful use he wishes to make of it? It cannot be said that he invites or allures children, because no such intention in fact exists, nor that he sets a trap for the innocent and unwary. The law does not impose a duty upon the landowner to take special precautions for a

class of persons, a doctrine which, if carried to its logical conclusion, would, as was said in Gillespie v. McGowan, 100 Pa. St., 144, 'charge the duty of the protection of children upon every member of the community except their parents.' In Delaware, etc. R. Co. v. Reich, 61 N. J. L., 635, 40 Atl. Rep., 682, it was said by Gummere, J.: 'The viciousness of the reasoning which fixes the liability on the landowner because the child is attracted lies in the assumption that what operates as a temptation to a person of immature mind is, in effect, an invitation. Such an assumption is unwarranted.' "

In the case of *Erie Railway Co.* v. *Hilt,* 247 U. S., 97, 62 Law Ed., 1003, the Supreme Court of the United States holds:

> "There is no ground for the argument that plaintiff was invited upon the tracks. Temptation is not always invitation. (Citing cases.) In this case, too, the plaintiff was not moved by the temptation, if any, offered by the cars, but by the wish to recover his marble. Therefore, it is unnecessary to consider whether an express invitation would have affected the case, or what conclusion properly could be drawn from the fact that children had played in that neighborhood before and sometimes had been ordered away, etc."

We submit that the foregoing is peculiarly applicable herein when it is recalled that it cannot be claimed that John Troglia was lured or attracted by the pond in the absence of any evidence that he had any knowledge of its existence prior to the time he arrived upon its bank carrying his gun. That there is any evidence of an invitation extended to him we deny.

> "Vacant brickyards and open lots exist on all sides of the city. There are streams and pools of water where children may be drowned; there are any quantities of surface where they may be injured. To compel the owners of such property either to inclose it or to fill up their ponds and level the surface so that trespassers may not be injured would be an oppressive rule. The rule does not require us to enforce any such principle even where the trespassers are children. We all know that boys of eight years of age indulge in athletic sports. They fish, shoot, swim and climb trees. All of these amusements are attended with danger and accidents frequently occur. It is part of the boy's nature to trespass especially where there is tempting fruit; yet I never heard that it was the duty of the owner of a fruit tree to cut it down because a boy trespasser may possibly fall from its branches."
>
> *Gillespie* v. *McGowan,* 100 Pennsylvania, 149.

In *Peters* v. *Bowman,* 115 Cal., 345, 47 Pac., 113, it appeared that the defendant permitted a pond to remain on his premises unguarded and unfenced. A boy of eleven while floating on a raft fell off and was drowned. Therein, the court, although it recognized and approved the "turntable cases," said:

> "A body of water—either standing as in ponds or lakes, or running as in rivers and creeks, or

ebbing and flowing, as on the shores of seas and bays—is a natural object incident to all countries which are not deserts. Such a body of water may be found in or close to nearly every city or town in the land; the danger of drowning in it is an apparent open danger, the knowledge of which is common to all; and there is no just view consistent with recognized rights of property owners, which would compel one owning land upon which such water, or part of it, stands or flows, to fill it up, or surround it with an impenetrable wall. However, general reasoning on the subject is unnecessary because adjudicated cases have determined the question adversely to appellant's contention. No case has been cited where damages have been successfully recovered for the death of a child drowned in a pond on private premises who had gone there without invitation; while it has been repeatedly held that in such a case no damages can be recovered. * * *

"There are streams and pools of water where children may be drowned; there are any quantities of surface where they may be injured. To compel the owners of such property either to inclose it, or to fill up their ponds and level the surface so that trespassers may not be injured, would be an oppressive rule. The law does not require us to enforce any such principle, even where the trespassers are children. We all know that boys of eight years indulge in athletic sports. They fish, shoot, swim, and climb trees. All of these amusements are attended with danger, and accidents frequently occur. It is a part of the boy's nature to trespass, especially where there is tempting fruit; yet I have never heard that it was the duty of the owner of a tree to cut it down because a boy trespasser might possibly fall from its branches. Yet the principle contended for by the plaintiff would bring us to this absurdity, if carried to its logical conclusion. Moreover, it would charge the duty of the protection of children upon every member of the community except their parents."

In *Ritz v. Wheeling* (W. Va.), 31 S. E., 993, the court said:

> "Ought a farmer be liable for failing to put a picket fence around his pond necessary for his cattle? If he does not, some little boy will climb the fence into the farmer's field, drown in the pond, and sue the farmer, on the same principle. The dam that contains water to turn the mill wheel, having a path around it shaded with willows, is very alluring to the child and the man. Must the miller inclose it? The canal, with its tow-path and frogs, is very attractive to the little boy or girl, and dangerous, too. If a child drown in it, is the company liable? How many more instances of things useful in lawful business, and withal very attractive to children, and very dangerous, might be put? And the rule contended for says that, if the thing causing the injury be attractive or seductive, the liability attends it. How many things are, or may be, so to children? 'A child's will is the wind's will.' Almost everything will attract some child. The pretty horse, or the bright red mowing machine, or the pond in the farmer's field, the millpond, canal, the

railroad cars, the moving carriage in the street, electric works, and infinite other things, attract the child as well as the city's reservoir. To what things is the rule to be limited? And where will not the curiosity, the thoughtlessness and the agile feet of the truant boy carry him? He climbs into the high barn and the high cherry tree. Are they, too, to be watched and guarded against him? As was well said in *Gillespie* v. *McGowan,* 100 Pa., 144, 45 Am. Rep., 365, this rule 'would charge the duty of the protection of children upon every member of the community except their parents.' A very onerous duty!"

In *Stendall* v. *Boyd* (Minn.), 75 N. W., 735, the court said:

"The doctrine of the turntable cases is the exception to the rule of non-liability of a land owner for accidents from visible causes to trespassers on his premises. If the exception is to be extended to this case, then the rule of non-liability as to tresspassers must be abrogated as to children and every owner of the property must at his peril make his premises child-proof. If the owner must guard an artificial pond on his premises so as to prevent injury to children who may be attracted to it, he must on the same principle guard a natural pond; and if the latter, why not a brook or creek, for all water is equally alluring to children? If he fenced in his stone quarry after it fills with water so that children cannot reach it —a well nigh impossible task—why should he not be required to do it before, for a stone quarry with its steep and irregular sides might well be an attractive and dangerous place to children? It would seem that there is no middle ground and that the doctrine of the turntable cases ought to be limited to cases of attractive and dangerous machinery. * * * We are of the opinion that the doctrine of the turntable cases ought not to be applied to this case. With the exception of Pekin v. McMahon, 39 N. E. Rep., 484, the courts of last resort, including those which recognize the doctrine of the turntable cases, have uniformly denied the liability of a land owner for injuries to trespassing children by reason of open and unguarded ponds and excavations upon his premises."

In *Klix* v. *Nieman* (Wis.), 32 N. W., 223, the court says:

"If the defendant was bound to fence or guard the pond, upon what principle or ground does this obligation rest? There can be no liability unless it was his duty to fence the pond. It surely is not the duty of an owner to guard or fence every dangerous hole or pond or stream of water on his premises for the protection of persons going upon his land who had no right to go there. No such rule of law is laid down in the books and it would be most unreasonable to so hold."

In *Thompson* v. *Illinois Central Railroad Co.,* 63 So., 185 (Miss.), which was a case involving the death of a minor in a pond upon the theory that the same constituted an attractive nuisance, the court said:

"Of course, one could have anticipated the possibility of this sad event; but we think the danger was comparatively remote. Scattered over the length and breadth of the land are innumerable ponds and lakes, artificial and natural; and occasionally a boy or man loses his life while wading or bathing in such a body of water. If, as a matter of fact, the owners of fish ponds, mill ponds, gin ponds, and other artificial bodies, wherein it is possible that boys may be drowned, can be held guilty of actionable negligence unless they inclose or guard the same, few will be able to maintain these utilities and to our minds an intolerable condition will be created."

"To say that a property owner must guard against such injury to a trespassing boy, simply because it is possible for him in a venturesome spirit to climb into the zone of danger, would be intolerable. In every dooryard and on every street side are shade and ornamental trees. To climb trees is as natural to the average boy as to a squirrel. Such sport is always attended with danger that the climber may lose his hold or break a branch and fall to his severe injury. Not infrequently it may bring him to an elevation where he is exposed to contact with wires carrying electric currents of greater or less intensity. If he falls and breaks his bones, or if he receives a stunning shock of electricity, ought the owner of the tree to be held liable in damages because he did not guard it against the approach of the lad, or because he did not give notice or warning in some way of the dangers to be apprehended in climbing it? No court has ever gone to such an extent, and the establishment of such rule would render the ownership of real estate a very undesirable investment."

> *Anderson* v. *Fort Dodge, etc. Ry. Co.* (Ia.), 130 N. W., 391.

"It is a matter of common knowledge that alluring and attractive flumes, such as the one in question in this case, carrying running water are extensively used in this territory not only by miners in the necessary and proper conduct of their business but by farmers in the necessary diversion and application of the public streams to a beneficial use upon their lands in the cultivation of their crops. Not only flumes, but irrigation ditches, large and small, similar in purpose, construction, and use, and equally dangerous and alluring to the child, are to be found throughout the territory wherever cultivation of the land is carried on, and such conduits, practically impossible to render harmless, are indispensable for the maintenance of life and prosperity. There is no distinction that can properly be drawn for liability for injuries received by a child from any of such various means of diversion or use of water. Both as a matter of law and as a matter of public policy, we feel that the so-called 'turntable doctrine' should not be extended to cover such a case as is here presented."

> *Salladay* v. *Old Dominion, etc. Co.* (Ariz.), 100 Pac., 442.

"The pond appears to be of like character, and, although made by the city, is virtually a reproduction of the ponds found in nature, and nature does not maintain attractive nuisances. That there always is possible danger of a child going upon the ice or falling into the water is true; but such an accident is as likely to occur on any like pond in nature. It has been said that there is possible danger in every step of life from the cradle to the grave, although the danger may not be foreseen. Every tree that stands in the park or in the city presents the possible danger that some boy may climb it and fall to his injury, or even death. Ordinary care requires only that means be taken to avoid such dangers as are reasonably to be apprehended—probable dangers, not possible dangers. The imminence of the danger is ordinarily the measure of care to be taken to avoid it. There seems no reason in this case to hold the city liable which would not have been equally cogent had the boy, in going to or from school, gone through a neighbor's pasture, with the owner's consent, and met a like fate upon a pond therein. We know of no rule that imposes higher care upon a city than upon an individual."

Harper v. *City of Topeka* (Kan.), 139 Pac., 1019.

This case is the latest decision of the Supreme Court of Kansas discovered by us and very clearly overrules earlier Kansas cases' relied on by plaintiff in error.

In the case of *Wheeling* v. *Harvey* (Ohio), 83 N. E., 66 annotated, in 19 L. R. A. (N. S.), page 1136, may be found collated many decisions bearing specifically upon the question as to whether ponds or reservoirs constitute attractive nuisances. Therein are cited the case of City of Pekin v. McMahon, 39 N. E., 484; Price v. Atchison Water Co., 58 Kan., 551, 50 Pac., 450; Kansas City v. Siese, 71 Kan., 283, 80 Pac., 626; Franks v. Southern Cotton Oil Co., 58 S. E., 960, 12 L. R. A. (N. S.), 468—all of which are cited or discussed in the brief of plaintiff in error. It appears that the Supreme Court of Illinois has repudiated the rule laid down in the City of Pekin v. McMahon. Following the citation of these cases are collated a large number of decisions repudiating the rule and reasoning which sustain the doctrine that a pond or reservoir is an attractive nuisance. And the writer of the annotation observes:

> "In the majority of cases, however, the attempt to extend the attractive nuisance doctrine to the dangers of the class discussed" (namely, ponds or reservoirs) "under this subdivision of the note has been unsuccessful."

We invite the attention of the court to the dissenting opinion in the case of *Kansas City* v. *Siese,* supra, which, following the case of *Price* v. *Atchison Water Co.,* supra, holds that a pond or reservoir constitutes an attractive nuisance.

> "In my judgment the Price case carries the principle of the turntable cases far beyond the danger limit. That if in the future the principle there announced shall be followed, we shall adjudge the owner of an apple tree, from which an adventurous boy shall fall and sustain injury, in

> his effort to reach a big, red apple attractively displayed on its branches, guilty of maintaining an attractive nuisance and answerable therefor in damages; or one, for the purpose of affording water for his stock or to run his mill, shall maintain a pond, guilty to the same extent. The claim that cases like the one at bar are governed by the principle of the turntable cases to my mind is against reason and the vast weight of authority." Citing cases.

In the note found on page 200, in Vol. 7, American and English Annotated Cases, it is held:

> "In accord with the doctrine of the reported cases the large majority of the decisions including some which recognize the doctrine of the turntable cases deny the liability of the landowner for injuries to trespassing children by reason of open and unguarded ponds and excavations upon his premises." Citing cases.

In the case of *Barnhart* v. *Chicago, Milwaukee & St. Paul* (Wash.), 154 Pac., 441, it is held:

> "That a pond caused by flood water collecting in a depression on a railroad company's right-of-way is not an attractive nuisance so as to make the railroad company liable for the death of an eight-year-old boy drowned while playing upon a raft on the pond."

See also:

Schwartz v. *Akron Water Works Co.* (Ohio), 83 N. E., 66;

Capp v. *St. Louis* (Mo.), 158 S. W., 616;

Charvoz v. *Salt Lake City* (Utah), 131 Pac., 901;
Johnson v. *Atlas Supply Co.* (Texas), 183 S. W. 31;
Green v. *Linton,* 27 N. Y. Supp., 891;
Von Almens, Adm'r v. *City of Louisville* (Ky.), 202 S. W., 880;
Ryan v. *Towar* (Mich.), 87 N. W., 644;
Riggle v. *Lens* (Ore.), 142 Pac., 346;
City of Omaha v. *Bowman* (Mo.), 40 L. R. A., 531;
La Grande v. *Wilkesbarre, etc.,* 10 Pennsylvania Sup. Ct., 12;
Missouri K. & T. R. Co. v. *Dobbins,* 40 S. W., 861;
McCabe v. *American Woolen Co.*, 124 Fed., 283; affirmed 132 Fed., 1006;
Arnold v. *St. Louis* (Mo.), 53 S. W., 900;
Dobbins v. *Missouri K. & T. Ry. Co.* (Texas), 38 L. R. A., 573;
City of Rome v. *Cheney* (Ga.), 55 L. R. A., 221.

"A pond is not to be treated as an attractive danger within the meaning of the turntable cases."

Smith v. *Jacob Dold Packing Co.,* 82 Mo. App., 9;
Cooper v. *Overton* (Tenn.), 52 S. W., 183.

"A landowner is not liable to trespassers even when those trespassers are children of tender years, for maintaining upon his land an unfenced or unguarded pond, the existence of which is apparent and well known."

Sullivan v. *Huidekoper,* 27 App. D. C., 154;
Overholt v. *Vieths* (Mo.), 6 S. W., 74;
Charlebois v. *Goebic, etc.* (Mich.), 51 N. W., 812;
Polk v. *Laurel Hill Cemetery Assn.* (Cal.), 174 Pac., 414.

As disclosed by the record the deceased minor son of plaintiff in error resided in Meaderville and went to school in McQueen Addition—points at least a mile away from the pond in question. Consequently, it is not a case of a reservoir immediately adjoining a highway habitually frequented by children. Not only John Troglia, but all of the other boys who frequented the spot for the purpose of swimming resided at points far distant therefrom. Under the circumstances the case of *Hanna, Adm'r* v. *Iowa Central Railway Co.,* 129 Ill. App., 134, finds application:

"The claim for damages is based upon a doctrine which is broadly stated by counsel for appellant in their brief as follows: 'As a rule, a trespasser cannot recover damages for an injury, suffered while wrongfully on the premises of another; but while this is the general rule, there is also a well recognized exception to it, which permits a child of tender years, when attracted upon the premises of another and there injured, to recover damages.' And it is argued by counsel that in this case the pond where the accident happened 'was so constructed with reference to its depth, location and attractive character as to impose upon defendant in error the duty of so guarding the pond that children of tender years might not be attracted and allured to the pond, and there come in contact with the danger, or meet the accident which befell plaintiff in error intestate.' This pond did not obtrude itself upon Carl Burch as an attraction and an allurement. It was remote from any street or highway on which he had a right to be or travel; and its allurements and attractions, whatever they may have been, were only presented to those who deliberately and designedly sought them out. Carl Burch could not have come in contact with them except by going nearly or quite a mile and a half from his home. If he took the route that seems generally to have been taken by the boys who went to the pond, he would only reach the swimming hole where the accident occurred by walking more than a third of a mile along and over a network of railway tracks which should have operated as a warning at every stop. A boy who would deliberately brave such dangers for the sake of a swim would hardly be deterred from that pleasure by any ordinary fence or gate.

"It is contended that Carl Burch was a child of such tender years that the attraction and allurement of the pond, remote though it was in point of distance, were irresistible to him on account of his lack of experience and immaturity of mind and judgment. As already stated, he was twelve years and seventeen days old at the time of the accident. Some testimony was introduced showing that his parentage was humble, that he was reared in a home possessng few books and little culture, and that he was behind the average child of his age in his studies. It does not seem to us that this testimony showed, or even tended to show want of native intelligence. It is a matter of common knowledge that the bookish or scholarly boy is not always the most intelligent, especially in regard to the phenomena and aspects presented by nature.

"In the case of Heimann v. Kinnare, 190 Ill., 156, the court said: 'In American and English Encyclopedia of Law (Vol. 7, 2 ed., 409) it is said there can be no recovery if the injury came from a danger fully apprehended by the infant, and of which he had assumed the risks, having the capacity to comprehend and avoid danger; and if a minor had reached years of discretion and is fully capable of comprehending danger and using sufficient care to avoid it, he may be guilty of contributory negligence as a matter of law.'

"Without referring to the numerous Illinois cases cited by our Supreme Court in support of this doctrine, it will be sufficient to say here that the principle thus laid down seems to us sound and wholesome. There is nothing in this record contravening the legal presumption that Carl Burch, a boy more than twelve years old, had 'the capacity to comprehend and avoid' the danger he incurred in going upon a floating log in water where he had been several times before. Fully comprehending the danger, and not using sufficient care and self-restraint to avoid it, he was 'guilty of contributory negligence, as a matter of law.'

"Appellant complains of some rulings in the court below as to the admissions of testimony. These rulings might have been erroneous, had it been the duty of appellee to take measures to prevent the boys of Monmouth from going to the pond to swim; but in the absence of any duty to take such measures, the errors, if any there were, worked no harm to appellant.

"We are of opinion that for the two reasons above stated the peremptory instruction of the court below directing the jury to find the defendant not guilty, was properly given.

"The judgment of the lower court is, therefore, affirmed."

Hanna, Adm'r v. *Iowa Central Railway Co.*, 129 Illinois Appellate Court Reports, 134-139.

It is argued that because the defendant in error erected danger signs near the pond, such act constituted an open admission that the pond was a dangerous instrumentality particularly alluring to minor children (Brief of plaintiff in error, pp. 23-24). Upon the face of the record it was not incumbent upon defendant in error to erect such signs, and the mere gratuitous assumption of a self-imposed duty not required by law does not constitute actionable negligence, if such duty is not performed.

Barney v. *Hannibal & St. Joseph Ry. Co.*, 26 L. R. A., 847.

Opposing counsel cite the cases of *Mason* v. *Northern Pacific Ry. Co.*, 45 Mont., 474, and *Conway* v. *Monidah Trust*, 47 Mont., 269, on the strength of which they contend that the trial court was precluded from granting the motion for a directed verdict herein solely because John Troglia was eleven years of age; but counsel overlook the fact that under the theory of this case it was incumbent on plaintiff in error to prove that John Troglia was too young to appreciate the danger of going into the pond and that he was, as a matter of fact, lured to his death by the pond in question.

The case of *Mason* v. *Northern Pacific Ry. Co.*, was not brought under the doctrine of attractive nuisances and none of the rules applicable to such an action is involved or discussed therein.

Likewise, the *Conway Case, supra,* was not one involving the rule under discussion. It was brought to recover for injuries sustained by a minor who fell down a shaft unguarded or fenced as required by City Ordinance. It constituted a hidden trap. None of the essentials of pleading or proof in an attractive nuisance case were therein involved or referred to. On the other hand, the case of *Gates* v. *Northern Pacific Ry. Co.*, 37 Mont., 103, *supra,* clearly announces the rule that in such a case as the one at bar, where lack of appreciation of danger due to immaturity is a vital issue, a boy of eleven years of age and shown to be bright, strong and athletic is deemed to possess adequate intelligence to know and appreciate the danger of going into the water. It is not an inflexible rule of law that simply because the record discloses that a boy is eleven years of age, he is to be held as too young to appreciate the danger of going into a pond or tampering with fire.

In the case of *Nicolosi* v. *Clark* (Cal.), 147 Pac., 971, it is held that a boy of ten years of age, not alleged to be deficient in intellect and understanding, will be held as a matter of law chargeable with knowledge that he has no right to take things from an open implement box of a contractor on a street and so be guilty of an unwarranted trespass in so doing, barring right of recovery for injury by dynamite caps so taken.

Mr. Thompson, in his Commentaries on the Law of Negligence, Vol. 1' Section 1051, discussing "accidents ascribed to childish inexperience, indiscretion and misfortune," cites cases wherein he justifies the decisions of courts denying recovery to boys of the age of John Troglia, who were injured as a result of accidents of the character described by him.

A discussion of contributory negligence on the part of John Troglia is beside the mark, until there is, first of all, substantial evidence of negligence on the part of the defendant in error. Of this we assert there is none.

We submit that this is clearly a case which can only be classified as an accident or one due to childish indiscretion on the part of the deceased Troglia. The record discloses that immediately prior to his death he had been in the pond off and on for a period of two hours (R., p. 55), and that he was fond of seeing how long he could stay under water (R., p. 65). It further discloses that he swam from the lower part to the east part and then he shouted for help a couple of times (R., p. 93). The witness Fabatz thought he was only playing in the water when he was drowning; "that he was only playing when he was calling for help, because the witness knew he was a good swimmer" (R., p. 95). That from prolonged submersion in the pond while engaged in the pastime of seeing how long he could stay under the water, he became exhausted is clear. To hold that under all of the circumstances the defendant in error was guilty of actionable negligence proximately contributing to his untimely end is sustained neither by law, reason nor justice, and we submit that the judgment of the lower court should be affirmed.

Respectfully submitted,

KREMER, SANDERS & KREMER,
Attorneys for Defendant in Error.

No. 3516

/ 3

United States

Circuit Court of Appeals

For the Ninth Circuit.

EDWARD WHITE, as Commissioner of Immigration for the Port of San Francisco,

Appellant,

vs.

CHAN WY SHEUNG,

Transcript of Record.

Upon Appeal from the Southern Division of the United States District Court for the Northern District of California, First Division.

Filmer Bros. Co. Print, 330 Jackson St., S F., Cal.

No. 3516

United States
Circuit Court of Appeals
For the Ninth Circuit.

EDWARD WHITE, as Commissioner of Immigration for the Port of San Francisco,

Appellant,

vs.

CHAN WY SHEUNG,

Transcript of Record.

Upon Appeal from the Southern Division of the United States District Court for the Northern District of California, First Division.

Filmer Bros. Co. Print, 330 Jackson St, S F., Cal.

INDEX TO THE PRINTED TRANSCRIPT OF RECORD.

[Clerk's Note: When deemed likely to be of an important nature, errors or doubtful matters appearing in the original certified record are printed literally in italic; and, likewise, cancelled matter appearing in the original certified record is printed and cancelled herein accordingly. When possible, an omission from the text is indicated by printing in italic the two words between which the omission seems to occur.]

Names and Addresses of Attorneys of Record.

For Petition and Appellee:

JOSEPH P. FALLON, Esq., San Francisco, Cal.

For Respondent and Appellant:

UNITED STATES ATTORNEY, San Francisco, Cal.

In the Southern Division of the United States District Court for the Northern District of California, First Division.

No. 16,672.

In the Matter of CHAN WY SHEUNG, on Habeas Corpus.

Praecipe for Transcript of Record.

To the Clerk of Said Court:

Sir: Please make copies of the following papers to be used in preparing transcript on appeal:

1. Petition for Writ of Habeas Corpus.
2. Order to Show Cause.
3. Demurrer to Petition.
4. Order Overruling Demurrer and Directing that Writ of Habeas Corpus Issue Returnable November 22, 1919.
5. Writ of Habeas Corpus and Marshal's Return of Service.
6. Return to Writ of Habeas Corpus.
7. Order Discharging Petitioner, dated Nov. 22, 1919.
8. Notice of Appeal.

9. Petition for Appeal.
10. Assignment of Errors.
11. Order Allowing Appeal.
12. Citation on Appeal.
13. Stipulation of Attorneys and Order of the Court that Respondent's Exhibits "A," "B" and "C," being the record of the Bureau of Immigration, be transferred to the United States Circuit Court of Appeals for the Ninth Circuit, to be considered in their original form, and without being transcribed or copied.

ANNETTE ABBOTT ADAMS,
United States Attorney.
BEN F. GEIS,
Asst. United States Attorney.

[Endorsed]: Filed at 11 o'clock and 45 Min. A. M. Jun. 9, 1920. W. B. Maling, Clerk. By C. M. Taylor, Deputy Clerk. [1*]

In the Southern Division of the United States District Court for the Northern District of California, First Division.

No. 16,672.

In the Matter of CHAN WY SHEUNG, on Habeas Corpus.

*Page-number appearing at foot of page of original certified Transcript of Record.

Petition for a Writ of Habeas Corpus.

To the Honorable, the Southern Division of the United States District Court, for the Northern District of California, First Division.

The petition of Jew Shep respectfully shows:

I.

That your petitioner is a Chinese person and a citizen of the United States, and a resident of the City and County of San Francisco and Northern District of California.

II.

That Chan Wy Sheung, the detained person, on whose behalf this petition is made, is the natural son of Chan Young (Ngeung), a native-born citizen of the United States, and as such is entitled to enter the United States.

That the said Shan Wy Sheung, hereinafter in this petition referred to as the "detained," is unlawfully imprisoned, detained, confined and restrained of his liberty by Edward White, Commissioner of Immigration for the Port of San Francisco at the Immigration Station at Angel Island, County of Marin, State and Northern District of California; that said imprisonment, detention, confinement and restraint are illegal, and that the illegality thereof consists in this, to wit: That it is claimed by the [2] said Commissioner that the said detained is a Chinese person and an alien not subject or entitled to admission into the United States under the terms and provisions of the Acts of Congress of May 6, 1882, July 4, 1884, November 3, 1893, and the Act of Congress of April 29, 1902, as amended and re-enacted by Section 5 of the Deficiency Act of April 7, 1904, which said acts are commonly known and referred to as the Chinese Exclusion or Restriction Acts; and that he, the said Commissioner, intends to deport the said detained Chan Wy Sheung away from and out of the United States to the Republic of China.

That the said Commissioner claims that the said detained arrived at the port of San Francisco on or about the 23d day of July, 1918, on the steamship "Tenyo Maru," and thereupon made application to enter into the United States as a citizen of the United States by virtue of being the foreign-born son of Chan Young (Ngeung), now deceased, who was a native-born citizen of the United States, and that the application of the said detained to enter the United States as a citizen thereof by virtue of being the foreign-born son of a native-born citizen of the United States was denied by the said Commissioner of Immigration, and that appeal was thereupon taken from the excluding decision of the said Commissioner of Immigration to the Secretary of the Department of Labor and that the said Secretary thereafter dismissed the said appeal. That it is claimed by the said Commissioner that in all of the proceedings had herein the said detained was accorded a full and fair hearing; that the action of the said Commissioner and said Secretary was taken and made by them in the proper exercise of the discretion committed to them by the statutes in such cases made and provided and in accordance with the regulations promulgated under the authority contained in said statutes. [3]

But, on the contrary, your petitioner, on his information and belief alleges that the hearing and proceedings had herein and the action of the said Commissioner and the action of the said Secretary and officials acting thereunder, was and is in excess of the authority committed to them by law and in this behalf your petitioner alleges:

That the detained arrived at the port of San Francisco July 23, 1918, and made application to enter the United States as a citizen thereof by reason of being the foreign-born son of Chan Young (Ngeung), a native-born citizen of the United States; that said application was denied by the immigration officials at the port of San Francisco; that thereafter an appeal was taken therefrom to the Secretary of Labor, and said Secretary of Labor sustained the decision of the port officials and dismissed said appeal; that thereafter a petition for a writ of habeas corpus was filed for and on behalf of the detained in the above-entitled court and said court ordered a writ of habeas corpus to issue; that in the return to said writ filed in said court the respondent prayed that the same be referred back to the Department of Labor for further and proper proceedings; that the petitioner for the detained in view of the detained's long confinement and the unavoidable delay in the decision of the Court consented and did make a motion that the matter be referred back to the Department of Labor, and that the writ be dismissed without prejudice to the detained; that thereafter and after further hearing had thereon before the Department of Labor the detained was again denied admission by the said immigration officials and said Secretary of Labor.

That your petitioner alleges upon information and belief that the relationship of father and son is fully established and is so conceded to be by the said immigration officials, and that the [4] adverse action of said officials and the said Secretary of Labor is based solely upon the alleged lack of proof of the father's nativity, notwithstanding the fact that proof was offered in 1899 of said nativity and the father was duly admitted as a native-born citizen of the United States; and that said proof fully satisfied the officials then in control; that since said year of 1899 the father has brought to and was permitted to land, two sons who were admitted as citizens of the United States and who are now residents thereof; that the said Chan Young (Ngeung), father of said detained, died in the year 1912 or six years before the hearing had thereon; that to deny the said detained admission after the repeated findings of prior officials of said Department of Labor that the said Chan Young (Ngeung) was in truth and fact a native-born citizen of the United States, especially when the said Chan Young (Ngeung) is now dead and unable to defend the said right, is an abuse of the discretion committed to them by law, and their finding is without the letter and the spirit of the law.

That your petitioner further alleges that the evidence submitted upon the application of the said detained to enter the United States was of such a conclusive kind and character and was of such legal weight and sufficiency that it was an abuse of discretion not to be guided thereby; and that no evidence was introduced that would warrant the said Department of Labor officials in denying the nativity of the father and the right of the said detained to enter the United States.

That your petitioner was informed that said decision to deport the detained was reached September 18, 1919, and the same would take place at 1 o'clock September 19, 1919, unless stayed by an order of this Honorable Court. [5]

That your petitioner has not in his possession any part of the record or testimony submitted upon the examination of the case of the said detained under the direction of the said Commissioner of Immigration, or any copy of the reports rendered thereon, nor copies of the proceedings had before the Secretary of Labor at Washington, and the surrender of the said detained having been requested for the purpose of his deportation by virtue of the action of the Secretary of Labor as aforesaid, and a copy of the said proceedings being in the possession of the said Commissioner, your petitioner does therefore stipulate that when a copy of the said immigration record is brought before this Court and produced by the immigration authorities, in accordance with their custom and practice in cases of this character, that your petitioner will then and there agree, and asks that the said immigration record so presented, be deemed and considered part and parcel of this petition, with the same force and effect as if filed herewith.

WHEREFORE, your petitioner prays that a writ of habeas corpus issue herein as prayed for, directed to the Commissioner, and directing him to hold the body of the said detained within the jurisdiction of this Court, and to present the body of the said detained before this Court, at a time and place to be specified in said order, together with the time and cause of his detention so that the same may be inquired into, all to the end that the said detained may be permitted to enter the United States and take up his residence therein as a citizen of the United States, having a lawful right to said privilege, and that he may thereafter go hence without day.

Dated San Francisco, Cal., September 18, 1919.

JOSEPH P. FALLON,
Attorney for Petitioner. [6]

State of California,
City and County of San Francisco,—ss.

Jew Shep, being first duly sworn, deposes and says:

That he is the petitioner named in the foregoing petition; that he had heard read the same and knows the contents thereof; that the same is true of his own knowledge, except as to those matters therein stated on his information and belief, and as to matters he believes it to be true.

JEW SHEP.

Subscribed and sworn to before me this 18th day of September, 1919.

[Seal of the Notary] WM. E. CHARD,
Notary Public, in and for the City and County of San Francisco, State of California.

[Endorsed]: Filed Sep. 17, 1919. W. B. Maling, Clerk. By C. W. Calbreath, Deputy Clerk. [7]

In the Southern Division of the United States District Court for the Northern District of California, First Division.

No. 16,672.

In the Matter of CHAN WY SHEUNG, on Habeas Corpus.

Order to Show Cause.

Upon reading and filing the verified petition of Jew Shep praying for the issuance of the writ of habeas corpus,—

IT IS HEREBY ORDERED that Edward White, as Commissioner of Immigration at the port of San Francisco, at Angel Island, be and appear before the above-entitled court, Department Number One thereof, on Saturday, the 27th day of September, 1919, to show cause, if any he has, why a writ of habeas corpus should not issue in this matter and the petition granted as prayed, and this at the hour of 10 o'clock of said day; and

IT IS FURTHER ORDERED, that said Chan Wy Sheung be not removed from the jurisdiction of this Court until further order of this Court; and

IT IS FURTHER ORDERED, that a copy of this order be served upon said Edward White or such other person having the said Chan Wy Sheung in custody as an officer of said Edward White.

Dated September 18, 1919.

M. T. DOOLING,
United States District Judge.

[Endorsed]: Filed Sep. 18, 1919. W. B. Maling, Clerk. By C. W. Calbreath, Deputy Clerk. [8]

In the Southern Division of the United States District Court for the Northern District of California, First Division.

No. 11,672.

In the Matter of CHAN WY SHEUNG, on Habeas Corpus.

Demurrer to Petition for Writ of Habeas Corpus.

Now comes the respondent, Edward White, Commissioner of Immigration at the port of San Francisco, in the State and Northern District of California, and demurs to the petition for a writ of habeas corpus in the above-entitled cause and for grounds of demurrer alleges:

I.

That the said petition does not state facts sufficient to entitle petitioner to the issuance of a writ of habeas corpus, or for any relief thereon.

II.

That said petition is insufficient in that the statements therein relative to the record of the testimony taken on the trial of the said applicant are conclusions of law, and not statements of the ultimate facts.

WHEREFORE, respondent prays that the writ of habeas corpus be denied.

ANNETTE ABBOTT ADAMS,
United States Attorney,
BEN F. GEIS,
Asst. United States Attorney,
Attorneys for Respondent.

[Endorsed]: Filed Nov. 15, 1919. W. B. Maling, Clerk. By C. W. Calbreath, Deputy Clerk. [9]

In the Southern Division of the United States District Court for the Northern District of California, First Division.

No. 16,672.

In the Matter of CHAN WY SHEUNG, on Habeas Corpus.

(Opinion and Order Overruling Demurrer and for Writ to Issue.)

JOSEPH P. FALLON, Esq., Attorney for Petitioner.

ANNETTE ABBOTT ADAMS, United States Attorney, and BEN. F. GEIS, Esq., Assistant United States Attorney, Attorneys for Repondent.

RUDKIN, District Judge.

The facts in this case are substantially as follows: Chan Young, the father of the present applicant, was admitted to the United States in December, 1899, as a native-born citizen, after a full hearing before the proper department. The testimony introduced on that hearing, consisting of the testimony of the then applicant, his father and at least one other witness familiar with the time and place of the applicant's birth, showed without contradiction that the applicant was born at 751 Sacramento Street, San Francisco, State of California, in the year 1875. In the year 1909 or 1910 Chan Way Bon, a son of Chan Young, was admitted as the son of a native-born citizen and in 1917 Chan Way Ging, another son was likewise admitted as the son of a native-born citizen. It is conceded by the Government that the present applicant is a brother of the two last-named [10] Chinese and a son of Chan Young who, as already stated, was formally admitted to the United States as a native-born citizen twenty years ago. Chan Young died in San Francisco in 1912, having resided continuously in the United States from the time of his admission up to the time of his death. The grandfather is likewise dead. The denial of the admission in this case was based upon the fact that the father of the applicant under the name of Chun Wan Mong on the 2d of June, 1899, filed a statement and declaration for registration at Victoria, British Columbia, stating that he was born at Ding Boy, Sun Woy District, China, and that he was then of the age of twenty-five years. There was likewise offered in evidence at the present hearing a certified copy of an application for a certificate of residence made by Chin Wong the grandfather of the applicant on the 10th day of April, 1894, stating, among other things, that the applicant arrived in the United States in

May, 1876. Based upon these two certificates or statements it is argued by the Government that the father of the applicant was not a citizen of the United States and that the statement of the grandfather that he arrived in the United States in 1876 precludes the idea that his son was born here in 1875. There was grave doubts in my mind whether either of these statements or certificates are competent or admissible as against the applicant. There is also a grave doubt in my mind as to whether the declaration made at Victoria was actually made by the father of the applicant. There is no testimony in the record tending to identify him as the person who made the declaration, and while the declaration shows that the applicant arrived at Victoria by the steamship "Umatilla," [11] there is other testimony tending to show that he *is* fact arrived by the steamer "Walla Walla." But, in any event, it occurs to me that the department should be bound in this matter by its own prior adjudications made at a time when the witnesses who had knowledge of the facts were living and able and competent to testify, and that it would be gross injustice to exclude the applicant now after the death of his father and his grandfather when it is utterly impossible to explain or contradict the *ex parte* statements offered in evidence against him. As to the declaration of the grandfather, it was not in evidence before the department and perhaps should not be considered but in any event, it seems to me, entirely too much importance is attached to the matter of dates. As showing the *case* with which dates may be confused or misstated I need only refer to the record in this case to show that it is stated in the brief of counsel for the Government and the memorandum prepared for the Secretary that the application of the grandfather was dated April 13th, 1894, whereas the certified copy shows that it was dated April 10th. Furthermore, the testimony given by the grandfather in 1899 showed that he had been a resident of the United States for thirty years, which would carry him back to the sixties and away beyond the birth of the applicant. I am fully aware of the limited power of the courts in matters of this kind and of the force and effect that must be given to the findings of the department, but I am of the opinion that the question here presented is one of law rather than of fact, and I cannot sanction the injustice that would result from excluding the applicant from the country at this late day under the circumstances [12] disclosed by this record. The decisions of the department after a full hearing should be given some effect and should not be overturned or set aside in subsequent cases upon any such pretext or for any such reasons as are here assigned.

The demurrer is, therefore, overruled and the writ of habeas corpus will issue as prayed, returnable November 22d, 1919, at 10 o'clock A. M.

November 20th, 1919.

[Endorsed]: Filed Nov. 20, 1919. W. B. Maling, Clerk. By C. W. Calbreath, Deputy Clerk. [13]

In the Southern Division of the United States District Court for the Northern District of California, First Division.

No. 16,672.

In the Matter of CHAN WY SHEUNG, on Habeas Corpus.

Writ of Habeas Corpus.

The President of the United States of America, to the Commissioner of Immigration, Port of San Francisco, California, Angel Island, Calif., GREETING:

YOU ARE HEREBY COMMANDED that you have the body of the said person by you imprisoned and detained, as it is said, together with the time and cause of such imprisonment and detention, by whatsoever name the said person shall be called or charged, before the Honorable FRANK H. RUDKIN, Judge of the United States District Court for the Northern District of California, at the courtroom of said court, in the city and county of San Francisco, California, on the 22d day of November, A. D. 1919, at 10 o'clock A. M., to do and recieve what shall then and there be considered in the premises.

AND HAVE YOU THEN AND THERE THIS WRIT.

WITNESS, the Honorable FRANK H. RUDKIN, Judge of the said District Court, and the seal thereof at San Francisco, in said District, on the 20th day of November, A. D. 1919.

[Seal] WALTER B. MALING,
Clerk.
By C. W. Calbreath,
Deputy Clerk.

JOSEPH P. FALLON,
Attorney for Petitioner. [14]

Return on Service of Writ.

United States of America,
Nor. District of Cal.,—ss.

I hereby certify and return that I served the annexed writ of habeas corpus on the therein named Commissioner of Immigration by mailing a true and correct copy thereof to Edward White, Comr. of Immigration, personally, at Angel Island, in said District, on the 20th day of November, A. D. 1919.

J. B. HOLOHAN,
U. S. Marshal.
By G. A. White,
Deputy.

[Endorsed]: Filed Nov. 21, 1919. W. B. Maling, Clerk. By C. W. Calbreath, Deputy Clerk. [15]

In the Southern Division of the United States District Court for the Northern District of California, First Division.

No. 16,672.

In the Matter of CHAN WY SHEUNG, on Habeas Corpus.

Return to Writ of Habeas Corpus.

Comes now Edward White, Commissioner of Immigration at the port of San Francisco, by P. A. Robbins, Immigrant Inspector, and in return to said petition for a writ of habeas corpus, admits, denies and alleges as follows:

I.

Admits that Chan Wy Sheung the detained, is the natural born son of Chan Young (Ngeung).

II.

Denies that Chan Young (Ngeung) is or ever was a native-born citizen of the United States, but in this connection alleges the fact to be that the said Chan Young (Ngeung) was born in King Boy village, Sun Woy District, China.

III.

Denies that Chan Wy Sheung is entitled to enter the United States as the natural-born son of said Chan Young (Ngeung) or for any other reason or at all entitled to enter the United States.

IV.

Denies that Chan Wy Sheung referred to as the detained is unlawfully imprisoned, detained, confined and restrained or is unlawfully imprisoned, or detained, or confined or restrained of his liberty by Edward White, [16] Commissioner of Immigration for the port of San Francisco or by any other person or persons whatever at the Immigration station at Angel Island, County of Marin, State and Northern District of California or elsewhere or at all so imprisoned or detained or confined or restrained, but in this connection alleges the facts respecting the imprisonment, detention, confinement and restraint of the said Chan Wy Sheung to be that the said Chan Wy Sheung is detained by the said Commissioner of Immigration at the Immigration station at Angel Island, County of Marin, State and Northern District of California for deportation to China pursuant to and under the authority of an order of deportation regularly and lawfully made by John W. Abercrombie, Acting Secretary of Labor, after a careful consideration of all the facts and evidence in the case presented to him upon appeal from the decision of the Board of Special Inquiry denying the application of the said Chan Wy Sheung to enter the United States after a full, fair and complete hearing of all the evidence submitted on behalf of the said Chan Wy Sheung.

V.

Denies that the hearing and proceedings or the hearing or proceedings had herein and the action of the said Commissioner and the action of the said Secretary and officials acting thereunder or the action of the said Commissioner or the action of the said Secretary or the officials acting thereunder was and is or was or is, in excess of the authority committed to them by law, but in this connection alleges the fact to be that the hearing and proceedings had and the action of the said Commissioner and the said Secretary and the said officials, was and is under and pursuant to the authority committed to them by law. [17]

VI.

Denies that the action of the said Commissioner or the action of the said Secretary or the officials acting thereunder in denying the said detained admission into the United States was or is an abuse of the discretion committed to them by law but in this connection alleges the fact to be, that decisions of the said Commissioner, the said Secretary and the officials acting thereunder are not *res judicata,* and that the evidence on which the said Commissioner, Secretary and officials acting thereunder acted in denying said detained admission into the United States was and is competent, proper and sufficient evidence showing that Chan Young (Ngeung) was not born in the United States and in so deciding said Immigration officials did not abuse the discretion committed to them by law.

VII.

Denies that the finding of the said Commissioner or the said Secretary of Labor or the officials acting thereunder was or is without the letter or spirit of the law.

VIII.

Denies that the evidence submitted upon the application of said detained to enter the United States was or is of such a conclusive kind or character or was of such legal weight or sufficiency that it was an abuse of discretion to deny the application of said detained to enter the United States.

IX.

Denies that the said Commissioner, or said Secretary or the officials acting thereunder or either or any of them were not guided by the evidence submitted and before said officials upon the application of the said [18] detained to enter the United States.

X.

Denies that no evidence was introduced that would warrant the said Department of Labor officials in denying the nativity of the father Chang Young (Ngeung) or the right of the said detained to enter the United States, but in this connection alleges the fact to be that there was evidence introduced that would and did warrant the said Department of Labor officials in denying the nativity of the father and the right of the said detained to enter the United States.

WHEREFORE, respondent prays that the said petition be denied and said Chan Wy Sheung be remanded to the custody of respondent for deportation and for such other and further relief as to this Court seems equitable and just.

ANNETTE ABBOTT ADAMS,
United States Attorney.

BEN F. GEIS,
Asst. United States Attorney. [19]

United States of America,
Northern District of California,
City and County of San Francisco,—ss.

P. A. Robbins, being first duly sworn, deposes and says: That he is a Chinese and Immigrant Inspector connected with the Immigration Service for the port of San Francisco, and has been specially directed to appear for and represent the respondent, Edward White, Commissioner of Immigration, in the within entitled matter; that he is familiar with all the facts set forth in the within return to the writ of habeas corpus and knows the contents thereof; that of affiant's knowledge the matters set forth in the return to the writ of habeas corpus are true, excepting those matters which are stated on information and belief, and that as to those matters he believes it to be true.

P. A. ROBBINS.

Subscribed and sworn to before me this 22d day of November, 1919.

[Seal] C. W. CALBREATH,
Deputy Clerk of the United States District Court, Northern District of California.

[Endorsed]: Filed Nov. 22, 1919. W. B. Maling, Clerk. By C. M. Taylor, Deputy Clerk. [20]

In the Southern Division of the United States District Court for the Northern District of California, First Division.

No. 16,672.

In the Matter of CHAN WY SHEUNG on Habeas Corpus.

Order Discharging Detained.

This matter having been regularly brought on for hearing upon the issues joined herein, and the same having been duly heard and submitted, and due consideration having been thereon had, it is by the Court now here ordered, that the said named person in whose behalf the writ of habeas corpus was sued out is illegally restrained of his liberty, as alleged in the petition herein, and that he be, and he is hereby discharged from the custody from which he has been produced, and that he go hence without day.

Entered this 22d day of November, A. D. 1919.

[Seal] WALTER B. MALING,
Clerk.
By C. W. Calbreath,
Deputy Clerk.

[Endorsed]: Filed Nov. 22, 1919. W. B. Maling, Clerk. By C. W. Calbreath, Deputy Clerk. [21]

In the Southern Division of the United States District Court for the Northern District of California, First Division.

No. 16,672.

EDWARD WHITE, as Commissioner of Immigration at the Port of San Francisco,
Appellant,

vs.

CHAN WY SHEUNG,
Appellee.

Notice of Appeal.

To the Clerk of the Above-entitled Court, to Chan Wy Sheung and to Joseph P. Fallon, Esq., His Attorney.

You and each of you will please take notice that Edward White, Commissioner of Immigration at the port of San Francisco, appellant herein, hereby appeals to the United States Circuit Court of Appeals for the Ninth Circuit, from an order and judgment made and entered herein on the 22d day of November, 1919, setting aside the return to the petition for a writ of habeas corpus, and discharging the said Chan Wy Sheung from the custody of the said Edward White, Commissioner of Immigration at the port of San Francisco, and appellant herein.

Dated this 18th day of May, 1920.

ANNETTE ABBOTT ADAMS,
United States Attorney,
BEN F. GEIS,
Asst. United States Attorney,
Attorneys for Appellant.

Due service and receipt of a copy of the within admitted this 18th day of May, 1920.

JOSEPH P. FALLON,
Atty. for Appellee.

[Endorsed]: Filed May 18, 1920. W. B. Maling, Clerk. By C. W. Calbreath, Deputy Clerk. [22]

In the Southern Division of the United States District Court for the Northern District of California, First Division.

No. 16,672.

EDWARD WHITE, as Commissioner of Immigration at the Port of San Francisco,

Appellant,

vs.

CHAN WY SHEUNG,

Appellee.

Petition for Appeal.

To the Honorable M. T. DOOLING, Judge of the District Court of the United States for the Northern District of California.

Edward White, as Commissioner of Immigration at the port of San Francisco, appellant herein, feeling aggrieved by the order and judgment made and entered in the above-entitled cause on the 22d day of November, 1919, discharging Chan Wy Sheung from the custody of said appellant, does hereby appeal from said order and judgment to the United States Circuit Court of Appeals for the Ninth Circuit, for the reasons set forth in the assignment of errors filed herewith.

WHEREFORE, petitioner prays that his appeal be allowed and that citation be issued, as provided by law, and that a transcript of the record, proceedings and documents, and all of the papers upon which said order and judgment were based, duly authenticated, be sent to the United States Circuit Court of Appeals for the Ninth Circuit, under the rules of such Court and in accordance with the law in such case made and provided.

Dated this 18th day of May, 1920.

ANNETTE ABBOTT ADAMS,
United States Attorney.

BEN F. GEIS,
Asst. United States Attorney.

Due service and receipt of a copy of the within admitted this 18th day of May, 1920.

JOSEPH P. FALLON,
Atty. for Appellee.

[Endorsed]: Filed May 18, 1920. W. B. Maling, Clerk. By C. W. Calbreath, Deputy Clerk, [23]

In the Southern Division of the United States District Court for the Northern District of California, First Division.

No. 16,672.

EDWARD WHITE, as Commissioner of Immigration at the Port of San Francisco,

Appellant,

vs.

CHAN WY SHEUNG,

Appellee.

Assignment of Errors.

Comes now Edward White, Commissioner of Immigration at the port of San Francisco, respondent in the above-entitled cause, and appellant in the appeal to the United States Circuit Court of Appeals for the Ninth Circuit, taken herein by his attorneys, Annette A. Adams, United States Attorney, and Ben F. Geis, Assistant United States Attorney, and files the following assignment of errors upon which he will rely in the prosecution of his appeal in the above-entitled cause to the United States Circuit Court of Appeals for the Ninth Circuit, from the order and judgment made by this Honorable Court on the 22d day of November, 1919.

I.

That the Court erred in granting the writ of habeas

corpus and discharging the alien Chan Wy Sheung from the custody of Edward White, Commissioner of Immigration at the port of San Francisco.

II.

That the Court erred in holding that it had jurisdiction to issue the writ of habeas corpus in the above-entitled cause as prayed for in the petition of said Chan Wy Sheung for a writ of habeas corpus. [24]

III.

That the Court erred in holding that the allegations set forth in the petition for writ of habeas corpus were sufficient in law to justify the granting and issuing of a writ of habeas corpus.

IV.

That the Court erred in finding that the evidence upon which the Secretary of Labor issued the order of deportation for the said Chan Wy Sheung was insufficient in character.

V.

That the Court erred in holding that Chan Wy Sheung was unlawfully imprisoned, detained, confined and restrained of his liberty by Edward White, Commissioner of Immigration at the port of San Francisco.

VI.

That the Court erred in holding that the evidence taken at the hearings accorded that said Chan Wy Sheung before the immigration officials was insufficient to justify the said respondent Edward White to hold, detain or deport the said Chan Wy Sheung.

VII.

That the Court erred in holding that Chan Young,

the alleged father of the said Chan Wy Sheung, was a citizen of the United States.

VIII.

That the Court erred in holding that Chan Wy Sheung was a citizen of the United States and as such citizen entitled to enter the United States.

IX.

That the Court erred in determining as a question of fact that Chan Wy Sheung was a citizen of the United States as against the decision of the Board of Special Inquiry and the Secretary of Labor that the said Chan Wy Sheung was not a [25] citizen of the United States.

X.

That the Court erred in holding there was not sufficient evidence that Chan Wy Sheung was not a citizen of the United States.

XI.

That the Court erred in holding that there was an abuse of discretion on the part of the Board of Special Inquiry and the Secretary of Labor in denying the said Chan Wy Sheung the right to enter the United States.

XII.

That the Court erred in holding that the hearing or hearings accorded the said Chan Wy Sheung by the immigration officials was or were unfair.

WHEREFORE, appellant prays that the said order and judgment of the United States District Court, for the Northern District of California, made and entered herein, in the office of the clerk of said court, on the said 22d day of November, 1919, setting aside the return to the petition for a writ of habeas corpus, and discharging the said Chan Wy Sheung from the custody of Edward White, Commissioner of Immigration, be reversed, and that the said Chan Wy Sheung be remanded to the custody of said Commissioner of Immigration.

Dated this 18th day of May, 1920.

ANNETTE ABBOTT ADAMS,
United States Attorney.
BEN F. GEIS,
Asst. United States Attorney,
Attorneys for Appellant.

Due service and copy of the within admitted this 18th day of May, 1920.

JOSEPH P. FALLON,
Atty. for Appellee.

[Endorsed]: Filed May 18, 1920. W. B. Maling, Clerk. By C. W. Calbreath, Deputy Clerk. [26]

In the Southern Division of the United States District Court for the Northern District of California, First Division.

No. 16,672.

EDWARD WHITE, as Commissioner of Immigration at the Port of San Francisco,

Appellant,

vs.

CHAN WY SHEUNG,

Appellee.

Order Allowing Appeal.

On motion of Annette A. Adams, United States Attorney, and Ben F. Geis, Assistant United States Attorney, attorneys for appellant in the above-entitled cause,—

IT IS HEREBY ORDERED, that an appeal to the United States Circuit Court of Appeals for the Ninth Circuit, from the order and judgment of November 22, 1919, heretofore made and entered herein, be, and the same is hereby allowed, and that a certified transcript of the records, testimony, exhibits, stipulations and all proceedings be forthwith transmitted to the said United States Circuit Court of Appeals for the Ninth Circuit, in the manner and time proscribed by law.

Dated, this 18th day of May, 1920.

M. T. DOOLING,
Judge of the District Court.

Due service and receipt of a copy of the within admitted this 18th day of May, 1920.

JOSEPH P. FALLON,
Atty. for Appellee.

[Endorsed]: Filed May 18, 1920. W. B. Maling, Clerk. By C. W. Calbreath, Deputy Clerk. [27]

In the Southern Division of the United States District Court, for the Northern District of California, First Division.

No. 16,672.

In the Matter of CHAN WY SHEUNG on Habeas Corpus.

Stipulation (for Transmitting Original Exhibits to Appellate Court).

It is hereby stipulated and agreed by and between the respective parties in the above-entitled cause that the records of the Immigration Service, which were filed in the above-entitled court as Respondent's Exhibits "A" "B," and "C" and which were made a part of respondent's return to the petition for a writ of habeas corpus in said cause, may be transferred, their original form and without being transcribed or copied, to the United States Circuit Court of Appeals for the Ninth Circuit, and the said records of the immigration service are and may there be considered as a part of respondent's return to the said petition for a writ of habeas corpus, and the record in determining this cause on appeal to the said United States Circuit Court of Appeals for the Ninth Circuit, without objection on the part of either of the said respective parties.

Dated this 18th day of May, 1920.

ANNETTE ABBOTT ADAMS,
United States Attorney,
BEN F. GEIS,
Asst. United States Attorney,
Attorneys for Appellee.
JOSEPH P. FALLON,
Attorney for Petitioner.

Due service and receipt of a copy of the within acknowledged this 18th day of May, 1920.

JOSEPH P. FALLON,
Atty. for Appellee.

[Endorsed]: Filed May 18, 1920. W. B. Maling, Clerk. By C. W. Calbreath, Deputy Clerk. [28]

In the Southern Division of the United States District Court, for the Northern District of California, First Division.

No. 16,672.

In the Matter of CHAN WY SHEUNG on Habeas Corpus.

Order Transmitting Original Exhibits to Appellate Court.

It appearing to the Court that it is both necessary and proper that the records of the Immigration Service referred to in the above stipulation should be inspected in the United States Circuit Court of Appeals for the Ninth Circuit, in determining the appeal of the said cause, the same having been filed and considered as stated in this court:

IT IS THEREFORE ORDERED that the said records be transferred in their original form by the clerk of this *court the* clerk of the United States Circuit Court of Appeals for the Ninth Circuit, to be retained by said clerk until the appeal in the above-entitled cause is properly disposed of, at which time the same are to be returned to the clerk of the above-entitled court.

Dated this 18 day of May, 1920.

M. T. DOOLING,
United States District Judge.

Due service and receipt of a copy of the within admitted this 18th day of May, 1920.

JOSEPH P. FALLON,
Atty. for Appellee.

[Endorsed]: Filed May 18, 1920. W. B. Maling, Clerk. By C. W. Calbreath, Deputy Clerk. [29]

Certificate of Clerk U. S. District Court to Transcript on Appeal.

I, Walter B. Maling, Clerk of the District Court of the United States, for the Northern District of California, do hereby certify that the foregoing 29 pages, numbered from 1 to 29, inclusive, contain a full, true, and correct transcript of certain records and proceedings, in the Matter of Chan Wy Sheung, on Habeas Corpus, No. 16,672, as the same now remain on file and of record in this office; said transcript having been prepared pursuant to and in accordance with the Praecipe for Transcript of Record (copy of which is embodied herein), and the instructions of the attorney for appellant herein.

I further certify that the cost for preparing and certifying to the foregoing transcript on appeal is the sum of Eleven Dollars and Thirty-five Cents ($11.35).

Attached hereto is the original Citation on Appeal, issued herein (page 31).

IN WITNESS WHEREOF, I have hereunto set my hand and affixed the seal of said District Court, this 25th day of June, A. D. 1920.

[Seal] WALTER B. MALING,
Clerk.
By C. M. Taylor,
Deputy Clerk. [30]

(Citation on Appeal.)

UNITED STATES OF AMERICA,—ss.

The President of the United States, to Chan Wy Sheung and to His Attorney, Joseph P. Fallon, Esq., GREETING:

You are hereby cited and admonished to be and appear at a United States Circuit Court of Appeals for the Ninth Circuit, to be holden at the city of San Francisco, in the State of California, within thirty days from the date hereof, pursuant to an order allowing an appeal, of record in the clerk's office of the United States District Court for the Northern District of California, Southern Division, First Division, wherein Edward White, as Commissioner of

Immigration for the port of San Francisco is appellant and you are appellee, to show cause, if any there be, why the decree rendered against the said appellant, as in the said order allowing appeal mentioned, should not be corrected, and why speedy justice should not be done to the parties in that behalf.

WITNESS, the Honorable M. T. DOOLING, United States District Judge for the Northern District of California, this 18th day of May, A. D. 1920.

M. T. DOOLING,
United States District Judge. [31]

[Endorsed]: No. 16,672. United States District Court for the Northern District of California, Southern Div., First Div. Edward White, Commissioner of Immigration, Appellant, vs. Chan Wy Sheung. Citation on Appeal. Filed May 19, 1920. W. B. Maling, Clerk. By C. M. Taylor, Deputy Clerk.

Due service and receipt of a copy of the within admitted this 19th day of May, 1920.

JOSEPH P. FALLON,
Atty. for Appellee.

[Endorsed]: No. 3516. United States Circuit Court of Appeals for the Ninth Circuit. Edward White, as Commissioner of Immigration for the Port of San Francisco, Appellant, vs. Chan Wy Sheung, Appellee. Transcript of Record. Upon Appeal from the Southern Division of the United States District Court for the Northern District of California, First Division.

Filed June 25, 1920.

F. D. MONCKTON,

Clerk of the United States Circuit Court of Appeals for the Ninth Circuit.

By Paul P. O'Brien,

Deputy Clerk.

In the Southern Division of the United States District Court, for the Northern District of California, First Division.

No. 16,672.

EDWARD WHITE, as Commissioner of Immigration at the Port of San Francisco,

Appellant,

vs.

CHAN WY SHEUNG,

Appellee.

Order Extending Time to Docket Case.

Good cause appearing therefor and upon motion of Ben F. Geis, Assistant United States Attorney, attorney for respondent and appellant herein:

IT IS HEREBY ORDERED that the time *within to* docket the appeal taken herein in the office of the Clerk of the U. S. Circuit Court of Appeals for the Ninth Circuit may be and the same is hereby extended for the period of thirty days from and after the 17th day of June, 1920.

Dated San Francisco, Calif., June 12, 1920.

M. T. DOOLING,
United States Dist. Judge.

Service of the foregoing order and receipt of a copy thereof is hereby admitted this 14th day of June, 1920.

JOSEPH P. FALLON,
Attorney for Appellee.

[Endorsed]: No. 3516. United States Circuit Court of Appeals for the Ninth Circuit. No. 16,672. In the Southern Division of the District Court of the United States for the Northern District of California, First Division. Edward White, as Commissioner of Immigration at the Port of San Francisco vs. Chan Wy Sheung, on Habeas Corpus. Order Extending Time to Docket Case. Filed June 14, 1920. F. D. Monckton, Clerk. Re-filed June 25, 1920. By F. D. Monckton, Clerk.

No. 3516

IN THE

United States Circuit Court of Appeals

For the Ninth Circuit

EDWARD WHITE, as Commissioner of Immigration for the Port of San Francisco,

Appellant,

vs.

CHAN WY SHEUNG,

Appellee.

APPELLANT'S BRIEF

FRANK M. SILVA,
United States Attorney.

BEN F. GEIS,
Assistant U. S. Attorney,
Attorneys for Appellant.

Neal, Stratford & Kerr, S. F. —7867

No. 3516

IN THE

United States Circuit Court of Appeals

For the Ninth Circuit

EDWARD WHITE, as Commissioner of Immigration for the Port of San Francisco,

Appellant,

vs.

CHAN WY SHEUNG,

Appellee.

APPELLANT'S BRIEF

STATEMENT OF FACTS.

This is an appeal from the judgment of the United States District Court for the Southern Division of the Northern District of California, First Division, made and entered on the 22nd day of November, 1919, discharging on writ of habeas corpus Chan Wy Sheung, the appellee herein.

Chan Wy Sheung is a Chinese person twenty-three years of age, born in Gin Boy Village, China (Ex. A, p. 26), where he has always lived (Ex. A, p. 24).

He claims to be the foreign born son of Chan Young (See affidavits Ex. A. pp. 1 and 2) alias Chan Ngeung, alias Chan Woon Mung (Ex. A. p. 26), an alleged native born citizen of the United States, and therefore claims the right of entry into the United States as a citizen thereof.

He was denied admission after a hearing before a Board of Special Inquiry, from whose decision an appeal was taken to the Secretary of Labor at Washington, D. C., where the decision of said Board was affirmed and the alien ordered deported.

He claims that his alleged father died in San Francisco March 3, 1912 (Ex. A, p. 26, Ex. B, p. 77). He testifies that he has two brothers, Chan Wy Won and Chan Wy Ging, who were admitted into the United States December, 1909; and July or August, 1917, respectively (Ex. A, pp. 25-26), the latter being a witness in the present case (Ex. A, p. 35).

The Immigration records at Angel Island show that Chan Wy Bon, Number 10375/115 arrived at the port of San Francisco on the SS "Korea" December 26, 1909, and was admitted January 1, 1910, as the son of a native (Ex. B, p. 49) and that Chan Wy Ging, Number 16366/6-24, arrived at the same port July 20, 1917, and was also admitted as the son of a native August 28, 1917 (Ex. B, p. 36), the prior landed brother, Chan Wy Bon, appearing as a witness (Ex. B, p. 14) and also furnishing an affidavit (Ex. B, p. 2).

Both Chan Wy Ging and Chan Wy Bon testified that their father, Chan Young, was dead (Ex. B, pp. 22 and 14).

In the case of Chan Wy Bon the alleged father, Chan Young, alias Chan Woon Mung, appeared as a witness (Ex. B, p. 44) and testified that he was born in the United States, K. S. 1-4-29 (June 2, 1875).

The said Chan Young presented as evidence of his right to be and remain in the United States the affidavit of his alleged father, Chan Wong, subscribed and sworn to December 6, 1899, bearing the endorsement of J. P. Jackson, Collector of Customs, showing he was landed December 26, 1899, ex SS "Umatilla" December 23, 1899, San Francisco, California (Ex. B, p. 55), and in the upper right hand corner thereof bearing the following endorsement:

> "1/2/10 appeared as father of Number 115 'Korea' December 26/09 M."

This endorsement has reference to the case of Chan Wy Bon (Ex. B, p. 49), in which Chan Young appeared as a witness (Ex. B, p. 44). A copy of said affidavit is also a part of the record (Ex. B, p. 58) in the case of the alleged father, Chan Young, an applicant for admission in 1899 (Ex. B, p. 75).

The relationship between the applicant and his alleged father is not questioned (Ex. A, p. 55) and there is no doubt that the alleged father is the Chan

Young who was admitted at this port December 26, 1899 (Ex. B, pp. 75 and 55).

Chan Wy Sheung was denied admission for the reason that both the Board of Special Inquiry and the Secretary of Labor found from the evidence that the alleged father, Chan Young, was not a citizen of the United States. (Ex. A, pp. 40 and 63).

ARGUMENT.

Twelve errors are assigned in the appeal on this case but the Government will argue chiefly the ninth error so assigned, to-wit:

> "That the Court erred in determining as a question of fact that Chan Wy Sheung was a citizen of the United States as against the decision of the Board of Special Inquiry and the Secretary of Labor; that said Chan Wy Sheung was not a citizen of the United States."

Whether or not Chan Wy Sheung is entitled to enter the United States as a citizen thereof depends solely and entirely upon the fact whether or not his alleged father, Chan Young, is or is not a citizen of the United States by reason of birth therein.

It is true that the proof of his (Chan Young's) citizenship was satisfactory to the Collector of Customs who admitted him as a citizen December 26, 1899 (Ex. B, p. 75).

It was upon this same proof of Chan Young's citizenship that the son, Chan Wy Bon (Ex. B, p.

49) was admitted January 14, 1910, the examining inspector who handled the case reporting as follows:

> "The status of the father and the essential trip was established by papers taken from the files of our office (Chan Young 'Umatilla' December 23, 1899, landed December 26, 1899.) No prior testimony with reference to marriage. In view of the foregoing recommend admission."

In the case of Chan Wy Ging, a son, admitted October 28, 1917 (Ex. B, p. 36) the same proof was relied upon as appears from the record.

> "The alleged father's American nativity was established to the satisfaction of the Collector of Customs in 1899 and again conceded in 1909 when Chan Wy Bon was landed."

In the present case, however, the Immigration officials were not satisfied as to the citizenship of the alleged father, Chan Young, alias Chan Woon Mung, and requested that an investigation be made at Victoria, B. C. (Ex. A, p. 8), the port from which he sailed when he applied for admission in 1899 (Ex. B, p. 61). In reply to this request the inspector in charge at Victoria, B. C., reported as follows:

> "Inclosed herewith Canadian form C.I. 4 statement and declaration of registration showing that Chin Won Mong landed here on the S.S. 'Umatilla' June 2, 1899. The Canadian records also show that he sailed from here on the S.S. 'Umatilla' for San Francisco December 20, 1899, under the name of Chan Young.

You will note that this alien landed here June 2, 1899, on the 'Umatilla' from San Francisco, paid the required $50 head tax, and was admitted to Canada as a laborer; also that his last place of domicile was given as Hong Kong, China, and birthplace Gin Boy Village, China. While the Dominion Immigration records do not show what vessel he arrived on from the Orient, they are of the opinion that he came from China via San Francisco in bond. Their records also show that he returned to San Francisco December 20, the same year, under the name of Chin Young, but the records give no explanation why he left here under a different name."

The manifest record of the SS "Gaelic" of May 22, 1899, shows that one Chun Won Mong, Grocer, China, age 25, in transit from Victoria departed on SS "Walla Walla" May 26, 1899, water transit, no papers (Ex. A, p. 11).

It was contended on behalf of petitioner in the court below that this could not be the father of the present applicant, as the Canadian records show that he arrived on the SS "Umatilla". It is possible, however, that when the notation was made on the manifest that the SS "Walla Walla" was the vessel scheduled for that day and that the SS "Umatilla" was substituted therefor and the notation on the manifest not changed accordingly. Be this as it may, the point is not material. The Canadian records show that Chan Woon Mong admitted there on June 2, 1899, to whom the certificate refers, sailed from Victoria, B.C. on the SS "Umatilla" for San Francisco December 20, 1899 under the name of Chin Yong (Ex. A, p. 10). The Immigration record at this port shows that Chin Yong arrived at San Francisco ex SS "Umatilla" December 23, 1899, and was admitted December 26, 1899. (Ex. B, p. 75).

At that time he testified that he was twenty-five years old, born in San Francisco at 751 Sacramento Street, second floor, in K.S first year 1875 (Ex. B, p. 62). That he went to Victoria this year, second or third month, where he worked in a cannery; that he paid head tax and received a certificate for it which he left with friends in Canada.

Two witnesses, Chun Wong, his alleged father, (Ex. B, p. 70) and Jang Yet (Ex. B, p. 65) testified in his behalf.

Chun Wong testified that he had lived in this country thirty years; that he was engaged as general laborer; that he had a certificate of residence Number 70815, laborer, dated San Francisco, April 13, 1894. That his wife, Ng Leung, lived in Gin Boy Village, China; that he had one son, Chun Yung, twenty-five years old, and who had just come from Victoria on the Steamer; that said son was born K. S. first year (1875) in San Francisco, 751 Sacramento Street, second floor (Ex. B, p. 70). That Chan Young left China the third month this year and went to Victoria (Ex. B, p. 69).

Jang Yet testified that he had known Chun Wong more than twenty years since he came in K. S. first year (1875); that he knew his wife Ng Shee then living in Ging Buey Village; that he had one son, Chun Yung, 25 years old, born 751 Sacramento Street; that he was learning to run a sewing machine at his (Chun Young's) father's place at that time, and that he was here two months before he, Chun Young, was born. It was on this evidence that the Collector of Customs admitted Chan Young, the father of the present applicant, in 1899.

As against this evidence we now have in the present case the record of Chan Young's, alias Chan Woon Mung's admission at the port of Victoria, B. C., June 2, 1899, wherein he testified that he was twenty-five years old, born at Gin Boy Village, District of Sun Woy. That he was a laborer; that his last place of domicile was Hong Kong, and that he paid a tax of $50 at the time of his entry (Ex. B, p. 76).

Respondent's Exhibit C is a certified copy of the original application of Chin Wong for a certificate of residence under the Act of May 5, 1892 as amended by the Act of 1893.

On the outside of this certificate appear the figures 14415, underneath which appear the figures 70815. The first of these figures 14415 refers to the number of the application, and the figures 70815 to the number of the certificate issued as a result of said application. The certificate so issued bears the same number 70815 as the one produced by Chun Wong when he appeared as a witness for his son, Chan Young, in 1899 (Ex. B, p. 70).

In this application for certificate of residence Chin Wong or Chin Young on April 10, 1894, testified under oath that he arrived in the United States in May, 1876, at the port of San Francisco per steamer, or nearly a year subsequent to the date on which it is claimed his alleged son, Chan Young, was born. The affidavit of Chan Wong (Ex. B, p. 58) gives the exact date of Chan Wong's birth in the United States as Kuong Suey first year, fourth month, and twenty-ninth day, or June 2, 1875, according to American reckoning. Chan Wong's witnesses to said application, Chan Jow, on the second page of said application testified under oath on April 10, 1894, that said Chin Wong arrived in the United States in May, 1876, per steamer.

Neither the Canadian record of Chan Woon Mung's admission at Victoria, B. C. in 1899 (Ex. B, p. 76) nor the application of his alleged father, Chin Wong, for a certificate of residence was before the Collector of Customs when Chan Young was admitted in 1899, nor were they before the Commissioner of Immigration when his alleged sons, Chan Wy Bon and Chan Wy Ging were admitted in 1910 and 1917 respectively. If this evidence had been before them, or if this evidence had been before the officers handling this case at the time they were under consideration, it is fair to presume that none of the applicants would have been admitted, for if Chin Wong first came to this country in 1876 he could not have had a son born here in 1875 as claimed.

Which testimony is entitled to the most credence, that of Chan Wong, the alleged father of Chan Young, that he had a son born here in 1875, or his statement that he first came to this country in 1876, which would preclude the possibility of his having a son born here in 1875 as claimed.

There was no motive for his testifying to anything other than the truth when he made his application for a certificate of residence April 10, 1894. It was otherwise, however, when he testified in 1899 as he wanted to have his son, Chan Young, admitted as a citizen. He had apparently forgotten his earlier testimony and it was necessary to fix a date and place of birth within this country concerning which all the witnesses could agree.

This contradictory testimony of the alleged father, Chan Wong, together with the testimony of Chan Woon Mong given at the time of his admission at Victoria, B. C., June 2, 1899 (Ex. B, p. 76), who is shown by the Canadian records to be the same person who left there under the name Chan Young December 20, 1899, ex SS "Umatilla" for San Francisco (Ex. A, p. 10) and was admitted at this port December 26, 1899 (Ex. B, p. 75), that he was born in Gin Boy Village is, it seems to us, conclusive proof of the fact that the father of the present applicant, Chan Wy Sheung, variously known and referred to as Chan Ngeung, Chan Woon Mung, and Chan Young was not born in the United States as claimed, and that his admission as such in 1899 was gained by fraud.

The entry of Chan Wy Bon and Chan Wy Ging was made possible by reason of the fraud perpetrated by their alleged father and the grandfather, and the present applicant now seeks to enter the United States by a perpetuation of that fraud.

Does the fraud thus perpetrated upon the Government ripen into a right and thereby estop the Government from denying admission to a Chinese person whose claim to entry is based on such a palpable fraud.

The court below, in its opinion and order overruling the demurrer, after stating the facts says:

> "The denial of the admission in this case was based upon the fact that the father of the applicant under the name of Chan Woon Mung on the 2nd of June, 1899, filed a statement and declaration for registration at Victoria, B. C. stating that he was born at King Boy Village, Sun Woy District, China, and that he was then of the age of twenty-five years. There was likewise offered in evidence at the present hearing a certified copy of an application for a certificate of residence made by Chin Wung, the grandfather of the applicant, on the 10th day of April, 1894, stating, among other things, that the applicant arrived in the United States in May, 1876. Based upon these two certificates

or statements it is argued by the Government that the father of the applicant was not a citizen of the United States, and that the statement of the grandfather that he arrived in the United States in 1876 precludes the idea that his son was born here in 1875. There are grave doubts in my mind whether either of these statements or certificates are competent or admissible as against the applicant. There is also grave doubt in my mind as to whether the declaration made at Victoria was actually made by the father of the applicant. There is no testimony in the record tending to identify him as the person who made the declaration and while the declaration shows that the applicant arrived at Victoria by the SS "Umatilla" there is also other testimony tending to show that he in fact arrived by the Steamer "Walla Walla". But, in any event, it occurs to me that the department should be bound in this matter by its own prior adjudications made at a time when the witnesses who had knowledge of the fact were living and able and competent to testify, and that it would be gross injustice to exclude the applicant now after the death of his father and his grandfather, when it is utterly impossible to explain or contradict the ex parte statements offered in evidence against him. As to the declaration of the grandfather, it was not in evidence before the department, and perhaps should not be considered, but, in any event, it seems to me entirely too much importance is attached to the matter of dates.

As showing the ease with which dates may be confused or misstated I need only refer to the record in this case to show that it is stated in the brief of counsel for the Government and the memorandum prepared for the Secretary that the application of the grandfather was dated April 13, 1894, whereas the certified copy shows that it was dated April 10.''

As to whether the statements or certificates referred to are competent or admissible as against the appellant we believe that it is now well settled that in hearings before the Immigration Department they are not governed by the strict rules of evidence or by the rules of procedure and practice which obtain in courts of law. The due process of law requirement is met, if they are given the fair, though summary hearing required by the law and the rules and regulations promulgated by the Secretary.

Healy vs. *Backus* 221 Fed. 358
Choy Gum vs. *Backus* 223 Fed. 487.

It is not open to the courts to consider the admissibility or weight of the evidence other than to determine whether there is any evidence at all to support the findings of the Immigration authorities. In the case of White vs. Gregory, 213 Fed. 768-770, this court, speaking through his Honor Judge Morrow, says:

> ''In reaching this conclusion the officers gave the alien the hearing provided by the statute. This is as far as the court can go in examining such proceedings. It will not inquire into the sufficienty of probative facts or consider the reasons for the conclusions reached by the officers.''

It seems to us that there can be no doubt about the declaration made at Victoria being made by the father of the present applicant. The Canadian records show that the person admitted at that port on June 2, 1899, under the name of Chin Woon Mong (Ex. B, p. 76) was the same person who returned to San Francisco December 20, 1899, under the name of Chin Young (Ex. A, pp. 10 and 9). This evidence is further corroborated by the testimony of Chan Young himself when an applicant for admission in 1899. At that time he testified as follows:

Q. Where did you live in Victoria?

A. Lived at Yuen Lung & Co. where my friends are.

Q. Did you pay head tax when you landed at Victoria?

A. Yes, I paid that and have certificate for it.

Q. Where is your certificate?

A. In Victoria at my friend's place.

Q. Suppose you are not landed, how do you expect to get back to Victoria without your certificate?

A. If I am not landed I have asked my friend to send certificate down.

Q. Did you get any papers in leaving Victoria that will entitle you to go back there?

A. (Applicant produced a card Number 3120). I had an understanding with Lee Mung

Geu, Custom House Interpreter at Victoria, that I should receive my certificate from him if not landed here.

Q. Was it he who gave you this card?

A. Yes, he gave me that.

Q. Have you a receipt for the head tax you paid when you first landed at Victoria?

A. That is with the firm of Yuen Lung & Co. in Victoria. (Ex. B, p. 61).

The rules and regulations of the Canadian Government relative to Chinese laborers who have been admitted thereto desiring to leave Canada and return, require that they receive a permit to leave and that they must return within one year, a provision similar to that in relation to Chinese laborers residing in the United States. The card produced by the applicant at the time he gave his testimony is a card bearing the number referring to the applicant's case, showing that he had been given a permit to leave Canada and return thereto within one year. Whether or not he is the same Chin Woon Mong whom the Immigration records at this station show to have gone to Canada on the SS "Walla Walla" it seems to us is immaterial, but the explanation heretofore offered why the manifest bore the notation showing that he departed on the "Walla Walla" seems to us reasonable.

As to whether or not the department should be bound by its prior adjudication of the citizenship of the alleged father in this case, we submit that it is only when the decision of the Immigration authorities excludes an alien from admission that such decision is final; decisions in favor of the right to enter are not conclusive on the United States. If this were not so an alien who entered in violation of the law could not later be arrested and deported for being in the United States in violation of law.

> *How Moy* vs. *North* 183 Fed. 89
> *Hoo Choy* vs. *North* 183 Fed. 92
> *Li Sing* vs. *United States* 180 U. S. 486, 45 L. Ed. 634.

Such decisions and findings of the Immigration authorities are not res judicata and are not binding upon said authorities. In the case of *Pearson* vs. *Williams* 202 U. S. 281- 285, 50 L. Ed. 1029-1031, the court says:

> "The Board is an instrument of the Executive Power not a court. It is made up, as we have mentioned, of the Immigration officials in the service of subordinates of the Commissioner of Immigration, whose duties are declared to be administrative by Section 23. Decisions of a similar type long have been recognized as decisions of the Executive Department and cannot constitute res judicata in a technical sense."

As to whether the declaration of the grandfather was in evidence before the department, it is true that the present certified copy introduced as Exhibit "C" was not before the department when the case was considered, but the original from which this certified copy was made was in the hands of the department and it appears from the memorandum prepared for the Acting Secretary that said record was then considered. Said memorandum shows as follows:

> "The records of the Chinese Certificate Division show that when in 1894 the alleged father of Chan Young applied for laborer's registration certificate he stated that he first arrived in the United States in 1876, while it will be noted that the claim is made that Chan Young, who is the alleged father of the present applicant, was born here in 1875." (Ex. A, p. 54).

As to the confusion and misstatement of dates referred to in the opinion, we confidently believe that an inspection of the records in this case will disclose that the learned Judge below was mistaken in his findings that:

> "It is stated in the brief of counsel for the Government and the memorandum prepared for the Secretary that the application of the grandfather was dated April 13, 1894, whereas the certified copy shows that it was dated April 10."

The following is quoted from pages 1 and 2 of the Government's brief, filed when the case was heard in the Court below:

> "Chan Young's alleged father, Chan Wong, at the time of his examination December 23, 1899, produced a *certificate of residence Number 70815, issued to him at San Francisco, California, April 13, 1894.* (Ex. B, p. 70).
>
> A duplicate of said certificate and the original application therefor is now on file in the Bureau

of Immigration, Department of Labor, Washington, D. C. A certified copy of said original application appears as respondent's Exhibit "C" in this case. In said original application for a certificate of residence the said Chan Wong testified under oath that he first arrived in the United States by steamer in May, 1876, and his identifying witness, Chan Jow, also testified that the said Chan Wong arrived in the United States on said date. This being true, his alleged son, father of the present petitioner, could not have been born in the United States in 1875 as claimed. * * * * *

Their testimony on December 23, 1899, when Chin Young was an applicant for admission into the United States as the native born son of said Chan Wong is in direct opposition of the testimony of Chan Wong and his identifying witness *in his application for a certificate of residence April 10, 1894."*

The application of the alleged father or of the alleged grandfather for a certificate of residence is referred to in the Bureau memorandum (Ex. A, p. 54) as follows:

"The records of the Chinese Division show that when in 1894 the alleged father of Chan Young applied for laborer's registration certificate he stated that he first arrived in the United States in 1876, while it will be noted that the claim is made that Chan Young, who is the alleged father of the present applicant, was born here in 1875."

No reference is made in this ~~document~~ Comment on the application to the month or day of the month in 1894 when this application was made.

The petition herein alleges unfairness on the part of the Board of Special Inquiry in the examination of the applicant, and an abuse of discretion on the part of said Board of Special Inquiry and the Secretary of Labor in denying the said applicant admission into the United States.

AS TO UNFAIRNESS.

Chan Wy Sheung, the appellee herein, arrived at the port of San Francisco, California, on the SS "Tenyo Maru" July 23, 1918, and made application to enter the United States claiming to be the foreign born son of Chan Young, an alleged native born citizen of the United States. In support of said application he presented the affidavits of Jew Fook Tei and Chan Wy Ging (Ex. A, pp. 1 and 2).

The case was first heard before a single Immigrant inspector and the application to enter denied by the Commissioner of Immigration. From the decision of said Commissioner an appeal was taken to the Secretary of Labor, Washington, D. C., who affirmed said Commissioner's excluding decision and ordered the applicant's deportation. Thereafter, to-wit: January 23, 1919, a petition for writ of habeas corpus number 16497 was filed in the Court Below and an order to show cause issued. Thereafter, to-wit: July 13, 1919, on motion of counsel for petitioner and with the consent of respondent's attorney, the habeas corpus proceedings then pending were dismissed without prejudice on condition that petitioner be given a hearing before a Board of Special Inquiry, following the rule laid down by this court in the case of *Quon Hing Sun,* 254 Fed. 402.

A Board of Special Inquiry was convened July 15, 1919, at which time the testimony of Chan Wy Ging (Ex. A, p. 35), Jew Fook Tai (Ex. A, p. 28), and Chan Wy Sheung (Ex. A, p. 26) was taken in shorthand, transcribed in typewriting, and made a part of the record in this case. At the conclusion of the hearing the Board of Special Inquiry not being satisfied that applicant's alleged father was a citizen of the United States, voted to defer further action of the case for ten days to permit the introduction of additional evidence in accordance with Rule 5 of the Regulations governing the admission of Chinese, and the applicant was so advised (Ex. A, p. 19).

The attorney of record was notified in writing July 16, 1919, that

> "The Board of Special Inquiry is unable to conclude that this applicant is entitled to land, the claimed citizenship of the alleged father not having been established to its satisfaction"

and allowed ten days within which to submit additional evidence. (Ex. A, p. 36).

Thereafter, to-wit: July 16, 1919, the attorney of record advised in writing that he had no further evidence to offer, waived the time allowed for its presentation (Ex. A, p. 38) and filed notice of appeal to the Secretary of Labor (Ex. A, p. 37).

Thereafter, to-wit: July 22, 1919, the Board of Special Inquiry denied the application of the said Chan Wy Sheung to enter the United States and he was so advised. (Ex. A, pp. 41, 40 and 39).

Thereafter, to-wit: July 23, 1919, the attorney of record (Ex. A, p. 43) and the Consul General for China (Ex. A, p. 42) were advised of the action of the Board of Special Inquiry.

Thereafter, to-wit: July 24, 1919, the attorney of record was given full opportunity to review the entire record in the case as appears from his receipt therefor (Ex. A, p. 45).

Thereafter, to-wit: August 4, 1919, the entire record was forwarded to the Secretary of Labor, Washington, D. C. on appeal (Ex. A, p. 48).

The applicant was represented before the Department in Washington, D. C., by Attorney M. Walton Hendry, who on August 15, 1919, was notified in writing that the record was ready for his inspection and he would be allowed ten days within which to review same and file a brief (Ex. A, p. 49).

Thereafter, to-wit: September 3, 1919, at the request of Attorney Hendry, the time within which he might inspect the record and submit brief was extended to September 10, 1919.

Thereafter, to-wit: September 10, 1919, a brief on behalf of Chan Wy Sheung was filed by Attorney Hendry, and thereafter, to-wit: September 11, 1919, said attorney was granted an oral hearing before the Acting Secretary, as appears from the notation on the margin of said brief (Ex. A, p. 62).

Thereafter, to-wit: September 16, 1919, the Acting Secretary of Labor, after a careful consideration of all the evidence adduced (Ex. A, pp. 55 and 63) dismissed said appeal and directed that the applicant be deported (Ex. A, pp. 64 and 65).

We submit in this connection, and firmly believe that the court will find from inspection of the record, that every opportunity was afforded applicant to present any and all evidence in support of his claim, and that all the witnesses so presented were fully and fairly heard, and that there is nothing in the record which at all justifies the claim of unfairness.

AS TO ABUSE OF DISCRETION.

We confidently urge and believe that the action of the Secretary of Labor in denying applicant the right to enter the United States and ordering his deportation is justified by the facts disclosed in the record, and to hold that such order and finding is a manifest abuse of the discretion committed to the Secretary by the statute would be to substitute the discretion of the court for that of the Secretary.

Abuse of discretion is defined by Corpus Juris as follows:

"A discretion exercised to an end or purpose not justified by, and clearly against reason and evidence; a clearly erroneous conclusion and judgment—one that is clearly against the logic and effect of such facts as are presented in support of the application, against the reasonable and probable deductions to be drawn from the facts disclosed upon the hearing." 1 C. J. 372.

ABUSE JUSTIFYING INTERFERENCE.

"The 'abuse of discretion', to justify interference with the exercise of discretionary power, implies not merely error of judgment, but perversity of will, passion, prejudice, partiality or moral delinquency. 29 Ind. A. 395; 62 N. E. 107-111."

1 C. J. 372.

"The exercise of an honest judgment, however erroneous it may appear to be, is not an abuse of discretion. Abuse of discretion and especially gross and palpable abuse of discretion, which are terms ordinarily employed to justify an interference with the exercise of discretionary power, implies not merely error of judgment, but perversity of will, passion, prejudice, partiality or moral delinquency. 29 N. Y. 418, 431."

1 C. J. 372.

"Difference in judicial opinion is not synonymous with abuse of judicial discretion. 62 N. J. L. 380, 383."

1 C. J. 372.

In the case of *Ekiu* vs. *United States,* 142 U. S. 660, the Court says:

> "And Congress may, if it sees fit, as in the statutes in question in United States vs. Jung Ah Lung just cited, authorize the Courts to investigate and ascertain the facts on which the right to land depends. But, on the other hand, the final determination of these facts may be entrusted by Congress to executive officers; and in such a case, as in all others in which a statute gives a discretionary power to an officer, to be exercised by him upon his own opinion of certain facts, he is made the sole and exclusive judge of the existence of those facts, and no other tribunal, unless expressly authorized by law to do so, is at liberty to re-examine or contravert the sufficiency of the evidence on which he acted."

In *United States* vs. *Ju Toy,* 198 U. S. 253, the Court says:

> "It is established, as we have said, that the Act purports to make the decision of the Department final, whatever the ground on which the right to enter the country is claimed, as well when it is citizenship as when it is domicile and the belonging to the class excepted from the Exclusion Acts."

In *Lou Wah Suey* vs. *Backus,* 225 U. S. 460, (56 L. Ed. 1167) which seems to be the latest case in point, the Court, speaking through Mr. Justice Day says:

"A series of decisions in this Court has settled that such hearings before executive officers may be made conclusive when fairly conducted. In order to successfully attack by judicial proceedings the conclusions and orders made upon such hearings, it must be shown that the proceedings were manifestly unfair, that the action of the executive officers was such as to prevent a fair investigation, or that there was a *manifest abuse of the discretion committed to them by the statute. In other cases the order of the executive officers within the authority of the statute is final.* U. S. vs. Jy Toy, 198 U. S. 253, 49 L. Ed. 1040, 25 Sup. Ct. Rep. 644; Chin Yow vs. U. S. 208 U. S. 8, 52 L. Ed. 369, 28 Sup. Ct. Rep. 201; Tang Tum vs. Edsell, 223 U. S. 673."

In the case of *Chin Low* vs. *U. S.,* 208 U. S. 8, the Court says: (52 L. Ed. 369).

"The question is, whether he is entitled to habeas corpus in such a case. * * * * If the petitioner was not denied a fair opportunity to produce the evidence that he desired, or a fair though summary hearing, the case can proceed no farther. These facts are the foundation of the jurisdiction of the District Court, if it has any jurisdiction at all. It must not be supposed that the mere allegation of the facts open the merits of the case, whether those facts are proved or not. And by way of caution, *we may add, that jurisdiction would not be established simply by proving that the Commissioner and the Department of Commerce and Labor did not accept certain sworn statements as true, even though no contrary or impeaching testimony* *was adduced.* But supposing that it could be shown to the satisfaction of the District Judge that the petitioner had been allowed nothing but the semblance of a hearing as we assume to be alleged, the question is, we repeat, whether habeas corpus may not be used to give the petitioner the hearing that he has been denied. * * * * But unless and until it is proven to the satisfaction of the Judge that a hearing properly so called, was denied, the merits of the case are not open."

We take this to be the true rule and earnestly insist that the record clearly shows that appellant was not denied the opportunity of a fair hearing.

This Court, in the case of Jeung Bock Hong, 258 Fed. 23, held as follows:

> "We cannot say that the proceedings were manifestly unfair or that the actions of the executive officers were such as to prevent a fair investigation or that there was a manifest abuse of the discretion committed to them by the statute. In such cases, the order of the executive officers within the authority of the statute is final."

Respectfully submitted,

FRANK M. SILVA,
United States Attorney.

BEN F. GEIS,
Asst. United States Attorney.

No. 3516

IN THE

United States Circuit Court of Appeals

For the Ninth Circuit

EDWARD WHITE, as Commissioner of Immigration for the Port of San Francisco,
Appellant,

vs.

CHAN WY SHEUNG,
Appellee.

BRIEF FOR APPELLEE.

JOSEPH P. FALLON,
Attorney for Appellee.

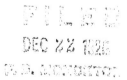

...SH PRINTING CO.

No. 3516

IN THE

United States Circuit Court of Appeals

For the Ninth Circuit

EDWARD WHITE, as Commissioner of Immigration for the Port of San Francisco,
Appellant,

vs.

CHAN WY SHEUNG,
Appellee.

BRIEF FOR APPELLEE.

The opening statement of the case by the appellant is substantially correct, to wit: That the appellee is the son of Chan Young. That the citizenship of Chan Young has been conceded by the Department of Labor on three prior occasions. These prior adjudications are now set aside and the citizenship of the father, Chan Young, is denied and the son is ordered deported.

The points raised by the Department of Labor in rendering this adverse decision are based upon two certificates executed over twenty years ago. The points are as follows:

First. Whether the father in this case, Chan Young, is the same man who signed a certificate of registration in Victoria, B. C., an exhibit in this case;

Second. Whether the facts stated in said certificate are true and conclusive as to the place of birth of the father; and

Third. Whether the grandfather made a statement that he came to the United States in 1876, which, if true, would preclude the possibility of the birth of his son, the father of the appellee, in the United States.

As to the first point, the facts are that the man in said certificate arrived in Victoria, B. C., SS. Umatilla June 2, 1899, and the Canton records state that it is their belief that this man arrived on said steamer to Victoria via San Francisco. A search was made upon the records at San Francisco to determine whether this was the case. The San Francisco records show that one Chun Wan Mong, which name corresponds with the name of the man in said certificate, arived at San Francisco on the SS. Gaelic May 22, 1899, and departed on the SS. Walla Walla May 26. Chinese transits for Victoria departed on the Umatilla May 30, 1899, and the manifest of the SS. China May 29, 1899, shows that 44 transits for Vancouver departed on the SS. Umatilla May 31, 1899. Further, the manifest of the SS. Peking May 8, 1899, shows that one Chan Wong, age 48, departed on the Umatilla May 16, 1899, for Victoria.

The evidence in this case taken in 1899 shows by the testimony of all witnesses that the father went from China to Victoria, B. C., the second or third month of the year 1899, but there is nothing to indicate that he came by way of San Francisco, and as the records of the San Francisco and Victoria offices disagree as to the steamer he departed on from San Francisco, we are certainly in a quandary as to whether he came direct to Victoria by way of San Francisco or by some other port, or direct. Therefore in order to determine that the man named in the certificate is the same man, it is necessary to presume that the records of the San Francisco office are incorrect. But what right have we to assume that the records of this office are incorrect any more than we have a right to assume that the records of the Victoria office are incorrect? Why would it not be just as fair to assume that, although the man named in the certificate did arrive June 2nd by way of the Umatilla, the Victoria records were in error in not showing that the Chun Wan Mong named by the San Francisco office as the party on the Walla Walla failed to arrive by said steamer in Victoria. The father might have been the man named as departing on the Walla Walla and the Victoria office been in error in not noting his name on their manifests, and there might have been two men departing on the Walla Walla, one named Chun Won Mong and the other named Chin Way Mong, the man named in the certificate. There is evidence in this identical case of two Chinamen having the same name. For instance, you will note that the manifest of the steamship City of Peking shows one Chan Wong in transit for Victoria by way of Umatilla May 16, 1899. It is manifest and clear therefore that it is necessary to resort to presumption in this case to determine whether the father is the same person as named in the certificate, and for reasons hereafter to be cited it is submitted that it is not fair at this late date under the circumstances of this case to resort to any presumption.

Further attention is called to the fact that the certificate in question shows that the last place of residence of the man who signed the same was Hong Kong, China, but the testimony taken in 1899 fails to disclose the fact that the father in this case was ever in business or ever domiciled in Hong Kong. The testimony of the father, as well as his father, shows that after the father completed his schooling in the home village, he then went into business in a store in the Nom How village, and that he was in that store for some time until the store burned. Further, in the testimony of the father in the old case, he produces a laborer's card No. 3120 which he had received from the Victoria office, but it will be noted that the number of this card fails to correspond with the number of the certificate in question, which would also tend to show that the father is not the man who signed that certificate.

Further, your attention is called to the statements on the reverse of this certificate, giving a description of the man, as having a pitted face, scar on right jaw and scar on left eyelid. A photograph of the father may be seen in the case of his prior landed son, Chan Way Bon No. 10375-115, but there appears to be nothing whatever in this photograph to answer to the above description, which would seem to be conclusive evidence that the father is not the man named in said certificate; and right here it is in order to state that this fact brings out more than any other the unfairness of questioning the citizenship of the father at this time. The records show that the father is dead and therefore there is no way to determine definitely except by the photograph above mentioned, that the father does not answer the description heretofore given. If he were alive it would be an easy matter to determine whether he answered this description, but the Department waits until he is dead, after recognizing his citizenship in three instances, to raise this question. It is certainly highly unfair.

Your attention is further invited to the signature on the certificate, and the signature of the father on the affidavit in the case of his prior landed son Chan Way Bon No. 10375-115. I submit that there is no more similarity between these signatures than between my signature and either of them. It does not require an expert, but a layman can see that there is no similarity in the handwriting of the men who signed these two papers referred to.

Further, your attention is called to the fact that the testimony in 1899 shows by all witnesses that the father came into Victoria in the second or third month, which at the latest would be the month of April, and which of course does not correspond with the date of the arrival of the man named in the certificate.

It is submitted that all of the above circumstances and facts not only throw serious doubt as to the identity in question, but are facts far more convincing of the lack of identity than the other points mentioned by appellant are of identity. But certainly, to say the least, all of these facts destroy any ground for holding that the identity is reasonably established.

The second point is whether even if the identity is established, the facts stated in this certificate can be taken as conclusive evidence of the place of the birth of the father. In taking up this point there is just one question that we would like to put first of all to appellant. Would the Department of Labor, in the absence of any other evidence, take a similar certificate as sufficient to establish the birthplace of a Chinaman? Never in the world. As a rule in deciding a case upon circumstantial evidence, the Court resorts to some motive, but where is the motive here? What object would this man have in stating in signing the certificate that he was born in China when he was intending to apply for admission on the ground of citizenship in this country? We have already shown that the certificate is in error in one respect, viz, the last place of residence, and if it is in error in one respect, why could it not be in this? If the certificate was signed by the father in this case, it is very manifest that he understood that he was merely giving the place from which he had come and not the place of his birth, and here again we are confronted with difficulty, because the man is now dead; we cannot ask him any questions; we cannot call in any witness who might have been present when he signed the certificate, because he, being dead, cannot give us the names of such witnesses.

Further, your attention is called to the fact that the certificates are the only evidence in this case, if we can consider them evidence, because it is not in the form of testimony sworn to that the father was born in China. We have the sworn testimony of the father when he was landed in this country and when one of his prior sons was admitted, exactly where he was born in this country and we also have the testimony of the father of his father as to whether he was born in this country and also the testimony of a witness who was working for the father's father at the time and who testified of his birth in this country. And in addition we have the death certificate filed in this case in 1912, six years before the present question was raised, signed by a disinterested witness, setting forth the fact that the father was born in this country, and it is submitted that this evidence is certainly stronger than the certificates which, without any direct evidence of their authenticity, are not admissible as evidence by the rules of the law of evidence, especially under all the circumstances of this case, and we repeat and insist that it is highly unfair and unjust to hold that these certificates even if under the circumstances herein mentioned should be sufficient to rebut all of the real evidence and the sworn testimony above mentioned, and to cause the Department to reverse its decision three times made on the question of citizenship.

At the time the applicant in this case sailed for this country he knew, as the Department had held in three instances, that his father was a citizen of this country, and it seems to us that it is highly unfair for the Government to hold out this fact as true, thus inducing this man to go to the expense of coming to this country and, after he arrives here, inform him that they have now made investigations and that their former decisions were incorrect, in spite of the fact that the Department has had twenty years to make the same investigation and could have obtained the same information that they now have twenty years ago.

The next point raised is that the grandfather's registration certificate sets forth that he came to the United States in 1876. When one considers the methods employed at the time of the registration it might easily be concluded that a mistake was made. A Chinese in registering would state the time of his arrival in the Chinese language and the same would be translated into English by either an interpreter or the registration clerk, and in translating the Chinese calendar the greatest care must be taken. In the case of Quan Hing Sun this Court has held "That it must distinctly appear that the Department was not influenced in its decisions by any considerations unauthorized by law", and cites a number of cases to that effect.

Ex parte Quan Hing Sun, 254 Fed. 402.

It is a plain rule of law that no decision of any Court once rendered can be reopened upon newly discovered evidence if that evidence could by reasonable diligence have been discovered before said decision was rendered, and especially is that true when the main witness in the case has since died. Further, no Court would under any circumstances or upon the discovery of any evidence allow a decision to be opened up twenty years after it was rendered. As the new evidence now relied upon in this case could have been discovered twenty years ago with reasonable diligence and the man against whom it is offered is dead there is no authority in law for admitting such evidence and the decision of the Department influenced by the consideration of such evidence would be a decision influenced by considerations unauthorized by law.

Further, said certificates are inadmissible in accordance with the rules of law for the reason that there is no proof offered in this case to show that they were signed by the father. The Department has not produced a single witness to prove that the man signed these certificates or even that the man whose name appears upon it signed it. Before these certificates would be admissible in any Court it would be necessary to prove the signature by witness, not by presumption. The law will admit no instrument in writing as evidence on presumption, but the signature must be proved before it is admitted as evidence.

> Wright v. Taylor, 30 Fed. Cases 18,096;
> Richmond etc. R. C. v. Jones, 72 Ala. 218;
> Lane v. Farmer, 13 Ark. 63;
> Wharton on Evidence, 2nd Ed., Sec. 689.

Not only has the Department failed to prove the signature as required by law or to prove the authenticity of the certificates, but on the other hand there are a number of facts as hereinbefore pointed out, such as comparison of the signature on this certificate with the father's signature on the affidavit in his son's case, supra, and the absence of any of the distinguishing marks mentioned in the certificates on the father's photograph, etc., which are convincing evidence to the contrary. As it is plain therefore that said certificates are inadmissible by the rules of law to prove the facts stated on their face, it is plain a decision of the Department based upon the consideration of such certificates as proper evidence would be influenced by considerations unauthorized by law and it is submitted therefore that the Department cannot consider said certificates as evidence. In the case of Owe Sam Goon, 235 Fed. 654, this Court said:

> "The rule of law respecting evidence demands of a party seeking to establish a fact that he produce the best evidence available to him. Greenleaf on Evidence (16 Ed.), Sec. 81; Wigmore on Evidence, Sec. 1173; Jones on Evidence, Vol. 2, Sec. 212. And this is the identical rule prescribed by the Department of Labor for the examination of the case of an alien charged with being subject to arrest and deportation under the Immigration Act. Of course, this means that the best evidence must be proper evidence. Jones on Evidence, supra; Ex parte Owe Sam Goon, 235 Fed. 654."

The Bureau seems to proceed upon the theory that these Chinese cases may be decided upon evidence inadmissible according to the rules of law, but it is plain, as in the case of Quan Hing Sun, supra, that the Department must not be influenced in its decisions by considerations *unauthorized by law* and it is submitted therefore that as said certificates are inadmissible under the rules of law there is no new evidence in this case and the applicant is entitled to land. The Department of Labor has held that the rules of evidence must be considered as illustrated by the fact that it has repeatedly held that hearsay evidence is inadmissible. In the case of Owe Sam Goon, supra, this Court further says:

> "As has been repeatedly stated, it is not our function to weigh the evidence in this class of cases, but we may properly consider the jurisdictional question of law, whether there was evidence to sustain the conclusion that the accused was in the United States in violation of law and subject to deportation under Section 21 of the Immigration Act. In the absence

of the best evidence to sustain the same, we may also conclude that the order of deportation was arbitrary and unfair, and subject to judicial review."

United States v. Jue Toy, 198 U. S. 253, 260; 25 Sup. Ct. 644, 40 L. Ed. 1140;

Chin Yow v. United States, 208 U. S. 8, 12, 28;

Sup. Ct. 201, 52 L. Ed. 369;

In re Chan Kam, 232 Fed. 855, 857 and cases cited therein.

If the father were alive and arrested, charged with being in or seeking re-entry from abroad entitled to have his right determined by a judicial inquiry with all its assurances and sanctions, and the strict rules of law would obtain. I invite the Court's attention on this point to the recent decision of the United States Supreme Court in the case of Edward White v. Chin Fong, 40 Supreme Court Advance Opinions, June 15, 1920. The Court said:

"But this overlooks the difference in the security of judicial over administrative action, to which we have adverted, and which this Court has declared, and in the present case, the right that had been adjudged, and had been exercised upon the adjudication."

If this be true in the father's case, it applies with equal force to that of the son when the only evidence adduced is that which could be invoked against the father if he were alive and when the son's claim is based upon the right that had been adjudged and had been exercised in reliance upon the adjudications.

But besides the applicant's legal rights to land in this case, common plain justice should entitle him to land. The applicant's father is dead. The Department has held three times that the father was a citizen of the United States. It has been twenty years since the Department decided upon the citizenship of the father, and the Department by not revising said decision induced this applicant to go to the expense of coming to this country, notwithstanding the fact that the Department could by reasonable diligence have discovered the same evidence twenty years ago while the father was alive and in a position probably to refute said evidence upon which it is now sought to reverse the former decisions. This plainly is not fair. It is not just and is in violation of the plain principles of law heretofore cited.

We respectfully urge that the judgment of the District Court be sustained.

Dated, San Francisco,
December 20, 1920.

Respectfully submitted,

JOSEPH P. FALLON,
Attorney for Appellee.

No. 3517

IN THE

United States Circuit Court of Appeals

For the Ninth Circuit

ALBERT YOUNG,

Plaintiff in Error,

vs.

THE UNITED STATES OF AMERICA,

Defendant in Error.

BRIEF FOR PLAINTIFF IN ERROR.

CLARENCE W. MORRIS,
CHAUNCEY F. TRAMUTOLO,
WILLIAM F. HERRON,
Attorneys for Plaintiff in Error.

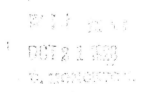

PERNAU-WALSH PRINTING CO.

No. 3517.

IN THE

United States Circuit Court of Appeals

For the Ninth Circuit

ALBERT YOUNG, *Plaintiff in Error,* vs. THE UNITED STATES OF AMERICA, *Defendant in Error.*	}

BRIEF FOR PLAINTIFF IN ERROR.

Statement of the Case.

The plaintiff in error and one Walter Dekau were charged by an information filed November 28, 1919, in the Southern Division of the United States District Court for the Northern District of California, with violating section 3 of the act commonly known as the "National Prohibition Act". The charging part of the information alleges:

> "That Walter Dekau and Albert Young, hereinafter called the defendants, heretofore, to wit, on the twentieth day of November, in the year of our Lord one thousand nine hundred and nineteen, at San Francisco, in the Southern Division of the Northern District of

> California, then and there being, did then and there, in violation of section 3 of the act of October 28, 1919, known as the 'National Prohibition Act', unlawfully, willfully and knowingly maintain a public and common nuisance in that they did unlawfully, willfully and knowingly sell and keep for sale for beverage purposes on the premises at Number 2965 Sixteenth street in San Francisco aforesaid, certain intoxicating liquor, to wit, whiskey" (Transcript of Record, p. 3).

Upon the trial of the cause both of the defendants were convicted. Thereafter their counsel moved for a new trial upon the grounds:

1. That the verdict is against the law.

2. That the verdict was not sustained by the evidence.

3. That the verdict was against the weight of the evidence.

At the same time the defendants moved in arrest of judgment upon the grounds:

1. That the information does not state facts sufficient to constitute an offense against the laws of the United States.

2. That the court had no jurisdiction to try the case.

3. That section 3 of title I of the so-called "National Prohibition Act" is unconstitutional in that it is not within the power of Congress to deprive this or any other state of its police powers (Transcript of Record, pp. 31-32).

Both of these motions were denied by the court, which thereupon passed judgment and sentence of fine and imprisonment upon both defendants. From this judgment the plaintiff in error prosecutes this writ.

Specification of Errors.

In seeking a reversal of this judgment the plaintiff in error relies upon the following errors committed by the trial court:

(1) That the evidence introduced and received at the trial of this cause was wholly insufficient to warrant a verdict of guilty as to the plaintiff in error, and that the trial court therefore erred in denying a motion for an instructed verdict of not guilty as to the plaintiff in error made by his counsel at the conclusion of the trial.

(2) That the information upon which plaintiff in error was convicted does not state facts sufficient to charge plaintiff in error with having committed any crime or offense aginst the laws of the United States and that therefore the trial court erred in denying plaintiff in error's motion in arrest of judgment.

(3) That the trial court also erred in denying the said motion in arrest of judgment for the reason that the court below had no jurisdiction to try the cause, the prosecution being not by indictment but by information.

I.

Brief of the Argument.

THE EVIDENCE WAS INSUFFICIENT TO JUSTIFY A CONVICTION.

In discussing this phase of the case we shall set forth a synopsis of the evidence as it appears in the record.

One R. W. Gloss, whose testimony will be found in the Transcript, pages 10-15, testified that he was a Deputy Collector of Internal Revenue, assigned for the enforcement of the War Time Prohibition Act. About 5:30 o'clock in the evening of November 20, 1919, he visited the place of business of the plaintiff in error at San Francisco in company with another deputy collector. This place of business was a saloon. At the end of the bar there was a private office, and as the witness entered he saw a man drinking a drink. The bartender came up to the cash register *with the cash* in his hand and rang up twenty-five cents. The officers took the glass away from the bartender and both of them smelled the glass and it smelled like whiskey. In the private office an overcoat was hanging, in the pocket of which there was a bottle of whiskey. The witness did not see the bartender serve liquor out of the bottle, but he saw him put the bottle back in the overcoat pocket. Young, the plaintiff in error, was not on the premises at the time, but was at home, and the bartender referred to in this testimony was Dekau, the plaintiff in error's co-defendant. The officers made a search of the premises and did not find any liquor other than that contained in the bottle in the overcoat pocket. The license of the saloon stood in the name of the plaintiff in error.

Similar testimony was given by the witness J. P. Doyle, the other deputy collector, who visited the premises on the occasion referred to, with the previous witness. He also testified that Mr. Young was not in the saloon at the time of the alleged sale (Transcript, p. 17).

Walter Dekau, charged in the information as W. Dekan, the co-defendant of plaintiff in error, took the stand in his own behalf. Besides denying that he made any sale of liquor on the occasion in question, and stating that the liquor found in the bottle in the overcoat pocket was liquor which he brought to the saloon when he went to work, for his own personal use, he gave the following testimony:

> "Q. Have you ever received any instructions from Mr. Young, the proprietor of the saloon, with reference to your conduct in the sale of liquor to anyone?
> A. He gave me orders not to sell any.
> Q. If there was any liquor sold on those premises on that particular day, it would have been sold against Mr. Young's consent?
> A. Yes, sir" (Transcript of Record, pp. 20-21).

Albert Young, the plaintiff in error, called as a witness in his own behalf, testified that on the day in question he had been in San Mateo, and did not arrive at the saloon until eight o'clock in the evening. He further testified that he never kept any whiskey on the premises; that he instructed his bartenders to serve no hard liquor, "to take no chances, just to serve soft drinks" (Transcript, pp. 24-25).

This testimony given by the defendants was absolutely uncontradicted. No other witnesses were produced by either side, and the foregoing constitutes an accurate synopsis of all the evidence produced at the trial.

At the conclusion of the case, defendants' counsel moved the court to instruct the jury to acquit the plaintiff in error on the ground that the government had not established any case against him. This motion was denied by the trial judge, and this refusal is assigned as error. Thus we are brought to the question of the sufficiency of the evidence to justify the verdict.

It must be borne in mind at the outset that the defendants were not charged in the information with making an illegal sale of liquor. The charge laid against them was that of maintaining a public and common nuisance

> "in that they did unlawfully, willfully and knowingly sell and keep for sale for beverage purposes, certain intoxicating liquor, to wit, whiskey."

It must further be borne in mind that the government's case establishes only this much: that the defendant Dekau, during the absence of plaintiff in error, made one sale of liquor from a bottle which he had in his overcoat pocket; that a search of the premises by the officers failed to discover any other liquor thereon (Transcript, p. 15); that plaintiff in error had given positive instructions to his employees that they were not to sell any liquor. In view of this, it must be apparent, we submit, that the evidence was wholly insufficient to justify the jury in convicting the plaintiff in error. In this behalf we most respectfully call the attention of the court to the following considerations:

FIRST. There is not in the record a scintilla of evidence, either direct or circumstantial, which tends in the remotest degree to show that plaintiff in error authorized or had the slightest knowledge of the one illegal sale proved by the government.

SECOND. There is not in the record a word of testimony to show that any other sales had ever been made on the premises; neither is there any other evidence that tends to show, either directly or by inference, that the proprietor of the saloon had knowledge that any liquor was ever on the premises.

THIRD. On the contrary, the uncontradicted evidence is that the only sale proven was made against the express instructions of plaintiff in error, and during his absence from the saloon.

Had there been evidence of other sales, or had the officers found a quantity of liquor stored or kept on the premises, the jury *might* then have been justified in drawing the inference that the proprietor had knowledge of the commission on the premises of such illegal acts. But to hold him criminally liable for maintaining a nuisance because his bartender, during his absence, made one illegal sale from a bottle, not kept on the premises, but carried in by the bartender in his overcoat pocket, would be to perpetrate a glaring injustice. To use the language of the learned Justice Cooper of the California District Court of Appeal:

> "But the sages of the law and the learned judges have established the rule that the independent acts and declarations of one man shall not be evidence against another. It is sufficient for everyone to answer for his own sins, and not for the sins of his neighbor."
>
> People v. Schmitz, 7 Cal. App. 355.

The fact that the relationship of master and servant existed between plaintiff in error and his co-defendant does not strengthen the government's case in the slightest degree. The vicarious liability which attaches to a master in civil cases for the acts of a servant while acting within the scope of his employment cannot be invoked in criminal cases. The rule of *respondeat superior* has no application here. Proof of express authorization is necessary before the employer can be held criminally liable, and such proof was not forthcoming in the case at bar.

The cases are uniform to this effect. We will call the attention of the court to a few of them. In People v. Green, 22 Cal. App. 45, 50, it is said:

> "The civil doctrine that a principal is bound by the acts of his agent within the scope of the latter's authority has no application to criminal law (1 McLain on Criminal Law, sec. 188). While false pretenses may be made to (*by?*) an agent of (*to?*) the person defrauded, yet when made by an agent they must be directly authorized or consented to in order to hold the principal, for authority to do a criminal act will not be presumed (1 McLain on Criminal Law, sec. 683)."

Commonwealth v. Stevens, 155 Mass. 291, 29 N. E. 508, was a prosecution for illegally selling liquor to a minor. The evidence showed that the sale was made by the clerk of the defendant. The court says:

> "The criminal liability of a master for the act of his servant does not extend so far as his civil liability, inasmuch as he cannot be held criminally for what the servant does contrary to his orders, and without authority, express or implied, merely because it is in the course of his business, and within the scope of the servant's employment; but he would be civilly liable for a tort of this kind (George v. Gobey, 128 Mass. 289; Roberge v. Burnham, 124 Mass. 277)."

In Grant Bros. Const. Co. v. United States, 13 Ariz. 388, 114 Pac. 955, it is said:

> "This act, a statute of the United States, being penal in its consequences, must be strictly construed, and as knowledge is the principal and indispensable ingredient of the offense, the government, the plaintiff in the case, must be held to proof of such knowledge or to proof of circumstances from which it might be fairly

inferred. Unless the evidence, therefore, affords proof of knowledge by the construction company, or proof of circumstances from which such knowledge may be fairly inferred; of the acts of Carney and his associates, the construction company cannot be held liable for such acts of Carney, for the master or principal is not liable criminally for the unlawful acts of his agent or servant, though such unlawful act be committed in the master's business, unless such unlawful act was directed by him or knowingly assented to or acquiesced in."

In State v. Henaghan, 73 West Virginia 706, 81 S. E. 539, we read:

> "The relation of principal and agent, or of employer and employee, is not recognized in the criminal law. By that law, every man must stand for himself."

In cases involving the alleged illegal sale of liquor, the decisions are uniform to the effect that the master is not criminally liable for illegal sales made by his clerk, servant or agent, without his knowledge or consent, express or implied, or in his absence and in disobedience to his commands or instructions. For example, under the Iowa statute relating to liquor nuisances, it was held that one is not liable criminally for an unlawful sale made without his knowledge and consent by his clerk.

State v. Hayes, 67 Iowa 27; 24 N. W. 575;

See also to the same effect:

Grosch v. Centralia, 6 Ill. App. 107;
Lathrope v. State, 51 Ind. 192;
Wadsworth v. State (Texas), 34 S. W. 934.

Thus it has been held that a conviction of selling intoxicating liquor without a license cannot rest upon the evidence merely that the person who made the sale was the defendant's clerk, in the absence of any evidence that defendant authorized the sale or participated therein.

Daniel v. State, 149 Ala. 44; 43 S. 22;
Seibert v. State, 40 Ala. 60.

To warrant a conviction for sales made by defendant's bartender in violation of the law, it must appear that defendant gave no orders not to make such sales, or that if such orders were given they were not in good faith.

Commonwealth v. Tittlow, 28 Pa. Co. Ct. 341;

In the Rhode Island case of State v. Burke, 15 R. I. 324, 4 Atl. 761, it was held that one cannot be convicted of maintaining a liquor nuisance by proof of sales on Sunday by an agent without proof of knowledge on the part of defendant, and without proof of authority, either express or implied.

In view of the evidence in the case at bar and the undoubted and unquestionable principles of law applicable thereto, we respectfully submit that the trial court should have instructed the jury to acquit the plaintiff in error. There is not in the entire record a scintilla of evidence to sustain the conviction as to him.

II.

THE INFORMATION CHARGES NO CRIME AGAINST THE UNITED STATES.

The information in this cause will be found on page 3 of the Transcript. The charging part thereof is set forth in the Statement of Facts which forms the introductory portion of this brief. The informtion, it will be noted, contains no statement of any of the facts constituting the alleged offense. It merely alleges, without giving any particulars whatsoever, that the defendants did sell and keep for sale certain intoxicating liquor. No particulars whatever are given. There is nothing to inform the defendants as to the charge which they would be called upon to meet, and they were plainly entitled to more specific information as to the particulars of the offense charged than is furnished them by the accusatory paper on file herein. Furthermore, the information is fatally defective in failing to aver that either of the defendants was the owner, or in the possession of, or had any control of any kind or character over the premises therein named. There is specific adjudication upon this question. In the case of State v. Nickerson (Kansas), 2 Pac. 654, the defendant was prosecuted for a common nuisance in selling and keeping for sale intoxicating beverages. The Kansas statute, which seems to be the prototype of the common nuisance section of the so-called Volstead Act, declared and denounced as a public and common nuisance premises upon which alcoholic liquors were sold, kept for sale, given away or furnished. We quote the language used by the Supreme Court of Kansas relative to an information far more specific than the one in the case at bar:

> "The first question arises upon the information, which, omitting the caption and verification, reads as follows:
>
> 'In the name and by the authority of the State of Kansas, I, G. W. Hurd, county attorney in and for said county, do now give here the court to understand and be informed that the above-named defendants, Maurice Robecker and Benjamin Nickerson, at divers days and times between the first day of June, 1881, and the time of filing this information, in a certain wooden building on lot 91, on Main street, known as Billiard Parlor, in the city of Solomon, in said county of Dickinson and State of Kansas, then and there being, did then and there and still continue to unlawfully sell, barter, and give away and keep for sale, barter, and use, spirituous, malt, vinous, fermented, and other intoxicating liquors, without taking out and having any permit or legal authority therefor, to the common nuisance of all the people of the State of Kansas, there lawfully being, and contrary to the statutes in such cases made and provided.
>
> 'G. W. Hurd, County Attorney.'
>
> "Does this charge an offense under section 13 of the prohibitory law, or one under section 7, or none at all? It would seem that the pleader intended to prosecute under section 13, but we are constrained to hold that it fails to state an offense under that section. At least, it states one only impliedly and by indirection, which is not good in criminal pleading. The section declares that all places where liquor is sold, etc., are common nuisances, and the owner or keeper thereof shall upon conviction be adjudged guilty

> of maintaining, etc. In other words, the party must be the owner or keeper of the place in which the liquor is sold, and it is immaterial whether he owns or has control of the liquor itself. Now, the charge is that he kept and sold liquor in the place; not that he owned or kept the place. Doubtless, proof that he kept and sold liquor in the place would sustain a finding that he was the keeper of the place; but still that is only evidence, and not the fact to be proved, and in criminal pleadings the ultimate fact and not the evidence of it must be charged. Directness and certainty must always be insisted upon in criminal matters. Thus, and thus only, can there be a certainty that a party complained of knows exactly what is charged against him, and what he msut be prepared to try. Thus, and thus only, can the protection which is due to every person charged with a criminal violation of law be secured."

A mere reading of the statute under which the plaintiff in error was prosecuted is sufficient to demonstrate the force of our contention. Section 3 of Title I of the "National Prohibition Act", upon which the information is based, reads as follows:

> "Section 3. Any room, house, building, boat, vehicle, structure, or place of any kind where intoxicating liquor is sold manufactured, kept for sale, or bartered in violation of the War Prohibition Act, and all intoxicating liquor and all property kept and used in maintaining such a place, is hereby declared to be a public and common nuisance, and any person who maintains or assists in maintaining such public and common nuisance shall be guilty of a misdemeanor, and upon conviction thereof shall be fined not less than $100 nor more than $1000, or be imprisoned for not less

> than thirty days or more than one year, or both. If a person has knowledge that his property is occupied or used in violation of the provisions of the War Prohibition Act and suffers the same to be so used, such property shall be subject to a lien for, and may be sold to pay, all fines and costs assessed against the occupant of such building or property for any violation of the War Prohibition Act occurring after the passage thereof, which said lien shall attach from the time of the filing of notice of the commencement of the suit in the office where the records of the transfer of real estate are kept; and any such lien may be established and enforced by legal action instituted for that purpose in any court having jurisdiction. Any violation of this title upon any leased premises by the lessee or occupant thereof shall, at the option of the lessor, work a forfeiture of the lease."

Now what is the crime denounced by the foregoing section of the statute? The crime consists not in the selling of the liquor, but in the maintaining of the place where liquor is sold, manufactured or kept for sale.

Obviously a stranger to the premises—a guest of the owner, perhaps, or a trespasser—could not be guilty of maintaining a nuisance because he would have no control over the premises. The .crime denounced by the foregoing section of the statute can be committed only by the owner or occupant, or by somebody having possession or control over the property. This is not alleged in the information.

Furthermore, the information nowhere alleges any facts from which it is made to appear that a nuisance in fact existed. Before any place can be a nuisance it must be common; it must have acquired a *status*. The information does not charge more than one sale on one particular day; and the evidence produced shows only one sale. The decisions are almost uniform to the effect that a single sale of liquor is not sufficient to constitute a nuisance. Thus, in State v. McIntosh (1903), 98 Me. 397, 57 Atl. 83, an indictment under a statute charging the defendant with keeping and maintaining a liquor nuisance, it is held that

> "one or more unlawful sales of intoxicating liquor in a place does not necessarily, and as a matter of law, make that place a common nuisance. The place must be habitually, commonly used for the purpose before it becomes a common nuisance."

The statute involved in this case provided that

> "all places used for the illegal sale or keeping of intoxicating liquors, all houses, shops or places where intoxicating liquors are sold for tippling purposes, all places of resort where intoxicating liquors are kept, sold, given away, drank or dispensed, in any manner not provided for by law, are common nuisances."

It had been held previous to the decision in State v. McIntosh (Me.), supra, that two sales would not as a matter of law constitute a house a nuisance, the court stating that

> "the evidence of such sales would be competent for the jury to consider upon the issue whether or not the house was habitually employed by the defendant for the purpose of selling contrary to law. And if it satisfied them beyond

> reasonable doubt that the defendant was in the habit of so selling therein, they might so find. The weight or value of such testimony was within their exclusive province, and it was erroneous for the court to fix the weight or value which they should give it."
>
> State v. Stanley (1892), 84 Me. 555; 24 Atl. 983.

In Com. v. Patterson (1885), 138 Mass. 498, 5 Am. Crim. Rep. 329, a complaint

> "for keeping and maintaining a common nuisance, to wit, a certain tenement used for the illegal sale and illegal keeping of intoxicating liquors",

the defendant, who had a license to sell liquors to be drunk on the premises, was shown to have made two sales, on two separate occasions, of liquor which was carried away from the premises. The jury were instructed

> "that if the defendant was proprietor of the saloon, and made either of the two illegal sales that were testified to, they must return a verdict of guilty."

The Supreme Court, in commenting upon this instruction, states:

> "This went too far; for, even if a single sale was sufficient evidence to warrant a conviction on this complaint, it certainly did not of itself constitute the offense set forth, or amount to more than evidence for the jury on which they might convict. A building cannot be said to be used for the illegal sale of intoxicating liquors, within the meaning of the Public Statutes, chap. 101, sec. 6, which makes it a nuisance, nor can the proprietor be said to

> keep or maintain such common nuisance within sec. 7 on the strength of a single casual sale, made without premeditation in the course of a lawful business. Not only do the words 'used' and 'keep' or 'maintain' import a certain degree of permanence, but the same idea is usually a part of the conception of a nuisance."

In this behalf we further call the attention of the court to the witty, brilliant and unanswerable dissenting opinion of Justice Robinson of the Supreme Court of North Dakota in Scott v. State, 163 N. W. 813:

> "One swallow does not make a summer; one love affair does not make a bawdyhouse. The house must be kept as a resort for illegal and immoral purposes; the wrong must be common or it is not a common nuisance and the legislature cannot make it otherwise. It is perfectly absurd to say that the keeping of a house wherein one, two, or three drinks are sold or given away is the keeping of a common nuisance.
>
> In Cana of Gallilee there was a wedding feast, and the mother of Jesus was there, and both Jesus and his disciples were called to the marriage, and when they wanted wine the mother of Jesus said unto the servants: 'Fill the water pots with water'. And they filled them up to the brim. Then he said unto them: 'Draw out now, and bear unto the governor of the feast'. And they bear it. When the ruler of the feast had tasted the water that was made wine, and knew not whence it was, the governor of the feast said to the bridegroom: 'Every man at the beginning doth set forth good wine, and when men have well drunk then that which is worse, but thou hast kept the good wine until now'. This beginning of miracles did Jesus in Cana of Galilee and manifested forth his glory.

It cannot be truly said that any person at that feast was guilty of keeping or maintaining a common nuisance, or that in North Dakota the recurrence of such a marriage feast would constitute the keeping or maintaining of a common nuisance. In Scripture drunkenness is everywhere denounced, but on occasions the drinking of wine and even strong drink is commended. Thus we did read: 'Give strong drink to him that is ready to perish and wine to those that be heavy of heart. Let him drink and forget his poverty and remember his misery no more'. 'Go thy way, eat thy bread with joy, and drink thy wine with a merry heart, for God now accepteth thy works'. He brought forth food out of the earth and wine that maketh glad the heart of man.

And the Apostle Paul writes to the Apostle Timothy: 'Drink no longer water, but use a little wine for thy stomach's sake and thine often infirmities'.

It is right to forbid the sale of drinks to Indians, minors, to some persons of Celtic blood, and to any person who does not know enough to care for himself and his family; but to forbid a taste of wine, beer, ale, or Dublin stout to an Anglo-Saxon or a Teuton, why, that is cruelty. And cruelty, thou art a wickedness.

The majority opinion says it is virtually conceded that if the testimony as stated be true, it is sufficient to establish the crime alleged. That is a grave mistake. There is no such foolish and false concession, and if there were, it would in no way justify the court in sustaining the conviction. The testimony wholly fails to show that the defendant kept a disorderly house or a common nuisance, or a house in any way given to the sale or drinking of intoxicating liquors, or that he did an injury to any person. Under the rulings of the court,

> were Christ to come to this state and to keep a house and to repeat the miracle of the marriage feast, he might be convicted and sentenced to the state's prison. That is neither law nor gospel.
>
> It is a matter of regret that in some cases judges are too ready to give a narrow and cold-blooded construction to drastic statutes and to impose on others burdens grievous to be borne, which they themselves touch not with one of their fingers.
>
> At the Grand Pacific I have a nice, exclusive bachelor apartment ($45 a month). Now, if the governor, the bishop, or one of the justices call on me and I open a bottle of foamy Dublin stout, my elixir of life, and for his stomach's sake or for good fellowship give him a glass and join him in a drink with a thousand earnest wishes for his health and happiness, does that make my nice, exclusive apartment a common nuisance? If I call on the good bishop, and he treat me to a glass or a bottle of wine, does that turn his palace into a common nuisance? If not, then is there one law for the palace and another law for the cottage? In administering the law we should never forget that the primary purpose of law and government is to build up, and not to pull down; to assure the right of all to enjoy and defend life and liberty, to acquire, possess, and protect property, and to pursue and obtain safety and happiness."

Since the information does not charge and since the evidence does not show more than one sale, we respectfully submit that the plaintiff in error could not have been guilty of maintaining a common nuisance. The information by reason of its failure to charge any facts showing that the premises were habitually used for illegal sales, fails to charge the commission of the crime attempted to be charged. Accordingly, since he was convicted upon an accusation that did not charge any crime, the plaintiff in error's motion in arrest of judgment was well taken, and should have been granted by the court below.

III.

THE COURT BELOW HAD NO JURISDICTION TO TRY THE INFORMATION.

It is our contention that prosecution of offenses under the "National Prohibition Act" by information is unconstitutional, and even if constitutional, is contrary to the express prohibitions of the act itself.

> "No person shall be held to answer for a capital, or otherwise infamous crime, unless on a presentment or indictment of a Grand Jury." (Constitution: Am. V.)

Even if it be held that the crime of which plaintiff in error was convicted was not an "infamous crime", still the provisions of the Prohibition Act seem to inhibit the filing of informations, and to contemplate prosecutions by indictment alone. Section 2 of the act provides:

> "The Commissioner of Internal Revenue, his assistants, agents, and inspectors, shall investigate and report violations of the War Prohibition Act to the United States Attorney for the district in which committed, who shall be

> charged with the duty of prosecuting, subject to the direction of the Attorney General, the offenders as in the case of other offenses against laws of the United States; and such Commissioner of Internal Revenue, his assistants, agents, and inspectors may swear out warrants before United States Commissioners or other officers or courts authorized to issue the same for the apprehension of such offenders, subject to the control of the United States Attorney, conduct the prosecution at the committing trial *for the purpose of having the offenders held for the action of a Grand Jury.*"

The act confers no authority to file informations on the United States Attorney, and obviously can have no other meaning than that proceedings against offenders must be by indictment.

It is respectfully submitted that the judgment should be reversed.

Dated, San Francisco,
October 20, 1920.

Clarence W. Morris,
Chauncey F. Tramutolo,
William F. Herron,
Attorneys for Plaintiff in Error.

IN THE

United States Circuit Court of Appeals

For the Ninth Circuit

ALBERT YOUNG,

Plaintiff in Error,

vs.

THE UNITED STATES OF AMERICA,

Defendant in Error.

REPLY BRIEF OF DEFENDANT IN ERROR.

FRANK M. SILVA,
United States Attorney.

WILFORD H. TULLY,
Asst. United States Attorney.

Attorneys for Defendant in Error.

Neal, Stratford & Kerr, S. F. —8858

No. 3517.

IN THE

United States Circuit Court of Appeals

For the Ninth Circuit

ALBERT YOUNG,
Plaintiff in Error,

vs.

THE UNITED STATES OF AMERICA,
Defendant in Error.

REPLY BRIEF OF DEFENDANT IN ERROR.

STATEMENT OF FACTS.

The plaintiff in error, hereinafter called the defendant, and his bartender, Walter Dekau, were convicted in the United States District Court for the Northern District of California of maintaining a public nuisance in violation of Section 3 of the National Prohibition Act.

The defendant contends (1) that the evidence was insufficient to justify a conviction; (2) that the information does not charge a crime against the laws of the United States, and (3) that the court had no jurisdiction to try the defendant upon the information.

ARGUMENT.

I.

The evidence is sufficient to sustain the conviction of the defendant.

The information charges the defendant as follows:

> "NOW, THEREFORE, your informant present: THAT W. DEKAU and ALBERT YOUNG, hereinafter called the defendants, heretofore to-wit, on the twentieth day of November, in the year of our Lord one thousand nine hundred and nineteen, at San Francisco, in the Southern Division of the Northern District of California, then and there being, did then and there, in violation of Section 3 of the Act of October 28th, 1919, known as the 'National Prohibition Act,' unlawfully, wilfully and knowingly maintain a public and common nuisance in that they did unlawfully, wilfully and knowingly sell and keep for sale for beverage purposes on the premises at number 2965 Sixteenth Street in San Francisco aforesaid, certain intoxicating liquor, to-wit, whiskey.
>
> AGAINST the peace and dignity of the United States of America, and contrary to the form of the statute of the said United States of America in such case made and provided."

The information shows that the defendant and Dekau were charged jointly with maintaining a public nuisance. The record shows that the proprietor of the saloon was the defendant Young, and that he employed Dekau as a bartender.

Trans., page 24:

> "Q. You are the proprietor of the premises referred to in this case. A. Yes, sir.
>
> Q. Do you recognize this bottle which has been offered in evidence here?
>
> A. We used to have wine bottles like that around."

Trans., page 17:

> "Q. Who conducts this place? A. Albert Young.
>
> MR. MORRIS: There is no question about that, Mr. Young conducts the place."

Trans., page 18:

> "Q. On or about November 20, were you employed by Mr. Young as a bartender in the saloon at Mission and 16th Street? A. Yes, sir."

The record also shows that intoxicating liquor was sold by the bartender Dekau at the premises and that the consideration involved in the transaction went to the benefit of the defendant Young.

Trans., page 11:

> "As I came up to the bar I saw a man drinking a drink and the bartender came up to the cash register with the cash in his hand, and rang up twenty-five cents; Deputy Collector Doyle

took this glass away from the bartender and we both smelled of the glass, and it smelled of whiskey."

Trans., pages 15-16:

> "I went in and there was a man drinking whiskey; he came to the bartender, Mr. Dekau, at that time he could not get into the little room, because the door was locked; it was a Yale lock, and he came around, he was behind the bar; Mr. Dekau went to the cash register and he rang up 25c; I took the glass and smelled of it. There was two parties standing outside of the bar, one by the name of McKey and another fellow that happened to work down at the Motor Taxi Company.
>
> Q. Did you see the liquor served?
>
> A. I saw the liquor served.
>
> Q. From the bottle? A. From the bottle.
>
> Q. You saw the 25c passed over the bar?
>
> A. Yes, sir."

The record thus shows that the defendant not only maintained the place which constituted the nuisance, but employed the man who sold the liquor, and received the profit arising out of maintaining the nuisance. To permit a proprietor to escape under such circumstances would render the Act nugatory as to the person who ought to be punished. The court in the case of Carroll v. State, 3 Atl. 29 (Md.) very aptly said:

"If the principal makes such sale at his peril, and is not excusable because he did not know or was deceived, for the reason that he was bound to know, and, if he was not certain, should decline to sell or take the hazard, it cannot be that, by setting another to do his work, and occupying himself elsewhere and otherwise, he can reap the benefit of his agent's sales, and escape the consequences of the agent's conduct. It would be impossible to effectually enforce a statute of this kind if that were allowed, and no license would ever be suppressed."

Where the evidence shows that the unlawful sale of liquor was made in the defendant's shop or place of business by his agent, that fact alone raises a presumption that the defendant authorized, or knew of it and consented to it.

Black on Intoxicating Liquor, section 371.

Commonwealth v. Perry, 148 Mass. 160—19 N. E. 212:

"Knowlton, J. In each of these three cases the only question is whether there was sufficient evidence to warrant a verdict of guilty. The testimony of the witness Dickerson was substantially the same in each. It tended to show a sale of pure alcohol, made by a clerk of the defendant, in the regular course of the defendant's business. That was sufficient to warrant a finding that the sale was authorized by the defendant. *Com.* v. *Locke,* 145 Mass. 401, 14 N. E. Rep. 621; *Com.* v. *Briant,* 142 Mass. 463, 8 N. E. Rep. 338; *Com.* v. *Holmes,* 119 Mass. 195."

Fullwood v. State, 7 So. 432 (Miss.)

"If appellant was the owner of the bar on the steamer Katie Robins, and intoxicating liquor was sold by a person apparently in charge thereof, as clerk or agent, the sale was, in the absence of any countervailing testimony, to be taken as a sale by the defendant; and, since there was no such countervailing evidence, the instruction given in behalf of the state was not error."

Also:

State v. Wentworth, 65 Me. 234.
Com. v. Nichols, 10 Metc. (Man.) 259.
Molihan v. State, 30 Ind. 266.

Where the defense is that the agent violated a direction or instruction requiring him not to make illegal sales, the question, whether or not such order was so given, is for the jury to determine.

State v. Wentworth, 65 Me. 234.
Com. v. Rooks, 150 Mass. 59—22 N. E. 436.

The jury in the case at bar has decided against the defendant upon his defense that the sale was unauthorized. The fact that the money paid for the liquor went into the cash register of the defendant would raise a conflict in the evidence so far as the testimony of the defendant and his bartender went concerning the instructions given.

II.

The information in the case at bar does state a crime against the laws of the United States.

Section 3 of Title I of the National Prohibition Act, under which the defendant was charged, provides:

> "Any room, house, building, boat, vehicle, structure or place of any kind where intoxicating liquor is sold, manufactured, kept for sale, or bartered in violation of the War Prohibition Act, and all intoxicating liquor and all property kept and used in maintaining such a place, is hereby declared to be a public and common nuisance, and any person who maintains or assists in maintaining such public and common nuisance shall be guilty of a misdemeanor, and upon conviction thereof shall be fined not less than $100 nor more than $1,000, or be imprisoned for not less than thirty days or more than one year, or both. If a person has knowledge that his property is occupied or used in violation of the provisions of the War Prohibition Act and suffers the same to be so used, such property shall be subject to a lien for and may be sold to pay all fines and costs assessed against the occupant of such building or property for any violation of the War Prohibition Act occurring after the passage hereof, which said lien shall attach from the time of the filing of notice of the commencement of the suit in the office where the records of the transfer of real estate are kept; and any such lien may be established and enforced by legal action instituted for that pur-

pose in any court having jurisdiction. Any violation of this title upon any leased premises by the lessee or occupant thereof shall, at the option of the lessor, work a forfeiture of the lease."

The information charges the defendant as follows:

"NOW, THEREFORE, your informant presents: THAT W. DEKAU and ALBERT YOUNG, hereinafter called the defendants, heretofore to-wit, on the twentieth day of November, in the year of our Lord one thousand nine hundred and nineteen, at San Francisco, in the Southern Division of the Northern District of California, then and there being, did then and there, in violation of Section 3 of the Act of October 28th, 1919, known as the 'National Prohibition Act,' unlawfully, wilfully and knowingly maintain a public and common nuisance in that they did unlawfully, wilfully and knowingly sell and keep for sale for beverage purposes on the premises at number 2965 Sixteenth Street in San Francisco aforesaid, certain intoxicating liquor, to-wit, whiskey.

AGAINST the peace and dignity of the United States of America, and contrary to the form of the statute of the said United States of America in such case made and provided."

An information which describes the offense in the words of the statute is sufficient.

Skinner v. State, 120 Ind. 127—22 N. E. 115.

"The general rule is that an indictment describing the offense in the language used by the statute in defining it is sufficient. State v. Bougher, 3 Blackf. 307; Pelts v. State, Id. 28;

Marble v. State, 13 Ind. 362; Malone v. State, 14 Ind. 219; Stuckmyer v. State, 29 Ind. 20; Shinn v. State, 68 Ind. 423; State v. Allisbach, 69 Ind. 50; Howard v. State, 87 Ind. 68; Toops v. State, 92 Ind. 13; State v. Miller, 98 Ind. 70; State v. Berdetta, 73 Ind. 185. Some of the exceptions are where the statute creating the offense charged contains language which embraces acts evidently not intended to be made criminal, and cases where it was the evident intention of the legislature that reference should be had to the common law for a complete definition of the offense declared by the statute. Schmidt v. State, 78 Ind. 41; Moore, Crim. Law, Sec. 171; Anderson v. State, 7 Ohio, 539; Mains v. Sta , supra. The case of Mains v. State falls within the latter exception. The statute under consideration does, in our opinion, create and fully define the offense for which the appellant was prosecuted. *It declares that whoever keeps a place where intoxicating liquors are sold, bartered, given away, or suffered to be drunk in a disorderly manner, to the annoyance or injury of any part of the citizens of this state, shall be fined,* etc. *In such case we think it sufficient, in charging the violation of such statute, to follow the language of the legislature in defining the offense.* We think the indictment above set out charges a public offense, and that the court did not err in overruling the motion in arrest of judgment."

Also:

State v. Welch, 7 Atl. 475 (Me.).
Com. v. Ferden, 141 Mass. 28, 6 N. E. 239.
Com. v. Ryan, 136 Mass. 436.

The information does not charge the defendant with "the selling of liquor," as intimated in defendant's brief, but it charges that he did "in violation of Section 3 of the Act of October 28, 1919, known as the National Prohibition Act, unlawfully, wilfully and knowingly maintain a public and common nuisance in that," etc.

Section 32 of the Act provides that it is not necessary to set out the details of the act complained of, but that it is sufficient to allege that the act complained of was prohibited and unlawful.

Section 32, National Prohibition Act follows:

> "It shall not be necessary in any affidavit, information, or indictment to give the name of the purchaser or to include any defensive negative averments, but it shall be sufficient to state that the act complained of was then and there prohibited and unlawful, but this provision shall not be construed to preclude the trial court from directing the furnishing the defendant a bill of particulars when it deems it proper to do so."

Where the statute and not the common law defines the character of the nuisance as in the case at bar, the repetition, or frequency, of illicit sales is not the test by which to determine the character of the place as a nuisance. The maintaining of a place where liquor is sold or kept for sale in violation of law is the act of the defendant creating the nuisance, and a single sale will warrant a conviction upon a charge for maintaining such a nuisance.

State v. Pierce, 65 Iowa 85, 21 N. W. 195.

"Counsel for defendant takes exception to this instruction. His position is that to render the place a nuisance, under the section quoted above, the drunkenness, etc., must be either carried on or permitted to be carried on there; that is, there must be a recurrence at the place of the acts enumerated in the section, or some of them, in order to make it a nuisance, and that it would not be given that character by a single transaction; but that, under the instructions, defendant might be convicted on proof that he permitted said acts to be done at his place on a single occasion. We think, however, that this position is not correct. The construction put upon the section by the district court gives to the language its natural and fair meaning. The people of a community may be greatly disturbed and annoyed by a single assemblage of drunken men in their midst, or by fighting and quarreling there, although it should occur but once. The object of the statute is to protect them from the disturbance and annoyance which would be occasioned by the occurrence of such events in their midst; and the evident intention of the legislature in enacting it was to provide for the punishment of men who should permit such acts to be done in buildings or places under their control to the disturbance of others."

State v. Reyelts, 74 Io. 499—38 N. W. 377.

"The district court rightly directed the jury that a single sale would warrant a conviction for the nuisance. The keeping of intoxicating liquors, with the intent to sell them contrary to law, is the act of defendant creating the nuisance. One sale will disclose the unlawful intent as well as the keeping. Hence upon one unlawful sale a conviction may be had for nuisance. This we understand is the recognized rule in this state.

III.

The District Court had jurisdiction to try the information.

A violation of the National Prohibition Act is a misdemeanor, and it is well settled that misdemeanors may be prosecuted by information.

United States v. Thompson, 251 U. S. 414.
United States v. Wells, 225 Fed. 320.
Weeks v. United States, 216 Fed. 320.

The fifth amendment to the Constitution upon which the defendant attempts to base his argument is specifically limited in its terms to infamous crimes and not applicable to misdemeanors.

The National Prohibition Act itself contemplates that prosecutions will be instituted by informations.

Section 32 of Act of October 28, 1919:

"In any affidavit, *information*, or indictment for the violation of this Act, separate offenses may be united in separate counts and the defendant may be tried on all at one trial and the penalty for all offenses may be imposed."

It is respectfully submitted that the judgment should be affirmed.

FRANK M. SILVA,
United States Attorney.

WILFORD H. TULLY,
Asst. United States Attorney.

18

United States

Circuit Court of Appeals

For the Ninth Circuit.

THE WEST SIDE IRRIGATING COMPANY, a Corporation,

Appellant,

vs.

THE UNITED STATES OF AMERICA,

Appellee.

Transcript of Record.

Upon Appeal from the United States District Court for the Eastern District of Washington, Southern Division.

FILED
JUL 24 1920
F. D. MONCKTON,
CLERK.

Filmer Bros. Co. Print, 330 Jackson St., S. F., Cal.

United States
Circuit Court of Appeals
For the Ninth Circuit.

THE WEST SIDE IRRIGATING COMPANY, a Corporation,

Appellant,

vs.

THE UNITED STATES OF AMERICA,

Appellee.

Transcript of Record.

Upon Appeal from the United States District Court for the Eastern District of Washington, Southern Division.

Filmer Bros. Co. Print, 330 Jackson St., S. F., Cal.

INDEX TO THE PRINTED TRANSCRIPT OF RECORD.

[Clerk's Note: When deemed likely to be of an important nature, errors or doubtful matters appearing in the original certified record are printed literally in italic; and, likewise, cancelled matter appearing in the original certified record is printed and cancelled herein accordingly. When possible, an omission from the text is indicated by printing in italic the two words between which the omission seems to occur.]

Index. Page

Names and Addresses of Attorneys of Record.

CARROLL B. GRAVES, Central Building, Seattle, Washington,

HARTMAN & HARTMAN, Burk Building, Seattle, Washington,

Attorneys for Appellant.

FRANCIS A. GARRECHT, Federal Building, Spokane, Washington,

E. W. BARR, Yakima, Wash.,

Attorneys for Appellees. [2*]

In the District Court of the United States for the Eastern District of Washington, Southern Division.

No. 741.

THE WEST SIDE IRRIGATING COMPANY, a Corporation,

Petitioner,

vs.

UNITED STATES OF AMERICA,

Respondent.

Petition for Leave to File Complaint to Vacate Judgment.

To the Honorable the Judge of said Court:

Comes now your petitioner, The West Side Irrigating Company, a corporation of the State of Washington, and respectfully shows unto the Court as follows, to wit:

---

*Page-number appearing at foot of page of original certified Transcript of Record.

I.

That the said petitioner is a corporation duly formed and existing under and by virtue of the laws of Washington with its principal place of business at Ellensburg in said State, and that it was incorporated for the purpose of appropriating and using water for irrigation purposes taken from the Yakima River and distributing the same to its stockholders, and has been in such business uninterruptedly since on or about the first day of July, 1890. That on the fifteenth day of October, 1917, judgment of the United States District Court for the Eastern District of Washington, Southern Division, holding terms at Yakima, in favor of the United States of America as plaintiff and against the West Side Irrigating Company as defendant, was affirmed on an appeal from the above-entitled court, all as recorded in Volume 246 of Federal Reporter at page 212, and [3] upon a *remittitur* from said United States Circuit Court of Appeals being received at Yakima, Washington, the judgment of the lower court entered on the nineteenth day of February, 1916, was thereby affirmed, but no action has been taken thereon since the entry of judgment.

II.

That at the time of the incorporation of said petitioner in 1889, it appropriated water for irrigating purposes from the Yakima River in the County of Kittitas, in said State of Washington, in the amount of four thousand miner's inches and commenced the use thereof during the summer of 1890, and since said date and up to the present time has been in uninterrupted and constant use of the water so appropriated, taking all thereof that it required for the purposes of its business and in supplying its stockholders up to the amount of four thousand miner's inches, and at no time since said date and up to this time has such right of user been interfered with by any person or persons whomsoever and has so adversely used the same up to and including the present date.

III.

That on or about the twenty-first day of October, 1905, the said respondent sent to the petitioner and its officers a duly authorized agent and employee, one T. H. Noble, who solicited the said petitioner to enter into an agreement in writing by which the water by it appropriated should be measured by cubic feet per second of flow instead of being determined by *cubic feet per second of flow instead of being determined by* miner's inches as the same was originally taken and the usual way of measurement in the neighborhood, and after negotiating with the said Noble and taking his statements and representations, he being a hydraulic engineer of skill and attainment, the said [4] petitioner was induced to and did enter into an agreement by which the water to be used in the conduct of its business should be eighty cubic feet per second, and the contract was so executed, and at the time the said petitioner and its officers believed, and were led to that conclusion by the statements made by the agent of the United States, that when they received eighty cubic feet per second of water it was equivalent to four thousand miner's inches as by the petitioner appropriated, and the mistake and error was not discovered until the summer of 1908 when the said Noble, then being in the employ of the State of Washington in doing hydraulic and irrigation work, came again to the petitioner and its officers, when, having discovered the mistake about that time, the said petitioner informed the said Noble of the mistake made and protested against being bound by the agreement as made, for the reason that a mistake had been made and the petitioner had been deprived of a valuable right and of sufficient water to supply its stockholders, as the amount appropriated is necessary therefor in order to produce the crops of the stockholders covering about seven thousand acres and in grass, grains and other crops such as are grown by irrigation in said district, and all of the land in a high state of cultivation.

IV.

That the petitioner discovered when the protest was made on the date aforesaid and about that time that four thousand miner's inches of water flow as determined by the custom and the decision of the Honorable Superior Court in and for the said County of Kittitas, where the rule was announced and [5] followed in the said district, would require a much larger amount than eighty cubic feet per second and not sufficient to protect and mature the crops growing in the district aforesaid.

V.

That the petitioner, after having protested, believed that its rights were fully protected and that it would not be disturbed in any way, and that it would be entitled and permitted peaceably to use the amount of water by it appropriated and that the respondent would be duly informed by the said Noble, and the said petitioner believed and understood that when it gave the notice to the said Noble, who was in charge of the irrigation matters upon the Yakima River and the chief therein, nothing further would be required of it in order to protect its rights, and that when said action was determined by this Court it was urged by the learned counsel for the respondent that because the protest against the effectiveness of the agreement aforesaid limiting the amount of water had not been communicated to the respondent, then and thereupon because of remaining silent, the said protest became of no effect, and the said Circuit Court of Appeals stated in its opinion as follows:

> "The stockholders gave no notice to any officer of the United States that they repudiated the contract, but on the contrary by their silence they ratified the same";

which conclusion and the argument producing the same caused the said case to be determined adversely to this petitioner, which petitioner alleges would not have occurred if all of the facts had been presented which were not then known to this petitioner.

VI.

That after said cause brought by the United States as aforesaid had been appealed to the United States Circuit Court [6] of Appeals and for the first time, and information which it could not have before obtained, the said petitioner learned that immediately after the protest was lodged with the said Noble as aforesaid, he, the said Noble, then and there communicated the fact of said protest to the officer of the United States in charge of all of its irrigation affairs in the entire Yakima Valley in said State of Washington, which office was at Yakima, in said district, and informed the said agent in charge of the same of the alleged mistake and of the intention of the said petitioner and its stockholders to refuse to stand and abide by said agreement because of mistake and misunderstanding, the said discovery, being on or about the 18th day of June, 1918, and that at the time of the trial of said cause the said agent in chief of said reclamation service in said district was in court and upon the stand as a witness, but did not disclose the fact of notice, but kept the same from the Court and this petitioner, and had he disclosed the fact the action would have been determined differently as shown by the decision of the United States Circuit Court of Appeals.

VII.

That the said petitioner was diligent in the preparation of its cause of action and that it believed it had protected its rights and was taken completely by surprise when the respondent denied any notice of such protest and then believed that no such notice had been received and only by mere accident discovered it later on, and that if a new trial is granted it will be able to produce the testimony to fully convince the Court that it should prevail.

VIII.

That the said petitioner has been in the open, notorious [7] and continuous use of all the water appropriated by it when needed without let, hinddrance or protest from any person or persons whomsoever and by adverse user is entitled to have its rights adjudicated by which it shall be entitled in the future to use in the past the entire four thousand miner's inches of water when the same is necessary and required, and that it will be able to prove all of its rights as herein claimed and set forth and for which it asks a new trial, by T. A. Noble, J. H. Prater, F. A. Strande, Mitchell Stevens and John Burch, C. T. Kenneth and W. A. Stevens, who will be in court as witnesses when said action is heard again in the United States District Court for the Eastern District of Washington, Southern Division. That by reason of the judgment and decree made as aforesaid if the same is put into effect (altho it has never been enforced but may be at any time), this petitioner and its stockholders have been greatly damaged and will be irreparably damaged if the decree is allowed to be enforced.

IX.

That the said respondent is the user and seller of water taken from the Yakima River and its tributaries, not in its sovereign capacity but in a private capacity in a business way, the same as individuals or local corporations of the State use water for irrigating purposes, having obtained the right, as individuals and corporations do and must, from the State of Washington for engaging in said business, and has no rights or more rights than those enjoyed and taken under the laws of the State of Washington, the said Yakima River and its tributaries being purely intrastate streams. [8]

X.

That upon petition duly presented to the United States Circuit Court of Appeals for the Ninth Circuit, where said judgment was affirmed on appeal as hereinabove mentioned, your petitioner was, by order of said Court entered on the 3d day of September, 1919, granted permission to present and file within petition in the above-entitled court for leave to have said judgment reviewed and the cause reheard in said court and 10 days allowed within which to file said petition herein, and the same is presented and filed herewith within the time as specified.

WHEREFORE, your petitioner prays for decree of this Court granting leave to file its bill of complaint herein to obtain a review and a rehearing of the former judgment, upon the ground of newly discovered evidence and adverse user, and for such order and decree as shall be proper and meet in the premises.

CARROLL B. GRAVES,
HARTMAN & HARTMAN,
Attorneys for Petitioner.

State of Washington,
County of King,—ss.

Mitchell Stevens, being first duly sworn, on oath says: He is vice-president of the West Side Irrigating Company, the aforesaid petitioner, and makes this verification for and on behalf of said corporation. That he has read the foregoing petition, knows the contents thereof, and that the same is true as he verily believes.

MITCHELL STEVENS.

Subscribed and sworn to before me this 3d day of September, 1919.

HAROLD H. HARTMAN,
Notary Public in and for the State of Washington,
Residing at Seattle.

Filed in the U. S. District Court, Eastern District of Washington, September 5, 1919. Wm. H. Hare. By C. Roy King, Deputy. [9]

In the District Court of the United States for the Eastern District of Washington, Southern Division.

No. 741.

THE WEST SIDE IRRIGATING COMPANY, a Corporation,

Petitioner,

vs.

UNITED STATES OF AMERICA,

Respondent.

Order Granting Leave to File Bill of Complaint to Vacate Judgment.

This cause coming on to be heard *ex parte* this day upon presentation of the petition for relief to file complaint to vacate judgment, the said petitioner appearing by its attorneys upon the petition and the Court, being fully advised in the premises, finds that the United States Circuit Court of Appeals for the Ninth Circuit on the 3d day of September, 1919, granted leave to present this petition to the undersigned Judge and, after consideration,—

IT IS ORDERED that the petition aforesaid be received and the same, with this order and other papers, shall be filed with the clerk of the court at Yakima, Washington, and the petitioner is hereby granted and given authority to file its bill of complaint for a new trial in this cause with the clerk aforesaid and, upon filing the same, the clerk shall issue the usual process and deliver the same for service upon the respondent aforesaid, to be served in the usual and ordinary way with the usual time as prescribed by the rules of this court for the respondent named aforesaid to be and appear in and defend said cause according to the rules of this court.

Done and signed this 3d day of September, 1919.

FRANK H. RUDKIN,
Judge of said District Court.

Filed in the U. S. District Court, Eastern District of Washington. Sept. 5, 1919. Wm. H. Hare, Clerk. By C. Roy King, Deputy. [10]

In the District Court of the United States for the Eastern District of Washington, Southern Division.

No. 741.

THE WEST SIDE IRRIGATING COMPANY, a Corporation,

Plaintiff,

vs.

UNITED STATES OF AMERICA,

Defendant.

Motion for Leave to Amend Bill of Complaint.

Now comes the plaintiff and moves the Court for leave to file its second amended bill of complaint, herewith presented.

Dated this 8th day of April, A. D. 1920.

HARTMAN & HARTMAN,
CARROLL B. GRAVES,
Attorneys for Plaintiff,

Filed in the U. S. District Court, Eastern District of Washington, April 10, 1920. W. H. Hare, Clerk. [11]

In the District Court of the United States, for the Eastern Division of Washington, Southern Division.

No. 741.

THE WEST SIDE IRRIGATING COMPANY, a Corporation,

Plaintiff,

vs.

UNITED STATES OF AMERICA,

Defendant.

Stipulation in re Amended Bill of Complaint.

IT IS STIPULATED AND AGREED, between the plaintiff, by its attorneys, Carroll B. Graves and Hartman & Hartman, and the defendant by its attorney, Francis A. Garrecht, that the plaintiff may file an amended bill of complaint in this action, to stand in the place of the one already filed, and that the defendant shall be given twenty (20) days in which to answer the same, and a further time, if a request is so made by the defendant in writing to the attorneys for plaintiff.

Dated, Sept. 27th, 1919.

CARROLL B. GRAVES,
HARTMAN & HARTMAN,
Attorneys for Plaintiff,
FRANCIS A. GARRECHT,

Filed March 23, 1920. W. H. Hare, Clerk. [12]

In the District Court of the United States, for the Eastern District of Washington, Southern Division.

No. 741.

THE WEST SIDE IRRIGATING COMPANY, a Corporation,

Plaintiff,

vs.

UNITED STATES OF AMERICA,

Defendant.

Order Allowing Filing of Second Amended Complaint.

Upon the application of plaintiff therefor, it is ORDERED: That the plaintiff may file its second amended bill of complaint, which said amended bill of complaint has been served upon the attorneys for the defendant and tendered for filing with the plaintiff's application.

Dated this 10th day of April, A. D. 1920.

FRANK H. RUDKIN,
Judge. [13]

In the District Court of the United States, for the Eastern District of Washington, Southern Division.

No. 741.

THE WEST SIDE IRRIGATING COMPANY, a Corporation,

Plaintiff,

vs.

UNITED STATES OF AMERICA,

Defendant.

Second Amended Bill of Complaint.

Comes now the said plaintiff above named and by leave of Court first had and obtained, files this its amended bill in equity in the nature of a bill or review of the judgment hereinafter referred to, and for cause of action states as follows:

I.

That the said plaintiff is a corporation duly formed and existing under and by virtue of the laws of Washington, with its principal place of business at Ellensburg in said State, and that it was incorporated for the purpose of appropriating and using water for irrigation purposes taken from the Yakima River, and distributing the same to its stockholders, and has been in such business uninterruptedly since on or about the 1st day of July, 1890, and that on the 15th day of October, 1917, judgment of the United States District Court for the Eastern District of Washington, Southern Division, holding terms at Yakima, in favor of the United States of America as plaintiff and against the West Side Irrigating Company as defendant, was affirmed on an appeal from the above-entitled court, all as recorded in Volume 246 of Federal Reporter at page 212, and upon a *remittitur* from said United [14] States Circuit Court of Appeals being received at Yakima, Washington, the judgment of the lower court entered on the 19th day of February, 1916, was thereby affirmed, but no action has been taken thereon since the entry of the judgment.

II.

That at the time of the incorporation of said plaintiff in 1889, it appropriated water for irrigating purposes from the Yakima River in the County of Kittitas in said State of Washington, in the amount of four thousand miner's inches, at the user's distribution boxes, and commenced the use thereof during the summer of 1890, and since said date and up to the present time has been in uninterrupted and constant use of the water so appropriated, taking all thereof that it required for the purpose of its business and in supplying its stockholders up to the amount of four thousand miner's inches, at the user's distribution boxes, and at no time since said date and up to this time has such right of user been interfered with by any person or persons whomsoever and has so adversely used the same up to and including the present date.

III.

That on or about the 21st day of October, 1905, the said respondent sent to the plaintiff and its officers a duly authorized agent and employee, one T.

A. Noble, who solicited the said plaintiff to enter into an agreement in writing by which the water by it appropriated should be measured by cubic feet per second, of flow, instead of being determined by miner's inches as the same was originally taken and the usual way of measurement in the neighborhood, and after negotiating with the said Noble and taking his statements and representations, he being a hydraulic engineer of skill and attainment, the said plaintiff was induced to and did enter [15] into an agreement by which the water to be used in the conduct of its business should be eight cubic feet per second, and the contract was so executed, and at the time the said plaintiff and its officers believed, and were led to that conclusion by the statements made by the agent of the United States, that when they received eighty cubic feet per second of water it was equivalent to four thousand miner's inches at the users' distribution boxes, as by the plaintiff appropriated, and used when necessary, and the mistake and error was not discovered until the summer of of 1908 when the said Noble, then being in the employ of the State of Washington in doing hydraulic and irrigation work, but not then known to be so engaged by the plaintiff, came again to the plaintiff, and its officers, when having discovered the mistake about that time, the said plaintiff informed the said Noble of the mistake made and protested against being bound by the agreement as made, for the reason that a mistake had been made and the plaintiff had been deprived of a valuable right and of sufficient water to supply its stockholders as the amount appropriated is necessary therefor, in order to produce the crops of the stockholders, covering about seven thousand acres and in grass, grains and other crops, such as are grown by irrigation in said district, and all of the land then being in a high state of cultivation, and that notwithstanding the fact that the said Noble was at said time in the employ of the State of Washington, the plaintiff believed that he was with and employed by the Reclamation Service of the United States, and did not know to the contrary, until this cause was being tried in the United States District Court during the year 1914.

IV.

That the plaintiff discovered when the protest was made [16] on the date aforesaid, and about that time, that four thousand miner's inches of water flow, at the users' distribution boxes, as determined by the custom and the decision of the Honorable Superior Court in and for the said County of Kittitas, where the rule was announced and long followed in the said district, would require a much larger amount than eighty cubic feet per second, which was not sufficient to protect and mature the crops growing in the district aforesaid.

V.

That the plaintiff, after having protested, believed that its rights were fully protected and that it would not be disturbed in any way, and that it would be entitled and permitted peaceably to use the amount of water by it appropriated and that the defendant would be duly informed by the said Noble, and the said plaintiff believed and understood *what* when it gave the notice to the said Noble, who was in charge of the irrigation matters upon the Yakima River, and the chief therein, nothing further would be required of it in order to protect its rights, and that when said action was determined by this Court it was urged by the learned counsel for the defendant that because the protest against the effectiveness and binding force of the agreement aforesaid, limiting the amount of water, had not been communicated to the defendant, then and thereupon because of remaining silent the said protest became of no effect, and because of such conclusion the said Circuit Court of Appeals stated in its opinion as follows:

> "The stockholders gave no notice to any officer of the United States that they repudiated the contract but on the contrary by their silence they ratified the same"; and also "and there is no convincing evidence of a mistake on the part of the appellant or its stockholders."

which conclusion and the argument producing the same caused the said case to be determined adversely to this plaintiff, which [17] plaintiff alleges would not have occurred if all of the facts promptly disavowing the unauthorized acts of the corporate officers had been presented which were not then known, nor could they have been known, to this plaintiff.

VI.

That in the trial of the cause, and when taking the testimony, the said Noble was called as a witness by the United States, and he there testified from the witness-stand, and upon leaving the stand, at the suggestion of counsel for plaintiff, the vice-president of the plaintiff Mitchell Stevens, immediately inquired of the said Noble if he did not notify the Reclamation Service about the protest and rights claimed in the summer of 1908 aforesaid, and thereupon the said Noble answered he had no such recollection, or words to that effect, and thereupon the said Stevens communicated this fact to his counsel, Carroll B. Graves, who was at the attorney's table, in the courtroom, where the testimony was being taken, of the answer that had been made, and the matter was then dismissed, believing that the said Noble had not communicated the fact to the officers of the Reclamation Service at Yakima or elsewhere.

VII.

That after said cause, brought by the United States as aforesaid, had been appealed to the United States Circuit Court of Appeals and for the first time, and information which it could not have before obtained, the said plaintiff learned that immediately after the protest was lodged with the said Noble as aforesaid, he, the said Noble, then and there communicated the fact of said protest to the officer of the United States in charge of all its irrigation affairs in the entire Yakima Valley in said State of Washington, which office was [18] at Yakima, in said district, and informed the said agent in charge of the same of the alleged mistake and of the intention of the said plaintiff and its stockholders to refuse to stand and abide by said agreement because of mistake and misunderstanding, the said discovery being on or about the 18th day of June, 1918, and that at the time of the trial of said cause the said agent in chief of said reclamation service in said district was in court, and upon the stand as a witness, but did not disclose the fact of notice but kept the same from the Court and this plaintiff, and had he disclosed the fact the action would have been determined differently as shown by the decision of the United States Circuit Court of Appeals.

VIII.

That the said plaintiff was diligent in the preparation of its cause of action, and that it believed it had protected its rights and was taken completely by surprise when the defendant failed to admit receiving notice of such protest and showed by the witness Noble that he was not an officer of the United States Reclamation Service at the time the protest was made to him, and then believed that no such notice had been received and only by mere accident discovered it later on, and that if a new trial is granted it will be able to produce the testimony to fully convince the Court that it should prevail, and that the said T. A. Noble is a resident and citizen of the State of Washington, and has resided therein for more than thirty years last past, and that he will be produced as a witness on any new trial granted and will testify substantially as follows:

That during the years 1905 and 1906, he was in the employ of the Reclamation Service of the United States engaged on the Yakima River Projects of the said Reclamation [19] Service, and in his capacity had conferences with the officers and shareholders of the plaintiff company and was a party to securing the so-called "limiting agreement," whereby the plaintiff was induced to limit the use of its water to 80 cubic feet per second of time. That the said Noble left the employ of said Reclamation Service on the 1st day of January, 1907, but continued to reside at North Yakima, Washington; and that, in the year 1908, he was appointed by the Superior Court of Kittitas County as a Water Commissioner under the laws of the State of Washington for the counties of Kittitas and Yakima, and in the discharge of his duties, in the month of July, 1908, he went to the county of Kittitas for the purpose of regulating the flow of water from the Yakima River into the various canals, and while there he discussed the said limiting agreement with officers of the plaintiff company, and the said officers then and there stated that said company and its stockholders had been misled by their misunderstanding and by misrepresentation as to the effect of said agreement, and that they had understood and been given to understand that the amount placed in the agreement was equal to 4,000 inches of water according to the method used by the plaintiff company and as estimated and calculated by the plaintiff company and its stockholders theretofore, and that a mistake had been made and that the plaintiff company and its stockholders would not be bound by the limiting agreement, and protested against their being so bound because of the mistake aforesaid and the fact that they had been misled, and that they had used and would insist upon using the amount of 4,000 inches as measured by them through the distribution boxes of the stockholders, and that at about the time of the conversation aforesaid, the said Noble measured the amount of water taken by the plaintiff, and that it exceeded [20] 80 cubic feet per second of time, and immediately thereafter he went to North Yakima to the Chief Officer of the Reclamation Service on the Yakima River projects, Charles H. Swigart, and related to him the interview had with the officers of the plaintiff company, and that the company was taking an amount in excess of 80 cubic feet per second, and that the officers of the plaintiff had protested and stated to the said Noble as aforesaid and that the plaintiff and its officers proposed to resist any attempt to reduce the amount of water to be taken by them to 80 cubic feet per second; and thereupon the said Swigart advised the said Noble not to proceed to enforce the said limiting agreement and to let the matter go as it was. That he, the said Noble, remembers that upon the trial of the case aforesaid he was a witness and that one Mitchell Stevens, an officer for the plaintiff company, inquired after he had left the stand, if he, the said Noble, did not convey the statement and protest made to him by the officers of the company, but the said Noble remarked that he didn't remember about it, and the incident at that time had passed from his mind. That long after said trial, to wit, in the summer of 1918, the said Mitchell Stevens called upon the said Noble concerning certain business, and after several conferences about other business matters, and after discussing what had occurred and what had been said by the officers of plaintiff company, the said Noble finally was able to recall that the things hereinbefore stated had been done and said. That at the time the said Noble went to Kittitas County in 1908 as aforesaid, he did so for the purpose of enforcing the limitations prescribed by the said limiting agreement, and that the only parties interested in such enforcement were the Reclamation Service and its officers, and upon the statement of said [21] Swigart that nothing further should be done in the matter, the said Noble made no attempt to enforce said limiting agreement against the plaintiff, and that the only reason why said agreement was not attempted to be enforced by the said Noble as Water Commissioner aforesaid was because of having conveyed to the said Swigart the statements and protests made by the officers of the plaintiff company and the request of said Swigart not to proceed further after he had received the information so given him by the said Noble.

IX.

That the said plaintiff has been in the open, notorious and continuous use of all of the water appropriated by it when needed without let, hinderance or protest from any person or persons whomsoever, and by adverse user is entitled to have its rights adjudicated by which it shall be entitled in the future to use as in the past, the entire 4,000 miner's inches of water measured at the users' boxes, when the same is necessary and required upon the District served, and that it will be able to prove all of its rights as herein claimed and set forth and for which it asks a new trial, by T. A. Noble, J. H. Prater, F. A. Strandle, Mitchell Stevens, and John Burch, C. F. Kenneth, and W. A. Stevens, who will be in court as witnesses when said action is heard again in the United States District Court for the Eastern District of Washington, Southern Division. That if the judgment and decree hereinbefore mentioned shall be continued in full force and effect and the plaintiff and its stockholders thereby perpetually limited to the use of 80 cubic feet of water per second of time, measured as prescribed by said decree, they will be greatly and irreparably damaged.

X.

That, because of the suppression of the fact by the defendant [22] of having had notice of said protest and reservation of rights, as fully set forth aforesaid, a manifest fraud and injustice was and has been visited upon and against the said plaintiff, to its great damage and detriment, and three years have not elapsed since the discovery of said fraud, and of the proof to right the wrong suffered. That, upon discovering the new evidence hereinbefore stated and suppressed as hereinbefore alleged, the plaintiff did not immediately file its bill of review; but, because of a change in the officers in charge of the Reclamation Service in the Yakima River projects, and believing that as agents of the United States such officers would endeavor to right the wrong imposed upon the plaintiff, it stated the newly discovered evidence to the officers then in charge, and the plaintiff was led to believe and believed that its application for redress was being favorably considered by the defendant and that plaintiff's application presented a matter of merit and equity to be considered by the defendant; and thereupon, plans and methods were discussed orally and by correspondence to the end that an adjustment might be made abviating further trial or litigation, and such negotiations resulted in petitions being presented to defendant's departments and arguments being made thereon. That all of said matters were so pending at the time action was taken in the United States Circuit Court of Appeals resulting in the order allowing the plaintiff to file its original bill in this cause, and such action was taken by the plaintiff because it feared the loss of its rights by reason of the delays in the negotiations had with the defendant; and that the reason action was not sooner taken by the plaintiff and the original bill herein sooner filed was because the plaintiff and its officers were led to believe that on account of the injury which [23] had been done to the plaintiff by suppressing the new evidence aforesaid, it would be relieved from the wrong it had sustained by the decree without applying to this Court for redress and that the matter would be settled and adjusted without further contest or litigation.

XI.

That the said defendant is the user and seller of water taken from the Yakima River and its tributaries, not in its sovereign capacity, but in a private capacity, in a business *say,* the same as individuals or local corporations of the State of Washington for engaging in said business, and has no rights or more rights than those enjoyed and taken under the laws of the State of Washington, the said Yakima River and its tributaries being purely an intrastate stream.

XII.

That by reason of the discovery of the said new matter the said judgment ought to be reviewed and reversed, and this plaintiff granted a decree of this court affirming its right to all of the water by it originally appropriated and by it used without let or hindrance, since the time of the appropriation, so far as the same so appropriated, has been required for conducting the affairs of the plaintiff.

XIII.

That the plaintiff has had to expend for itself and is liable for a large bill of costs and expenses, and must expend a large amount still in costs, in preserving and defending its rights, all of which would not have been necessary or required if the defendant had not so suppressed the facts, which otherwise would have given a decree in plaintiff's favor, and because of the wrong done and fraud suffered, the said defendant should be adjudged to pay and required to [24] repay the same, and all thereof, to the plaintiff.

XIV.

That at no time since the rendition of the decree in said case No. 228, or the affirmance thereof by the Circuit Court of Appeals, has the defendant herein in any manner or form, by notice or otherwise, attempted or tried to enforce the decree, or any thereof, or in any manner interfere with the rights of the said plaintiff and its shareholders.

WHEREFORE, the said plaintiff prays:

(a) That said action be reviewed, considered, and a decree entered upon and in conformity with the newly discovered evidence and rights set forth herein, and that testimony be received and taken under consideration, to aid the Court in conclusion:

(b) That the judgment heretofore rendered be reversed and set aside:

(c) That said cause of action may be heard on such new and supplemental matters and facts as may be offered, at the same time that it is reheard upon said original complaint;

(d) That plaintiff be allowed and permitted to amend its answer filed in the original cause, to comport to the facts hereinbefore set forth, and that the plaintiff be awarded judgment and decree of this court for the settling and determining of all of its rights to the water appropriated and used, as set forth in the complaint, and for all thereof, without protest, molestation or interference on the part of the defendant, or anyone acting through, by, or for it;

(e) That plaintiff may have and recover its costs and damages herein, and, [25]

(f) That plaintiff may have such other and further relief as shall be deemed just and equitable.

CARROLL L. B. GRAVES,
HARTMAN & HARTMAN,
Attorneys for Plaintiff.

State of Washington,
County of King,—ss.

Mitchell Stevens, being first duly sworn, on oath says: That he is vice-president of the West Side Irrigating Company, the aforesaid plaintiff, and makes this verification for and on behalf of said company; that he has read the foregoing second amended complaint, knows the contents thereof and that the same is true, as he verily believes.

MITCHELL STEVENS.

Subscribed and sworn to before me this 7th day of April, 1920.

HAROLD H. HARTMAN,
Notary Public in and for the State of Washington,
Residing at Seattle.

Filed in the U. S. District Court, Eastern District of Washington, April 10, 1920. W. H. Hare, Clerk. [26]

In the District Court of the United States, for the Eastern District of Washington, Southern Division.

No. 741.

THE WEST SIDE IRRIGATING COMPANY, a Corporation,

Plaintiff,

vs.

THE UNITED STATES OF AMERICA,

Defendant.

Motion to Dismiss Second Amended Bill of Complaint.

Comes now the defendant in the above-entitled action and moves the Court to dismiss plaintiff's second amended bill of complaint and application to vacate the judgment entered on the 15th day of October, 1917, in the Circuit Court of Appeals for the Ninth

Circuit, affirming a judgment of the United States District Court for the Eastern District of Washington, Southern Division, in favor of the United States of America, as plaintiff, and against the West Side Irrigating Company, as defendant, and to deny plaintiff's application for relief, for the following reasons:

1. That the facts set forth in plaintiff's second amended bill of complaint are not sufficient to require this defendant to answer herein.

2. That plaintiff's said second amended bill of complaint is without equity and plaintiff is not entitled to any relief.

3. That said second amended bill of complaint, in its first paragraph, refers to the judgment of this Court heretofore rendered and to the judgment of the Circuit Court of Appeals for the Ninth Circuit, affirming said judgment on appeal, and by reference embodies the proceedings [27] had therein, of which this Court will take judicial knowledge, and it affirmatively appears therefrom that plaintiff seeks relief herein upon grounds different and variant from those asserted in the original case.

4. That further comparison of the second amended bill of complaint with the record in the original cause referred to in paragraph one of said second amended complaint, shows that the representations upon which relief is now sought are not true in this: That the suggestions of fraud set forth in the second amended bill of complaint are based upon the statements that one, Charles H. Swigart, chief officer of the Reclamation Service, was present in court and upon the witness-stand at the previous trial, and failed to dis-

close the evidence alleged to have been suppressed, when the record in the former trial conclusively shows that said Charles H. Swigart was never a witness in said case at all.

5. That the allegation in said second amended bill of complaint that plaintiff was misled by its officers or agents is not sufficient to amount to an allegation of fraud, and is inadequately pleaded; the allegations that the officers of the Government suppressed evidence being mere gratuitous conclusions, based in the most favorable view upon the carelessness and inexcusable neglect of plaintiff in not having discovered the evidence alleged to have been suppressed; that plaintiff herein, on said former trial, made no effort whatever to support any allegation that the company had given notice to the United States of the renunciation of the contract, either by questioning T. A. Noble, who was a witness, or by calling said Charles H. Swigart, Supervising Engineer of the United States Reclamation Service, who was not a witness. [28]

6. That the said matter alleged as newly discovered evidence is cumulative, immaterial and not controlling, and that there is ample in the record to sustain the findings and decisions made by the District Court and the Circuit Court of Appeals in said cause on other grounds than those stated in the second amended bill of complaint; that even if the facts set forth in the second amended bill of complaint, which are alleged to show an attempt to give notice of the renunciation of the contract, had in fact been communicated to the United States as stated, it clearly

appears that this so-called notice was casual, incidental, informal and by hearsay only, and entirely fails to meet that clear, unmistakable, unequivocal, absolute and final renunciation which the law required as a basis for the abrogation of a contract.

7. That conceding the allegations of the second amended bill of complaint, it appears from the stipulation in the record that the attempted renunciation was made too late to be available as an abrogation of contract, for the reason that it conclusively appears from the undisputed evidence offered in the former case, referred to in paragraph one of said second amended bill of complaint, that at the time of the alleged notice, the said contract was no longer executory as regards the United States; but that the United States, prior thereto, had expended vast sums in reliance upon the contract, and further, that the Government could not again be placed in the position it was before the contract was signed, and would, therefore, have been entitled to disregard said notice, even if given, as alleged in said second amended complaint, and would be at liberty to treat the contract as still binding and institute its action as it did. [29]

8. That the alleged newly discovered evidence set forth in the second amended bill of complaint seeks to abrogate the defense of estoppel; but the allegations thereof would not avail the plaintiff corporation for that purpose, since the stipulation of the parties in the record in the former action, referred to in paragraph one of plaintiff's second amended bill of complaint, conclusively shows that prior to the alleged notice of renunciation claimed to have been

given to T. A. Noble, the Secretary of the Interior, had already approved the Yakima Project and purchased the irrigation system for the Sunnyside Unit thereof and expended large sums in reliance upon plaintiff's contract and those of others of similar tenor:

9. That the plaintiff herein is guilty of laches in bringing its action for relief from the judgment heretofore rendered; that the uncontradicted evidence in the transcript of record in the former trial referred to in paragraph one of plaintiff's second amended bill of complaint herein conclusively shows that this plaintiff corporation had knowledge that the contract in question limited it to the use of a less amount of water than it now claims it understood was to be its portion as early as in January, 1906, and at said time had determined to resist the enforcement of the agreement; but according to its own showing, as set forth in the second amended complaint herein, it failed and neglected and made no effort to notify the United States, or any of its agents or supposed agents, of this fixed intent to rescind or repudiate the contract until the summer of 1908, at which time the Government had already expended approximately $1,263,000.00, all of which was sufficient to warrant the findings made by the Court, in the former action and sustained by its judgment. [30]

10. That plaintiff herein is further guilty of laches in bringing its action for relief from the judgment heretofore rendered, as it appears from the second amended complaint that the opinion of the Circuit Court of Appeals was rendered October 5, 1917; that

plaintiff became acquainted with the facts set forth in said second amended bill of complaint as early as June, 1918, and the facts set forth as justification for the delay in bringing the action for relief are not sufficient to relieve the plaintiff from the imputation of laches.

11. It affirmatively appears from said second amended bill of complaint that said plaintiff has failed, neglected and refused to conform to the decree of the Court entered herein, and said application for relief is an abuse of the administration of justice, applied for in the hope of protracting the litigation and for the purpose of delaying the enforcement of the decree.

FRANCIS A. GARRECHT,
United States Attorney.

Filed April 10, 1920. W. H. Hare, Clerk. [31]

In the District Court of the United States for the Eastern District of Washington, Southern Division.

No. 741.

THE WEST SIDE IRRIGATING COMPANY, a Corporation,

Plaintiff,

vs.

UNITED STATES OF AMERICA,

Defendant.

Order and Judgment Granting Motion to Dismiss.

The plaintiff having filed herein its second amended bill of complaint, and the defendant, by its attorneys, having moved to dismiss said second amended bill of complaint, said motion being in the nature of a demurrer to said second amended bill, and the same having been submitted to the Court, it is

ORDERED: That said motion to dismiss be, and the same is hereby sustained; and the plaintiff having declined to plead further and electing to stand on said second amended bill of complaint, it is

ORDERED, ADJUDGED and DECREED that second amended bill of complaint be, and the same is hereby dismissed, and the above-entitled action and proceeding be, and the same hereby is dismissed.

To the above ruling and judgment of the court, the plaintiff excepts and such exception is allowed.

Dated this 12th day of April, A. D. 1920.

FRANK H. RUDKIN,
Judge.

Filed April 12th, 1920. W. H. Hare, Clerk. [32]

In the District Court of the United States for the Eastern District of Washington, Southern Division.

No. 741.

THE WEST SIDE IRRIGATING COMPANY, a Corporation,

Plaintiff,

vs.

THE UNITED STATES OF AMERICA,

Defendant.

Petition for Allowance of Appeal.

The above-named plaintiff in the above-entitled cause feeling itself aggrieved by the judgment and decree rendered against it in said cause, on the 12th day of April, 1920, prays the Court to allow it an appeal from the said judgment and decree to the United States Circuit Court of Appeals, for the Ninth Circuit, and to fix *in* an order allowing said appeal and the amount of the bond required for costs.

JOHN P. HARTMAN,
CARROLL B. GRAVES,
Attorneys for Plaintiff.

Due service and receipt of copy of foregoing petition is hereby acknowledged this 14th day of June, 1920.

F. A. GARRECHT,
Attorneys for Defendant.
By C. H. L.

Filed in the U. S. District Court, Eastern District of Washington, June, 12, 1920. W. H. Hare, Clerk. [33]

In the District Court of the United States for the Eastern District of Washington, Southern Division.

No. 741.

THE WEST SIDE IRRIGATING COMPANY, a Corporation,

Plaintiff,

vs.

THE UNITED STATES OF AMERICA,

Defendant.

Assignment of Errors.

Plaintiff assigns as errors, upon which it will reply in the United States Circuit Court of Appeals for reversal of the decree and judgment of the Trial Court, the following:

I.

The Trial Court erred in holding that the second amended complaint herein does not state facts sufficient to constitute a cause of action, nor facts sufficient to entitle plaintiff to the relief sought, and in granting defendant's motion to dismiss the same.

II.

The Trial Court erred in dismissing the second amended complaint upon the ground of laches and want of equity.

III.

The Trial Court erred in rendering and entering its decree dismissing this action and giving judgment against plaintiff for costs.

JOHN P. HARTMAN,
CARROLL B. GRAVES,
Attorneys for Plaintiff.

Due service and receipt of copy of foregoing Assignment of Errors is hereby acknowledged this 14th day of June, 1920.

F. A. GARRECHT,
By C. H. L.
Attorneys for Defendant.

Filed in the U. S. District Court, Eastern District of Washington, June 12, 1920. W. H. Hare, Clerk. [34]

In the District Court of the United States for the Eastern District of Washington, Southern Division.

No. 741.

THE WEST SIDE IRRIGATING COMPANY, a Corporation,

Plaintiff,

vs.

THE UNITED STATES OF AMERICA,

Defendant.

Order Allowing Appeal.

This cause coming on to be heard upon the petition of the plaintiff herein, for an allowance of the appeal from the decree and judgment rendered herein on the 12th day of April, 1920, and the Court having heard said petition and the assignments of error having been filed herein,—

IT IS ORDERED that the said appeal be and the same is hereby allowed, and the plaintiff and appellant shall give a cost bond on appeal for the sum of Two Hundred Dollars.

Dated, this 12th day of June, 1920.

FRANK H. RUDKIN,
Judge.

Filed in the U. S. District Court, Eastern District of Washington, June 12, 1920. W. H. Hare, Clerk. [35]

In the District Court of the United States for the Eastern District of Washington, Southern Division.

No. 741.

THE WEST SIDE IRRIGATING COMPANY, a Corporation,

Plaintiff,

vs.

THE UNITED STATES OF AMERICA,

Defendant.

Citation.

To the United States of America, GREETING:

You are hereby cited and admonished to be and appear at the United States Circuit Court of Appeals for the 9th Circuit, to be holden at the city of San

Francisco, California, within thirty (30) days from the date hereof, pursuant to an order allowing an appeal entered in the clerk's office for the Eastern District of Washington, Southern Division, in that certain suit No. 741, wherein the West Side Irrigating Company is plaintiff and appellant, and United States of America is defendant and appellee, to show cause, if any there be, why the decree of dismissal of said cause and judgment against plaintiff for costs should not be corrected and why speedy justice should not be done to the parties in that behalf.

WITNESS Honorable ———, Chief Justice of the Supreme Court of the United States, this 12th day of June, 1920.

FRANK H. RUDKIN,
Judge.

Due service of foregoing citation is admitted this 14th day of June, 1920.

F. A. GARRECHT,
By C. H. L.,
Attorney for Defendant. [36]

In the District Court of the United States for the Eastern District of Washington, Southern Division.

No. 741.

THE WEST SIDE IRRIGATING COMPANY, a Corporation,

Plaintiff,

vs.

THE UNITED STATES OF AMERICA,

Defendant.

Bond on Appeal.

KNOW ALL MEN BY THESE PRESENTS, that we, The West Side Irrigating Company, a corporation, as principal, and Mitchell Stevens, John A. Yearwood, J. H. Prater, and G. W. Weaver, as sureties, are held and firmly bound unto the United States of America, in the full and just sum of Two Hundred Dollars, to be paid to the said defendant, to which payment well and truly to be made we bind ourselves, our heirs, executors, administrators, successors and assigns, jointly and severally, firmly by these presents.

Sealed with our seals, and dated this 4th day of June, 1920.

WHEREAS, lately at a session of the United States District Court for the Eastern District of Washington, Southern Division, in a suit pending in said court between the above-named plaintiff and the above-named defendant, a decree and judgment was rendered in said cause, dismissing said cause with costs, against the above-named plaintiff; and

WHEREAS, said plaintiff has sustained from said court an order allowing an appeal to the United States Circuit Court of Appeals for the 9th Circuit, to reverse the aforesaid decree and judgment rendered on the 12th day of April, 1920, and a Citation directing the above-named defendant and appellee is about to be issued citing and admonishing the said defendant to appear at the [37] United States Circuit Court of Appeals for the 9th Circuit, to be holden at San Francisco, California.

Now, the condition of the above obligation is such that, if the above-named plaintiff shall prosecute said appeal to effect, and shall answer all costs which shall be awarded against it if it shall fail to make good its plea, then the above obligation shall be null and void; otherwise it shall remain in full force and virtue.

WEST SIDE IRRIGATING COMPANY,
By MITCHELL STEVENS,
Vice-president.

State of Washington,
County of Kittitas,—ss.

Mitchell Stevens and John A. Yearwood and J. H. Prater and G. W. Weaver, being first duly sworn, on oath, each for himself says, that he is a resident and citizen of said county and state, and one of the sureties in the foregoing bond; that he is worth in his own individual right, above all debts, liabilities and exemptions, the sum of above Two Thousand ($2,000.00) Dollars, subject to levy by execution, that he is neither sheriff, court officer, nor attorney at law, is a freeholder of said county, and state, and an elector thereof.

MITCHELL STEVENS.
JOHN A. YEARWOOD.
J. H. PRATER.
G. W. WEAVER.

Subscribed and sworn to before me this 11th day of June, 1920.

A. T. GREGORY,
Notary Public in and for the State of Washington
Residing at ———.

Approved as to form and sufficiency of sureties this 12th day of June, 1920.

FRANK H. RUDKIN,
Judge.

Filed in the U. S. District Court, Eastern District of Washington. June 12, 1920. W. H. Hare, Clerk. [38]

In the District Court of the United States for the Eastern District of Washington, Southern Division.

No. 741.

THE WEST SIDE IRRIGATING COMPANY, a Corporation,

Plaintiff,

vs.

THE UNITED STATES OF AMERICA,

Defendant.

Order Striking Motion to Dismiss Amended Bill of Complaint, etc.

This cause coming on to be heard on the 23d day of March, 1920, at Yakima, upon the motion of the defendant to dismiss the plaintiff's amended bill of complaint, and application to vacate the judgment, and for other relief, as set forth in said pleading, the said plaintiff being represented by its attorneys Carroll B. Graves and Hartman & Hartman, and the defendant being represented by its attorneys Francis A. Garrecht and E. W. Burr, and the Court being fully advised in the premises, finds that the said motion, so called, is in conflict with the rules of pleading and practice and the general principles of law governing this court, because it is an attempt to try the merits of the action, and to bring matters before the court beyond the pleading, to wit, the amended complaint, and because thereof, the same should be stricken, except that the parties may proceed upon the same, and to be considered, as a general demurrer against the amended bill, and to be so argued and presented.

IT IS, THEREFORE, ORDERED that the said motion and all thereof be stricken and held for naught, except that the defendant may present under the pleading filed its demurrer, based upon the ground that the amended complaint does not state facts sufficient to constitute a cause of action, to which all counsel agree, and as such may be argued at this time.

Done in open court this 29th day of March, 1920.

FRANK H. RUDKIN,

Judge.

Filed in the U. S. District Court, Eastern District of Washington, March 30, 1920. Wm. H. Hare, Clerk. By Edward E. Cleaver, Deputy. [39]

In the District Court of the United States for the Eastern District of Washington, Southern Division.

No. 741.

THE WEST SIDE IRRIGATING COMPANY, a Corporation,

Plaintiff,

vs.

UNITED STATES OF AMERICA,

Defendant.

Amended Bill of Complaint.

Comes now the said plaintiff above named and by leave of Court first had and obtained, files this its amended bill in equity in the nature of a bill or review of the judgment hereinafter referred to and for cause of action states as follows:

I.

That the said plaintiff is a corporation duly formed and existing under and by virtue of the laws of Washington with its principal place of business at Ellensburg in said state, and that it was incorporated for the purpose of appropriating and using water for irrigation purposes taken from the Yakima River, and distributing the same to its stockholders, and has been in such business uninterruptedly since on or about the first day of July, 1890, and that on the fifteenth day of October, 1917, judgment of the United States District Court for the Eastern District of Washington, Southern Division, holding terms at Yakima, in favor of the United States of America as plaintiff and against the West Side Irrigating Company as defendant, was affirmed on an appeal from the above-entitled court, all as recorded in Volume 246 of Federal Reporter at page 212, and upon a *remittitur* from said United States Circuit Court of Appeals being received at Yakima, Washington, the judgment of the lower court entered on the nineteenth day of February, 1916, was thereby affirmed, but no action has been taken thereon since the [40] entry of the judgment.

II.

That at the time of the incorporation of said plaintiff in 1889, it appropriated water for irrigating purposes from the Yakima River in the County of Kittitas in said State of Washington, in the amount of four thousand miner's inches, at the users' distribution boxes, and commenced the use thereof during the summer of 1890, and since said date and up to the present time has been in uninterrupted and constant use of the water so appropriated, taking all thereof that it required for the purpose of its business and in supplying its stockholders up to the amount of four thousand miner's inches, at the users' distribution boxes, and at no time since said date and up to this time has such right of user been interfered with by any person or persons whomsoever and has so adversely used the same up to and including the present date.

III.

That on or about the twenty-first day of October, 1905, the said respondent sent to the plaintiff and its officers a duly authorized agent and employee, one T. A. Noble, who solicited the said plaintiff to enter into an agreement in writing by which the water by it appropriated should be measured by cubic feet per second of flow, instead of being determined by miner's inches as the same was originally taken and the usual way of measurement in the neighborhood, and after negotiating with the said Noble and taking his statements and representations, he being a hydraulic engineer of skill and attainment, the said plaintiff was induced to and did enter into an agreement by which the water to be used in the conduct of its business should be eighty cubic feet per second, and the contract was so executed, and at the time the said plaintiff and its officers believed, and were led to that conclusion by the statements made by the agent of the United States, [41] that when they received eighty cubic feet per second of water it was equivalent to four thousand miner's inches at the users' distribution boxes, as by the plaintiff appropriated, and used when necessary, and the mistake and error was not discovered until the summer of 1908 when the said Noble, then being in the employ of the State of Washington in doing hydraulic and irrigation work, but not then known to be so engaged by the plaintiff, came again to the plaintiff, and its officers, when, having discovered the mistake about that time, the said plaintiff informed the said Noble of the mistake made and protested against being bound by the agreement as made, for the reason that a mistake had been made and the plaintiff had been deprived of a valuable right and of sufficient water to supply its stockholders as the amount appropriated is necessary therefor, in order to produce the crops of the stockholders covering about seven thousand acres and in grass grains and other crops, such as are grown by irrigation in said district, and all of the land then being in a high state of cultivation, and that notwithstanding the fact that the said Noble was at said time in the employ of the State of Washington, the plaintiff believed that he was with and employed by the Reclamation Service of the United States, and did not know to the contrary, until this cause was being tried in the United States District Court during the year 1914.

IV.

That the plaintiff discovered when the protest was made on the date aforesaid, and about that time, that four thousand miner's inches of water flow, at the users' distribution boxes, as determined by the custom and the decision of the Honorable Superior Court in and for the said County of Kittitas, where the rule was announced and long followed in the said district, would require a much larger amount than eighty cubic feet per second, which was not sufficient to protect and mature the crops growing [42] in the district aforesaid.

V.

That the plaintiff, after having protested, believed

that its rights were fully protected and that it would not be disturbed in any way, and that it would be entitled and permitted peaceable to use the amount of water by it appropriated and that the defendant would be duly informed by the said Noble, and the said plaintiff believed and understood that when it gave the notice to the said Noble, who was in charge of the irrigation matters upon the Yakima River, and the chief therein, nothing further would be required of it in order to protect its rights, and that when said action was determined by this Court it was urged by the learned counsel for the defendant that because the protest against the effectiveness and binding force of the agreement aforesaid, limiting the amount of water, had not been communicated to the defendant, then and there upon because of remaining silent the said protest became of no effect, and because of such conclusion the said Circuit Court of Appeals stated in its opinion as follows:

> "The stockholders gave no notice to any officer of the United States that they repudiated the contract, but on the contrary, by their silence, they ratified the same";

which conclusion and the argument producing the same cause the said case to be determined adversely to this plaintiff, which plaintiff alleges would not have occurred if all of the facts had been presented which were not then known, nor could they have been known, to this plaintiff.

VI.

That in the trial of the cause, and when taking the testimony, the said Noble was called as a witness by the United States, and he there testified from the witness-stand, and upon leaving the stand, at the suggestion of counsel for plaintiff, the vice-president [43] of the plaintiff, Mitchell Stevens, immediately inquired of the said Noble if he did not notify the Reclamation Service about the protest and rights claimed in the summer of 1918 aforesaid, and thereupon the said Noble answered he had no such recollection, or words to that effect, and thereupon the said Stevens communicated this fact to his counsel, Carroll B. Graves, who was at the attorneys' table, in the courtroom, where the testimony was being taken, of the answer that had been made, and the matter was then dismissed, believing that the said Noble had not communicated the fact to the officers of the Reclamation Service at Yakima or elsewhere.

VII.

That after said cause, brought by the United States as aforesaid, had been appealed to the United States Circuit Court of Appeals and for the first time, and information which it could not have before obtained, the said plaintiff learned that immediately after the protest was lodged with the said Noble as aforesaid, he, the said Noble, then and there communicated the fact of said protest to the officer of the United States in charge of all of its irrigation affairs in the entire Yakima Valley in said State of Washington, which office was at Yakima, in said district, and informed the said agent in charge of the same of the alleged mistake and of the intention of the said plaintiff and its stockholders to refuse to stand and abide by said agreement because of mistake and misunderstanding, the said discovery being on or about the 18th day of June, 1918, and that at the time of the trial of said cause the said agent in chief of said Reclamation Service in said district was in court, and upon the stand as a witness, but did not disclose the fact of notice but kept the same from the Court and this plaintiff, and had he disclosed the fact the action would have been determined differently as shown by the decision of the United States Circuit Court of Appeals. [44]

VIII.

That said plaintiff was diligent in the preparation of its cause of action, and that it believed it had protected its rights and was taken completely by surprise when the defendant by its witness denied any notice of such protest, and that the witness Noble was not an officer of the United States Reclamation Service at the time the protest was made to him, and then believed that no such notice had been received and only by mere accident discovered it later on, and that if a new trial is granted it will be able to produce the testimony to fully convince the Court that it should prevail.

IX.

That the said plaintiff has been in the open, notorious and continuous use of all the water appropriated by it when needed without let, hindrance, or protest from any person or persons whomsoever, and by adverse user is entitled to have its rights adjudicated by which it shall be entitled in the future to used as in the past, the entire four thousand miner's inches of water measured at the users' boxes, when the same is necessary and required upon the district served, and that it will be able to prove all of its rights as herein claimed and set forth and for which it asks a new trial, by T. A. Noble, J. H. Prater, F. A. Strande, Mitchell Stevens, and John Burch, C. F. Kenneth, and W. A. Stevens, who will be in court as witnesses when said action is heard again in the United States District Court for the Eastern District of Washington, Southern Division, and that by reason of the judgment and decree made as aforesaid, if the same is put into effect (altho it has never been enforced but may be at any time), this plaintiff and its stockholders have been greatly damaged and will be irreparably damaged if the decree is allowed to be enforced. [45]

X.

That, because of the suppression of the fact by the defendant, of having had notice of said protest and reservation of rights, as fully set forth aforesaid, a manifest fraud and injustice was and has been visited upon and against the said plaintiff, to its great damage and detriment, and three years have not elapsed since the discovery of said fraud, and of the proof to right the wrong suffered.

XI.

That the said defendant is the user and seller of water taken from the Yakima River and its tributaries, not in its sovereign capacity, but in a private capacity, in a business way, the same as individuals or local corporations of the State of Washington for engaging in said business, and has no rights or more rights than those enjoyed and taken under the laws of the State of Washington, the said Yakima River and its tributaries being purely an intrastate stream.

XII.

That by reason of the discovery of the said new matter the said judgment ought to be reviewed and reversed, and this plaintiff granted a decree of this Court affirming its right to all of the water by it originally appropriated, and by it used without let or hindrance, since the time of the appropriation, so far as the same so appropriated has been required for conducting the affairs of the plaintiff.

XIII.

That the plaintiff has had to expend for itself and is liable for a large bill of costs and expenses, and must expend a large amount still in costs, in preserving and defending its rights, all of which would not have been necessary or required if the defendant had not so suppressed the facts, which otherwise would have given a decree in plaintiff's favor, and because of the wrong [46] done and fraud suffered, the said defendant should be adjudged to pay and required to repay the same, and all thereof, to the plaintiff.

XIV.

That at no time since the rendition of the decree in said case No. 228, or the affirmance thereof by the Circuit Court of Appeals, has the defendant herein in any manner or form by notice or otherwise, attempted or tried to enforce the decree, or any thereof, or in any manner interfere with the rights of the said plaintiff and its shareholders.

WHEREFORE, the said plaintiff prays:

(a) That said action be reviewed, considered, and a decree entered upon and in conformity with the newly discovered evidence and rights set forth herein, and that testimony be received and taken under consideration, to aid the Court in conclusion;

(b) That the judgment heretofore rendered be reversed and set aside;

(c) That said cause of action may be heard on such new and supplemental matters and facts as may be offered, at the same time that it is reheard upon said original complaint;

(d) That plaintiff be allowed and permitted to amend its answer filed in the original cause, to comport to the facts hereinbefore set forth, and that the plaintiff be awarded judgment and decree of this Court for the settling and determining of all of its rights to the water appropriated and used, as set forth in the complaint, and for all thereof, without protest, molestation or interference on the part of the defendant or anyone acting through, by, or for it;

(e) That plaintiff may have and recover its costs and damages herein; and,

(f) That plaintiff may have such other and further relief as shall be deemed just and equitable.

CARROLL B. GRAVES,
HARTMAN & HARTMAN,
Attorneys for Plaintiff.

Filed March 23, 1920. W. H. Hare, Clerk. [47]

In the District Court of the United States for the Eastern District of Washington, Southern Division.

No. 741.

THE WEST SIDE IRRIGATION COMPANY, a Corporation,

Plaintiff,

vs.

UNITED STATES OF AMERICA,

Defendant.

Opinion.

HARTMAN & HARTMAN and CARROLL B. GRAVES, for Plaintiff.

FRANCIS A. GARRECHT, U. S. Attorney, and E. W. BURR, District Counsel U. S. Reclamation Service, for Defendant.

RUDKIN, District Judge.

This is a bill in the nature of a bill of review to obtain a rehearing or reconsideration of a case finally determined by this Court and affirmed by the Circuit Court of Appeals.

United States v. West Side Irrigation Co., 230 Fed. 284.

West Side Irrigation Co. v. United States, 246 Fed. 212.

The parties are here reversed, but for convenience will be referred to as plaintiff and defendant as in the original proceeding. The suit was originally brought to restrain the defendant from diverting water from the Yakima River in violation of a certain limiting agreement, a copy of which is set forth in the two opinions referred to. A final decree was entered in favor of the plaintiff in accordance with the prayer of the complaint. The opinion of the Circuit Court of Appeals affirming the decree was filed on the 15th day of October, 1917, and the mandate or *remittitur* from that court was filed in the District Court on the [48] 28th day of November, 1917. On the 3d day of September, 1919, an order was entered in the Appellate Court granting the defendant permission to present to the District Court the present bill of complaint and to apply to that Court for leave to file the same. On the same date a *pro forma* order was entered in this court permitting the filing of the bill and directing process to issue. Pursuant to this order the bill was filed, and the case is now before the Court on motion to dismiss the bill as amended by stipulation, for want of sufficient facts, for want of equity, and upon the ground of laches. A statement of the issues determined on the final hearing in the trial and appellate courts, together with a statement of the newly discovered evidence, will dispose of the case without further argument or comment. The issues are thus stated in the opinion of the Trial Court;

> "It is conceded throughout the testimony that the defendant has diverted water from the river in excess of 80 cubic feet per second of time, and it asserts the right to do so upon three grounds: First, because the limiting agreement was *ultra vires* and void; second, because the

water should be measured at the several points where it is diverted from the canal by the different stockholders or users, and not at the intake of the canal, or at least that such was the understanding of the defendant; and, third, that the defendant at all times claimed the right to divert and use 4,000 inches of water measured according to the system or module adopted by it; that it was represented to the defendant that 80 cubic feet per second was the equivalent of the 4,000 inches thus measured, while in truth and in fact the 4,000 inches as measured by the defendant is the equivalent of upwards of 90 cubic feet per second; and it is claimed that the difference between the 80 cubic feet per second, measured at the intake, and the 4,000 inches as measured by the defendant at the points of delivery to the different stockholders, is 24.6 cubic feet per second. In other words, the defendant claims and asserts the right to divert from the river 104.6 cubic feet per second, while the government claims that it is limited to 80 cubic feet per second."

The Trial Court then held that the defense of *ultra vires* could not prevail for two reasons: First, because no such defense was interposed by answer; and second, because the stockholders had notice of the limiting agreement soon after its execution, and it then became their imperative duty either to abide by the agreement, [49] or promptly disavow the unauthorized acts of the corporate officers and bring notice of such disavowal home to the Government or to some authorized officer of the Government. The Court further found that there was no mistake of fact, either as to the place of measurement or as to quantity of water, and that the agreement was founded upon an adequate consideration.

Some new questions seem to have been raised in the Circuit Court of Appeals. That Court held: First, that there was no merit in the contention that the complaint was insufficient to state a cause of action, in that it did not show that the United States or anyone in privity with it had been deprived of the use of water or had sustained a present injury; second, that there was no merit in the contention that the United States had no authority to maintain the action; and disposed of the claim of mistake in the following language:

> "The suggestion that the agreement was founded upon mistake cannot avail the appellant. There is no evidence whatever that there was a mutual mistake. And there is no convincing evidence of a mistake on the part of the appellant or its stockholders. And if, indeed, there was a mistake on their part, they waived the right to assert it by their subsequent silence. There is no plea of mistake in the answer to the complaint. The whole defense of the appellant as pleaded rests upon its construction and conception of the terms of the agreement itself."

The Court further held that there were two answers to the claim on the part of the defendant that the limiting agreement was void.

"First, that no such defense is pleaded in the answer; and second, that the stockholders gave no notice to any officer of the United States that they repudiated the contract, but, on the contrary, by their silence they ratified the same."

The claim of newly discovered evidence is substantially this: One T. A. Noble was an officer of the Reclamation Service of the United States on the 21st day of October, 1905, when the limiting agreement was executed; at that time the defendant believed that the 80 cubic feet of water per second was the equivalent of 4,000 inches measured at the distributing boxes of the different [50] users and did not discover the mistake until the summer of 1908; at the time of such discovery the defendant informed Noble thereof and entered a protest against being bound by the agreement as made, for the reason that it deprived the defendant of valuable rights and of sufficient water to supply its stockholders; at the time of the giving of such notice the defendant erroneously believed that Noble was still in the employ of the United States, and did not discover that Noble was not then in the employ of the United States until he testified on the trial of this case some seven or eight years later; when Noble left the witness-stand he was asked by one of the officers of the defendant whether he had conveyed the information thus given him to the officers of the Reclamation Service, and he answered in the negative; the defendant has since discovered that this information was in fact conveyed by Noble to the officers of the Reclamation Service, "and that if a new trial is granted it will be able to produce testimony to fully convince the Court that it should prevail." It is further claimed that the plaintiff suppressed testimony at the original trial, and was therefore guilty of fraud.

Assuming that all this testimony is newly discovered, and assuming further that it was all before the court on the former hearing, in what conceivable way could it change the result? There were only two issues in the case upon which the proffered testimony could have the slightest bearing. First, on the question whether the limiting agreement was obligatory upon the defendant; and second, whether the execution of that agreement was the result of mistake, either as the place of measurement or quantity of water to be diverted. The first issue was decided against the defendant upon two grounds: First, because no such defense was made at the trial, or rather, presented by the answer; and second, because "the stockholders gave no notice to any officer of the [51]
United States that they repudiated the contract, but, on the contrary, by their silence they ratified the same."

The newly discovered evidence has no bearing upon this latter issue, because it is not claimed that either Noble or the Reclamation Service was notified that the contract was executed without authority, and in that respect the record upon which the former decision was based has not been changed. Noble was simply notified that the defendant claimed that there was a mistake of fact as a result of which it was deprived of water to which it was lawfully entitled, but inasmuch as both courts found that there was no such mistake how can this notice avail the defendant, or how could the new evidence change the result? On the question of mistake the Circuit Court of Appeals likewise found against the defendant on several grounds, namely:

> "There is no evidence whatever that there was a mutual mistake. And there is no convincing evidence of a mistake on the part of the appellant or its stockholders. And if, indeed, there was a mistake on their part, they waived the right to assert it by answer to the complaint. The whole defense of the appellant as pleaded rests upon its construction and conception of the terms of the agreement itself."

The decree was therefore affirmed on several grounds, and the silence of the defendant was only incidentally referred to. Indeed, in the view of the Trial Court and the Appellate Court the issue now sought to be raised was not presented by the pleadings in the original case, and the defendant is merely seeking a trial *de novo* on an entirely new theory, utterly disregarding the former trial and the finality of the former decision. For this reason alone the bill of complaint is entirely insufficient. Again, the newly discovered evidence was brought to the attention of the defendant fifteen months before the present proceedings were instituted, and such delay alone is sufficient to defeat the application. Under the statutes of this state a judgment may be vacated for certain [52] reasons within one year, but the Supreme Court has uniformly held that the moving party must act with diligence even within the year.

> Nelson v. Nelson, 56 Wash. 571, and cases cited.

And while the decision of the state court is not absolutely controlling here, the rule announced is a fundamental one.

What has already been said fully answers the charge of fraud. Furthermore, I am not aware that any obligation rested upon the Government to prove any part of the case of its adversary. As said by the Supreme Court in McDougall vs. Walling, 21 Wash. 478:

> "It cannot be the rule that a judgment can be attacked for fraud because in the trial the prevailing party defendant failed to voluntarily disclose the weakness of his defense, or some evidence which would tend to overthrow his defense. Ordinarily, the pleadings must determine what issues will be tried; and it has never seemed to be the practice that a party must disclose to his adversary what his testimony will be, or that he must suggest testimony for his adversary."

It is apparently insisted at this time that the Court has already passed upon the sufficiency of the showing as to the newly discovered evidence in permitting the bill to be filed, and that that question is now foreclosed. If counsel is correct in this, the error of the Court in permitting the bill to be filed without notice to the adverse party becomes at once apparent. But in any view of the case the position is untenable.

Even had the Court passed directly upon that question at an earlier stage of the trial the Court has still full jurisdiction of the case and it is its plain duty to correct the palpable error thus committed. I may say in conclusion that I deemed it best to dispose of the application upon its merits, rather than upon technical questions of procedure advanced at the hearing. Perhaps the better practice is to sign an order requiring adverse party to show cause why the bill should not be filed, but whether the sufficiency of the showing made be determined before or after the filing of the bill is a matter of form rather than of substance.

The motion to dismiss is sustained. [53]

In the District Court of the United States for the Eastern District of Washington, Southern Division.

No. 741.

THE WEST SIDE IRRIGATION COMPANY, a Corporation,

Plaintiff,

vs.

UNITED STATES OF AMERICA,

Defendant.

Memorandum Opinion.

HARTMAN & HARTMAN and CARROLL B. GRAVES, for Plaintiff.

FRANCIS A. GARRECHT, U. S. District Attorney, and E. W. BURR, District Counsel U. S. Reclamation Service, for Defendant.

RUDKIN, District Judge.

The plaintiff has asked leave to file a second amended bill of complaint in this case, stipulating that the bill as amended may be considered by the Court on motion to dismiss without further argument. I assume that the amendment is proposed solely for the purpose of making a record for the Appellate Court, as the changes do not meet or obviate the defects found in the former bills. The motion for leave to amend is granted, and the motion to dismiss interposed by the Government will be sustained.

Let a final decree be entered accordingly.

Filed April 12th, 1920. W. H. Hare, Clerk. [54]

In the District Court of the United States for the Eastern District of Washington, Southern Division.

No. 741.

THE WEST SIDE IRRIGATING COMPANY, a Corporation,

Plaintiff,

vs.

UNITED STATES OF AMERICA,

Defendant.

Praecipe for Transcript of Record.

To the Honorable, the Clerk of said Court:

Comes now the plaintiff by its attorneys of record and requests you to make a transcript for appeal of this case to the Circuit Court of Appeals, pursuant to order made, and include therein (omitting, however, formal matters from any page or record where not needed to give the Court information), the following:

1. Petition for leave to file bill.
2. Order of Court allowing filing of bill.
3. Application of plaintiff to file amended bill.
4. Order of Court allowing filing of amended bill.
5. Application of plaintiff to file second amended bill.
6. Order of Court allowing filing second amended bill.
7. Second amended bill.
8. Motion of defendant to dismiss second amended bill.
9. Order sustaining motion dismissing bill and granting judgment.
10. Petition for appeal.
11. Assignment of errors.
12. Order of Court allowing appeal.
13. Citation.
14. Bond on appeal.

Dated this 17th day of June, 1920.

CARROLL B. GRAVES,
HARTMAN & HARTMAN,
Attorneys for Defendant.

REQUESTED BY DEFENDANT.

Amended Complaint, filed March 23, 1920.
Opinion, filed March 30, 1920.
Opinion, filed April 12, 1920.

FRANCIS A. GARRECHT,
Attorney for Defendant. [55]

Certificate of Clerk U. S. District Court to Transcript of Record.

United States of America,
Eastern District of Washington,—ss.

I, W. H. Hare, Clerk of the District Court of the United States for the Eastern District of Washington, do hereby certify that the foregoing typewritten pages to be a full, true, correct and complete copy of the record and all proceedings had in said action as called for in the praecipe for a transcript of the record herein, as the same remains of record and on file in the office of the clerk of said court; and that the same constitutes the record on appeal from the order, judgment and decree of said District Court of the United States for the Eastern District of Washington, to the Circuit Court of Appeals for the Ninth Judicial Circuit.

I further certify that I hereto attach and herewith transmit the original citation issued in this cause.

I further certify that the cost of preparing and certifying the foregoing transcript is the sum of ($25.85) Twenty-five Dollars and Eighty-five Cents, and that the same has been paid to me by attorneys for the appellant.

IN WITNESS WHEREOF, I have hereunto set my hand and affixed the seal of said court at the city of Spokane, in said district, this 29th day of June, A. D. 1920, the Independence of the United States of America the one hundred and forty-fourth.

[Seal] W. H. HARE,
Clerk. [56]

[Endorsed]: No. 3518. United States Circuit Court of Appeals for the Ninth Circuit. The West Side Irrigating Company, a Corporation, Appellant, vs. The United States of America, Appellee. Transcript of Record. Upon Appeal from the United States District Court for the Eastern District of Washington, Southern Division.

Filed July 1, 1920.

F. D. MONCKTON,

Clerk of the United States Circuit Court of Appeals for the Ninth Circuit.

By Paul P. O'Brien,

Deputy Clerk.

No. 3518

United States Circuit Court of Appeals
For The Ninth Circuit

THE WEST SIDE IRRIGATING COMPANY, a Corporation,

Appellant,

—vs.—

THE UNITED STATES OF AMERICA,

Appellee.

Appeal From the United States District Court for the Eastern District of Washington Southern Division.

HON. FRANK H. RUDKIN, Presiding.

BRIEF OF APPELLANT

CARROLL B. GRAVES,
606-8 Central Bldg., Seattle, Wash.,

HARTMAN & HARTMAN,
300-6 Burke Bldg., Seattle, Wash.,

Attorneys for Appellant.

No. 3518

United States Circuit Court of Appeals

For The Ninth Circuit

THE WEST SIDE IRRIGATING COMPANY, a Corporation,

Appellant,

—vs.—

THE UNITED STATES OF AMERICA,

Appellee.

Appeal From the United States District Court for the Eastern District of Washington Southern Division.

HON. FRANK H. RUDKIN, Presiding.

BRIEF OF APPELLANT

CARROLL B. GRAVES,
606-8 Central Bldg., Seattle, Wash.,

HARTMAN & HARTMAN,
300-6 Burke Bldg., Seattle, Wash.,

Attorneys for Appellant.

United States Circuit Court of Appeals
For The Ninth Circuit

THE WEST SIDE IRRIGATING COMPANY, a Corporation,

Appellant,

—vs.—

THE UNITED STATES OF AMERICA,

Appellee.

Appeal From the United States District Court for the Eastern District of Washington Southern Division.

HON. FRANK H. RUDKIN, Presiding.

BRIEF OF APPELLANT

STATEMENT OF THE CASE.

This is a Bill in the nature of a bill of review of the decree of the District Court for the Eastern District of Washington, Southern Division, rendered February 19th, 1916, affirmed by the Circuit Court of Appeals for the Ninth Circuit October 15th, 1917, in favor of the United States of America and against West Side Irrigation Company, whereby appellant was enjoined from diverting from the Yakima river in excess of 80 cubic feet per second of water, as specified in the so-called "limiting agreement" of October 21st, 1905, which appellant was induced to sign, upon the representation of the United States Reclamation Service that it correctly expressed the amount of water appropriated by appellant. The Bill of Complaint was filed September 5th, 1919, pursuant to leave granted on petition of appellant herein, and by order of the Circuit Court of Appeals entered on the 3rd day of September, 1919. The Second Amended Complaint in condensed form is as follows:

Second Amended Complaint.

I.

Appellant is a corporation under the laws of Washington, carrying on irrigation, and recites the judgment of the District Court, affirmed by the Circuit Court of Appeals, and that no action has been taken thereon since the entry of said judgment.

II.

Appellant appropriated and has constantly used since 1890 4000 miner's inches of water taken from the Yakima River, in the County of Kittitas, Washington, measured at the users' distribution boxes, which it has used without interference up to the present date.

III.

That on October 21, 1905, appellant entered into an agreement in writing, at the solicitation of T. A. Noble, agent and representative of appellee, by which the water appropriated by it should be measured in cubic feet per second of flow, instead of miner's inches, which was expressed in said agreement as 80 cubic feet per second, which appellant was led to believe by the said T. A. Noble, who was a hydraulic engineer of skill and attainment, was the equivalent of the water it was appropriating, to-wit, 4000 miner's inches at the service boxes, and appellant limited to the use of the flow of water so measured in cubic feet per second, and in the summer of 1908 appellant discovered that a mistake had been made, and notified the said Noble and protested against being bound by said agreement, repudiating said agreement, which would deprive appellant of sufficient water to supply its stockholders, as the amount appropriated is necessary to produce the crops of the stockholders covering about seven thousand acres in grass, grains and other crops, all of which land was in a high state of cultivation, and although the said Noble was then in the employ of the State of Washington in irrigation work, appellant believed that he was with and employed by the United States Reclamation Service, and did not know the contrary until the trial in 1914.

IV.

That appellant discovered when the protest was made that four thousand miner's inches of water measured at the users' distribution boxes, would require a much larger amount than eighty cubic feet per second, which was not sufficient to protect and mature the crops.

V.

That appellant believed its rights had been fully protected by notifying the said Noble, by whom appellee would be duly informed of its protest, but upon the trial of the case the court held that the protest had not been communicated to appellee, but that appellant ratified the agreement by remaining silent, which conclusion caused the case to be determined adversely to appellant, which would not have occurred if the facts regarding the prompt disavowal and repudiation of the agreement had been presented, but they were unknown and could not be known at that time to appellant.

VI.

That upon the trial, Noble was questioned by the vice-president of appellant, on leaving the witness stand, at the suggestion of appellant's counsel, as to whether he did not notify the Reclamation Service about the protest and rights claimed in the summer of 1908, and thereupon Noble answered that he had no such recollection or words to that effect, and upon communicating this to counsel for appellant the matter was not pressed further, as it was believed that Noble had not communicated the facts to the Reclamation Service.

VII.

That after the case was appealed to the Circuit Court of Appeals, appellant learned for the first time that immediately after the protest was lodged with Noble as aforesaid, he then and there communicated the fact to the officer of the United States in charge of all irrigation affairs in the entire Yakima Valley in the State of Washington, and informed him of the mistake and the intention of the appellant and its stockholders to refuse to stand and abide by the agreement because of mistake and misunderstanding, which discovery was made on or about June 18th, 1918, and said agent in chief was in court and on the stand as a witness, and did not disclose the fact of notice, and had he done so the decision would have been different.

VIII.

That appellant was taken by surprise when it was showed by the witness Noble that he was not an officer of the Reclamation Service at the time the protest was made to him, and that T. A. Noble will be produced as a witness on any new trial, and will testify that in 1905 and 1906 he was in the employ of the Reclamation Service on Yakima River projects, and conferred with the officers and stockholders of appellant, and was a party to securing the "limiting agreement," whereby appellant was induced to limit the use of its water to 80 cubic feet per second of time; that he left the employment of the Reclamation Service Jan. 1st, 1907, and in 1908 was appointed State Water Commissioner for Kittitas and Yakima Counties, and closely associated with the Reclamation Service and in the discharge of his duties in July, 1908, went to the County of Kittitas for the purpose of regulating the flow of waters from the Yakima River in to the various canals, and while there discussed the "limiting agreement" with the officers of appellant, who stated that the company had been misled by their misunderstanding and by misrepresentation as to the effect of said agreement, and they had understood and been given to understand that the amount placed in the agreement was equal to 4000 inches of water according to the method used by appellant, and a mistake had been made, and appellant and its stockholders would not be bound by the "limiting agreement," and protested against their being so bound because of the mistake and the fact that they had been misled, and that they had used and would insist upon using the amount of 4000 inches as measured by them through the distribution boxes of the stockholders, and at that time Noble measured the water taken by appellant and found that it exceeded 80 cubic feet per second, and immediately thereafter went to North Yakima to the Chief Officer of the Reclamation Service on the Yakima River projects, Charles H. Swigart, and related to him the interview had with the officers of the company, and that the company was taking in excess of 80 cubic feet per second, and had protested and stated to said Noble as aforesaid, and proposed to resist any attempt to reduce the amount of water to be taken by them to 80 cubic feet per second, and thereupon Swigart advised Noble not to proceed to enforce the agreement, but let the matter go as it was; that Noble was a witness on the trial, and was asked by Mitchell Stevens, an officer of appellant after he had left the stand, if he the said Noble did not convey the statement and protest made to him, but the said Noble remarked that he didn't remember about it; that long after the trial in the summer of 1918, the said Mitchell Stevens called on Noble, and after discussing what had occurred and been said, the said Noble finally was able to recall that the things hereinbefore stated had been done and said, and the reason the agreement was not enforced was because of the information conveyed to Swigart and his request not to proceed further.

IX.

That appellant has been in the open, notorious and continuous use of all the water appropriated by it when needed, without let, hindrance or protest from any person or persons whomsoever, and by adverse user is entitled to have its rights adjudicated entitling it to the use in future as in the past of the entire 4000 miner's inches of water measured at the users' boxes, and it will be able to prove all its rights, and for which it claims a new trial, by T. A. Noble, J. H. Prater, F. A. Strandle, Mitchell Stevens, and John Burch, C. F. Kenneth, and W. A. Stevens, who will be in court as witnesses when said action is heard again in the District Court; that if the judgment is continued in force and effect appellant and its stockholders will be greatly and irreparably damaged.

X.

That because of suppression of the fact by appellee of having had notice of said protest and reservation of rights, a manifest fraud and injustice was visited upon appellant, and three years have not elapsed since the discovery of the fraud, and of the proof to right the wrong suffered; that upon discovering the new evidence hereinbefore stated appellant did not immediately file its bill of review, but because of change in the officers in charge of the Reclamation Srvice, and believing that its application for redress was being favorably considered, and plans and methods were discussed orally and by correspondence to the end that an adjustment might be made obviating further litigation, and such negotiations resulted in petitions being presented to the federal departments and arguments being made thereon; that all said matters were pending at the time action was taken in the United States Circuit Court of Appeals for an order allowing appellant to file its bill in this cause, and such action was taken because appellant feared the loss of its rights by delays in the negotiations, and the reason action was not taken sooner was because appellant and its officers were led to believe that on account of the injury done by suppressing the new evidence it would be relieved from the wrong it had sustained by the decree without applying to this Court for redress, and the matter settled without further litigation.

XI.

That appellee is a user and seller of water taken from the Yakima River not in its sovereign capacity, but in a private capacity, in a business way, the same as individuals or private corporations of the State of Washington, and has no rights other than those enjoyed under the laws of the State of Washington, the said Yakima River being purely an intrastate stream.

XII.

That by reason of the discovery of said new matter, the judgment ought to be reviewed and reversed, and appellant granted a decree affirming its right to all of the water by it originally appropriated and by it used since the time of appropriation, and all of which is required for conducting its affairs.

XIII.

That appellant has been put to large expense in defending its rights, because of the wrong and fraud suffered, and appellee should be required to pay the same and all thereof to appellant.

XIV.

That appellee has never attempted to enforce said decree.

PRAYER for review of said action and a decree in conformity with the newly discovered evidence, that said judgment be reversed and set aside, that the action be heard on such new and supplementary matters as may be offered, at the same time it is reheard upon said original complaint, that appellant have leave to amend its answer in the original cause, to comport with the facts hereinbefore set forth, and be awarded a decree settling its rights to the water appropriated and used as set forth in the complaint, without interference on the part of appellee, that it may recover its costs, and for such other relief as may be equitable. (Record, pp. 14-28.)

On April 10th, 1920, appellee filed its Motion to Dismiss the Second Amended Bill of Complaint, which was briefly as follows:

Motion to Dismiss Second Amended Bill of Complaint.

Motion to dismiss the second amended complaint, and deny all application for relief thereunder, on the following grounds:

1. Insufficient facts to require an answer.
2. Want of equity.
3. That the court will take judicial notice of the record in the case in which the judgment was entered, which is sought to be vacated, and by reference thereto, it appears that appellant seeks relief upon grounds different and variant from those asserted in the original case.
4. The record in the former trial shows that Charles H. Swigart was never a witness in that case, in which respect the representations made are not true.
5. That the allegations of fraud are inadequately pleaded, and appellant made no effort on the former trial to support any allegation that the company had given notice to the Reclamation Service of renunciation of the contract.
6. That the alleged newly discovered evidence is cumulative, immaterial and not controlling, and there is ample to sustain the decree on other grounds, and if the facts alleged to show notice of renunciation of the agree-

ment had in fact been communicated to the United States as stated, the notice was casual, incidental, informal and hearsay only, and not sufficient to form basis for abrogation of contract.

7. That the abrogation of contract came too late because it appears from evidence on former trial that the United States had prior thereto expended vast sums in reliance on the contract, and Government could not be placed in position it was before the contract was signed, and would be entitled to disregard said notice.

8. Stipulation in former action shows that prior to alleged notice of renunciation the Secretary of the Interior had approved the Yakima Project, and expended large sums in reliance of appellant's contract and those of others of similar tenor.

9. That record on former trial shows that appellant had knowledge that the contract limited its use to an amount of water less than it claims as early as January, 1906, and it is guilty of laches in failing to notify the United States until the summer of 1908, at which time the Government had already expended $1,263,000.00.

10. That appellant is further guilty of laches in bringing this action, as it became acquainted with the facts set forth in the second amended bill of complaint as early as June,

1918, and the facts set forth as justification for the delay are not sufficient to relieve from imputation of laches.

11. That said application is an abuse of the administration of justice, in the hope of protracting litigation.

(Record pp. 28-33.)

On April 12th, 1920, the District Court rendered its order and judgment dismissing the second amended bill of complaint, and that the action be dismissed, to which ruling and judgment of the Court, appellant excepted and an exception was duly allowed. (Record. p. 34.)

SPECIFICATION OF ERRORS.

The District Court erred and its judgment was erroneous in the following particulars:

I.

The Court erred in holding that the second amended complaint herein does not state facts sufficient to constitute a cause of action, nor facts sufficient to entitle appellant to the relief sought, and in granting the motion to dismiss the same.

II.

The Court erred in dismissing the second amended complaint upon the ground of laches and want of equity.

III.

The Court erred in rendering and entering its decree dismissing this action and giving judgment against this appellant.

ARGUMENT.

The decree of the Circuit Court of Appeals affirming the judgment sought to be vacated, was rendered October 15th, 1917. By reference to the Second Amended Complaint, it will be seen that it was the summer of 1918 before appellant discovered that the so-called "limiting agreement" had been promptly disavowed as soon as it became known that it did not express the facts. At that time, Mitchell Stevens, the Vice-President of the company, called upon Mr. T. A. Noble, and the details were discussed, whereupon Mr. Noble did remember that immediately after the protest made to him in 1908, he had gone to Charles H. Swigart, Chief Officer of the Reclamation Service on the Yakima River projects, and related to him the interview had with the officers of the company, that the company was using in excess of 80 cubic feet of water, and would resist any efforts to restrict them to less than their appropriation, for the reason that the agreement did not correctly state the facts, and they were misled by the Reclamation Service as to the measure of water which would supply them with the quantity they were entitled to. It will be remembered that on the trial in the District Court, Mr. Noble went on the witness stand, and as he left the stand was interrogated at suggestion of counsel for appellant, and could not then recall that he had communicated these facts to the Reclamation Service, and therefore it seemed useless to plead the disavowal of the contract, and from the evidence as then presented it seemed true that appellant had never protested against the agreement to the Government itself. As Mr. Noble was the water commissioner at the time the protest was made to him, the officers of the company took it for granted that he was the proper official to notify of their position. One of the grounds upon which the Circuit Court of Appeals relied in arriving at its judgment, was the failure to communicate this protest to the Government, whereby it was held that appellant had ratified the agreement.

The discovery of this new and important evidence places the whole matter in a different light. Instead of a binding agreement, which the courts held was not subject to the construction placed upon it by appellant, the company is now in position to prove that there was never any agreement at all, for the reason that the so-called agreement was promptly disavowed as soon as appellant knew what it meant. Appellant at no time thought or understood that it was in any way parting with any of its property.

There is no question but that the Government was responsible for the statement of 80 cubic feet per second as the amount limited to appellant in the agreement, and that the federal officers or agents responsible therefor knew it was intended to represent the amount of water measured at the users' boxes as 4000 miner's inches, and that appellant's officers relied upon the superior technical knowledge and good faith of the federal agents, when they assured appellant's officers that they would get that amount of water if the agreement read 80 cubic feet per second. It is likewise certain that such representations were false, and the correct equivalent would have been about 105 cubic feet per second. These facts appellant has alleged in its second amended complaint, and is prepared to substantiate by proper evidence.

Not only does the second amended bill of complaint seek relief because of fraudulent misrepresentations in obtaining the signature of appellant to the "limiting agreement," but by the newly discovered evidence it conclusively appears that there was no agreement in existence upon which to base the court's decree, because as soon as the truth had been discovered appellant promptly disavowed the agreement, stating to the Reclamation Service through Mr. Noble that the contract was void because unauthorized and secured through misunderstanding of measurements therein stated, and this protest and disavowal was immediately communicated to the United States Reclamation Service, and the chief officer in charge thereof, to whom the communication was made, concluded to leave appellant in the enjoyment of its rights, and not to molest it.

Another feature of the trial of the case, which does not add anything to the equity and good conscience of appellee, to say the least, was not only its silence as to receiving notice of protest, but when it became apparent that appellant could not prove any actual notice, counsel for the Government made the utmost of such failure of evidence, and emphasized to the highest degree, noting specifically in five different places in their brief, such failure, and thus it became the most cogent reason of the Circuit Court of Appeals for affirming the judgment, that appellant had ratified the contract by its silence.

We do not claim any intentional bad faith on the part of appellee, but we do state that it has obtained a judgment taking appellant's property without its consent, and without compensation, and that it is not in position to avail itself of that purely technical advantage on the ground of estoppel, which is the only theory upon which such judgment can be sustained.

The misrepresentations referred to above and reasons given, were all communicated to the federal Reclamation officer, as shown by the newly discovered evidence, as alleged in the second amended complaint, and yet the District Court has dismissed the case on motion, because it says, the newly discovered evidence was immaterial, since it was determined on the previous trial that there was no mistake anyway. We believe, in view of this evidence, that we are entitled to prove that there was a mistake, and false representations as well, and that the appellant disavowed the contract because thereof, and the Government accepted the same as a renunciation and abrogation of the agreement.

In rejecting the newly discovered evidence, on the ground that the original decree found that there was no mistake, the court was in error, inasmuch as the only mistake considered in that case was the question of mistaken construction of the agreement, while the mistake pointed out here is a mistake of fact—that appellant was induced to sign an agreement supposed to state correctly the amount of water it was appropriating, while it actually limited appellant to a quantity much less than that. The Opinion of the District Court itself disposes of its own conclusion in that respect, in the following language:

> "Indeed, in the view of the Trial Court and the Appellate Court the issue now sought to be raised was not presented by the pleadings in the original case, and the defendant is merely seeking a trial *de novo* on an entirely new theory."

But that is no reason why the bill of complaint is insufficient. The authorities do not sustain the decision on that point.

The new matter may be concerning a point not in issue in the original cause, provided that it be connected with the subject-matter of the bill.

> Foster's Federal Practice (3rd Ed.) Sec. 355, Vol 1, pp. 789-90.
>
> *Partridge vs. Osborne*, 6 Russ. 195.
>
> *United States vs. Sampeyreac*, Hempst. 118.

Matter discovered after the decree has been made, though not capable of being used as evidence of anything which was previously in issue in the cause, but constitutes an entirely new issue, may be the subject of a bill of review.

Fletcher's Equity Pl. & Pr., Sec. 922, pp. 981-2.

Story Eq. Pl. Sec. 416.

Dan. Ch. Pl. 1577.

The newly discovered evidence is, therefore, entirely relevant and material, and sufficient to sustain the bill in this case, as it shows that appellant promptly disavowed the so-called "limiting agreement," upon discovering that it had signed an instrument which did not express the true intention and agreement between the parties, and was therefore no contract at all.

There is no contract where a party takes advantage of mistake, by accepting an offer which does not express the real intention of the other party.

Page on Contracts, Vol. 1, Sec. 86, pp. 144-145.

It has been generally held, that where the seller either over or under estimates the quantity of the subject-matter of the sale, and he is in position to know the quantity, or from a reasonably accurate estimate thereof, and the purchaser is not, if the seller falsely and fraudulently over or under estimates the same, and such estimate is relied upon by the purchaser, it constitutes a fraud.

Cases cited in Note, 45 L. R. A. (NS) p. 243.

Misrepresentation of material facts, although innocently made, if acted upon by the other party to his detriment, will constitute sufficient ground for rescission and cancellation in equity.

9 C. J. 1169.

Mistake of fact by one party to contract constitutes ground for rescission.

9 C. J. 1167-8.

The only fraud necessary to sustain the judgment is such as may be inferred from failure of defendant to correct the mistake of plaintiff, known to or suspected by the former.

Wilson vs. Moriarty, 88 Cal. 207, 212; 26 Pac. 85.

Mistake of fact sufficient to avoid contract, even though neither party guilty of fraud, and this even though the apparent obligations of the parties have been fully performed.

9 C. J. 1166-7.

A mistake similar to that complained of here is also good ground for a bill of review. A mistake in the figuring because of data accidentally overlooked is ground for a bill of review.

34 Cyc. 1707.

Now, it plainly appears from the Second Amended Complaint, that appellant had appropriated and was in the actual use of 4,000 miner's inches of water, measured at the users' distribution boxes, at the time the "limiting agreement" was signed, and that by the newly discovered evidence of T. A. Noble, it will be able to prove not only that appellant's protest and refusal to comply with the agreement was duly communicated to the Reclamation Service immediately upon discovery of the mistake, but also the nature of the mistake, namely, that 80 cubic feet per second at the intake was not equivalent to 4,000 miner's inches as measured by appellant, or, no matter how it was measured, that it was not a correct estimate of the flow of water appellant had appropriated and was using, and which it was intended to represent. Appellant will be able to prove that there had been no possible increase in the diversion of water to its canal during the three years from the time of signing the agreement to the date of protest, which was the quantity appropriated, and intended to be defined by the agreement, in other words, conclusive proof that the agreement was based on a mistaken estimate. That was not the question in issue on the former trial, although it is vital to the decision. The question there raised was, whether 80 cubic feet per second fixed in the agreement, was intended to represent a measurement taken at the intake or at distribution point—a question of construction of contract. We can not deny that the court determined that question, and held that the contract must be construed to mean 80 cubic feet at the intake. No matter how erroneous appellant may consider that conclusion to be, it seems that we are precluded from going behind that finding of the court on the former trial. But the mistake of fact on which appellant's protest was based was not in issue in that case, was not set up in the pleadings, and was not decided in the sense that it is not now open to review upon the newly discovered evidence. Nevertheless, it is so connected with the subject-matter of that case, that it is vital to the decision, and the decree can not stand, unless it is determined adversely to appellant. Appellant went right on using the same amount of water it had always diverted from the time of signing the agreement down to the date of protest, and in so doing believed that it was in all things complying with the agreement itself, and when it was notified by Mr. Noble that he was going to enforce the agreement by cutting down their flow of water very materially, appellant and its trustees protested promptly and emphatically. The doctrine of estoppel can not be asserted against appellant under those circumstances. We earnestly contend that appellant should not be denied a new trial on these important questions, because of the decision arrived at under the original pleadings, and certainly its bill of review should not have been dismissed without at least a full hearing on the merits. It is a question of great importance, affecting many property owners, and valuable rights. The Reclamation Service has not by any means cleared itself of the imputation of unfairness in this transaction, and it would be inequitable to deny these people every opportunity to maintain their rights which equity will allow. And be it remembered that appellee is not here acting in its sovereign capacity but as a user of water like any citizen of the state and could not have acted at all in using water but for the permission granted by the legislature of the state of Washington. See Sec. 6411 R. & B. Code of Washington.

Another point: The District Court dismissed the question of ultra vires, with the remark that the newly discovered evidence had not changed the situation in that regard. We think it has materially. The court in the former trial held that the contract was not ambiguous, and must be upheld, because the officers of appellant, signed it, notwithstanding it takes property of the stockholders which they never authorized, because they are estopped by acquiescence and failure to renounce the unauthorized act. It was not necessary to state in so many words, that the officers were not authorized to sign the agreement, even if the court held that they must be regarded in law as having intended to do what they actually did, that is, agreed to in writing. There was never any pretense that the stockholders gave the officers of appellant discretionary power. This legal inference can not be extended to the stockholders, who never authorized it, and protested as soon as they knew what the officers had signed, or what the Government claimed it was, no matter in what words that protest was expressed. They can not be estopped on the ground of acquiescence, even though they did not state in their protest want of authority. It is sufficient that they protested, and have continued to protest all the time, and have lived up to their protest by refusing to comply with the agreement. Having protested against the agreement itself, they can not be held to have ratified the act of their officers in signing it, solely upon the ground that they did not specifically disclaim their authority to do so. Ratification assumes that the agent had no authority, but the principal becomes bound by adopting the unauthorized contract itself. The newly discovered evidence shows that this was not done in the case at bar.

Ratification, in the law of principal and agent, is the adoption and confirmation by one of an act or contract performed or entered into in his behalf by another, who, at the time, assumed to act as his agent without authority to do so.

Lexington v. Lafayette County Bank, 165 Mo. 671; 65 S. W. 943.

Reid v. Field, 83 Va. 26.

Ft. Scott Nat. Bank v. Drake, 29 Kan. 311, at 323.

Ansonia v. Cooper, 64 Conn. 536, at 544.

Heyn v. O'Hagen, 60 Mich. 150, at 156; 26 N. W. 861.

II.

There can be no valid reason, as it seems to counsel for appellant, whereby the judgment may be sustained on the ground of laches. The allegations of the second amended complaint completely negative that conclusion. It does not appear that delay in bringing suit has prejudiced appellee in any way.

The defense of laches to defeat the right to rescind a contract for fraud will not be entertained unless it is made to appear that it would be inequitable to deny it.

Davis v. Louisville Trust Co., 181 Fed. 10; 104 C. C. A. 24; 30 L. R. A. (N. S.) 1011.

It is alleged that immediately after discovery of the new evidence, there was a change in the officers of the Reclamation Service, and the facts were laid before the new officials that appellant was led to believe its application was being favorably considered, plans and methods were discussed, which led to filing petitions with federal departments, and arguments made thereon, which matters were pending when appellant applied for leave to file its bill of review, which was finally done because of the delay in the negotiations with the Government; that action was not taken sooner because appellant had reasonable grounds to believe that matters would be adjusted without further litigation.

There is no arbitrary bar by lapse of time to filing a bill of review based on new matter.

16 Cyc. 522, and cases cited.

On the question of laches and bearing directly thereon the doctrine is set forth in our favor as found in

9 C. J. 1203 (Sec. 4).

13 C. J. 601 (§ 623).

The question of diligence was disposed of by granting leave to file the bill of review, both by the Circuit Court of Appeals and the District Court. There was nothing before the court on the motion to dismiss, which was not before it then. That order is a judicial determination, not to be set aside without cause.

In the case of a bill of review based on newly discovered evidence, the question of diligence is necessarily a preliminary one upon which it is not necessary to join issue by the pleadings, but which is to be considered and passed upon at the time application is made for leave to file the bill, and having been once disposed of when the bill is allowed, it will not again be considered on the final hearing.

Kelley Bros. and Spielman v. Diamond Drill & Machine Co., 142 Fed. 868, affirmed, *Birdsboro Steel Foundry & Machine Co. v. Kelley Bros & Spielman*, 147 Fed. 713; 78 C. C. A. 101.

Lewellen v. Mackworth, 2 Ark. 40.

Hodges v. Mullikin, 1 Bland. Ch. 503.

Crawford v. Smith, 93 Va. 628; 25 S. E. 235, 657.

It has been said that the question of diligence is preliminary, and having been disposed of by permission to file the bill it will not again be considered on the final hearing, if not improvidently granted.

Foster's Federal Practice, Vol. 2, 1409.

There is absolutely nothing from which laches may be inferred on the part of appellant, and it seems a manifest abuse of discretion of the court in dismissing the bill on that ground. If anyone has slept on his rights, it is appellee. The judgment sought to be set aside remains unenforced, and no attempt has ever been made to carry it into execution. That corroborates the allegations concerning pendency of negotiations commenced upon discovery of the new evidence. Appellee certainly has not suffered because of the delay.

Several paragraphs of the motion are directed to the point that appellant's attempted renunciation of contract came too late, after the Government had expended large sums in developing the project. There is no showing on that account, which amounts to an estoppel. In the first place, procuring the "limiting agreement" in this instance was not one of the prerequisite conditions required by the Department of the Interior before undertaking the reclamation project. It was neither the adjustment of a conflicting claim, nor determination of a suit pending. Far from being a conflicting claim, it is undisputed that the agreement was intended to preserve all rights claimed by appellant, and relinquishing none.

In the second place, no matter how much money the Government has expended in developing the project, there is not the slightest ground for inference that it would not have been done, if the agreement had not been obtained from appellant, or that appellee relied thereon to its detriment. Anyway considering the large amount appropriated by respondent the water here in question is so small as to make the Reclamation Service's claim for damage ridiculous.

Thirdly, it does not appear that anyone was injured by the delay, although that would not be a defense in this action in any event.

And in this connection, may we not ask, who will be injured if the bill of review should finally prevail? What injury can result from depriving one of something he never had? On the other hand, if appellant is denied a hearing, it will be forcibly dispossessed of property it has enjoyed continuously for over twenty years, and the seven thousand acres of cultivated farm lands of its numerous stockholders will be immediately stripped of more than a quarter of their value, their crops will be sacrificed, and many of them ruined. And yet it is proposed, that appellant be denied even a hearing on its bill of review, because it was guilty of laches in attempting to adjust its rights out of court, and during all that time appellee could have enforced the judgment it had obtained at any moment, but has never made any attempt to do so.

Finally, we call attention to the failure of the case in 56 Wash. cited in the opinion of the court, to sustain the rule there laid down. It was an application to modify a judgment for mere variance between the complaint and judgment. The Washington statute, which the District Court refers to, cited in 56 Wash., and found in Secs. 466 and 467 Rem. Code of Washington, is inapplicable to an application to review a judgment on the ground of newly discovered evidence, and affords no basis for the Court's decision, even by analogy.

III.

To recapitulate: The newly discovered evidence will show that when notified that the "limiting agreement" would be enforced by curtailing appellant's right to divert the quantity of water it was using, its officers immediately protested on behalf of the stockholders, and refused to comply with the agreement, because they were never authorized and never intended to sign an agreement, which would surrender any right which they claimed, and it will be proved, first, that when the agreement was signed they were entitled to the full amount of water in use at the time of protest, and since that time, to-wit, the total flow of water then and now required to irrigate the lands under appellant's canals, which the evidence will prove conclusively has been a constant quantity at all times from a date prior to the signing of said agreement, and second, that the only agreement between the parties was one limiting appellant to that amount of water, and when the agent of the Reclamation Service called upon the stockholders to give a definite estimate of amount they claimed and were appropriating, that was very clearly given as 4,000 miner's inches, measured at the users' distribution boxes, as determined by the custom and decision of the Superior Court of Kittitas County, and when it was defined in the agreement by the Reclamation Service as 80 cubic feet per second, which was not equivalent to the amount agreed upon, that act was unauthorized, and the discrepancy was unknown to appellant or its stockholders until the protest was made in the summer of 1908, and appellant has at all times maintained the right to divert the original amount of water notwithstanding the so-called "limiting agreement;" that appellant was misled on the former trial by Mr. Noble's inability to recall the notice of disavowal promptly communicated to the Reclamation Service at the time it was made, and thereby appellant was unable to present the evidence on the trial, and the only result attained with a construction of the agreement favorable to the Government; that from that moment down to the filing of the Bill of Review, appellant has been unremitting in its endeavors to obtain relief from the judgment entered, by negotiations with the Reclamation Service, petitions to the Department of the Interior, and Executive Officers of the United States, and was led to believe by the federal authorities that matters could be satisfactorily adjusted without litigation; that appellant has been guilty of no laches, has done nothing which amounts to an estoppel of its rights, and there is no want of equity in its bill; while appellee, on the other hand secured appellant's signature, in the first place, to a document contrary to its clearly expressed intention and understanding at the time, confirmed that understanding by acquiescing therein for years, and when it finally did undertake to enforce the agreement, took an unconscionable advantage of appellant's inability to prove its disavowal of the agreement at the time, and obtained a judgment against appellant upholding the contract as ratified by failure to repudiate it, and has finally lulled appellant by a hope of amicable adjustment out of court, which has resulted in a delay, which the District Court has made the ground upon which it has dismissed the bill of complaint in this proceeding, and rendered the judgment appealed from.

It is respectfully submitted, that the judgment of the District Court should be reversed, and that the cause may proceed to hearing upon the second amended bill of complaint.

Respectfully submitted,

CARROLL B. GRAVES and
HARTMAN & HARTMAN,
Attorneys for Appellant.

No. 3518.

United States Circuit Court of Appeals For the Ninth Circuit

THE WEST SIDE IRRIGATING COMPANY, a corporation,
Appellant,
vs.
THE UNITED STATES OF AMERICA,
Appellee.

Appeal From the United States District Court for the Eastern District of Washington, Southern Division.

HON. FRANK H. RUDKIN, *Presiding.*

Brief of Appellee

FRANCIS A. GARRECHT,
United States Attorney,
Federal Bldg., Spokane, Wash.

SHAW & BORDEN CO. 189601

United States
Circuit Court of Appeals
For the Ninth Circuit

THE WEST SIDE IRRIGATING COMPANY, a corporation,
Appellant,

vs.

THE UNITED STATES OF AMERICA,
Appellee.

Appeal From the United States District Court for the Eastern District of Washington, Southern Division.

HON. FRANK H. RUDKIN, *Presiding.*

Brief of Appellee

STATEMENT

A resume of the facts established in the former trial of this case will be helpful in determining the merits of this appeal.

As early as 1903 the entire low water flow of the Yakima River had been exhausted. Alleged appropriations exceeded by a considerable amount the flow of the river.

In 1905 there had developed a shortage of water with a resultant conflict of claims. Litigation had been begun, into which the West Side Irrigating Company would naturally have been drawn, and which ultimately and inevitably would have involved all claimants of water rights in the Yakima River.

The Secretary of the Interior was being importuned by the local people to take up the Yakima Project and extend irrigation thereunder through the storage of flood waters. Responding to this request, on December 12, 1905, the Secretary notified the Geological Survey, then in charge of the work of the Reclamation Service, of certain conditions which he considered it was necessary for the water users to meet before the United States would approve the Yakima Project.

One of these conditions was that the local people should first secure from the appropriators on the river written agreements reducing the several amounts of their alleged appropriations so that the total claim would aggregate an amount not exceeding the low water flow of the river.

This matter was taken up by the Commercial Clubs of the Valley and a vigorous campaign was conducted among the water users for the purpose of securing compromises of the different claims and reducing them sufficiently to meet the requirements of the Government. Public meetings were held and committees of citizens were appointed to adjust conflicting claims and secure concessions of rights. The settlement of the amount of the water for insertion in each instrument was left with the committees and the water claimants.

As a result of this campaign the Yakima Valley people secured some fifty separate agreements limiting rights to the use of the water of the Yakima River in accordance with the Government's suggestion, one of which agreements was executed by the West Side Irrigating Company.

This agreement bears date October 21, 1905, and among other things states:

> Whereas, no irrigation project to be undertaken by the United States within the said watershed can be recommended as feasible unless the quantity of water to which each present water user from the Yakima River and its tributaries is entitled *be first definitely ascertained and agreed to,* and, whereas, the undersigned *claim* certain quantities of water from the Yakima River and its tributaries and *are willing to limit their claim* to the said water to the quantity of water designated in the following schedule.

The schedule provided for a delivery from April to September, inclusive, of 80 cubic feet of water per second and during the month of October of 34 cubic feet per second.

This agreement further states that this company "does *limit* its respective rights of appropriation from said Yakima River and its tributaries to the above specified amount" and it also provides "that it is hereby understood and agreed that the *limita-*

tion of water rights as herein specified *is made as a compromise* in order to secure the benefits above referred to."

Following the execution of the above mentioned limiting agreement, and on March 27, 1906, the Secretary of the Interior authorized the construction of the Yakima Project, and thereafter expended large sums of money thereon before any suggestion was made to the United States by anyone that there was a misunderstanding regarding any of these agreements. At the time of the former trial of the case the project expenditures of the Government had reached the sum of $7,420,000.00.

Thus the West Side Irrigating Company, in very plain and simple language, specifically agreed to reduce its claim as a compromise and for the purpose of securing the benefits of a Government Irrigation Project. Nevertheless, after the United States, relying upon this and other limiting agreements, had expended large sums of money upon this project the West Side Irrigating Company declined to be bound by the agreement; and on June 25, 1912, the United States brought its action in the District Court for the Eastern District of Washington, to enjoin the company from diverting any water in excess of the amount named in the agreement. Thereupon the company went into court with the contention that it never had intended to reduce its claim, and furthermore that it must have 4000 inches or 80 second feet of water at its lateral measuring boxes, rather than at the intake of its canal, the point where its appropriation under the law must necessarily be.

The facts and law of the case were presented with great care and detail, and February 19, 1916, a decision was handed down in the case upholding the contentions of the Government and the validity of the agreement (230 Fed. 284). The West Side Irrigating Company appealed from this decision, to this court, and on October 15, 1917, the judgment of the lower court was affirmed (245 Fed. 212). After waiting nearly two years the company filed a petition to reopen the case upon the ground of newly discovered evidence. Upon motion duly made, the amended bill of complaint was dismissed, and, likewise, the second amended bill of complaint, from which order this appeal has been taken.

Several issues, which have already been passed upon by the court, are again urged upon its attention. It is very earnestly insisted that previous to the execution of the agreement the corporation diverted at the river more than 80-second feet. The figures of the hydrographers of the Geological Survey, which were presented at the trial, show, however, that in 1904 and 1905 the company, on no single day, was running water into its ditch equal to 80-second feet and that the average during the height of the season was between 65 and 75 feet.

At the trial Mitchell Stevens, vice-president of the corporation and the official who executed the agreement, who was the principal witness at the trial and who made the affidavits accompanying the petition for a rehearing herein, gave testimony indicating that he knew of these measurements being made, and that they were used as a basis for determining the amount of water to which the company was entitled.

If for any reason the water flowing in the ditch during these two years, was less than usual the officers and members of the company knew it then, and could have given the discrepancy with much greater accuracy than they can now; but no objections were made at the time and not at all until many years after the company had determined to resist the enforcement of the agreement.

All pertinent matters presented by the second amended bill of complaint, with the single exception of showing whether one Noble gave a certain notice to the Reclamation Service officials in 1908, relative to the contention of the West Side Irrigating Company that a mistake had been made, were presented at the trial of the case, and the last named point is the only new matter brought before the court by this petition for a review.

ARGUMENT.

I.

The claims of the West Side Irrigating Company are entirely without merit, and the attitude of its active agencies has been so lacking in frankness as almost to amount to duplicity and this conduct has characterized this litigant from the beginning.

The petition for bill of review was addressed to this court and an order entered thereon. Later, leave of the District Court to file the bill of complaint was procured, all without notice to appellee, which was unfair and not in accord with correct proceedure.

Having induced the court to permit the filing of its bill of complaint without any showing whatever and without notice to the opposite party, appellant now insists that the court's favor restricts its power to dismiss the bill on motion.

Bills of review have been dismissed because leave to file the same was improvidently granted.

> 2 *Foster,* Sec. 488, p. 1409;
> *Hopkins v. Hebard,* 235 U. S. 291; 194 Fed. 301;
> *Accord v. Western Pocahontas Corp.,* 156. Fed. 989.

The proceedings on a petition to rehear in a court of original jurisdiction are not, or should not be, conducted *ex parte.* The proper course is to file the petition with the Clerk of the proper court, and obtain from the judge an order on the adversary party to appear at the following rule day, or some other stated day, and show cause why the prayer of the petition should not be granted.

10 *R. C. L.*, Sec. 352, p. 564.

Inasmuch as the petition for a rehearing is not an *ex parte* proceeding, counter affidavits may be received by the court in order that the court may be fully advised as to whether or not due diligence was indulged in by the petitioning party, and whether or not the evidence sought to be introduced was material.

Sheeler vs. Alexander, 211 Fed. Rep. 546.

After filing this petition for a rehearing and the affidavits, he should then obtain an order upon the adverse party to show cause at some later date why his prayer for a rehearing should not be granted.

Sheeler v. Alexander, 211 Fed. 547.

The petition for leave must set forth the grounds on which it is based and ask permission to file the bill. It must be upon notice to the adverse party to show cause against the application.

Counter affidavits may be introduced denying the allegations of the petition or the moving affidavits.

16 *Cyc.*, 524.

The findings of the court on the application for leave to file the bill of review are not conclusive on the court at the subsequent hearing on the bill.

When the bill of review has been improperly filed, the proper mode of objecting is by motion to strike it from the files, and not by demurrer.

16 *Cyc.* 524.

Originally, the rule was that a Court of Equity could not amend its decree, or re-hear the cause after the final decree had been enrolled. This principal was, however, changed by one of Lord Bacon's ordinances. It being in derogation of the principle of the common law, the ordinance is to be strictly construed, and bills of review are not entertained otherwise than in conformity with the conditions as stated therein.

Bills of review are, therefore, not specially favored in equity.

10 *R. C. L.*, p. 568, Sec. 356;
Purcell v. Miner, 4 Wall 513; 71 U. S. 520.

II.

It affirmatively appears from the second amended bill of complaint that appellant has failed, neglected and refused to conform to the decree of the court entered herein, and the said application for relief is an abuse of the administration of justice, applied for in the hope of protracting the litigation and for the purpose of delaying enforcement of the decree.

In no other case within our experience has any party to an action commended itself for violating the court's decree, or gone further in effrontery by expressly claiming consideration and rights because of refusal to comply with a court's injunction.

This alone should have precluded the granting of the petition for a rehearing.

To entitle a person to bring a bill of review, it is necessary that he should have obeyed or performed the decree, as if it be for land that the possession be yielded.

> Sec. 449, page 1410, *Foster's Fed. Practice,* Vol. 2.

To the same effect:

> *Simpkin's Fed. Suit in Equity,* 3rd. Ed. (Bill of review, p. 608).
> 16 *Cyc.* 524.

If there are circumstances which ought to constitute an exception to the general rule requiring a person to perform, he must show them to the court, and obtain an order relieving him from performance before filing the bill.

The object of this rule requiring performance of a decree as a condition precedent to the right to maintain a bill of review is to prevent abuse in the administration of justice by the filing of such bills solely for delay and vexation or otherwise protracting the litigation to the discouragement and distress of the adverse party.

10 *R. C. L.*, page 576, Sec. 363, citing:
Ricker v. Powell, 100 U. S. 108;
Willamette Iron Bridge Co. v. Hatch, 19 Fed. 348;
Kimmerly v. Arms, 40 Fed. 555.

III.

Where the petitioner in an application for a bill of review is guilty of laches the bill should be dismissed.

The opinion of the Circuit Court of Appeals was rendered October 5, 1917.

The Mandate was filed in the District Court November 28, 1917.

According to the affidavit of Mitchell Stevens, vice-president of the company, he became acquainted with the facts upon which the petition is based June 18th, 1918.

The application for review was not made to the Circuit Court of Appeals until the 3rd day of September, 1919.

Application for leave to file such a bill must be promptly made after the discovery of the new evidence; and any laches in this respect on the part of the party aggrieved by the decree will be fatal.

Central Trust Co. v. Grant Locomotive Works, 135 U. S. 207.
Jorgensen v. Young, 136 Fed. 378.

We concede that the statutes of the State regulating proceedings of this kind are not binding on Federal Courts; but the practice followed might be persuasive in determining whether proper diligence was exercised.

Sec. 464, Remington and Ballinger's Code, provides:

> The superior court in which a judgment has been rendered * * * shall have power after the term (time) at which such judgment was made, to vacate or modify such judgment. * * *
>
> 4. For fraud practiced by the successful party in obtaining the judgment or order.

Sec. 465:

> When the grounds for a new trial could not with reasonable diligence have been discovered before, but are discovered after the term (time); when the * * * decision was rendered * * * the application may be made by petition filed as in other cases not later than *after the discovery.* * * *
>
> The facts stated in the petition shall be considered as denied without answer, * * * but no motion shall be filed *more than one year after* the final judgment was rendered.

Sec. 467:

> The proceedings to obtain the benefit of subdivision 4 of Section 464, shall be by petition, verified by affidavit, setting forth the judgment, * * * the facts or errors constituting a cause to vacate or modify it, and if the party is a defendant, the facts constituting a defense to the action; and such proceedings must be commenced *within one year after* the judgment

There is no showing of the exercise of any reasonable diligence by the corporation, either at the trial or since, of any endeavor to have Mr. Noble recollect that he had notified some official of the Reclamation Service of the conversation alleged to have taken place between him and Mitchell Stevens. No official of the company appears to have interviewed Mr. Noble on the subject from the day of the trial, March 22, 1915, until June 18, 1918. What restoratives were applied to make Mr. Noble's memory more acute in 1918 than it was three years before are not mentioned and the reason for not having tried to revive his recollection before the final determination of the case by the courts also is not stated.

The Government is not responsible for the failure of Mr. Noble to advise Mitchell Stevens of any action he may now claim he took as to giving notice to any one, and the appellant is not entitled to relief, unless it first shows that the Government procured and was instrumental in procuring any false statement made by Noble to Stevens.

Where jurisdiction of the party and the case is not denied, the mere fact that he expected the testimony of an important witness would be in his favor; whereas, in the trial the witness testified the other way, will not support a plea that the judgment was fraudulently obtained.

> *Wier vs. Vaile*, 65 Cal. 466 (4 Pac. 422), cited in 23 *Cyc.*, p. 1590.

A comparison of the second amended bill of complaint with the record in the original case referred to in paragraph one of said second amended bill of complaint, shows that the representations upon which relief is now sought is not true in this: That the suggestions of fraud set forth are based upon the statements that one Chas. H. Swigart, chief officer of the Reclamation Service, was present in court and upon the witness stand at the trial, and failed to disclose the evidence alleged to have been suppressed, when the records in the former trial conclusively show that said Chas. H. Swigart was never a witness in said case at all.

Further, the allegation in said second amended bill of complaint that plaintiff was misled by its officers or agents, is not sufficient to amount to an allegation of fraud, and is inadequately pleaded; the allegations that the officers of the Government suppressed evidence being mere gratitious conclusions, based in the most favorable view upon the carelessness and inexcusable neglect of appellant in not having discovered the evidence alleged to have been suppressed; that appellant, on said former trial, made no effort whatever to support any allegation that the Company had given notice to the United States of the renunciation of the contract, either by questioning T. A. Noble, who was a witness, or by calling said Charles H. Swigart, Supervising Engineer of the United States Reclamation Service, who was not a witness.

It may be that the foregoing points of objection to the bill of review may be classified as technical. In declining to pass on them in the court below, Judge Rudkin, in his opinion, said: "I may say in conclusion that I deem it best to dispose of the application upon its merits, rather than upon technical questions of procedure." We know that it is the disposition of courts, at the present time, not to permit mere technicality of procedure to interfere with the rights of parties, and this is as it should be. But when the litigant has received every consideration and the case has been tried upon its merits and the applicant for relief fails, refuses and declines to abide by the judgment of the courts, patience ceases to be a virtue and in keeping with their own dignity, in the interest of orderly procedure and generally that there might be an end to the litigation, courts should consider objections which are well founded in the law, even though they appear to have a technical aspect.

IV.

Passing now to what may be termed the merits of this case on this appeal.

A bill of review for newly discovered evidence is not favored by the courts. Its allowance is not a matter of right in the party, but rests in the sound discretion of the court to be exercised cautiously and sparingly and only under circumstances that demonstrate it to be indispensable to the merits and justice of the cause.

10 *R. C. L.,* Sec. 362, page 575.

To the same effect is:

Craig vs. Smith, 100 U. S. 233.

It must be noted, too, that the court is not absolutely bound to grant relief either for error apparent or for newly discovered evidence, even though it appears that a different decree should have been granted.

10 *R. C. L.,* page 569, Sec. 357.

If the circumstances have so changed that it appears inequitable to disturb the decree, or if for any reason the court deems it inadvisable to disturb it, relief will not be granted.

Ricker vs. Powell, 100 U. S. 104.

As pointed out in the opinion of the lower court, the matter alleged as newly discovered evidence is not controlling and there was ample in the record on other grounds to sustain the findings and decisions made by the District Court and the Circuit Court of Appeals.

"Indeed," as the opinion goes on to say, "in the view of the Trial Court and Appellate Court the issue now sought to be raised was not presented by the pleadings in the original case, and the defendant is merely seeking a trial *de novo* on an entirely new theory, utterly disregarding the former trial and the finality of the former decision. For this reason alone the bill of complaint is entirely insufficient."

Even if the facts set forth in the second amended bill of complaint, which are alleged to show an attempt to give notice of the renunciation of the agreement, had in fact been communicated to the officer of the Reclamation Service as claimed, it unmistakably appears that the so-called notice was casual, incidental, informal and by hearsay only.

The notice and conversation which it is now claimed that Mr. Noble had with Mr. Swigart was so vague and uncertain that it made so little impression on Mr. Noble's mind that three or four years of memory cultivation was necessary to enable him to recall it at all.

It appears from the transcript of record of the trial of this case that even Mr. Stevens with his facile memory could not say whether it occurred in 1906 or 1907 and the approximate date could only be arrived at by the fact that it occurred after Mr. Noble had become a Water Commissioner for Yakima County, which was not before the season of 1908. The substance of what was said at the time is given by Mr. Noble as follows (p. 191):

> A. "Mr. Stevens and I had other business together; I gave him some advice as to putting in concrete head gates; the most of our conversation was along that line. I don't recall that very much was said about their limiting agreement. I believe I did tell him that they were diverting more than they had stated in

> that agreement, and I believe that Mr. Stevens told me that they felt that they had a right to divert more and they did not feel bound by that agreement. That is as near as I can recollect the substance of our conversation referring to this matter."

We say this is a weak basis upon which to abrogate this important agreement when the law declares that the renunciation of a contract must be distinct and unequivocal.

13 *Corpus Juris,* 654.

Conceding, for the purposes of argument, that this conversation or notice that the corporation did not deem itself bound by the agreement, was actually communicated to the officer of the Reclamation Service, it appears from the record that it was then too late to be available as an abrogation of the contract, for the reason that it conclusively appears from the undisputed evidence offered at the trial that at the time of this alleged notice, the contract was no longer executory as regards the United States, which had, prior thereto, expended vast sums in reliance upon the agreement; and, further, the Government could not then be placed in the position it was before the signing of the contract, and would, therefore, be entitled to disregard said notice, even if given, and would have the liberty to treat the contract as binding and institute its action as it did.

Nor does the alleged newly discovered evidence abrogate the Government's defense of estoppel, and the allegations thereof do not avail appellant for that purpose, since the stipulation of the parties in the record of the former action, conclusively shows that long before the alleged notice of renunciation had even been given to T. A. Noble, the Secretary of the Interior had already approved the Yakima Project and purchased the irrigating system for the Sunnyside Unit thereof and expended large sums in reliance upon this and the other similar agreements.

It is not even suggested that appellant tried to to notify the Government at any time prior to July, 1908. This of itself is an indication of bad faith. The uncontradicted evidence at the former trial conclusively shows that this corporation had knowledge of the agreement which was executed October 21, 1905, on resolution of its Board of Directors. Within two months from that time dissatisfaction arose and by January 2, 1906, the corporation at a stockholders' meeting had definitely resolved not to be bound by the agreement. Almost immediately the corporation employed counsel and has acted under legal advice since. But according to its own showing it failed and neglected and made no effort to notify the United States, or any of its agents or supposed agents of this fixed determination to rescind or repudiate the contract until the summer of 1908, and even then the only notice given was to an agent of the State and it was not clear and unequivocal. Furthermore, by that time the

Government had expended approximately $1,263,-000.00, which of itself is sufficient to warrant the courts in sustaining the agreement.

There would be no end to suits if the indulgence asked for in this case were permitted. The alleged discovery of new evidence after the entry of the decree, even after the final appeal, that witness Noble would now testify that he communicated to Mr. Swigart the conversation he had with Mr. Stevens is plainly insufficient in itself. But beyond that it is based upon the very fact that the witnesses' memory is indistinct and uncertain. Mr. Noble was asked about this matter at the former trial and he could not then remember.

The mischief which would result is well pointed out in the brief of counsel published in the case of *Southard vs. Russell,* 16 Howard 564, which later received sanction in the decision.

> "This court, after the most careful research, cannot find one case reported in which a bill of review has been allowed on the discovery of new witnesses to prove a fact which had before been in issue, although there are many where bills of review have been sustained on the discovery of records and other writings relating to the title which was generally put in issue. The distinction is very material. Written evidence cannot be easily corrupted; and if it had been discovered before the former hearing, the presumption is strong that it would have been produced to prevent further litigation and expense. New witnesses, it is granted, may also be discovered without subornation, but they may easily be procured by

it, and the danger of admitting them renders it highly impolitic." "If, then, whenever a new witness or witnesses can, honestly or by subornation, be found whose testimony may probably change a decree in chancery or an award, a bill of review is received, when will there be an end of litigation? And particularly will it not render our contests for land almost literally endless? What stability or certainty can there be in the tenure of property? The dangers and mischief to society are too great to be endured."

Respass v. McClanahan, etc., Hand. (Ky.) 347.

The action of the trial court in granting or refusing an application to open, vacate or set aside a judgment is, generally speaking, within the sound judicial discretion of such court, and its action will not be disturbed by an appellate court except for a clear abuse of discretion.

15 *R. C. L.* 720, Sec. 174.

After this matter has been so thoroughly considered we think this court should not put the Government to the delay, expense and loss incident to a retrial upon the showing made.

Respectfully,

FRANCIS A. GARRECHT,

United States Attorney, for Appellee.

No. 3518

United States Circuit Court of Appeals

For The Ninth Circuit

THE WEST SIDE IRRIGATING COMPANY, a corporation, *Appellant*,

—vs.—

THE UNITED STATES OF AMERICA, *Appellee*.

APPEAL FROM THE UNITED STATES DISTRICT COURT FOR THE EASTERN DISTRICT OF WASHINGTON, SOUTHERN DIVISION.

HON. FRANK H. RUDKIN, *Presiding*.

REPLY BRIEF OF APPELLANT

CARROLL B. GRAVES,
606-8 Central, Bldg., Seattle, Wash.

HARTMAN & HARTMAN,
300-6 Burke Bldg., Seattle, Wash.
Attorneys for Appellant.

THE ARGUS PRESS. SEATTLE

No. 3518

United States Circuit Court of Appeals

For The Ninth Circuit

THE WEST SIDE IRRIGATING COMPANY, a corporation, *Appellant*,

—vs.—

THE UNITED STATES OF AMERICA, *Appellee*.

APPEAL FROM THE UNITED STATES DISTRICT COURT FOR THE EASTERN DISTRICT OF WASHINGTON, SOUTHERN DIVISION.

HON. FRANK H. RUDKIN, *Presiding*.

REPLY BRIEF OF APPELLANT

CARROLL B. GRAVES,
606-8 Central, Bldg., Seattle, Wash.

HARTMAN & HARTMAN,
300-6 Burke Bldg., Seattle, Wash.
Attorneys for Appellant.

THE ARGUS PRESS, SEATTLE

No. 3518

United States Circuit Court of Appeals

For The Ninth Circuit

THE WEST SIDE IRRIGATING COMPANY, a corporation, *Appellant,*

—vs.—

THE UNITED STATES OF AMERICA, *Appellee.*

APPEAL FROM THE UNITED STATES DISTRICT COURT FOR THE EASTERN DISTRICT OF WASHINGTON, SOUTHERN DIVISION.

HON. FRANK H. RUDKIN, *Presiding.*

REPLY BRIEF OF APPELLANT

STATEMENT

We vigorously assail the statement of appellee for the reason that it is an astonishing departure from well recognized rules, and an attempt to drag into a consideration of the points at issue matters not under consideration and which cannot be considered under the record here.

A statement is "the very lock and key to set open

the windows" of the case to be considered. Inaccuracy of statement, or a statement of matters which do not appear from the record in the case, however they may occur, inevitably tend to invalidate the conclusion drawn therefrom. Aside from ethical or legal considerations, accuracy is not achieved and the real points to be determined are obscured if the statement be given consideration.

The amended bill of complaint and second bill of complaint were attacked, not by answer, but by a motion to dismiss. This motion was not confined to urging any defense arising upon the face of the bill, but went further and by statement and argument contained in the motion, attempted to do the very thing which is again attempted in the statement at bar. See motion, p. 28, printed record.

Upon motion therefor, an order was made in the district court striking all parts of said motion except that portion which was based upon the ground that the amended complaint did not state facts sufficient to constitute a cause of action, and by agreement the motion was so argued. Printed record, p. 43. The final order and judgment granting this motion to dismiss expressly limited the order as having been made upon the motion as though it were a demurrer. Printed record p. 34.

It was within the right of appellee to have filed an answer to the bill and brought into the case all the material and relevant facts which may have been desired and which do not appear upon the face of the bill of complaint. The appellee did not chose so to do, but elected to urge a motion to dismiss in the nature of a demurrer, and the case is brought here in that situation. The obvious and ill-advised attempt to bring into the consideration of the motion or demurrer, facts not apparent from the face of the bill, is an act subject to criticism and which sound practice will not condone.

In considering a motion to dismiss, the pleadings alone are involved.

New Equity Rule 29.

Hosler vs. Ireland, 219 Fed. 490, 135 C. C. A. 201.

Answering the part of appellee's statement deemed part of the record that appellee sought to secure agreements from appropriators reducing the amounts of their alleged appropriations, it has departed from the admitted facts in the case, that the Government sought only to avail itself of the surplus storage waters, and solicited agreements which would fix the maximum amount of water claimed by each appropriator. There is not the slightest foundation for the suggestion that appellant was asked to sign an agreement reducing its appropriation. On the contrary it was undisputed that appellant claimed the full amount, and signed the agreement solely because it understood it was so specified therein.

Again, appellee says in its brief, that the Secretary of the Interior required certain conditions to be met before the United States would approve the Yakima Project, and one of these was that written agreements be secured reducing the amounts of alleged appropriations. Now, as this document is not before the court, we are at a disadvantage, as we are likewise concerning much of the statement and argument of counsel for appellee based upon alleged circumstances wholly outside of the record. But the only conditions we can find that appellee relied upon in the original case, as contained in the notice of the Secretary of the Interior are as follows:

> "First. The adjustment of all conflicting claims of those who are appropriating water from the Yakima River or any other body of water, for irrigation, power or any other purpose.
>
> "Second. The determination of all suits now pending to prevent the diversion of water from the Yakima River to the Yakima Indian Reservation, and any and all other litigation that in any way tends to embarrass or restrict the appropriation of the waters from said river or any other body of water needed for the irrigation of the lands under said proposed projects."

There was neither any conflict between the claim of appellant and any other appropriator, nor was appellant involved in any litigation whatever. The right of appellant to the amount of water it claimed then and claims now was unquestioned. In plain language, appellant was simply induced to sign the agreement when it was off-guard, whereby it was held to have parted with rights it was never asked to surrender and never intended to. Nor did it ever receive any consideration or benefit therefor, but has only continued to use its own water, which has uniformly flowed through its canal for more than twenty years.

We do not agree with counsel for appellee in the assertion that issues here have been passed upon in the original case. And the testimony in that case as to measurements taken by the Geological Survey on some other issue are not controlling. Nor were such measurements any reliable test of the water appropriated and being used by appellant, as the evidence in that case, as well as much more accurate evidence now available, shows that the measurements were taken when the normal flow of water in appellant's canal was materially diminished for other reasons.

Correction should also be made of the statement on page 5 of appellee's brief, to the effect that this is an appeal from the order dismissing the amended bill of complaint and likewise the second amended bill. The motion of appellee to dismiss the amended bill of complaint was stricken on motion of appellant (Tr. pp. 43-44). The second amended bill of complaint was filed thereafter, and appellee's motion to dismiss was granted.

ARGUMENT

We are not going to enlarge upon the argument already made, but only to touch upon one or two things in the argument for appellee, which seem to require it.

Notwithstanding appellee complains that the order granting leave to file the bill of review was *ex parte*, and no opportunity given to file counter affidavits, it will be remembered that appellee did not file any counter affidavits, or make any showing whatever in contravention of the right to file a bill of review, but moved to dismiss the same on mere informal allegations of the evidence adduced upon the trial of the original case. There was nothing before the court upon which to base its order of dismissal, which was not before it when leave was granted to file the bill of review, and therefore no proper reason or grounds for overruling the order first entered.

Regarding the alleged rule requiring one bringing a bill of review to perform the decree in some cases, it is not applicable here. As counsel explains, it is invoked in any event only against bills filed solely for delay and vexation, of which it would be outrageous to accuse this appellant, after it has struggled for years to obtain redress from the Government in the shape of annulling the erroneous judgment, and all the time appellee has stood by without attempting to enforce the judgment, because of appellant's constant efforts, until departmental delays compelled it to bring the bill of re-

ADDITIONAL AUTHORITIES FOR REPLY BRIEF
IN CASE NO. 3518, UNITED STATES
CIRCUIT COURT OF APPEALS.

IRRIGATING COMPANY VS. UNITED STATES.

here has been no change in circumstances bills
reform instruments because of mistake after a c
le lapse of time (16 Cyc. 158) Essex vs. Day
rs) 52 Conn. 483. Lockwood vs. White, 65 Vt. 4

ears was held not a bar to an attack on a compr
rs. Sap. 81 Ala. 525, 16 Cyc. 158, Note 72.

cence of plaintiff in a conflicting claim canno
by the court where no circumstances appear
on plaintiff for assertion of his rights.
159.

ADDITIONAL AUTHORITIES FOR REPLY BRIEF
IN CASE NO. 3518, UNITED STATES
CIRCUIT COURT OF APPEALS.

IRRIGATING COMPANY VS. UNITED STATES.

here has been no change in circumstances bills w
reform instruments because of mistake after a co
e lapse of time (16 Cyc. 158) Essex vs. Day
s) 52 Conn. 483. Lockwood vs. White, 65 Vt. 46

ears was held not a bar to an attack on a compro
. Sap. 81 Ala. 525, 16 Cyc. 158, Note 72.

ence of plaintiff in a conflicting claim cannot
red by the court where no circumstances appear
n plaintiff for assertion of his rights.
159.

view for fear of losing its rights by such delays. Not only has appellant thus shown good reason why performance was waived, but it has sought to preserve its right by prescription and adverse possession as against appellee, and still claims and asserts such rights. The rule does not operate where good reason is shown for non-performance, or when performance would extinguish some right which the party has at law.

15 Cyc. 525;

Griggs vs. Gear, 8 Ill. 2;

Massie vs. Graham, 16 Fed. Cas. No. 9,263, 3 McLean, 41.

On page 12 of appellee's brief, sections of the Code of the State of Washington are set forth in part, taken from statutes of procedure under our state laws in cases of motions for new trial and vacation of judgments, usually required to be filed within one year. Counsel for appellee admit that the statutes quoted do not govern in this case. They are, therefore wholly inapplicable here. In fact, they have no bearing on the case at all. In view of the gravity of the situation which confronts appellant, to urge such an argument seems untimely, if not even trifling with the real questions at issue.

For counsel for appellee to stigmatize appellant's application as effrontery to the court, is unjust and uncalled for and especially when appellee's rights are inferior and subsequent to appellant's. Many farmers in this community face loss and ruin, if they shall be deprived of the water, which is absolutely necessary to cultivate and mature their crops. Property rights which have been so long enjoyed should not be disturbed without gravest consideration. Counsel for appellant have endeavored, as best they may, to deal with a difficult situation, in order that the rights of appellant may be acknowledged and restored. There is no thought of effrontery, but only a sincere desire to have justice done, and that a fair trial of this matter may be had to the fullest extent. Impughning motives and casting aspersions does not conduce towards a just ending or right a wrong sustained. With this thought in view, we respectfully submit the case to the consideration of the court.

Respectfully submitted,

CARROLL B. GRAVES and
HARTMAN & HARTMAN,
Attorneys for Appellant.

No. 3518.

In the United States Circuit Court of Appeals

For The Ninth Circuit

WEST SIDE IRRIGATING CO., *Appellant,*

vs.

UNITED STATES OF AMERICA, *Appellee.*

APPEAL FROM THE UNITED STATES DISTRICT COURT FOR THE EASTERN DISTRICT OF WASHINGTON, SOUTHERN DIVISION.

HON. FRANK H. RUDKIN, *Presiding.*

PETITION FOR REHEARING AND SUPPORTING BRIEF

CARROLL B. GRAVES and
HARTMAN & HARTMAN,
Attorneys for Petitioner.

300-306 Burke Bldg., Seattle, Wash.

THE ARGUS PRESS, SEATTLE

No. 3518.

In the United States Circuit Court of Appeals

For The Ninth Circuit

WEST SIDE IRRIGATING CO., *Appellant,*

vs.

UNITED STATES OF AMERICA, *Appellee.*

APPEAL FROM THE UNITED STATES DISTRICT COURT FOR THE EASTERN DISTRICT OF WASHINGTON, SOUTHERN DIVISION.

HON. FRANK H. RUDKIN, *Presiding.*

PETITION FOR REHEARING AND SUPPORTING BRIEF

CARROLL B. GRAVES and
HARTMAN & HARTMAN,
Attorneys for Petitioner.

300-306 Burke Bldg., Seattle, Wash.

THE ARGUS PRESS, SEATTLE

No. 3518.

In the United States Circuit Court of Appeals For The Ninth Circuit

WEST SIDE IRRIGATING COMPANY, *Appellant,* vs. UNITED STATES OF AMERICA, *Apellee.*	No. 3518 PETITION FOR REHEARING

APPEAL FROM THE UNITED STATES DISTRICT COURT FOR THE EASTERN DISTRICT OF WASHINGTON, SOUTHERN DIVISION.

HON. FRANK H. RUDKIN, *Presiding.*

PETITION FOR REHEARING

Comes now the Appellant by its attorneys, Carroll B. Graves and Hartman & Hartman, and moves the Court herein for a rehearing and permission for reargument of this cause for the reasons and upon the grounds as follows:

I.

That the opinion rendered is not in conformity

with and based upon the admitted facts presented by the record and diverges therefrom.

II.

That the decision as rendered is not in conformity with the weight of authority in this, that it is contrary to the rules and principles of equity governing the issues as joined.

III.

That by the opinion, it seems that a digression has been had from the proceedings taken below in this, that the so-called motion of Appellee was, by the Lower Court, treated only as a demurrer to the bill on the general ground and all other parts thereof stricken and disregarded, while in the opinion it appears that the Court has given consideration to the allegations in the so-called motion, which allegations are, and as considered would be, in the nature of an answer joining an issue and calling for a trial upon the merits, by the *nise prius* court.

IV.

That the equities in the case have not received due consideration in that the Appellant has never acquiesced in the original judgment and that no prejudice has been shown to have been suffered by the Appellee because of delay or want of diligence in filing the bill herein and under the admitted case Appellee is not prejudiced or injured.

V.

That by the admitted allegations of the bill under the record the uncontradicted fact is presented to this Court, that it must be assumed, in the absence of any allegations to the contrary, if the water in dispute was not used by the Appellant it runs into many ditches of private ownership with unadjudicated rights, over whom the Reclamation Service has no power or authority, nor the State, until all rights are adjudicated, and thereby, and because thereof, great injury would accrue to the Appellant and no damage to the Appellee.

VI.

That notwithstanding, the undisputed record shows that Appellant is entitled to cancellation of the so-called Limiting Agreement because of mistake—notice of same and repudiation both by actual notice and by Appellant's conduct fully understood, by Reclamation Service; and therefore the decision in this case will deprive the Appellant of the relief prayed for on the ground that the notice of revocation of the contract given to the Appellee was not technically definite or sufficient and Appellant should be granted such relief in this action.

VII.

That it is shown by the record that fraud has been practiced by which the Appellant was injured, if the judgment rendered shall be enforced, and no opportunity given for redress.

VIII.

That an error of law has been committed in holding that the mistake pointed out at time of agreement had to be mutual.

IX.

That there is no mutuality of remedy. In the resolution of the board of directors quoted in this decision it does not say "Provided the government should complete the irrigation project as stated by the court—but, provided the government completes the High Line Canal." This "High Line Canal" referred to was a contemplated or proposed canal in Kittitas County just above the canal of the West Side Irrigating Company's Canal and the wastage and seepage from such a project would have materially benefited the West Side Irrigation Canal by directly wasting into it. But no such canal is now even projected or contemplated by the Government and it is the general concensus of opinion that it never will be built by either the Government or private parties on the West Side of the Yakima River in Kittitas County. So that beside the question of mutuality of remedy, it is absurd to say that the Appellant could compel the Appellee to carry out this or any other proposed project. There is, therefore, apparent want of equity in going outside the record and not confining this decision to the record as presented to the Court.

X.

That if the decision shall stand, remain and be enforced, the Appellant will be deprived of its property without due process of law, the Constitution of the United States will be violated and be disregarded, and the Supreme law of the land held for naught.

Wherefore, the Petitioner prays that your Honors may take under consideration the grounds alleged above, order and direct a rehearing and reargument of this cause and set the time therefor, and in presenting this petition, as a part thereof, and to sustain the same, the Petitioner respectfully submits and calls the Court's attention to its brief thereon hereinafter following.

That an order may be made and entered directing and allowing the Appellant to serve copies of the petition and brief on Appellee, and that such other and further orders may be made as shall be just and right.

WEST SIDE IRRIGATING COMPANY.

By CARROLL B. GRAVES and

HARTMAN & HARTMAN,

Its Attorneys.

300-306 Burke Bldg., Seattle, Wash.

We, the undersigned, attorneys of record and counsel for West Side Irrigating Company, Petitioner aforesaid, do hereby certify and state that in our judgment and opinion the Petition for a rehearing is well founded in law and that it is not interposed, filed or urged for the purpose of delay or to hinder the orderly procedure of justice.

Dated at Seattle, Washington, this 26th day of January, 1921.

CARROLL B. GRAVES,
HARTMAN & HARTMAN,

No. 3518.

In the United States Circuit Court of Appeals For The Ninth Circuit

WEST SIDE IRRIGATING COMPANY, *Appellant,* vs. UNITED STATES OF AMERICA, *Apellee.*	No. 3518 BRIEF UPON THE PETITION FOR REHEARING

APPEAL FROM THE UNITED STATES DISTRICT COURT FOR THE EASTERN DISTRICT OF WASHINGTON, SOUTHERN DIVISION.

HON. FRANK H. RUDKIN, *Presiding.*

BRIEF UPON THE PETITION FOR REHEARING

The Petitioner, West Side Irrigating Company prays the indulgence of the Court in filing a supplemental brief in support of the Petition for Rehearing and respectfully urges the Court to consider the same in connection not only with the Petition but because of an issue of grounds set forth in the brief. An eminent American statesman of our early period once said, "Nothing is ever settled until it is settled right." We firmly believe that if this cause finally rests upon the decision rendered on the 3rd of January last that it will not be settled in accordance with this axiom which has become a part of our supreme law as though within our sacred constitution.

ARGUMENT.

I.

1. It is with considerable trepidation that we approach the argument for a rehearing of this cause. When an action has been presented more than once to a Court, it becomes more or less irksome, particularly to the Court, to further consider any argument because most of us conclude that all the reasons ought to have been presented in the first instance.

However, we are conscious of the fact, after a more careful study of the whole situation, that we did not present all that should have been presented to the Court as reasons why the Appellant should have prevailed. For our admitted dereliction may we now, humbly confessing, make amends.

We believed that there was no contract at all and, therefore, upon the argument, presented the cause from that viewpoint. The Court, however, has arrived at a different conclusion. Without prejudice to this position, we now readily see that we should have gone further and shown that even if there was a contract existing, nevertheless because of the strong allegations in the bill by the Appellee admitted, because of the general demurrer, for these reasons, if for no other, a reversal should be had in order that the facts may be presented and a trial had upon the facts and not allow the case to be concluded upon a theory contrary to and in violation of the rules of equity.

Naturally counsel for Appellee would be tempted to present extrinsic facts, because they were denied the right to present an issue upon the tendered motion which they made and did, both in the written and oral argument, go outside of the record and drag in outside and extrinsic matters, which would be pertinent at a trial on an issue of facts, *but not otherwise.* This having been done, counsel for Appellant to a certain extent did not meet it, nor do we now think we should have so done. All this gives a false coloring and must of necessity have had some effect upon the Court.

We emphasize this because it is apparent that even the Court itself, which it should charge to counsel, has gone outside of the admitted case presented and presumed a state of facts to exist which are admitted not to exist. For instance, it is alleged that Swigert was a witness. This is admitted by Appellee, yet the Court bases some of its reasons for reversal upon the conclusion that Swigert was not a witness. By using the allegation in the rejected motion only, could this have been so determined as a fact. We use this as an illustration to show that counsel for Appellee, did not hew to the line as they should have done, and believe these are reasons that will strongly appeal to any one why, if not a different decision shall be reached, at least a rehearing shall be granted to give counsel the right to correct the wrong impression which may have been made.

2. Under well reasoned cases of the Supreme Court this whole proceeding is a case in equity purely and that must be kept in view at all times. It seems to us that the Court has overlooked this fact and has treated the action from the viewpoint of the code pleadings under technical law rules.

We are persuaded that there has been fatal error all through this proceeding, as well in the judgment of the District Court, as in the opinion of the Court of Appeals, in disposing of the fundamental ground of mistake as one determined by the judgment sought to be vacated. The opinion of the Court in that case has been cited several times as settling this issue, holding that there was no satisfactory evidence of a mistake in that case. But the mistake there considered was the belief of the West Side Irrigating Company that the contract was intended to limit the water diverted to 80 cubic feet at the distribution boxes, whereas it was held that the contract plainly meant at the point of intake.

That was the only question of mistake at issue in that case, which was wholly one turning on construction of the meaning of the contract. That can not be held a determination of whether or not the evidence now offered is sufficient, because we offer to prove that appellant repudiated the contract because it understood and was so advised by the agent of appellee that 80 cubic feet at the intake was equivalent to 4,000 miners inches at the distribution boxes. Certainly the sufficiency of that evidence has not been passed upon before. In fact the materiality and binding force of it if proved must be admitted.

The opinion takes the position that the question of mistake and fraud, so strongly relied on in this action, was decided in the former case, but it is certain that the point was never in issue in that case or at any time until the question was presented here. Both courts have heretofore intimated to the contrary but such *was not* pleaded in the answer.

Thus a new and distinct question is presented calling for equitable interpretation only, and to which law rules have no application. Such are too harsh in equity cases.

The opinion lays stress upon the fact that the moving party waited an undue time after discovering what Mr. Noble had testified to on or about the 18th day of June, 1918. Ample reason is pleaded, and under the pleadings admitted, why the delay occurred. Negotiations were pending between the parties by letters, conferences and otherwise (paragraph X of the Second Amended Bill, Record p. 24) and these negotiations were not completed when the action was commenced because the Irrigating Company did not dare wait longer. More, under the Washington Statute, which governs, if there is no Federal Rule, the Appellant has three years from June 18th, 1918, to bring its action (Remington's Code, Par. 159). This being an equitable proceeding, it is by the pleadings admitted, that the Appellant acted in the best of faith, therefore it should be rewarded rather than punished for this delay.

3. By inference, from the opinion rendered, we draw the conclusion that the Court may have the feeling that the Appellant is seeking to trifle with orderly Court procedure. Such is farthest from the minds of any of the parties. We beg to assure the Court that no such thought has ever entered the mind of either litigant or counsel. The Appellant and its shareholders are fighting desperately, as it is very apparent, to protect all they have and that which they have enjoyed so long. And why should they not so contend? Would they, under the circumstances, be true if they should do otherwise. Their homes and their firesides are at stake. They have been persistent and insistent we admit, but that is the spirit which should accentuate every good and high class citizen and red blooded American. If the water, which they have so long enjoyed and

owned, is without any consideration taken away from them and allowed to run waste and to other parties not parties to this suit, their rights are seriously imperiled, their property values threatened and at least greatly damaged if not ruined and their property taken without due process of law and in violation of the Federal Constitution. If this insistence and persistence damaged any one or any party whomsoever it might be different. But such course does not and cannot damage any one. Equity certainly, therefore, will come to the rescue.

True the Appellee, by answer, might plead facts, although not at any time having so intimated, that it would be damaged by the loss of this water. If so, that comes upon the trial of the issue. We can not so presume under the issue as now presented. And it is time enough to meet such an issue if and when it arises.

This cause was tried and determined upon a demurrer to the bill and thereby everything in the bill admitted to be true. This condition can not and must not be departed from without violating all rules of procedure. We note, however, that the Court refers to a statement, which is allowable only in an answer, in the so-called motion. Such statement was expressly eliminated by the order of the District Judge, and it must be kept in mind that Judge Rudkin specifically stated and ordered that he would hear and consider the pleading interposed as a general demurrer to the bill, and not otherwise. To take any other view is unfair to the trial judge, to all the parties, to all well considered procedure, and to this Court itself. We know it was not the intention of the Court to overlook the fact that the bill is challenged by a demurrer and allow the allegations, in the so-called motion which would be denied on pleadings, to have any weight or to influence the Court, but this seems a fair deduction on reading the opinion. This it seems to us alone, even conceding there are no other grounds, demands a setting aside of the opinion and calling for a reargument. Of course this may have occurred possibly, because Appellant may not have made its cause clear, and further this Court may be impatient because of the persistencies as indicated. In any event a mistake has been made and now no one is concerned who made it, but all are concerned in helping to make the correction.

True, we do not insist that Mr. Swigert or anybody in charge of the Reclamation Service desired to purposely, intentionally, fraudulently and deliberately deceive the Appellant who is and long has been an owner, holder and user of the public waters by lawful appropriation, superior to any rights of the Appellee, whose rights were conferred by the State Legislature in 1905 (Session Laws 19, pp. 180-2). But everyone knows well that there is *actual fraud* and *constructive fraud.* No matter which kind is practiced the redress remedy is the same in each. We do insist and so plead, and it is admitted by the Appellee that a *constructive fraud* was perpetrated upon the Appellant, and that is what we want to meet and have a chance to try the issue squarely and fairly in open Court, and upon the facts being presented if we are wrong, the costs will be paid and that is the end. Fraud is always fraud whether actual or constructive. The fraud charged can be met only by proof and it seems to us passing strange that the Reclamation Service is unwilling to come out in the open and face the charge in a Court trial upon an issue squarely drawn.

4. In considering the closing part of the opinion, we are convinced that the Court has not kept in mind the fact that the Appellee is not here in its sovereign capacity, but in a private business capacity on an exact parity and on the same standing, with the Appellant. This Appellee admits by its demurrer. The case of *U. S. vs. Strang* from the Supreme Court decided January 3rd, 1921, aids us in this position. We appreciate that we have so long regarded the United States as appearing in Court only in its sovereign capacity that we forget to assign it to its proper place when it does appear as a competitor with individuals, in a private capacity as a business concern, a position which it has assumed only in the last few years under the pressure of a strong desire for a parental form of government.

Under stress of circumstances, the Appellee in

its activities has more and more departed from its merely political or governmental functions and invaded many fields heretofore occupied wholely by personal enterprise, and when it does it must and shall abide by the rules imposed upon the citizen when carrying on similar enterprises.

It is only in these later days that the United States has gone into a general business outside of perfoming the parts required of the sovereign. We naturally should give an artificial advantage to the Appellee when acting in its sovereign capacity, but that disappears absolutely, and should and does disappear absolutely, when it goes into competition in ordinary business enterprises with private individual and corporate enterprises.

5. The review is denied because it is claimed there is want of diligence in discovering the evidence of carrying home the notice of protest to the Reclamation Service prior to the trial. This position is not tenable. It is inequitable and a violation of conscience, to deny Appellant relief on this ground. The Reclamation Service occupied a fiduciary relation as to the water users, and it was not merely a case of refraining from disclosing testimony, of facts material to the opposing party, but the Appellee made positive claim of want of notice of protest and strong argument in its brief, before both courts, on that point. The Appellee was an agent for other water users than Appellant's shareholders, having advanced money for

ditch and impounding construction and seeking to have its money returned later. In fact, it was and is a mortgagee operating for other water users than the Appellant until its money advanced is paid by the users, when all its direction ceases.

Moreover, there was and is no proof of any material injury or injustice to the Appellee by reason of the delay or want of discovery, while great damage and injustice is admitted to Appellant. Therefore, under all equity rules and under such admitted facts the right to remedy the wrong can not, must not, and shall not be denied. In equity the strict rules of law must always be subservient to justice and good conscience. We fear in this case this rule, unconsciously, has been disregarded and not applied.

5. It is held that the protest made, after the contract was deliberately ended, was not formal and/or definite. Such conclusion ignores the fact that Appellant has never complied or been required to comply with the judgment. It repudiated the so-called contract or limiting agreement the first time compliance was demanded and has never been molested in all the past thirty (30) years, in the full use and enjoyment of the water by it owned and appropriated. Repudiation may not have been pleaded in the former trial. However, that is entirely immaterial, but the *Appellee has never been at any time in doubt about the attitude of the Appellant.* This fact is plain, outstand-

ing, considered, admitted and fully understood at all times. To hold that the Appellant acquiesced, notwithstanding the newly discovered evidence, is highly artificial and technical, and not substantial justice or equity. It is allowing the rigor of the law to undo right. It visits a manifest injustice upon one without considering rights, *and* while invoking such a harsh rule no benefit accrues to the Appellee. Wrong, sometimes, may be suffered and by law enforced, if thereby another is greatly benefited. But that harsh rule cannot be even invoked here. All the admitted facts, measured by the rules, forbid.

7. We trust we will not be deemed objectionable if we say that the whole decision seems to rest on technicalities and not equity. We can quite understand why the Court may for the time being have reached such a conclusion and under the theory that there must be an end of proceedings. But in this case we insist that we have not trespassed upon patience, that we have not gone beyond our rights, that we are within all equity rules, and that conscience and the best good for all is on our side.

After all, the only questions, arising on the demurrer before the court, are whether or not the newly discovered evidence and issues presented are material, and if so, is Appellant estopped from applying for a bill of review on that ground?

That they are material must be admitted, when

it is remembered that the judgment sought to be vacated in its last analysis rested upon the rejection of the issues now raised, first, because not raised by the pleadings in that case, and second, because of acquiescence on the part of Appellant by failure to notify the United States of its repudiation of the contract, which deficiency in the evidence the newly discovered evidence supplies. It is true the court holds the notice was not formal, but this is a demurrer, and formal notice might and can be proved under the allegations of the bill.

Then is appellant estopped? With any convincing reason, it can not for a moment be argued that it has done anything to acquiesce in or comply with the decree, or in any way estopped itself from maintaining a position it has asserted at all times. But it is held that Appellant was not diligent in obtaining the newly discovered evidence from Mr. Noble by interrogating him on the witness stand, or before the trial, instead of immediately after he left the stand. It must be remembered that the question of repudiation was not in issue then, as Appellant was proceeding on the theory that the contract when properly construed expressed its understanding and agreement. In any event, Appellant is here denied relief, not for want of diligence, as we are constrained to view it, but for failure to do much more than was required under the circumstances; more than sanctioned proceedings in and under any circumstances require or ever invoke.

II.

1. Admit for argument's sake that the contract was not repudiated and, therefore, is in existence subject to the right of cancellation for fraud in obtaining it.

Then, we insist that the demurrer must be overruled for three reasons.

1st. Because the allegations of the Second Amended Bill show that the notice given was sufficiently definite to constitute abrogation of contract as between the parties and, therefore, there was no contract in existence to be enforced by the judgment here sought to be vacated unless fraud shall be enthroned, and

2nd. Even if the Court should not hold that the contract was thus abrogated by act of the parties, the bill must be sustained in the form of an action for rescission of that contract, which relief was denied on the former trial because of failure to overcome the presumption of ratification and acquiescence, owing wholly to the want of evidence, then in possession of the Appellee, but not discovered nor could it be discovered by the Appellant until after the final judgment was rendered, and which the Court has already found in this proceeding is amply sufficient to justify review and rehearing of the whole case; and,

3rd. This whole question is one that can be

reached only by answer, and cannot be passed upon by way of demurrer directed against the bill.

In our brief we have cited many authorities. But the Court seems to place its conclusions on its own rules, reasoned out. Often this is best and so far we have followed this course. However, it will, we trust, aid the Court to quote new authorities, bearing upon the new points earnestly made. And we are most earnestly pleading here for the cause is desperate if Appellant loses. Its loss can not be recouped. The waters of the Yakima River are all appropriated and this Appellant has not the finances or credit to go into the high mountains and create impounding reservoirs.

On this second point suggested above the authorities hold that a plea of laches in discovering fraud is not a good defense and that no notice of disaffirmance is necessary further than the bringing of a suit for rescission upon the grounds of fraud.

Note the following:

> One induced by false representations to deal with another under circumstances permitting rescission of the contract for fraud does not, within the limitations of statute, lose any remedy to redress the wrong by mere delay to act prior to receiving knowledge of the facts or failure by reason of want of ordinary diligence to obtain such knowledge.

Hall vs. Bank of Baldwin, 127 N. W. 969, 143 Wis. 303.

Notice of disaffirmance is not required, when rescission is based and claimed on grounds of fraud.

Wolf vs. N. W. Nat'l. City Bank, 170 App. Div. 565, 156 N. Y. S. 575.

Where rescission is sought in equity, the rule of the best considered cases is that notice of disaffirmance by complainant is not a prerequisite to relief, but that the institution of the suit constitutes sufficient notice of complainant's election to rescind the contract, and no prior notice need be given.

9 C. J. 1207.

Bringing an action to rescind a contract for fraud is sufficient notice of election to rescind.

Lufkin vs. Cutting, 225 Mass. 599, 114 N. E. 822.

The necessity of giving notice upon the rescission of a contract exists only when the party rescinding has received some benefit or advantage from the contract, which he must surrender before he can claim to rescind.

Ripley vs. Hazelton, 3 Daly (N .Y. 329).

2. Further authorities may be cited, as bearing upon the charge of laches against the plaintiff, particularly in view of defendant's conduct in withholding the facts unknown to plaintiff, and even misleading the plaintiff at the time of the trial, as follows:

No duty to make inquiry arises, where de-

> fendant has so conducted himself to plaintiff's knowledge as to lull him into a sense of security and justify him in believing no mistake has been made.
>
> 25 Cyc. 1197.

This doctrine is most pertinent when applied to the admitted facts in this case. The conduct of Appellee at all times, in making investigations and otherwise was such that it did lull the Appellant and its shareholders into a sense of security, and it was justified in believing that it was entitled to and would not be molested, in holding all the water, rights and property, which it had so long enjoyed and owned.

Note further the rule:

> It has been said that the matter upon the discovery of which a bill of review is based, if previously known to the other party must be of such a nature that he was not in conscience obliged to have discovered it to the Court; and if it was known to him and such as in conscience he ought to have discovered, he obtained the decree by fraud, and it ought to be set aside by an original bill.
>
> Foster's Federal Practice, Vol. 2, p. 1408 (5th Ed.).
>
> No act of a party will amount to a confirmation of a fraudulent transaction, or acquiescence therein, unless done with full knowledge of the fraud.
>
> 6 Cyc. 305.

Inasmuch as plaintiff acted promptly, in renouncing under the contract, upon discovering the proof for the misrepresentation in calculating the flow of water, there can be no estoppel for anything done by Appellee prior thereto.

> Estoppel by improvements made with the acquiescence of the other, cannot arise against one ignorant of his rights at the time.
>
> 48 L. R. A. (N. S.) 772 (note 2).

We cite this authority in the event the Court may take judicial notice of Appellee's improvements but otherwise it is not in point.

> A party defrauded in a contract will not be debarred of his rights unless his delay to assert them amounts to a waiver, or he consciously does some act which will prevent the other party from being put in as good a position as he was before.
>
> *Martin vs. Ash.*, 20 Mich. 166.

The doctrine announced in the Martin case applies with special force here. The silence of Appellee and its cloaking the fact of knowledge of the protest, and, at least by outward show, pretending that it did not have the notice, prevented the Appellant from otherwise protecting itself. This alone is sufficient for rehearing and reversal.

> In a suit for formal rescission in equity, it is not a condition precedent to bringing the suit, that the defrauding party be placed in *statu quo.*

Page on Contracts, Vol. 1, p. 220.

Fraud is clearly, specifically and truly stated and, for the time being, by the demurrer admitted. The rule is, and we think nothing to the contrary, as follows:

> A judgment obtained by fraud will always be set aside when the Court's attention is called thereto.
>
> *Metcalf vs. Williams*, 104 U. S. 93, 95, 26 L. Ed. 665-666.
>
> *National Surety Co. vs. State Bank of Humboldt*, 120 Fed. 593.
>
> *Aldrich vs. Crump*, 128 Fed. 984.
>
> *Sanford vs. White*, 132 Fed. 531.

This is a strong doctrine but salutary. It is right and certainly has application at this time.

The 120 Fed. noted above, after citing with approval many decisions of the Supreme Court of the United States and other Courts, lays down the rule governing questions of this kind and naming the elements which must be complied with in order that relief shall be granted as follows:

> "The indispensable elements of such a cause of action are (1) a judgment which ought not, in equity and good conscience, to be enforced; (2) a good defense to the alleged cause of action on which the judgment is founded; (3) fraud, accident, or mistake which prevented the defendant in the judgment from obtaining the benefit of his defense; (4) the absence of

fault or negligence on the part of the defendant; and (5) the absence of any adequate remedy at law."

National Surety Co. vs. State Bank, 120 Fed. 599.

Appellant's relief sought falls within all the rules laid down and for that reason a different conclusion should be reached. Even if the fraud charge is eliminated then under this case under the ground of accident and mistake the remedy will lie. The allegations of the bill are ample and sufficient therefor.

May we call the Court's attention specifically to the Metcalf case in the 104 U. S. above and quote therefrom the following (the italicized words being ours and not as in the opinion):

> When a party has been deprived of his right by *fraud, accident,* or *mistake,* and has no remedy at law, a court of equity will grant relief. Perhaps in view of the equitable control over their own judgments which courts of law have assumed in modern times, the judgment might have been set aside, on motion, for the cause set forth in the bill; but if this were true, the remedy in equity would still be open; and the fact that the court declined to exercise the power upon motion, rendered the resort to a bill necessary and proper. Formerly bills in equity were constantly filed to obtain new

> trials in actions at law, a practice which still obtains in Kentucky, and perhaps in some other jurisdictions; but the firmly settled practice by which courts of law entertain motions for new trial, and the dislike of one court unnecessarily to interfere with proceedings in another, has caused an almost total disuse of that jurisdiction. Courts of equity, however, still entertain bills to set aside judgments obtained by fraud, accident, or mistake.
>
> *Metcalf vs. Williams*, 104 U. S. 95-96.

We quote this opinion for three reasons, as follows:

1st. Because Appellee in the Lower Court questioned the right to proceed as we did proceed, and

2nd. Because it clearly shows that the Appellant is within its rights.

3rd. Because to deny the right of trial as claimed by the Appellant and admitted by Appellee, would be taking property and property rights without due process of law and in violation of the Constitution of the United States.

III.

Bearing upon the question of fraud, mistake, misrepresentation, misunderstanding and similar points, all having a bearing upon this case, we desire to call the Court's attention to the following from Cyc.:

6 Vol. p. 286.

9 Vol. pp. 388 and 395.

16 Vol. pp. 84-5.

36 Vol. pp. 600 and 603.

In

16 Cyc. 68

with numerous authorities sustaining the text, we find that where relief is given because of mistake of one party alone, it is where it is induced by the conduct of one party, or where the other party seeks unconsciously to take advantage. This principle it would seem to us applies here.

There was a mutuality of mistake, for we want to put it no harsher than that, so far as Mr. Noble is concerned. He seemed to think, or at least said, that 80 second feet was the same as 4,000 miners inches, and induced the Appellant and its Trustees to so believe. Had they not so thought they never would have acted. This is a tryable issue as will appear by the following citations from Cyc. and the numerous authorities there quoted, to-wit:

16 Vol. p. 71.

36 Vol. pp. 604-5 and 608.

It would seem to appear from the opinion in this cause that the Court has treated the controversy as one in law and not equity. We think there is no question under the Supreme Court decision cited, but what this is an action in equity purely fusing if not contrary to the principles involved; and that being admitted the opinion at least is conthis affording a strong reason why the rehearing must be had.

We submit this whole cause with confidence in our position and firm in the belief that the rehearing will be granted, and upon a rehearing more time allowed than is usually given under the rules in which to present this most important question. Not only are Appellant's stockholders involved, but many other of the small ditch owners and users through the State of Washington and other states, where the Reclamation Service is engaged in irrigation, are likewise involved. Then further it involves the sacred right of taking property without compensation and due process of law.

Respectfully submitted,

CARROLL B. GRAVES and
HARTMAN & HARTMAN,
Attorneys for Appellant.

300-306 Burke Bldg., Seattle, Wash.

Lightning Source UK Ltd.
Milton Keynes UK
UKHW010628110219
337000UK00006B/149/P

9 780260 60